DUE

DEFENDING THE ISLAND

DEFENDING THE ISLAND

Caesar to the Armada

Norman Longmate

HUTCHINSON
London Sydney Auckland Johannesburg

Hutchinson & Co (Publishers) Ltd
An imprint of Century Hutchinson Ltd
Brookmount House, 62–65 Chandos Place, London WC2N 4NW

Century Hutchinson Australia (Pty) Ltd
89–91 Albion Street, Surry Hills, NSW 2010

Century Hutchinson Group (NZ) Ltd
PO Box 40–086, 32–34 View Road, Glenfield, Auckland 10

Century Hutchinson Group (SA) Pty Ltd
PO Box 337, Bergvlei, 2012 South Africa

First published in 1989

© Norman Longmate 1989

Set in Bembo 10½/12
by Input Typesetting Ltd., London
Printed and bound by Mackays of Chatham, Kent

ISBN 0 09 170910 5

331444

CONTENTS

BOOK 3: ENGLAND VERSUS ROME

FOREWORD

Fear of a foreign invasion of the British Isles has troubled the minds of successive generations of their inhabitants, and especially of Englishmen, for though the attack has often come through Wales, Scotland or Ireland England has always been the ultimate target. Throughout the sixteen and a half centuries covered by this volume the risk of invasion was ever-present and for much of it hardly a decade passed without an attack from the continent being either feared, contemplated, or attempted, while on the South Coast actual landings were at some periods almost an annual event. Limitations of space have inevitably defeated my original intention of recording, wherever possible in the words of contemporaries, every occasion on which any enemy has set foot on our shores, but I have none the less included far more, and described them in much greater detail, than any previous work in this field. (Most such books have, indeed, been very slight; and the last two-volume invasion history, on a much more modest scale than the present one, appeared more than a century ago.) 'Invasion' I have defined as any operation which involves foreigners under arms landing on British soil against the wishes of the ruling government. This includes successful landings in force, followed by occupation and a change of ruler; major attacks ultimately followed by withdrawal; attempts which failed at an earlier stage, through military defeat or for other reasons; short-term raids, when an enemy spent only a few hours or days ashore; so-called *tentatives*, where elaborate preparations came in the end to nothing; and 'friendly invasions' or 'invasions by invitation', when an enemy responded to an appeal for assistance from within the country, or a partly foreign army supported a claimant to the English throne. I have also covered a number of invasion alarms, which often involved as much dismay and disruption as real attempts.

Although invasions of the British Isles were often a consequence of English operations on the continent, and most weapons and military techniques relevant to invasions were developed primarily in foreign wars, or in internal rebellions and their suppression, the need to keep the text to a reasonable length has precluded dealing with these subjects in detail. I have, however, tried to explain as fully as space has allowed *why* invasions occurred, especially when they resulted not from the tedious squabbles between king and nobility of which so much medieval history consists, but from such causes as the English claim to the French throne or hostile relations between the ruling English sovereign and the papacy. I have thus found myself writing a far more wide-ranging book than the basically military history I had intended, while constantly being compelled to omit much interesting material on grounds of publishing practicality rather than irrelevance. I have tried none the less to retain, and to establish the truth of, some of the familiar legends associated with the invasion story, from Alfred's burning of the cakes to Drake's determination to finish his game of bowls. A truly comprehensive history of the invasions of England could easily rival in length Gibbon's *Decline and Fall of the Roman Empire*, which runs to around 1,350,000 words. *Defending the Island*, which will consist of two volumes of 200,000 words each, is by comparison distinctly slight, but is none the less four times the length of the single, short volume originally commissioned, and the research for the two volumes, and the writing of the first, have already taken some five years.

For most of the period covered here the language used by the chroniclers was not English and even when it did become the universal tongue it was far from standardized. The quotations in the earlier chapters have been translated into modern English, while those from around 1500, which can, with a little effort, be understood by the modern reader, have been retained in the original, though I have made some minor changes to improve readability, like substituting 'u' for 'v' where necessary. The original punctuation has also been altered where it seemed clumsy or misleading. In the case of names, of places and persons, which throughout this period were often rendered, even in the same sentence, in many different ways, I have opted for what seems the most generally accepted form, while giving the alternatives in parenthesis.

I have tried to identify, and indicate precisely in the text, the location of all the sites and villages mentioned, about which many previous writers have been remarkably vague. Except in the case of Wales, where the names then adopted could claim some earlier authority, I have used throughout the historic names of the counties during the period covered by this book, not those imposed on the country in 1974.

No proper calendar existed in England in the early years of the period covered by my story, and by the end most of Europe was using a different one from that in use in England, which did not come into line with her neighbours until September 1752. I have followed throughout the 'Julian' calendar still in use in England in 1603, though with some cross-references in the Armada chapters to the Gregorian calendar adopted by Spain in 1582.

My principal debt, at this halfway point in what has proved a far longer and more arduous task than I anticipated, is to Mr Anthony Whittome of Century Hutchinson, who has shown a sympathetic understanding of the reasons for the successive increases in length, and delays in delivery of the manuscript, for which I have pleaded. I am also grateful to Miss Gabrielle Allen, who undertook the picture research, to Mr Rodney Paull, who drew the maps, and to Mr Alex McIntosh who copy-edited the manuscript and, as an experienced amateur sailor, was able to prevent my repeating the errors about winds and tides which appear in so many accounts of naval operations by non-specialists. I acknowledge with thanks the help of those who undertook research for me, though the real fruits of their labours will not be apparent till Volume II: Mrs Venetia Abdalla, formerly Miss Venetia Compton; Miss Pat Burstall; Miss Eve Cottingham; Miss Liz Dwiar; Miss Julie Hornsby; and my daughter, Miss Jill Longmate. The obscurities of Laurence Minot's poems were kindly unravelled for me by Mr Julian Roberts, of the Bodleian Library, Oxford, and by Miss Anne Lutyens-Humfrey, formerly of Cambridge. Miss Sonia Anderson of the Royal Commission on Historical Manuscripts helped me on a number of archival points, and Dr Carole Rawcliffe, of the History of Parliament project, supplied me with much helpful material on Tudor defence legislation. Dr Jack Jones, formerly Curator of the Carisbrooke Castle Museum, and Mr Anthony Cantwell, of St Helens, Ryde, gave me useful information about the Isle of Wight. I am particularly grateful to Mr Bryan Harris who made many helpful suggestions as to how the text might be edited and took the photograph of the author which appears on the dust jacket. I also owe thanks to many museum curators, librarians and private individuals who gave assistance of various kinds and to my fellow-members of the Fortress Study Group and of the United Kingdom Fortifications Club, who provided a fund of specialist knowledge and rekindled my enthusiasm when it began to flag.

All this assistance will be more fully, and appropriately, acknowledged in the second volume of *Defending the Island*. This is provisionally entitled *After the Armada* and will cover the years from 1603 to 1945. It is hoped that it will appear during 1990, the fiftieth anniversary of the last great invasion threat – a reminder that the danger described in this book is by no means a remote and distant one but a constantly recurring feature of our heritage and history.

N.R.L.   October 1988

BOOK 1
BEFORE THE CONQUEST

I

AN UNKNOWN COUNTRY

He also invaded Britain, a hitherto unknown country.

Suetonius, Julius Caesar, *recalling 55 BC*

In the beginning was the sea. *Rule Britannia*, written in 1740, boasted of a time

When Britain first, at heaven's command,
Arose from out the azure main

but the truth was less dramatic. The white cliffs which were to be its landmark and bulwark and the long chalk uplands which culminated in them emerged only slowly from the sea-bed as one inch of lime-laden ooze was laid upon another every thousand years. The final separation of the island from the adjoining landmass came remarkably late in the geological timescale, less than 7000 years ago, when the 'land bridge' across the English Channel finally subsided beneath the waves. Henceforward the sea was to be the dominant influence on all the inhabitants of the island, even those who never saw it. From the moment when an invader's pen casts the first light upon it, the story of Great Britain is a maritime one. The sea has founded and fortified, shaped and sheltered all.

Although those who had formerly come on foot, in search of game or pasture land, now had to travel by boat the influx of peoples from the adjoining continent continued throughout the centuries before Christ as the Romans tightened their grip on one area after another and inter-tribal wars encouraged mass migration. By half-way through the first century BC at least twenty major tribes, with numerous sub-divisions and many scattered enclaves of earlier inhabitants, occupied mainland Britain, amounting to perhaps a quarter of a million people. Sometimes their names commemorated the areas they came from like the Parisii, from the Seine valley, who settled in what was to become Yorkshire, sometimes they survive here like the Dumnonii and Durotriges whose descendants became Devonians or Dorsetmen. One of the largest tribes, settling in the border area of present-day Wales, the Prython or Brython, may have given their name to the whole nation; the first recorded visitor, a Greek from Marseilles, landed in the 'Pretanic Isle' around the year 325 BC. The island's other name, Albion, probably comes from the white cliffs: 'alba' is Latin for 'white'.

About the British Isles around 60 BC there seemed little to attract an invader. Most of the country was still covered with thick forest, with swamps in the lower-lying areas. In little woodland clearings and on windswept hilltops, or in the valleys alongside rivers, clustered small communities of mutually distrustful tribes, occasionally cooperating, sometimes fighting, but mainly living out their dull, damp laborious lives barely aware of each other's existence. Theirs was a deeply primitive society, permeated by insecurity, terrorized rather than consoled by a bloodthirsty religion – one group at least, in Gloucestershire, had the still unexplained habit of eating their womenfolk – wholly dependent on the seasons, for both food and comfort. They lived in pits sunk in the ground or grass-thatched mud and timber huts. Apart from the mysterious stone circles built centuries before for worship, their only other buildings were earthen hill forts erected to protect their goods and cattle, some vast, elaborate, structures, many consisting of little more than a ditch-encircled stretch of woodland.

As yet nothing remotely approaching a single kingdom with a recognized capital existed but the accidents of geography had made Salisbury Plain the centre of such civilization as there was. This great, well-drained chalk plateau offered ideal conditions for settlement and a natural communications centre, as three great chalk ridges spread out from it, to the Wash to the Straits of Dover and to Beachy Head – all potential invasion routes into England, though as yet no one had looked at the country in this light.

The Romans calculated dates *ab urbe condita*, 'from the founding of the city'. By AUC 699, 55 BC by the Christian calendar adopted later, the Roman Empire covered most of the known world, stretching nearly 3000 miles from the Atlantic coast of modern Portugal to the distant frontier of Syria, and from Carthage and Alexandria to the North Sea coast of Germany. Rome was almost exactly the geographical, as well as the political and cultural, centre of this huge area.

Every Roman citizen could in theory reach high office but Julius Caesar started a long way up the ladder, being born in Rome itself, in July of 100 BC, into a patrician, i.e. noble, family, nephew of the then consul, the highest office in the state. Well educated and intelligent, he attracted attention early, and by the time he assumed the formal symbol of manhood, the *toga virilis*, at sixteen, was already, according to a

Roman historian, 'tall, fair and well-built'. He married in the same year, and for a second time not long after, when his first wife died, but rapidly became notorious for his affairs, which culminated when he was 52 in his relationship with the 21-year-old Cleopatra, Queen of Egypt, with whom he may have contemplated founding a new dynasty.

Caesar's career really began in his teens when he joined the staff of the *propraetor*, or resident governor, of the Roman province in Asia. A second mission followed. This time he was captured by pirates, and, according to the biographer Plutarch writing a century later, 'When these men at first demanded of him 20 talents for his ransom, he laughed at them for not understanding the value of their prisoner and voluntarily engaged to give them 50.' The incident is characteristic of the man. So is the sequel. Once set free Caesar led a punitive expedition which captured the pirates and crucified them.

At the age of 26 Caesar received public recognition as one of the 24 military tribunes – a formal honour – and was appointed to the College of Pontiffs, responsible for the state's religious observances. Eleven years later, now 37, after a period in Spain as *quaestor*, a form of itinerant judge-cum-administrator, he became *pontifex maximus*, or high priest, for life, though he was indifferent to religion except to buttress the authority of the state.

By 61 BC Caesar was in command of the Roman forces in Southern Gaul, a turbulent part of the still-expanding empire. In the next four years he really established his reputation as an outstandingly able military commander, controlling from his base at Lyons, to use its later name, a force of nearly 50,000 of the best soldiers in the world.

The year 57 BC saw the subjugation of the Belgae, whose name survives in modern Belgium, and who were believed to be organizing a vast conspiracy against the Romans. Caesar then turned his attention to the rebellious Venetii in the north-west corner of Gaul in and around Cape Finisterre. The final encounter, in Quiberon Bay, in which the Venetii were totally defeated by a Roman fleet carrying foot soldiers, he watched from the surrounding cliffs. The turning point came when the Roman infantry, wielding 'long poles, not unlike the grappling hooks used in sieges', tore down the rigging of the enemy ships. 'After that', he commented, 'it was a soldier's battle'. For centuries to come warfare at sea was to be universally regarded as merely an extension of fighting on land.

In the early months of 55 BC Caesar was fully preoccupied with throwing back, with heavy slaughter, the unfortunate German tribes forced into Gaul because, as they explained, 'we were expelled from our homes'. To this he retorted unfeelingly that 'It was not reasonable for men who had been unable to protect their own territory to expect to occupy other people's.' He pursued the wretched refugees back across the river, probably because no previous Roman general had done so: contemporaries had already identified the outstanding trait in his character as ambition.

His success against the Germans led to public celebrations in his honour in Rome and this in turn encouraged him to contemplate new conquests. Beyond the narrow strip of blue water which washed the shores of now subject Gaul, the white cliffs of a largely unknown, still untamed island beckoned. No real military reason existed for attacking it. The Romans already possessed a vast empire stretching from Asia and Africa across Europe to the Channel; Britain was a remote and primitive place with little to attract them. Caesar's own explanation is unconvincing:

> It was now near the end of summer and winter sets in early in those parts, because all that coast of Gaul faces north. Nevertheless Caesar made active preparations for an expedition to Britain, because he knew that in almost all the Gallic campaigns the Gauls had received reinforcements from the Britons. Even if there was not time for a campaign that season, he thought it would be of great advantage to him merely to visit the island, to see what its inhabitants were like, and to make himself acquainted with the lie of the land, the harbours, and the landing-places.

The real reasons for this first invasion of Britain were at once deeper and simpler. Caesar, like every Roman general, needed to keep his name before the public. He needed, as well as hungered for, personal glory. He had an army and, since the defeat of the Venetii, a fleet. Why not use them? Britain was invaded not because it was dangerous or important, but because it was there.

When Caesar set out to gather information about his objective he can have found few sources to help him. The full extent of his knowledge several years later he tidily summarized in his *Gallic Wars*, written after two long visits. In 55 BC he must have known much less:

> The island is triangular, with one side facing Gaul. One corner of this side, on the coast of Kent, is the landing-place for nearly all the ships from Gaul, and points east; the lower corner points south. The length of this side is about 475 miles. Another side faces west, towards Spain. In this direction is Ireland, which is supposed to be half the size of Britain, and lies at the same distance from it as Gaul. Midway across is the Isle of Man, and it is believed that there are also a number of smaller islands . . . This side of Britain, according to the natives' estimate, is 665 miles long. The third side faces north; no land lies

opposite it, but its eastern corner points roughly in the direction of Germany. Its length is estimated at 760 miles. Thus the whole island is 1900 miles in circumference.

Although he misplaced Ireland to the south of England instead of to the west Caesar's estimates do great credit to his topographical intelligence service. The all-important fact, that Britain is a triangular-shaped island close to France, he got right and its dimensions not wildly amiss: the 'base line', from the South Foreland, just east of Dover, to Land's End is actually 330 miles [531 km] long, the eastern coast, from South Foreland to the northern tip of Scotland, 560 miles [900 km], and the side furthest from France, from Land's End to Dunnet Head, just west of John o' Groats, is 600 miles [965 km]. The actual coastline, with its bays and inlets, headlands and promontories, is, of course, much longer: 7110 miles [11,440 km] by modern measurement. Of this England and Wales account for 2410 miles [3877 km], of which today about one-tenth is mudflats and marshland; in Caesar's day it will have been far more. Scotland's coast extends over 2500 [4022] and Ireland's (seen as a single geographical unit) covers the remaining 2200 [3540].

A few square miles of land have been reclaimed from the sea since Caesar's time, and elsewhere the sea has receded over the centuries leaving former ports well inland. Overall, however, Britain's coastline has changed little since the first invaders sighted it and its essential character inland has changed not at all. Its outstanding feature is that almost all the higher ground lies to the left of a line drawn from the present-day Middlesborough to Gloucester, and all the lower, sometimes almost flat, land to its right. There are hills, like the Chilterns and Cotswolds in the 'lowland' area, and long stretches of high ground, like the Berkshire Downs and Exmoor, but none likely to deter an invader. The Cheviots form a natural boundary to the north of England and the Cambrian mountains shut off what is now Wales, while England itself is split in two for about half its length by the solid backbone of the Pennine Chain. No spot in Britain is more than 75 miles [120 km] from tidal water, but the island presents by no means an easy target to unwanted visitors. Nowhere is the surrounding sea more than 300 feet [90 m] deep, and along many stretches of coast it is too shallow for any but the smallest ships. Much of Scotland, Wales, north-west England, and both shores of the great south-west peninsula, present to the mariner mile upon mile of cruelly inhospitable cliffs, occasionally broken by little harbours too small to shelter a large fleet.

Caesar was well aware how pitifully scanty was his knowledge of the country where his legions might soon be fighting and, busy himself in collecting ships and troops, sent a trusted subordinate, Gaius Volusenus, 'to make a general reconnaissance and return as soon as he could'. Once he had done so, after a four-day absence, the expedition prepared to set sail.

It had taken eight legions to pacify Gaul; Caesar assigned to his expedition against England only two, the Tenth and his favourite unit, the Seventh, a total of about 10,000 men, mainly infantry, but supported by a few archers and slingers.*

Embarking the infantry on 80 transports, and making ready the escorting warships, fully taxed the resources of Caesar's main port, almost certainly Boulogne. The cavalry, probably numbering about 250, were loaded into another 18 transports eight miles [13 km] further along the coast, at a spot called Ambleteuse.

During the afternoon and early evening of 24 August 55 BC the last troops filed on board the large boats with the broad sails tossing gently on the swell in Boulogne harbour, no doubt apprehensive about the voyage and landing ahead.

'After the completion of these arrangements, Caesar took advantage of favourable weather and set sail about midnight.' Thus he recorded the start of this first attempt to invade Britain. Of his thoughts as he stood on board his command ship he has left no record, but they must have been optimistic. At 45 he was at the peak of his powers, the conqueror of Gaul, idol of the most powerful army in the world, on his way to conquer a new, previously untamed, land.

Already, unknown to him, things had started to go wrong. The cavalry had made such a hash of embarking that by the time they did set sail 'their transports', as he later wrote, 'were carried back to land by the tide.' Then the wind changed keeping them in harbour. 'The booted ones', as the Roman infantry described themselves, were on their own.

Dawn, later the favoured time for amphibious assaults, found the fleet still in mid-Channel and when they did approach the shore the sight was far from reassuring:

> Caesar himself reached Britain with the first ships about nine o'clock in the morning and saw the enemy's forces posted on all the hills. The lie of the land at this point was such that javelins could be hurled from the cliffs right on to the narrow beach enclosed between them and the sea. Caesar thought this a quite unsuitable place for landing, and therefore rode at anchor until three o'clock, in order to give the rest of the ships time to come up. Meanwhile he assembled the generals and military tribunes [young noblemen sent by the Senate to gain military experience] and, telling them what he had learned from Volusenus,

*For a fuller account of the organization of the Roman army see Chapter 3, page 31.

explained his plans. He warned them that the exigencies of warfare, and particularly of naval operations, in which things move rapidly and the situation is constantly changing, required the instant execution of every order. On dismissing the officers he found that both wind and tidal currents were in his favour. He therefore gave the signal for weighing anchor and, after proceeding about seven miles ran his ships aground on an evenly sloping beach, free from obstacles.*

News of Caesar's approach faced the British with the same dilemma that was to confront their successors for the next two thousand years. Did they try to destroy the enemy piecemeal on the beaches, where he might enjoy local superiority? Or did they husband their strength and gather reinforcements for a decisive counter-attack later? On this occasion the decision was taken for them. Lacking any central command structure, and with no guarantee that the tribes further inland would support them, the Britons had no real option except to fight where they stood. Caesar himself described what followed:

The natives, on realizing his intention, had sent forward their cavalry and a number of the chariots which they are accustomed to use in war . . . The rest of the troops followed close behind and were ready to oppose the landing. The Romans were faced with very grave difficulties. The size of the ships made it impossible to run them aground except in fairly deep water; and soldiers, unfamiliar with the ground, with their hands full, and weighed down by the heavy burden of their arms, had at the same time to jump down from the ships, get a footing in the waves, and fight the enemy, who, standing on dry land or advancing only a short way into the water, fought with all their limbs unencumbered and on perfectly familiar ground, boldly hurling javelins and galloping their horses, which were trained to this kind of work. These perils frightened our soldiers, who were quite unaccustomed to battle of this kind, with the result that they did not show the same alacrity and enthusiasm as they usually did in battles on dry land.

Caesar ordered the warships – which were swifter and easier to handle than the transports, and likely to impress the natives more by their unfamiliar appearance – to be removed a short distance from the others and then to be rowed hard and run ashore on the enemy's right flank, from which position slings, bows and artillery [i.e. stone-hurling catapults] could be used by men on deck to drive them back. This manoeuvre was highly successful. Scared by the strange shape of

*For a detailed study of Caesar's actual landing place see Vine pp. 95–6 and 137.

the warships, the motion of the oars and the unfamiliar machines, the natives halted and then retreated a little.

Caesar's use of the classic tactic of surprise had proved effective but the battle was still in doubt. The eagles of the two legions were still on board. Carried into battle by the senior centurion, protected by a special unit, the gold and silver eagle was at once the legion's 'colours' and rallying point, whose capture represented an irremediable blot on its reputation.

As the Romans still hesitated, chiefly on account of the depth of water, the man who carried the eagle of the Tenth Legion, after praying to the gods that his action might bring good luck to the legion, cried in a loud voice, 'Jump down, comrades, unless you want to surrender our eagle to the enemy. I, at any rate, mean to do my duty to my country and my general.' With these words he leapt out of the ship and advanced towards the enemy with the eagle in his hands. At this the soldiers, exhorting each other not to submit to such a disgrace, jumped with one accord from the ship, and the men from the next ships, when they saw them, followed them and advanced against the enemy.

Both sides fought hard. But as the Romans could not keep their ranks or get a firm foothold or follow their proper standards, and men from different ships fell in under the first standard they came across, great confusion resulted. The enemy knew all the shallows and when they saw from the beach small parties of soldiers disembarking one by one, they galloped up and attacked them at a disadvantage, surrounding them with superior numbers, while others would throw javelins at the right flank of a whole group.

It was time for Caesar to intervene again.

Caesar therefore ordered the warships' boats and the scouting vessels to be loaded with troops, so that he could send help to any point where he saw the men in difficulties. As soon as the soldiers had got a footing on the beach and had waited for all their comrades to join them, they charged the enemy and put them to flight, but could not pursue very far, because the cavalry had not been able to hold their course and make the island.

In blaming his lack of mounted troops for his inability to follow up the retreating enemy Caesar was being no more than just to himself: this was the cavalry's traditional role. But what he had already achieved proved sufficient.

The defeated enemy, as soon as they rallied after their flight, hastened to send an embassy to ask for peace, promising to give hostages and carry out Caesar's commands . . . Caesar reproached them for making war on him without provocation, after sending envoys to the continent of their own accord to sue for peace, but said that he would pardon their ignorance and demanded hostages. Some of these they handed over at once; the rest they said would have to be fetched from a distance and should be delivered in a few days' time. Meanwhile they bade their men return to the fields, and the chiefs began to come from all parts to solicit Caesar's favour for themselves and their tribes.

The missing cavalry had still not turned up and on the fourth day after Caesar's arrival the 18 transports carrying them, which had at last got out of Ambleteuse, were frustratingly whisked away again.

When they were approaching Britain and were visible from the camp, such a violent storm suddenly arose that none of them could hold its course. Some were driven back to their starting-point; others, at great peril, were swept westwards to the south of the island. In spite of the danger they cast anchor, but as they were being filled with water by the waves, they were forced to stand out to sea into the darkness of the night and return to the continent.

This was not to be the last time that an invading fleet was forced back to its base without even unloading its cargo, and the Romans were now to pay an even higher price for their ignorance of conditions in the Channel.

It happened to be full moon that night, at which time the Atlantic tides are particularly high – a fact unknown to the Romans. The result was that the warships used in the crossing, which had been beached, were waterlogged, and the transports, which were riding at anchor, were knocked about by the storm, without the soldiers having any chance of interfering to save them. A number of ships were shattered, and the rest, having lost their cables, anchors, and the remainder of their tackle, were unusable, which naturally threw the whole army into great consternation; for they had no other vessels in which they could return, nor any materials for repairing the fleet, and, since it had been generally understood that they were to return to Gaul for the winter, they had not provided themselves with a stock of grain for wintering in Britain.

The British, having assembled after the battle to carry out Caesar's terms for surrender, now decided to resume fighting and to try to drag hostilities out into the winter, for reasons Caesar himself explained.

If this army was conquered or prevented from returning, they felt confident, that no-one would come across to invade Britain. Accordingly, after renewing their promises of mutual loyalty, they slipped away one by one from the camp and secretly called up once more the men who had returned to the fields.

The Britons, meanwhile, did their best to lull their recent enemies into a false sense of security. 'Britons were still working in the fields, while others were actually going backwards and forwards to the camp' and the first sign of trouble was 'an unusually large cloud of dust' from the direction in which the Seventh Legion had gone foraging:

> Caesar immediately guessed the truth . . . and ordered the cohorts [sub-divisions of a legion] on guard duty to set out with him in the direction indicated, two of the others to relieve them, and the rest to arm immediately. After going some way he saw that the Legion was hard pressed by enemy forces and holding its ground with difficulty, packed closely and pelted with missiles from all directions; for as the corn had already been cut everywhere except in one place, the enemy had expected that our men would go there and had hidden by night in the woods. Then, when the soldiers were scattered and busy cutting corn, with their arms laid down, they had made a sudden attack, killing a few and throwing the rest into confusion before they could form up, and also surrounding them with cavalry and chariots.

The masterly deployment of these fighting vehicles took the Romans by surprise: they had found nothing comparable in Gaul. Caesar, no mean judge, was impressed by their occupants' skill, perfected no doubt in many an inter-tribal war and effective enough to come close to routing his best Legion:

> In chariot fighting the Britons begin by driving all over the field hurling javelins, and generally the terror inspired by the horses and the noise of the wheels are sufficient to throw their opponents' ranks into disorder. Then, after making their way between the squadrons of their own cavalry, they jump down from the chariots and engage on foot. In the meantime their charioteers retire a short distance from the battle and place the chariots in such a position that their masters, if hard pressed by numbers, have an easy means of retreat to their own lines. Thus they combine the mobility of cavalry with the staying power of infantry; and by daily training and practice they attain such proficiency that even on a steep incline they are able to control the horses at full gallop and to check and turn them in a moment. They can run along the chariot pole, stand on the yoke and get back into the chariot as quick as lightning.

The men of the 7th Legion were unnerved by these tactics and it was just at the right moment that Caesar came to their rescue. At his approach the enemy halted and the soldiers recovered from their alarm. But as he considered the situation too hazardous for attacking or engaging in battle, he stayed where he was, and after a short interval led the legions back to camp.

The British climate, a constant ally of the islanders, now put a stop to further operations: 'There followed several days of continuous bad weather, which kept our men in camp and also prevented the enemy from attacking.'

His enemy, used to such conditions, put the lull to good use:

During this time the natives sent messengers in all directions, who informed their people of the small numbers of our troops and pointed out what a good opportunity they had of getting booty and liberating themselves for ever, if they could drive the Romans from their camp. By this means they quickly collected a large force of infantry and cavalry, which advanced towards the camp. Caesar foresaw that what had happened before would happen again; even if the enemy were beaten their speed would enable them to escape out of harm's way.

The shadowy, if not shady, figure of Commius, an envoy whom Caesar had sent to negotiate with the Britons, now turned up again, giving the Romans new heart and an invaluable reinforcement, which Caesar immediately put to good use. He knew by now that his enemy were formidable in irregular fighting but in an encounter battle on a site of his choosing the result was likely to be different.

Having luckily obtained about 30 horsemen whom Commius had brought across he drew up the legions in battle formation in front of the camp. Before the engagement had lasted long the enemy were overpowered and took to flight. The Romans pursued as far as their strength enabled them to run, killing a number of the fugitives, and then set fire to all the buildings over a wide area and returned to camp. The same day envoys came to Caesar to sue for peace. He demanded twice as many hostages as before and ordered these to be brought to the continent as the equinox was close at hand and he thought it better not to expose his damaged ships to the dangers of a voyage in wintry weather. Taking advantage of a favourable wind he set sail shortly after midnight and the whole fleet reached the continent safely.

The expedition, however, was not to end as smoothly as these words suggested, for 'two transports . . . failed to make the same harbours as the rest and were carried a little farther south'. The men on board, coming ashore in the territory of a hostile tribe, only escaped being massacred when 'Caesar sent all the cavalry to their aid'.

This inglorious ending to the summer's campaign spoke for itself. This first attempt to subdue the British had begun with a mishap, continued with a serious rebuff and ended in near-disaster. The public thanksgiving of 20 days which the Senate decreed was unmerited. He had visibly failed to tame the Britons and was lucky to have got most of his force safely home.

The historian Seutonius, writing more than a century later, remained unimpressed, dismissing Caesar's achievement very briefly: 'Caesar invaded Britain, a hitherto unknown country, and defeated the natives, from whom he exacted a large sum of money as well as hostages for good behaviour.'

2

AN ELEPHANT IN KENT

Caesar had with him a very large elephant . . . The Britons were terrified at the sight of this huge and unknown beast.

Polyaenus, Stratagems of War, *recalling 54 BC*

When in the late Spring of 54 BC, AUC 700, Caesar returned to Northern France it was already late in the year to start a major campaign, but he found preparations for his second assault on Britain well advanced.

> On his arrival he made a tour of all the winter camps and found that, in spite of a serious shortage of materials, the men had worked with such enthusiasm that they had built and equipped six hundred vessels of the type [previously] described and twenty-eight warships. These would all be ready for launching in a few days. Caesar congratulated the soldiers and the officers who had superintended the work, gave them further instructions and ordered all the ships to be assembled at Portus Itius [almost certainly Boulogne], the starting point for the easiest crossing to Britain, a run of about thirty miles.

Although it seemed for the moment secure, Gaul remained a potential danger, and Caesar left behind there no fewer than 'three legions and two thousand cavalry, with orders to guard the ports, provide for a supply of corn' and 'watch events'. This large rearguard also deprived Caesar of his ablest subordinate, Labienus, left behind to command it, but the force now crossing the Channel was still nearly three times the size of the earlier expeditionary force. It consisted of five legions, totalling about 25,000 men, mainly infantry but with the usual supporting arms, and – so badly missed last time – 2000 cavalry. The 540 transports built or bought by the Roman army were supplemented by 200 privately-owned ships, which may have contained merchants hoping to establish trading links once the island was subdued, or the 'camp followers' who accompanied armies on every major campaign, to provide for their needs and comforts.

The great fleet stood out to sea on an ebb tide, its sails filled by a gentle south-westerly breeze just before dusk around 8 p.m., on 6 July 54 BC, a brave sight in the dying rays of the evening sun. Caesar was no doubt vastly relieved to have left his recent troubles behind him, but before long he heard a new and alarming sound, the ominous flapping of empty sails.

> About midnight the wind dropped, with the result that he was driven far out of his course by the tidal current and at daybreak saw Britain left behind on the port side.

The whole Roman fleet was being swept up Channel into the North Sea, far from its intended objective. Now the wisdom of Caesar's decision to equip his ships with oars as well as sails was strikingly vindicated:

> When the set of the current changed he went with it, and rowed hard to make the part of the island where he had found the best landing places the year before. The soldiers worked splendidly and by continuous rowing enabled the heavily laden transports to keep up with the warships. When the whole fleet reached Britain about midday, no enemy was to be seen. Caesar discovered afterwards from prisoners that, although large numbers had assembled at the spot, they were frightened by the sight of so many ships and had quitted the shore to conceal themselves on higher ground.

This explanation is not necessarily correct. As later events were to confirm, the British in 54 BC were much better equipped to work together than in the previous year and may consciously have decided to oppose the enemy in force once he had landed rather than attack him piecemeal on the beaches. Treachery, too, as so often in this period, may also have played a part.

Whatever the explanation, Caesar, recalling the reception the year before, can hardly have believed his eyes as, in the early afternoon of 7 July 54 BC his huge army was able to disembark and form up ashore unharassed. The precise spot remains uncertain but was 'an open shore of soft sand' near Deal or Walmer, close to where he had landed previously. Having chosen a site for his base camp and assigned a force to protect it, Caesar decided to exploit success and attack at once without allowing his men a night's rest after their crossing.

> On learning from prisoners where the enemy were posted he left ten cohorts [i.e. 5000 men] and three hundred cavalry on the coast to guard the fleet and marched against the Britons shortly after midnight . . . A night march of about 12 miles brought Caesar in sight of the enemy, who advanced to a river with their cavalry and chariots and

tried to bar his way by attacking from a position on higher ground. Repulsed by his cavalry they hid in the woods, where they occupied a well-fortified post of great natural strength, previously prepared, no doubt . . . since all the entrances were blocked by felled trees laid close together. Scattered parties made skirmishing attacks out of the woods, trying to prevent the Romans from penetrating the defences. But the soldiers of the 7th Legion, locking their shields together over their heads and piling up the earth against the fortifications, captured the place and drove them out of the woods at the cost of only a few wounded. Caesar forbade them to pursue far, however, because he did not know the ground and because he wanted to devote the remaining hours of the day to the fortification of his camp.

So far all had gone well for Caesar. But, just as in the previous year, the weather now took a hand.

The next morning he sent out a force of infantry and cavalry in three columns to pursue the fleeing enemy. They had advanced some way and were in sight of the nearest fugitives, when dispatch riders brought news . . . of a great storm in the night, by which nearly all the ships had been damaged or cast ashore: the anchors and cables had not held and the sailors and their captains could not cope with such a violent gale, so that many vessels were disabled by running foul of one another. Caesar at once ordered the legions and cavalry to be halted and recalled. He himself went back to the beach, where with his own eyes he saw pretty much what the messengers and the dispatch described.

By the time he got back to the front the military situation had deteriorated. The Britons, it emerged, had made good use of the breathing space afforded them by the storm, for 'he found that larger British forces had now been assembled from all sides by Cassivellaunus, to whom the chief command and direction of the campaign had been entrusted by common consent.' This marked a most notable surrender of sovereignty by the normally fiercely independent and feuding tribes. It also meant that Caesar was going to have to penetrate far further into the country than he had done so far, for this new leader's 'territory', Caesar recorded, 'is separated from the maritime tribes by a river called the Thames and lies about 75 miles from the sea'. If Caesar had any illusions that his initial victory would bring about a rapid surrender he speedily lost them. Once again, Roman professionalism triumphed in every set-piece battle, but the victors were hounded and harassed whenever they moved forward:

The British cavalry and charioteers had a fierce encounter with our cavalry on the march, but our men had the best of it everywhere and drove them into the woods and hills, killing a good many, but also incurring some casualties themselves by a too eager pursuit. The enemy waited for a time and then, while our soldiers were off their guard and busy fortifying the camp, suddenly dashed out of the woods, swooped upon the outpost on duty in front of the camp and started a violent battle. Caesar sent two cohorts – the first of their respective legions [i.e. about 2000 men, as 'first' cohorts were double the normal size] – to the rescue, and these took up a position close together; but the men were unnerved by the unfamiliar tactics and the enemy very daringly broke through between them and got away unhurt . . . The attack was eventually repulsed by throwing in some more cohorts.

The Romans were now learning, the hard way, that they had sacrificed mobility to the need for personal protection. 'It was seen,' admitted Caesar, 'that our troops were too heavily weighted by their armour to deal with such an enemy: they could not pursue them when they retreated and dare not get separated from their standards.' Even more worrying, although the chariots had lost their novelty value, their handling remained extraordinarily effective:

The cavalry, too, found it very dangerous work fighting the chario-teers; for the Britons would generally give ground on purpose and after drawing them some distance from the legions would jump down from their chariots and fight on foot, with the odds in their favour. In engaging their cavalry our men were not much better off; their tactics were such that the danger was exactly the same for both pursuers and pursued.

The battle outside the camp, and the successful withdrawal which followed it, seem to have emboldened the Catuvellauni and their allies to fresh efforts on a larger scale:

Next day the enemy took up a position on the hills at a distance from the camp. They showed themselves now only in small parties and harassed our cavalry with less vigour than the day before. But at midday, when Caesar had sent three legions and all the cavalry on a foraging expedition . . . they suddenly swooped down on them from all sides, pressing their attack right up to the standards of the legions. The legionaries drove them off by a strong counter-attack and continued to pursue until the cavalry, emboldened by the support of the legions which they saw close behind them, made a charge that sent the natives flying headlong. A great many were killed and the rest were given no chance of rallying or making a stand or jumping from their chariots. This rout caused the immediate dispersal of the forces that had assembled from various tribes to Cassivellaunus's aid, and the Britons never again joined battle with their whole strength.★

The Great Stour, which is generally identified as the first river crossed by Caesar, had not proved much of an obstacle to the Romans; the Britons must have had higher hopes of the Thames. Even here, however, guided by excellent local intelligence, Caesar succeeded in finding the most vulnerable section of this natural defence line.

> The river is fordable at one point only and even there with difficulty. At this place he found large enemy forces drawn up on the opposite bank. The bank was also fenced by sharp stakes fixed along the edge, and he was told by prisoners and deserters that similar ones were concealed in the river-bed. He sent the cavalry across first and then at once ordered the infantry to follow. But the infantry went with such speed and impetuosity, although they had only their heads above water, that they attacked at the same moment as the cavalry. The enemy was overpowered and fled from the river-bank.

The British collapse is more easily explained if one accepts a story not mentioned by Caesar but preserved by a second-century historian:

> Caesar had with him a very large elephant, an animal which the Britons had never encountered before, and he had armoured it with iron scales. Upon its back he had put a large tower containing archers and slingers and he had sent it ahead into the river. The Britons were terrified at the sight of this huge and unknown beast, from the tower on whose back came a volley of arrows and stones, and one and all – men, horses and chariots – they turned tail and fled. Through the terror inspired by this single animal, the Romans were able to cross the river in safety.

> One biographer of Caesar has helpfully concluded that the elephant must have been Indian because African bush elephants were untamable and African forest elephants, such as Hannibal had used to cross the Alps 150 years before, were too small to support a howdah. Other writers, disappointingly, ignore the animal or suggest it belongs to some much later occasion and about its fate the records are silent.

> The point where Caesar got his army across the Thames, with or without an escorting elephant, is still not finally established. The Venerable Bede, around AD 730, stated that 'traces of these stakes can still be seen; cased in lead and thick as a man's thigh, they were fitted immovably in the river-bed'. William Camden, whose classic *Britannia*

★For a detailed study of Caesar's line of march see Vine *op. cit.*

appeared in 1586, identified the spot as the 'Koway' or 'Conway' Stakes, where the river was still barely six feet [2 m] deep at low tide. Recent writers have tended to favour Brentford in West London, just upstream from Kew Bridge, apparently on account of its name, and attempts have also been made, inconclusively, but not on the face of it unreasonably, to demonstrate that the Thames could be forded at Westminster, in the very heart of modern London.

About what happened after the Thames had been forded there is no uncertainty, thanks to Caesar himself:

Cassivellaunus had now given up all hope of fighting a pitched battle. Disbanding the greater part of his troops, he retained only some 4000 charioteers, with whom he watched our line of march. He would retire a short way from the route and hide in dense thickets, driving the inhabitants and cattle from the open country into the woods wherever he knew we intended to pass. If ever our cavalry incautiously ventured too far away in plundering and devastating the country, he would send all his charioteers out of the woods by well-known lanes and pathways and deliver very formidable attacks, hoping by this means to make them afraid to go far afield. Caesar was thus compelled to keep the cavalry in touch with the column of infantry and to let the enemy off with such devastation and burning as could be done under the protection of the legionaries – tired as they often were with marching.

The British tactics, to wage a guerrilla war, were clearly effective but insufficient by themselves to force the Romans to turn back. Perhaps Cassivellaunus hoped that, with the winter approaching – it must by now have been around early August – the Romans would before long withdraw of their own accord, as they had done a year earlier. In any case, with the legions invariably triumphant in the open field, and their success in assaulting fixed defences, as at Bigbury, already established, there was little else he could do. But in the end he was beaten by the desertion of his natural allies, and the shameful betrayal of the British cause by the man known ever afterwards as the 'Black Traitor' Mandubracius. His real name was Avarwy and he was probably the son of the recently dead king of the Trinovantes, who occupied Essex and southern Suffolk, and according to Caesar, 'had gone over to the continent to put himself under Caesar's protection, having fled for his life when his father the king of the Trinovantes was killed by Cassivellaunus'. He travelled back to his native country with Caesar, possibly to serve as chief interpreter and negotiator with the British, as well as potential puppet-king, under Roman control, of his old tribe.

During this march envoys arrived from the Trinovantes, about the strongest tribe in south-eastern Britain . . . The envoys promised to surrender and obey Caesar's commands and asked him to protect Mandubracius from Cassivellaunus and send him home to rule his people as king. Caesar demanded forty hostages and grain for his troops and then allowed Mandubracius to go. The Trinovantes promptly sent the required number of hostages and the grain.

The capitulation of the Trinovantes, aided perhaps by lingering envy and fear of Cassivellaunus's notoriously belligerent tribe, the Catuvellauni, started an understandable landslide of defections.

When they saw that the Trinovantes had been protected against Cassivellaunus and spared any injury on the part of the Roman troops, several other tribes, the Cenimagni, Segontiaci, Ancalites, Bibroci and Cassi, sent embassies and surrendered. From them Caesar learnt that he was not far from Cassivellaunus's stronghold, which was protected by forests and marshes and had been filled with a large number of men and cattle . . . He marched to the place with his legions and found that it was of great natural strength and excellently fortified.

Caesar was more fortunate in his informants than subsequent historians; the location of Cassivellaunus's capital remains uncertain, but is generally thought to have been Wheathampstead, in modern Hertfordshire, above five miles [8 km] north of St Albans on the River Lea, where remains still exist of a 100-acre [40-ha.] site surrounded by a ditch, 100 feet [30 m] wide and 30 feet [9 m] deep. Up to now Caesar had not been greatly impressed by the defences he had encountered. 'The British,' he commented, 'apply the term "strongholds" to densely wooded spots fortified with a rampart and trench.' For Cassivellaunus's capital, however, he felt some respect:

He marched to the place with his legions and found that it was of great natural strength and excellently fortified. Nevertheless he proceeded to assault it on two sides. After a short time the enemy proved unable to resist the violent attack of the legions and rushed out of the fortress on another side. A quantity of cattle was found there, and many of the fugitives were captured or killed.

Cassivellaunus himself escaped. While the Roman threat to his base had been developing he had been organizing a major counter-attack on a totally different front, 85 miles [137 km] away as the crow flies:

While these operations were proceeding in his territory, Cassivellaunus sent envoys to Kent ordering the four kings of that region, Cingetorix, Carvilius, Taximagulus and Segovax, to collect all their troops and make a surprise attack on the naval camp. When these forces appeared the Romans made a sortie, in which without suffering any loss they killed a great many of them and captured Lugotorix, a leader of noble birth.

The defeat of this unexpected assault may have owed something to Caesar himself, for around 5 August he had visited the base camp near Deal, which may have led to its local defences being strengthened. Its failure finally took the heart out of the British:

> On receiving news of this action, Cassivellaunus, alarmed by so many reverses, by the devastation of his country, and above all by the defection of his allies, sent envoys to Caesar to obtain terms of surrender, employing Commius as an intermediary. Caesar had decided to return to the continent for the winter, for fear any sudden rising should break out in Gaul. The summer, too, was nearly over, and he knew that the Britons could easily hold out for the short time that remained. Accordingly he granted Cassivellaunus's request for terms, demanding hostages, fixing an annual tribute to be paid by the Britons to the Roman government, and strictly forbidding Cassivel-launus to molest Mandubracius or the Trinovantes.

Agreement once reached, Caesar wasted no time:

> As soon as the hostages were delivered he led the army back to the coast, where he found the ships repaired. He had them launched, and as he had a large number of prisoners, and some of the ships had been destroyed by the storm, decided to make the return voyage in two trips. Of all these large fleets, not a single ship with troops on board was lost, while very few of the vessels coming over empty from the continent [built by Labienus in response to Caesar's earlier appeal] reached their destination. After waiting a long time for them in vain, Caesar was afraid of being prevented from sailing by the approaching season of the equinox and so had to pack the men more tightly than usual on the ships he had. The sea becoming very calm, he set sail late in the evening and brought all the fleet safely to land at dawn.

Thus ingloriously, and uncomfortably, on or about 27 September 54 BC, ended the second attempt to invade Britain. Had the British surrendered earlier, the expedition might have ushered in a permanent occupation. As it was, Caesar probably planned to return to complete the business later, but he never did. The campaign was clearly a failure. The Senate failed to award him any form of public thanksgiving, much less the coveted 'triumph' given Rome's greatest heroes on their return from the wars, and the opinion rapidly gained ground that Britain was barely worth conquering. The influential writer and politician, Marcus Tullius Cicero, whose own brother, Quintus, served in Britain, summed up the verdict of Roman society. 'It is now known,' he had written to a friend, even before the second expedition had sailed, 'that there is not a pennyweight of silver in the whole island and no hope of plunder except in the form of slaves.' Now Caesar, Cicero observed, was returning home with nothing to show for his losses and exertions, except some 'tribute' and the usual hostages.

Though the Roman mob rejoiced in the sight of seeing British captives in chains, and in Caesar's presentation to the goddess Venus of a chaplet of his favourite pearls – the only real fruits of the expedition – it became the received opinion among educated Romans that Britain was not worth acquiring.

The murder of Caesar in 44 BC granted the British Isles a long reprieve from the threat of invasion. Cut down as he arrived to address the Senate about yet another overseas campaign, in Asia, his two somewhat pointless expeditions to Britain were not mentioned in the posthumous indictment his assassins delivered against him. The Roman public talked constantly of a fresh expedition being prepared but it never sailed although one of the most famous Roman poets, Virgil, in the *Georgics*, published in 30 BC, described enthusiastically 'the crimson curtain' at the theatre 'rising embroidered with the figures of Britons' and boasted how 'the ends of the earth pay tribute', but the only Britons to be seen in Rome were emissaries from the still independent tribes, which had long ago defaulted on the annual levy they were supposed to send. In 34 BC, according to a contemporary historian, the emperor Augustus actually set out to invade Britain 'to outdo the feats of his adoptive father', i.e. Caesar, but a revolt elsewhere caused him to change his mind. Horace, in a work published around 30 BC, predicted that 'Augustus will be held a god among us when the Britons and the dangerous Persians have been added to the empire,' but it seemed that Augustus was going to have to wait for deification, for when, in 27 BC he tried again, he got no further than Gaul.

The following year Augustus was still breathing fire and slaughter at the Britons but once again his mighty vengeance remained unleashed, this time because of a rising in Northern Italy and a new war in Spain. So it continued; always there was some good reason for not actually setting sail and after AD 14 Augustus's successor, Tiberius, adopted a deliberate policy of non-expansion. Significantly, in AD 16, when some Roman soldiers were shipwrecked on the coast of Britain, they were returned to the continent unharmed.

Throughout the 80 years after Caesar's departure during which the British were left untroubled by foreign invasion, they made rapid progress towards developing a more orderly, even near-civilized, way of life. Cassivellaunus had made no attempt to rebuild his shattered capital but had created an entirely new one near where St Albans was soon to be built. His tribe, the powerful Catuvellauni, had consolidated their pre-eminent position in spite of their recent defeat, and spread in all directions until they controlled Cambridgeshire, Northamptonshire, Bedfordshire, Buckinghamshire, Middlesex and even eastern Oxford-shire and north-east Surrey. Another tribe altogether, the Coritani, were strong in the Midlands and North, including Leicestershire, Notting-hamshire, Lincolnshire and South Yorkshire. The Dobunni, outside the 'Belgic' group, were to be found in Hereford and Worcestershire, Warwickshire, Gloucestershire and west Oxfordshire and even as far south as Somerset. Also well-established in their respective areas were the Durotriges of Dorset, the Dumnonii of Devon, the Brigantes, who occupied most of the north, except the area around the Humber, which belonged to the Parisi, and the Iceni of Norfolk and north-west Suffolk. Little was known of the tribes in Wales. Tribal boundaries were still fluid and uncertain and distrust of one's neighbours widespread, as the continued proliferation of hill forts testified, but Roman goods dating from this period suggest a society stable enough for extensive commerce with the continent, and a number of rulers had established their own coinage, a sure mark of communal progress. The geographer Strabo, writing around 26 BC, provides the first list of British exports: gold, silver, slaves, hunting-dogs, grain, cattle, iron and hides. The Britons in return imported ivory, amber and glass, and – not mentioned by Strabo – wine, oil and pottery. This valuable trade must have been an important factor making, on the British side, for peace. To the Romans it was different, making a further invasion more attractive.

In AD 39–40 the Romans were given a new pretext for interference when the son of the king of Caesar's old adversaries, the Catuvellauni, was expelled by his father for some unspecified offence – conceivably for being too pro-Roman – and led a group of supporters across the Channel to seek sanctuary in the Roman empire. The emperor Gaius, better known as Caligula, in power from AD 37 to 41, has been euphemistically described as 'eccentric'; he was in fact a sadistic monster, now best remembered for having made his horse a consul and having declared himself a god; he was, not before time, assassinated and proved mortal. This unworthy successor to the great Caesar chose to regard the arrival of a handful of malcontents and runaways from Britain as a great victory, as Suetonius, born later that century, in AD 75, caustically described:

Gaius . . . wrote an extravagant despatch to Rome as if the whole island had surrendered to him, and ordered the couriers not to dismount from their post-chaise on reaching the outskirts of the city but make straight for the Forum and the Senate House, and take his letter to the Temple of Mars the Avenger for personal delivery to the Consuls in the presence of the entire Senate.

Preparations for what was to prove the most ludicrous and short-lived attempt to invade Britain were now undertaken:

In the end, he drew up his army in battle array facing the Channel and moved the arrow-casting machines and other artillery into position as though he intended to bring the campaign to a close. No one had the least notion what was in his mind when he gave the order: 'Gather sea-shells!' He referred to the shells as 'plunder from the ocean, due to the Capitol and to the Palace', and made the troops fill their helmets and tunic-laps with them; commemorating this victory by the erection of a tall lighthouse . . . in which fires were to be kept going all night as a guide to ships. Then he promised every soldier a bounty of four gold pieces, and told them: 'Go happy, go rich!' as though he had been excessively generous.

The 'tentative' of AD 40, to use a term coined by a later French writer to describe a planned invasion that never materialized, cannot be dismissed merely as the antics of a lunatic. Troops had clearly been assembled, ships collected and Caligula had done his best, in his own inimitable way, to endear himself to his men:

After reaching his headquarters, Gaius showed how keen and severe a commander-in-chief he intended to be by ignominiously dismissing any general who was late in bringing along from various places the auxiliaries he required. Then, when he reviewed the legions, he discharged many veteran leading-centurions on grounds of age and incapacity, though some had only a few more days of their service to run; and, calling the remainder a pack of greedy fellows, scaled down their retirement bonus to sixty gold pieces apiece.

Caligula was assassinated in AD 41, at the age of 29. His uncle, Claudius, widely regarded in Rome as a joke, was found by a guard cowering behind a curtain and with no other claimant on hand, found himself, no doubt to his astonishment, proclaimed emperor. More generous than the dead Caligula, he promptly 'promised every man 150 gold pieces'.

Claudius was no Julius Caesar but he was well aware that the safest way to ensure he did not suffer his predecessor's fate was to conduct a victorious campaign overseas and, thanks to Caligula's abortive 'seashell' invasion, the plans, shipping, port facilities and what would now be called the infrastructure for a major expedition already existed. So, too, did a convenient, more or less permanent *casus belli*, in the inter-tribal warfare endemic in the British Isles, as the greatest historian of the century, Tacitus, born in AD 55, later described:

> Once the Britons were obedient to kings; now they are torn apart by the warring parties of different leaders. There is, of course, from our point of view nothing more useful than if, when we are facing more than one strong enemy, they do not act in concert. It is very rare that two or more British tribes will come together to repel a common danger. They fight separately and are defeated separately.

The final, precipitating, factor was probably, as in Caesar's day, the fact that there were troops to spare. Although Spain, the Rhine and the Danube were now adequately guarded, two new legions had recently been formed, giving Claudius the opportunity, with minimum risk, to cut a dash where his predecessors had failed.

That the British might be entitled to live out their lives under their own rulers never seems to have entered into the Romans' consideration. 'Forget not, Roman,' declares the father of the supposed founder of Rome in the *Aeneid*, written around 20 BC, 'that it is your special genius to rule the peoples; to impose the ways of peace, to spare the defeated, and to crush those proud men who will not submit.' Outside the privileged circle of Roman citizenship they recognized only two categories of people, the recalcitrant and proud, *superbi*, and the dependent and despised, *subiecti*. The Britons, having belonged to the former were now, if Claudius had his way, to be demoted to the latter.

3
AN EASY TRIUMPH

He decided that Britain was the country where a real triumph could be most readily earned.

Suetonius, Claudius, *recalling AD 43*

Claudius's invasion of Britain, though he left others to direct it, was carefully planned. Leading the initial assault were two legions now known, semi-officially, by nicknames as well as numbers: II Augusta, from Strasbourg, named after the emperor who had raised it, and XX Valeria Victrix, from Cologne, whose title acknowledged the victories it had achieved under Valerius. Sailing with them, or directly afterwards, were XIV Gemina or 'twin', one of two formed from a single legion, drawn from Mainz, and IX Hispana, which had formerly served in Spain.

These were all experienced units, 'blooded' in recent fighting, and the commanders were selected with equal care. In supreme command was Aulus Plautius, a former consul and successful governor of Pannonia [now part of Hungary] an unruly province he had tamed, whose subordinates included a future emperor, Vespasian. Under their command, in addition to the 20,000 'regulars' of the legions, were about the same number of 'auxiliaries' recruited from the warlike peoples the Romans had conquered but now usually serving under Roman officers. They were commonly employed as archers, some units being wholly or partially mounted, or as cavalry.

The expedition of AD 43 almost ended before it had begun, for Aulus Plautius had no sooner got his men together and announced their destination than he found he had a mutiny on his hands. Dreading the sea and what lay beyond it the men refused to embark. Their embarrassed general had to send to Rome for help and Claudius despatched his chief secretary, Narcissus, as his personal spokesman, an inspired choice as it turned out. Narcissus was not a Roman citizen by birth but a freed slave and as he climbed up on the platform to address the legionaries someone started up the chant of 'Io, Saturnalia!', the cry with which slaves greeted each other during the feast of that name when the normal social order was overturned. The whole assembly dissolved in laughter and after it had calmed down there was no more trouble.

This third invasion, lacking a Caesar, is much less well-documented than its predecessors. It *is* known that the whole task force was split into three, and that after some, unspecified, difficulties on the crossing, one landing was probably near Chichester, and another somewhere near Richborough, between Ramsgate and Sandwich, about five miles [8 km] beyond Deal, where the Romans established their main camp and naval base. The site of the third landing, possibly a mere diversionary feint, is unknown.

Caesar's problem had been to get ashore and then fend off the Britons. Plautius's was that he could not bring them to battle. Cassivellaunus's successor, Cunobelinus, died before the Romans arrived, and command rested on his two anti-Roman sons – a third, as already mentioned, had deserted to the enemy – Caratacus [or Caraetacus], probably in charge in Kent, and Togodumnus in Hampshire. What followed was in many ways like 54 BC over again. The first major stand came along the River Medway, where men from inland reinforced the remnants of the two recently defeated armies. The battle, most unusually, lasted two days. On the first day the Britons were twice caught unawares by outflanking forces which unexpectedly got across the river undetected. First a 'Celtic' – presumably an 'auxiliary' or renegade British – unit crossed the river and killed the horses of the British charioteers, so that they could neither fight nor retreat; second, a force of regular legionaries assaulted them, under the command of Vespasian and his brother. On the second day the Britons came close to capturing one of the senior Roman officers, which so infuriated him that he led a violent counter-attack, driving them back in headlong retreat.

No attempt seems to have been made to hold the Thames. The Romans' 'auxiliary' cavalry swam across, the foot soldiers got over the river dryshod by a bridge, perhaps built by their field engineers. The British were harassed as they withdrew and, though the Romans lost some men in the marshes of the Lea Valley, continued to retreat into Essex where they turned and fought a delaying action.

About this time, though the details are unknown, Togodumnus was killed, and resistance began to stiffen, causing Plautius to abandon the pursuit and even, it seems, to pull back his men behind the Thames. He, as previously instructed, sent for the emperor, Claudius, who, once the real fighting was over wanted to be there to claim the credit for final victory: to secure a 'triumph' was the real object of the whole exercise.

It must have taken at least two months for him to arrive from Rome and the Roman sources are contradictory about what followed. That he arrived with the maximum pomp, accompanied by his own praetorian guard, is indisputable, but whether he saw any fighting is more doubtful. The best chronicler of the invasion says that he led a successful, opposed, crossing of the Thames, but as the Britons had not been able to defend it several months earlier a purely technical 'assault', with the emperor in front, seems more likely. At all events Claudius, a politician rather than a general, achieved precisely what he had set out to do. He marched in triumph into Colchester and received the submission of many of the tribes; he dictated terms of peace to the vanquished within the enemy capital, henceforward the centre of a new Roman province with Plautius as its governor; he was repeatedly hailed by the troops as *imperator*, a term reserved for victorious generals; and after 16 agreeable ego-boosting days was on his way back to Rome where he duly enjoyed his 'triumph' and had a majestic arch erected boasting that eleven kings had submitted to him without the loss of a single life, a 'Roman' life being understood. In Britain an even more striking monument was planned, a vast temple in its new Roman capital, Colchester, where Claudius was to be worshipped as a god.

Suetonius, writing in the next century was more impressed by Claudius's 'triumph' than by its cause:

> Claudius's sole campaign was of no great importance. The Senate had already voted him triumphal regalia, but he . . . decided that Britain was the country where a real triumph could be most readily earned. Its conquest had not been attempted since Julius Caesar's day . . . He marched north through Gaul until reaching Gesoriacum [Boulogne]; crossed the Channel from there and was back in Rome six months later. He had fought no battles and suffered no casualties, but reduced a large part of the island to submission. His triumph was a very splendid one and among those he invited to witness it were his provincial governors and certain exiles as well. The emblems of his victory included the naval crown [decorated with ships' prows] representing the crossing and conquest . . . of the ocean, which he put on the Palace gable beside the civic crown [of oak-leaves, awarded for saving citizens' lives]. His wife, Messalina, followed the chariot in a covered carriage and behind her marched the generals who had won triumphal regalia in Britain.

A Roman civilian might have supposed that the whole of Britain was now securely within the Roman Empire. A soldier serving there might have been more inclined to remark that it was now all over – bar the fighting. The invaders were now indeed well established ashore and the original bridgehead had broadened into such a large lodgement area that it was unlikely they could be expelled by force. They had already extended Rome's authority far further than Caesar had done, over most of southern England, as far west as Hertfordshire, where Cassivellaunus's former capital was about to be transformed into Roman Verulamium, later St Albans, and as far north as the more recent capital at Colchester, now Camulodunum. They enjoyed possession of the already important trading post and river crossing called Londinium and with a first-class port at Richborough (Rutupiae) their lines of communication with Gaul seemed secure. They had never yet, however, spent a winter in England and lurking somewhere – perhaps in the forests of the Midlands or the fens of East Anglia – was the still uncaptured Caratacus, with even more formidable, since unknown, enemies in the mountains of Wales and the distant uplands of Yorkshire and Dorset. As the grim northern winter came down in the months after Claudius's flying visit the final issue by no means seemed decided. The Romans occupied, at most, less than half of England, and a line drawn diagonally from the Wash to near present-day Bournemouth on the Channel marked the limits of their conquest. All now depended on the legions, easily outnumbered by the Britons but forming the most highly-trained and professional fighting force in the world.

In most countries, in most centuries, to serve as a conscript soldier was regarded as a misfortune and to volunteer to serve as one a disgrace. This was never true of the Roman Army, which offered to the poor man status, security and the chance of riches. Until not long before Caesar's time only men aged 17 to 46 who possessed some property were accepted as recruits. They provided their own arms and armour. Then, under Caesar's uncle, Marius, the rules were relaxed. Henceforward any Roman citizen could volunteer, irrespective of his wealth, and the legions were established on a permanent basis and offered a career for life, with regular pay and, more important, the hope of plunder, so that men enlisted eagerly under a general with a record of past victories. The rate of pay, 225 denarii a year, later raised to 300, was supplemented by a special grant, or 'donative', when a new emperor took office. As in every army compulsory deductions meant that a soldier saw little of his pay in cash. Apart from clothing and food a proportion of one's pay had to be saved, while each legion also had its own, voluntary, savings bank, and a burial club, to which contribution was compulsory. Pay was sometimes in arrears but there was not, until late on in the empire's history, any lack of recruits to sign on for 20 years plus another five as a 'veteran', or, under a change introduced in the first century AD, for a full 25 years with the colours. The Roman army offered attractive post-retirement benefits to its soldiers – a discharge bonus of 3000 denarii, or a grant of land, along with his accumulated savings. The sizeable plot of land provided was commonly on the frontiers of the empire or near one of its strongholds, so that the veteran helped to establish a permanent Roman presence and to provide a trained reserve in case of emergency.

Although there were many minor changes, the force which invaded Britain in AD 43 was in essentials the same as Caesar's and was to remain so throughout the Roman occupation. The basic formation, both for command purposes and administration, and the focus of a soldier's loyalty, was the legion, of roughly 5000 men: the number varied at different dates from 4800 to 6000 men and its actual strength might be smaller than its official establishment. About one-sixth were tradesmen who would bear arms only in dire emergency: engineers, architects, masons, clerks, cooks, bargemen, medical orderlies, pioneers. The fighting men themselves embraced several specialisms, including the *gaesati*, or spearmen, the *sagittarii*, or archers, and – sometimes mounted – the *exploratores* or scouts.

The legion was sub-divided into ten cohorts, the 'first cohort', a crack unit, being nearly double the size of the rest, with a fighting strength of about 800 as against the usual 480. The cohorts were split up into 'centuries', originally 100 men, now nearer 80, under the command of a centurion, so that there were 59 centuries in a legion. The centuries were further sub-divided into ten units of eight men each, known as *conturbernia* because they shared a tent, a useful arrangement which encouraged unit loyalty. In action, a man looked first for his tent-mates, then for the cohort's distinctive standard and then for his legion's eagle, while listening for commands from his centurion's voice or the commander's trumpet.

In the Roman army the foot-soldier was king. A legion's 120 mounted men, in four *turmae* around 30 strong, were scouts and messengers rather than true cavalry. These were of humbler status, usually drawn from the *auxilia*, serving in *alae*, or wings, of 16 *turmae*, being on paper – the actual strength was usually less – 512 strong, though at least one deployed in Britain was twice this size. The auxiliaries were also sometimes sub-divided into mounted cohorts, of *cohors equitata*, of about 80 men, and *cohors peditata*, or infantry, made up of six centuries of 80 men each. In the course of time the auxiliaries came to outnumber the regular legionaries and to share their privileges. Before Augustus raised the first auxiliaries, in the long reign which ended in AD 14, only Roman citizens had been allowed to serve in the Roman army, but the new force drew on all the provinces administered by Rome, and though it accepted volunteers, was kept up to strength by conscription.

The auxiliaries had good reason to feel disgruntled at their treatment; the infantry were paid one-third, the cavalry only two-thirds of what a Roman legionary received, but a man who completed 25 years service qualified for Roman citizenship and even its retrospective grant to his children, which meant that his sons could become legionaries.

The quality of recruits was high. In the Claudian, and post-Claudian, period no one below 5 ft 10 in [1.77 m] was accepted for the first cohort, and no one below 5 ft 7 in [1.7 m] for the rest and a man had to be of free birth and good character; illegitimacy, provided one's father was a soldier, was no bar. The normal age limits on joining were 18 to 23, but recruits as young as 13 and as old as 36 were sometimes accepted. Later, standards slipped. By the reign of Diocletian (AD 284–305) the lower height limit had become general even for first cohorts, recruits were accepted between 19 and 35 and – an ominous sign – were branded on enlistment to discourage desertion.

The Romans had an elaborate military hierarchy. The lowest rank of NCOs, *immunes*, so called because they were exempt from fatigues, were technicians and clerks, but received no extra pay. Next came the *principales*, with from 50 to 100 per cent more than the ordinary legionary. They provided the standard-bearers in the cohorts and were expected to give a lead in battle. Above them were the *duplicarii*, each of whom received double pay and was second-in-command of a century. The structure in auxiliary units was similar.

Each legion included 60 officers, roughly one to each 100 men, though the name 'centurion' embraced various ranks from the junior lieutenants or *primi ordines* up to a single *primuspilus*, equivalent to a full colonel. One specialist, the *cornicularius*, was in charge of the legion's headquarters staff and there was a permanent orderly officer, the *benificarius*. Above this level were non-regimental officers, often men of social standing and political influence in Rome but not career soldiers. The commander of a legion had served as a senator in Rome and was known as the legionary legate, or *legatus legionis*; earlier in life he would have been a military tribune, i.e. a young man of standing attached to a senior commander to gain military experience. The military tribunes came in two versions, 'broad-striped' and 'narrow-striped'. The former were short-term 'attachees' sponsored by the senate – a senator wore a broad strip on his toga – the latter were career officers gaining command experience, the two groups together providing the legion's commanding officer with his staff.

Provided he did everything 'by the book', even a poor commander fighting, as the Romans always were, against less sophisticated forces, was unlikely to stumble into a major disaster. Being surprised at night was, for example, almost ruled out since the regulations, religiously adhered to, required a temporary fort to be built, to a set pattern, whenever a detachment halted for the night. The site for this 'marching camp' would be selected by surveyors sent on ahead and the troops when they arrived would immediately dig out a ditch three feet [1 m] wide and deep and raise an earth rampart around five feet [1.5 m] high, to be topped with the stakes – two per man – carried by the legionaries. The rolled-up leather tents carried by the unit's mules would then be erected, also according to a standard layout. The centurion's smaller, but single, tent was placed at the end of the eight containing his 'century', the commander's more impressive one in the centre. Ovens, latrines and rubbish pits were all discreetly built or dug in regular, predetermined places. Marching camps designed for more than overnight occupation would be larger and stronger.

To a heavily-burdened foot soldier, tramping wearily into the night's resting place after a long day's march over the windswept fells, having then to turn to with his spade must have been anything but welcome, but constant practice made the legions quick and adept. In one campaign, in Asia, despite the hot climate, four legions between them built nearly five miles [8 km] of earth ramparts in only three days.

Although the legionary's trade was an innately dangerous one everything possible had been done to lessen the risks to which he was exposed. Centurions and standard bearers, who were in particular danger, usually wore chain mail, but the ordinary foot soldier was almost as well protected by a strong but flexible cuirass, consisting of metal plates at back and front and over his shoulders held together by leather straps. Above this was a helmet, made of bronze or iron with a curved guard at the back to protect the neck, while the lower part of his body was protected by an apron of metal-bound thongs worn like a sporran, and his feet by heavily-studded boots shaped like sandals. In close combat he could protect himself with his *scutum*, a large, curved, rectangular shield, which could also be used as a weapon.

Every legionary carried two javelins (*pila*) about seven feet long, which could kill a man at 30 yards [27 m], and were deliberately made with an iron shaft which bent on impact, so that, once stuck in an enemy shield, it could neither be dislodged nor pulled out and thrown back. The unfortunate bearer of the shield would therefore be forced to discard it and the legionary would then close in to finish him off with his *gladius*, a short, two-feet [0.6-m] long sword with a wide blade and point, designed to be used for thrusting with a stabbing motion, not all-round slashing. A wound two inches [5 cm] deep from a *gladius* was often fatal and, if that failed, or the legionary was apparently disarmed, he still had his *pugio*, or dagger.

Auxilia were more cheaply equipped, sometimes with 'mail' armour formed by a series of linked rings, more often by 'scale', consisting of overlapping metal strips sewn on to a fabric or leather backing to form a shirt reaching to the thigh, slit at the sides for cavalrymen. Both cavalry and infantry wore helmets but the latter also carried a flat oval or hexagonal shield. The cavalry were armed with a longer sword designed for slashing not thrusting, the *spatha*, and three spears which could also be used as lances.

To engage the enemy at longer range every legion contained a small contingent of archers, some of whom might be mounted. They were armed with a short bow strengthened with horn. In hand-to-hand fighting they used a short axe. Slings, of which more will be said later, were also used to hurl stones, by soldiers specially trained in this art.

Artillery was important in the conquest of the British Isles since the Britons lacked any answer to it, and, properly sited in permanent fortifications, it enabled a small Roman garrison to hold down large stretches of countryside. The 'field artillery' of the Roman army, which travelled with it, consisted largely of *catapultae*, mounted on carts drawn by mules. These were outsize bows made of animal gut which, by turning the handspikes on a wheel, could be tightened sufficiently to hurl a heavy javelin 1000 yards [920 m]. Equally mobile and dangerous was the *cheiroballista*, a spring gun operated by twisted sinews in metal drums, given tension by the use of levers and firing 12-in [30-cm] long metal-tipped bolts. Vespasian's Second Legion (II Augusta) alone may have had as many as 60 and used them to devastating effect. The Romans also deployed heavy siege artillery, though getting this into position was a massive undertaking only contemplated as a last resort, and its fire – unlike that of the *catapultae* and *ballistae* – was extremely inaccurate. The weapon the Romans used was the onager, meaning 'wild ass', so-called because of its violent kick. The onager consisted of a heavy beam supported at one end between two uprights and forced down at the other by a rope fastened to a winch. When the firing catch was released the beam shot upwards hurling a stone weighing a hundredweight [112 lb or 50 kg] up to a quarter of a mile [440 yards or 400 m].

To confront this fearsome fighting force no single 'British army' existed. Even the most aggressive tribe could not keep its menfolk permanently under arms and campaigning had to be fitted in between the more compelling imperatives of seedtime and harvest. The only full-time soldiers were the charioteers, the aristocrats of their communities, who could leave others to till their land for them. Caesar had testified to their surprise and shock value but they were not so successful against determined infantry drawn up in regular formations and the hillier terrain of the north and west was far less suited to their use than the plains and gentler slopes of the south and east. Contrary to legend, they probably did not have scythe-like blades* attached to their wheels and their chief use in the long campaign now beginning was to ferry a few warriors rapidly into and out of battle. The charioteers were immensely skilled but the ordinary British foot soldier was for all practical purposes untrained, especially in manoeuvring in action. With troops unaccustomed to acting together, and with no real command structure or communications system all the chieftain in charge could do was draw up a simple plan which everyone could understand and stick to it, almost irrespective of how events developed. Exploiting a sudden opportunity for an attack was usually beyond him, while in a defensive battle on anything like equal terms his men were bound to be outclassed. A few, exceptionally well-off, noblemen owned helmets and shields, but most Britons turned out to fight in nothing but a pair of trousers, or even stark naked to facilitate swimming rivers. Their chief weapon was a long sword, designed for 'slashing' rather than 'thrusting' so that it needed room to be used to full effect and was little use in what was later called the *mêlée*, when ranks were broken in a general free-for-all. Before this hand-to-hand stage was reached they used javelins, bows – though little mention is made of them – and, their only real distance weapon, slings, which in expert hands could hurl a two-ounce [60-gm] rounded stone up to 200 yards [180 m] with remarkable accuracy. Stocks of pebbles from nearby beaches have been found in the remains of houses in settlements of the period, including no fewer than 20,000 in a single mound at Maiden Castle in Dorset.

It was fortresses such as this to which the Britons now looked for survival. Britain was rich in hill forts, some going back to the Bronze Age, around 850 BC, though the main period of building, and the strengthening of those constructed earlier, began around 500 BC and ended abruptly with the main Roman invasion.

Initially created to shelter a tribe against its envious neighbours the hill forts now had to provide long-term protection against invaders. A few were well-sited for this, the so-called 'promontory' forts, accessible only from the land on a high, projecting peninsula and surrounded on three sides by tall cliffs and the sea. The Cornish coasts contained many such strongholds – hard to take by assault but almost impossible to escape from – and still provide some fine examples, like Maen Castle near Land's End. A few were also built on similarly isolated sites above river valleys. The overwhelming majority of the 3000 hill forts which still survive, about half of them in Scotland, were of the 'contour' type, where a ditch was dug out to follow the contour line round the summit

*Although some early writers mention the scythe, none of the best sources, including Caesar, do so and its existence is not supported by archaeological evidence.

of a hill, or sometimes the whole of it. The fortification might consist of a single ditch and bank enclosing an area no more than 70 yards [60 m] across covering less than an acre [0.4 ha.], but there were far more elaborate works with six or seven successive lines of defence, as at Old Oswestry in Shropshire. The majority lay between these extremes, occupying from one to 30 acres [0.4–12 ha.]. The men who undertook these huge projects, with no engineering knowledge and only the most primitive tools, had no textbooks or training to guide them, only a mass of willing labour spurred on by fear. The basic thinking behind the design was simple; the enemy could not be kept at a distance so he must be trapped in the ditch outside the ramparts from which he could be assailed with spears and stones. The building process was equally straightforward. As earth was dug out to form the ditch it was piled up behind it to form a rampart or *glacis*, sometimes topped by a wooden fence for additional protection. In the strongest forts there might be a further wall, of earth or stones, held in place by wooden revetments, with a path behind them wide enough for a man to patrol. To protect the entrance a separate outwork would be built to cover the main gateway, or there might be a staggered way which forced an attacker to slow down. The gateway itself was blocked by tree-trunks, barricades of thorn bushes or heavy gates pivoting on solid uprights, and sometimes topped by a catwalk for look-outs. Occasionally there were other deterrents. At one fort at Bredon Hill in Worcestershire, six severed heads were displayed over the gate, but the results were disappointing; archaeological evidence – 64 mutilated bodies inside the earthworks – shows that the defenders were finally overwhelmed.

The strongest forts presented the attacker with a steeply sloping wall 40 feet [12 m] high between the bottom of the ditch and the top of the rampart behind it. Most were less ambitious in scale but might have other refinements, as at Ladle Hill, near Kingsclere in Hampshire, where the material dug out was carefully graded to use the largest pieces of chalk as the foundations of the rampart, though the plan proved too complicated and the fort remained unfinished. Experiments in similar soil at Overton Down in Wiltshire, using, as the builders of the earlier forts did, picks made of deer antlers, shovels made of oxen's shoulder blades and wicker baskets to remove the spoil have demonstrated that one energetic male can build 12 cubic feet [0.3 cu. m.] of ditch and rampart in a day, but by the first century AD iron was commonplace and progress must have been much faster. If properly organized gangs were used, a medium-sized fort of about eight acres [3.2 ha.] could have been enclosed by a single ditch backed by a bank in about four months.

The hill forts were very unevenly distributed, mainly following the upland pattern of southern England, though there were smaller concentrations in Kent and Essex, in Derbyshire and West Yorkshire, and in a broad strip along the Welsh borders. Some sites have now disappeared for ever, or, conceivably, have not been discovered, but in Devon and Cornwall alone remains exist of 294, while the 'frontier' counties have sizeable numbers: Shropshire 43, Herefordshire 28, Gloucestershire 60, and Powys (formerly Montgomeryshire, Radnorshire and Brecknockshire) 105. These are mainly small. The really large and elaborate forts are almost all in Wessex; Hampshire has 50, Wiltshire 49, Dorset 31.

Thus, following the invasion of AD 43 the Romans were confronted by a dozen substantial forts along the ridge of the Marlborough Downs in Wiltshire, from Ashdown to Devizes, and across the highest section of Salisbury Plain from Upavon near Pewsey to Warminster, followed by others near Wilton and Shaftesbury in Dorset. Just outside modern Dorchester was the still unspoilt and spectacular Maiden Castle, where four successive circles of banks and ditches enclosed an area nearly 700 yards [600 m] by 300 [275 m]. The way towards it was commanded by several almost as imposing. Two, Hambledon Hill and Hod Hill, crowned the high ground beside what is now the road from Shaftesbury to Blandford Forum, the latter, excavation suggests, having rows of round huts arranged along winding streets, some with walled courtyards used for stabling horses. There was probably a catwalk over the main gateway at the end of a tunnel-like entrance, and the resident chieftain occupied a larger hut than his subjects, near the centre of the enclosure. Beyond Blandford, on the road to the coast, was a third major fort, Spettisbury Rings.

Precisely when, and in what order, these hitherto almost impregnable fortresses fell is uncertain, but it was probably early on in Aulus Plautius's invasion and perhaps even before Claudius arrived. A seaborne landing in Dorset by the Second Legion seems unlikely, since they had sailed with the first wave of assault troops, but they may have marched along the coast from Southampton, attacking Maiden Castle first and then working their way inland, rather than following the more obvious route south-west from Wiltshire across Salisbury Plain. The whole operation, in which the culture and liberty of an ancient people was extinguished in a few weeks, is cursorily, almost casually, dismissed by Suetonius in his biography of the general directing it:

Vespasian . . . proceeded to Britain, where he fought 30 battles, subjugated two warlike tribes, and captured more than 20 towns, besides the entire Isle of Vectis [i.e. Wight].

No eye-witness account exists of any of these attacks and even the archaeological evidence is scanty. We do not know whether it was a glorious autumn day as the legions spread out over the springy green hillside to storm Maiden Castle or whether the dank Dorset mist or a grey winter drizzle engulfed it. What we do know is that Vespasian probably swept the defenders of the successive lines of ramparts with ballista fire, to which they had no answer, and then attacked the weaker, eastern entrance. The smoke from huts outside the gate, to which he set fire, provided a smokescreen, under cover of which the legionaries, sword in hand, moved remorselessly forward. A fierce battle followed. Thirty-eight skeletons have been unearthed near the entrance, presumably buried where they fell, all with deep head wounds – nine of them, in the case of one man who must have put up a terrific fight for his life. The gates were finally destroyed, a standard Roman practice when a town was taken, and a large breach driven through the walls.

At Spettisbury Rings, the next place to be subdued, if the Romans advanced inland, as suggested earlier, resistance was no less ferocious, as the remains of the 80 bodies, many bearing sword wounds, later recovered from an earth-filled ditch testify. Hod Hill, possibly the capital of the Durotriges if this was not at Dorchester, may have put up a less prolonged resistance, for no signs remain of a struggle around the gates. The occupants may have been cowed and battered into surrender by a sustained bombardment, for the Romans erected a tower 600 yards [540 m] away and mounted on it *catapultae* or *ballistae* which put down a devastating fire on the interior of the fort; the chief's hut, in the centre, was apparently their aiming-point, for eight metal bolts were later found within its foundations. Here, unusually, the Romans permanently occupied the heights they had gained, building a small fort within the walls, and mounting artillery on platforms to command the approaches. The legions then resumed their advance westward to subdue what was probably the second tribe mentioned by Suetonius, the Dumnonii. Worlebury, near Weston-super-Mare, in Somerset, where 18 skeletons have been found, and Hembury, near Honiton in Devon, were probably conquered by the seemingly invincible Second Legion. By then its commander was apparently back in Rome, for he took part in Claudius's great triumph in AD 44, and his chief of staff was awarded the 'mural crown' for his capture of so many fortresses.

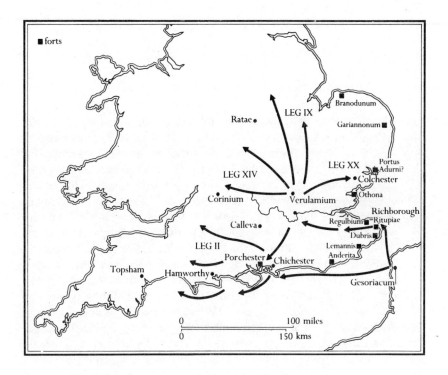

The coming of Rome. Roman landings and lines of advance 43 AD, and forts built later.

4

A DISTURBED AND PERILOUS STATE

Neither before nor since has Britain ever been in a more disturbed and perilous state.

Tacitus, Agricola, *recalling AD 61*

After the departure of Claudius late in AD 43 the legions pressed on remorselessly in all directions. Vespasian's II Augusta, having tamed Wiltshire and Dorset, now turned its attention to the Dumnonii of Devon and Cornwall. It may, by AD 47, have reached Exeter; ten years later, after its commander had been showered with honours on his return to Rome, where he eventually became emperor (AD 69–79), II Augusta, or its successors, built a permanent fort at Nanstallon, near Bodmin. The absorption of the whole south and west of England into the Empire was complete. The Ninth Legion marched north-east through Cambridgeshire and round the edge of the still undrained Fens. It then pushed on to Lincoln and, possibly after a detour via Leicester and the Midlands, when Plautius left England, in autumn AD 47, may already have reached the Humber. Legion XIV had meanwhile, it appears, been sent north-west into Shropshire, subduing en route the area around Cirencester in the Cotswolds, perhaps supported by Legion XX, which then became the left 'prong' of an advance into Wales via Gloucester.

The precise pattern of occupation during this third stage of the invasion, when the Romans had clearly come to stay, is hard to chart since legions were often split into detachments called 'vexillations', used to hold down areas already conquered, or where no real resistance was expected. The limit of Roman penetration by this time was a line running from near Topsham in Devon via Cirencester, Leicester and Lincoln to the Humber near Burton at the mouth of the Trent, soon to be marked out for most of its length by a major Roman road, the Fosse Way. From this backbone roads were built by the legions, aided by gangs of British forced labourers, to connect up the forts and towns which became the visible signs of Rome's supremacy.

The roads, many built in the first half-century after AD 43, were crucial in securing and retaining Rome's grip on the island. Plunging straight as a legionary's arrow across hill and river, through waste and woodland, the routes they followed still remain the most widespread legacy the occupation left behind. Although the roads were not paved, layers of smaller gravel-like stones were laid upon the larger rocks beneath, providing a surface usable in all seasons and well-provided with bridges and paved fords. Ultimately 5000 miles [8000 km] of road, usually 20–24 feet [6–8.3 m] wide, were built, but the road system was already taking shape by around AD 47. London, with its bridge, was soon the most important communications centre in the country, from which Watling Street ran north-west to Wroxeter. Another road, which later became the Portway, ran south-west to Silchester and, in due course, Dorchester; and Ermine Street ran north to Lincoln and, when the legions fought their way to it, the Humber, York and – after dividing at Piercebridge – to Carlisle and Corbridge on the Scottish border.

To Aulus Plautius, when he returned to Rome at the end of his period as first governor of the province in AD 47, it must have seemed that Britannia was now secure. Claudius, who had already seized most of the credit, was grateful. 'He granted Aulus Plautius an ovation' – a formal honour inferior only to a 'triumph', which was reserved for the imperial family – Suetonius recorded, 'going out to meet him when he entered the city and courteously giving him the wall' – i.e. the place of honour – 'on his way up to the Capitol and down again.'

Aulus Plautius was followed by Ostorius Scapula, 'both of them fine soldiers', according to Tacitus. It was the settlement imposed by Ostorius on hitherto friendly peoples who had peacefully accepted Roman over-lordship that now precipitated far more serious trouble. To maintain their far-flung empire the Romans had always relied on securing the cooperation of the most influential rulers in the captured territories wherever they would agree to preside over 'client-kingdoms'. The main factor in the fierce and widespread opposition the Romans now encountered, however, was – as so often in war – the inspiring leadership of an outstanding personality, Caratacus, worthy son of a famous father, a natural soldier, who since his defeat at the hands of Aulus Plautius back in AD 43 had merely been biding his time in the natural fastness of the Welsh mountains. His leadership, skilful enough to reconcile the normally feuding tribes into a formidable anti-Roman force and popular enough to enable him to challenge the enemy in one tribal area after another, transformed a series of local risings into something approaching a national rebellion:

Next Ostorius invaded Silurian territory [i.e. the area around the Severn where Gloucestershire adjoins South Wales]. The natural ferocity of the inhabitants was intensified by their belief in the prowess of Caratacus, whose many undefeated battles – and even many victories – had made him pre-eminent among British chieftains. His deficiency in strength was compensated by superior cunning and topographical knowledge. Transferring the war to the country of the Ordovices [i.e. Central Wales], he was joined by everyone who found the prospect of a Roman peace alarming. Then Caratacus staked his fate on a battle. He selected a site where numerous factors – notably approaches and escape-routes – helped him and impeded us. On one side there were steep hills. Wherever the gradient was gentler, stones were piled into a kind of rampart. And at his front there was a river without easy crossings. The defences were strongly manned.

The site of this epic battle remains a mystery, though probably on the Severn, but, thanks to Tacitus, its course is not in dispute:

The British chieftains went round their men, encouraging and heartening them to be unafraid and optimistic . . . Caratacus, as he hastened to one point and another, stressed that this was the day, this the battle, which would either win back their freedom or enslave them for ever. He invoked their ancestors, who by routing Julius Caesar had valorously preserved their present descendants from Roman officials and taxes – and their wives and children from defilement. These exhortations were applauded. Then every man swore by his tribal oath that no enemy weapons would make them yield – and no wounds either.

This eagerness dismayed the Roman commander, disconcerted as he already was by the river-barrier, the fortifications supplementing it, the overhanging cliffs and the ferocious crowds of defenders at every point. But our soldiers shouted for battle, clamouring that courage could overcome everything; and their leaders spoke to the same effect, to encourage them further.

After a reconnaissance to detect vulnerable and invulnerable points, Ostorius led his enthusiastic soldiers forward. They crossed the river without difficulty, and reached the rampart. But then, in an exchange of missiles, they came off worse in wounds and casualties. However, under a roof of locked shields, the Romans demolished the crude and clumsy stone embankment, and in the subsequent fight at close quarters the natives were driven to the hill-tops. Our troops pursued them closely. While light-armed auxiliaries attacked with javelins, the heavy regular infantry advanced in close formation. The British, unprotected by breastplates or helmets, were thrown into disorder. If they stood up to the auxiliaries they were cut down by the swords and spears of the regulars, and if they faced the latter they succumbed to the auxiliaries' broadswords and pikes. It was a great victory. Caratacus's wife and daughter were captured; his brother surrendered.

Caratacus, forging another link in the legend that surrounded him, escaped and fled north into the territory of the Brigantes, who had a long anti-Roman tradition, but whose sovereign, Cartimandua, had recently made her peace with Rome. Tacitus describes the sequel: 'He was arrested and handed over to the conquerors.'

When Caratacus reached Rome, in AD 51, he was, though a prisoner, regarded as a hero and, looking round at the splendours of Imperial Rome, is said to have asked: 'Why, when you had all this, did you covet our poor huts?' Caratacus's brave example had inspired a whole series of new risings against the Romans in Britain, as Tacitus frankly chronicled:

> Battle followed battle. They were mostly guerrilla fights, in woods and bogs. Some were accidental – the results of chance encounters. Others were planned with calculated bravery. The motives were hatred or plunder. Sometimes these engagements were ordered by the generals; sometimes they knew nothing of them.
>
> The Silures were exceptionally stubborn. They were enraged by a much-repeated saying of the Roman commander that they must be utterly exterminated . . . Two auxiliary battalions, which their greedy commanders had taken plundering with insufficient precautions, fell into a trap laid by the Silures. Then they began, by gifts of spoils and prisoners, to tempt other tribes to join their rebellion.
>
> At this point, exhausted by his anxious responsibilities, Ostorius died. The enemy exulted that so considerable a general, if not defeated in battle, had at least been eliminated by warfare. On hearing of the governor's death the emperor, not wanting to leave the province masterless, appointed Aulus Didius Gallus to take over.

Tacitus, who clearly disliked Didius, describes with relish what followed:

> Didius made for Britain rapidly. But he found a further deterioration. For in the interval a Roman brigade . . . had suffered a reverse. Reports were magnified. The enemy magnified them, to frighten the new general; and the new general magnified them to increase his glory if he won, and improve his excuse if resistance proved unbreakable. Again the damage was due to the Silures; until deterred by Didius's arrival, they plundered far and wide.

Didius had barely been replaced by Quintus Veranius in AD 58, supposedly a 'strong man', famous for a successful campaign in the mountains of Southern Turkey, when the latter, too, died, worn out by his struggles with the Welsh tribes. *His* successor, C. Suetonius Paulinus – confusingly he is referred to by both names – also arrived with an impressive record won in the Atlas mountains of Morocco, and immediately turned his attention to North Wales, which had beaten both his predecessors.

After two years campaigning spent in successfully marching his forces through that most inhospitable of regions, Paulinus felt ready to attack Anglesey, called by the Romans Mona, the centre of the Druid religion, which had 'given sanctuary to many refugees' says Tacitus. Many myths have gathered round the Druids, but the Romans believed, probably with some justice, that they had given to the British resistance the character of a holy war, and good military reasons existed for trying to eliminate it.

Tacitus admirably described the epic battle which followed:

Flat-bottomed boats were built to contend with the shifting shallows and these took the infantry across. Then came the cavalry; some utilized fords, but in deeper water the men swam beside their horses. The enemy lined the shore in a dense armed mass. Among them were black-robed women with dishevelled hair like Furies, brandishing torches. Close by stood Druids, raising their hands to heaven and screaming dreadful curses. This weird spectacle awed the Roman soldiers into a sort of paralysis. They stood still – and presented themselves as a target. But then they urged each other (and were urged by the general) not to fear a horde of fanatical women. Onward pressed their standards and they bore down their opponents, enveloping them in the flames of their own torches. Suetonius garrisoned the conquered island. The groves devoted to Mona's barbarous superstitions he demolished. For it was their religion to drench their altars in the blood of prisoners and consult their gods by means of human entrails.

Suetonius Paulinus was not left long to enjoy his victory. He was still on the far side of the Menai Straits, consolidating his hold on the newly conquered island, when news reached him of a rising on the far side of the country. The Iceni of Norfolk, after an unsuccessful rebellion in the early days of Roman rule, had settled down to live in reasonable harmony with the invaders under their king Prasutagus. Now he had died: whether in AD 59 or early in AD 61 is uncertain. He left his throne to his widow, Boudicca,* with their two daughters as her heirs, making the Roman emperor a joint heir as a device to try and guarantee them their inherit-

*The traditional form 'Boadicea' seems to derive from a copying error. I have followed Peter Salway, *Roman Britain*, published 1981, in favouring 'Boudicca', but some writers I have quoted prefer 'Boudica'.

ance. The attempt, a familiar legalistic fiction, failed. The Romans chose to regard the special relationship which Prasutagus had enjoyed as ending with his death; the royal line was considered extinguished; Iceni citizens were conscripted into the Roman army, to serve against their fellow Britons; and the ill-judged legacy to Nero, who had succeeded to the imperial throne in AD 54, was treated by the local Romans, as Tacitus admitted, as a licence to do what they liked with the royal family and their property:

> Kingdom and household alike were plundered like prizes of war, the one by Roman officers, the other by Roman slaves. As a beginning, his [i.e. Prasutagus's] widow Boudicca was flogged and their daughters raped. The Icenian chiefs were deprived of their hereditary estates as if the Romans had been given the whole country. The king's own relatives were treated like slaves. And the humiliated Iceni feared still worse, now that they had been reduced to provincial [i.e. ordinary colonial] status. So they rebelled.

What converted a serious but isolated tribal rising into a near-national rebellion was that the Romans, neglecting their own precept to 'divide and rule', had dealt with equal insensitivity with another basically friendly tribe, the Trinovantes of Essex. The unfortunate residents of Colchester, in addition to the taxes common throughout the empire, were subjected to constant demands to support the vast temple raised to Claudius's memory, while the 'colony' of discharged soldiers requiring land was ever expanding. Tacitus was under no illusions about the Trinovantes' grievances:

> They particularly hated the Roman ex-soldiers who had recently established a settlement at Camulodunum. The settlers drove the Trinovantes* from their homes and land and called them prisoners and slaves. The troops encouraged the settlers' outrages, since . . . they looked forward to similar licence for themselves. Moreover, the temple erected to the divine Claudius was a blatant stronghold of alien rule, and its observances were a pretext to make the natives appointed as its priests drain the whole country dry.

Though the Roman historians later garnished their stories of the great revolt with colourful tales of omens and portents the storm when it broke seems to have taken the local commanders by surprise. Colchester, the scene of surrender 17 years before, was the first place to feel the Britons' fury:

---

*Trinobantes in the original. I have followed the form adopted by Salway, as with other names.

It seemed easy to destroy the settlement; for it had no walls. That was a matter which the Roman commanders, thinking of amenities rather than needs, had neglected. At this juncture, for no visible reason, the Statue of Victory at Camulodunum fell down – with its back turned, as though it were fleeing the enemy. Delirious women chanted of destruction at hand. They cried that in the local senate-house outlandish yells had been heard; the theatre had echoed with shrieks; at the mouth of the Thames a phantom settlement had been seen in ruins. A blood-red colour in the sea, too, and shapes like human corpses left by the ebb tide, were interpreted hopefully by the Britons – and with terror by the settlers.

With no military commander nearby they turned to the governor's civilian colleague and chief financial officer, the hated provincial procurator, Decianus Catus, whose ruthless greed had helped to precipitate the present outbreak.

He sent them barely two hundred men, incompletely armed. There was also a small garrison on the spot. Reliance was placed on the temple's protection. Misled by secret pro-rebels, who hampered their plans, they dispensed with rampart or trench. They omitted also to evacuate old people and women and thus leave only fighting men behind . . .

Then a native horde surrounded them. When all else had been ravaged or burnt, the garrison concentrated itself in the temple. After two days' siege it fell by storm. The Ninth Roman division . . . attempted to relieve the town, but was stopped by the victorious Britons and routed. Its entire infantry force was massacred, while the commander escaped to his camp with his cavalry and sheltered behind its defences . . . Catus Decianus, horrified by the catastrophe and by his unpopularity, withdrew to Gaul.

The camp to which the routed commander withdrew with his cavalry was probably that of the 'vexillation' at Longthorpe near Peterborough, which shows signs of desperate efforts to strengthen its fortifications around this time. About the seriousness of the situation Tacitus, looking back years later when writing the biography of an officer then serving as a 'broad-stripe' military tribune in one of Suetonius's legions, was in no doubt:

Neither before nor since has Britain ever been in a more disturbed and perilous state. Veterans had been massacred, colonies burned to the ground, armies cut off. They had to fight for their lives before they could think of victory.

The defeat of a legion in the field by mere barbarians was almost unprecedented; so was the loss of a large area like East Anglia. But whatever his defects as a governor Suetonius was not lacking in physical courage nor in the moral courage to take unpalatable decisions, as Tacitus confirms:

> Suetonius, undismayed, marched through disaffected territory to Londinium. This town did not rank as a Roman settlement, but was an important centre for business-men and merchandise. At first, he hesitated whether to stand and fight there. Eventually, his numerical inferiority – and the price only too clearly paid by the divisional commander's rashness [i.e. in attacking superior forces in East Anglia] – decided him to sacrifice the single city of Londinium to save the province as a whole. Unmoved by lamentations and appeals, Suetonius gave the signal for departure.

Hardening his heart, never very difficult for a Roman officer, and ignoring the tears and pleas of the abandoned civilians, since only those fit enough to travel with the army were able to accompany him, Suetonius set off back along Watling Street towards the Midlands. The layers of ashes discovered centuries later amid the foundations of ruined Roman buildings bear mute witness to what happened after his departure, while Tacitus briefly dismisses the fate of their former occupants: 'Those who stayed because they were women, or old, or attached to the place, were slaughtered by the enemy.'

On his way north Suetonius stopped briefly at the next important Roman town, Verulamium, which was near the site of the capital which Cassivellaunus had built a century before. Now his descendants were to have their revenge, for Suetonius took the same hard decision as he had done in London and with the same inevitable result: 'Verulamium,' records Tacitus succinctly, 'suffered the same fate.'

When there were no Roman civilians left to kill, the British horde – it was accompanied by so many non-combatants it could hardly be called an army – set off in pursuit of Suetonius. Success seems to have bred confidence, but in any case they had no real choice; until the governor and his legions had been decisively beaten no hope existed of driving out the hated occupiers for good. The historians who are the sources for these events disagree as to whether Suetonius turned to fight willingly or reluctantly. Probably he would have preferred to wait, but, hard pressed by the enemy advance guard and with no hope of further supplies, he made the tactical decision to accept battle on ground of his own choosing. He may have been influenced by the unwelcome news which had come in from Exeter,* that the Second Legion would not be coming to reinforce him, although the west was apparently tranquil.

The reasons for the Second Legion's defection throw an interesting light on the Roman command system. By ill chance the legate normally in command at Exeter was away and his nominal second-in command was a well-born but inexperienced 'broad-stripe' tribune of around 20, usually concerned with administrative matters, Poenius Postumus. He does not seem to have consulted the most experienced soldier in the camp, the camp commandant, who, according to the usual practice, would have been a former chief centurion who had 'come up the hard way' and was socially his inferior. No doubt fearful of weakening his own garrison Poenius decided to play for safety and leave his men where they were.

Once he realized no help would be coming from the west, Suetonius, commanding a force of about 10,000 men, drawn from the Fourteenth Legion, detachments of the Twentieth and some locally based auxiliaries, 'decided', according to Tacitus, 'to attack without further delay'. The exact spot remains unknown, but Mancetter, near Atherstone in Warwickshire, about ten miles [16 km] north of Coventry, and about a hundred [160 km] from London, has been suggested, where a steep escarpment of rock with a wide plain in front approaches Watling Street.

He chose a position in a defile with a wood behind him. There could be no enemy, he knew, except at his front, where there was open country without cover for ambushes. Suetonius drew up his regular troops in close order, with the light-armed auxiliaries at their flanks and the cavalry massed on the wings. On the British side, cavalry and infantry bands seethed over a wide area in unprecedented numbers. Their confidence was such that they brought their wives with them to see the victory, installing them in carts stationed at the edge of the battlefield.

Now at last, after more than a century of defeat and withdrawal, surrender and humiliation, the British were to meet the Romans in open battle. Both sides, even if Tacitus has improved on what was actually said, knew that it was a decisive moment, a fight to a finish. For Boudicca, her back still perhaps bearing the scars of the brutal beating she had received for the sole crime of being a British queen, it was the climax of a brave and eventful life. Her age is unknown but the Greek historian Cassius Dio described her as being 'possessed of greater

---

*Collingwood places the Second Legion at Gloucester but admits there is no evidence of a legionary fortress there. Other writers (e.g. Falkus and Salway) prefer Exeter, where more recent research has revealed such a camp. Exeter seems more likely but Legion II may well have had a detachment elsewhere.

intelligence than often belongs to women' and painted a striking, if unreliable, picture of her appearance that fateful morning:

> In stature she was very tall, in appearance most terrifying, in the glance of her eye most fierce, and her voice was harsh; a great mass of the tawniest hair fell to her hips; around her neck was a large golden necklace; and she wore a tunic of divers colours over which a thick mantle was fastened with a brooch. This was her invariable attire.

According to Tacitus, Suetonius had mustered 'nearly 10,000 armed men', but recent estimates put the true total, including cavalry, at 11–13,000 and Boudicca's army at perhaps 100,000; Cassius Dio's figure of 230,000, excluding non-combatants, is universally accepted as absurd. In training and discipline, however, the balance of advantage was very different. So too, it must be said, it was in generalship, while the Britons were fighting on terrain of the Romans' choosing which would favour the very type of close-quarter combat at which the legionaries excelled.

> Suetonius confidently gave the signal for battle. At first the regular troops stood their ground. Keeping to the defile as a natural defence, they launched their javelins accurately at the approaching enemy. Then, in wedge formation, they burst forward. So did the auxiliary infantry. The cavalry, too, with lances extended, demolished all serious resistance. The remaining Britons fled with difficulty since their ring of wagons blocked the outlets. The Romans did not spare even the women. Baggage animals too, transfixed with weapons, added to the heaps of dead. It was a glorious victory, comparable with bygone triumphs. According to one report almost eighty thousand Britons fell. Our own casualties were about four hundred dead and a slightly larger number of wounded.

The British casualty figures were certainly exaggerated, even allowing for the slaughter of the panic-stricken families fleeing from the field pursued by battle-maddened legionaries; in another major battle, much later, even Tacitus only claims 10,000 British dead for the loss of 360 Romans, which seems more realistic. The final death toll included two who did not die on the battlefield. According to Tacitus, 'Boudicca poisoned herself', though Dio says that she fell ill and died, to be given a rich burial by her still loyal subjects. As for Poenius Postumus, acting commander of the absent Second Legion, on hearing of what had happened he 'stabbed himself to death because he had cheated his formation of its share in the victory'.

5

THE TRIBES BEYOND THE FORTH

In the summer in which his sixth year of office began Agricola enveloped the tribes beyond the Forth.

Tacitus, Agricola, *recalling AD 83*

The crushing of the great rebellion of AD 60–61 left most of England quiescent. By AD 67 the island seemed peaceful enough for Nero to withdraw the Fourteenth Legion, which had defeated Boudicca, to the continent and, though it briefly returned later, it was finally removed for good. With the overthrow, and suicide, of Nero in AD 69 and the outbreak of civil war between rival contenders for the imperial throne, Britain ceased to occupy a significant place in Roman affairs and it was only with the emergence in AD 69 of Vespasian as emperor, a post he was to hold for the next ten years, that the conquest of the still untamed areas was resumed. Early in AD 71, in good time for the campaigning season, Vespasian, who had himself played a leading part in the invasion of AD 43, appointed a new governor, Petillius Cerialis, also a veteran of operations in England, where he had commanded the Ninth Legion during earlier campaigns in the north. With him came a new legion, II Adiutrix, raised by Vespasian from former marines at Ravenna. The military establishment in Britain was now back to its full strength of four legions, based, though with detachments often elsewhere, at Wroxeter, in Shropshire, Gloucester – possibly with a secondary depot at Exeter – Lincoln and, an entirely new location, York, where Cerialis installed his old unit, the Ninth, in a brand-new fortress, well placed for a further advance northwards and for reinforcement by sea, since the Ouse was navigable to that point by fair-sized vessels.

Cerialis was succeeded, after the normal three-year tour of duty, by an even more distinguished soldier, Julius Frontinus, a lawyer and administrator of distinction rather than a mere soldier, who wisely adopted a more enlightened policy towards the tribes he defeated than his predecessors.

To succeed him, in AD 78, Vespasian selected another soldier who knew the country, Gnaeus Julius Agricola, who had witnessed Boudicca's rebellion as a young military tribune in his early twenties and had later commanded the Twentieth Legion, based on Gloucester, in his early thirties. The good sense that led him to choose a historian as his daughter's husband was to ensure that posterity was aware of his achievements, for the favoured bridegroom, Tacitus, was to write a flattering biography of his father-in-law, the only governor of Britain so commemorated.

Of what lay beyond the Cheviot Hills, which form a natural barrier running from what is now the Solway Firth to the North Sea, little was known and the Romans may originally have intended to draw their northern frontier at this point. Nothing was more unsettling, however, than for a newly-subdued tribe to have turbulent neighbours and the invasion of Scotland was therefore undertaken not merely to extend the Roman empire but as a preventive strike against the potentially marauding Scots.

Agricola began the campaign in his third year as governor, AD 80. By now he was accustomed to British weather, no doubt echoing Tacitus's harsh judgement: 'The climate is wretched, with its frequent rains and mists.' About the unexplored country now being opened up by the Roman army he was little more encouraging. 'The general shape of Britain,' he explained, 'has been compared . . . to an elongated diamond or a double-headed axe. Such indeed is its shape south of Caledonia . . . But when you go farther north you find a huge and shapeless tract of country, jutting out to form what is actually the most distant coastline, and finally tapering into a kind of wedge.' The Romans now knew for certain, however, that the 'wedge' did end, for a Roman fleet had recently circumnavigated the whole British mainland and had confirmed and 'thus established', what Caesar had merely guessed, 'the fact that Britain was an island' and the same ships had 'discovered and subjugated the Orkney Islands, hitherto unknown'.

Scotland alone was quite enough to keep the northern legions busy and in AD 83 they launched the major offensive for which the campaigns of earlier years had merely been laying the foundations. Never afraid of amphibious operations Tacitus now made use of a weapon the Scots did not possess, his fleet, demonstrating even more strikingly than Caesar that whoever had command of the sea controlled Britain.

In the summer in which his sixth year of office began, Agricola enveloped the tribes beyond the Forth. Fearing a general rising of the northern nations and threatening movements by the enemy on land, he used his fleet to reconnoitre the harbours . . . The war was pushed forward simultaneously by land and sea; and infantry, cavalry and marines, often meeting in the same camp, would mess and make merry together. They boasted, as soldiers will, of their several exploits and adventures, and matched the perilous depths of woods and ravines against the hazards of storms and waves, victories on land against the conquest of the ocean.

In getting the various arms of his task force to work so harmoniously together Agricola had achieved another 'first' for the British Isles and almost, also, a 'last'. Army and navy were seldom to cooperate so amicably again and inter-service rivalry, if not open hostility, features large in British invasion history. For the moment, the effect of Agricola's ships was demoralizing if not decisive: 'The Britons . . . as was learned from prisoners, were dismayed by the appearance of the fleet; now that the secret places of their sea were opened up, they felt that their last refuge in defeat was closed against them.'

The Roman army probably spent the winter in Scotland, in small fortified camps in the long valley known as Strathmore between the mountains of Perth and the Ochil and Sidlaw hills or in a larger base on the River Tay. In the following summer, AD 84, Agricola launched what was intended to be a decisive offensive, immersing himself in planning it, according to Tacitus, 'to distract his mind from its sorrow'; he had just heard of the death of his infant son. His opponents, too, had mustered every man they could for a fight to a finish. Both sides realized that the coming battle would settle whether Scotland was to retain its independence or become merely the bleakest, most remote section of a totally subjugated Britannia.

The campaign began like the previous year's, though this time the legions were supported by some renegade Britons who had clearly decided that the Romans had come to stay. There was another difference. The Scottish tribes, instead of the hit-and-run attacks and night raids on which they had so far relied, had found a leader and were prepared to stand and fight in the open field – the very tactic that had proved disastrous to every British commander in the past, from Cassivellaunus to Boudicca.

So the stage was set by Agricola for what was to prove the last great set-piece battle between Romans and Britons:

He sent his fleet ahead to plunder at various points and thus spread uncertainty and terror; then, with an army marching light, which he had reinforced with some of the bravest of the Britons who had proved their loyalty by long years of submission, he reached Mount Graupius, which he found occupied by the enemy. The Britons were, in fact, undaunted by the loss of the previous battle, and were ready for either revenge or enslavement. They had realized at last that the common danger must be warded off by united action, and had sent round embassies and drawn up treaties to rally the full force of all their states. Already more than 30,000 men could be seen, and still they came flocking to the colours – all the young men, and famous warriors whose 'old age was fresh and green'*, every man wearing the decorations he had earned.

Mons Graupius was almost certainly Bennachie, 1733 feet [528 m] high, an outstanding peak even in the mountainous country where it stands, about five miles west of Inverurie and about 20 miles from Aberdeen: a reminder of how far into the Highlands the Romans had now penetrated.

Including the turncoat Britons and at least two full legions, each of them 5000 strong, Agricola's forces cannot in fact have been far short of the enemy total and in military skill they were vastly superior, as soon became evident:

> The fighting began with exchanges of missiles and the Britons showed both steadiness and skill in parrying our spears with their huge swords or catching them on their little shields, while they themselves rained volleys on us. At last Agricola called upon four cohorts of Batavians [Germans from the Rhineland] and two of Tungrians [another German tribe, formerly the *Germani*] to close and fight it out at sword's point. These old soldiers had been well drilled in sword-fighting, while the enemy were awkward at it, with their small shields and unwieldy swords, especially as the latter, having no points, were quite unsuitable for a cut-and-thrust struggle at close quarters. The Batavians, raining blow after blow, striking them with the bosses of their shields, and stabbing them in the face, felled the Britons posted on the plain and pushed on up the hillsides. This provoked the other cohorts to attack with vigour and kill the nearest of the enemy. Many Britons were left behind half dead or even unwounded, owing to the very speed of our victory. Our cavalry squadrons, meanwhile, had routed the war chariots, and now plunged into the infantry battle. Their first onslaught was terrifying, but the solid ranks of the enemy and the roughness of the ground soon brought them to a standstill . . . Our infantry had only a precarious foothold and were being jostled by the horses' flanks; and often a runaway chariot, or riderless horses careering about wildly in their terror, came plunging into the ranks from the side or in head-on collision.

So far it had been a soldiers' battle. Now it became a general's:

> The Britons on the hill-tops had so far taken no part in the action and

*A well-known tag from Virgil, *The Aeneid*, 6, 304.

had leisure to note with contempt the smallness of our numbers. They were now starting to descend gradually and envelop our victorious rear. But Agricola, who had expected just such a move, threw in their path four squadrons of cavalry which he was keeping in hand for emergencies and turned their spirited charge into a disorderly rout. The tactics of the Britons now recoiled on themselves. Our squadrons, obedient to orders, rode round from the front of the battle and fell upon the enemy in the rear. The open plain now presented a grim, awe-inspiring spectacle. Our horsemen kept pursuing them, wounding some, making prisoners of others, and then killing them as new enemies appeared. On the British side . . . whole groups, though they had weapons in their hands, fled before inferior numbers; else-where, unarmed men deliberately charged to face certain death. Equipment, bodies and mangled limbs lay all around on the blood-stained earth; and even the vanquished now and then recovered their fury and their courage. When they reached the woods, they rallied and profited by their local knowledge to ambush the first rash pursuers. Our men's over-confidence might even have led to serious disaster. But Agricola was everywhere at once. He ordered strong cohorts of light infantry to ring the woods like hunters. When the thickets were denser, dismounted troopers went in to scour them; where they thinned out, the cavalry did the work. At length, when they saw our troops, re-formed and steady, renewing the pursuit, the Britons turned and ran. They no longer kept formation or looked to see where their comrades were, but scattering and deliberately keeping apart from each other they penetrated far into trackless wilds. The pursuit went on till night fell and our soldiers were tired of killing. Of the enemy some 10,000 fell; on our side, 360 men.

And so at last Agricola had the decisive victory he had sought – or so, for the moment, it seemed. For Britain it was the end of serious resistance to Roman rule, at least over most of the province; for Agricola it marked the end of his career. That winter he was recalled to Rome and grudgingly granted 'the customary decorations of a triumph, the honour of a complimentary statue and . . . a highly flattering address', but there was no formal procession, since the Emperor Domitian was intensely jealous of his subordinate's success and considered that 'the qualities of a good general should be the monopoly of the emperor.' After being repeatedly passed over for further office, even though after various disasters in the field 'public opinion began to clamour for Agricola to take command', he settled down to a life of retirement, ended by death in AD 93, at the age of 54. He left behind him an England largely reconciled to Roman rule, a Wales subdued, and a Scotland apparently – but it soon turned out, only apparently – tamed.

Agricola was credited in his time as governor with having built 60 forts, not all of them in Scotland, and 1300 miles [2000 km] of roads, although some of this work was probably done by his successor. In England the temporary wooden forts which had housed the legions were now replaced by stone structures, barracks for a long-term presence rather than defensive posts for an invading army. Their chosen sites – Chester, for Legion XX, York for Legion IX, Caerleon in Monmouth-shire for II Augusta, much of which was a little later moved further north, reflected their belief that England offered little risk of internal disturbance, though there were 'colonies' of discharged veterans in East Anglia and the Severn area, at Lincoln and Gloucester. All told the garrison in Britain amounted to about 55,000 men, of whom about 16,800 were first-class regulars, 360 cavalry. The rest were auxiliaries, divided into about 68 units, 16 of which were cavalry. Unless sent north they saw little action.

The period from AD 96 to AD 180 is known as the era of 'the Five Good Emperors', a remarkable phenomenon in Roman history, and under their rule Britain flourished. The road network had from the first been designed to serve military purposes and stations for changing horses, and posting-houses, for providing transport to places in the surrounding countryside, were set up at regular intervals, providing a system more advanced than anything the British Isles was to enjoy for more than a thousand years to come. Along the roads sped the Imperial Post, carrying official messengers and favoured individuals, at an average speed of 50 miles a day, though a really important person could, in emergency, achieve far better results. Early in the first century AD, though not in Britain, the Emperor Tiberius was said to have covered 200 miles in 24 hours, but even an average journey from Britain to Rome took only 25 days.

Communications, in the message-carrying sense, remained primitive, for most messages could travel no faster than a man could ride. Signal posts were established on some watchtowers, both on the coast and inland, on which flags or other symbols could be hoisted, or flares burned, to convey military intelligence, but these must have been unreliable in bad weather and of limited use after dark.

Some time around AD 120 serious fighting occurred in Britain. Its cause, and course, are unknown but it was almost certainly due to an invasion, no doubt short-lived, from the north, for when, in AD 122, the Emperor Hadrian arrived in Britain on a tour of inspection he concentrated his attention on the Scottish border. Unlike Claudius, the last Roman emperor to visit Britain, Hadrian was a doer rather than a boaster, interested in every aspect of his vast inheritance, including the welfare of the races the Romans held subject. A remarkably versatile, cultivated figure, Hadrian was himself a painter and poet, an able architect and enthusiastic builder, of towns as well as fortifications. He had already had extensive military experience at many levels, from junior officer to military governor, when in AD 117, he became emperor at the age of 41. He immediately set out on a five-year tour of all Rome's far-flung possessions, during which he took the bold decision that Scotland should henceforward be written off; the official frontier line should follow the route already recognized in practice as the British frontier. Hadrian travelled the whole 80 miles or so of the Stanegate himself, possibly on foot: a friend refers jocularly to his 'walking through Britain'. At some points the frontier was moved from the valley up on to the surrounding hills, or transferred from the south side to the ridge on the north. At the western end the existing minor defensive line was carried further along the south shore of the Solway Firth to Bowness, where the firth becomes too deep to ford; at the eastern end a new bridge and fort were erected at Newcastle. Between these two points Hadrian ordered the building of a solid continuous wall, of stone for its first 40 miles [64 km], where this material was readily available, till it reached the River Irthing, near present-day Gilsland, about 16 miles [26 km] east of Carlisle, then of turf or clay for another 30 miles [48 km] to Bowness. During construction the wall was extended by another four miles [6.4 km] from Newcastle down-river to Wallsend, making its total length nearly 80 Roman miles, slightly less by British measurement, as one Roman mile was 1000 double paces, or 1611 English yards, against the 1760 [1.61 km] of the British. The turf wall was fairly soon, though precisely when is not known, replaced by a stone one, sometimes built in front of it, and a line of forts was also added for 50 miles [80 km] down the coast from the Solway Firth, where an easy sea crossing from Scotland remained possible.

Even while building was in progress the width of the Wall was reduced, but it remained a massive undertaking, especially for men relying on muscle power with only the simplest of mechanical aids. By far the most elaborate such work attempted anywhere by the Romans, it remains the longest continuous defensive line ever constructed in the British Isles. The stone section was 10 feet [3 m], later reduced to 8 feet [2.4 m] wide at the base, 15 to 20 feet [4.5–6 m] high from ground to parapet, solidly built of local stone round a rubble and mortar core. In front was a ditch, of varying depth and width, but at some points 30 feet [9.1 m] across. The turf wall, before it was replaced, was 20 feet [6 m] wide, 12 feet [3.6 m] high, also with a ditch. Throughout its length the Wall was protected by forts, a mile apart, now known as 'mile-castles', which housed the garrison, 150 strong, with two signal turrets between the forts, i.e. about one-third of a Roman mile [490 m] apart, to shelter sentries or pass messages. Behind the Wall ran the *vallum*, a huge ditch 20 to 40 feet [6–12 km] wide and 10 feet [3 m] deep, with sloping sides, so that its base was 8 feet [2.4 m] across. On both sides 30 feet [9.1 m] away from the edges of the ditch – space technically known as 'the berm' – the excavated earth was heaped in a continuous rampart 20 feet [6 m] high, the whole *vallum* area occupying a strip of land 120 feet [36 m] broad, stretching from coast to coast without a break, apart from causeways provided by the forts. The purpose of the *vallum* remains obscure, though it may have been an elaborate customs line with no military purpose, or built to prevent hostile or dishonest natives damaging the wall or stealing the wagons and stores left outside the forts.

Hadrian had brought with him a new legion, VI Victrix, based at York, to bring Britain back to its normal establishment of four, and this seems to have worked full-time on building the Wall, while the Second and Twentieth Legions are also known to have laboured on the windswept Northumberland hillsides with pick and spade, cart and crane. The task was prodigious. The Wall contained over two million cubic yards [1.5 million cubic m] of material, quarried and cut locally in Northumberland but in Cumberland having to be brought from miles away, and nothing was skimped. Bridges and gateways, as well as the main works, were clearly intended to be as impressive in appearance as they were solid in strength. Another two million cubic yards of soil and rubble had to be excavated to form its ditch, which was driven remorselessly through solid rock as well as earth and chalk. The *vallum*, everywhere following the line of the Wall, absorbed, it has been estimated, another million man-days of labour.

The Roman army now reaped a rich harvest from the inclusion of engineers and similar specialists in every legion and the constant training in building work its campaigning methods provided for every soldier. Each century employed on the Wall was given a specific section – usually about 40 yards [37 m] – to complete, or a specific part of a fort, each unit no doubt striving to keep up with its neighbours.

Hadrian's Wall was never intended as a fighting platform, like the battlements of a castle or the ramparts of a hill fort, but as an extended observation post, with its walk seven to eight feet [2.1–2.4 m] wide running along its whole length, reached by ladders every 500 yards [457 m] and stairways every Roman mile [1.5 km]. Here, too, were the small 'fortlets' or mile-castles, with accommodation for about 30 men and entrances at the front as well as behind the Wall, so that the garrison could sally forth to tackle marauding parties approaching it.

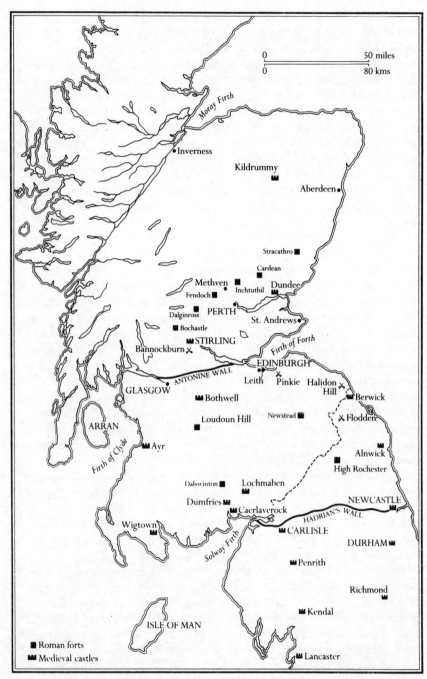

0   50 miles
0   80 kms

Moray Firth

• Inverness

Kildrummy

Aberdeen •

Stracathro ■

Cardean ■

Methven •   Inchtuthil ■   Dundee

Fendoch ■

Dalginross   ■ PERTH

■ Bochastle   St. Andrews •

STIRLING

Bannockburn ✕   *Firth of Forth*

EDINBURGH

ANTONINE WALL   Leith   Pinkie ✕   Halidon ✕
GLASGOW   Hill
       Bothwell   Berwick

ARRAN   Loudoun Hill   Newstead ■   ✕ Flodden

Firth of Clyde   ■ Ayr   Alnwick ■
                          High Rochester

Dalswinton ■   Lochmaben

Dumfries   NEWCASTLE

Wigtown   Caerlaverock   *HADRIAN'S WALL*

CARLISLE

              Solway Firth   DURHAM

                   Penrith

                   Richmond

ISLE OF MAN   Kendal

■ Roman forts   Lancaster
▥ Medieval castles

Scotland and the Borders 43 AD–1603.

Hadrian's Wall took at least five years to build, perhaps, if the outworks along the Cumberland coast and the replacement of the original turf by masonry along its whole length are included, as long as ten or eleven. It was, however, well under way before Aulus Pretorius left Britain, around AD 126, having, it is believed, supervised most of the work himself. On Hadrian's death, in AD 138, his chosen successor, Antoninus Pius, found he had inherited Hadrian's problems along with his crown, as the same writer, in his biography of Antoninus, briefly recorded: 'He conquered the Britons through his legate Lollius Urbicus, another wall, of turf, being set up when the barbarians had been driven back.'

Antoninus himself never visited the country and the credit for what became known as the Antonine Wall, such as it is, belongs to Lollius Urbicus, governor of the province from around AD 138 to 144. He arrived from Lower Germany with a great reputation for energetic action and now attempted to succeed where Agricola had failed and claim Southern Scotland permanently for Rome. Using Hadrian's Wall as a base and source of troops instead of as an established front line, new expeditions, between AD 140 and 142, were sent plunging forward into the Border country and the Scottish lowlands, and a new supply depot was established at Corbridge on the Tyne, just behind the Wall. This latter had clearly done its intended work and northern England was now considered secure enough for the frontier to be moved forward, to the next natural line, between the Firths of Forth and Clyde. Here a much more modest barrier was erected, skilfully sited to command the best possible view, but consisting throughout of turf, on a stone base 14 feet [4.3 m] wide, behind a ditch 40 feet [12 m] wide and 10 feet [3 m] deep. There was no *vallum* and Antonine's Wall was only 37 miles [60 km] long, half the length of Hadrian's, with 19 much smaller forts – 1–6 acres [0.64–2.4 hectares] in area – spread out at intervals of about two miles [3.2 km]. The largest, at Mumrills, between Falkirk and the Firth of Forth, accommodated the commandant and his staff; the rest mainly housed small detachments, none containing more than 500 men. The legions may have supplied perhaps one-third of the total garrison, auxiliary units the rest, with a total force, at its peak, of 6–7000 men, employed, in contrast to those on Hadrian's Wall, both as patrols and as the fighting reserve.

The Antonine Wall, with earthen ramparts round the forts replacing stone walls, and timber gateways the elaborate stone entrances Hadrian had favoured, was in every respect a cut-price version of the original and, apart from a few platforms for beacon fires, no provision was made for signalling, and no mile-castles were built. More serious still, the line was not extended along either shore to its rear, so that it could easily be outflanked by an enemy equipped with boats. On the other hand it included some refinements not included further south, like the 'lilies', sharpened stakes in hidden pits, of which evidence has been found at Rough Castle, west of Falkirk, near modern Bonnybridge – a device which the Scots were later to make their own.

With six strong working parties, two from each legion, labouring to build it, instead of the less efficient 'century' system adopted by Hadrian, Antonine's Wall was rapidly finished and by early AD 143 was in commission. Two walls, however, proved weaker than one. The detailed course of events over the next half-century or so is still a mystery, but if – and even this is uncertain – the Romans tried to hold both walls simultaneously, they failed. The written sources are vague, the archaeological findings, as usual, contradictory. One solid fact in a morass of speculation is that in AD 175 the Emperor Marcus Aurelius, more renowned as a philosopher than as a soldier, sent 5500 cavalry to Britain, a huge number suggesting some sudden emergency. The Antonine Wall was abandoned at least once, probably around AD 154, then re-occupied, only to be abandoned again about AD 163. Archaeology reveals that it was wrecked once more, though whether by the retreating Romans or the advancing Scots it cannot tell us. Roman writers who refer merely to 'the Wall' make confusion worse.

In 208 the Emperor Severus arrived in northern England to lead a new campaign against the Scots. 'Small of stature but powerful . . . mentally . . . very keen and very vigorous', according to the historian Dio, he established his rear base at Corbridge, between Hexham and Newcastle, about two miles [3.2 km] behind Hadrian's Wall, and then thrust the legions forward across the Wall, over the Cheviot Hills and River Tweed, through the Scottish lowlands and across the Firth of Forth into Fife, which forms a promontory between the Firth of Forth and the Firth of Tay. Here a forward camp for his striking force was set up, at Carpow, near modern Dunfermline, supported by a naval base at Cramond on the far side of the Forth, mid-way between present-day Edinburgh and the Forth Bridge.

Severus, in spite of his failing health – he had for years been a martyr to gout – penetrated deep into the Highlands and perhaps as far as the Moray Firth, for forts from his period have been found beyond Aberdeen. But on 4 February AD 211, aged 65, he died at York, the first Roman emperor to end his life on British soil. His final charge to his two sons, who were always quarrelling, 'Be harmonious, enrich the soldiers and scorn all other men,' was ignored. The elder, Caracalla, murdered his brother and, possibly after one final campaign, gave up all his father's hard-won gains: 'With the enemy he came to terms, withdrew from their territory and abandoned the forts.'

This peaceful interlude was followed by another civil war among the Romans. In AD 285 the Emperor Diocletian assumed the title of *Britannicus Maximus*, or 'overlord of the British', while his junior co-emperor, Maximian, took responsibility for the western part of the empire and appointed as chief of the *Classis Britannica*, or British fleet, a former pilot from the Low Countries, M. Mausaeus Carausius. 'British fleet' was a misnomer. Although there were some naval bases in Britain the warships in the Channel were commanded from Boulogne and their main duty was protecting the coast from what is now Belgium to Brittany from piracy and plunder-seeking raids by Germans from further north. Carausius soon became suspected of being in league with these adventurers, and, in Edward Gibbon's words, when justice seemed about to catch up with him, 'he sailed over to Britain, persuaded the legions and the auxiliaries which guarded that island to embrace his party' and proclaimed himself emperor.

After an unsuccessful engagement at sea the two existing emperors accepted Carausius as one of themselves, and from AD 287 to 293 Britain remained Carausius's private empire. He was murdered by his own chief minister, Allectus, who for the next three years, from AD 293 to 296, took the title of emperor for himself.

In AD 296, more than 250 years after Claudius's invasion, the Romans launched another amphibious assault on the British Isles, this time to overthrow the usurper Allectus and bring the province back into the empire. The true emperor, Constantius, divided his fleet into two, himself apparently sailing with the smaller force from Boulogne to somewhere on the south-east coast. The main body of transports sailed from Le Havre with his second-in-command, Asclepiodotus. The weather was bad with a beam wind liable to drive them up-Channel, but then a fog came down and the enemy fleet slipped by unseen while Allectus's ships, now blind, waited to pounce on it as it stood into the Solent or the Sussex shore. Asclepiodotus must have landed somewhere between present-day Brighton and Portland, probably around Southampton, and immediately burnt his boats before setting out towards London. Constantius, meanwhile, had crossed from Boulogne, probably to that stretch of coast near Deal the Romans had favoured before. Allectus seems to have decided that Asclepiodotus posed the greater threat and hurried to engage him before all his forces were assembled, pinioned like every defender of England upon that perpetual dilemma, whether to deal with each lodgement at once but piecemeal, or wait to collect sufficient strength for a major counter-attack. The site and course of the resulting battle are unknown, but not its outcome. A professional 'panegyrist' later acclaimed Constantius's victory, which was not really his, but his second-in-command's:

Fleeing from you he ran straight into your forces . . . having seen you
behind him so overwhelmed Allectus that he rushed headlong to his
death . . . so deranged with shock that he neither drew up his troops
into a proper array for battle nor . . . organized all the units he was
collecting together into an effective force. Instead, quite forgetting all
this massive preparation, he hurled himself into battle with only the
old authors of the conspiracy [i.e. his usurpation of power] and some
regiments of barbarian mercenaries. Thus . . . while the Roman
empire triumphed hardly a Roman citizen was killed.

With Allectus defeated and dead Britain was reincorporated in the
empire. Constantius's men arrived in London in time to prevent Allectus's defeated troops from sacking it on their way home. The relieved,
and reprieved, citizens, British and Roman, had 'the pleasure,' wrote a
Roman historian, 'of witnessing the slaughter, as if it were a public
show' and a gold medallion was struck to show a figure representing
London kneeling outside its gates in homage to the victorious Constantius, 'restorer of the eternal light' of Roman rule.

With the legions and the auxiliary units fighting each other in the
south, Hadrian's Wall was again overrun, whether by a series of relatively
minor raids or by an engulfing wave remains uncertain. Much rebuilding
followed and in AD 305 Constantius, now sole emperor, led a new
invasion deep into Scotland well beyond the Forth–Clyde line, possibly
with the support of a fleet, as in Agricola's day. Once again the terrain
proved almost as troublesome as the enemy, who are, for the first time,
identified as 'Picts', a term which seems to include both the Highland
tribes and those known earlier as Caledonians.

Despite the Picts, the Romans managed to rebuild the damaged
sections of Hadrian's Wall and to strengthen the walls of Chester and
York, where Constantius died, like Severus before him, in AD 306.
Like Severus he was succeeded by his son, who had been serving with
him against the Scots, and has become known as Constantine the Great.
The usual civil war followed his appointment and at one time six rival
emperors were ruling simultaneously, but by AD 324 he had emerged
the victor and, having moved the imperial capital eastwards, to the
city renamed Constantinople, survived – a remarkable record – to die
naturally at the age of 63, in AD 337.

During Constantine's reign a reorganization of the empire, already
begun in other areas, was extended to Britain, which now became one
of twelve imperial dioceses, its head, or *vicarius*, being responsible to the
official who ruled Spain and Gaul. At the same time it was split into
four, instead of two, units. These were *Britannia Secunda*, centred on
York, between Hadrian's Wall and the Humber/Mersey line; *Britannia*

Prima covering Wales and the South-West, with its capital at Cirencester; *Flavia Caesariensis*, taking in East Anglia and the Midlands, commanded from Lincoln; and *Maxima Caesariensis*, east of a line running almost due north from the Solent, with headquarters in London. The army was split into a locally-based garrison, with purely defensive duties within the province, and a field army, in which cavalry now became the senior arm.

Constantine left the British Isles another, more enduring, legacy than these reforms. How Christianity reached them is unknown but around AD 304 the Britons acquired their first saint, Saint Alban, according to tradition a Roman soldier martyred for giving shelter to a fugitive priest at Verulamium. Eleven years later, Constantine ended all persecution of the Christians and, in AD 324, Christianity became a state religion. It was to survive, not least in the abbey church and cathedral town of St Albans, long after Verulamium, and the whole panoply of Roman rule, were but a memory.

6

THE HOSTILE OARS

When . . . the sea foamed under hostile oars you, Stilicho, fortified me.

Speech in honour of the Roman general Stilicho, AD 400

Invincible as they knew themselves to be on land, the Romans at first gave little priority to protecting Britain against seaborne invasion. Not long after Claudius's invasion in AD 43, however, the so-called British fleet, or *Classis Britannica*, was established, with bases on both sides of the Channel, and around AD 100 a fortress was erected at Dover, with a lighthouse 80 feet [24 m] high on the cliffs.

The real creator of England's coastal defences, however, was probably the breakaway commander, and self-styled emperor, Carausius, who, in pursuance of his brief to keep the Saxon pirates along the east coast in check, built, or extended, a series of fortresses extending as far north as the Wash and as far south as Skegness and Dunwich, both later destroyed by coastal erosion. Later, around AD 290, having himself invaded England by the short sea-route, Carausius turned his attention to the south-east, in his attempt to exclude the imperial armies, who, none the less, as has been seen, launched a successful invasion and overthrew him. His successors inherited the series of fortresses he had rebuilt and strengthened all round the coast of Kent and Sussex.

The Romans had already recognized one of the basic principles of maritime defence, that a harbour needs to be protected from assault from the land as well as from the sea. Working southwards from the Wash, the first Roman fortress an invader would have encountered was at Brancaster [*Branodunum*] about six miles [10 km] from Hunstanton and about three [5 km] from Burnham Market, probably serving as a base for coastal patrols, though now, thanks to coastal erosion, a mile [1.6 km] inland. As late as the seventeenth century, its walls still stood 12 feet [3.7 m] high and 10 feet [3 m] thick, backed by a rampart 20 feet [6 m] wide, and fronted by a ditch more than 40 feet [13.5 m] wide and 8 feet [2.4 m] deep. The fort was of relatively simple design, about 180 yards [168 m] square without towers or bastions, a 'fortified barracks' to use a later term, rather than a strongpoint designed to survive a determined siege.

Almost in the centre of the great curve where the east coast stretches out into the North Sea was Burgh Castle, about 40 miles [64 km] as the crow flies, rather more as the legion marched, from Brancaster and roughly the same distance from the next link in the chain, Walton Castle. Burgh Castle, once, it is thought, *Garriannom* [or *Gariannonum*], is on high ground sloping down to the River Waveney, a tributary of the Yare, about four miles [6.4 km] inland from Great Yarmouth, and is also no longer in sight of the sea. In Roman times it must have presented a formidable obstacle, roughly rectangular in shape, with an east wall 220 yards [200 m] long, running parallel to the high ground which forms a natural barrier overlooking the harbour to the west, and north and south walls 100 yards [90 m] long, built of split flints and tiles round a 'concrete', i.e. rubble and mortar, core.

Some 40 miles [64 km] further round the coast stood Walton Castle, believed to be the Romans' *Portus Adurni*. Walton, at that time 100 feet [30 m] above sea level, was built near present-day Felixstowe, just west of the mouth of the River Deben and separated by the estuary of two other important rivers, the Orwell, which leads up to modern Ipswich, and the Stour, which penetrates deep into Essex, from the port of Harwich. The remains of Walton Castle were sketched in 1623 and described in 1732 – "'tis 100 yards long, 5 feet above ground, 12 feet broad at each end and turned with an angle'. It may once have commanded the approaches to a good harbour, but has long since vanished into the sea.

Bradwell-on-Sea, about 12 miles [20 km] east of Maldon in Essex (not to be confused with other places of the same name), was probably *Othona* to the Romans. The very location which made it formidable, on a promontory on the south side of the mouth of the River Blackwater, exposed it to the ravages of the waves, but enough remains to show that it was a solid, roughly rectangular construction, 160 yards [150 m] long on the west or landward side and rather under 100 [90 m] on the west, these two sides being further protected by a ditch, while the south side rests against a mound. The whole site covered about 5 acres [2 hectares] and as late as 1865 the walls were still 'upwards of 14 feet [5 m] thick', with projecting bastions at the corners.

The Thames, which had made London by far the largest Roman city in England, was also a potential source of weakness, pointing, like a somewhat wavering arrow, into the very vitals of the kingdom. To protect the approaches to it the Romans constructed a large, almost square, fort with rounded corners, about 200 yards [180 m] by 190 [175 m], at *Regulbium*, now known as Reculver, about two miles [3 km] east of Herne Bay on the Kent side of the estuary. The building was in a simple style, with walls nine and a half feet [3 m] thick, with an earthen bank behind, but without bastions and with only simple defences at the gateways. It was probably built early in the occupation to guard the ships bringing in supplies to Claudius's troops, rebuilt, used by Carausius, then again disused until during the fourth century the revival of the seaborne menace led to its being used again.

About eight miles [13 km] south-east of Reculver was its twin fortress, Richborough [*Rutupiae*], far more imposing, overlooking the area now known as Sandwich Bay and the Downs, and very close to the beaches where both Caesar and Claudius had landed. The sea gives as well as takes away, and while half of Reculver has been washed away, Richborough now lies a mile or so inland, midway between Sandwich and Ramsgate. Its history encapsulates that of Rome in Britain. First, a monument to its conqueror, Claudius, was built; then a small fort to protect its garrison; finally, much later, around AD 230, large-scale fortifications to keep out a foreign enemy, with banks and earthworks. Later still, perhaps between AD 275 and 300, the ramparts gave way to stone walls, 10 feet [3 m] thick and 25 feet [7.5 m] high, topped by turrets and surrounded by two deep ditches, enclosing an area of about an acre [0.4 hectare] in extent. The residents did not lack comforts and amenities. There was a bathhouse and assembly hall as well as a temple and wooden barrack blocks, long since perished, for the garrison. Eventually, too, perhaps early in the fifth century, a Christian church appeared of timber and daub.

Apart from the early watchtower, already mentioned, two successive, partly overlapping, forts were built at Dover [*Dubris*], the first a simple affair intended to protect the *Classis Britannica*, the second, far more imposing, built on high ground to the south-west of the then harbour, complete with earth bank behind, to give the defenders access to the top of the wall – about 160 yards [150 m] long and seven feet [2.4 m] thick on the seaward side, making use of the white chalk which had first caught the Romans' eye in the surrounding cliffs: the fort built to protect the fleet had been less than half the width and lacked even a rampart.

Stutfall Castle, at Lympne [Lemannis], near Hythe, 13 miles [21 km] down the coast was an unusual, pentagon, shape, on the slope of a steep hill dropping down to marshland and the sea. It overlooks Romney Marsh and was of fairly standard dimensions, with six lengths of wall about 11 feet [3.5 m] thick, of rubble faced with Kentish ragstone, the longest stretching for nearly 220 yards [200 m]. Towers at the angles of the walls provided for covering fire, but divine protection was invoked, too; an altar was later pressed into service to help form the platform for the gate.

Probably later than most of the others in the chain, around AD 340 a large fort was built at Pevensey [*Anderita*], roughly midway between Lympne and the next fort and now about three miles [5 km] up the coast from Eastbourne. It is close to a beach still offering an attractive landing place for shallow-draught vessels and in Roman times must have commanded a harbour on an estuary which has now silted up. The fort is, unusually, oval in shape, occupying slightly higher ground in a low-lying and marshy area, linked to the mainland by a single road. The whole site is about 320 yards [290 m] by 160 [150 m] and, like almost everything the Romans did, Pevensey was built to last. The foundations rested in a trench five yards [4.5 m] wide – in which were packed a layer of flints and clay two feet [0.6 m] thick – and another one and a half to three feet [0.5–1 m] thick, with oak beams driven into them, with above a criss-cross structure of beams. On this was laid some seven inches [0.2 m] of mortar, then two courses of stones, on which the wall of flint and concrete rubble was raised, four yards [3.7 m] in depth, with facings of brown ironstone and green sandstone, giving it a striking patchwork appearance.

The most important south coast harbour of all was Portsmouth, a large triangular area of landlocked water with a narrow, easily defensible, entrance. Along the inland base of the triangle the Romans built, at sea level, their finest fortress, still one of the best-preserved in northern Europe, Portchester, a site so strategically important that, like many others, it was to be used by later generations of defenders. Originally 13 feet [4 m] thick and nearly 20 feet [6 m] high, the walls, made of flints bound by mortar and interspersed with tile-courses, are protected on one and a half sides by the sea, on the rest by deep ditches. They form a giant square, nearly 200 yards [180 m] long on each side, enclosing an area of nearly ten acres [4 hectares], providing ample space for the infantry who garrisoned it. Twenty external towers, at intervals of about 33 yards [30 m], linked by battlements, and two defended gateways, flanked by watchtowers, increased Portchester's strength and give it more in common with the castles which were to follow it – one indeed in a corner of Portchester itself – than the simpler fortified camps which had preceded it.

A subject of controversy throughout the centuries which followed the Roman occupation was the effectiveness of shore-based artillery against ships. Room certainly existed within all their larger forts to operate the fearsome stone-hurling onagers with which the army was equipped, but it seems unlikely they would have been accurate enough to hit a small, moving target. As for the lighter *catapultae* and *ballistae*, which fired stones or metal darts and other anti-personnel weapons, the turrets and towers on some of the coastal forts may have been designed to accommodate them, and – though some experts question this – the openings up to two feet [0.6 m] wide cut in some external walls, as at Burgh Castle, were probably intended for this purpose.

Disappointingly, no account exists of any such encounter, but the seriousness with which the threat from the sea was regarded is made clear by the appointment, perhaps around AD 300, certainly by AD 350, of a single commander known as the Count of the Saxon Shore. The term 'Saxon Shore' clearly covers the whole series of forts just described, all of which (excluding Portchester) are listed in a famous document, the *Notitia Dignitatum*, probably dating from around AD 420, though only surviving in a fifteenth-century copy. The Count's headquarters were probably at Richborough and beyond the furthest major fort in the chain, at Brancaster, or possibly Skegness, he may have controlled a series of signal towers along what is now the Yorkshire coast, at Huntcliff, Goldsborough, Ravenscar, Scarborough and Filey. These were essentially fortified coastguard stations, 90–100 feet [27–30 m] high, protected by a stone wall, rampart and ditch, and big enough to mount a small catapult for self-protection on their corner bastions. Their main purpose, however, was to provide news of a coming attack, to the legions at York or the Roman warships based in the River Humber.

The main field army in Britain, needed to repel any serious invasion, was under the control of a separate officer, the *Dux Britanniarum* – roughly, Commander-in-Chief of the Britons – but the Count of the Saxon Shore was responsible for the units manning at least nine of the ten forts mentioned earlier, details for Portchester being absent. They came from all over the Roman empire and included troops of various arms, perhaps because by now the authorities in Britain were glad to scrape together whatever men they could for these basically static duties. The more mobile formations seem to have been assigned to East Anglia, where the distances to be covered were largest and sizeable enemy detachments might get ashore. A reconnaissance unit of *exploratores* was based at Walton, a Jugoslav cavalry unit at Brancaster, and another, of Spanish horsemen, at Burgh Castle.

The Saxon shore forts, with their adjoining harbours, probably served as bases for light patrolling vessels intended to give warning of an impending attack rather than for the larger units; heavier warships were probably concentrated on the French side of the Channel. A fourth-century writer describes light craft powered by forty oarsmen, and nicknamed 'Picts', after the Romans' near-invisible adversaries in Scotland – the ships' hulls and sails, and the men's clothes and faces, being painted sea-green to make them almost impossible to see at a distance.

While the Saxon shore forts were being built or strengthened the

Romans began, for the first time, to take seriously the 'back-door' threat from across the Irish Sea. New fortifications were built some time between AD 300 and AD 400 at Lancaster on the north-west coast of England and at Cardiff in South Wales, to which the legion formerly based at Caerleon may have been transferred. A small fort was built to protect the harbour at Holyhead on Holy Isle, just off the far shore of Anglesey, and the fortress above Caernavon, overlooking the Menai Strait, was abandoned in favour of a new one closer to the shore. Then the Romans had planned to use Wales and the Lancastrian coast as a jumping-off place to invade Ireland; now they built to keep out the Irish, or, as they were then known, the Scots, who by around AD 350, and perhaps much earlier, were attacking the island in two directions, straight across the Irish Sea into what is now Lancashire, and north-east into Scotland, which eventually acquired their name as raids gave way to invasion and invasion to settlement. The old name of Caledonians, for those north of Hadrian's Wall, now increasingly gave way to 'Picts', until 'the Picts and the Scots' came to sum up the twin dangers, from Scotland and from Ireland, threatening the Romans' hold on England and Wales.★

For centuries the Roman Empire had traded on its opponents' rivalry towards each other. Now at last the Picts and the Scots, the Franks – from Franconia in Germany – and the Saxons, had learned their lesson, combining in AD 367–8 in what an indignant Roman historian called 'the barbarian conspiracy'. The Picts and Scots united to overrun Hadrian's Wall. The German tribes descended on the coast of Gaul and probably also south-east England. It was a well-planned, skilfully coordinated attack. The emperor Valentinian, hurrying back from Germany to deal with trouble in France, was intercepted by a messenger bearing grim tidings. The *Dux Britanniarum*, in command of the main British garrison, had been killed; so had the Count of the Saxon Shore, responsible for its naval defence; and, it soon emerged, the whole south-east was overrun with rebels or invaders, London was virtually besieged and the northern counties wholly lost.

It was the most serious crisis for more than 300 years and Valentinian's initial response was fumbling and inept. First one officer was sent and recalled, then another. Eventually an adequate force was assembled, of four experienced units from the main field-army, and an able general, Theodosius, father of a future emperor, selected. Landing, apparently unchallenged, at Richborough, Theodosius advanced towards London, rounding up or dispersing the enemy detachments as he went, their

★'Pict' was probably a Roman version of the Celtic 'Priteni', meaning 'painted' or 'tattooed'.

movements slowed down by prisoners and booty. On the 'barbarian' side whatever unity and discipline had been achieved earlier seem to have broken down in the intoxication of success and the temptation of undreamed-of plunder.

A long campaign, in which Theodosius made his way steadily northward like all his predecessors, followed, and by AD 369 Britain was securely back within the empire. But a few years later the commander of the army, Magnus Maximus, who had stayed in Britain and, in AD 382, won another victory over the Picts and Scots, led his best troops across the Channel to make his own bid for the imperial throne.

Thus, only a year or two after being refortified and reoccupied, the key defences of Britain were once again emptied of men, or fatally weakened. Hadrian's Wall was stripped of most of its troops, the Welsh forts given up, as the Twentieth Legion left Chester for the Continent, the new stronghold at Portchester denuded of men as its garrison crossed the Channel to fight for Maximus. The defence of the island now rested on a few auxiliary units and on foreign tribes settled in sensitive areas; at least one German settlement of this kind took place, probably near Hadrian's Wall, their own king being given the rank of tribune.

The darkness of near-anarchy was now descending on Britain and later British chroniclers are a better guide, poor though they are, than Roman historians. What one describes as the first Pictish War now occurred; the Irish who had for decades been raiding the more remote areas of Wales now began to make permanent lodgements there; the watchtowers on the Yorkshire coast, built or restored by Theodosius, were probably overrun at this time, either by Saxons now ravaging the coast or Pictish bands venturing southward unchallenged. Two bodies discovered in the ruins of one watchtower many centuries later, at Goldsborough near Whitby, tell their own story; one sentinel had been stabbed in the back, the other had fallen on the body of a large dog – perhaps installed by the guards to provide additional warning.

Roman rule in some form may have continued to function, at least in the Midlands and south and west of England, even after Maximus's departure in AD 383, and some time after he was defeated, in AD 388, probably in 389 or 390, Britain was reincorporated in the empire. In AD 395 Theodosius the Great died, to be succeeded in the west by his son Honorius, aged eleven, though the real ruler was the regent, Flavius Stilicho, husband of Theodosius's niece, a 'barbarian' Vandal by origin, but a highly successful diplomat and already, at 36, a successful and energetic commander. Whether or not Stilicho himself crossed to Britain to direct operations in what became known as the second Pictish War is uncertain, but by AD 398 the country was again secure enough for some units to be recalled to the Continent, and for some of the less important forts to be evacuated.

Stilicho, like Agricola before him, was fortunate enough to have his achievements written up at the time, in his case by a sycophantic court poet, Claudius Claudianus (Claudian). In AD 399 Claudian writes that news is awaited of 'the Saxon conquered, the Ocean calmed, the Pict broken and Britain secure'. By January AD 400 in a court masque in the emperor's honour Britannia made an appearance as a dishevelled, roughly-clad barbarian, delivering a eulogy in honour of her deliverer:

> When I too was about to succumb to the attack of neighbouring peoples – for the Scots had raised all Ireland against me and the sea foamed under hostile oars – you, Stilicho, fortified me. This was to such effect that I no longer fear the weapons of the Scots nor tremble at the Pict, nor along all my shore do I look for the approaching Saxons on each uncertain wind.

The fate of the province of Britannia was now settled not on the banks of the Humber or Thames but those of the Tiber, for though the imperial court had retreated to Milan and then to Ravenna, Rome itself was still the real heart of the western empire. The tribes beyond the frontiers, whom the Romans had for so long treated with arrogant contempt, were now pressing in upon it on all sides. At the very end of AD 406 the Germans poured in hordes across the Rhine which Caesar had, 450 years before, claimed as a boundary which none but Romans had the right to cross. They were, for the moment, driven back, but not for long and while they were ravaging Gaul, and other intruders were challenging the legions in Spain, in AD 408 the most serious attack yet was launched on Britain, apparently by the Saxons. Constantine III, co-emperor responsible for its defence, was himself besieged in the far south of France, at Arles. No tribute reached Italy from Britain, no money arrived in Britain, which had lost its own mint 20 years before, to finance the occupation; the last coins subsequently found in any numbers had been struck in Rome before AD 402.

Its troops unpaid, its peoples ungoverned, its contacts with both Ravenna and Arles broken, Britain was on its own. In AD 409 the one general who might have saved Rome as he had, briefly, saved Britain, Stilicho, was executed for alleged treason to a government now stumbling towards disaster. In AD 410 the most formidable of all its enemies, Alaric the Goth, ending its eight centuries of immunity from foreign occupation, stormed and sacked Rome. The always complicated, often sordid, history of the city still had several centuries to run, but AD 410 has traditionally been accepted as the year the occupation of Britain, which had begun 367 years before, ended. Effective Roman control over

the whole of England and Wales had probably ceased several years
earlier; relics of Roman administration may have lingered on in some
areas for several decades, perhaps even to around AD 450. But AD 410
was the turning point, the year in which the Emperor Honorius issued
an imperial rescript warning such authorities as remained in the island
that they must now look to their own defence, though even these facts
are disputed. The instructions to Britain, it has been suggested, may
have been only a routine exhortation regularly addressed to cities under
threat, and perhaps it was not *Britannicus* which was meant, but *Bruttium*
or *Brettia* in Italy. Whatever the truth about the directive, it is from
around this time that Britain could no longer be claimed as part of the
empire, and that no central authority existed to protect it, the real test,
Caesar himself had argued, of any state's credibility.

7

THE GROANS OF THE BRITONS

To Aeutius, now consul for the third time: The groans of the Britons.

Appeal from English resident in Rome, c. 446

Two hundred years of obscurity followed the ending of the Roman occupation, and another four hundred of confusion. About who occupied Britain little argument is needed; about how and when our ignorance remains almost complete. The only contemporary source, *About the Destruction of the Britons*, by a presumed monk, Gildas – mistakenly, the reader cannot but feel, 'surnamed "Sapiens" or the Wise' – was written around AD 546, probably in the West Country; it is basically a religious tract, of a fiercely partisan kind. To Gildas the Romans were 'our illustrious defenders', finally driven out by the ingratitude of their subjects, it being, 'a proverb far and wide, that the Britons are neither brave in war nor faithful in time of peace':

> The Romans, therefore, left the country, giving notice that they could no longer be harassed by such laborious expeditions, nor suffer the Roman standards, with so large and brave an army, to be worn out by fighting against these unwarlike, plundering vagabonds.

Another native writer, Nennius, probably a Welshman, writing his *History of the Britons* at some unknown date, probably around AD 796, took an equally jaundiced, if more modest, view. 'Being dull in intellect and rude of speech . . . I, Nennius, have endeavoured to write some extracts which the dullness of the British nation had cast away.'

Several medieval chroniclers attempted to reconstruct the history of this dark period, possibly using near-contemporary accounts which have since disappeared, the most important being Geoffrey of Monmouth, writing around 1136, when he became a bishop, though his *History of the Kings of Britain* combines possibly reliable fact with obviously fictional magical prophecies. Amid this sorry catalogue of credulity and fabrication two works stand out: The Venerable Bede's *History of the English*

Church and People, completed in his monk's cell in Jarrow in AD 731, and the *Anglo-Saxon Chronicle*, not kept as a contemporary record until about AD 891, but including, in some versions, a brief account of earlier periods. Although some dates are clearly wrong and such unlikely events as 'fiery dragons were seen flying in the air' are recorded, it is still a uniquely valuable source, the seminal, pioneering, work of recording events as they happened, as Bede is the first of British historians, examining them later.

From the written materials, inadequate, muddled, contradictory as they are, one incontrovertible fact emerges. Between approximately AD 400 and 800*, England, though not Wales and Scotland, was subject to a whole series of invasions, which led eventually to the newcomers occupying the whole country, overthrowing or coming to terms with its existing rulers, and intermarrying with their subjects. A Celtic people, to which some admixture of Roman blood, and a lesser amount from other parts of the Roman Empire, had been added, became an Anglo-Saxon one, predominantly Germanic in origin and with a new, Germanic, language. Both Romans and British tended to use the single term 'Saxons' to describe these new settlers†, but three major groups can be distinguished, the Jutes from the north of present-day Jutland, the Angles from southern Jutland and the future Schleswig-Holstein and the Saxons from the North Sea coastline between the mouths of the Elbe and the Rhine. A letter written from a Roman citizen to a friend serving on anti-Saxon duties in the Channel around this time pays these enemies an impressive tribute§:

> Your foe is of all foes the fiercest. He attacks unexpectedly; if you expect him, he makes his escape; he despises those who seek to block his path; he overthrows those who are off their guard; he cuts off any enemy whom he follows; while, for himself, he never fails to escape when he is forced to fly. And more than this, to these men a shipwreck is a school of seamanship rather than a matter of dread . . . For since a storm throws those whom they wish to attack off their guard, while it hinders themselves in the midst of wrecks and sea-beaten rocks in the hope of making profit out of the very tempest.

The Saxons' poetry confirmed this outsider's judgement. 'The blast of the tempest,' ran one set of verses, 'aids our oars, the bellowing of the

---

*As the practice of dating years from the birth of Christ was adopted during the Anglo-Saxon period, 'AD' is omitted from subsequent dates in this book.

†See Myres, p. 105, for confirmation of the unreliability of this term. 'To the frightened provincial the precise ethnology of those who looted his villa was a matter of indifference. Angles or Jutes, they were all Saxons to him.'

§Quoted by J. R. Green, *The Making of England*, pp. 16–17.

heaven, the howling of the thunder hurts us not; the hurricane is our servant and drives us where we wish to go.' The British, now accustomed to a more settled, peaceful life, were no match for such fearsome foes, but the first challenge, once Roman protection was removed, came from another quarter, as Gildas recorded:

> No sooner were they gone, than the Picts and Scots, like worms which in the heat of midday come forth from their holes, hastily land from their canoes . . . differing from one another in manners, but inspired with the same avidity for blood . . . Moreover, having heard of the departure of our friends, and their resolution never to return, they seized with greater boldness than before on all the country towards the extreme north as far as the wall. To oppose them there was placed on the heights a garrison equally slow to fight and ill adapted to run away, a panic-stricken company, who slumbered away days and nights on their unprofitable watch . . . Our wretched countrymen were dragged from the wall and dashed against the ground . . . Their brothers and children . . . left their cities, abandoned the protection of the wall, and dispersed themselves in flight more desperately than before. The enemy . . . pursued them with more unrelenting cruelty than before, and butchered our countrymen like sheep, so that their habitations were like those of savage beasts.

Gildas had probably got the details wrong; he was always liable to confuse the Antonine Wall with Hadrian's Wall and both are known to have been given up long before this. Nevertheless some serious incursions by the Picts and Scots did occur at this time, as a far more reliable witness, the Venerable Bede, confirms. Western Christendom was at this time being troubled by the Pelagian heresy, which questioned the doctrine of original sin, and in or soon after 429 the future St Germanus was sent from Gaul to preach against it.

A Frenchman by birth, Germanus had been educated at Rome and become a successful barrister and then Roman governor of a large part of Gaul, before he was, reputedly against his will, ordained, whereupon his whole character changed and he became a dedicated and saintly pastor. He was aged about 51 on reaching England and, having sorted out the Pelagians and obligingly performed a miracle, restoring sight to a blind girl, was, with a fellow bishop, on his way home when he suddenly found his earlier reputation, as a military leader, had caught up with him, as Bede describes:

> Meanwhile the Saxons and Picts joined forces and made war on the Britons . . . and the latter feared that their strength was unequal to the challenge, they called on the saintly bishops for help. They came at

once . . . and put such heart into the timid people that their presence was worth a large army . . . It also happened that the holy season of Lent was beginning, and was so reverently kept under the bishops' direction that the people came each day for instruction and flocked to receive the grace of baptism. Whereas they had formerly despaired of human strength, all now trusted in the power of God . . .

After the Feast of Easter . . . Germanus promised to direct the battle in person. He picked out the most active men and, having surveyed the surrounding country, observed a valley among the hills lying in the direction from which he expected the enemy to approach. Here he stationed the untried forces under his own orders . . . Suddenly Germanus, raising the standard, called upon them all to join him in a mighty shout. While the enemy advanced confidently, expecting to take the Britons unawares, the bishops three times shouted 'Alleluia!' The whole army joined in this shout, until the surrounding hills echoed with the sound. The enemy column panicked, thinking that the very rocks and sky were falling on them, and were so terrified that they could not run fast enough. Throwing away their weapons in headlong flight, they were well content to escape naked, while many in their hasty flight were drowned in a river which they tried to cross. So the innocent British army saw its defeats avenged and . . . the bishops overcame the enemy without bloodshed.

The 'alleluia victory', as it became known, has been claimed for Maesgarmon, the 'Field of German', at Mold in Flintshire, where a nearby church is dedicated to the victor, a possible location if the Picts and Scots, landing in Colwyn Bay or along the Dee Estuary, were the enemy, rather than the Saxons. In any case, Germanus returned to Gaul and the peace he had gained did not endure for long. His lugubrious fellow-cleric, Gildas, describes the next stage in the disintegration of Roman Britain with his usual gloomy relish:

The whole country was entirely destitute of provisions, save such as could be procured in the chase. Again, therefore, the wretched remnant, sending to Aetius, a powerful Roman citizen, address him as follows: 'To Aetius, now consul for the third time: the groans of the Britons'. And again a little further, thus, 'The barbarians drive us to the sea; the sea throws us back on the barbarians; thus two modes of death await us. We are either slain or drowned.'

The 'groans of the Britons' appeal must have occurred, if the reading of 'Aetius' in Gildas's ambiguous original is correct, in or soon after 446. It produced no response and, as Gildas happily reported, conditions then seem to have gone from bad to worse:

> The audacious invaders therefore return to their winter quarters, determined before long again to return and plunder. And then, too, the Picts for the first time seated themselves at the extremity of the island, where they afterwards continued, occasionally plundering and wasting the country.

So far, the leaders of the various British communities, as Gildas commented, had shown little capacity to act together:

> It has always been a custom with our nation as it is at present [i.e. about 550] to be impotent in repelling foreign foes, but bold and invincible in raising civil war.

Now, however, there seems to have been a change of heart, though Gildas naturally puts the worst possible gloss on it:

> Then all the councillors, together with that proud tyrant Gurthrigern, the British king, were so blinded that, as a protection to their country, they sealed its doom by inviting in among them (like wolves into the sheep-fold), the fierce and impious Saxons, a race hateful both to God and men, to repel the invasions of the northern nations. Nothing was ever so pernicious to our country, nothing was ever so unlucky. What palpable darkness must have enveloped their minds – darkness desperate and cruel! Those very people who, when absent, they dreaded more than death itself, were invited to reside, as one may say, under the selfsame roof.

The more usual form of the name of the British king mentioned by Gildas is Vortigern, who may have come from the Gloucester area, and all sources agree about the invitation and its results, though Nennius dates it as '447 years after the passion of Christ'. AD 447, i.e. after the *birth* of Christ, seems more likely. This almost agrees with the *Anglo-Saxon Chronicle*:

> 449 . . . Hengist* and Horsa, invited by Vortigern, king of the Britons, came to Britain at a place which is called Ypwinesfleot, at first to help the Britons, but later they fought against them.

The spot where the newcomers landed, rendered differently in various versions of the *Chronicle*, is agreed to have been Ebbsfleet, in the Isle of

---

*Both in the translation quoted here and in the extract which follows the name appears as 'Hengest', but I have adopted the more familiar form, used by both Collingwood and Salway.

Thanet, now half a mile inland from Pegwell Bay, and roughly midway between Sandwich and Ramsgate.

Hengist's force of mercenaries, which probably consisted of Jutes, though another version of the *Chronicle* describes them as Angles, is said to have arrived in three ships so can have numbered only a few hundred. They were obviously, however, first-class fighting men and at first loyally carried out their contract: 'King Vortigern gave them land to the south-east . . . on condition that they fought against the Picts. They then fought against the Picts and had victory wherever they came.'

The *Anglo-Saxon Chronicle* recounts what followed:

> 449. Then they sent to Angel [i.e. the land of the Angles]; ordered [their kinsfolk] to send more aid and to be told of the worthlessness of the Britons and of the excellence of the land. They then at once sent hither a larger force to help the others. These men came from three nations of Germany: from the Old Saxons, from the Angles, from the Jutes.

A breach between the Britons and their supposed protectors was not long in coming and the explanation that Gildas offers has the ring of truth:

> The barbarians being thus introduced as soldiers into the island, to encounter, as they falsely said, any dangers in defence of their hospitable entertainers, obtain an allowance of provisions, which, for some time being plentifully bestowed, stopped their doggish mouths. Yet they complain that their monthly supplies are not furnished in sufficient abundance and they industriously aggravate each occasion of quarrel, saying that unless more liberality is shown them, they will break the treaty and plunder the whole island. In a short time, they follow up their threats with deeds.

The rapid growth of the Saxon presence in the south-east of Britain (though its dates must be treated with caution) is recorded by the *Anglo-Saxon* Chronicle:

> 457. In this year Hengist and Aesc fought against the Britons at a place which is called Crechanford and there slew four thousand men; and the Britons then forsook Kent and fled to London in great terror.
> 465. In this year Hengist and Aesc fought against the Welsh near Wippedesfleot and there slew twelve Welsh nobles.
> 473. In this year Hengist and Aesc fought against the Welsh and captured innumerable spoils, and the Welsh fled from the English like fire.
> 477. In this year Aelle came to Britain and his three sons, Cymen,

Wlencing and Cissa . . . at the place which is called Cymenesora and there slew many Welsh and drove some to flight into the wood which is called Andredesleg.

For 'Welsh' one can probably read 'British', i.e. the Celtic, pre-Saxon occupants of the British Isles, and many of the places named have been identified with reasonable certainty. Hengist's victory in 457 was probably at Crayford in Kent, his presumed ally, Aelle, landed on Selsey Bill, in Sussex, and the defeated British took refuge in the great wooded area of the Sussex Weald. The Saxon settlement was clearly expanding in all directions and all set to become permanent. In 488, according to the *Chronicle*, Hengist's son Aesc succeeded him on his new throne, the start of a reign of 34 years. By 491 Aelle, who had arrived after Hengist, was rivalling his success, assisted by one of *his* sons, even managing to dislodge the British from a strongly fortified position:

491. In this year Aelle and Cissas besieged Andredesceaster [i.e. the Roman fort at Pevensey] and slew all the inhabitants; there was not even one Briton left there.

News of the rich and easy pickings to be had across the water must by now have spread far and wide among the German tribes for every few years saw new chieftains arriving on the South Coast:

495. In this year two princes, Cerdic and Cynric his son, came to Britain with five ships at the place which is called Cerdicesora and the same day they fought against the Welsh.
501. In this year Port and his two sons . . . came with two ships to Britain at the place which is called Portesmuda and immediately seized land and slew a young Briton, a very noble man.

Those superb natural harbours which should have given the British a series of powerful bases for their ships were now the highways used by their enemies to encompass their destruction. Cerdicesora, for example, where two waves of invaders landed, is probably near Totton at the head of Southampton Water and Portesmuda is almost certainly Portsmouth. But the Britons did not succeed without a struggle, as even Gildas admits:

The discomfited people, wandering in the woods, began to feel the effects of a severe famine, which compelled many of them without delay to yield themselves up to their cruel persecutors, to obtain subsistence; others of them, however, lying hid in mountain caves and woods, continually sallied out from thence to renew the war. And then it was, for the first time, that they overthrew their enemies, who had for so many years been living in their country . . . The boldness of the enemy was for a while checked.

Unfortunately, as Gildas goes on to complain, 'the enemy left our people, but the people did not leave their sins'. Hence the subsequent destruction, of which he provides the nearest we have to an eye-witness account:

> For the fire of vengeance, justly kindled by former crimes [i.e. the sins of the Britons which Gildas had been denouncing], spread from sea to sea, fed by the hands of our foes in the east, and did not cease, until, destroying the neighbouring towns and lands, it reached the other side of the island, and dipped its red and savage tongue in the western ocean . . . All the columns were levelled with the ground by the frequent strokes of the battering-ram, all the husbandmen routed, together with their bishops, priests and people, whilst the sword gleamed, and the flames crackled around them on every side. Lamentable to behold, in the midst of the streets lay the tops of lofty towers, fragments of human bodies . . . with no chance of being buried, save in the ruins of the houses or in the ravening bellies of wild beasts and birds . . . Some, therefore, of the miserable remnant, being taken in the mountains, were murdered in great numbers; others, constrained by famine, came and yielded themselves to be slaves for ever to their foes, running the risk of being instantly slain . . . Others, committing the safeguard of their lives, which were in continual jeopardy, to the mountains, precipices, thickly wooded forests and to the rocks of the seas . . . remained still in their country.

This melancholy tale of what happened between approximately 450 and 500, though it may have started earlier and undoubtedly continued later, is borne out by the evidence of archaeology. In this half century Roman towns were abandoned, the villas deserted, apart perhaps from a few squatters camping out within the walls as they crumbled into ruin, the forts and watchtowers – Pevensey seems to have been a rare exception – left to the inroads of weed and weather. Sometimes the Britons reoccupied their old hill forts, not apparently for protection – there was no new building at this time – but simply as a convenient site for their huts; mostly they formed new settlements in woodland clearings or by the rivers, hoping the apparently invincible invaders would leave them in peace or agree to be bought off. Urban society and any form of municipal government ceased. The great strongholds of Roman influence became as though they had never been; London itself is not mentioned in any contemporary source between 457 and 604; Colchester and Rochester, Winchester and Silchester temporarily vanish from the pages of history, not due to military attack – there are no signs of their being stormed – but to their population deserting them as trade collapsed and famine and disease carried off those who tried to eke out a living amid the ruins. Archaeology confirms the ending of urban life. In Verulamium, occupied longer than most towns, one still habitable house became a barn. In Cirencester unburied bodies lay in the now silent main street. In Wroxeter people apparently took refuge in the heating channels below the town baths and there died. By around 450 the process was probably already well advanced, by 500 almost complete.

Around this time the British made their last great effort to preserve their independence. Whom they chose as their leader is, like so much else in the Dark Ages, uncertain, and whether one sustained attempt at resistance was made, or two, led respectively by the survivor of a Roman, or Romano-British family, and a native-born Briton. Gildas, writing of events within living memory, links the name of the former to a battle allegedly fought by the latter 44 years earlier, a valuable clue if, as suggested earlier, Gildas was writing around or a little before 550.

> An opportunity happening, when these most cruel robbers were returned home, the poor remnants of our nation (to whom flocked from divers places round about our miserable countrymen as fast as bees to their hives . . .) . . . that they might not be brought to utter destruction, took arms under the conduct of Ambrosius Aurelianus, a modest man, whom of all the Roman nation was then alone in the confusion of this troubled period by chance left alive. His parents, who for their merit were adorned with the purple, had been slain in these same broils and now his progeny, in these our days, although shamefully degenerated from the worthiness of their ancestors, provoke to battle their cruel conquerors, and by the goodness of our Lord obtain the victory. After this, sometimes our countrymen, sometimes the enemy, won the field . . . until the year of the siege of Bath-hill, when took place almost the last, though not the least, slaughter of our cruel foes.

Nennius hinders rather than helps by referring to an 'Ambrosius, who was the great king among the kings of Britain' of whom 'the natives had cause of dread', but is, however, much more explicit about the nation's other possible leader:

> Then it was, that the magnanimous Arthur, with all the kings and military force of Britain, fought against the Saxons. And though there were many more noble than himself, yet he was twelve times chosen their commander and was as often conqueror . . . The twelfth was a most severe contest, when Arthur penetrated to the hill of Badon. In

this engagement, 940 fell by his hand alone, no one but the Lord affording him assistance. In all these engagements the Britons were successful.

Gildas does not mention Arthur* but his 'Bath-hill' is clearly Nennius's 'Mount Badon', and persistent tradition identifies Arthur with the West Country. Some enthusiasts have even identified the site of Arthur's supposed capital, 'Camelot', as Cadbury Castle, at Sparkford in Somerset, about five miles [8 km] south of Castle Cary, where an abandoned hill fort was undoubtedly refortified at this time. A new wall of earth and rubble, strengthened by timber framing, was added to the four existing ramparts, which formed a perimeter 1200 yards [1100 m] long, and enclosed an area 18 yards [7.3 hectares] in extent, enough to give shelter to 1000 men. If this *was* Arthur's headquarters it could have kept in touch, by means of beacons, with a string of other forts or vantage points which may have been reoccupied, stretching as far west as Dinas Powys near Cardiff in South Wales. Arthur's name also occurs in several places not far away, including Arthur's Stone, near Hay on Wye, and Carreg Coetan Arthur (Arthur's Table) at Newport on the coast.

King Arthur's very existence is doubted by some responsible historians; the Venerable Bede does not mention him, while that notorious literary liar, Geoffrey of Monmouth, by contrast, devotes nearly fifty pages to Arthur's exploits, in which he not merely 'makes the Saxons his tributaries', which may well be true, but 'adds to his government Ireland, Iceland . . . and the Orkneys' and 'subdues Norway . . . Aquitaine and Gaule'. To the same world of fantasy belong mysterious swords, round tables and saintly knights, practising a code of chivalry not to be established for another 500 years.†

The Battle of Mount Badon forms a rare island of fact in a sea of uncertainty, though doubt still surrounds its exact date, place and nature. It was fought, however, at some point between 491 and 516§, perhaps around 500, and somewhere in the West Country, most probably on a hill close to Bath, though Liddington Castle, close to the Ridgeway, just south of Swindon in Wiltshire, and Banbury Rings near Wimborne Minster in Dorset, are other possibilities. That, as Bede says, 'the Britons made a considerable slaughter of the invaders' seems certain, as does the

---

*One very obscure passage refers to 'the bear' – Celtic *artos* – but the suggestion that he had Arthur in mind seems very far-fetched.

†Myres, p. 16, admirably summarizes the present state of knowledge. 'If we add anything to the bare statement that Arthur may have lived and fought the Saxons, we pass at once from history to romance.'

§Myres, Appendix III, pp. 222–3, sets out in detail the case for assigning it to the period 490–516 and the reasons why no greater precision is possible.

sequel, that this was a great British victory which held the Saxons in check for a whole generation.

In spite of Arthur's success, the *Anglo-Saxon Chronicle* (perhaps misdating events which occurred either earlier or later), records both further expansion by the invaders who had already arrived and fresh landings by new groups of conquerors:

508. In this year Cerdic and Cynric slew a Welsh king . . . and 5000 men with him . . .

514. In this year the West Saxons, Stuf and Wihtgar, came to Britain with three ships at the place which is called Cerdicesora, and fought against the Britons and put them to flight.

519. In this year Cerdic and Cynric obtained the kingdom of the West Saxons and the same year they fought against the Britons at a place now called Certicesford. And from that day on the princes of the West Saxons have reigned.

Certicesford, presumably named after the powerful Cerdic, has been tentatively identified as Charford on the River Avon, about eight miles [13 km] west of Salisbury, on the track leading from the coast to Old Sarum. Soon afterwards, around 520 if legend is to be trusted, Arthur himself was killed in battle, possibly fighting a rebellious break-away unit within his own command. Thereafter, the Saxons were able to consolidate their existing gains and make free with former British territory. In 534, according to the *Anglo-Saxon Chronicle*, Cerdic and his son Cynric 'gave all the Isle of Wight' to two of their relatives, after one of whom, Wihtgar, it may conceivably have been named.

Whatever Arthur had achieved was clearly not permanent. Gildas, probably writing around 550 and mournful to the last, records one final melancholy fact: 'Neither to this day are the cities of our country inhabited as before, but being forsaken and overthrown still lie desolate.'

Thereafter the *Anglo-Saxon Chronicle* continues year by year the sad tale. In 552 Cynric, we are told, 'put the Britons to flight' at Old Sarum near Salisbury, the site of a hill fort in the heart of Wiltshire and a major centre from Roman times onward. Four years later, in 556, Cynric is another 30 miles inland, at Barbury Castle, another reoccupied hill fort, near Swindon, when a new name appears as his ally, Cealwin, who soon receives his reward:

560. In this year Cealwin obtained the kingdom in Wessex.

By 577 Cealwin was himself being helped by another Saxon king, Cuthwine, perhaps his brother, and they proved a formidable combination:

577. In this year Cuthwine and Cealwin fought against the Britons and slew three kings . . . at the place which is called Dyrham; and they captured three cities, Gloucester, Cirencester and Bath.

The 'three cities', if Gildas is to be believed, must by now have been deserted, but the Saxons had clearly cut the country in half and reached the River Severn as well as seizing the strategic point on it where the Romans had once based a legion. Dyrham is now generally accepted as being close to the modern village of that name, which lies seven miles [11 km] north of Bath. The likeliest site is Hinton Hill, which rises 600 feet [180 m] just to the north of Dyrham, though the name of Dyrham Camp was only given much later to the fort on the top.

Even less is recorded about the Battle of Dyrham than about that at Mount Badon less than ten miles away, but it is possible the Saxons charged down the hill on their enemy below and this time there was no Arthur to rally the defenders. The slaughter of the three kings suggests that the British were surrounded and overwhelmed, too weak to win, too hard-pressed to fly. Much of the island was still unconquered, but Dyrham seems to have been the end of sustained, large-scale resistance. After nearly two hundred years of treaty-making and compromise, resistance and defeat, England had fallen to a new invader.

8

THE RAVAGES OF HEATHEN MEN

In this year . . . the ravages of heathen men miserably destroyed God's church on Lindisfarne, with plunder and slaughter.

The Anglo-Saxon Chronicle, *recalling 793*

By around the year 600 the Saxons had clearly come to stay.

The various kingdoms were mainly named after the tribes which had settled them, within which eventually one would emerge supreme. The south and west of the country, excluding the peninsula of Devon and Cornwall, was the home of the West Saxons, which became Wessex. Across the middle of the country, the kingdom of Mercia was eventually to give its name to the area which included the Middle Saxons' Middlesex and the East Saxons' Essex. In the northern half of the country several separate kingdoms were also to merge into one, Northumbria, largely thanks to the work of King Ethelfrith, who reigned between about 593 and 616, as Bede describes:

> About this time, Ethelfrith,* a very powerful and ambitious king, ruled the kingdom of the Northumbrians. He ravaged the Britons more cruelly than all other English leaders . . . He overran a greater area than any other king . . . exterminating or enslaving the inhabitants, making their lands either tributary to the English or ready for English settlement . . .
>
> Alarmed at his advance, Aidan, king of those Scots who lived in Britain, came against him with a large and strong army, but was defeated and fled with very few, having lost almost his entire army at a famous place known as Degsastan . . . From that day until the present, no king of the Scots in Britain has dared to do battle with the English.

Degsastan is probably Dawston in Liddesdale, just west of the border

---

*Bede renders the name as Ethelfrid and the *Anglo-Saxon Chronicle* as Ethelfrith. Since names at this time were spelt in many ways I have used the form which seems easiest for the reader.

between Roxburgh and Northumberland. Greater certainty surrounds the site of Ethelfrith's next major battle, about 615, this time against the Welsh, against whom he advanced either due south from Carlisle or westward into Mercian territory, at Chester.

In 616 or 617 Ethelfrith was himself killed in a battle against a third enemy, the king of the East Angles. A long period of internal conflict followed, with Northumbria and Mercia each in turn defeating the other but with only one major encounter with an outside army, the Picts, against whom King Ecgfrith of Northumbria, temporarily in the ascendant, led an army in 685, apparently in the hope of making southern Scotland part of his territory. Like their forebears when faced by the Romans the Picts let the terrain fight for them, retreating deep into the hills of Angus, ten miles beyond the Firth of Tay. Here at Nechtansmere, named after the Scottish king Nechtan, close to Dunnichen, south-east of Forfar, the advancing English were trapped against the shore of a loch and Ecgfrith and the bodyguard surrounding him were cut down. This was the last attempt to conquer Scotland. During the next century civil war between the kingdoms which together made up the patchwork of Anglo-Saxon England continued but the limits of English power, one of them the Welsh border, another a line stretching roughly from Exeter to Minehead★ along the line of the River Exe, were settled.

The Christian Church was at this time much the most important unifying force in England, and when its people next tookup arms against an invader it was as a Christian people fighting against heathens. During the two centuries of turmoil after the decay of Roman rule the faith had largely been lost, but in 597 thanks to Pope Gregory, who remarked of the fair-haired youths he saw in a Roman slave market, 'Not Angles but angels', the future Saint Augustine was sent with a band of monks to convert the Saxon King Ethelbert of Kent, who had married a foreign, Christian wife. This invasion, via the Isle of Thanét, rapidly succeeded. Before Augustine's death, in 604, he had been consecrated 'Bishop of the English' and the church had been divided into two provinces, of Canterbury and York, sub-divided into dioceses, on the pattern which continues to this day. In 625 King Edwin of Northumbria married a Kentish princess who took her religion with her as an invisible dowry. Her husband and all his household became Christian, soon followed by the rest of Northumbria and within the next generation the new religion had been accepted through all three major kingdoms, apart from a few pagan enclaves like Sussex and the Isle of Wight. In 664, at the Synod of Whitby, the 'Church in England' – not yet the 'Church of England', a most important distinction – decided to commit itself totally to the

★The reference here, as elsewhere, is to the future site of the places named.

leadership of Rome, instead of the Celtic church, much nearer home, which had a much less centralized and hierarchical structure. The king of Northumberland, presiding at the Synod, is said to have given his vote for Rome for fear St Peter might bar the gates of heaven against him and the result was that Britain would, for the foreseeable future, enjoy a common religion and retain at least some links with the rest of Europe.

The Saxons relied for protection more on their known prowess on the battlefield than on defensive works, but King Ethelbald, who reigned for 41 years during the 'golden age' of Mercian supremacy, regularly issued charters to newly-founded churches relieving them of all financial burdens except the maintenance of bridges and fortresses in their areas, a regular requirement in all such documents for centuries to come whoever the recipient. The charters granted to the new ports and *burhs*, i.e. boroughs, by later Saxon monarchs imposed specific obligations to keep its walls in repair, sometimes in return for the right to levy a toll on all goods changing hands in the local market. Little is known of such defences, which were probably of a very primitive nature, but the Saxons did leave behind one major work of fortification, built by the king who ruled Mercia between Ethelbald's death in 757 and his own in 796, and this will be described in a moment.

The name Mercia was derived from 'March', or borderlands, while 'Welsh' in Saxon meant 'foreigner' and covered all those earlier known as Britons, who had fled from either the Roman or Anglo-Saxon advance. Though the occupants of Wales quarrelled among each other, as no doubt did the other surviving Britons, in Cornwall and Stathclyde, an independent kingdom on the Solway Firth around modern Dumfries, they united in posing a constant threat to the security of Mercia. One Welsh king, Eliseg, said to have been descended from Vortigern, proved particularly troublesome, and having 'seized the inheritance of Powys' – possibly in modern Shropshire – according to a surviving memorial, 'held it from the power of the English for nine years with fire and sword'. To keep Eliseg and his forebears and successors out, the Mercians at first built ditches backed by banks of earth on the lowland roads favoured by the Welsh, to provide a vantage point for sentinels as much as a fighting platform. They included one substantial barrier, Wat's Dyke, 38 miles [60 km] long, from Holywell, about four miles [6.4 km] north-west of Flint on the River Dee, to the hill fort at Old Oswestry in Shropshire, about three miles [5 km] west of Ellesmere.

The building of Wat's Dyke, which covered only about a quarter of the Welsh border, proved merely a dress rehearsal for a far more ambitious project, thus described by the biographer of a later Saxon king, writing in the next century:

There was in Mercia, in recent times, a certain valiant king, who was feared by all the kings and neighbouring states around. His name was Offa and it was he who had the great rampart made from sea to sea between Britain and Wales.

'The great rampart', known as Offa's Dyke, served as an unmistakable frontier between England and Wales, rather than for purely defensive purposes. The single bank and ditch, together 60 feet [18 m] wide, stretch for 81 miles [130 km] between the Irish Sea and the Bristol Channel, wherever there is no natural barrier of wood or water. Some stretches run undeviatingly for 12 miles [20 km] testifying to the engineering skill of Offa's unlettered henchmen.

The real danger to Anglo-Saxon England, as to Romano-British society before it, was invasion by sea. In 787, according to the *Anglo-Saxon Chronicle*, the very year after Offa's death, a new and sinister sight was witnessed on the coast: 'In this year . . . came for the first time, three ships of Norwegians from Hörthaland; these were the first ships of the Danes to come to England.'

Far more details are given by the chronicler Ethelwerd, writing a century later:

> Whilst the pious king Bertric was reigning over the western parts of the English, and the innocent people . . . were enjoying themselves in tranquillity and yoking their oxen to the plough, suddenly there arrived on the coast a fleet of Danes, not large, but of three ships only . . . When this became known, the king's officer, who was already stopping in the town of Dorchester, leaped on his horse and galloped forwards with a few men to the port, thinking that they were merchants rather than enemies and, commanding them in an authoritative tone, ordered them to be made to go to the royal city; but he was slain on the spot by them, and all who were with him.

This unfortunate official, trying, very properly, to collect the customs due to his royal master, was the first victim of a new series of marauders whose name was soon to strike terror in the hearts of all who heard it. The term 'Danes' or 'Northmen' or 'Vikings' – the word came from the *viks*, or creeks, where they sheltered between raids – was used indiscriminately to describe them, though these first, unwelcomed visitors, if the *Chronicle* can be trusted, were from the area around Hardanger Fiord, not far from modern Bergen. It was also the Norwegians who from this time onward attacked, and later occupied, the Shetland and Orkney Islands, and sailed round the north of Scotland to assault the Hebrides and the Isle of Man. As news of the undefended riches on the far shore spread, the Danes, from about 835 onwards, set off in their turn to attack the east coast of England or to turn down-Channel to come ashore in the south and south-west. A large force, probably from both Norway and Denmark, also established themselves on the facing shore of France, giving the area a new name, Normandy, land of the Norsemen.

As with the Saxons, the threat was slow to develop. Six years after that first appearance at Portland in the west of Wessex another Viking fleet appeared 400 miles away in the far north of Northumbria – not, according to the *Anglo-Saxon Chronicle*, without the usual warning signs:

> 793. In this year dire portents appeared over Northumbria and sorely frightened the people. They consisted of immense whirlwinds and flashes of lightning and fiery dragons were seen flying in the air . . . A little after that in the same year . . . the ravages of heathen men miserably destroyed God's church on Lindisfarne, with plunder and slaughter.*

Lindisfarne, on Holy Island, was one of the most sacred places of the English church, constantly mentioned by Bede. Now his own former home was to provide a target:

> 794. Northumbria was ravaged by the heathen and Ecgfrith's monastery at Donemup [i.e. Jarrow] looted.

This time at least the English, aided by nature, seem to have attacked the invaders:

> One of their leaders was slain, and some of their ships besides were shattered by storms; and many of them were drowned there, and some came ashore and alive and were at once slain at the river mouth.

The new century started badly. In 802 the former Celtic shrine of Iona, off the Isle of Mull in the Inner hebrides, was sacked, a preliminary to a subsequent descent on Ireland.

To contemporaries it must have seemed that their religion itself was being singled out for attack by these new barbarians. The great scholar Alcuin of York looked back with nostalgia on what seemed the peaceful past: 'For almost 350 years we and our fathers have dwelt in this fair land and never have such times appeared in Britain like these we now endure from a pagan people.'

The truth was that monasteries in isolated spots, occupied by an unarmed band of monks and often filled with valuable jewels and plate, made natural targets. Never can prayer have been more fervently said in

---

*Between 756 and 845, due to a copyist's error, events in the original *Chronicle* are dated two to three years too early. I have used the corrected dates here.

monastic chancel and choir than the one now added to the Litany: 'From the fury of the Northmen, Good Lord deliver us.'

The sight of a Viking ship as it approached the shore must have been impressive as well as terrifying. First, if the wind was on-shore, one would make out the single square sail, set amidships, with its broad, brightly coloured stripes. Soon the slim open boat would come into view, its overlapping oak planks painted black, with its prow, carved in the shape of a dragon, riding high above the waves. Then the shields of the crew, painted alternately yellow and black, could be distinguished, where they hung in rows along the bulwarks as their owners bent to the oars, up to 30 or 35 on either side. Finally the men themselves would become visible, grim-faced below tall curved helmets and, in the later invasions, wearing chain-mail shirts. As they leapt ashore, any watcher who had not yet fled would see that they were armed with huge battle-axes, swung with both hands, bows and swords. Sometimes they brought horses with them, mostly they seized what they needed, before advancing, not as a disorderly pirate rabble, but in an organized force which could be formed into wedge-shaped units for fighting if any were rash enough to offer resistance.

After the first Viking raids on England a lull followed as they turned their attention in other directions, while England was preoccupied with internal conflict, as King Egbert, who ascended the throne of Wessex in 809, steadily established it as the dominant power. After defeating the surviving Britons of 'West Wales', i.e. Cornwall, he settled accounts with Mercia, at the Battle of Ellandun in 825, at a spot variously identified as being just south of Swindon, at Wroughton in Wiltshire, or at Amesbury. The unity achieved by force of arms did not continue but the time when Saxon England could afford the self-indulgence of civil war was running out. Ten years after Ellandun the *Anglo-Saxon Chronicle* had more alarming tidings to record:

> 835. In this year the heathen devastated Sheppey.
> 836. In this year King Egbert fought againt 25 ships' companies at Carhampton; and great slaughter was made there, and the Danes had possession of the place of slaughter.

In these two attacks nearly two hundred miles apart there was, for those with eyes to read, a real warning sign instead of 'the light seen frequently in the sky' beloved of the chroniclers. The Isle of Sheppey, in the Thames estuary, was a natural enough landing point for intruders from the North Sea, but Carhampton, just inland from Bridgwater Bay on the west coast of Somerset, was probably attacked by Northmen based in Ireland or the off-shore islands on the west coast of Scotland, so that the country was now exposed to simultaneous assault on all sides.

Two years later there was another ominous development, though victory on this occasion went to the Saxons:

838. In this year a great pirate host came to Cornwall, and they [the Danes and the Britons of Cornwall] united, and continued fighting against Egbert, King of Wessex. Then he made an expedition against them, and fought against them at Hingston Down, and there put to flight both Britons and Danes.

The location of this battlefield is not known and in the following year Egbert died, but his son Ethelwulf* proved a worthy successor and seems to have inspired the leading members of his nobility, or ealdormen, with his same drive and courage:

840. In this year ealdorman Wulfheard fought at Southampton against 35 ships' companies and made great slaughter there and won the victory . . . And ealdorman Ethelhelm fought against the Danes at Portland with the men of Dorset and the ealdorman was slain, and the Danes had possession of the place of slaughter.

Firm statistics about the number of 'Danes', as the Vikings were now known, involved in the various raids are lacking, but the remains of a Viking ship found in Norway, suggest that it could not have been handled by less than 60–70 men, nor have accommodated many more than 100. Seventy-two feet [22 m] long, 17 feet [5.2 m] wide, and displacing up to 30–40 tons, the traditional Viking ship had an extraordinarily shallow draught of only three feet [1 m], so that it could ground high enough up most beaches for its crew to leap directly ashore, and easily navigate the numerous inlets and rivers along the English coastline. As news spread across the plains of Jutland into the Baltic and up the Norwegian fiords that gold and fine clothes, women and slaves, were to be found for the taking on the far side of the North Sea, to join an expedition or two was coming to be regarded as almost a test of manhood. Like successful Roman generals, Viking leaders who returned weighed down with plunder attracted retinues of followers, eager to serve under such men as Ivar the Boneless, son of Ragnar Leather-breeches, and Eric Bloodaxe.

The first Viking attack via the Thames seems to have followed an earlier action in Kent:

842. In this year there was great slaughter in London, and in *Cantwic* [presumably Canterbury] and in Rochester.

The next year brought further troubles in the west:

*Æthelwulf in the original.

843. In this year King Ethelwulf fought at Carhampton against 35 ships' companies and the Danes had possession of the place of slaughter.

The enemy then seem to have left the English mainland undisturbed for five years, when cooperation between the populations of adjoining countries produced a happier result about 20 miles further east, near modern Burnham:

848. In this year ealdorman Earnwulf with the men of Somerset and Bishop Ealstan and ealdorman Osric with the men of Dorset fought against a Danish host at the mouth of the River Parret and made great slaughter there and won the victory.

But in 850 came a new and highly ominous development: 'And the heathen stayed in Thanet over the winter.'

Five years later the Danes again wintered in England, this time in the Isle of Sheppey, in the Thames estuary, much nearer London than Thanet. By 860 the capital of Wessex, only ten miles [16 km] from Southampton Water, was being attacked, a disagreeable welcome to the throne for the new king, Ethelbert*:

In his reign a great pirate host landed and stormed Winchester. And against the host fought ealdorman Osric with the men of Hampshire and ealdorman Ethelwulf with the men of Berkshire and put the host to flight, and had possession of the place of slaughter.

This victory apparently brought southern England some years of peace, but the next entry in the *Anglo-Saxon Chronicle*, ten years later, recorded an alarming new development, the payment of blackmail:

865. In this year the heathen host remained in Thanet, and made peace with the Kentishmen; and the Kentishmen promised them money in return for the peace.

The same year by our reckoning† saw the succession to the throne of Ethelbert's brother, Ethelred I – not to be confused with Ethelred the Unready – and the arrival of another large invading force, a hundred miles [160 km] to the north: 'And this same year came a great heathen host to England and took winter quarters from the East Anglians, and there were provided with horses and they made peace with them.'

It was now the turn of Northumbria, already weakened by a feud between two rival kings:

*Aethelberht in the original.
†The *Anglo-Saxon Chronicle* dates these events in 866, but its year probably began on 24 September. They clearly occurred before 31 December by our calendar.

866. In this year the host went from East Anglia over the mouth of the Humber to York in Northumbria; and there was great dissension of the people among themselves . . . It was late in the year when they set about making war against the host, nevertheless they gathered great levies and went to attack the host at York and stormed the city, and some of them got inside; and immense slaughter was made of the Northumbrians there, some inside, some outside, and both the [Northumbrian] kings were slain, and the remnant made peace with the host.

The sack of York has been dated as occurring on 21 March 867 and marked with deepest humiliation yet. The Danes – displaying a sophistication at odds with their basic brutality – set up a puppet ruler in Northumbria, and now settled down for the winter in Mercia, safe from attack from the rear. But at last for the English, too, there were encouraging signs. During 868 the King of Wessex's brother, Alfred, of whom more will be heard, married the daughter of a Mercian ealdorman, and the two kingdoms began to act together, as a Saxon cleric, Bishop Asser, writing later in the same century, describes:

In the same year [i.e 867–8] the Viking army left Northumbria, came to Mercia and reached Nottingham; and they spent the winter that year in the same place. Immediately upon their arrival there, Burgred, King of the Mercians, and all the leading men of that people sent messengers to Ethelred, king of the West Saxons, and to his brother Alfred, humbly requesting that they help them, so that they would be able to fight against the Viking army; they obtained this easily. For the brothers . . . gathered an immense army from every part of their kingdom, went to Mercia and arrived at Nottingham, single-mindedly seeking battle.

The 'great army' of the Saxons now seemed about to confront the invaders' dreaded 'hosts', but the result was an anti-climax.

Since the Vikings, protected by the defences of the stronghold, refused to give battle, and since the Christians were unable to breach the wall, peace was established between the Mercians and the Vikings, and the two brothers, Ethelred and Alfred, returned home with their forces.

A chance to crush the enemy had been lost, for the Danes could not have resisted an indefinite siege and Mercia, perhaps judging that their allies from Wessex would eventually have to leave, probably bought the invaders off, with gold and food. The locals must have watched with vast relief as the longships sailed back down the Trent while the rest of the enemy army 'rode back to Northumbria and went to the city of York, and remained there for a whole year'.

If the Mercians thought they had now seen the last of the intruders they were soon disillusioned. The Danes now had a convenient base from which to attack their neighbours. The first to suffer were the North Folk and South Folk of East Anglia, as the clerical writer previously quoted records:

> In the year of the Lord's Incarnation 870 . . . the Viking army mentioned above passed through Mercia to East Anglia and spent the winter there at a place called Thetford. In the same year, Edmund, king of the East Angles, fought fiercely against that army. But, alas, he was killed there with a large number of his men, and the Vikings rejoiced triumphantly; the enemy were masters of the battlefield, and they subjected that entire province to their authority.

The ravaging of East Anglia seems to have caused particular horror. The best account was compiled a century later by a French writer, who claimed to have gathered his facts from an archbishop who had heard them from the king's armour bearer★:

> Having raked together their booty, Inguar [a Viking leader] left on the spot Hubba, his associate in cruelty, and approaching suddenly with a great fleet landed by stealth at a city in that region, entered it before the citizens were aware of his approach and set it on fire. Boys and men, old and young, whom he encountered in the streets of the city, were killed; and he paid no respect to the chastity of wife or maid. Husband and wife lay dead or dying together, on their thresholds; the babe, snatched from its mother's breast, was . . . slaughtered before her eyes. An impious soldier scoured the town in fury, athirst for every crime by which pleasure could be given to the tyrant who, from sheer love of cruelty, had given orders for the massacre.

Edmund is said to have been summoned from Kent to take over the throne of East Anglia and on his defeat the Danes are reputed to have offered him peace if he would hand over half his treasure and become their vassal. He replied that he would only do so if his new overlord agreed to become a Christian, whereupon he was scourged and then murdered, on or about 20 November 870, being tied to a tree and bombarded with arrows. His body, thrown carelessly into woodland, was tracked down, according to legend, by a grey wolf and then removed to the monastery erected in his honour at St Edmundsbury, now Bury St Edmunds, where the abbey remains can still be seen.

★I.e. the Abbot of Fleury, quoted by Hodgkin, Vol. II, p. 532.

Edmund was being regarded locally as a saint within 40 years of his death, and was later canonized. He became the first of the real, as distinct from the mythical, national heroes to inspire later generations of his countrymen.

9

WORTHY KING ALFRED

I desired to live worthily as long as I lived.

King Alfred, writing c. *895*

By the autumn of 870 only Wessex, the richest and most highly developed part of the country, was still independent, but the Danes did not intend that it should remain so for long. A Welsh clergyman resident in Wessex, the future Bishop Asser, in an account written only 20 years later, described what happened as 870 came to a close and the new year began:

> In the year of the Lord's Incarnation 871 . . . the Viking army of hateful memory left East Anglia, went to the kingdom of the West Saxons, and came to the royal estate called Reading (situated on the southern bank of the River Thames, in the district called Berkshire). On the third day after their arrival there, two of their earls, with a great part of the force, rode out for plunder, while the others constructed a rampart between the two rivers Thames and Kennet, on the right-hand [southern] side of the royal estate. Ethelwulf, ealdorman of Berkshire, confronted them with his followers at a place called Englefield, and battle was joined there resolutely on both sides. When both sides had held out there for a long time, and when one of the Viking earls had been killed and a great part of the army overthrown, the others took to flight and the Christians won the victory and were masters of the battlefield.

Englefield is seven miles [11 km] west of the point where the Danes had dug in and they were presumably probing the defences in that direction as well as collecting food for the coming winter. The Danish base occupied a strong position within the confluence of the Thames and Kennet, but the Saxon commanders decided to attack while the morale of the freshly-blooded troops was still high:

Four days after these things had happened there [i.e. at Englefield], King Ethelred and his brother Alfred combined forces, assembled an army, and went to Reading. When they had reached the gate of the stronghold by hacking and cutting down all the Vikings whom they had found outside, the Vikings fought no less keenly; like wolves they burst out of all the gates and joined battle with all their might. Both sides fought there for a long time and fought fiercely, but alas, the Christians eventually turned their backs, and the Vikings won the victory and were masters of the battlefield.

Among the victims at the battle of Reading was the recent victor of Englefield, ealdorman Ethelwulf, and it says much for the spirit of the men he had led, and for the resolution of the two royal brothers, that they did not abandon the struggle. The encounter at Reading, like that at Englefield, seems instead to have stiffened their resolution and there now followed an even fiercer confrontation. Its precise location is still in doubt. The traditional site, close to White Horse Hill near Uffington, about ten miles [16 km] east of Swindon, is now less favoured than one about half a mile [0.8 km] south of Lowbury Hill, two miles [3.2 km] north-east of the village of Compton, and 12 [19] west of Reading. Both are high on the Berkshire downs in the very heart of Wessex and the latter lies on the ancient Ridgeway, down which, it seems likely, the Danes were advancing westwards when the Saxons barred their way, inspired, according to Asser, by the humiliating memory of having 'turned their backs' at Reading:

The Christians were aroused by the grief and shame of this and four days later, with all their might and in a determined frame of mind, they advanced against the Viking army at a place called Ashdown . . . But the Vikings, splitting up into two divisions, organized shield-walls of equal size (for they then had two kings and a large number of earls), assigning the core of the army to the two kings and the rest to all the earls. When the Christians saw this, they too split up the army into two divisions in exactly the same way, and established shield-walls no less keenly.

It seems likely that Alfred's division took up its position on one side of the Ridgeway, facing east, and his brother's on the other. Now, however, the latter's piety, which Bishop Asser could hardly criticize, seemed about to lose the battle before it had even begun.

Alfred and his men reached the battlefield sooner and in better order; for his brother, King Ethelred, was still in his tent at prayer, hearing mass and declaring firmly that he would not . . . forsake divine service for that of men . . . Since the Vikings were ready and had reached the battlefield more quickly, Alfred . . . finally deployed the Christian forces against the hostile armies . . . even though the king had not yet come, and acting courageously, like a wild boar . . . when he had closed up the shield-wall in proper order, he moved his army without delay against the enemy.

Alfred's tactics were wholly orthodox: a steady advance by shield-protected swordsmen moving remorselessly forward in a single line. But the Saxons, perhaps because of delay in taking up their position, were at a disadvantage, as Asser reports:

The battlefield was not equally advantageous to both contending parties. The Vikings had taken the higher position first, and the Christians were deploying their battle-line from a lower position. A rather small and solitary thorn-tree . . . grew there, around which the opposing armies clashed violently, with loud shouting from all, one side acting wrongfully and the other side set to fight for life, loved ones and country.

How long the battle lasted, and at what point Ethelred at last got up off his knees and joined in, we do not know, though the daylight must have begun to fade early for it was undoubtedly mid-winter – possibly 8 January 871. Much blood must have been spilt on the green downland turf below that grey sky before, suddenly it seems, it was all over:

When both sides had been fighting to and fro, resolutely and exceedingly ferociously, for quite a long time, the Vikings . . . were unable to withstand the Christians' onslaught any longer; and when a great part of their forces had fallen, they took to ignominious flight. One of the two Viking kings and five earls were cut down in that place, and many thousands on the Viking side were slain there, too – or, rather, over the whole broad expanse of Ashdown, scattered everywhere, far and wide . . . and the entire Viking army was put to flight, right on till nightfall and into the following day, until such time as they reached the stronghold from which they had come. The Christians followed them till nightfall, cutting them down on all sides.

The Battle of Ashdown must for the moment have seemed decisive, but before the month was out the Danes felt confident enough to venture out in strength again, to a point about eleven miles [17 km] south of Reading.

A further fourteen days after these things had happened there, King Ethelred, together with his brother Alfred, combined their forces for a battle against the Vikings, and went to Basing. They clashed violently on all fronts, but after a long struggle the Vikings gained the victory and were masters in the battlefield. When the battle was over, another Viking army came from overseas and attached itself to the band.

In mid-April 871 King Ethelred died. Now all depended on Alfred, born at Wantage in 849. With five brothers, as well as an elder sister, Alfred had seemed unlikely to inherit the throne and he was a serious, bookish, child, who, having mastered all the available Anglo-Saxon works, lamented that there was no one in all Wessex learned enough to teach him the 'liberal arts' such as Latin literature. His recreation was learning poetry, as well as the psalms and daily services, by heart. Alfred was a martyr to two painful and at times crippling illnesses, one known to be piles, the other probably a gastric complaint, but no evidence exists that his sufferings ever affected his judgement or the sweetness of his disposition and there was no question of his not succeeding Ethelred, as Bishop Asser confirms:

> Alfred . . . took over the government of the whole kingdom as soon as his brother had died, with the approval of divine will and according to the unanimous wish of all the inhabitants of the kingdom. Indeed, he could easily have taken it over with the consent of all while his brother Ethelred was alive, had he considered himself worthy to do so, for he surpassed all his brothers both in wisdom and in all good habits; and in particular he was a great warrior and victorious in virtually all battles.

And so the epic struggle that was to make Alfred the idol alike of his own people and posterity began. 871 was known to later historians as 'The year of battles'. Their heavy defeat at Ashdown in January had not checked the Danes for long. By May they had reached the very heart of Wessex, close to the Wiltshire/Dorset border, at Wilton, four miles [6 km] west of Salisbury, nearly 50 miles [80 km] from their winter base at Reading. During the year the army of Wessex fought another eight actions, and at best, as Bishop Asser records, 'the Saxons made peace with the Vikings, on condition that they would leave them; and this the Vikings did.'

So far Alfred had done no more than force the invaders to march off to make a nuisance of themselves elsewhere. This they duly did, settling in London until the Mercians in turn bought them off, 'with immense tribute' according to a contemporary charter, whereupon they moved on to Northumbria. The winter of 872-3 was spent at Rorksey in the Lindsey district, ten miles [16 km] north-west of Lincoln, and the following winter they set up their camp about 30 miles [48 km] further south, at Repton, also on the River Trent, some five miles [8 km] above the future site of Burton, on the Staffordshire/Derbyshire border.

Late in 874 or early in 875 a major new development occurred. The Danish 'host' was divided, a sign that it now had little fear of any force that might be brought against it, at least in the Midlands and the North.

> In the year. . . . 875 . . . the Viking army left Repton and split up into two bands. One band, under Halfdan, set out for the province of the Northumbrians, and spent the winter there beside the river Tyne; it subdued the entire province of the Northumbrians and also ravaged the Picts and the men of Strathclyde. The other band, under three Viking kings (Guthrum, Oscetel and Anwend), went to a place called Cambridge, and spent the winter there.
>
> In . . . 876 . . . the Viking army left Cambridge by night; they went to a fortified site called Wareham . . . situated in the district called . . . Dorset in English, between the two rivers Frome and Tarrant, in a very secure position except on the west, where it is joined to the mainland.

From Wareham raiding parties seem to have sallied out to plunder the surrounding area: according to Ethelwerd, 'they ravaged the greater part of the province.' Alfred proved powerless to stop these murderous excursions and, probably after several months of sporadic fighting, realized he must, as he had done five years before, come to terms:

> King Alfred firmly made a treaty with the army, the condition being that they should leave him; the army, without any dispute, gave him as many picked hostages as he alone chose, and they also took an oath . . . that they would immediately leave his kingdom.

Promises, however, meant little to the Vikings as the all-too-predictable sequel demonstrates: 'One night, practising their usual treachery . . . they broke the treaty, killed all the hostages they had, and turning away, they went unexpectedly to another place, called Exeter . . . There they spent the winter.'

Exeter, protected by a river, with the open sea only a few miles away, was as strong a position as Wareham, and far deeper into Wessex, but now, not for the last time, the weather came to the rescue of the embattled English. In that summer of 877, recorded the *Chronicle*, 'the pirate host sailed west about, and they were caught in a great storm at sea, and there off Swanage 120 ships were lost.' As many as 5000 men may have perished and no doubt this encouraged the garrison of the camp at Exeter to make peace again. For a few months they kept their word, withdrawing to Mercia which, like Northumbria, was divided up between their various kings, though their puppet, Ceolwulf, was allowed to keep what they did not want. The invaders began to put down roots in the Midlands, with the establishment of fortified centres in Derby, Nottingham, Lincoln, Stamford and Leicester, later known collectively as 'the Five Boroughs'. But Wessex was not to be left in peace for long, as the *Anglo-Saxon Chronicle* recorded: 'In this year [878] the host went secretly in midwinter after Twelfth Night to Chippenham, and rode over Wessex and occupied it and drove a great part of the inhabitants oversea, and of the rest they reduced the greater part to submission, except Alfred the king.'

Now, in the opening months of 878, the fortunes of Wessex reached their nadir, its peoples oppressed or driven into exile – even if 'oversea', as some interpretations suggest, merely meant crossing the Bristol Channel – its leader a hunted fugitive, deserted except for a small bodyguard, as his biographer describes:

> King Alfred, with his small band of nobles and also with certain soldiers and thegns, was leading a restless life in great distress amid the woody and marshy places of Somerset. He had nothing to live on except what he could forage by frequent raids, either secretly or even openly, from the Vikings, as well as from the Christians who had submitted to the Vikings' authority.

Some time around Easter, celebrated in 878 on 23 March, after weeks of wandering from place to place, Alfred took refuge in the 'island' of Athelney in West Somerset, a stretch of low-lying ground near the village of the same name, to the east of the road which now runs from Bridgwater to Taunton. Athelney was protected by swampy marshes which became impassable after heavy rain and was conveniently sited for the king's headquarters, lying roughly midway between Chippenham and Exeter, and not far from his birthplace, Wantage and the royal estates at Chippenham, and Faringdon, where he could expect to find support. The wet and wooded countryside around was just the type of area armies tried to avoid and thus ideally suited to a fugitive monarch.

In this dark hour, with Britain and the Christian faith apparently about to be overwhelmed, was born the legend of Alfred as national hero, the epitome of those qualities of courage and steadfastness in adversity generations of Englishmen liked to claim as their own. Already by the twelfth century he was being described as 'England's shepherd' or 'England's darling', by the sixteenth he had become 'Alfred the Great', in the seventeenth he was 'deliverer', in the nineteenth he was 'watchman'. The most famous story attached to Alfred's name was first mentioned in a saint's biography 300 years later, but only given wide currency when Archbishop Parker of Canterbury, in Elizabeth I's reign, inserted it into his edition of Asser's *Life of Alfred*, in 1574. This famous tale recounts how Alfred took refuge during his Athelney period with a poor herdsman's wife who set him to watch the cakes she was baking before an open fire, and scolded him when, preoccupied with his own problems, he allowed them to burn, a reproof he meekly accepted. Another engaging anecdote, first set down in the fourteenth century and generally accepted after Thomas Fuller had recorded it as fact in 1655, had Alfred wandering in the Danish camp 'disguised under the habit of a fiddler', where 'he discovered their condition and some of their intentions'.

Whatever the reasons, the year 878, having begun in disaster, ended in triumph. The first sign that the tide was about to turn came soon after the seizure of Chippenham by Guthrum, when another Danish army appeared far to the west, on the other side of Wessex. Now it was the enemy's turn to suffer a disagreeable surprise, as Bishop Asser related with holy relish:

> In the same year the brother of Ivar and Halfdan sailed with 23 ships from Dyfed [i.e. South-Wales] (where he had spent the winter), after slaughtering many of the Christians there, and came to Devon; there . . . he met an unhappy death with 1200 men, at the hands of the king's thegns, and in front of the stronghold at *Cynuit*. For many of the king's thegns, with their followers, had shut themselves up for safety inside this stronghold . . . The Vikings . . . made no attempt to storm it, since . . . that place is very secure from every direction except the east . . . Instead they began to besiege it, thinking that those men would soon give way, forced by hunger, thirst and the siege . . . But it did not turn out as they thought. For the Christians, long before they were liable to suffer want in any way, were divinely inspired and, judging it much better to gain either death or victory, burst out unexpectedly at dawn against the Vikings and by virtue of their aggressiveness, from the very outset they overwhelmed the enemy . . . together with their king, a few escaping by flight to the ships.

Asser, who actually visited the site of this important sortie, one of the most decisive in the history of siege warfare, does not mention one intriguing detail, recorded by a twelfth-century chronicler:

> They captured no little spoil. And among it they took the banner which they call the Raven. Men say that the three sisters of Inguar . . . the daughters of Lothbrok [i.e. Ragnar Leatherbreeches], wove that banner and did the whole of it in a single day. Moreover men say that in every battle in which that banner went before them, the raven in the middle of the design seemed to flutter as though it were alive, if

they were going to have the victory. But if they were about to be beaten in the coming fight it would hang down without moving.*

The raven – said to have been associated with the god Woden – was to continue to feature in accounts of similar battles for more than a century. What prediction it gave before this West Country battle is unrecorded, but the place is generally accepted as Countisbury, a hill just east of the coastal town of Lynmouth on the Somerset/Devon border.

Alfred was not present at Countisbury, but still in the background, biding his time. Now came the moment for which the fugitive king had been waiting and working, the opportunity to expel the invader and reclaim his kingdom:

> Presently, in the seventh week after Easter [i.e. 4-10 May 878] he rode to Egbert's Stone, which is in the eastern part of Selwood Forest . . . and there all the inhabitants of Somerset and Wiltshire and all the inhabitants of Hampshire – those who had not sailed overseas† for fear of the Vikings – joined up with them. When they saw the king, receiving him (not surprisingly) as if one restored to life after suffering such great tribulations, they were filled with immense joy. They made camp there for one night. At the break of the following dawn the king struck camp and came to a place called Iley and made camp there for one night.

The precise location of Egbert's Stone, where the warriors of Wessex acclaimed their monarch before going out to do battle against the Danes, is uncertain. The likeliest spot is near Penselwood, midway between Wincanton and Mere, where Somerset, Dorset and Wiltshire meet – a natural rallying-point. ('Alfred's Tower', near Stourton, about two miles [3 km] further north, was not erected until around 1720.) 'A place called Iley' is almost certainly the present Eastleigh Wood, at Sutton Veny, two miles [3 km] south-east of Warminster in Wiltshire, and about 13 miles [21 km] from Penselwood, a fair day's march for a newly assembled army.

As the Saxons advanced towards Chippenham the Danes came out to meet them, barring their way high on the Wiltshire downs at Ethandun (or Ethandune), probably close to the present village of Edington, about 13 miles [21 km] south of Chippenham and about seven [11 km] due north of Sutton Veny. Bishop Asser describes the epic encounter which followed:

*Quoted by Hodgkin II/566 from 'Annals of St Neots', attributed to W. M. Stevenson edn of 'Asser's Life of King Alfred', 1904.

†As in an earlier reference (see page 101 above) 'overseas' may here mean crossing a large estuary, in this case Southampton Water.

When the next morning dawned he moved his forces and came to a place called Edington, and fighting fiercely with a compact shield-wall against the entire Viking army, he persevered resolutely for a long time; at length he gained the victory through God's will. He destroyed the Vikings with great slaughter, and pursued those who fled as far as the stronghold, hacking them down; he seized everything which he found outside the stronghold – men (whom he killed immediately), horses and cattle – and boldly made camp in front of the gates of the Viking stronghold with all his army.

A fortnight's siege proved sufficient for the Danes. Capitulation followed, more complete than any achieved before:

When he had been there for 14 days the Vikings, thoroughly terrified by hunger, cold and fear, and in the end by despair, sought peace on this condition: the king should take as many chosen hostages as he wanted from them and give none to them; never before . . . had they made peace with anyone on such terms. When he had heard their embassy, the king (as is his wont) was moved to compassion and took as many chosen hostages from them as he wanted. When they had been handed over, the Vikings swore in addition that they would leave his kingdom immediately, and Guthrum, their king, promised to accept Christianity and to receive baptism at King Alfred's hand. Three weeks later Guthrum . . . with thirty of the best men from his army, came to Alfred at a place called Aller, near Athelney. King Alfred raised him from the holy font of baptism, receiving him as his adopted son.

The treaty of Wedmore, named after a village about eight miles west of modern Wells in Somerset, ended the Saxon/Viking war, though too much should not be made of his baptism; one Viking chief, on a similar occasion, complained cynically that he had 'gone through this washing' twenty times already. But, for a time at least the peace was kept.

Alfred made remarkable use of the breathing space which he had won for himself and his people. For 14 years after 880, though minor incursions continued, Wessex remained free from major invasions. During this period, and to a lesser extent thereafter when he was once again embattled, Alfred undertook a series of reforms and innovations. Even the least military served a patriotic purpose, encouraging a sense of national identity, strengthening Alfred's control over every part of his kingdom, and giving to the struggle against the Danes the character of a spiritual crusade against barbarism.

He also provided the machinery whereby resistance might be made effective. The shire became, and remained, the essential administrative

Saxons vs. Vikings. Danish invasion routes 789–900 and King Alfred's fortified towns.

unit, first of Wessex then of the rest of the country, the authority through which taxes were raised, justice dispensed and troops levied. An assembly of wise men, the *witenagemot*, which bishops, ealdormen and other local dignitaries attended on a rotation system, provided advice to the king and conveyed decisions reached centrally on such matters as the construction of fortifications and the raising of money; half the state's income was earmarked for maintaining the forces and financing new building, the rest being allocated to spiritual, educational and charitable purposes.

Alfred's own conception of this task was set out in the notes he added to his own translation of Boethius's *Consolation of Philosophy*, written in Latin around the year 520 and still in print:

I desired to live worthily as long as I lived and to leave after my life, to the men who should come after me, the memory of me in good works . . . A man cannot work on any enterprise without resources. In the case of the king, the resources and tools with which to rule are that he have his land fully manned; he must have praying men, fighting men and working men.

What Wessex needed most after his great victory at Edington in 878 and the subsequent expulsion of the Danes was fighting men. Their numbers were increased, and their effectiveness improved, in three ways, by reforming the Saxon *fyrd*, or main part-time army, by creating fortified towns, or *burhs*, and by building a fleet.

The *fyrd* was in two parts. The select *fyrd*, drawn from, or financed by, the better-off, might have to serve at any time. The great *fyrd*, called out only in time of war, consisted of the larger landowners, or *thegns*, 'twelve-hynd' men, the 'hynd' or 'hide' being the standard unit of land measurement, some minor yeomen, or 'six-hynd men', and the great mass of ordinary freemen or *ceorls*. Serfs were not required to bear arms, because, with so little to lose, they might desert to the enemy. Many exemptions must also have been made to allow the vital work of the countryside to continue and Alfred seems to have pioneered what was later known as 'the linked battalion' system. 'The king,' comments the *Anglo-Saxon Chronicle* on a later campaign, 'had divided his levies into two sections, so that there was always half at home and half on active service, with the exception of those men whose duty it was to man the fortresses.'

The fortresses, or, more accurately, the fortified towns or *burhs*, were the second of Alfred's great military innovations, designed, on the soundest of military principles, to reduce the need for an army by substituting wood and stone for men. The Danes themselves, as Alfred had had ample evidence, were well able to erect temporary fortifications, but Alfred's scheme was far more ambitious. The works involved were much stronger; a permanent force of *burhware*, 'the men who keep the burhs', was earmarked to garrison the selected towns, exempt from normal service in the *fyrd*; and, above all, for the first time, a systematic plan was drawn up, identifying the danger spots and setting out the area which each fortified town was expected to protect.

About 30 places were ultimately earmarked as *burhs*, though the work did not really get under way until about 890 and even then was not always completed satisfactorily. The main line of defence along Wessex's northern frontier began at Gloucester and then followed the path of the Thames, with fortresses at Oxford, Wallingford, London and, on the other side of the river, Southwark. There were then a series on, or close to, the most exposed part of the coast, at Rochester, Canterbury, Dover, Hastings, Lewes and Chichester, with others at Portchester, where the former Roman defences were repaired, and Christchurch (then known as Twyneham) to guard the Solent. Wareham and Exeter were now both fortified, with another *burh*, the furthest west in the chain, being set up at Lydford in mid-Devon, on the western edge of Dartmoor, close to the Cornish border. Athelney, where Alfred had once hidden, was now fortified as a *burh*, as were Pilton, about four miles [6 km] from Wells in Somerset, Watchet, on the adjoining coast in the middle of what is now Bridgwater Bay, Axbridge, a few miles further north and about seven miles [11 km] from the same stretch of coast, and Bath, where the surviving Roman walls were pressed into service. Both Chippenham and Cirencester, where the Danish 'host' had so recently halted, were now fortified, as were Shaftesbury, Wilton and Winchester, the nearest to a capital that Alfred possessed.

Although a man of ingenious mind and even, in a small way, an inventor – a new type of lantern is credited to his design – Alfred made no real contribution to military architecture. Where Roman defences still stood the Saxons made use of them. Where a convenient promontory existed, as at Lydford and Christchurch, the Saxons dug out a ditch, and erected an earthwork rampart. At Wareham and Wallingford, where the ground was less favourable, the earthen wall was built in a rectangle and faced with wood or stone.

Building the *burh* defences must have been a formidable undertaking; the wall at Wallingford, for example, was a full 3000 yards [2700 m] in circumference. The residents, and those of the surrounding countryside, were required to maintain the walls once built, based on its length in hides, each man being assigned about four feet [1.125 m] to keep in repair and, when necessary, patrol. The principle that a town, rather than the central government, was responsible for its own defences, was to endure for many centuries to come.

Alfred has been somewhat romantically described as 'the father of the Royal Navy', a claim to which an entry in the *Anglo-Saxon Chronicle* for 882 lends support:

> And the same year King Alfred went out to sea with ships and fought against four ships' companies of Danes, and captured two of the ships, and slew the men; and two surrendered to him, and the men were badly cut about and severely wounded before they surrendered.

In 885 Alfred's infant navy fought another successful action:

> In the same year Alfred . . . transferred his fleet . . . from Kent to East Anglia in order to plunder that area. When they arrived at the mouth of the River Stour, 13 Viking ships rigged for battle immediately advanced . . . A sea-battle was joined; there was savage fighting everywhere. All the Vikings were killed and all their ships (together with all their booty) were captured.

The year after the naval battle at Stourmouth, i.e. in 886, Wessex firmly took control of the largest and most important city in the island, which stood in a key strategic position on the border between that kingdom and Mercia. Bishop Asser recorded the event:

> In this same year, Alfred, king of the Anglo-Saxons, restored the city of London splendidly – after so many towns had been burned and so many people slaughtered – and made it habitable again; he entrusted it to . . . Ethelred, ealdorman of the Mercians. All the Angles and Saxons – those who had formerly been scattered everywhere and were not in captivity with the Vikings – turned willingly to King Alfred.

From being a possible source of dissension between Wessex and Mercia, London henceforward became the linch-pin which bound them together. It is on these foundations, and the *Anglo-Saxon Chronicle* for 886, which says that 'all the English people submitted to him, except those who were in captivity to the Danes', that later descriptions of Alfred as the first king of England are based.

The Danes, whether peaceful or militant, remained an alien presence, but the utmost Alfred could hope to do was to confine them to the extensive area known as the Danelaw, within which their own laws applied. Probably after the indecisive battles of 886, Alfred drew up a major treaty with Guthrum laying down in detail the boundary line between the Danelaw and the Saxon kingdoms. The frontier line ran along the Thames, then up the River Lea to its source, then in a straight line to Bedford, and from there along the banks of the River Ouse to Watling Street, between Tamworth in Staffordshire and Passenham in Northamptonshire, so that the country was split roughly along a diagonal line drawn between London and Chester. The Danelaw represented a huge foreign enclave within England, covering around one-third of the country – excluding Wales and Scotland – from the Tees to the Humber estuary, and from the Trent to the Thames, embracing part of Yorkshire, the whole of Lincolnshire and East Anglia and most of the East Midlands, with the frontier line extending from Lichfield, through Repton, to Nottingham and present-day Goole. No future invader, with one exception, was to secure so much, and though Alfred had saved Wessex, and preserved the Christian faith, he had had to pay a heavy price.

Guthrum kept loyally to his word until his death in 890, but he had no power to restrain the Danes now on the Continent, who in 892 decided to cut their losses in mainland Europe and seek supposedly easier victories and a permanent place of settlement across the Channel. Some ships carried women and children, but the two armies the Danes assembled were still far larger than any previously encountered, and the smaller had a commander with a fearsome reputation, Haesten, who

25 years before had personally killed in a single battle two Frankish commanders, and was a veteran of many of the Vikings' most impressive exploits.

Alfred now faced his last, and greatest, challenge, as the *Anglo-Saxon Chronicle* evidently recognized:

892. In this year the great host . . . went again from the east kingdom [i.e. of the German King Arnulf] westward to Boulogne, and were there provided with ships so that they crossed in one voyage, horses and all, and then came up into the mouth of the Lympne with 250 ships. That estuary is in East Kent, at the east end of the great forest we call Andraed [i.e. the Weald] . . . They pulled their ships upstream as far as the forest, four miles from the entrance to the estuary, and there stormed a fort within the fen; occupying it were a few peasants and it was half built.

While, probably around October 892, the main Danish force was digging in around Appledore, in southern Kent, a second landing was made about 20 miles [32 km] to the north, via another already classic invasion route: 'Soon after this Haesten came with 80 ships into the mouth of the Thames and made himself a fort at Milton Royal.'

Milton Royal was on the banks of the River Swale, behind the Isle of Sheppey, the enemy ships having apparently sailed in round the Isle of Thanet. Haesten was clearly acting in concert with the unnamed leader of the main Viking force, suggesting a growing sophistication in the Danes' strategy. The two camps between them were obviously designed to dominate the whole of East Kent and provide a bridgehead more than 40 miles [64 km] across, stretching from the Thames to the Sussex coast and 25 miles [40 km] deep, providing a vast base for plundering the east coast and for receiving reinforcements from France or even Norway.

No alternative now remained but war and, in the spring or early summer of 893 the Saxons' first move was to try to prevent the two newly arrived enemy armies joining forces:

Then King Alfred gathered his levies and marched so that he was encamped between the two hosts, at a convenient distance from the stronghold in the forest and the stronghold on the water so that he could overtake either if they wished to make for any open country. Then afterwards they moved through the woods in gangs and bands, wherever the margin was left unguarded; and almost every day other troops, both from the levies and also from the forts went to attack them, either by day or by night . . . Only twice did the host come out from the camps in full force; on the one occasion when they first landed, before the levies were mustered, and on the other occasion when they wished to evacuate those positions. They had then seized much plunder and wished to carry that northwards across the Thames into Essex, to meet the ships. Then the levies rode and intercepted them and fought against them at Farnham, and put the host to flight and recovered the plunder; and they fled across the Thames without using any ford, then up by the Colne on to an island.

Farnham, in Surrey, close to the Hampshire border, was 70 miles [112 km] from Appledore but near the western extremity of the Andred's Weald, and the Danes were now granted a respite. The section of the *fyrd* on duty was due to go home and its replacement had not yet taken over, so that a siege of the island on the Colne had to be abandoned. The residents of the Danelaw now demonstrated that their loyalty was to their compatriots, not to the king of their adopted land:

> When he was on his way thither and the other levies were on their way home, the Danes remaining behind in their position because their king had been wounded in the fight and could not be moved, the Danes dwelling in Northumbria and East Anglia assembled about 100 ships which sailed south about and about 40 ships which sailed north about and besieged a fort in Devonshire on the Bristol Channel; and those which sailed south about besieged Exeter. When the king learned of this, he marched west towards Exeter with all the levies, with the exception of a very inconsiderable part who continued eastward.

Alfred had had no option but to divide his forces, for now a third danger had developed. Haesten, last heard of at Milton in Kent, had, it seems, sent an advance guard to Benfleet in Essex, probably during the truce secured by the baptism of his sons. He had then decided to transfer his main force there, and the main Danish army, checked at Farnham, had apparently moved on from the temporary camp at Colne to the same site.

The fort at Benfleet was on a spit of land by the Thames, easily protected by earthworks; once the enemy were firmly established there they were likely to be exceedingly difficult to dislodge. But Alfred's son Edward, and his son-in-law Ealdorman Ethelred, were equal to the challenge.

> Then they [the English] advanced and put that host to flight, stormed the fort, and seized everything inside it, both property and women and also children and conveyed them all into London; and all the ships they either broke up or burned up or brought to London or to Rochester.

It had been an unrewarding year for the Danes and soon afterwards, during 894, they were on the move again, only to become victims of their own predatory behaviour:

> In this year, the host moved from Wirral into Wales; they were unable to remain there because they had been deprived of both the cattle and corn which had been plundered. Then again they moved from Wales with the plunder they had taken there, marching across Northumbria and East Anglia so that the levies were unable to get at them, until they reached east Essex, on an island out at sea called Mersea.

The expedition was now back almost at its starting point, for Mersea Island, at the mouth of the River Colne, about seven miles [11 km] due south of Colchester by land, was only about 22 miles [35 km] south-east of their old base at Benfleet. A further campaign followed in 895 but the Danes faced increasing resistance, although Alfred remained too weak to destroy their army and had to be content to harry it back into the Danelaw. At last, however, it seemed that they had had enough of invading Wessex:

> The following summer [i.e. 896] the host dispersed, some to East Anglia, some to Northumbria, and those without stock [i.e. without families or possessions to keep them in England] got themselves ships there, and sailed south oversea to the Seine. The host, by the mercy of God, had not altogether utterly crushed the English people.

It was probably about this time that he undertook the second stage of his naval building programme:

> Then King Alfred ordered warships to be built to meet the Danish ships; they were almost twice as long as the others, some had 60 oars, some more; they were both swifter, steadier, and with more freeboard than the others: they were built neither after the Frisian design, nor after the Danish, but as it seemed to himself that they could be most serviceable.

Precisely what type of vessel Alfred constructed remains obscure, but it was certainly the first built in England specifically as a warship. It clearly outclassed the Viking longships in size and speed, and provided a more stable fighting-platform from which to launch arrows and spears, while its greater height gave it a tactical advantage in fighting at close quarters.
Alfred's fleet now proved its worth:

> On one occasion the same year [896] came six ships to the Isle of Wight and did much harm there, both in Devon and almost everywhere along the coast. Then the king ordered nine of the new ships to put out, and they blockaded the entrance from the open sea against their escape.

Then the Danes sailed out with three ships against them, and three of their ships were beached on dry land at the upper end of the harbour and the crews had gone off inland. Then the English seized two of the three ships at the entrance to the estuary, and slew the men, but the other escaped; in her also all but five were slain; and they escaped because the ships of the others were aground . . . When the tide had ebbed many furlongs from the ships, the Danes went from the three ships to the other three which were stranded on their side and then there they fought. There were slain . . . 62 . . . English and Frisians, and 120 of the Danes. The tide, however, came first to the Danish ships, before the Christians could push off theirs, and hence they rowed away out to sea. They were so sorely crippled that they were unable to row past Sussex, but there the sea cast two of them ashore; the men were led to the king at Winchester, and he had them hanged there. The men who were on the single ship reached East Anglia badly wounded.

So on a Hampshire gallows, and in a battered ship, laden with wounded, limping back to the safety of the Danelaw, ended the Danes' last great attempt to subdue Alfred's kingdom during his lifetime. The battle on the shore, probably at Poole harbour in Dorset, was in some ways the greatest of all his victories, for it pointed the way to the island's future inviolability, through mastery of the element which had exposed her to almost incessant attack for the past half-century. The Danelaw, and the lasting threat it provided, remained, but Alfred had saved Wessex, and thereby England. He was still only 50 when he died, perhaps of the plague, probably of sheer exhaustion. The *Anglo-Saxon Chronicle* gave him a brief obituary which hardly did him justice, though the king, a modest man, might have appreciated it:

In this year died Alfred, son of Ethelwulf, six nights before All Hallows' Day [i.e. on 26 October 899]. He was king over all England except that part which was under Danish domination, and he ruled the kingdom twenty-eight and a half years.

IO

BUYING OFF THE SPEAR

In this year it was decided for the first time to pay tribute to the Danes because of the great terror they inspired along the sea coast.

The Anglo-Saxon Chronicle, *991*

King Alfred had prevented his country from being overwhelmed by its invaders but for more than a century after his death the struggle for mastery of the island continued. The Danes were relatively weakly established in East Anglia, though it was part of the Danelaw, but firmly in control in the East Midlands, dominated by their Five Boroughs, and increasingly powerful in the north-west, in an area stretching roughly between modern Manchester and Carlisle and covering about one-third of the distance between the Lancashire and Yorkshire coasts. These Northumbrian Norwegians came from Ireland, a seemingly inexhaustible reservoir of new settlers, but in the long run an even greater threat was posed by the new Viking state across the Channel, where a whole new kingdom was founded by Rolf, or Rollo, the Ganger; being too tall to ride the small northern horses he had to 'gang', i.e. walk, on foot. In 913 the king of the West Franks was forced to come to terms with the marauding Danes and offered them a province of their own, with land on either side of the Seine and a capital at Rouen. In return Rollo agreed to be baptized, under a new name, becoming Robert, first Duke of Normandy, and to marry the French king's daughter. Before long the newcomers vastly extended their territory and became more French than the French, adopting their language and becoming known as Normans, a name destined to be writ large in British history.

The two great military reforms accomplished by Alfred, the reorganization of the *fyrd* into two forces, and the building of *burhs* as local strongholds, now began to bear their richest fruit. The new King Edward the Elder and his sister not merely fortified towns within their own territory, to prevent the enemy marauding at will, but also built new fortresses in and around the Danelaw, a process in which Ethelfled, described by the *Anglo-Saxon Chronicle* as the 'Lady of the Mercians', was at least as active as her brother. For the next few years the *Anglo-Saxon Chronicle* is full of stories of raids and fortress-building, but there seem to have been no major invasions nor any decisive engagements. Again and again, however, the fortified towns proved their worth, not merely as places of refuge, but as secure bases from which the garrisons ventured out to harass any invading force weak enough to attack.

Protecting the whole coastline was impossible but even here Edward had some notable successes, as in 915:

> The king had arranged that the coast should be guarded against them along the southern shore of the Severn estuary, from Cornwall in the west eastwards as far as the mouth of the Avon, with the result that they durst not land anywhere in that region. However, they landed secretly by night on two separate occasions, once east of Watchet and again at Porlock, and on each occasion the English struck them so that only those few escaped who were able to swim out to the ships. They [i.e. the rest] encamped out on the island of Steepholme until the time came that they were very short of food, and many men perished of hunger, since they were unable to obtain provisions; then they went thence to Dyfed [i.e. South Wales] and thence to Ireland.

Edward's sister, meanwhile, was proving equally successful further north. Shortly before she died, in 917, she had seized Derby and Leicester, two of the famous 'Five Boroughs', which commanded the surrounding countryside, sometimes almost to the limits of the shires later named after them. Her brother, Edward, advancing north into the Danelaw proper, had already occupied Witham and Maldon close to the Essex coast, and Hertford and Bedford further inland, while he went on, as Ethelfled was making her great move forward, to take back into English hands two more of the five boroughs, at Nottingham and Lincoln, along with Colchester and Northampton.

Edward had no intention of allowing his sister's death to halt the progress of taming the Danes. Mercia, already subordinate to Wessex, was now annexed to it and the *Anglo-Saxon Chronicle* recorded the astonishing climax to his achievement, a mere quarter-century after his father had bequeathed to him a country half-occupied by dangerous aliens and surrounded by potential enemies:

> 924. In this year King Edward was accepted as 'father and lord' by the king of the Scots and his people, by King Regnald and all the Northumbrians, also by the king of the Strathclyde Welsh and all his subjects.

Edward the Elder did not live long to enjoy his triumph. He died in the same year and his son Elfwerd survived him by only 16 days. The new king, Athelstan, was happily more robust and carried on his father's expansionist policy:

> 934. In this year King Athelstan invaded Scotland both with a land and naval force, and harried much of the country.

It was perhaps this alarmingly effective demonstration of the power of the newly-united English that finally drove Athelstan's enemies into forming a coalition against him under the formidable leadership of the Viking Olaf, who that year became the Viking ruler in Dublin and of all his countrymen in eastern Ireland. Olaf's father had been driven out of Northumbria by Athelstan and the invasion from across the Irish Sea which Olaf mounted, aided by a confederacy of Scots, Welsh and Anglo-Danes resident in Britain, was on a huge scale. According to the medieval chronicler William of Malmesbury, a monastic librarian writing around the year 1125, a huge armada of 615 ships sailed up the Humber, presumably after travelling north-about round Scotland, to join a great land-based force assembled from Scotland and north-west England. Estimates of the size of Olaf's army range from an improbable 20,000 to an inconceivable 60,000, but whatever the true total it was met by a joint Wessex-Mercian forces under Athelstan. One of the two epic battles of the century followed. The site, Brunanburh, remains unidentified, though the suggestions include Burnswark in Dumfrieshire, four miles [6 km] south-east of Lockerbie and about 20 [32 km] north-west of Carlisle, Bromborough on the River Mersey in Cheshire, and, by a modern writer, 'a location between Derby and Rotherham'.

The battle of Brunanburh began at dawn, the Mercians, under their own commanders, advancing against the Danes, the Saxons from Wessex charging the Scots. The resulting struggle, a fierce, hand-to-hand no-holds-barred affair, involved vast slaughter on both sides and dragged on all day. Victory when it came was decisive and, for once, properly exploited, with the Saxon horsemen hunting down and hacking to pieces the Danes and Scots who fled from the field. To record the great event the *Anglo-Saxon Chronicle* for 937 lapsed into verse, its compiler presumably transcribing the work of an unknown contemporary poet:

> In this year King Athelstan, lord of warriors,
> Ring-giver of men, with his brother prince Edmund,
> Won undying glory with the edges of swords,
> In warfare around *Brunanburh*.
> With their hammered blades, the sons of Edward
> Clove the shield-wall and hacked the linden bucklers,
> As was instinctive in them, from their ancestry,

To defend their land, their treasures and their homes,
In frequent battle against each enemy.

The anonymous poet described with relish how each section of the great
coalition met its end:

The foemen were laid low: the Scots
And the host from the ships fell doomed. The field
Grew dark with the blood of men after the sun,
Rose high in the morning, above the horizon.
There lay many a warrior
Of the men of the North, torn by spears,
Shot o'er his shield; likewise many a Scot
Sated with battle, lay lifeless.

The sorry Norsemen who escaped the spears
Set out upon the sea . . . making for Dublin
O'er deep waters, in ships with nailed sides
Ashamed and shameless back to Ireland.

Athelstan's death late in 939 was followed by a new invasion by Irish
Vikings, seeking revenge for Brunanburh. The new king, Athelstan's
brother Edmund, had fought there, as a 16-year-old. Now eighteen,
Edmund managed to intercept Olaf's army at Leicester, but under the
treaty which followed was forced to surrender all his dead brother's
gains and the area between Watling Street and Northumbria, covering
Leicestershire, Derbyshire, Nottinghamshire and Lincolnshire, was now
restored to Danish rule. Olaf made the customary gesture of being
baptized, but in the following year, 941, it became all too clear that this
had not brought any change of heart, for he again invaded Northumbria
beyond the River Tees and even sacked a church near Dunbar.

Edmund was killed, in May 946, in a manner more Viking than
English, stabbed to death in mid-feast by a thief he had banished. His
sons were mere infants, so he was, in the sensible Saxon fashion,
succeeded by his brother, Eadred. By the time of King Eadred's death in
955, although Cumbria had been abandoned to the Scots, Northumbria
was safely within the overlordship of Wessex under an earl answerable
to the king, and the titles Eadred had adopted – 'King of the Anglo-
Saxons', 'Lord of All Albion', even, most grandiose of all, 'Caesar of the
whole of Britain' – were a statement of fact rather than of pious
aspiration.

The disastrous two-year reign of Eadred's 15-year-old nephew,
Eadwig, known because of his beauty as the 'all-fair', was followed by

that of his brother Edgar, from 959 to 975, later regarded as a halcyon interlude in English history.

King Edgar was succeeded by his eldest son. Edward, born to his first wife, and, in 878, by Edward's half-brother, Ethelred, aged ten. The new reign, according to an anonymous monk writing a few years later, began in high promise:

> King Ethelred, the illustrious atheling [i.e. royal prince or heir apparent], was consecrated to the supreme dignity of the kingdom . . . and there was great rejoicing at his consecration. For he was young in years, graceful in manners, beautiful in face and comely in appearance.

But Ethelred proved, tragically for his country, to be both the longest-reigning and the feeblest monarch of all Alfred's line. Self-indulgent, cruel, distrustful and, above all, perpetually vacillating between one policy and another, he was to go down to posterity as Ethelred the Redeless, i.e. the man of no counsel, or Ethelred Unraed, the uncounselled, converted over the centuries into Ethelred the Unready.

It was Ethelred's misfortune that his accession should have coincided with a new burst of restless, ruthless activity among the Scandinavian peoples. A Danish chieftain, Harold Gormsson, later known as Harold Bluetooth, had recently, as he himself boasted, 'won for himself all Denmark and Norway and made the Danes Christians', a conversion which, somewhat ironically, was to endanger Christian England, for many of his subjects refused to abandon their old faith and instead set off overseas. For the compilers of the *Anglo-Saxon Chronicle*, if any remembered the distant and dangerous past, it must have been like old times come again:

> 980. In this year . . . Southampton was ravaged by a pirate host and most of the citizens slain or taken prisoner. In the same year the island of Thanet was harried; and . . . Cheshire was harried by a pirate host from the north.
>
> 981. In this year Padstow was laid waste; and in the same year much destruction was done everywhere along the coast, both in Devon and Cornwall . . .
>
> 982. In this year three pirate crews landed in Dorset and ravaged in Portland . . .
>
> 987. In this year Watchet was ravaged.
>
> 988. In this year Goda, the Devonshire thane, was slain and many with him.

The fierce resistance the West Country men put up on this occasion became a legend, recalled with pride by the biographer of the then Archbishop of York, writing around the year 1000.

A very severe battle took place in the west, in which our countrymen, who are called Devonshiremen, strongly resisted and obtained the victory of a holy triumph, thus gaining glory. Many of our side fell, more of theirs, for of our men, a most brave thegn, Streonwold by name, was killed, with some others, who preferred to end their lives by a warlike death than to live in shame.

Soon other parts of the coast were being attacked as the *Anglo-Saxon Chronicle* makes clear:

> 991. In this year came Anlaf with 93 ships to Folkestone and harried outside, and sailed thence to Sandwich, and thence to Ipswich, over-running all the countryside and so on to Maldon.

'Anlaf' was Olaf Tryggvason, who later became king of Norway, and both the size of his fleet and his successive attacks on Kent, Suffolk and Essex revealed a danger far worse than any so far encountered by Ethelred. The stage was set for the second great set-piece battle of the century, the Battle of Maldon.

If Ethelred, now aged 18, was present at Maldon the fact is unrecorded and the unchallenged hero, and victim, of the day was the local ealdorman, a veteran of earlier Viking raids who had held his high office for 25 years. Now he faced the same enemy again, as the *Chronicle* recorded: 'Ealdorman Byrhtnoth came to meet them with his levies and fought them.'

The Norwegians – whether the Danes were also involved is uncertain – had taken up a very strong position, of a kind they had so often occupied before, on the island of Northey, which lies rather under two miles [3 km] down-river from Maldon, linked by a causeway which still exists – the island itself has become a bird sanctuary – to the land. As the River Blackwater, then as now, is tidal, it could only be crossed at low tide. The two armies confronted each other on either side of the water as they waited for its level to fall, an ideal situation in which to exchange offers of peace, or threats, and to deliver grandiose morale-boosting speeches. A detailed, and conceivably accurate, account of these exchanges, and of the subsequent encounter, survives in *The Battle of Maldon*, a magnificent contemporary poem, possibly written by an eye-witness:

> The Viking herald stood on the river's brim,
> Scornful, haughty words the sea-pirate spoke.
> 'I come,' said he, 'from bold sea-warriors. Send us at once
> Gifts as a ransom; 'twill be best for you in the end
> To buy off our onslaught, rather than to stand
> The strength of our spear charge. No need is there of fight

1 Fixed defences, Roman style: Hadrian's Wall in Northumberland

2 Fixed defences, British style: Maiden Castle, Dorset

3　The conquerors of
　Britain. *left*: Caesar
4　*Below left*: Claudius
5　*Below right*:
　Hadrian

6 Rulers of England: *Above left*: Alfred
7   *Above right:* Edgar
8   *Below left:* Cnut
9   *Below right:* Edward the Confessor

10   'In frequent battle'. *Top*: Saxons fighting the Vikings
11   *Bottom*: Saxons fighting the Danes at Stamford
                             Bridge

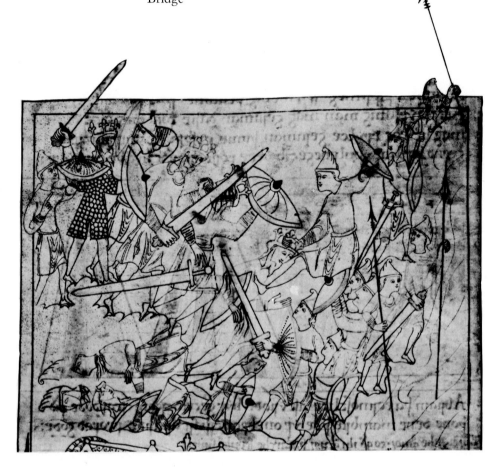

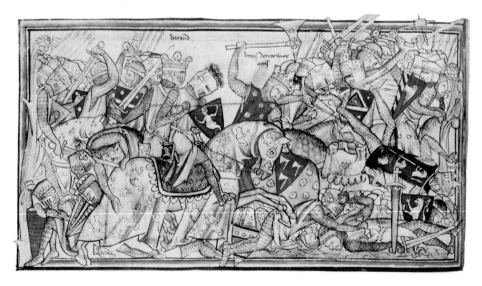

12   The end of Saxon England. Two scenes from the Bayeux Tapestry depicting the
13   death of King Harold

14 Warfare, Norman style.
Top left: An early siege engine
15 *Top right:* Defending a castle with missiles
16 *Above:* A seaborne attack on a coastal fort
17 *Right:* Storming the battlements

18   A very English weapon. Longbows in action during a siege
19   Archery practice

20 'Lords of the English sea'. A small ship action. An illustration from a 13th century military treatise, *De re militari*

21 A big ship battle. Sluys, 1340

If ye but agree. For gold ye shall have peace . . .
Take ye your peace and we
With all our booty will put out to sea, sail from these coasts
And ever hold faith and friendship, at peace with you for aye.'

The English commander did not reply, as well he might, that earlier generations of his people had heard similar promises before. He struck instead, according to the anonymous poet, a nobler note:

Then Byrhtnoth answered, his voice in anger rose,
His shield he waved,
He shook his ashen spear-shaft and in rage his voice rang out.
'Hear then, thou sea-wolf, the answer of my folk.
The tribute we will give shall be the point of spear,
The keen, envenomed point, the thin ground edge, the battle-gear
That shall in fight destroy ye. Go, thou pirates' herald,
Send thou this message of deep-seated hate.
Here stand I, an earl, stand with my men
To hold this land against ye, this land and its people,
For Ethelred my king. In war shall ye heathen be crushed.
Think ye we'd shame, since ye have come so far,
To buy our peace with gold? No! In the cut and thrust
Of sword and spear, we'll pay in full our ransom.'

If Byrhtnoth actually, as the poet implies, withdrew the advance-guard on the causeway to allow the enemy to assemble in strength on the mainland, it seems an act of military folly. There may, however, have been strategic sense in what seemed tactical madness, for if contained on Thorney Island the Vikings would no doubt eventually have sailed off to harass some other section of the coast, while if brought to battle they might be crushed for good. More puzzling is the Saxons' failure to fall upon the enemy while they were most vulnerable, as they waded ashore, or, for that matter, to storm the island themselves. If the Danes, as the poem confirms, could cross the river at low tide – 'The sea-wolves,' says the poet, 'waded through the flood, west o'er the shining water' – what prevented the Saxons doing the same?

The Viking hosts with shields aloft strode through the Panta [i.e. River Blackwater], climbed up the bank . . .
Flashed from the fingers the sharp-filed spear,
Whipped from the humming string the arrow keen and hard,
Shield clashed with spear, bitter was the battle rush.
Strong men on each side fell to earth.

Wounded twice, Byrhtnoth was rescued by a young man described as

'King Ethelred's thane': the king himself, now 23, preferred to fight by proxy. Finally, overwhelmed in close combat, Byrhtnoth dies a holy, hero's death:

> There fell from his grip the gold-hilted sword, no more could he
> hold
> The fine steel again, no more his weapons wield.
> Then cried he aloud, the grey-bearded fighter, encouraged his men,
> Bade them fight on, keep heart and face the foe.

In spite of a final rally by the bravest of the Saxons Maldon field was lost. As the evening shadows crept over the flat wastes of the Essex shore and the tide began to come in, bearing away the bodies of the fallen, some of the Saxons:

> Rushed from the battle and made for the forests
> Sought the fastness of the woods and saved their lives.

Although the Danes had been badly mauled it was the Saxons who had suffered a decisive defeat, and the *Anglo-Saxon Chronicle* recorded what followed: 'Afterwards peace was made with them and the king stood sponsor for him [i.e. Olaf] at confirmation.'

There was, however, a far more dangerous development. 'Buy off the spear, or bear it,' ran a Saxon proverb. Bearing the spear having proved unendurable, Ethelred now opted, as the *Chronicle* describes, for the alternative: 'In the same year [991] it was decided for the first time to pay tribute to the Danes on account of the atrocities they wrought along the sea coast. On this first occasion it amounted to ten thousand pounds.'

By the end of 991* Ethelred had negotiated a full-scale treaty with the Danes under which Olaf Tryggvason undertook to protect Ethelred's kingdom against any other Viking army that might attack it. Rules were laid down for arbitration of disputes between Englishmen and Vikings and – the real nub of the matter – Ethelred confirmed that £22,000 in gold and silver had been paid the invaders in return for peace.

A melancholy sequence of attack, betrayal and defeat now set in, with each year bringing worse tidings than the last and with the tedious repetition of English humiliation and impotence varied only by the change of location as the enemy, finding the whole island at their mercy, turned their brutal attention to one area after another. The total failure of Ethelred's costly and grovelling subservience after Maldon was finally revealed in 994, only three years later, when his supposed protector, Olaf Tryggvason, now reappeared under his true colours, in alliance

---

*994 according to some accounts. I have followed Stenton, p. 372 fn 1, which gives reasons for preferring the earlier date.

with a new and hardly less formidable foe, Swein, son of King Harold of Denmark.

> 994. In this year on the Nativity of St Mary [8 September] came Anlaf [i.e. Olaf] and Swein to London with 94 ships, and kept up an unceasing attack on the city and they purposed moreover to set it on fire, but there they suffered greater loss and injury than they ever thought possible that any garrison would inflict upon them . . . They went away, doing as much harm as any host was capable of doing in burning, harrying and slaughter, both along the coast and in Essex, Kent, Sussex and Hampshire. Finally they got themselves horses, and rode far and wide wherever they pleased, and continued to do unspeakable damage.

Ethelred's response was very different from what King Alfred's had been in similar circumstances. He knew only one answer to defeat: capitulation:

> Then the king and his councillors agreed to send to them, offering tribute and supplies, if they would desist from harrying. This they agreed to, and the whole host came to Southampton, and there took up winter-quarters, and were provisioned from the whole kingdom of Wessex and paid £16,000. Then the king sent Bishop Aelfheah and ealdorman Ethelweard to seek King Anlaf, hostages being sent meanwhile to the ships; and Anlaf was conducted with great ceremony to the king at Andover. The king stood sponsor for him at confirmation and gave him royal gifts; and Anlaf then promised, and also kept his word, that he would never come again to England with warlike intent.

That Olaf should have observed his side of the bargain was indeed remarkable enough to merit recording, though probably due to the fact that not long afterwards he became involved elsewhere and subsequently became king of Norway. The English had, however, whatever the reasons, secured two years of peace, a bargain at the price, but in 997 other Northmen returned, in greater strength than ever, and, for the first time, apparently acting on a continuous, coordinated plan which marked out one coastal area after another for systematic plundering:

> In this year the host went round Devonshire into the mouth of the Severn, and there harried, both in Cornwall, Wales and Devon and landed at Watchet; they wrought great havoc by burning and killing people and then went back round Land's End to the south side, and entered the estuary of the Tamar, and so up it until they came to Lydford [i.e. Lydford, Devon, about ten miles [16 km] east of

Launceston, not Lydford, Somerset]. There they burned and slew everything they met, and burnt to the ground Ordwulf's abbey church at Tavistock, carrying off an indescribable amount of plunder with them to the ships.

Manifestly, 'buying off the spear' had failed. All that had changed was that the enemy were now bargaining from even greater strength than before:

1002. In this year the king and his councillors decided to pay tribute to the fleet and to make peace, on condition that they ceased from their evil deeds. The king sent ealdorman Leofsige to the fleet and he, at the command of the king and his councillors, arranged a truce with them, and that they should receive maintenance and tribute. This was accepted and they were paid £24,000.

This latest humiliation, which all too clearly presaged similar blackmail to come, was followed by Ethelred's first real attack on the Danes in a treacherous massacre:

In the same year the king gave orders for all the Danish people who were in England to be slain on St Brice's day [13 November], because the king had been told that they wished to deprive him of his life by treachery, and all his councillors after him, and then seize his kingdom.

The St Brice's Day massacre had the very reverse of the intended effect. It infuriated the Danes who escaped it, without intimidating them, and prompted King Swein of Denmark to resolve to avenge his sister, Gunnhild, who had been living in England, and was among the victims. Swein Forkbeard, as he was known, held sway, through puppet rulers, over much of Norway as well as Jutland and the adjoining islands, and had defeated that same Olaf Tryggvason who had been so sore a trial to the English Saxons in the past. In the same year Ethelred married his second wife, Emma, sister of Duke Richard II of Normandy, and known to the chroniclers as 'the lady'. Instead of bringing her adopted homeland fresh allies she proved instead a source of fresh weakness and the marriage connection with Normandy was to have lasting and unforeseen consequences. Meanwhile, in 1003, with treason encouraging cowardice, and cowardice opening the door to defeat, the fortunes of Ethelred's unhappy country seemed to have reached their nadir:

In this year Exeter was destroyed through Hugh, the French fellow, whom the Lady [i.e. Queen Emma] had appointed as her reeve; the host utterly laid waste the borough and seized much plunder there.

It was not until 1005 that the Danes finally set sail for home, but they returned in 1006 and again the next year when 'tribute money amounting to £30,000 was paid to the hostile host', sufficient to ensure that for the rest of 1007 the land was left in peace, and in 1008, another Viking-free year, Ethelred at last began to react more positively to the still ever-present threat.

> 1008. In this year the king gave orders that ships should be speedily built throughout the whole of England; namely one large warship from each three hundred hides and a cutter from every ten hides, while every eight hides were to provide a helmet and a corselet.
> 1009. In this year the ships . . . were made ready, and there were more of them . . . than there had ever been before in England in the days of any king. They were all brought together off Sandwich to be stationed there to protect this realm against every invading host.

Now, however, Ethelred's efforts were to be frustrated by a fierce squabble among the noblemen commanding his new navy, which ended in one man playing the Viking and leading 20 ships 'harrying everywhere along the south coast' while most of the remaining eight, which set off in pursuit of the traitor, were wrecked 'by a storm worse than anyone could remember'. The compiler of the *Anglo-Saxon Chronicle* had once again only a tale of disaster to record:

> When news of the fate of these ships reached the rest of the fleet under the command of the king, then it was as if everything was in confusion, for the king, the ealdormen and the chief councillors went home, abandoning the ships thus irresponsibly. Then those who remained with the ships brought them back to London, thus inconsiderately allowing the effort of the whole nation to come to naught, so that the threat to the Danes, upon which the whole of England had set its hopes, turned out to be no more potent than this.

The Viking attacks had been accompanied by much casual, indifferent cruelty, but few atrocities of sadistic violence undertaken for its own sake are recorded. In the campaign which began in the autumn of 1011, however, the invaders were to commit their worst, or most publicized, outrage since the martyrdom of King Edmund 140 years earlier.* The story began with the sacking of the most holy place in England:

> In this same year, between the Nativity of St Mary [8 September] and Michaelmas [29 September] they besieged Canterbury and made their way in through treachery . . . And there they seized the Archbishop Aelfheah [i.e. Alphege] and . . . all those in holy orders, both men and women, that were in the borough . . . They remained in the

*See Chapter 8, page 94.

borough as long as they wished; and when they had searched it thoroughly, then they went to their ships, taking the archbishop with them.

For seven months the Danes kept the saintly Alphege a prisoner, until his captivity reached a tragic conclusion:

The host became greatly incensed against the bishop, because he was not willing to offer them any money and forbad any ransome to be given for him. Moreover they were very drunk, for wine had been brought to them from the south. Then they took the bishop, and led him to their tribunal, on Saturday evening within the octave of Easter [19 April], and pelted him to death with bones and the heads of cattle; and one of them smote him on the skull with the iron of an axe, so that with the blow he sank down and his holy blood fell upon the earth, and his holy soul was sent forth to God's kingdom.

Sixty years after his death Alphege was to be canonized, but he left a more immediate legacy to his country, for the commander of a substantial part of the Viking fleet, Thorkell the Tall, was so disgusted by the drunken butchery at Greenwich, that he switched sides immediately peace was concluded: 'When the tribute was paid, and oaths of peace were sworn, then the host dispersed as widely as before it had been concentrated. Then 45 ships transferred their allegiance to the king, and promised him to guard this land, on condition that he fed and clothed them.'

This unexpected bonus of a ready-made navy proved unable to stave off the final disasters of Ethelred's reign. King Swein of Denmark was soon on the move again and Thorkell's defection provided an excuse, if any were needed, for a new attack on England. According to the Danish writer known as the Encomiast, from the *Encomium*, or uncritical biography, he wrote of Queen Emma, the initiative for this latest attack came from the warriors surrounding King Swein: 'The soldiers of the above-mentioned king, confident that they would profit by the firm steadfastness of their lord, decided to persuade him, who was already meditating the same plan, to invade England, and add it to the bounds of his empire by war.'

Swein prudently left behind his younger son to rule in his stead, but 'took the elder in his own company':

And so, everything being duly arranged, he reviewed the comrades of his expedition and . . . went to his ship surrounded by armed soldiery. There was no delay; on all sides men were proceeding to the shore, and a variety of armed men were on every side. When at length they were all gathered, they went on board the towered ships, having picked out by observation each man his own leader on the brazen prows. On one side lions moulded in gold were to be seen on the ships, on the other birds on the tops of the masts. Here there were glittering men of solid gold or silver nearly comparable to live ones, there bulls with necks raised high and legs outstretched . . . The royal vessel excelled the others in beauty as much as the king preceded the soldiers in . . . dignity . . . Placing their confidence in such a fleet, when the signal was suddenly given, they set out gladly and . . . placed themselves round about the royal vessel . . . some in front and some behind. The blue water, smitten by many oars, might be seen foaming far and wide, and the sunlight, cast back in the gleam of metal, spread a double radiance in the air.

The *Anglo-Saxon Chronicle* completed the story of the apparently remorseless process by which the independent England created by Alfred was overwhelmed:

1013 . . . In the same year, before the month of August, came King Swein with his fleet to Sandwich, and very soon after went round East Anglia into the mouth of the Humber, and so up along the Trent until he came to Gainsborough. Then Earl Uhtred and all Northumbria straightway submitted to him, and all the people of Lindsey, and then the people belonging to the Five Boroughs, and soon afterwards all the Danes to the north of Watling Street; and he was given hostages from every shire.

Thereafter the citizens of London submitted and gave hostages, because they were afraid he would destroy them. Then Swein demanded tribute in full and supplies for his host during the winter, and Thurkil demanded the same for the host that lay at Greenwich, yet despite this they went harrying as often as they pleased. At this time nothing went right for this nation, neither in the south nor in the north.

The chronicler's exasperated despair was understandable, but all was not yet quite lost. Thanks to the Norman connection established by his second marriage Ethelred's queen Emma and sons, Edward and Alfred, 'crossed the sea to her brother Richard', an exile in which the king himself soon joined them: 'Then at Christmas the king left the fleet for the Isle of Wight and remained there for that festival, afterwards crossing the sea to Richard.'

England was now a Danish province, ruled by a Danish king by right of conquest. Swein's triumph proved, however, remarkably brief for on 2 February 1014 he died. His obvious successor, his second son, was already in England, left behind in command of the ships in the Trent, and, as the *Chronicle* reported, 'the fleet all chose Cnut as king', but

Swein's death revived the flagging patriotism of Ethelred's former ministers, though their message to their absent sovereign in France was more pragmatic in tone than romantic: 'Then all the councillors, both spiritual and temporal, advised that King Ethelred should be sent for, declaring that no lord was dearer to them than their rightful lord, if only he would govern his kingdom more justly than he had done in the past.'

It was now up to Ethelred to prove that times really had changed. Cnut was at Gainsborough in Lindsey, the area of Lincolnshire between the Trent and the Humber from which he had drawn much of his support, and he had, as the *Anglo-Saxon Chronicle* reported, made an agreement with 'the people of Lindsey to supply him with horses and then set out together and harry'. Instead, however, it was the Saxons who did the harrying, with Viking ruthlessness, and the Danes who found themselves on the defensive:

> Then King Ethelred came with levies at full strength into Lindsey before they were prepared and they made raids and slew every human being they could find. Cnut put to sea with his fleet, and the unhappy people were thus left in the lurch by him: he sailed southward until he came to Sandwich, and there put ashore the hostages which had been given to his father, and cut off their hands and noses.

After this final act of spite Cnut sailed back to Denmark, leaving Ethelred to enjoy the unfamiliar taste of victory, though he still had to buy off his ally Thorkell, whose fleet remained at Greenwich, with another £21,000. Then, for 16 months, from the end of April 1014 until the end of August 1015, England was at peace. This unusual calm was ended by Ethelred's eldest son, Prince Edmund, who, with his father's connivance, marched into the Danelaw, killed its two leading thegns and forcibly married the widow of one of them. The *Anglo-Saxon Chronicle* recorded what followed:

> 1015. Before the Nativity of St Mary [8 September], the prince proceeded from the west and went north to the Five Boroughs . . . and the people all submitted to him.

Edmund was not left to enjoy his conquest for long. Cnut, now aged 23, having left his elder brother to rule in Denmark, was already on his way back to England to seize what he regarded as his own inheritance. He was accompanied by his formidable brother-in-law, Eric, a veteran commander of great reputation, while Thorkell the Tall, instead of protecting Ethelred, now turned up in Denmark with nine warships to join the new expedition.

The force which Cnut finally mustered was probably the largest ever to descend on England. Three European sources put the number of vessels at 200, 960 and 1000 respectively and 'the Encomiast' quoted earlier boasted that they carried the very flower of the Danish and Norwegian races: 'In the whole force there could be found no serf, no freedman, none of ignoble birth, none weak with old age. All were nobles, all vigorous with the strength of complete manhood, fit for all manner of battle, and so swift on foot that they despised the fleetness of cavalry':

> Here was so great a quantity of arms, that one of those ships would have very abundantly supplied weapons, if they had been lacking, to all the rest. Furthermore, there were there so many kinds of shields, that you would have believed that troops of all nations were present. So great, also, was the ornamentation of the ships, that the eyes of the beholders were dazzled, and to those looking from afar they seemed of flame rather than of wood . . . Gold shone on the prows, silver also flashed on the variously shaped ships. So great, in fact, was the magnificence of the fleet, that if its lord had desired to conquer any people, the ships alone would have terrified the enemy, before the warriors whom they carried joined battle at all . . . And so the force. . . . having unfastened the anchors and ropes from the shore, boarded the lofty ships and put to sea, and swept the waves with such impetus, that you would have thought that they were flying over the water in winged ships, which hardly creaked, heavy as the sea was.
>
> And so in good order and with a favourable wind they touched at Sandwich . . . and after they had dropped anchor, scouts went ashore in boats, and having made a very rapid examination of the immediate neighbourhood, returned to the familiar ships, and reported to the king that thousands of opponents were present in readiness. For the natives, burning most fiercely to renew the war against the king and the Danes, had assembled squadrons . . . and gathered together and acting as one pressed on.

The Danes wisely thought better of trying to land at Sandwich and sailed on down the coast to Poole. King Ethelred had now added physical infirmity to poor judgement and indecisiveness and was lying sick at Cosham, near Portsmouth, when the Danish fleet appeared in September 1015, making him a mere spectator of the events which followed. The *Chronicle* told the sad tale:

> Cnut came into Sandwich and straightway sailed round Kent to Wessex, until he came to the mouth of the Frome, and harried in Dorset and Wiltshire and Somerset . . . Then ealdorman Eadric gathered levies, and Prince Edmund gathered others in the north; and when they joined forces, the ealdorman intended to leave the prince

in the lurch, and for this reason they parted without giving battle and left the field clear for their foes. Then ealdorman Eadric won over forty ships from their allegiance to the king, and then did homage to Cnut. And the West Saxons submitted and gave hostages, and supplied the host with horses, and it remained there until Christmas.

The invading fleet and armies, in possession of the whole Midlands and North, and with little, it seemed, to fear in the South, now assembled for the final assault on London. And then suddenly, on 23 April 1016, 'after a life,' the *Anglo-Saxon Chronicle* charitably commented, 'of much hardship and many difficulties,' King Ethelred died.

I I

THE WHOLE REALM OF ENGLAND

In this year Cnut succeeded to the whole realm of England.

The Anglo-Saxon Chronicle, *1017*

Few kings can have faced a more threatening situation than Ethelred's son Edmund when, in 1016, at the age of about 35, he succeeded to the throne of England. Northumbria was lost, Mercia devastated and defenceless, and the victorious invader was already leading his fleet from its apparently impregnable base in Poole harbour up the Thames. The chief noblemen and clergy of Wessex considered the war already lost and met at Southampton to swear allegiance to Cnut as king of England in return for a formal promise of good government. But Edmund, known as Ironside because of his physical strength, was made of sterner stuff than his unlamented father. London still held out and he persuaded its chief citizens, and the country landowners who had taken refuge there, to proclaim him king. The *Chronicle* recorded the progress of the succeeding struggle on two fronts:

> Then at Rogation days [7–9 May], the [Danish] ships came to Greenwich, and within a short time went on to London. They dug a great channel on the south bank and dragged their ships to the west side of the bridge, and afterwards built earthworks outside the borough so that no one could get in or out, and attacked the borough repeatedly, but they withstood them valiantly.

Cnut's initial base was Greenwich, from which he moved his ships up-river to Bermondsey, where London Bridge, no doubt stoutly defended, barred further progress. He therefore outflanked it by a massive new canal, and thereby gained command of the whole upper Thames, while building a counter-earthwork outside the city walls on the south bank as a preliminary to cutting off all access to it.

London, however, still put up a stout defence and, according to the (male) English chronicler Florence of Worcester, who dates the start of the siege at about 7 May 1016, the Danes now decided to try instead to defeat the new king's army in the field:

> The citizens resisting them manfully drove them to a distance from the walls. Therefore, raising the siege for the present, and leaving part of the army to guard the ships, they made a forced march into Wessex, and allowed King Edmund Ironside no time to get together his army. However, with such troops as he was able to muster in so short a space of time, he boldly encountered them in Dorsetshire, giving them battle at a place called Pen, near Gillingham, where he defeated and put them to flight.

The battle at Pen, in fact Penselwood, in mid-Somerset, three miles [5 km] north-east of Wincanton, was only a minor one. A far more important encounter followed, at 'Scearstan', i.e. Sherston, about 40 miles [64 km] north of Penselwood and about five miles [8 km] west of Malmesbury, close to the Wiltshire/Gloucestershire border, where the Danes were victorious. This was in turn the prelude to an even greater confrontation.

Ashingdon, or Asandun, is the last of the great battles between Danes and Saxons for the mastery of England, begun at Ashdown in 871, and continuing through Ethandun in 878, Brunanburh in 937 and Maldon in 991. This final encounter took place near the village of Ashingdon about five miles [8 km] north of Southend-on-Sea. It was a full-scale, set-piece affair marked out by a greater display of tactics and more effective use of ground than in most of the earlier confrontations between invaders and invaded. Edmund's army outnumbered Cnut's, but his men, looking forward to going home again, were not in the same class as combat troops as the Danes, who had an even fiercer motivation; the English stood between them and their ships, moored in the River Crouch just to the north.

The *Anglo-Saxon Chronicle* gives little information about the course of the fighting but it has been reconstructed with reasonable certainty from other sources. Edmund's army spent the night of 17 October 1016 on Ashington Hill, only one and a half miles [2.5 km] from the Danes, who posted themselves on the hill at Canewdon, and then moved forward to occupy a ridge about 1000 yards [900 m] to the west. The Saxon forces were probably organized into three divisions, with Eadric's Mercians on the right flank and a little to the rear, with the legendary Ealdorman Ulfkell, the hero of many earlier battles, commanding the East Anglian contingent on the English left.

Edmund himself was with the main Wessex levies in the centre. The Danes' famous raven was said to have appeared on its normally empty banner and fluttered excitedly, as a portent of victory★, but it seems to have been generalship, and perhaps treason, which decided the issue. Edmund, taking the initiative, opened the battle by a downhill charge, but the going was easier on his left than on his right and gaps began to appear in the English line. As the real fighting began, Eadric's division, either from orders or, more probably, because he had already opted for treachery, remained ominously inactive, and continued to take no part in the action as the Danes advanced on their right.

Reading between the lines of the *Anglo-Saxon Chronicle*, it seems highly likely that he had contemplated treachery from the first: 'Then ealdorman Eadric did as he had so often done before: he and the *Magesaete* [from Herefordshire and south Shropshire] were the first to set the example of flight, and thus he betrayed his royal lord and the whole nation.'

But Edmund Ironside still lived and until he was dead or captured the invaders' victory was not complete. Like those first Britons who had fled before the Romans he now made for the Severn, perhaps contemplating a final stand in the Welsh mountains. His enemies followed close behind:

After this battle King Cnut proceeded with his host into Gloucester-shire, where he heard tell that Edmund the king was. Then ealdorman Eadric and the councillors who were present advised that the kings should come to terms; they exchanged hostages, and the kings met at Alney, and made a compact of mutual friendship, both with pledge and with oath, and fixed the amount of money to be paid to the host, and dispersed, having agreed that King Edmund should hold Wessex and Cnut Mercia.

Alney was an island in the Severn, near Deerhurst in Gloucestershire, about three miles [5 km] down-river from Tewkesbury. Edmund was only allowed to retain any part of his own kingdom on the payment of what was euphemistically called *Heregeld*, or 'army-tax', a distinct misnomer since it was, of course, the Danes' army which it financed; later it became known, more graphically, as *Danegeld*. Its payment had, however, hardly begun, when a totally unexpected development occurred: 'On St Andrew's day [30 November], King Edmund passed away.' The consequence was predictable:

1017. In this year Cnut succeeded to the whole realm of England.

The *Anglo-Saxon Chronicle* recorded the sequel

1018. In this year the following tribute was paid over all England; it amounted in all to £72,000, in addition to that which the citizens of

★See Chapter 9, p. 102.

London paid, which was £11,000. Part of the host returned to Denmark, and 40 ships remained with King Cnut.

The non-Danish parts of England were sufficiently peaceful not to need an army of occupation. Cnut's only permanent military force was provided by his housecarles, a combined bodyguard and standing army numbering perhaps 3–4000. They formed a military fraternity of which the king was himself a member and, according to legend, Cnut having slain one of the brotherhood in a moment of anger, duly knelt before the rest to plead for punishment and paid a large fine.

Known in Scandinavia as 'the Rich' 'the Mighty' and 'the Powerful', it is sad that Cnut should be best remembered in England for an incident that probably never happened, first described in a medieval chronicle less than a century later:

When at the summit of his power, he ordered a seat to be placed for him on the sea-shore when the tide was coming in; thus seated, he shouted to the flowing sea, 'Thou, too, art subject to my command, as the land on which I am seated is mine; and no one has ever resisted my commands with impunity. I command you, then, not to flow over my land, nor presume to wet the feet and the robe of your lord.' The tide, however, continuing to rise as usual, dashed over his feet and legs without respect to his royal person. Then the king leaped backwards, saying 'Let all men know how empty and worthless is the power of kings, for there is none worthy of the name, but He whom heaven, earth and the sea obey by eternal laws.'

For Cnut the tide finally came in on 12 November 1035 at Shaftesbury. His death, at about the age of 40, exposed England once again to dissension and possible invasion, for Harthacnut, his only legitimate son, was unable to leave Denmark, which was threatened by the rise of a hostile ruler in Norway.

Eventually Cnut's second wife fled across the channel to take refuge in Flanders and the son of Elfgifu of Northampton, Cnut's first and 'temporary wife', became de facto king of England as Harold I, though his mother was probably the real ruler. She did not enjoy her triumph for long for in 1039, Emma's son, Harthacnut, came to terms with King Magnus of Norway leaving him free to reclaim his British kingdom. He was at Bruges, collecting troops for the invasion of England from his mother's protector, Count Baldwin of Flanders, when news reached him that made it unnecessary. On 17 March 1040 King Harold I died and Harthacnut was invited to cross the Channel to succeed him. Two years later, while carousing at a wedding, he suddenly collapsed and his death rapidly followed.

Several claimants to the now vacant throne existed in Scandinavia but what really counted was being on the spot and a stronger candidate was already in England, Harthacnut's half-brother Edward, youngest son of Ethelred by Queen Emma. Edward's cause was championed by Earl Godwin and by the most influential of the bishops and thus, as the *Anglo-Saxon Chronicle* records, Harthacnut's untimely death was followed by the restoration of the English royal line: 'Before he was buried, the whole nation chose Edward to be king in London; and may he reign as long as God grants him.'

Edward, later known as Edward the Confessor*, eldest son of Ethelred the Unready and born in Oxfordshire, was unquestionably English, though he had spent most of his life in his mother's Normandy, only returning to his native land a year before he became its king at around the age of 40. He looked to Normandy for support against the powerful territorial magnates through whom Cnut had ruled and especially the mighty Earl Godwin of Wessex, whose daughter Edith married the king in 1045. A protracted and complicated power struggle followed between the pro-Norman party, the house of Godwin, posing as champions of the English interest, and the residual pro-Danish group, which included Edward's own mother, Emma, who with her second marriage, to Cnut, had become more Danish than the Danes.

That the island suffered only some minor attacks while thus divided against itself must be attributed to the weakness of its enemies, not to its own strength, though for several years after 1042 a very real threat existed of invasion by King Magnus of Norway, who claimed to have inherited the throne of England along with that of Denmark.

In 1044 Edward mobilized a fleet of 35 vessels off Kent in anticipation of a possible descent from Norway and the following year, 1045†, responded even more vigorously, as Florence of Worcester described: 'Edward, king of England, assembled a very powerful fleet at the port of Sandwich, to oppose Magnus, king of Norway, who threatened to invade England: but the expedition was abandoned in consequence of Swein, king of Denmark, having commenced hostilities against him.'

Although Magnus suceeded in defeating Swein and occupying Denmark he died in 1047, leaving Swein in possession of Denmark. The new king of Norway, Harold Hardrada, a famous warrior, 'stern in council', the meaning of his by-name, for the moment had his hands full

---

*See p. 137 for an explanation of this by-name.

†Stenton p. 421 attributes these two expeditions to 1045 and 1046, but Florence of Worcester does not mention the first and places the second in 1045. The dating in the *Anglo-Saxon Chronicle* is contradictory. Douglas and Greenaway p. 104 admit that, 'The dates given in the *Chronicle* present problems of some complexity', but settle for those used above.

and, in the words of Florence of Worcester, 'shortly afterwards', i.e. in 1048, 'sent ambassadors to King Edward, making offers of peace and amity, which were accepted'.

Not every Northman was yet ready to hang up his sword and helmet and the *Anglo-Saxon Chronicle* described in 1048 the reappearance of a once-familiar menace:

> In this same year Lothen and Yrling came to Sandwich with 25 ships and seized there indescribable booty, both in captives and in gold and silver, so that no one knew what it amounted to in all. They sailed then round Thanet, intending to do the same there, but the inhabitants bravely resisted, and refused to allow them to land and refused them water, and completely drove them off. They sailed thence to Essex, and harried here and took captives and whatever they could find, and sailed then east to Flanders and sold there the spoil they had taken, and thereafter sailed east whence they had come.

In the following year, 1049, the English fleet was called on twice to defend the homeland. The first encounter came with a force belonging to a former associate of Cnut's, Osgod Clapa, whom Edward had sent into exile and who, planning his revenge, had established himself with a fleet of 29 ships at Wulpe, north-west of Sluys on the Flemish coast. Florence of Worcester relates what followed:

> Osgod, taking with him his wife returned to Denmark with six ships; the rest sailed over to Essex, and returned with no small plunder, which they carried off from the neighbourhood of Eadulf's Ness; however, a violent tempest overtook and sunk all except two, which were captured at sea, and all on board perished.

Eadulf's Ness has been identified as the Naze, the headland just up the coast from Walton, and the *Anglo-Saxon Chronicle* says merely that Osgod Clapa's men 'did damage' or 'did evil' there. Worse was to follow as the chronicler Florence of Worcester describes:

> In the month of August of the same year, some Irish pirates, entering the mouth of the River Severn with 36 ships, landed at a place called Wylese-Eaxan and with the aid of Griffyth, king of South Wales, plundered in that neighbourhood and did considerable damage. Then, joining their forces, the king [i.e. Griffyth] and the pirates crossed the River Wye and burnt Dymeham, massacring all they found there. Aldred, Bishop of Worcester, with a few of the people of Gloucestershire and Herefordshire, flew to arms against them; but the Welshmen who were in their ranks, and had promised to be faithful to them, sent a messenger privately to King Griffyth, begging him to lose no

time in attacking the English; in consequence of which he hastened to the spot with his own followers and the Irish pirates, and falling on the English before daybreak, slew many of them and put the rest to flight.

From around this time Saxon England was subjected to a basically peaceful but none the less persistent invasion as Edward fell more and more under French influence, and attempts by the great, almost regal, Godwin family of Wessex to resist this development were to bring the country close to civil war.

Eventually the Godwins took refuge with Count Baldwin of Flanders, an endlessly hospitable figure always happy to receive refugees from across the Channel. Intoxicated by the feeling that he was for the first time truly master in his own house, King Edward exploited his victory with more enthusiasm than sense. Free now of Godwin's restraining, pro-English, influence, he invited in more and more Normans, showering them with patronage and visibly preferring their advice to that of his native-born counsellors. The climax, fraught with long-term consequences, came late in 1051 or early in 1052: 'After these occurrences, William, earl [in fact Duke] of Normandy, came over to England with a vast retinue of Normans. King Edward honourably entertained him and his companions, and on their return made them many valuable presents.'

During this visit it seems likely that Edward promised William – as he assuredly had no right to do – that the latter should succeed to the throne of England though no written agreement to this effect exists. The widespread resentment at Edward's francophile policy became clear in the summer of 1052, when Earl Godwin, the great enemy of French influence, returned to his native land in triumph. His attack, a 'friendly invasion' in that it undoubtedly engaged the support of many of his countrymen, took place simultaneously from two directions. Godwin himself, sailing from Bruges, after an abortive attempt to land at Pevensey, frustrated by bad weather, reached the Isle of Wight and then sailed on to Portland. His ablest son, Harold, and his brother, crossed from Ireland to the mouth of the Severn and 'landed on the borders of Somersetshire and Dorsetshire'. Here they fought a successful battle against local residents loyal to the king, before going on round Lands End to join their father. The combined fleet then sailed on up the Thames, reaching Southwark on 14 September 1052, but a battle was avoided, for 'nearly all shrunk from fighting against their kinsfolk and countrymen' and Godwin, having demonstrated what an invader could do when he enjoyed popular support, was restored to favour. He died only seven months later, in April 1053, and his son Harold became Earl of Wessex, Edward's most powerful subject and, as he soon proved, his best military commander. In a masterly series of campaigns he routed the Welsh king Gruffydd (or Gryffyth or Griffith) of South Wales, with results described by the *Anglo-Saxon Chronicle* for 1063:

> The inhabitants . . . then turned against Gruffydd, their king, and slew him, and brought his head to Harold, who put another king in his place.

It was probably in 1064 that an event occurred ignored by the English chroniclers, but made much of by the Norman ones, notably William of Jumieges, a well-placed source writing about 1070:

> Edward, king of the English, being . . . without an heir, sent Robert, Archbishop of Canterbury to the duke with a message appointing the duke as heir to the kingdom which God had entrusted to him. He also at a later time sent to the duke, Harold, the greatest of all the counts in his kingdom alike in riches and honour and power. This he did in order that Harold might guarantee the crown to the duke by his fealty and confirm the same with an oath according to Christian usage. When Harold set out on his mission he was borne along by the wind until he reached Ponthieu and there he fell into the hands of Guy, Count of Abbeville [in fact, Ponthieu], who straightway threw him with his retinue into prison. When the duke heard of this he sent messengers, and by force caused him to be released. Harold thereupon sojourned with the duke for some time, and performed fealty to him in respect of the kingdom with many oaths.

The Normans were to stick to this version of events through everything that followed. The Bayeux Tapestry, which was probably embroidered at about the same time as the chronicles*, provides for what it was worth – since all three were propagandist works – further confirmation, indeed nearly half of it is concerned with Harold's visit. The Tapestry shows, as the accompanying text explains, how William 'gave arms to Harold', i.e. accepted him as his vassal, and how 'William came to Bayeux where Harold took an oath to Duke William'. Harold is shown with a hand placed upon two reliquaries, presumably containing the bones of dead saints. The solemn oath thereby depicted is not spelt out but has always been assumed to be Harold's promise to assist William to obtain the throne of England.

What actually *did* happen is still a matter of conjecture. That Harold did undertake to support William's claim to succeed Edward seems likely, but whether such a promise was binding is questionable. If Harold, as some accounts suggest, had been shipwrecked and impri-

*See Chapter 13, p. 150.

soned, with no other means of getting home except cooperation with his host, he was in no position to bargain; if he was tricked, as others claimed, into swearing an exceptionally solemn oath by the surreptitious insertion of sacred relics into a supposedly empty box, the validity of the promise was clearly disputable. Could, in any case, such an undertaking, whether legitimately given or not, have any value, when the throne was not Harold's to bestow, but the Witan's, and stronger, hereditary claimants to it existed? Here were questions to keep the lawyers happily occupied for years and there are many other possibilities. Harold may have done what the Normans alleged, believing any price justified to secure William's friendship to protect England from the more immediate danger of an invasion by the King of Norway. Or he may have reasoned that he could always plead that he had given his word under duress, so that he was entitled to repudiate it.

Edward was to acquire the by-name of 'the Confessor', meaning *not* that he was forever on his knees but that he suffered for professing the Christian faith, and a century after his death he was, for no very good reason, canonized. Men looked back to his reign as a golden age, and Westminster Abbey, which he commissioned, provided him with a fitting memorial, as the *Anglo-Saxon Chronicle* recorded:

> King Edward came to Westminster towards Christmas and there had the abbey church consecrated which he himself had built to the glory of God . . . He passed away on the vigil of the Epiphany and was buried on the Epiphany [6 January 1066] in this same abbey church.

> A gracious ruler for twenty-four years
> He dispensed bounties and prosperous days
> Ruler of warriors . . . he ruled Welsh,
> Scots and also Britons too,
> Angles and Saxons and their champions.
>   So, surrounded by the cold sea wave,
> Lived those squires young and brave,
> Loyally obeying Edward their noble king.

Who now was to rule 'those squires young and brave'? The legitimate successor was Edgar 'the Atheling', or heir apparent, grandson of Edward the Confessor's brother, Edmund Ironside, but he was probably still a child and, with the country threatened from both Norway and Normandy it needed as its ruler the ablest soldier it could find. That made the choice of both the dying king and the Witan inevitable. The Earls of Wessex had achieved the final accolade despite the family's long record, now conveniently forgotten, for disloyalty and rebellion:

Yet did the wise king entrust his kingdom
To a man of high rank, to Harold himself,
The noble earl, who ever
Faithfully obeyed his noble lord
In words and deeds, neglecting nothing
Whereof the national king stood in need.

12

A FAR FROM TRANQUIL REIGN

In this year was Harold consecrated king, but was not to enjoy a tranquil reign.

The Anglo Saxon Chronicle, *1066*

So serious was the danger of invasion that the Witan endorsed Harold's selection as king with almost indecent haste, and he was consecrated on the very day of Edward the Confessor's funeral. The councillors were right to act swiftly. Harold's hated brother Tostig, driven into exile the previous year for oppressing his tenants, was only just across the Channel, in Flanders; William of Normandy and Harold (Harald) Hardrada of Norway not much further.

In its military arrangements Anglo-Saxon England in 1066 lagged behind its neighbours. For the defence of his kingdom by land Harold could look first to his 'housecarles', professional soldiers largely living about the court but sometimes dwelling on crown estates. The ordinary thegns, or landowners, small or large, also had an obligation to turn out when called, but the custom had developed of allowing them to send a substitute, or money in lieu. The nature of the obligation varied but often the owner of each five hides of land – roughly the area of a small village – was responsible for supplying a soldier or the cash to pay him, at the rate of 20 shillings for his two months' tour of duty, plus a subsistence allowance to feed and board him.

This somewhat crude system had worked reasonably well, though the royal army tended, as described earlier, to melt away when its part-time members had completed their two months in the field. Where King Harold was weakest was at sea. When he ascended the throne no full-time fleet existed, but various places on or near the South Coast were required to provide ships and seamen when needed in return for such privileges as being allowed to keep the fines raised in the local courts. Dover, Fordwich (on the River Stour, two miles [3 km] from Canterbury), Romney and Sandwich all had such obligations; so, too, it seems likely, did Hastings and Hythe. Boroughs a long way from the sea might also be financially responsible for providing sailors or, as with the select *fyrd*★, money in lieu under their charters. Warwick, for example, in the very heart of the Midlands, is known a little later in the century to have had to supply four sailors, or £4 in lieu, when the king required. Finally, the king had the traditional right to requisition merchant ships and crews for his navy when necessary, but the men involved were untrained in fighting and the method, which disrupted ordinary business, unpopular.

Harold enjoyed four months of peace after his accession in January 1066, well aware that with the spring and summer the ships of one at least of his three enemies, the renegade Earl Tostig, Hardrada of Norway or William of Normandy were likely to appear on the horizon. In the event he was to be attacked by all three. The most poetic version of the events which followed came from the pen of an Icelandic historian-cum-saga-collector, Snorre, or Snorri, Sturlason, whoses *Lives of the Norse Kings*, written around 1230, presents the story through Scandinavian eyes. He clearly relied on oral tradition, but his tale agrees substantially with that set down, more prosaically, by contemporary or near contemporary Norman and English chroniclers.

According to Sturlason, the first to move was Tostig [Tosti] who began his sinister campaign to secure the throne of England for himself, by trying to persuade King Swein of Denmark to espouse his cause. But Swein was unimpressed by Tostig's reminders of the great days of his uncle Cnut. 'I am so much less mighty than my kinsman Cnut,' Swein told Tostig candidly, 'that I find it hard to hold Denmark against the Norsemen.' But nothing could discourage a really determined traitor:

> Tosti the Jarl now turned another way; he arrived in Norway and went to King Harold . . . and asked the king to give him help to get his realm of England. The king said that the Norsemen had no wish to go to England and make war there when they had an English chief over them. 'Folk say,' he said, 'that the English are not altogether to be relied on.'
>
> Then said the jarl . . . 'I can make it so that most of the chiefs in England will be thy friends and helpers . . . All men know that there never was such a warrior born in the Northlands as thou, and it seems strange to me that thou wilt fight fifteen years to get Denmark but thou wilt not have England, which is now lying free for thee.'

This skilful, diplomatic approach duly succeeded:

> King Harald sent bidding through all Norway and called out a levy on half the people. This was much talked about, and there were many

★See p. 106.

guesses as to how it would go on the journey; some related and reckoned up all King Harald's great deeds and said that nothing would be impossible for him; but some said that England would be hard to win, for the folk were more numerous and the warriors who were called the thingmen troop [i.e. the royal household bodyguard] were so bold that one of them was better than two of Harald's best men.

While Harold Hardrada was preparing to launch his attack on England, Tostig, instead of waiting to coordinate his own assault with his new ally's went ahead independently, returning to Flanders to assemble his invasion force. That spring a particularly brilliant comet obligingly gave warning of impending trouble and then, as Florence of Worcester related, on 24 April, the anticipated disaster duly materialized:

> Soon afterwards, Earl Tosti returned from Flanders, and landed in the Isle of Wight; and, having compelled the islanders to give him pay and tribute, he departed, and plundered along the sea-coast, until he arrived at Sandwich. King Harold, who was then at London, having been informed of this, ordered a considerable fleet and a body of horse to be got ready, and prepared to go in person to the port of Sandwich. On receiving this intelligence, Tosti took some of the boatmen of the place, willing or unwilling, into his service, and departing thence, shaped his course for Lindsey, where he burnt several vills [i.e. small townships or large estates] and slew a number of men. Thereupon Edwin Earl of Mercia, and Morcar, Earl of Northumbria, flew to the spot with some troops and drove them out of that neighbourhood; and, on his departure, he repaired to Malcolm, King of the Scots, and remained with him during the whole summer.

While King Harold of England had been successfully repelling one enemy and preparing to challenge another, his third adversary, Harold Hardrada of Norway, had been assembling his fleet in the Solunder Islands, outside the Sognefiord. Snorre Sturlason recounts what followed: 'King Harald then sailed south with his followers to meet his army. There so great a force of men gathered together that King Harald had nearly two hundred ships*, besides supply ships and small ships.'

By the time Florence of Worcester came to tell the story the total had risen even higher:

> After these transactions, Harold Hardrada†, King of Norway . . . suddenly arrived at the mouth of the River Tyne, with a powerful fleet of more than five hundred great ships. Earl Tosti joined him

*Another reading of the same passage gives the number as 240.
†'Harfaager' in the original, a recognized mistake. King Harold Harfaager had died about 931.

with his fleet, as they had before agreed, and they made all sail into the Humber; and then, ascending the River Tyne against the current, landed their troops at a place called Richale [i.e. Riccall, nine miles [14 km] south of York].

Whatever the exact size of the force Harold Hardrada commanded he clearly intended a full-scale invasion. The news that reached Harold of England – Harold Godwinson, as he is sometimes called to distinguish him – soon after he got back to London from dealing with Tostig, that another enemy was already ashore 200 miles [320 km] to the north, presented him with an agonizing decision. The armies of his third enemy, Duke William, were still massed in Normandy, awaiting a favourable wind. Should the re-mustered English army be redeployed in Kent and Sussex, to meet an invasion which had not yet occurred, or be sent northwards to challenge an immediate, but in the long run perhaps less serious, danger?

Harold bravely, and, most commentators have considered, rightly, did not hesitate. 'As soon as King Harold received this news,' confirms Florence of Worcester, 'he marched with all expedition against Northumbria.' He had hardly disembarked, near London Bridge, before on Monday 18 September 1066, he was off again, this time on horseback, leading his little force of mounted men and infantry on an epic march which became a legend. While they were on the road news reached them that the Norwegians were already ashore on English soil and that King Harold and his men were behaving in the worst traditions of their Viking forebears. Snorre Sturlason describes his countrymen's behaviour with evident relish:

He went ashore and straightway harried and subdued the district; he was not withstood. After this King Harald went to Scarborough and fought with the townsmen. He went up the hill which is there and had a great pile built and set alight. And when the fire was blazing they took great forks and shot the burning wood into the town; then one house after another caught fire and the whole town surrendered. The Norsemen slew many men and took all the goods they could lay hands on. The Englishmen had then no other choice if they wished to keep alive, than to submit to King Harald.

This was not the first time Scarborough had suffered, indeed its name derived from the Old Norse for 'hare lip', the distinguishing mark of its Viking founder, and 'Stronghold'. Harold's success there seems to have whetted his appetite for further raids but at last signs appeared of British resistance:

After this King Harald went south along the coast with all his host and came to Holderness, where a troop of men came against them and where King Harald held battle and got the victory. After this King Harald went up the Humber, then up along the river and there came to land.

The British ships, heavily outnumbered, retreated up the Ouse, and then, it seems likely, up the River Wharfe to Tadcaster, ten miles [16 km] south-west of York, while the enemy disembarked unchallenged. The arrival of the Norwegians was already known in London, but for the moment all depended on the Northern earls, the young brothers Edwin and Morcar.

The English earls chose a strong position to bar the enemy advance on York, two miles [3.2 km] beyond the river crossing at the village of Fulford south of the city, with their right flank on the Ouse and their left on a ditch, surrounded by marshy ground, at Heslington, a little to the north-east, though the Norwegian saga-writer claims that it was the invaders who selected the site:

King Harald then went ashore and began to draw up his lines; one wing stood forth on the river bank, whilst the other went further inland towards a dike, where there was a deep wide marsh full of water. The jarls had their lines placed with the whole crowd of men down along the river. The king's standard was near the river, where the line was thick; towards the dike it was thinnest and the men there the least reliable.

The same chronicler confirms that the battle which followed was fiercely contested:

The jarls then came down along the dike and the wing of the Norsemen, which was towards the dike, fell back and the Englishmen went after them, thinking that the Norsemen would flee. And when King Harald saw that the Englishmen's wing was coming down upon them alongside the dike, he had the war blast blown and egged on his army eagerly; he had his standard, the Land-Waster, borne forth. Then the onset was so hard that everything gave way before them and there was a great loss of men in the jarls' army. The army quickly turned in flight, some fleeing up the river, others down, though most of the men leaped into the dike, where the fallen lay so thickly that the Norsemen could go dry-foot across the marsh.

Harold wasted no time in following up his success and there was for the moment little disposition to resist him, as the Norwegian chronicler makes clear:

After the battle . . . all the folk in the nearest districts submitted to

King Harald, but some fled. King Harald then went on his way to win the town [of York] and he brought his host to Stamford Bridge. But because the king had won so great a victory over great chiefs and a mighty army, all the folk were afraid and had no hope of withstanding him. Then the townsmen made this plan, that they should send toward the king and put themselves and likewise the town, into his power . . . On the Sunday [24 September 1066] King Harald went with all his arming to the town and they sat at a thing [i.e. council] outside the town and the townsmen came out to it. All the folk promised obedience to King Harald and as hostages they gave him the sons of all the foremost men, according to Tosti the Jarl's knowledge of all the men in the town. In the evening the king went to his ships after this easy victory and was very happy.

The Battle of Fulford has been overshadowed by the others which followed it, but the Norwegian losses, perhaps as high as a thousand men, seriously weakened Hardrada's army at the very start of the campaign. They may also have encouraged Hardrada, the senior partner in the alliance, to delay the next stage of his invasion until the reinforcements from York arrived, an important element in attracting more Englishmen to join them as they advanced south.

He left 150 hostages of his own as proof of his good faith and then withdrew to Stamford Bridge, eight miles [13 km] east of York, where four roads converged and the old Roman road crossed the River Derwent by a wooden bridge.

By Sunday 24 September, the day after the abject capitulation of York, Harold of England had reached Tadcaster, 185 miles [296 km] north of London and only 16 [26 km] from Stamford Bridge, his approach unsuspected by Hardrada, whose troops were still licking their wounds after the hard-won victory at Fulford, of which Harold must have learned while pressing northwards. The news, however, merely strengthened his resolve and he took the bold decision to seek battle at once, instead of pausing for his weary troops to have a good night's sleep, as Snorre Sturlason makes clear:

The same evening after sunset King Harold Godwinson came from the south to the town [of York] with a mighty army; he rode into the town by the wish and consent of all the townsmen. Then men were set at all the town gates and on all the highways so that news thereof should not come to the Norsemen; this army was in the town during the night.

The English army hurried north-east through the still-dark streets of York, taking the shortest route to bring them face to face with their enemy. Harold had achieved complete tactical surprise and only after having had his breakfast did Harold Hardrada muster his army, sending one-third of his men off to guard the expedition's ships, 15 miles [24 km] in the rear at Ricall, and ordering the rest to march with him to York via Stamford Bridge. Accounts of a meeting to exchange hostages at Stamford Bridge, mentioned by some sources, seem unreliable.

Among the men a holiday atmosphere prevailed and at first even the sight of a great cloud of dust rising in the early morning air, followed by the glint of sunlight on sword-blades and helmets, did nothing to dispel it:

> At this time there was very good weather and the sun was hot. The men left their brynies [i.e. breastplates] behind and went up with their shields, helmets and spears and with swords girded; many had bows and arrows also and they were very merry. But when they came near the town, a great army rode out against them; they saw the smoke from the horses, and fair shields and white brynies. The king stopped his army, called Tosti the Jarl to him and asked him what army that might be. The jarl answered and said that he thought that there might be trouble, but it might also be that they were some of his kinsmen seeking mercy and friendship and vowing the king help and trustiness in return. The king then said that they should first stop and get to know more about this army. They did so, and the army grew greater the nearer it came and it all looked like a sheet of ice when the weapons glistened.

When at last the truth of their situation dawned upon the treacherous Tostig he urged a retreat to the ships, but Harold would have none of it.

> Then said King Harald: 'I will choose another plan: to set three bold men on the swiftest horses and bid them ride as fast as they can and tell this to our men; then they will come quickly to our help, for the Englishmen shall have a sharp fight ere we bow down' . . . King Harald then had his standard, the Land-Waster, set up and . . . drew up his army; his line was long and not thick: both wings he bent back so that they came together and there was a wide ring, his standard was there and they were well-chosen men. In another place there was Tosti the Jarl with his troop; he too had a standard. The line was drawn up in this way because the king knew that the riders were wont to ride on in troops and straightway turn back. The king said that his troop and the jarl's troop should go where it was most needful and 'the bowmen shall also be there with them and they who stand foremost shall set their spear shafts in the earth and turn the points towards the riders' breasts, in case they ride on us; and they who

stand in the second rank shall set their spear points towards the horses' breasts.'

The absence of their usual armour seems to have affected the Norwegians' morale and the king himself is said to have lamented the loss of his mail coat, 'so long,' according to the saga-writer, 'that it stretched halfway down his legs and so strong that a weapon had never fastened on to it', in a verse scarcely calculated to raise his men's spirits:

Forth we go
In our lines
Without our brynies
Against blue edges.

The helmets shine;
I have no brynie.
Our shrouds now lie
Down on those ships.

Harold Hardrada seems to have selected Stamford Bridge as a convenient site for a camp rather than as a defensive position but he was quick to make the most of it when, unexpectedly, he found himself confronted by the main English army. The fighting probably took place around the bridge itself, which survived until 1727 and spanned the River Derwent 400 yards [370 m] upstream of its modern replacement. As Harold of England led his army forward Harold of Norway seems to have retreated behind the river, leaving a small picket on the far, west, bank to hold the crossing while he deployed his forces about 300 yards [270 m] behind it, in four divisions, three of them in an arc side by side, the fourth a little further forward in the centre, on rising ground since named Battle Flats.

To come to grips with the main enemy forces, the English, advancing in four sections in line behind each other, had to force the bridge. The *Anglo-Saxon Chronicle* describes how this was achieved:

Fierce fighting went on until late in the day . . . The Norwegians fled from the English, but there was one Norwegian who stood firm against the English forces, so that they could not cross the bridge nor clinch victory. An Englishman shot with an arrow but to no avail, and another went under the bridge and stabbed him through under the coat of mail.★

★The text from 'fled' onwards was not in the original but was added in the twelfth century, perhaps from some source now lost. This is, incidentally, the final entry in this particular version of the *Chronicle*. Anglo-Saxon England was drawing tumultously towards its close.

It was in fact merely the Norwegian advance guard which had retreated, as intended, but with the English across the river in force the real confrontation began, first with a bombardment from the English archers, then with a charge by Saxon infantry and possibly horsemen, leading to fierce hand-to-hand fighting.

Snorre Sturlason's account is probably accurate, apart from making more of the Norwegian king's personal exploits than warranted:

The battle began and the Englishmen rode forth against the Norsemen. The opposition was hard and it was not easy for the Englishmen to ride on to the Norsemen because of the archers, and so they rode in a ring round them . . . but . . . when they could do nothing, retreated from them. And when the Norsemen saw that they seemed to ride upon them without strength they went against them and wished to pursue the fleeing men. And when they had broken the shield line, the Englishmen rode upon them from all sides and threw spears and shot at them. And when King Harald Sigurdson saw that, he went forth into the strife where the weapon fighting was greatest. It was then the hardest of battles and many men fell in both armies. Then King Harald Sigurdson grew so heated that he rushed forth right out of the line and struck with both hands; then neither helm nor brynie could stand against him. All who were nearest turned away. Then . . . King Harald Sigurdson was wounded in the throat by an arrow. This was a fatal wound. He then fell and so did all the troop which went forth with him except those who turned back, and they held fast to the standard.

The final stage of the battle followed the arrival of the Norwegian reinforcements, determined, since their king had fallen, to save his banner, but exhausted after a round-trip on foot of 30 miles [48 km]:

Eystein Orre came up at the same moment from the ships with the men who were following him; they were all in full armour. Eystein then got King Harald's standard, the Land-Waster. The strife now began a third time and it was very hard; many Englishmen fell and they were near fleeing . . . Eystein's men had gone so heatedly from the ships that from the beginning they were so tired that they were almost unfit for battle when they came into it. But they were so mad that they did not protect themselves so long as they could stand up. They threw off their ring-brynies [i.e. body armour] and then it was easy for the Englishmen to find places to strike them. Some of them collapsed through exhaustion and died unwounded. Almost all the great men amongst the Norsemen had then fallen. It . . . grew dark in the evening before all the man-slaying was at an end.

Although 'Orre's storm', as the last-minute intervention by the contingent from Riccall became known, was to pass into Norse legend, Stamford Bridge was unquestionably a native victory. The *Anglo-Saxon Chronicle* was justly jubilant:

> That day a very stubborn battle was fought by both sides. There were slain Harold the Fairhaired [a mistake for Harold Hardrada] and Earl Tostig, and the remaining Norwegians were put to flight, while the English fiercely assailed their rear until some of them reached their ships: some were drowned, others burnt to death, and thus perished in various ways so that there were few survivors, and the English had possession of the place of slaughter. The king then gave quarter to Olaf, the son of the king of the Norwegians, to their bishop, to the jarl of Orkney [who had provided troops for Tostig], and to all those who were left aboard the ships. They then went inland to our king and swore oaths that they would ever maintain peace and friendship with this land; and the king let them sail home with 24 ships.

That so tiny a fleet was sufficient to carry home the survivors of Fulford and Stamford Bridge testifies to the completeness of the English success. So, too, does the fact that the men whom Harold allowed to leave in peace kept to their word and never troubled England again. But this final victory of Saxon England over its most persistent adversary had come too late. The *Anglo-Saxon Chronicle* entry for 1066 – 'In this year was Harold consecrated king, but was not to enjoy a tranquil reign' – proved to be an example of English understatement. For while Harold was still at York with his triumphant army news reached him, on 1 October 1066, that the third invader within five months had already landed on English soil.

13

A FATAL DAY FOR ENGLAND

This was a fatal day for England, a melancholy havoc of our dear country.

William of Malmesbury, recalling 14 October 1066

On 10 January 1066, or a date very close to it, Duke William of Normandy was, so legend has it, in the act of drawing his bow while hunting in the park of Quevilly, near Rouen, when a messenger arrived post-haste from England. He brought what the Normans always professed to have found astounding news: that Harold, son of Godwin, having promised William the throne of England on Edward the Confessor's death, had now ascended it himself. The Duke forthwith abandoned the chase and on 15 January sent a message to Harold asserting his own claim, which – though no record of this exists – was clearly rejected. William immediately began preparations for an invasion, an operation more thoroughly and systematically planned than any landing on English soil since the Roman assault under Claudius a thousand years earlier. The successive incursions of Celts and Jutes, Angles and Saxons, Danes and Norwegians had been by comparison, even when they led to permanent occupation, casual, almost accidental, affairs.

'William the Bastard', as he had hitherto been known, had been born, around 1027, to a tanner's daughter and outside wedlock, but his father, Robert, who in 1028 became Duke of Normandy, insisted on his barons swearing to recognize the child as his heir and at the age of seven or eight William duly succeeded him. A man of little education – it is uncertain if he could read or write – unwilling to shed blood except on the battlefield, he bitterly resented gibes at his humble origins; 30 citizens of one town who had hung out skins on its walls with shouts of 'Hides for the tanner' had their hands and feet cut off. By 1066, aged around 39, he was as ruler, statesman and soldier, at the height of his formidable powers.

If William of Poitiers is to be believed, the magic of William's name brought in men from a wide area. His reputation as a disciplinarian ensured that they were well-behaved, a far more substantial achievement, while his greatest diplomatic triumph was to secure the support of the pope, Alexander II. Although many cardinals argued that the Church ought not to endorse a claim, however just, which could only result in bloodshed, William was declared to be the rightful king of England and presented with a banner blessed by the pope and a ring containing a hair of St Peter.

This was the first invasion of England of which a pictorial record exists. The whole story of the expedition, including the events leading up to it, is told in the famous Tapestry, 77 yards [70 m] long by 20 inches [50 cm] high, commissioned soon afterwards by William's half-brother, Odo, Bishop of Bayeux, for display in his new cathedral. Embroidered in coloured wool on a linen base, it depicts in detail many of the events, such as Harold's alleged oath, already described, and clearly illustrates how William gives orders for a fleet to be built, followed by the felling of trees, the preparation of the planks and the assembly and launching of the vessels, stylized though they are – the largest ship holds no more than nine men and six horses. The tapestry also shows the finished ships being loaded, with weapons and barrels of wine, a commodity in which England was clearly expected to be deficient.

Intelligence about the situation in England cannot have been hard to come by for Edward the Confessor's reign had left his country littered with French-speaking Norman sympathizers. But even if William knew that the far shore now lay open to him since Harold's fleet had dispersed, on 8 September, he could not seize the opportunity, for the same wind which carried Harold Hardrada from Norway kept William's fleet pinioned in port. Day after day the knight's pennants and papal banner pointed to the land as a stiff onshore breeze seemed to mock the divine – or at any rate papal – assistance they had been promised. And when, on 12 September, the wind did change it almost brought disaster:

The whole fleet most carefully equipped had for long waited for a south wind at the mouth of the Dives and in the neighbouring ports, but now by a west wind it was driven thence towards the harbour of St Valery. But the prince, daunted neither by the delay, nor by the loss of ships, nor even by the craven flight of many who broke faith with him . . . prudently concealed his lack of supplies by increasing the daily rations and . . . caused those who had perished in the storm to be secretly buried. By varied exhortation he put courage into the fearful and confidence into those who were cast down. Also he made pious and fervent supplication that the wind which was still adverse might be made favourable to him, and to this end he caused to be brought outside the church the body of [St] Valery himself . . . And all those aspiring to set out on the invasion joined with him in this act of Christian humility.

St Valery is a very minor figure in church history whose name is not even included in the English calendar of saints, but his bones proved more efficacious than Alexander II's blessing or St Peter's hair. On Wednesday 27 September 1066, while in distant Yorkshire Harold and his troops were still recovering from the Battle of Stamford Bridge, fought two days before, the weather, which had been cold and wet for the past 15 days, at last changed. So, more importantly, did the wind; the eager crowds on the ground who each day had looked anxiously up at the weathercock on the tower of the minster of Saint Valery, at which William himself had been a frequent worshipper, at last had their reward:

At length the longed-for wind began to blow. All raised their hands and voices in thanks to heaven. Tumultuously encouraging one another they went on board with the utmost haste, and with eager joy began their perilous voyage. So extremely rapid was the launching that even while one was calling for his knight and another for his companion, most of them, forgetful alike of followers, companions or provisions, were only eager in their haste not to be left behind. The duke vehemently urged on board any that were slow, but cautious lest, if they reached the opposite coast before daybreak, they might have to disembark in confusion at a hostile or unknown port, he gave orders through a herald that when the vessels had reached the open sea they should tarry for a little, and cast their anchors not far from him until they saw a lantern displayed at the masthead of his ship. A trumpet then gave the signal for setting sail.

As the last trumpet notes died away the great fleet stood out to sea in the deepening twilight. The sun had set at 5.34 p.m. and William was anxious they should be out of the Somme estuary within an hour, to reduce the risk of collisions. After 9.15, when the crescent moon had also set, darkness must have covered the waters apart from the lanterns winking at the mastheads as the stationary ships tossed up and down on the waves. Sixty miles [96 km] ahead, on a straight course, lay the coast of Sussex.

How many ships took part in the crossing is uncertain; the Norman chroniclers, precise about so much, are on this and similar figures notably vague. A French poet, a century later, put the total fleet at 696, against 752 ships previously promised, but many of these, according to the classic history of the expedition were probably not proper transports, 'only large open boats with a single mast and sail, and with a smaller boat attached'. As for the size of the army they carried, many military historians have tried to calculate it, using such sources as the known size of cross-Channel expeditions later in the Middle Ages, when some ships carried up to 44 men, against the nine, plus horses, shown in the ships depicted in the Bayeux Tapestry. William of Poitiers quotes his hero as saying, of his opponent, 'I would not hesitate to oppose him with my own brave men even if I had only ten thousand of these instead of the sixty thousand I now command,' while another near-contemporary chronicler settles for 14,000. A late Victorian writer estimated 10,000 and an eminent general, on the basis of 400 ships carrying nine men with horses and 296 ships carrying 25 infantry or supply troops, argued in a military journal in 1907 for a total of 11,000, including sailors and non-combatants, giving a fighting force – though he does not say this – of perhaps 10,000.

William's ship soon outran its companions, as William of Poitiers explained: 'After a pause in the night the ships weighed anchor. That which carried the duke, more eager than the others for victory, quickly left the rest behind, as if held to its course by the will of its master.'

The mundane truth was that the *Mora* was less heavily laden than the rest of the fleet and also, probably, of superior design, for it was the personal gift of William's wife Matilda. It was moreover highly distinctive, with the replica of a gilded boy blowing on an ivory horn at its stern, in addition to the customary carved animal as a figurehead, and sails carrying a wide vertical yellow stripe, flanked by two in red. The ships of William's immediate entourage displayed a similar pattern, but in different colours.

The darkness, on Thursday 28 September 1066, began to fade around 5 a.m. and daylight – sunrise was at 6.4 a.m. – brought an unwelcome shock:

> In the morning an oarsman sent by the duke to the masthead was asked whether he could sight the following fleet but he replied that he could see nothing but sea and sky. Immediately the duke cast anchor. In order to appease among his companions any fear or apprehension he commanded a large repast for himself, and accompanying it with a bumper of spiced wine, he dined in good spirit as if he was in a room in his own house. Thus he imparted confidence to his followers, and made them feel sure that they would soon see again their fellows.

William's morale-boosting breakfast was soon justified: 'After it the oarsman was sent aloft for the second time and he exclaimed that he now saw four ships; afterwards, when he had climbed for the third time, he cried out that the numberless masts clustered together looked like trees in a forest.'

William had achieved his first victory; he had sailed his fleet across the Channel, together and unchallenged, and around 8.30 a.m. they reached the English coast at the intended spot. A second success, even more notable, followed: 'Thus, with a favourable wind, they all reached Pevensey, and there, without opposition, they freely disembarked.'

Already the expedition had proved more fortunate than Caesar's, which had had to fight its way ashore. Through no fault of their own, the English had been unable to exploit those few precious hours when an invading army was most vulnerable. The precise time of the landing has been calculated to be 'at the third hour', 8.57 a.m. by modern chronology, and the spot has been identified as Pevensey Levels, close to the later village of Pevensey, which lies in the middle of Pevensey Bay, with Hastings nine miles [14 km] to the east and Eastbourne five miles [8 km] to the south-west. Here a wide, flat shingle beach gives on to a flat, though water-intersected, low-lying area immediately behind the shore, close to where Pevensey Castle now stands.

Pevensey offered what every heavily equipped invading force required: long beaches where the foot soldiers could disembark and a harbour to handle the transport and weightier equipment. It had, however, some disadvantages: a solitary road inland, leading to Lewes and London, which could easily be blocked; and a landing area partly under water when the tide came in and too small to serve as a satis-factory base for such a huge army. The chroniclers' accounts are contra-dictory, but it seems likely that the *Mora* and a few supporting ships entered Pevensey harbour, which may have provided wharves, and that the rest of the fleet unloaded their troops, and perhaps horses, on the beach and shingle bank adjoining it. According to well-docu-mented tradition William himself was first ashore and slipped and fell full length as he stepped on to English soil. A groan went up from the bystanders at this ill omen, but William turned the incident to advantage, shouting as he lay outstretched: 'By the splendour of God, I have taken seizin of my kingdom, the earth of England is in my two hands.'

The archers, bow-strings and arrows at the ready, are said to have followed William ashore, and then the knights, formidable once properly armoured and mounted, but highly vulnerable until then. With the landing area secure, William energetically followed up his initial success, consolidating his hold on Pevensey and making a personal reconnaissance of the immediate environs. The smallness of his escort makes clear that little opposition was expected: 'William himself, with 25 knights and no more, went out to gain information about the neighbourhood and its inhabitants. Because of the roughness of the ground he had to return on foot, a matter doubtless for laughter.'

That his men felt able to laugh at him confirms the high morale in the Norman camp, and there is no reason to doubt another of the same chronicler's anecdotes:

> The Duke came back carrying on his shoulder, besides his own hauberk [i.e. short coat of chain-mail], that of William fitz Osbern, one of his companions. This man was famed for his bodily strength and courage, but it was the duke who relieved him in his necessity of the weight of his armour.

The chroniclers offer no explanation as to why William now decided to move his base camp about ten miles [16 km] up the coast to Hastings, which offered a strong defensive position where a range of hills runs right down to the sea, the high ground commanding the beaches to either side of it. Here William erected a temporary castle of earth and timber. Thanks to the Bayeux tapestry this was, we know, of the motte-and-bailey type soon to become a familiar part of the English landscape, consisting of a wooden structure on top of a mound, natural or man-made, surrounded by a ditch and rampart, topped by a fence. It was later to be replaced by a more permanent structure.

Either at Pevensey or, more probably, at Hastings, William discovered that only two of his ships had been lost, one of which, however, had carried a clerk-cum-soothsayer who had predicted that the voyage would be completed without mishap and that England would fall to the Normans without a blow being struck. William reacted robustly to this news. 'A poor diviner must he have been,' he commented, 'who could not divine the way and time of his own death.' The other missing ship probably ran aground at Romney, 16 miles [26 km] to the east, where the townsfolk massacred the crew to a man: the first Englishmen to shed Norman blood, and to demonstrate that the invasion was not to be a walk-over.

News of William's landing reached Harold in the middle of his victory celebrations at York, if a poet commissioned a century later to describe these events can be believed, and though in some details he is undoubtedly wrong this seems likely enough. The message was supposedly brought by a local thegn who hid himself behind a hill to watch the Normans disembarking, before making an epic day and night ride north with his alarming tale.

While the Normans waited for the English to respond to their landing raiding parties were sent out into the surrounding countryside. The Bayeux Tapestry shows a sad incident that must have been repeated many times over, a woman and child emerging hand-in-hand from a house which two Norman soldiers have just set on fire. News of these outrages, too, was rapidly carried to York.

Seldom can two armies have been as anxious to confront each other as those of Duke William and King Harold. Florence of Worcester, writing a little later, testifies to Harold's eagerness to come to grips with his enemy:

When the king might have supposed that all his enemies were quelled, he received intelligence of the arrival of William, earl of Normandy, with an innumerable host of horsemen, slingers, archers and foot soldiers . . . and that he had moored his fleet at a place called Pevensey. Thereupon the king led his army towards London by forced marches; and, although he was very sensible that some of the bravest men in England had fallen in the two [recent] battles, and that one half of his troops was not yet assembled, he did not hesitate to meet the enemy, in Sussex, without loss of time.

Harold can hardly have left Yorkshire before the morning of Monday 2 October at the earliest, but he was back in London by Thursday the fifth and while waiting for the levies he had called out to arrive made a pilgrimage to the church of the Holy Cross at Waltham, now Waltham Cross, on the northern outskirts of London, about 13 miles [21 km] from Westminster. The minster, founded by Harold himself, contained an alleged fragment of the true cross – hence the battle-cry 'Holy Cross!' chanted by Saxon soldiers – and the king promised the monks further endowments, and to rule justly and piously if God should give him victory in the coming battle. As Harold lay flat on his face before the Holy Cross itself, the head of Christ was said to have bowed downwards in acknowledgement of this royal homage and to have remained bent ever after.

According to the Norman chroniclers, Harold was urged by his brother Gyrth to let him, Gyrth, make the first attack since he had never sworn any form of oath to William, whether binding or not, and, if he were beaten, Harold could raise a new army from the troops still coming in. At the same time Gyrth suggested that they should lay waste the countryside between London and the coast, burning every house that might give the enemy shelter, trampling down every cornfield that might provide him with food, so that even if the Normans won the initial battle they would, as winter arrived, be starved into surrender. Harold's counsellors are said to have urged him to do as his brother advised, but found him adamantly opposed to postponing the decisive battle or to devastating the Sussex countryside. 'Never,' the Norman poet previously quoted reports him as saying, 'will I burn an English village or an English house; never will I harm the lands or the goods of any Englishman. How can I do hurt to the folk who are put under me to govern? How can I plunder and harass those whom I would fain see thrive under my rule?'

With these brave words the die was cast. On Wednesday 11 October, determined to fight on the Saturday, which had, he said, always been his lucky day, Harold led his army out of London, its numbers being swollen as they went by the great fyrd mustered from Sussex and Kent. After a gruelling 58-mile [93-km] march he was by nighfall on Friday 13 October only six miles [10 km] from Hastings. According to William of Poitiers the Normans received early warning of his advance, for 'trusty knights . . . sent out by the duke on patrol came back in haste to report the approach of the enemy.'

Harold had covered the journey back from York to London in only four days, travelling at the extraordinary rate of 49 miles [78 km] a day; even the foot soldiers must have completed it in no more than ten days, covering nearly 20 miles [32 km] in each day's march. Some may have straggled after him, but the main force coming from London marched at over 18 miles [29 km] a day to reach the hill where they bivouacked on Friday night, and where Harold, all surprise lost, now planned to bar William's route to London.

Harold's army, weary and travel-stained though it was, made an impressive sight as it deployed, and according to William of Poitiers, was of intimidating size:

> If any ancient writer had described the host of Harold, he would have said that at its passage the rivers became dry and the forests were turned into plains. From all the provinces of the English a vast host had gathered together. Some were moved by their zeal for Harold, but all were inspired by the love of their country which they desired, however unjustly, to defend against foreigners. The land of the Danes who were allied to them had also sent copious reinforcements.

Whether the English army outnumbered the Norman is highly dubious. A presumably impartial and certainly thorough German historian, writing 800 years later, put its strength at 6–7000 and many of these were untrained and almost unarmed, certainly inferior in both respects to the 60,000 of whom William boasted and the 10,000 or so fighting men, excluding non-combatant sailors and sutlers, he may actually have commanded. A recent military historian, taking into account all the known factors, thinks William's army may have numbered 8000 men in arms – others had been left behind to garrison Pevensey and the new castle at Hastings – against perhaps 8800 under Harold's command, figures which roughly agree with the average of the estimates made by eleven other writers on the subject.

By the standards of the time both armies, apart from the small peasant contingent in Harold's ranks, were well equipped. The two sides were not vastly different in appearance, apart from the presence among the Normans of a large proportion of heavily armed cavalry, totalling perhaps 3600, who fought on horseback, thanks to the introduction of the stirrup into Europe, but not into England, 300 years earlier. This meant that a mounted man could retain his seat while striking out at armed infantry, and these 'knights', with their attendant esquires and retainers, must have made a terrifying sight, able to lunge at the mere foot soldier with a lance or slash at him with a heavy sword and well protected by a conical metal helmet with nose-piece, a kite-shaped shield and a hauberk, or coat of chain-mail, starting below the neck but reaching to the knees. The timorous wore a second layer of protection beneath the hauberk, a heavy tunic padded with wool, called a gambeson.

The Norman infantry, paid professionals hired for the campaign, bore a superficial resemblance to Roman legionaries, with their sandals and legs encased in leather thongs, with above them leather jerkins and caps, or, for the more fortunate, chain shirts and iron caps. They hardly get a look-in in the Bayeux Tapestry but formed the bulk of William's army, and were a very formidable fighting force, with their short axes, spears, broad-swords and daggers. The designer of the Tapestry was more impressed by William's archers, whose short cross-bow was deadly at 50 yards [46 m], effective at 100 [90 m] and still troublesome at 150 [136 m]. One is shown firing from the saddle but most served on foot.

The English, however, fought dismounted, as they had always done. Their armour was almost identical to the Normans', and their weapons largely similar, though there were far fewer archers, to judge from the Bayeux Tapestry, and the most common armament was a club or javelin, or the already venerable broadsword. The humblest members of the fyrd carried forks or stakes, stone hatchets or hammers, or spear-like halberds on long wooden shafts whose exotic names – vouge, glaive and gisarme – concealed their derivation from agricultural implements. The most distinctive Saxon weapon was the long-handled axe, probably introduced by the Danes. It could only be wielded with both hands, which meant the user laying down his shield, but with it a strong man could bring down horse and rider with a single blow. This was Harold's chosen weapon. William preferred the mace, a club-like object with a metal head, favoured by the clergy – it was used by William's half-brother, Odo, Bishop of Bayeux, who thereby observed the Church's rule forbidding an ordained priest to shed blood.

William prepared for battle, so the chronicler says, probably with truth, in a suitably pious fashion, simultaneously managing to denigrate his opponent: 'The duke . . . attended mass with the greatest devotion . . . With great humility he hung round his neck the relics on which Harold had sworn the oath he had now broken, and whose protection he had therefore lost.'

Although William of Poitiers admits disarmingly 'no one has reported to us in detail the short harangue' to his troops, the words attributed to William sound convincing enough:

'Now is the time,' he said, 'for you to show your strength, and the courage that is yours. You fight,' he added, 'not merely for victory but also for survival. If you bear yourselves valiantly you will obtain victory, honour and riches. If not, you will be ruthlessly butchered, or else led ignominiously captive into the hands of pitiless enemies. There is no road for retreat. In front, your advance is blocked by an army and a hostile countryside; behind you, there is the sea where an enemy fleet bars your flight . . . The English have again and again fallen to the sword of an enemy . . . nor have they ever been famed as soldiers. The vigorous courage of a few men armed in a just cause . . . must prevail against a host of men unskilled in combat. Only be bold . . . and victory will gladden your hearts.'

Such was William's eloquence that eventually one of his noblemen had to ride up and remind him it was time to move. The knights, having ridden out from Hastings in a lighter outfit, now put on their full armour and exchanged their 'travelling' horses for the heavier war-horses on which they would go into action. William himself suffered an embarrassing mishap, putting on part of his coat of mail back-to-front, but laughed off what his followers regarded as a bad omen, remarking that, like the armour, its wearer would soon be turned round, from a duke into a king. One of his spies now came to report that he had seen the royal standard of England among the thickest ranks on the very summit of the opposing hill. On hearing this, William swore a vow that if he were victorious he would build a great minster on that very spot – thus helpfully identifying for later generations the precise location of the misleadingly named Battle of Hastings.

Harold had chosen as the assembly point for the troops from the south-eastern counties the hoar, i.e. old, apple tree on a hill close to the point where the track from Hastings joined the road to Rochester and London, or, if one turned left instead of right, led into the London to Lewes road, the two routes to the capital being respectively 64 and 61 miles [102 and 98 km] long. By modern reckoning the town which grew up nearby is 57 miles [91 km] from London and seven [11 km] north-west of Hastings. The battle was fought half a mile [800 m] south of the assembly point on the slopes leading up from a slight dip in the ground, between the ridges occupied by the two armies. The intervening area was dry in the centre but marshy where the land fell away on either side, and though the slope leading up to the English lines was gentle the sides of the spur were steep, making it almost impossible to outflank. Harold's command post was at the centre of the spur, where the prehistoric track from the coast crossed a local path known as the Wasingate.

The precise site of the battle and its misleading name have generated much discussion over the centuries. The 'hoar apple tree' where the English army assembled was on Caldbec Hill, a name still in use, 350 feet [107 m] high. William deployed his men on Pelham Hill, 225 feet [69 m] above sea level at its highest point. The ridge, 275 feet [84 m] high, along which the Saxons were massed was unnamed. As for the name of the battle, the medieval chroniclers placed it *in planis Hastinges*, i.e. in unwooded country, not necessarily level, near Hastings. One monkish chronicler, writing around 1140, has caused continuing confusion by referring to the site as Sanguelac, later anglicized into Senlac, apparently derived from Norman attempts to render the Saxon name Santlache, 'sandy area', or, in a grim play on words, *Sanguelac*, i.e. 'lake of blood'. In fact for nearly a century after 1066 the battle was invariably known as Hastings, after William's former base, and though today the town of Battle marks the site this traditional name is too well established to be altered.

The morning of Saturday 14 October 1066 was unusually light for the time of year. Dawn broke at 5.30 a.m. and by six the Normans must have been on the march. Soon afterwards, according to the Bayeux Tapestry, both commanders learned from their scouts of the approach of the enemy army and it was now that the donning of armour and delivery of speeches mentioned earlier must have occurred. William of Poitiers describes his namesake's 'approach to contact' with his enemy: 'He then advanced in good order with the papal banner which had been granted to him borne aloft at the head of his troops.' About 8 a.m. the leading Norman troops came into sight of the Saxons as they reached the ridge of Telham Hill and William, presumably seeing the battlefield for the first time, deployed his troops as far forward as he dared – just out of extreme arrow range – of the Saxon front line, on ground about 50 feet [15 m] lower.

The Saxons awaited them in ranks nine or ten deep, along a front of about 800 yards [730 m] mainly on level ground, but rising to about 60 feet [18 m] above the track leading across it from Hastings, and about 150 feet [46 m] above the marshy valley to either side. Below them there stretched an incline, nowhere more than one in 15, but still steep enough to make attacking difficult.

William had split his force into three, taking command himself, with his two half-brothers, of the largest, Norman, contingent in the centre, totalling perhaps 4300 men, placing on his left the Breton division, some 2100 strong, and on his right the combined French and Flemish division, numbering perhaps 1600. All three were arranged in the same way, as the chronicler explains:'In the van he placed foot-soldiers equipped with arrows and crossbows; in the second rank came the more heavily armed infantry clad in hauberks; and finally came the squadrons of knights in the midst of whom he rode himself . . . in such a position that he could give orders by hand or by voice.'

Now a diversion occurred. A minstrel or juggler called Taillefer, weary of his normally menial role or hungry for glory, begged permission to strike the first blow. When William agreed, Taillefer rode out between the two armies, singing ancient songs of long-dead heroes like Roland and Charlemagne, flinging his sword in the air and catching it again. He then charged the English lines, where he killed or wounded two men before being struck down himself.

Battle was now joined in earnest, in a scene immortalized by William of Poitiers:

> The duke and his men, in no way dismayed by the difficulty of the ground, came slowly up the hill, and the terrible sound of trumpets on both sides signalled the beginning of the battle. The eager boldness of the Normans gave them the advantage of attack . . . The Norman foot drawing nearer provoked the English by raining death and wounds upon them with their missiles. But the English resisted valiantly, each man according to his strength, and they hurled back spears and javelins and weapons of all kinds, together with axes and stones fastened to pieces of wood. You would have thought to see our men overwhelmed by the death-dealing weight of projectiles . . .
> The shouts both of the Normans and of the barbarians were drowned in the clash of arms and by the cries of the dying and for a long time the battle raged with the utmost fury.

A heavy battle-axe, swung with both hands by some huge enraged Saxon, must have been a fearsome weapon and the sight of their comrades being literally hewn to pieces around them was too much for the attackers: 'Then the foot-soldiers and the Breton knights, panic-stricken by the violence of the assault, broke in flight before the English and also the auxiliary troops on the left wing [gave way] and the whole army of the duke was in danger of retreat.'

The flight of the Bretons seems to have been due to that blind panic, following the sudden realization that one may at any moment be killed, which is liable to affect any troops in any battle, and William acted promptly to stop the rot:

Seeing a large part of the hostile host pursuing his own troops, the prince thrust himself in front of those in flight, shouting at them and threatening them with his spear. Staying their retreat, he took off his helmet, and, standing before them bareheaded, he cried: 'Look at me well. I am still alive and by the grace of God I shall yet prove victor. What is this madness which makes you fly, and what way is open for your retreat? You are allowing yourselves to be pursued and killed by men whom you could slaughter like cattle. You are throwing away victory and lasting glory, rushing into ruin and incurring abiding disgrace. And all for naught since by flight none of you can escape destruction.' With these words he restored their courage, and, leaping to the front and wielding his death-dealing sword, he defied the enemy . . . Inflamed by his ardour the Normans then surrounded several thousands of their pursuers and rapidly cut them down so that not one escaped.

Some time during the long afternoon there must have been a lull as the troops on either side seized what food and drink they could, attended to their horses, gathered up new stocks of missiles and re-formed ready to make or resist the next attack. At some point, ammunition wagons, like the one shown in the Bayeux Tapestry, must have arrived with fresh supplies of arrows, for William now ordered a fresh bombardment, not, like the initial one, aimed at the front ranks of the enemy, but fired high in the air so it fell on the men behind. This shower of missiles did deadly execution both among those who lacked armour, and those who were protected, for some plunged straight down through the defenders' helmets, while those who raised their shields above their heads exposed their bodies to sword and javelin. The Bayeux Tapestry shows some shields bristling, porcupine-like, with intercepted arrows, and a particularly fierce and accurate volley was launched at the group clustered round the king and his standard.

A persistent tradition attributes Harold's death to this salvo, but the text in the Bayeux Tapestry reads simply 'Harold Rex interfectus est', i.e. 'King Harold is killed', and covers three figures, one standing, the arrow victim, one on horseback, sword in hand, and one, apparently just cut down by the horseman, slumping to the ground. The probability is that this last is Harold, while even if the standing figure *were* Harold, he is *not* plucking an arrow from his eye, but as the original stitch holes show, removing one from his helmet just above it. The 'arrow in the eye' story first appears much later, in an otherwise obscure account of the battle written in 1099, after which it was taken up by other chroniclers and finally 'confirmed' by the nineteenth-century restorers of the original embroidery, who bent the arrow shaft to conform to the now accepted legend.

Around 3 p.m., or a little later, the fourth and decisive stage of the battle began. The Norman horsemen – some now reduced to fighting on foot because of the loss of their steeds – and infantry swung round to the western ridge, on the Saxon right, where the gradient was easier than elsewhere, and began to force their way along the crest, hacking away at all in their path. William, judging that the enemy left was also weakening, ordered the Franco-Flemish division on his own right to attack so that Harold's army was soon under pressure from two directions. Eventually four knights, led by Count Eustace of Boulogne, hacked their way to where Harold, according to the traditional version of events, already lay dying and seized their opportunity to behave in a thoroughly unknightly fashion. One stabbed the dying king in the chest, another cut off his head, and the other two had to content themselves with mutilating his body, cutting open his abdomen and chopping off his leg. Another, braver, band of 20 Normans pledged themselves to carry off the English standards, and though several were killed in the attempt, the English line was now pierced at many points and organized resistance was beginning to break up.

William of Poitiers vividly describes the closing stages of the great battle:

> Evening was now falling, and the English saw that they could not hold out much longer against the Normans. They knew they had lost a great part of their army, and they knew also that their king with two of his brothers and many of their greatest men had fallen. Those who remained were almost exhausted and they realized that they could expect no more help. They saw the Normans, whose numbers had not been much diminished, attack them with even greater fury than at the beginning of the battle, as if the day's fighting had actually increased their vigour. Dismayed . . . they began to fly as swiftly as they could, some on horseback, some on foot, some along the roads, but most over the trackless country . . . Many left their corpses in the depths of the forest, and others were found by their pursuers lying by the roadside . . . Although ignorant of the countryside the Normans eagerly carried on the pursuit, and striking the rebels in the back brought a happy end to this famous victory.

William's triumph was not yet complete. One final, if minor, engagement was still be fought as darkness began to descend on the Sussex fields and forests, probably on the rear, north, slope of Caldbec Hill, about a mile behind the main position. At this point a gentle gradient led suddenly to the edge of a steep-sided ravine, concealed by grass and crossed only by a narrow causeway, beyond which a piece of ground, 400 yards [366 m] long, offered a suitable site for a last desperate effort. Here, as William of Poitiers describes, was fought the final action of the Battle of Hastings:

> Some of those who retreated took courage to renew the struggle on more favourable ground . . . The duke, who was following the victorious standards, did not turn from his course when he saw these enemy troops rallying . . . With a harsh voice he called to Eustace of Boulogne, who with fifty knights was turning in flight and was about to give the signal for retreat. This man came up to the duke and said in his ear that he ought to retire since he would court death if he went forward. But at the very moment when he uttered the words Eustace was struck between the shoulders with such force that blood gushed out from his mouth and nose and, half dead, he only made his escape with the aid of his followers . . . In this dangerous phase of the battle many Norman nobles were killed since the nature of the ground did not permit them to display their prowess to full advantage.

This last, not unworthy, stand of Saxon England ended in defeat, but the Normans were forced to pay a heavy price for their final triumph and William had a cairn erected there to commemorate his hard-won victory, giving the hill the enduring name, among the Normans, of *Mountjoy*. Two hundred years later, however, it was still known to the English as *Maufosse*, from *Malfosse*, 'the evil ditch' – the point where their last hope of retaining their independence had irrevocably vanished.

The sun set on Saturday 14 October 1066 about 5 p.m. An hour later it was dark, and, if William of Poitiers is to be believed, in the gathering dusk the victorious William made his way back to the scene of his victory, perhaps wondering, like other commanders before and since, whether it had been worth the cost:

> The duke returned to the main battlefield, and he could not gaze without pity on the carnage . . . The bloodstained battle-ground was covered with the flower of the youth and nobility of England. The two brothers of the king were found near him, and Harold himself, stripped of all badges of honour, could not be identified by his face, but only by certain marks on his body. His corpse was brought into the duke's camp, and William gave it for burial to William, surnamed Malet, and not to Harold's mother, who offered for the body of her beloved son its weight in gold. For the duke thought it unseemly to receive money for such merchandise.

Harold's final resting place is still not known for certain but one story relates how the fragments of Harold's mutilated body were reassembled in a cloth and interred at Hastings, below a stone reading, with cruel irony:

> By command of the Duke, you rest here a King, O Harold, That you may be guardian still of the shore and sea.

The number of casualties is uncertain but modern estimates, based on the figures for other battles and the remarkable length of the Battle of Hastings, eight hours – three times as long as most at that period – favour a total of around 30 per cent killed or badly wounded. The English suffered even worse than the Normans. Not only had the cream of the nobility been lost, but lesser men of substance, like the sheriff and thegns of Berkshire, had been almost totally annihilated, while the monks of Winchester who had followed their abbot to the battlefield lay dead together, still wearing their holy habits beneath their armour.

Historians have differed ever since about the true significance of William's victory at Hastings, but as early as 1125 William of Malmesbury at least had no doubts:

> This was a fatal day for England, a melancholy havoc of our dear country, brought about by its passing under the domination of new lords.

BOOK 2
FROM HASTINGS TO MILFORD HAVEN

14
WILLIAM CAME AND CONQUERED

In this year came William and conquered England.

The Anglo-Saxon Chronicle, *1066*

William Duke of Normandy, not yet King of England, spent the night of Saturday 14 October 1066 on the battlefield which had brought him victory. He ordered his tent to be pitched where the fighting had been fiercest and his banner was planted where that of the vanquished Harold had flown only a few hours before. Having knelt to give thanks for his success, he took off his armour amid the applause of his troops, the dents in the shield and helmet revealing that he had fought as fiercely as any of them. Then he ate a hearty meal and slept soundly, untroubled by the dead still lying unburied all around or by warnings that some wounded Englishman might creep up on him in the darkness.

Sunday was devoted to the burial of the dead and on Monday William returned to his base camp at Hastings, to await the submission of the rest of those he now considered his lawful subjects.

He waited in vain. Such news as reached Hastings suggested that the nation's resistance was only just beginning. The greatest earls in the land, Edwin of Mercia and Morcar of Northumbria, still possessed formidable bodies of troops, the English fleet was still intact and London remained untaken, while an obvious claimant to the vacant throne was on hand, in the shape of Edgar, the atheling. Harold, it has been generally agreed since, had made a disastrous blunder in challenging William too soon, but this at least meant that many men had not yet been in action. The best troops, Harold's housecarles, were dead or defeated but large numbers of the fyrd had not yet been mobilized and if an energetic leader had emerged and the spirit of the country had been roused, William's already badly mauled army might still have been pushed back into the sea. Unfortunately, however, the English were divided. Earls Edwin and Morcar seem to have regarded Harold's death as an opportunity to re-assert the supremacy of their respective provinces over their long envied rival, Wessex, and to have retired in disgust when neither of them was offered the throne.

William had already accomplished the first military objective of any serious invader, the defeat of the enemy army in the field, resisting the temptation to make for 'political' targets such as Winchester, Canterbury or London. After five days at Hastings, resting his troops and waiting for the emissaries of surrender who never arrived, he left a small force, since estimated at 200, to garrison his camp there and set off to consolidate his victory. He probably had under his command about 5400 men, about one third of them cavalry, and their first task was to settle a small account: William was never the man to forgive and forget: 'He left Hastings in charge of a brave commander, and proceeded to Romney, where he punished at his pleasure those who had previously killed some of his men.'

News of his vengeance went ahead of him up the coast, as William of Poitiers describes:

> Then he marched to Dover, which had been reported impregnable and held by a large force. The English, stricken with fear at his approach, had confidence neither in their ramparts nor in the natural strength of the site, nor in the number of their troops. This castle is situated on a rock adjoining the sea and it is raised up by nature and so strongly fortified that it stands like a straight wall as high as an arrow's flight.
>
> Its side is washed by the sea. While the inhabitants were preparing to surrender unconditionally, our men, greedy for booty, set fire to the castle and the greater part of it was soon enveloped in flames. The duke, unwilling that those who had offered to surrender should suffer loss, gave them a recompense in money for the damage of the castle and their property . . . Having taken possession of the castle the duke spent eight days adding new fortifications to it.

Like Caesar, William made a sharp distinction between those who resisted, whom he treated without mercy, and those willing to surrender without a fight, to whom he was magnanimous, but on this occasion his generosity brought him little benefit:

> Owing to foul water and bad food his knights were there stricken with severe dysentery, and many were brought by weakness almost to the point of death. But this adversity did not daunt the duke. Posting a guard in Dover, he left there his sick and himself went forward to tame the enemies he had conquered. Not far from Dover the men of Canterbury came out to meet him in order that they might give him hostages and swear allegiance . . . The next day the duke

went on to the Broken Tower [apparently near Canterbury] and there he was stricken with the sickness that had previously afflicted his troops. Occupied with the general good and fearful lest his army should lack anything necessary to it, he would not brook delay for the sake of his health.

William was probably more ill than he cared to admit for he remained a whole month near Canterbury, leaving the news of his severity at Romsey and leniency at Dover to spread, and its implications to sink in. His mere name was sufficient by itself to cause fear and a few messengers sent to the town officials of Winchester were enough to secure its formal submission and the payment of tribute. Winchester was a notable prize for it was the ancient capital of Wessex and the home of Queen Edith, widow of Edward the Confessor, whose rightful heir William claimed to be. She sent William a personal gift and seems to have used her influence on his behalf. Certainly she made no move either to become a symbol of national resistance herself, or to press the claims to the throne of Edgar the atheling, whom the Witan had now elected as king.

Of Edgar himself little is known, though in 1066 he can still have been only 15 or 16 and far from being the mature, charismatic leader the situation required. William seems to have regarded him as a mere irrelevance and he plays no part in subsequent events.

Much effort has been devoted to trying to reconstruct the course of William's campaign between the beginning of November and Christmas Day 1066. All that is unquestionable is that after a long approach march across the North Downs, probably through Maidstone but stopping short of Leatherhead, a Norman army reached Southwark, and prepared to storm London bridge or to force a passage of the river elsewhere. William of Poitiers describes what followed:

> Its citizens could themselves supply a numerous and formidable force and they had now been joined by so many troops that they could hardly be housed even in this large town. Some of them indeed made a sortie, but an advance guard of 500 Norman knights bravely drove them back within the walls and then burnt all the buildings on this side of the river.

A lesser commander, with mid-winter approaching, might have tried to force the issue by a full-scale assault, but William was content to wait, as earlier in the campaign, while the threatened citizens thought over their situation, simply bypassing London and making a wide detour through Surrey, north Hampshire and Berkshire: 'The duke, who was following, went on without opposition, and having crossed the Thames by ford and bridge arrived at Wallingford.' Wallingford, 47 miles [75 km] from London, had been a fortress town since Alfred's time, and here, if anywhere, the Saxons needed to stand and fight for no better natural obstacle than the Thames existed. Even today it is 35 yards [32 m] wide at this point: in 1066 it was no doubt wider, but it already possesed both a ford and a bridge, and its defence was vital if the river line was to be held. Both, however, were yielded up without a spear being thrown and the enemy army crossed dry-shod from Wessex into Mercia.

William's stay at Wallingford brought further proof of the demoraliz-ation of his opponents: 'There the metropolitan bishop, Stigand, came to him and surrendered. He swore fealty and renounced the atheling whom he had rashly nominated as king.' With the defection of the Archbishop of Canterbury who had the best of reasons for resisting the Normans, the heart must have gone out of the young king's party. The intimidating and destructive march which the invaders now made through Oxfordshire, Bedfordshire and Hertfordshire, in a wide loop round the Chilterns as far north as St Neots and as far east as Hertford, possibly in two columns, which passed on either side of Bedford and came together again at Enfield, must have driven all but the most resolute to thoughts of surrender. One Norman chronicler, William of Jumieges, makes Wallingford the base from which the Norman army moves on to fight another battle:

> It was from there that he advanced against London. When the advance-guard of his army reached the central square of the City, they found there a large company of rebels who were ready to offer a fierce resistance to them. The Normans therefore engaged and inflicted upon the City a great mourning on account of the large numbers of young men and citizens whom they slew. At length the Londoners saw that they could hold out no longer. So they gave hostages and submitted themselves and all their possessions to their hereditary lord, to their most noble conqueror.

No other mention of this battle is on record, though this passage may be the origin of the title by which William later became known; 'King William the Conqueror' is first referred to in a charter dating from around 1130. Florence of Worcester gives a different account of the submission of London:

> Meanwhile, Earl William was laying waste Sussex, Kent, Hampshire, Surrey, Middlesex and Herefordshire [a mistake for Hertfordshire] and ceased not from burning vills and slaughtering the inhabitants, until he came to a vill called Beoreham, where Alfred, the archbishop [of York], Wulfstan, Bishop of Worcester, Walter, Bishop of Here-

ford, Edgar, the Atheling, the earls Edwin and Morcar, and some Londoners of the better sort, with many others, met him, and, giving hostages, made their submission and swore fealty to him.

'Beorham' has been identified as Berkhampsted or, more probably, as Little Berkhampsted, a village two miles [3 km] from Hertingfordbury and about 21 [34 km] from London. William of Poitiers's version of events is more dramatic:

> The duke [after Stigand's surrender] then proceeded on his way and when he was in sight of London the principal citizens came out to meet him. They surrendered themselves and their city into his hands, like the citizens of Canterbury before them, and gave him such hostages as he asked. Further, the bishops and the lay magnets begged him to assume the crown. 'We are accustomed to obey a king,' they said, 'and we desire to have a king as lord.'

Whatever the true facts within less than three months of William stepping ashore at Pevensey, he was crowned king of England in a ceremony described by William of Poitiers, and marred by a memorable misunderstanding:

> On the day appointed for the coronation William, the duke, was hallowed king by the . . . Archbishop of York . . . who set the royal crown upon the duke's head, and led him to the throne in the presence of a great company of bishops and abbots assembled in the church of St Peter the Apostle. [i.e. Westminster Abbey] . . . This was done on Christmas Day in the year of our Lord 1066. The duke had refused to be crowned by Stigand, Archbishop of Canterbury . . . The Archbishop of York . . . demanded of the English in a fitting oration whether it was their will that William should be crowned as their lord. All without the least hesitation shouted their joyous assent . . . The Bishop of Coutances in like manner addressed the Normans, and they showed the same eagerness as the English . . . Those who for safety were keeping guard outside the abbey, being armed and mounted, thought the shouting boded some ill, and so without reason they started to set fire to the city.

Six days later 1066, during which the country – if one included the uncrowned Edgar – had had four kings, reached its end, to be summed up by the *Anglo-Saxon Chronicle* with striking brevity:

> 1066. In this year came William and conquered England.

By March 1067 William felt confident enough that England was secure to go on a long visit to Normandy. He embarked at Pevensey, where he had landed only six months before, in ships bearing plain white sails in token of victory.

The mercenary troops hired for the campaign were paid off and all those Normans who wished to go home returned with him, plus a distinguished band of hostages-cum-guests. They included all those around whom resistance to his rule might have gathered in his absence, including the teenage Prince Edgar and the young earls Edwin and Morcar, not much older, who were admired for their boyish good looks and long fair curls and gold-embroidered robes. Also admired were the piles of gold and silver ornaments and gem-embroidered vestments, which William now displayed like one of his Viking forebears returning from a raid, and his progress through cheering crowds lining the streets of his capital, Rouen, could hardly have been bettered by Claudius's imperial triumph in Rome a thousand years before.

When William left England early in 1067 he entrusted its rule in his absence to two men particularly close to him, as Florence of Worcester describes:

> Lent drawing near [it began on 21 February] king William returned to Normandy . . . leaving his brother Odo, Bishop of Bayeux, and William Fitz-Osborne★ whom he had created Earl of Hereford, governors of England, with orders to build strong castles in suitable places.

Bishop Odo was given special responsibility for the south-east coast and established his headquarters at Dover Castle. Fitz-Osborne, who had been the seneschal, or steward, of William's household in Normandy, was required to keep a particular eye on Winchester and Canterbury, as well as the Welsh border area covered by his own earldom, and the North. William's chief fear at this stage was of an attack from Scandinavia, and Fitz-Osborne at first concentrated his attention on East Anglia, from a base at Norwich.

Opposition to the Normans was slow to develop and localized; nothing approaching Boudicca's great national revolt against the Romans ever materialized, but the Norman takeover was challenged in a small way in a number of places. It was almost certainly a rising on the Welsh Borders, led by a man known variously as Edric the Forester [i.e. 'man of the woods'] or Edric the Wild, which drew away Bishop Odo and the governor of Dover Castle from Kent, for they are said to have been 'beyond the Thames' when a far more serious outbreak occurred in their own territory, a domestic rebellion supported by a foreign invasion.

★This is how Thomas Forester renders the name in his edition of Florence of Worcester, but Freeman prefers 'Fitz-Osbern' and Stenton 'fitz Osbern'.

The invader was Count Eustace of Boulogne, who had fought on William's side at Hastings. A notorious turncoat, murderer and, what in that age seemed even worse, a coward, Eustace had fallen out with his former ally. and may have had some vague hope of holding Dover as a check on William's power. It was probably in mid-August or early September that news of Odo's absence was sent across the Channel to Eustace, who responded immediately. He was welcomed on landing, after a night voyage, by an enthusiastic body of locals who promised him extensive reinforcements if he cared to wait a day or two, but he decided to attack at once, at dawn. The defenders of Dover Castle put up such a stout resistance that Eustace ordered a retreat to the ships, whereupon the Normans threw open the gates and charged out in that traditional manoeuvre, a sortie. So hard was it pressed that someone, perhaps Eustace himself, raised the cry that Odo had returned and was leading an overwhelming force against them. The retreat became a rout. Some men were fatally wounded by blows from their own comrades or injured themselves on their own weapons, and when the shore was reached many more were drowned when they crowded so recklessly back on to their ships that the overloaded vessels sank. The British came off better, managing to hide in the surrounding countryside or to drive off their pursuers. Eustace himself, as everyone might have predicted, also got away and although a Norman council subsequently condemned him as an insurgent vassal, and confiscated his English estates, he managed within a year to be restored to William's favour, too important perhaps to alienate for good.

Soon after William's return from Normandy, on 6 December 1067, he faced new troubles in the West Country. Once the far west had housed the Celts who most fiercely resisted the Anglo-Saxons: now it had become the chief stronghold of English sentiment. Foreign merchants and the surrounding shires and towns were called on to form a great English alliance with the well-fortified cathedral city of Exeter, which formed a natural rallying point for all who opposed the Normans. Harold's mother Gytha had taken refuge there, probably with his three sons, now young men, and with the illegitimate twins born after his death to his charmingly-named mistress Edith Swan-Neck.

Exeter was not seeking to restore the house of Godwin, but to assert its municipal independence and ancient privileges. To William's demand that it swear allegiance to him the dominant party in the city replied, a little confusedly, 'We will take no oaths to the king: we will not receive him within our walls; but we are ready to pay to him the tribute which we have been used to pay to former kings.' William was not the man to bargain. 'It is not my custom,' he replied 'to receive my subjects on such conditions,' and now set off westward, devastating the Dorset towns through which he marched.

The effects on Wareham and Shaftesbury were still evident 20 years later. In Dorchester, the county town, only a few houses were left standing; at Bridport probably not a single one. This severity had its effect. The leading citizens of Exeter hurriedly offered total submission and sent William hostages, only to have their surrender disowned by the humbler townsfolk, who barred the gates and thronged the walls. When William rode round them with a force of 500 horsemen one of the defenders standing on the battlements 'went so far,' in the words of a Victorian historian, 'as to offer William and his followers an insult as unseemly as it was senseless' and – though he discreetly left its nature in the original Latin, here translated – 'discharged noise from his lower parts to show his contempt of the Normans'.

His reception infuriated William, who had one of the unfortunate hostages blinded in full view of the men manning the East Gate, but if he hoped this would encourage the besieged to capitulate without further bloodshed, the attempt failed. Exeter, protected by the River Exe to the south-west and by ravine-like ditches forming a natural moat around most of the rest, with strong walls and gates following the original Roman ground plan, held out for 18 days. One assault after another was repulsed and, controlling the river as they did with access to the sea, the defenders seemed likely to hold out indefinitely. In the end the city fell to superior Norman military skill, through the digging of a sap or tunnel which undermined the walls.

The fall of Exeter in 1068 was followed by the destruction of other towns which failed to learn the lessons of what had happened there. Lydford, then larger than Barnstaple, virtually ceased to exist after 40 of its 69 burgesses had lost their homes, while Barnstaple itself saw 23 houses pulled down out of 49.

William now considered his new realm sufficiently secure to summon his wife, Matilda, to join him, and at Whitsun, 11 May 1068, she was crowned queen in Westminster Abbey. Henceforward the country was, when its sovereign married, to have a king and queen, and even at times to have women monarchs, ruling in their own right – something never possible in France.

Around the end of 1068 William decided that the time had come to incorporate the most northerly part of England, consisting roughly of the modern counties of Northumberland and Durham, within his new kingdom. William selected as new earl of Northumberland a Flemish soldier called Robert of Comines, who set out confidently in early January 1069 with a force variously reckoned at from 500 to 900, ignoring warnings from the Bishop of Durham that the potential dissidents vastly outnumbered it. Having stirred up fresh hatred of the Normans by quite needlessly laying waste the countryside as he marched and casually killing some harmless peasants, Robert entered Durham unopposed, installing himself and his officers in the Bishop's Palace and encouraging his men, who were forcibly billeted on the citizens, to treat the city as if it had been taken by storm. Most of the local population probably would have fled but for the deep snow all around; now they were goaded into fighting back. During the night the gates were flung open to an army raised by the local native nobility and the Normans were, in the early hours of 28 January 1069, massacred as they slept or staggered sleepily to arms. Robert of Comines and his entourage were burned to death or hacked down as they tried to escape; only one wounded Norman survived to tell the tale.

Edgar the atheling, who had taken refuge with King Malcolm of Scotland, now crossed the Scottish border to claim his inheritance and marched on York, where the population turned out on his side to help besiege the newly completed, and bitterly hated, Norman castle. Its commander one of William's closest associates, William Malet, sent desperately to the king saying that unless a relieving force arrived soon he must surrender. In spite of the snow and the early darkness the Normans now marched north at such a rate that they took the besiegers of York Castle by surprise, with devastating results, and for eight days William remained in the town, inflicting fearful punishment upon its residents.

England had now to look elsewhere for liberation from Norman rule and turned to King Swein [or Sweyn or Swegen] of Denmark who was a nephew both of the famous Cnut and of the now exiled Queen Gytha. A large fleet and powerful army were assembled, with fighting men drawn not only from Denmark but from neighbouring areas like Friesland and Saxony, from Norway, and even from distant Poland.

Swein himself stayed at home but the expedition was commanded by several members of his family, assisted by English noblemen who had taken refuge in Denmark. William seems to have taken calmly its well publicized approach, filling in time hunting in the Forest of Dean in Gloucestershire, where he was well placed to resist Edric the Wild and his Welsh allies.

The enemy fleet was first sighted off Dover, where a landing was easily repulsed by Odo of Bayeux and Hugh de Montfort, and it was followed by another equally ineffective, at Sandwich, ten miles [16 km] further up the coast. The invaders next entered the estuary of the River Orwell, through what is now Harwich harbour, and landed near Ipswich, but were driven back to their ships with the loss of 30 men, not by the Normans but by what a Norman writer describes as 'the provincials'. This repulse, close to Thetford, where, in 1004, the legendary Ulfcytel had made his famous stand against an earlier King Swein, was followed by a much more serious attack on Norwich, defended by a renegade Englishman, Ralph, son of Ralph the Staller. He now routed the Danes before they could even attack the city. Cut down, driven into the River Yare, or sent in headlong flight back to their ships, the invaders now made for Yorkshire. Here their reception was very different: the whole countryside turned out to welcome them and, it is said, men poured joyfully, on foot or horseback, towards York to attack its hated castles, the seat and symbol of their oppressors.

The local Norman commander, William Malet, soon proved that he was no Odo of Bayeux, as Florence of Worcester reveals:

> The Normans, who garrisoned the forts, set fire to the adjacent houses, fearing that they might be of service to the Danes in filling up the trenches [i.e. bridging the moats around the castles]; and the flames spreading, destroyed the whole city, together with the monastery of St Peter. But they were speedily punished for this by an infliction of the divine vengeance; for on Monday the Danish fleet arrived before the city was entirely consumed, and the forts [having been] stormed the same day, and more than 3000 of the Normans killed (the lives of William Malet and his wife and two children, with very few others, being spared), the ships drew off laden with plunder.

News of the Danes' arrival had sparked off risings in various other parts of England, but they are ignored by the English chroniclers and little is known about them. From Somerset and Dorset a force was mustered to besiege the new castle of Montacute near Yeovil, an attempt serious enough for troops to be brought to defeat it from as far afield as London, Salisbury and Winchester. They undoubtedly included some Englishmen. Nor was this the only place where the vanquished fought for their captor. When the Britons of Devon and Cornwall, still untamed, attacked the city of Exeter, with its hated castle, the townsmen, faithful to their treaty with William, joined forces with the Norman garrison in manning the walls and united in a sortie which drove the besiegers into flight and a disastrous encounter with the Norman relieving force. Those taken prisoner were mutilated before being released, to become a walking warning against challenging Norman rule.

The Danes in the North remained unbeaten and, at the invitation of their English allies, planned to celebrate the mid-winter festival, around Christmas time, in York, but this time William decided that he would be the uninvited guest and led an army nearly 60 miles [96 km] due north from his headquarters at Nottingham to the River Aire, where, ten miles [16 km] south-east of Leeds, the town of Castleford now stands. The river was impassable and for three weeks, displaying that rare attribute of a successful general, patience, William waited on the right bank while his enemies lined the left. The idea of building his own bridge he rejected, fearing an enemy attack while his men were thus occupied, but he sent out reconnaissance patrols to find a ford. Eventually one was successful, the knight in charge possibly taking soundings with his spear until he found a section of the river bed firm and shallow enough for horsemen to get across. A force of 60 then forced a passage in the face of enemy opposition, followed by the whole army, which then made its way to York, 21 miles [33 km] away by the most direct route, but far longer by the roundabout one actually followed. This precaution proved unnecessary. The Anglo-Danish armies had scattered and not a javelin was flung as William reoccupied the ruined city.

The systematic devastation of Yorkshire and the adjoining counties which William now undertook is generally regarded as the outstanding blot on what was by the standards of the time, a relatively merciful career. This was no casual 'harrying', but a deliberate attempt to ruin a substantial area, both to punish its people for past misdeeds and to render them incapable of further rebellion. Above all, it was designed to discourage future opposition: if he could not reign by consent he would rule by terror.

Even one Norman chronicler was shocked into criticism*:

Never had William shown so great a cruelty. He gave way shamefully to this vice and did not trouble to restrain his resentment, striking down innocent and guilty alike with an equal fury. In the anger which carried him away, he caused to be assembled crops, herds and flocks, food and utensils of every kind, and burned them all. In this manner all the sources of life north of the Humber were destroyed. There followed in England a famine so serious and so widespread, the disasters of the famine were so frightful, that more than 100,000 individuals of all ages and both sexes perished.

Easter in 1070 was on 4 April and the three months between the two great Christian festivals must have seemed the longest, cruellest winter in living memory in Yorkshire and Durham and the areas of Cheshire, Shropshire, Staffordshire and Derbyshire which were also, though to a lesser extent, affected, and which still bore the scars 17 years later, when large stretches of countryside were still derelict. In William's own great survey of his possessions, begun 15 years later in 1085, the single word 'Waste' appears against entry after entry in the records of Yorkshire

---

*Quoted by Slocombe, p. 189.

land-holdings and Florence of Worcester tells the grim tale of what happened to the few survivors:

> In consequence of the ravages of the Normans . . . so severe a famine prevailed in most parts of the kingdom, but chiefly in Northumbria and the adjacent provinces, that men were driven to feed on the flesh of horses, dogs, cats and even of human beings.

After the subjugation of York, another Norman debt remained to be settled. The heavy January snow lay all about as William launched the next stage of his campaign, an advance into Durham. So narrow were some of the paths northward that the men often had to advance in single file and William himself was sometimes forced to dismount. The occupation of Durham – capture it could hardly be called, for there was no resistance – was like York all over again. When it was over only the walls of the great minster still stood, and they sheltered none but the dead and dying: the bishop and clergy and everyone else able to ride or run, had fled.

During January William made his way back to York over terrain previously considered impassable, crossing the snow-bound Pennines and negotiating deep valleys almost as impenetrable, amid ice and frost that obscured the track, killed many of the horses and drove William's army almost to mutiny. It was the toughest march of his whole career, an epic feat of will and endurance. Once William was lost in wild moorland as night fell, alone except for six escorting knights, but he survived to lead his travel-worn, half-frozen, grumbling troops back into York, and then, almost before they had had a chance to rest and recover, on to Chester.

To keep the border area quiet William assigned the earldom of Chester to a trusted Norman, Hugh of Avranches, nicknamed Hugh the Wolf, who though of ferocious temperament, was so overweight he had to be lifted into the saddle. He successfully conquered Flintshire and built a fortress at Rhuddlan, close to the coast of North Wales, near modern Rhyl, to ensure that both sides of the Dee were in safe hands. If fewer people died in those operations than in Yorkshire and Durham it was because many fled. The streets and churchyard of Evesham, in the furthest corner of Worcestershire, were choked with homeless refugees and though the still-English abbot of Evesham Abbey fed all he could, every day the monks had to bury five or six more fugitives from the conqueror's wrath.

The army which had harried the North and the Welsh borders was disbanded at Salisbury, all those mercenaries who wished being allowed to collect their pay and go home, though the men who had earlier wished to desert had to wait another 40 days before their release. The conquest of England was now complete: future fighting involved rising

Duke William's victory. The Normans' route to Hastings and the subjugation of southern England, 1066.

against an established government rather than defensive battles against an invader. Easter 1070, on 4 April, saw the final extinction of Anglo-Saxon England. William was formally recrowned King of England by three cardinals sent from Rome, while the last major survivor from pre-Norman times, Archbishop Stigand, was deposed and replaced by the Norman Lanfranc, William's close friend and counsellor.

The English church was henceforward as completely under William's control as the English state, and it was the appointment of a Norman 'strong-man' as head of the great religious institution at Peterborough, known as the Golden Borough, that sparked off the last real resistance to the Normans. The Danish fleet, whose leaders had come to terms with William the previous winter, was now established a long way from the Humber at Ely and in June 1070 was invited by the dissident locals to occupy Peterborough Abbey to save its treasures from the Normans, against the wishes of the monks. They did so in characteristic fashion.

When the new abbot arrived, at the head of 160 armed men, a somewhat unusual escort for an ecclesiastic taking possession of a religious community, he found the place in ruins and its sole occupant one sick monk, in the infirmary. Before long his authority was re-asserted and the Danes responsible, after a two-day appearance in the Thames, perhaps as a final threatening gesture, sailed off to Denmark, on 24 June 1070.

During the next ten years the Fenland area, still known today as the 'Isle of Ely', became a magnet and stronghold for all those not yet prepared to accept the Norman conquest. Among them were that famous pair Earl Edwin and his brother Earl Morcar, but the unquestioned leader of the 'outlaws', as the *Anglo-Saxon Chronicle* priggishly describes them, was a hitherto unknown thegn from Lincolnshire called Hereward.

Hereward 'the Wake', meaning 'watchful', a name first used three centuries later, is undoubtedly a historical figure though many of the 'facts' recorded about him are suspect. He is said, on good evidence, to have been short but well made, with long golden hair, an oval face and light-coloured eyes, and remarkably agile for his height. His wife, more dubiously, is believed to have been Flemish and skilled in magic. His contemporary biographer credits him with no more than 300 men, only 100 of them mounted, plus a few archers, and the largest estimate puts his forces no higher than 700, but with this comparative handful of followers he succeeded in defying the full might of the formidable William, and the combined *fyrd* of nine counties, for more than a year.

William set up his headquarters for the new campaign in his castle at Cambridge and was soon organizing a series of assaults by boat, from Brandon, on the Little Ouse, and from Reche, near the confluence of the River Cam and the Ouse, south-east of Ely. It proved impossible, however, to bring his full strength to bear in such operations and eventually he undertook a major feat of military engineering to enable his men to advance dry-shod. Florence of Worcester sets out the facts:

> Hereward, a man of great bravery, with many others, took ship and went to the Isle of Ely, intending to winter there. The king, hearing of this, blocked up every outlet on the eastern side of the island by means of his boatmen, and caused a bridge two miles long to be constructed on the western side.

To build this bridge, or causeway, vast stores of timber and hides were assembled and stone was brought by the boat-load from Cottenham, but less orthodox measures were not despised. William is said to have installed a witch in a wooden tower to demoralize the English by her spells but she proved ineffective; the tower, complete with sorceress, was speedily burned down. Like Alfred before him, stories are recorded of Hereward venturing in disguise into the enemy camp, posing as a potter and a fisherman, and he is said to have led various sorties against pro-Norman villages such as the hamlet of Burwell, ten miles [16 km] south of Ely. His own garrison was in the end, it seems likely, defeated by treachery rather than force of arms when the monks of Ely, perhaps recalling what Hereward's allies had done at Peterborough and eager to buy William's favour, betrayed the way in to the hitherto impregnable island. While the English were hemmed in on the east the main assault was probably delivered from the west along the causeway from Aldreth, about seven miles [11 km] south-west of Ely. Florence of Worcester describes the defenders' reaction: 'When they saw that they were thus shut in, they resisted no longer and all surrendered themselves to the king, except the brave Hereward, who escaped through the fens with a few others.'

By his own standards William treated the rebels mercifully. The rank and file were merely blinded or mutilated; Earl Morcar was kept in semi-captivity for the rest of his life; Earl Edwin escaped capture but was, mysteriously, killed by his own men six months later; and Hereward himself, having escaped to the Continent, later made his peace with William and may have died fighting for the Normans in France.

Hereward's revolt was crushed in the autumn of 1071. A year later, in mid-August 1072, William confronted his most dangerous external enemy, Malcolm of Scotland. Without waiting for the Scots to attack he led a large army, supported by a coastal fleet, across the Border and the Firth of Forth and, meeting little resistance, pressed on to the Tay. Here, at Abernethy, Malcolm acknowledged William as his overlord and, under a treaty of friendship, agreed to expel his own son-in-law, Edgar the atheling, the legitimate claimant in English eyes to the throne William had usurped. A little later, Edgar himself, having failed to find allies on the Continent, came to terms with William, settled for a pension and an estate in Hertfordshire and lived to enjoy a peaceful old age.

After his succession to the Danish throne in 1080 King Cnut began to plan another invasion to regain the empire over which his famous namesake had once ruled. Rumours circulated that year that a huge fleet was assembling in the Limfiord, north of Jutland, but it never appeared, though there was a serious disturbance in Northumbria, perhaps intended to coincide with the Danes' arrival. By 1085, however, Cnut had got together a formidable confederation including King Olaf of Norway, son of the famous Harold Hardrada, who promised 60 ships, and Robert, Count of Flanders, his own father-in-law, who offered 600, while Cnut himself is said to have assembled 1000.

Tired of waiting to set sail, the Danish troops first grumbled, then, when Cnut tried to restore discipline, mutinied. William was able to spend a peaceful Christmas at Gloucester and during 1086 Cnut was murdered by his own subjects.

To raise money to keep out the Danes a heavy Danegeld-style tax had been levied of 72 pence per hide of land, but so many estates had changed hands it was difficult to collect. Information was also needed on the capacity of different districts to provide quarters and subsistence for imported mercenaries. 'The king,' recorded one chronicler in 1085, 'had mickle thought and very deep speech with his Witan about this land, how it was set and by what men.' The result was 'The Description of all England', compiled during 1086 and now known as Domesday Book, an immensely detailed and unique record of men and land, horses and cattle, rents and obligations, of obvious military, as well as fiscal, value.

The possibility of invasion, aided by internal insurrection, may also have played a part in what seemed at the time a monstrously selfish action; the creation of the New Forest stretching from Salisbury to the sea over a distance of 30 miles [48 km] covers an area of 17,000 acres [7000 hectares]. The chroniclers disagree as to whether this meant the destruction of 60 parishes, or only half this number, and whether some were merely placed under the special Forest Law rather than physically obliterated. Even this was serious enough, for a man could legally be killed or blinded merely for snaring a rabbit or carrying a bow where Forest law applied. Primarily intended to assist William in indulging his passion for the chase, the creation of the New Forest also ensured that this area, a natural target for an invader, could not support a foreign army or conceal men plotting rebellion.

The Normans believed that the lack of fixed defences was largely responsible for the comparative ease with which they had conquered the island, as the chronicler Orderic Vitalis explained: 'The fortifications called castles by the Normans were scarcely known to the English provinces, and so the English – in spite of their courage and love of fighting – could put up only a weak resistance to their enemies.'

The new castles, built initially to hold down the English though later providing them with protection against external enemies, became the great, and hated, symbol of Norman oppression. The first, temporary, castles erected were of the 'motte and bailey' type, like the one raised at Hastings. A circular ditch was dug out and the earth from it used to form a mound within, reinforced with stones brought from outside, the alternating layers of stone and soil ultimately forming a cone 40 feet [12 m] or more high, with a flattened top which might be as small as 80 square yards feet [71 sq. m] or as large as half an acre [2000 sq. m]. As a second line of defence a wooden palisade, and sometimes a wooden tower, possibly on stilts, from which missiles could be hurled at assailants, was built on top of the mound. These two features, the central 'motte' or mound, and the outer area enclosed by the ditch, the 'bailey' or fortified courtyard, are common to almost all castles, though with many variations. There might, for example, be both an inner bailey and, separated from it by a further ditch, an outer bailey used to accommodate stables and other outbuildings, with an encircling ditch enclosing both baileys and the motte. The flimsy and vulnerable wooden tower which formed the heart of the first castle rapidly gave way to an immensly strong stone citadel, round or square, known as the great tower, the donjon, or, more expressively, as the keep, expected to hold out even if the outer defences were overwhelmed.

Unlike the old Saxon hill forts, or Alfred's burhs, designed to enclose a whole community within a fence and ditch or simple stone walls, the Norman castles were intended to house only a single lord and his retainers, plus a garrison large enough to overawe the surrounding countryside. Their presence was a continuing threat, and irritation, to the local population, and every rebellion tended to be followed by the erection of a castle, as at Exeter, Warwick and Nottingham, or by the addition of a second fortress to reinforce an existing one, as at York. All told the Normans built some 33 castles during the first, perilous five years of William's reign in England, and added nearly twice as many during the next 16, with a notable concentration in the Midlands, on the Welsh borders, and along the south and east coast. An outstanding example of castle design was the 'great tower', begun by the Thames in London in 1079, which formed a whole royal palace as well as a fortress. The keep was rectangular, nearly 100 feet [30 m] square, with walls 15 feet [4.5 m] thick at their broadest point, additional strength being provided by the old Roman walls of the city, forming the bailey defences. Colchester, another key point since Roman times, had an even longer keep, enclosing an area 150 feet [46 m] by 110 [34 m], three storeys high with corner turrets, and was designed to form the linch-pin of the East coast defences against a new Danish invasion.

On Thursday 9 September 1087 William I died, at the then respectable age of 61, his burial, at Caen, like his coronation at Westminster, being marked by some unseemly scenes. A fire broke out among the surrounding houses and a local citizen tried to forbid the burial on the ground that the site of the church had been stolen from his family. Eventually the dead king's body proved too large for its sarcophagus and could only be squeezed inside with a struggle. The *Anglo-Saxon Chronicle* in its obituary had some sharp words to say about the departed monarch:

> He caused castles to be built which were a sore burden to the poor. A hard man was the king.

15

NOTHING BUT STRIFE

In the days of this king there was nothing but strife, evil and robbery.

The Anglo-Saxon Chronicle, *1136, describing King Stephen's reign.*

For several centuries after the death of William I, England was seldom free from the threat of invasion, sometimes from across the channel, but more often from Wales and Scotland. On his deathbed the great Duke had bequeathed the Duchy of Normandy to his eldest son Robert of whom he had a low opinion, while reserving the kingdom of England for his second and favourite son, named after him but generally known by his nickname Rufus, or 'the Red' from his ruddy complexion. William's youngest son, Henry, received as his portion 5000 pounds of silver, immediately demonstrating his practical streak by weighing it out while his father still breathed. Rufus, now William II of England, equally unsentimental, set sail to claim his inheritance the instant he learned of William I's death, on 9 September 1087. By the 26th he had been crowned at Westminster, but he had hardly ascended the throne when he faced a whole series of invasions and rebellions in support of the claim of his brother Robert, nicknamed Curthose, to rule Normandy and England jointly, as his father had done. They were led by Odo of Bayeux, a notorious oppressor of the native population, whose support, Rufus realized, was crucial, as Henry of Huntingdon describes: 'The king therefore summoned an assembly of his English subjects and promised that he would restore the freedom of chase and of the woods and that he would confirm the ancient laws they loved.'

None of these promises was destined to be kept, but they served their purpose and Rufus showed sound strategic sense in dealing effectively with the situation in Kent, where Odo had raised an insurrection, and in Sussex, where Odo's henchman, Roger of Morton, had 'ravaged the country about Pevensey'.

For six weeks Rufus's lines encircled Pevensey, and his siege engines battered its walls, while the embattled garrison waited for the sight of

Norman transports on the horizon. But day followed day and none appeared. Eventually, according to Henry of Huntingdon, Robert sent forward a body of troops to support his friends, preparing himself to follow with a powerful army, but by now the fyrd in the coastal areas was fully mobilized and the result of this small-scale invasion on behalf of the Conqueror's eldest son – who himself stayed behind in Normandy – was a fiasco, all the more humiliating in that it took place at Hastings: 'The English, who guarded the sea, attacked the armed force, and immense numbers of them [i.e. the Normans] were either put to [the] sword or drowned. Whereupon those who were besieged in Pevensey Castle, provisions failing them, surrendered it to the king.'

The most discreditable episode in the whole story now followed:

Bishop Odo solemnly swore to depart the realm and deliver up his castle at Rochester. But when he came there with a party of the king's troops to cause it to be surrendered, Earl Eustace and the other great men who were in the city seized the king's officers, at the bishop's secret instigation, and threw them into prison.

According to Orderic Vitalis, this Medway town had been selected by the rebels as their base for good reason.

With careful forethought they chose the fortified town of Rochester as their base, so that if the king had not besieged them they could have broken out to plunder the two cities of London and Canterbury on either side of them, and have taken advantage of the sea . . . to send messengers for help without loss of time. But the energetic king anticipated their intention and in May blockaded the walled town with a great army, and by fortifying two siege-towers cut off the enemy's egress.

In the end having withstood all the missiles and arrows Rufus could hurl against them, Odo and his fellow traitors succumbed in July 1088 to a more mundane opponent:

In the town of Rochester a plague like one of the plagues of Egypt broke out . . . The men could not go outside the fortifications, and as disease spread many of them died from various infections. Consequently myriads of flies were generated in the rotting flesh of men and horses, and breeding rapidly in the heat of the summer and the breath of over-crowded men, they filled the eyes and nostrils of the besieged and contaminated their food and drink in a horrible way. The proud troop of rebels were so harassed by the torment of the flies that they could eat nothing either by day or night unless a great number of them took turns to protect their comrades' mouths by beating away the flies with whisks. In the end Odo of Bayeux and his accomplices could endure the siege no longer, and sent messengers to ask King William to make peace and receive the surrender of the town . . . The unhappy bishop . . . though he voiced dire threats . . . was banished from England and stripped of his vast possessions . . . he returned in confusion to Bayeux and never set foot in England again.

Rufus built only one major castle, but a vitally important one, Carlisle, though its most impressive feature, its mighty keep, was probably added later. His own contribution to military technology was to be of a different kind. On Thursday 2 August 1100, he was hunting in the New Forest near Brockenhurst when a local blacksmith delivered to him some custom-built arrows with metal tips, and the king obligingly handed two of them to a companion with a reputation as a good shot. The new, improved arrow did all that had been claimed for it, after the famous marksman had spotted a beast moving between himself and the king. Orderic Vitalis learned what followed:

Walter let fly an arrow. It sped swiftly over the beast's back, grazing the hair and mortally wounded the king, who was standing directly in its path. He fell to the ground and . . . died at once. Many were thrown into confusion and terrible shouts that the king was dead rang through the wood.

In the general panic one man, the king's younger brother Henry, kept his head: 'Henry galloped at top speed to Winchester castle where the royal treasure was and imperiously demanded the keys from the keepers as the lawful heir.'

The 32-year-old prince was only just in time. Hard on his heels arrived the treasurer who claimed the keys, and the crown, for Robert Curthose. Henry's robust response was to draw his sword in defence of his own right to succeed. According to William of Malmesbury, a chronicler writing between 1125 and 1142, probably while librarian at Malmesbury Abbey, by the time Rufus's body on a cart '. . . dripping with blood all the way', had reached Winchester the matter was settled. Three days later Henry I was crowned at Westminster Abbey.

An attempt to oust the new sovereign was almost inevitable, but it took the lackadaisical Robert of Normandy, now in his late forties, a year to get an expedition together. Henry responded with his usual energy. The fyrd was called out and mustered at Pevensey where the king himself tried to knock the raw recruits into shape, as William of Malmesbury describes:

Arriving at Portsmouth, he landed, divided and posted his forces over the whole district . . . Grateful to the inhabitants for their fidelity, and anxious for their safety, he frequently went through the ranks, instructing them how to elude the forocity of the cavalry by opposing their shields, and how to return their strokes. By this he made them voluntarily demand the fight, perfectly fearless of the Normans.

The external danger confronting Henry was more formidable than the half-hearted invasion from the same quarter with which his predecessor had had to deal, but the greatest threat, as then, came from internal betrayal, as Florence of Worcester makes clear:

> Robert, Earl [in fact Duke] of Normandy, having raised a large body of horsemen, archers and foot soldiers, assembled his ships [at a place] called . . . Ultres-port [i.e. Tréport]. The king, receiving intelligence of this ordered his boats-carles [i.e. the local boatmen, pressed into the royal service] to guard the sea, and to watch that no-one approached the coast of England from Normandy: while he himself, having collected an immense army from every part of England, encamped near Hastings in Sussex, concluding for certain that his brother would land in that quarter. The earl, however . . . tampered with the fidelity of some of the king's boats-carles, by promises of various kinds, that, throwing off their allegiance, they deserted to the earl and became his pilots to England. All being ready, he embarked with his army, and about . . . [1st August] landed at Portsmouth, and, immediately marching his army towards Winchester, pitched his camp on a suitable spot. Immediately that his arrival was known, some of the English nobles went over to him as they had before promised . . . The bishops, however, with the common soldiers and English people, stood by him resolutely, and were ready to a man to be led to battle for his cause.

Contrary to all expectation, Robert had thus got his men ashore in safety and well inland and Henry, outflanked, could merely set off to intercept him. He did so at Alton, 25 miles [40 km] from Portsmouth and about 50 [80 km] from London, but the decisive battle with Robert, so long overdue, was again postponed. An agreement was patched up between the contending brothers, under which the adherents of both rulers had their confiscated lands restored and Henry promised to pay his brother 3000 marks, i.e. 2000 pounds in silver a year*, to leave him in peace.

The final settlement with Robert was not long in coming. Henry finally put paid to the danger of invasions by attacking his brother in his own territory. The decisive battle was fought at Tinchebray [or Tinchebrai], 35 miles [56 km] east of Avranches on 28 September

*A silver mark consisted of 160 pennies and a pound weight of silver of 240, hence the later division of the pound sterling into 240 pence.

1106. In barely an hour an overwhelmingly English army defeated an overwhelmingly Norman one. Robert was taken prisoner and died in captivity in Cardiff 28 years later, aged 80.

Although the danger of invasion was now lifted, Henry greatly strengthened the former Saxon Shore fort at Portchester, near Portsmouth, adding a new stone wall and a four-storey keep. Further up the coast, at Rochester, a new keep was added to an existing castle, and at Dorset, to the west, Corfe Castle acquired a tall new tower. A regular feature of all these works was the addition of a cross-wall, to enable the rest of the castle to hold out even after part had fallen, and a porch, which had to be stormed before the besiegers could even attack the inner door beyond it.

The king had already survived at least two close shaves, a French sword-blow that forced his helmet into his forehead, and a Welsh arrow which violently struck his breast plate. He was destined to fall victim to a smaller adversary. At the age of 67, remarkably old for the time, he was, as Henry of Huntingdon explains, 'returning from hunting at St Denys [in Normandy]' when 'he partook of some lampreys, of which he was fond, though they always disagreed with him' – a piece of self-indulgence which proved fatal.

Henry I's death, on 1 December 1135, was followed by nearly 20 years of civil war, commonly described as 'the anarchy'. Although much fighting took place on English soil and both fortifications and military equipment were put to the test of operational use, it was essentially an internal struggle, though sometimes supported by outside invasion. Henry I's designated heir, the Empress Matilda, aged 33 when her father died, was an unpleasant woman, arrogant and greedy, who had left England when she was eight years old and had made a highly unpopular second marriage to Geoffrey, Count of Anjou. Most of the nobility, so ready to plead the sacred rights of inheritance where their own property was concerned, gladly ignored her claim in favour of that of a rival contender, Stephen of Blois, son of Henry's sister Adela and a French nobleman. Stephen, aged about 38, possessed the overwhelming advantage of being on the spot. He was also a far more attractive personality than his cousin, good-natured, generous and universally liked, though indecisive and ineffective. He responded energetically, however, to his uncle's death, took ship for England and, by Christmas, had been crowned by the Archbishop of Canterbury in London.

Stephen's real problems followed Matilda's arrival on, or about, 30 September 1139. The king had previously begun to make anti-invasion preparations on the south-east coast, but was called away to Marlborough in Wiltshire where the custodian of the castle had declared, a little prematurely, for the empress. In his absence Matilda had arrived at

Portsmouth with her brother Robert, who rode off to Bristol, the main centre of the pro-Matilda party. She had with her only a trifling force of 140 knights and though she established herself with Henry I's widow, the Queen dowager Adelaide, at Arundel Castle in Sussex, she could at this stage easily have been detained. Chivalrously, but absurdly, Stephen instead gave her a safe conduct to join her brother. It proved a disastrous mistake. Gloucester, followed by many other places, now declared for Matilda, and a full-scale civil war followed.

For the ordinary citizen it was a wretched time, as the *Anglo-Saxon Chronicle*, in one of its last entries, confirms:

> In the days of this king there was nothing but strife, evil and robbery, for quickly the great men who were traitors rose against him . . . When the traitors saw that Stephen was a good-humoured, kindly and easy going man who inflicted no punishment, then they committed all manner of horrible crimes . . . Every great man built him castles and held them against the king: and they filled the whole land with these castles. They sorely burdened the unhappy people of the country with forced labour on the castles; and when the castles were built, they filled them with devils and wicked men.

The end of the nation's long agony began to come in sight in October 1147 when Matilda's most powerful supporter in England, her illegitimate half-brother Robert of Gloucester, died, and in February 1148 Matilda herself withdrew across the Channel. The military tide was unmistakably swinging against her and she now placed her hopes on obtaining the succession to the English throne for her eldest son Henry, born at Le Mans in Maine in 1133. Henry had first set foot on English soil at the age of nine, when he landed at Wareham with a relief expedition sent to rescue his mother from Oxford, and at 14 he was back at the head of a small army of mercenaries, which he led, unsuccessfully, against two of Stephen's castles in the Gloucester area, Stephen, with extraordinary amiability, paying his travel expenses back to Anjou. In 1149, now 16, Henry got as far as Carlisle, where he planned a joint campaign with King David of Scotland, which came to nothing, but in 1151 he was invested with the dukedom of Normandy and later that year, on his father's death, also succeeded him as Count of Anjou. Nine months later, in May 1152, he made a brilliant marriage to the ex-wife of Louis VII of France, daughter and heir to the Duke of Aquitaine, a famous, black-eyed charmer, still only 30, who brought as her dowry nearly half of France.

A month after his wedding to Eleanor of Aquitaine Henry was making active preparations for what one chronicler called 'a sudden descent on

England', another of those 'friendly invasions' where the invader claimed to be acting on behalf of the English people.

The invasion season was well past, but Henry eventually mustered a force of 140 knights and 3000 foot soldiers, to be carried in 36 vessels, and in early January 1153 set sail from Barfleur, on the north-east tip of the Cotentin peninsula. His destination was Wareham in Dorset, 70 miles [120 km] away, a somewhat longer crossing than his great grandfather had attempted in 1066 under far more favourable conditions.

Henry's contemporaries were uncertain as to whether, in launching a cross-Channel invasion in mid-winter, the young man, still only 19, was exhibiting the rashness of youth or the daring of a natural commander. 'Both parties.' comments Henry of Huntingdon, 'were struck at his encountering the dangers of a tempestuous sea in mid-winter; what the one considered intrepidity, the other called rashness.' But fortune, as it always seemed to do with Henry, favoured the bold and he seems to have got his troops ashore without mishap.

Henry's immediate objective was to relieve the castle at Wallingford on the upper Thames, mid-way between Reading, 13 miles [21 km] downstream, and Oxford. Loyal to Matilda ever since her standard had first been raised, Wallingford lay about 80 miles [128 km] from Wareham by the most direct cross-country route, though substantially further by road. With great strategic insight Henry decided to relieve the pressure on it by attacking instead one of Stephen's strongholds, Malmesbury in Wiltshire, about 16 miles [26 km] nearer, a royalist intruder in a pro-Matilda area.

Even by the standards of an English January the weather was appalling, but Henry refused to be diverted from his plan, as Henry of Huntingdon admiringly testifies:

> The brave young prince, of all things disliking delay, collected his adherents, both those he found and those he brought with him, and laid siege to Malmesbury Castle . . . He presently took it by storm. After the place was taken, the strong keep, which could only be reduced by famine, was still held for the king who . . . lost no time in collecting all his forces and pitched his camp near Malmesbury.

Henry's attempt to bring the king to battle on ground of his own choosing had thus succeeded, but the royal forces outnumbered the invader's. Now however General Winter took a hand:

> The day after his arrival he [King Stephen] drew out his army in battle array. It included a great body of distinguished knights and made a splendid and formidable appearance, with its noble chiefs and their banners glistening with gold; but . . . the floodgates of heaven were

opened and heavy rain drove in their faces, with violent gusts of wind and severe cold, so that God himself appeared to fight for the duke . . .

The young duke's army trusted more to its valour than its numbers . . . It was drawn up on the bank of a stream of water, not far from the walls of the town . . . which was so flooded by the torrents of rain and snow that no-one could venture to ford it . . . The young and illustrious duke was at the head of his troops in splendid armour . . . He and his followers had the tempest of wind and rain at their backs, while it drove in the faces of the king and his army, so that they could hardly support their armour and handle their spears, dripping with wet . . . When neither party could cross the river and the king could no longer endure the severity of the weather, he marched back to London, his operation having failed and his discomfiture being complete.

While the Archbishop of Canterbury and the Bishop of Winchester tried to mediate between the two sides, the fighting went on. Henry captured Stamford and Nottingham, Stephen's son Eustace marched through Cambridgeshire inflicting widespread destruction, apparently in the hope of provoking Henry into a full-scale battle of the kind he had so far avoided. It was probably Eustace's sudden death, on 17 August 1153, that caused his father to lose heart and on 6 November 1153 the king and the duke met at Winchester to agree that Stephen should retain the crown for the rest of his life, but that Henry should succeed him. It was also agreed that all the illicit castles erected since Henry I's death should be destroyed. It was a sensible, practical arrangement, its results acclaimed by the *Anglo-Saxon Chronicle*: 'Soon there was a good and lasting peace such as had never been before, and the king was stronger than he had ever been. The Count [i.e. Henry of Anjou] went oversea [in fact at Easter 1154] and all the people loved him, for he administered justice fairly and made peace.'

This was almost the last entry in the often pessimistic *Chronicle*, the sole surviving version of which finally came to an end the following year, its task done. The England of Alfred was dead, its records no longer kept in its native tongue but in Latin or Norman French.

On 25 October Stephen, aged about 57, died. The dashing young prince who was crowned as his successor, Henry II, on 19 December 1154, was the first of the Angevins, also known as Plantagenets from the *Plante Genet* (*Planta Genista*), or flowering bloom, Henry's father Geoffrey had worn in his hat.

16

DESTROYING KING HENRY

We have not come to this country to sojourn
But to destroy King Henry, the old warrior.

Song of invading force of Flemings, 1173

With the accession of Henry II the Channel became an unwelcome ditch dividing one part of his vast dominions from another rather than a bulwark for the island's defence. Although the new king never did learn to speak English, far more is known about his appearance and personality than of most medieval monarchs. The chronicler Gerald of Wales (Giraldus Cambrensis), writing just after the king's death, gives a vivid portrait:

> His frame was stocky with a pronounced tendency to corpulence, due rather to nature than to indulgence . . . for in eating and drinking he was moderate and sparing. In times of war, which frequently threatened, he gave himself scarcely a modicum of quiet . . . and in times of peace he allowed himself neither tranquillity nor repose . . . He was rarely seen to sit down either before or after supper . . . He would wear out the whole court by continual standing.

Even less restless monarchs than Henry II felt uneasy when they were not fighting someone. The chronicler William of Newburgh, a near contemporary of the king, writing in a Yorkshire priory not later than 1197, remarks that the 'month of June' is a time 'when kings are wont to go to war'. Much of Henry's reign was to be spent in fighting, in Normandy, Ireland, Scotland and Wales, but the only foreign invasions were a result of the great tragedy of his life, his quarrel with his sons. 'Except by the sorrows his sons inflicted on him,' says the contemporary observer Walter Map, 'he reigned unconquered and unshaken.'

As so often, internal rebellion went hand in hand with foreign invasion. In 1173 the king's eldest son, Henry the Younger, having reached the age of 18, asked to be made the ruler of one of his three territories, England, Normandy or Anjou. When his father refused his son secured the support of several foreign monarchs as well as some of the leading English nobility. The most important was Earl Robert of Leicester, who landed at Walton in Suffolk on Michaelmas Day, 29 September 1173, with a formidable force of Flemings, the most notable mercenaries of their time and enthusiastic immigrants into other people's countries. This new contingent was distinctly unmartial, consisting mainly of weavers hoping for a prosperous future in England. They advanced dancing and singing a curious ditty:

> We have not come to this country to sojourn
> But to destroy King Henry, the old warrior,
> And to have his wool, for which we have a desire.

The Flemings, under Leicester's leadership, marched 30 miles [48 km] inland from Walton and captured a royal castle at Haughley, before setting off towards the earl's own castle, which he hoped to relieve. In command on the English side was the Constable of England, Humphrey de Bohun. He decided to bar the road leading north from Bury St Edmunds in an area about three miles [4.8 km] beyond the town and about one mile [1.6 km] short of the present town of Culford, at Fornham St Genevieve, about equidistant from the village of Fornham St Martin and Fornham All Saints*. The motley force which he assembled on 17 October 1173 was outnumbered four to one and consisted largely of peasants armed with pitchforks and flails, but the position was a strong one, bounded by marshes, and this rustic horde proved more than a match for the Flemings, as William of Newburgh recorded:

> The latter, unable to wheel either to the right or to the left, made a virtue of necessity and boldly pushed on with all speed using their cavalry as a screen. And so began a desperate battle, the king's troops fighting for glory and the rebels for safety; but victory fell to the royal army. The earl was taken captive with his wife, a woman of masculine disposition . . . together with almost all the cavalry, but nearly the whole host of infantry was annihilated.

On 15 May 1174 the advance guard of a second invading force landed at Whitsand at the mouth of the River Orwell in Suffolk, between present-day Harwich and Felixstowe. It was welcomed, according to William of Newburgh, by the Earl of Norfolk, Hugh Bigod, 'a powerful and crafty man'.

> With the guidance and cooperation of this same Hugh, the army advanced upon the city of Norwich and broke into it with very little

*Not, of course, Farnham, as stated by Hozier I p. 170, which is in Surrey.

trouble, since it was without a garrison and stricken with sudden panic. After pillaging its wealth the army returned to its camp laden with spoils.

On 7 July 1174 , in response to the pleadings of one of his counsellors sent by his colleagues from England the king reluctantly left Normandy, embarking at Barfleur despite the gale then raging. To the protestations of the ship's crew he bravely replied that if God wished him to restore peace in his kingdom He would protect him and by sunset, after a stormy but speedy crossing, he was in Southampton.

There was a fatalistic quality about the king's actions at this time; it was almost as though he wanted to be overthrown, as his punishment for causing the murder two years before of the Archbishop of Canterbury, Thomas à Becket. Instead of making his way immediately to one of the fronts – Northumbria, the Midlands and Norfolk – where men were actively in arms against him, or hurrying to Kent to strengthen its defences, Henry went instead to Canterbury, as William of Newburgh describes:

> He hastened thither as soon as he had landed, and prayed before the tomb of the blessed Archbishop Thomas, shedding copious tears. Having entered the chapter of the monks he prostrated himself on the ground and most humbly entreated their pardon; at his own urgent petition this man who stood so high in rank was beaten with rods by all the brethren in turn.

While the king was abasing himself at Canterbury the situation further north was being transformed. Hitherto King William of Scotland, who had invaded England in April, had largely been having things his own way; now, in a dramatic reversal of fortune, he was defeated and captured, at Alnwick in Northumberland, on 13 July★.

The capture of King William was really the end of the great conspiracy. Henry II now took the field in person; his mere arrival was enough to bring about the surrender of Huntingdon and when he reached Northampton his remaining enemies hurried there to capitulate. England was safe and by 8 August 1174 he was back in Barfleur, where his run of victories continued.

The year had been by any test a remarkable one, but Florence of Worcester put it in perspective in a marvellously concise summary:

> AD 1174. The Flemings coming over in aid of the king's son, burn Norwich. Richard, prior of Dover, is consecrated archbishop of

★Oman, I p. 400, inexplicably dates the battle as being fought on 13 June, an example of the innumerable difficulties confronting anyone writing on medieval history.

Canterbury by the lord pope. All the world is afflicted with coughs and colds.

Although there were some minor outbreaks of trouble on both sides of the Channel after 1174 the contemporary who styled Henry 'the greatest of the illustrious rulers of the world' was hardly exaggerating and the preamble to the royal charters which described him as 'king of the English, duke of the Normans, duke of the Aquitanians and count of the Angevins' was making a sober statement of fact. All this could not have been achieved, or if achieved preserved, without a talent for military organization and construction which were to leave their mark for generations, even centuries, to come.

The first great change was in the widespread use of mercenaries. Such troops, however, required to be paid, hence the introduction of scutage, the payment by each knight of a fixed sum in lieu of personal revenue, for each shield, or *scutum*, he should have supplied. (The customary amount was 2s 8d [£1.33] , or two marks, representing 40 days under arms at 8d [3p] a day, but he could still, if he chose, come in person instead of paying cash. The centralized administrative and judical system introduced by Henry II made it possible for the first time to lay down common scales for weapons and armour which every freeman was required to possess, and to enforce them through the network of justices, henceforward an essential element in local defence, who kept the king's peace in every shire. The Assize of Arms 1181 left no one in doubt about his obligations:

> Let every holder of a knight's fee have a hauberk [coat of chain mail], a helmet, a shield and a lance . . . Also, let every free layman, who holds chattels or rent to the value of 16 marks, have a hauberk, a helmet, a shield and a lance. Also, let every free layman who holds chattels or rent worth 10 marks have an aubergel [a cheaper version of the hauberk] and a headpiece of iron, and a lance. Also, let all burgesses and the whole body of freemen have quilted doublets and a headpiece of iron, and a lance.

It became the practice, though not under the Assize of Arms a legal obligation, for those required to possess arms to produce them at least once a year. This was the shire 'muster' which later became also an occasion for providing some elementary training in drill and weapon-handling. Henry II's famous Assize was the first statutory, as distinct from traditional, requirement laid on the freemen of Norman England to defend their country, The landless were exempt from what was regarded as a privilege more than a duty. 'The king commands,' ran the final sentence of the Assize, 'that no-one should be accepted for the oath of arms except a free man.'

Recent experience had demonstrated the value of the castle as an effective means of preventing an invader enjoying freedom of movement and both the Treaty of Winchester of 1153, which had guaranteed Henry the succession, and the subsequent agreements in 1174, following his defeat of the rebels and the Scots, had called for the destruction or surrender into trusted hands of castles belonging to the losing side. Henry built, however, or greatly strengthened, far more fortresses than he demolished and, unlike most commanders of the time, he was not over-awed by the supposed impregnability of even a minor castle if adequately garrisoned against existing methods of assault.

Siegecraft in the twelfth century had made little advance in either technique or equipment since Roman times. The aim was still, if forced to attack, to oppose a supposedly irresistible force to a hitherto immovable object. When, as commonly happened, the first storming parties, having filled up the surrounding ditch with rubble or earth, attempted to swarm over the walls on scaling ladders and were repulsed, the attacker, if famine could not be left to do its work, had resort either to trying to undermine the walls or to break through them. The accepted method for the first was to dig away at the most vulnerable corner of the walls, shoring them up, as the earth was scraped away, with wooden beams. These were then surrounded with straw and brushwood which was set alight, so that as the supports burned away the foundations of the wall collapsed, the device being known as a 'furnace' or a 'mine'. The great disadvantage, apart from the difficulty of finding a suitable spot where the miners could dig away undisturbed, was that mining could not be used when, as happened more often than not, a castle was built on high ground, with exposed approaches or on rock.

Often, therefore, the attackers turned to the ram or the bore, which relied wholly on brute force. The former was a huge tree trunk, fitted with a reinforced head, and hung by ropes from two uprights. It was hauled back as far as the suspension allowed by a working party of 40 to 60 men, then released to batter against the selected spot on the castle wall. The bore was sometimes known as a 'mouse', because it was intended to gnaw away at the castle ramparts, or as a 'cat', supposed to claw its way in, or as a 'hog', using its tusks against its enemy. It was lighter and easier to handle than the ram, and a shade more subtle, since it consisted of a heavy pole with an iron point, which was driven into the mortar between the stones in the fortress wall and levered about until a small hole was created. This was then gradually enlarged until there was room enough for an assault party to climb through, or a whole section of the wall collapsed.

The conventional counter-measures were to use, against the ram, powerful wooden forks shaped like an inverted 'Y', which trapped the unwieldy object and made it impossible to draw back or manoeuvre effectively, and to hang down crude palisades of wood, or sacking filled with straw, on which the initial impact was uselessly dissipated. These measures were commonly accompanied by a shower of missiles, sometimes including hot pitch or boiling oil. It therefore became customary to equip the soldiers handling the ram or bore with a mobile shelter or penthouse, frequently mounted on wheels or rollers, which totally enclosed them. Its sides, made of hides on a wooden frame, or hurdles, were sufficient protection against stones or spears while the roof, which needed to be fireproof, was made of stronger beams, covered with tiles or earth.

These crude and cumbersome devices were to be seen on the battlefield for centuries to come but far more attractive to Henry II was the mobile tower – he had taken one to Ireland in 1171 – an upright wooden construction from which an observer could see over the castle walls and missiles could be directed at any defenders who presented a sudden target. Attractive in theory, the tower was in practice vulnerable to bombardment by heavy missiles, or fire, and hard to use on any except firm, level ground. If a ditch were filled in so that the tower could be trundled right up to the walls it was liable to sink into the newly-dug earth, making it impossible to employ it for its other purpose, as an assault platform, from which a drawbridge could be lowered onto the top of the castle walls. The truth was that, although an exceptionally able and determined commander, like King Henry himself, might successfully capture a castle the balance of advantage still lay with the defence. In the duels between boulder-throwing 'artillery' the castle dweller was likely to come off best, and the assault party advancing with mantlets, consisting of stakes wattled together, over their heads, was little better protected than the Roman centurions who had formed a *testudo* with their shields.

Henry was responsible for three new castles at specially vulnerable points along the coast. At Scarborough, he confiscated the existing castle and built, between 1159 and 1168, an immensely strong new tower, on a rock said to be 'stupendous alike in height and area and surrounded by inaccessible cliffs rising out of the sea'. Once it had accommodated a Roman signal station and a Viking camp; now it was to survive, surrounded by its ditch cut through the solid rock, untaken for 500 years. At Orford, on the east coast, which towered over Hugh Bigod's Framlingham and other potential trouble spots, Henry built an equally strong castle on a previously unfortified site. It was finished just before the invasion of 1173, when neither native rebels nor invading Flemings dared attack it, and the novel design principles (to be described in a moment) which it incorporated were to have a lasting influence. Ten years after it was finished, work began on Henry's masterpiece, Dover Castle. By the time it was finished, two years after Henry's own death, £7000 had been spent on converting William I's old fortress into the finest in England, and one of the most powerful in Europe. Its real novelty, not fully displayed until the work was finally completed by Henry's grandson three reigns later, consisted in there being not merely one outer bailey wall but two, forming concentric lines of defence inside each other, and both enclosing the great inner keep. This formed a near-cube, with walls 100 feet [30 m] long, only a little more than its height. The keep had walls 17–21 feet [5–6.5 m] thick, and to approach it at all attackers would have to scale, or break through, first the outer wall – under fire from the inner wall – then the second wall, the curtain wall of the inner bailey, which was protected by 14 rectangular towers, including two pairs on either side of the gatehouses which could offer mutual support.

The Romans had made use of projecting towers to help protect any section of an outer wall which was threatened and the reintroduction of the idea in Henry II's reign seems to be due to the military architect on whom he relied, known as Maurice the Engineer. The other great step forward lay in the reinforcement and improved design of the keep. Traditionally, as remained the case at Dover, this had been rectangular but under Henry II the polygonal keep also came into fashion. The weakness of the four-sided keep was that its corners might be knocked away by missiles, or undermined, since there were areas of dead ground where an attacker was not in the defender's line of sight. At Orford, built on a 'green-field' site, the walls of the keep were no longer set at right angles to each other and received further protection from three adjoining turrets. Some later castles, like Chilham in Kent and Tickhill in Yorkshire, dispensed with the turrets as it began to be realized that the keep's shape should itself protect it, and ultimately the round keep, and semi-circular towers on the external bailey walls, were found to be more effective.

Against the ingratitude of one's children, and the approach of old age, no fortress, however powerful, could provide a defence. Henry II's closing years, when England was secure, were clouded by apprehension about the future, even after his eldest son, the faithless Henry, had died in 1183. Richard was the new heir apparent, but was soon engaged in a bitter quarrel with his father, while his younger brother, John, had already shown signs of unfitness for the throne, though he remained Henry's favourite. The king may have considered disinheriting Richard in John's favour but had still not done so when, on Thursday 6 July

1189, he died, at Chinon in Anjou. Combative to the last, he whispered in Richard's ear as his son hypocritically knelt to kiss him on his deathbed, 'may the Lord spare me until I have taken vengeance on you,' a prayer destined to remain unanswered.

17
KING JOHN IS ENRAGED

The King of England, being greatly enraged on account of the interdict, sent his sherriffs . . . to all quarters of England giving orders . . . to all priests to depart the kingdom immediately.

Chronicler Roger of Wendover, recalling 1208

During the reign of Richard I England remained free from invasion, although he barely merited the title of King of England, for he regarded it solely as a source of men and money for his military adventures overseas. 'I would sell London,' one chronicler reports him as saying, 'if I could find a suitable purchaser.' His accession, at the age of 31, coincided with a wave of international religious fervour. Already two great crusades had been launched to try and free the Holy Land from the domination of the infidel Turk. Now a Third Crusade was being clamoured for throughout Christendom, its attractions being admirably put by a contemporary French song-writer*:

> Now is the time when war and chivalry, the pursuits that are most pleasant in the world, can make us free of the happier world to come . . . King of France, King of England, make your peace with one another, and he who first consents to this shall have the higher honour in the eyes of the Eternal.

King Richard needed little persuasion. Before he even visited his newly-inherited kingdom he called on King Philip II of France, also known as Philip Augustus, to arrange that they go on crusade together, and having landed in England on 13 August 1189 he left it again, en route to Palestine, only four months later, on 12 December. Richard belatedly remembered that he was king of England in October 1192, when he sailed from Acre on the long journey home, only to be shipwrecked and, after many adventures, he ended up a prisoner of the Emperor Henry VI of Germany.

Richard's imprisonment was his brother's opportunity. As soon as the news reached England, John crossed to France to enter into an

*I.e. Pons de Capdueil quoted by Davis p. 287.

alliance with Philip II, who had arrived home safely from Palestine. John offered to do homage to him for all his brother's continental possessions and even for England itself in return for French support for his seizure of the English throne. Philip agreed and began to assemble a fleet at Witsand and to collect an army of Flemish mercenaries to embark in it for England. He also planned a diplomatic master-stroke, a marriage to the Danish princess Ingeborg, sister of King Cnut VI, who not only possessed a large fleet but had, through his famous namesake, some faint claim to the English throne.

News of his brother's attempt to oust him left Richard, still in Germany, remarkably undisturbed. 'My brother John,' he commented, 'is not the man to conquer a country if there is anyone to offer even the feeblest resistance.' John in fact faced the determined opposition of his own mother, Queen Eleanor, who, though over 70, was more than a match for her 26-year-old youngest son. Under her directions the chief royal officials, the two judiciars, in the opening months of 1193, rebuilt city walls, strengthened castles – more than 30 had money spent on them during the year – increased their garrisons and called out the fyrd to watch and protect the south coast. Meanwhile Philip II went ahead with his part of the plan and on 15 August 1193 married Ingeborg of Denmark, dreaming perhaps of another 1066, with the Norse and French invaders arriving simultaneously. These plans finally foundered on the wedding night. Philip is believed to have consummated the marriage but next morning announced that he wanted no more of his new wife and ordered her to go home. Eventually he found some obliging bishops to declare the marriage void, but the invasion of 1173 was off for good.

Richard was finally released on 4 February 1194 and landed at Sandwich on 13 March. On 12 May 1194 he set sail again to spend the rest of his life in more or less continuous warfare against the King of France or his own rebellious vassals. It was now that he built his most famous monument, Château Galliard, 'the saucy castle', on a key strategic point commanding the River Seine at Andeli. Here he constructed a stockade across the river, laid out a whole new town, now known as Petit-Andelys and erected on a 300-foot [90 m] high rock overlooking the river an apparently impregnable fortress protected by powerful outworks.

Richard would no doubt have been happy to be remembered by Château Galliard, a monument both to his obsession with things military and to the precedence he always·gave in his thinking to Normandy at the expense of England. He might also have almost welcomed his own means of death, which arrived, not in the heat of battle, but at least from an arrow, which struck him in the shoulder while he was enjoying an after-supper ride at Chalus in south-west France to watch a minor siege. He died twelve days later, on 7 April 1199, from gangrene following an operation to remove the bolt. He was 41 and in his ten-year reign had spent less than six months in England.

Although it was land warfare in which Richard I excelled, the need to make civilian vessels more suitable for military purposes also led to some advances in ship design. The 'bridge' did not originate for command purposes, but to facilitate boarding for hand-to-hand combat by 'bridging' the gap to the neighbouring vessel. Although built as transports, many ships acquired a fore-castle, a raised platform at the bow, and another elevated section at the stern, the 'aft-castle'. The section of the deck at the rear of the ship was known as the 'poop', the maritime equivalent of a castle's keep where the *retenue de poupe*, or poop guard, would hold out when a ship was successfully boarded, before sallying out to repel the intruders.

Few ships were big enough to support any form of artillery and the dominant aim in naval tactics was to get to close quarters with the enemy and seize an opposing ship by *coup de main*. While manoeuvring to do so, arrows, darts and stones, flung by hand or sling, all made useful missiles; somewhat more sophisticated was the use of soft soap, thrown down on to the enemy deck, to cause the opposing crew to slip, and three-pronged grappling irons called *triboli*, cast aboard to catch in woodwork or rigging. A two-edged weapon, since it might blow back in one's own face, was launching a cloud of quicklime to temporarily blind the enemy sailors and most dreaded of all, though more an eastern than a western weapon, was Greek fire. An English eyewitness, travelling with Richard I on the Third Crusade, noted that, when it landed, Greek fire burned with a bright flame, had an appalling smell and could only be extinguished by throwing sand or vinegar on it. The formula remained a secret but probably involved a mixture of saltpetre, sulphur and pitch, possibly heated with oil. The best defence was found to be draping hides or cloths soaked in vinegar or urine over vulnerable structures, but iron plates might be used when available. These also provided protection against the cruder type of fire-raising missile, consisting of tow soaked in oil and then fixed to the standard bolt or dart fired by an arbalest or cross-bow.

Richard I was considerably more interested in maritime matters than his predecessors. He seems to have known about the nautical compass, first mentioned, around 1190, by a French writer, though its origins were far older. The king encouraged the preparation and use of charts, while an improved rudder now began to replace the traditional steering oar lashed to the stern.

By now a regular hierarchy was developing on board ship. Under the ship's master, or *rector*, who probably also owned it, was a *contremaître*, or mate, and a bo'sun (boatswain), responsible for masts, sails and rigging, with, on the larger vessels, specialists such as a carpenter, a caulker, a steersman or lodesman, an *escrivain* or writer (a literate among men mainly illiterate), and an aptly-named 'tormentor', or surgeon. A large ship would include at least two trumpeters and perhaps a couple of drummers to sound signals in action and to entertain the crew in more peaceful times. Food for the ordinary crew members was probably at least as plentiful as on shore, though inevitably not fresh, the staples being salt fish, pickled meat, dried lentils and ships biscuit.

The basic method of assembling ships for national defence, which in Richard's case meant for carrying across the Channel or further afield, was by requiring named towns to provide a specified number, complete with crew. The Cinque Ports, already mentioned, of Hastings, Dover, Hythe, Romney and Sandwich, formed the backbone of the system, Winchelsea and Rye being added just after Richard's time, and other coastal towns being included as necessary. For the Third Crusade, in December 1189, the five original Cinque Ports supplied 33 ships, Shoreham and Southampton three each, and nine others were given by private individuals or the king himself. Two-thirds of the cost of the Cinque Port ships was met from the Exchequer; the rest fell on the citizens of the ports concerned. One at least had a crew of 60, but most ships probably had only 20 to 30. The standard rate of pay was 2d [1p] for an ordinary seaman and 4d [2p] for a steersman, which added up, with food and equipment, to a formidable amount; in the financial year from Michaelmas 1189 one official alone dealing with naval matters disbursed more than £5000. All told, including the 48 just mentioned, a fleet of around 100 vessels was finally assembled, though where the other 52 or so came from is uncertain.

The large fleets collected by Richard I had revealed the inadequacy of the existing harbours on the south-east coast and in 1194, as the Exchequer rolls recorded, 'It pleased the lord king Richard to build the town of Portsmouth.' A handful of cottages on the Hampshire coast were now granted a charter, and in the next five years large sums were spent on building houses, which were to remain royal property, on leasing out other building sites to encourage new settlers, and on erecting ramparts and a dock. The nation now had a base for a fleet which itself did not yet exist.

The reign of King John was to be in every respect different from that of his predecessor, a difference which extended even to the appearance of the new sovereign who, as already mentioned, succeeded his elder brother on 7 April 1199. King John was in all respects, even the physical – at 5 ft 5 in [1.64 m] tall he made an unimpressive showing – a man too small for his high position. He was 31, an age combining maturity with vigour, and had succeeded to an empire founded by the most respected monarch of the century, and recently defended by the most admired soldier.

The great defect in John's character, which was to lead to his subjects inviting an enemy to invade the country, was his cruelty. This shocked even an age that took savagery for granted. It was first made manifest soon after his accession when he captured his fifteen-year-old nephew, sometimes known as 'little Arthur', who had become a vassal of John's enemy Philip II, also known as Philip Augustus, of France. More significantly, many on both sides of the Channel considered Arthur, son of John's dead elder brother Geoffrey, to have a better claim to the throne than John himself. Precisely what did happen to Arthur once he fell into his uncle's hands is still uncertain, but the account given by a contemporary monastic chronicler in the *Annals of Margam* in Glamorgan, though disputed by some of John's admiring biographers, offers by far the likeliest explanation:

> After King John had captured Arthur and kept him alive in prison for some time, at length, in the castle of Rouen, after dinner on the Thursday before Easter [i.e. on 3 April 1203], when he was drunk and possessed by the devil, he slew him with his own hand, and tying a heavy stone to the body cast it into the Seine. It was discovered by a fisherman in his net, and being dragged to the bank and recognized, was taken for secret burial, in fear of the tyrant, to the prior of Bec.

After Arthur's murder nothing went right for John and the fatal flaw in his character that seemed to paralyse his faculties became increasingly evident. Any competent commander should have been able to hold Normandy, which bristled with well-fortified occupied castles, but John managed to lose it. Even Château Galliard fell on 6 March 1204 after a six-month siege, when Philip II's engineers managed to find a way into the outer fortifications through a chapel window and bring down a wall of the keep. One after another towns long famous in Norman, and more recently in English, history – Bayeux, Cherbourg, Barfleur – capitulated without a fight. On 24 June 1204 the capital of Normandy, Rouen, surrendered to the French invader. A great kingdom assembled over centuries had been thrown away in five years.

John's unpopularity following the loss of Normandy was compounded by the financial measures he introduced, some to finance his private indulgences, but many made necessary by rising prices and the needs of defence. It cost him up to 2s [10p] a day to hire a mercenary horseman, whom his father could have obtained for 8d [3p]. As a financial innovator and tax-gatherer John proved an outstanding success. Never had so much been collected, and so efficiently accounted for. The standard method of raising money for national defence, as already described, was by scutage, charged on each 'fee' of land held by a knight. Henry II during his 35-year reign had imposed only eight scutages, Richard I, in 10 years, only three. John, in 17 years, collected eleven and at a far higher rate, for where Henry had usually levied one mark [13s 4d or 66p] per knight's fee*, or at most two [£1 6s 8d or £1.33], and Richard 10s [50p] or £1, John demanded at various dates £1, two marks, two and a half marks [£1 13s 4d or £1.33] and £2.

Hardly anyone was not exposed to far heavier, and far more frequent, demands for money from King John than from any previous monarch. Many of his demands were justified; some were not, but both categories were resented. The distinction between the king's private needs and those of the nation was not understood. In the long run, not wholly with justice, it was John's constant demands for money, on top of his other misdeeds, which led to his alienation from his people and especially from the barons, on whose goodwill and support he depended. 'He was,' complained one monastic archivist,† 'a pillager of his subjects . . . They forsook him and, ultimately, little mourned his death.'

John had planned to send a major expedition to France in May 1205 but was unable to overcome the opposition of the barons, the nation's leading soldier, William the Marshal, Earl of Pembroke, and the Archbishop of Canterbury, Hubert Walter.

In his fury at being thwarted John wept tears of rage and frustration and it was hardly surprising that when, on 13 July 1205, Archbishop Hubert Walter died the king's reaction was jubilant. 'Now for the first time,' he exclaimed, 'I am King of England!'

By October 1206 most of Poitou had been regained and the need to protect the renewed link with the Continent gave a great impetus to the expansion and development of the navy. The nucleus of the nation's defences was still provided by the traditional 'ship service' rendered by the five Cinque Ports of Dover, Hastings, Hythe, Romney and Sandwich, and their two associated 'ancient towns' of Winchelsea and Rye, but they now shared their burden with a number of smaller places known as 'members' or, for lesser communities, 'limbs'. Dover, for example, claimed Folkestone and Faversham as corporate members, Margate, St John's, Goresend (now Birchington), Birchington Wood (now Woodchurch), St Peter's, Kingsdown and Ringwould, as 'limbs'. All told 'members' and 'limbs' raised the basic seven privileged places to a total of 39. With the emphasis now on the longer sea-crossing to Bordeaux and La Rochelle, however, for which larger ships and larger

---

*The mark survived as a unit of account, used in calculating solicitors' fees in amounts of 6 s 8 d upwards, until the advent of decimal currency in 1971.

†I.e. the author of The Annals of Barnwell, quoted by Warren, John p. 150.

harbours than the Cinque Ports and their associates were more suitable, it now made better sense to hire or 'arrest', i.e. requisition, larger vessels elsewhere, and, for full-time defence, to make use of a full-time navy so far as ships were concerned.

The backbone of the new force consisted of royal galleys. By 1205 a total of 46 (excluding five in Ireland), were stationed around the coast from Kings Lynn in Norfolk to Gloucester, commanding the western 'back door' into the island. A substantial building programme was also under way, £368 being spent in that year on the construction of galleys in London alone, while 20 new galleys and 34 other vessels for royal use were launched between 1209 and 1212. Already the installations at Portsmouth, first erected in the previous reign, were having to be expanded. The dockyard was steadily walled in, and warehouses for ropes and sails during the winter months and a new mole to facilitate loading and embarkation were also constructed. To man the king's ships, trained seamen were drawn when needed from the merchant fleet. They could be impressed but this was seldom necessary, since pay had recently risen to 3d a day [1.5p] for an ordinary sailor and 6d [3p] for a shipmaster. Sailors in the king's service also enjoyed a major bonus, the prospect of prize-money, one of the rare ways in which a poor man might become wealthy. The crew shared out up to half the value of a captured vessel and in one year alone, 1212, 13 French prizes were disposed of on the king's behalf. 'Never,' wrote one jubilant chronicler a year later, 'did so much booty come into England.'*

In the decade following the loss of Normandy a department identifiable as the Admiralty, though it did not yet bear the name, emerged for the first time. Already a distinction was being made between operational command and maintenance and supply of the fleet. The first Admiral of the Fleet, though not so described, was John's half-brother, William Longswood, Earl of Salisbury, a bastard son of Henry II, but far more important, because more permanent, was the administrative head of the infant navy. The first identifiable First Lord of the Admiralty, to use a much later term, was William de Wrotham, who in 1198 became custodian of the tin-mines of Devon and Cornwall, responsible for organizing the shipment of tin abroad. In 1204 he was promoted to be Canon of Wells and Archdeacon of Taunton and became one of the 'chief keepers of the ports', concerned with allocating to particular ports the galleys then being built for coastal defence. Within a year or so de Wrotham had become the supreme authority on all naval matters. He commissioned ships, partly paid for from the proceeds of the tin-mines, which he still controlled, it being a common medieval practice to allocate

*Quoted from the *Life of William the Marshal* by Warren, John p. 125.

specific sources of income to particular items of expenditure, recruited and paid seamen, handled, and collected the revenue from, the sale of prize cargoes, acted as a judge in maritime disputes, and ensured that the ports operated at maximum efficiency, for both trade and naval purposes. He advised the sheriff of Southampton, who was also responsible for Portsmouth, since the former was still the more important place*, on building the new mole there, saw that the new dockyard was safely walled in, and, turning his attention to Southampton Water, issued stern orders preventing the erection of dams and fish weirs which would obstruct the free passage of shipping. For the first time comprehensive records began to be kept of the movements of shipping, and the whole coast was sub-divided into administrative districts, each containing four or five harbours or anchorages.

If John's role as founder of the English navy is unexpected, it is even more surprising that it was in his reign that the claim was first advanced, or so later generations believed, that the English had some special, presumably God-given, right to regard the Channel – not yet known as the English Channel – as their special preserve. It was claimed in the seventeenth century, although the document cited as proof has since disappeared, that in 1200 John issued a royal proclamation from Hastings that all ships passing up or down *La Manche* must lower their sails as a mark of respect whenever they encountered a vessel in his service. This nautical form of rendering homage was later to provoke intense resentment and even war, but for the moment seems to have passed unremarked. Looking back it can be seen that the years from 1204 to 1206 were a turning-point. Before then the principal danger to the King of England had been land-based attack on his continental possessions; for the rest of John's reign, and ever afterwards, the greatest threat was to the homeland and came from the sea.

The second half of King John's reign was to be dominated by a quarrel with a ruler who commanded no armies but was still the most powerful individual in Europe, Pope Innocent III. It began with the death, already mentioned, of Hubert Walter, Archbishop of Canterbury, in July 1205. The pope selected as Hubert's successor, Stephen Langdon, an Englishman in his late forties, born in Lincolnshire, and now, after a distinguished career at the university of Paris, a cardinal at Rome. He was an admirable choice. After his experiences with Hubert Walter, however, John would consider no one but his own nominee – John de Gray, Bishop of Norwich, who had been his secretary. Eventually, to

*The 'fifteenth' on the value of goods handled in 1202 raised £712 from Southampton, second only to London's £836.

enforce his will the pope made use, in March 1208, of the second most fearful weapon in his spiritual armoury, as Roger of Wendover described:

> The bishops . . . not finding any repentance in the king . . . fearlessly fulfilled the duty required of them by the pope, and laid a general interdict on the whole of England . . . All church services ceased to be performed . . . with the exception only of confession, and the viaticum [i.e. rites for the dying] in cases of extremity, and the baptism of children. The bodies of the dead, too, were carried out of cities and towns, and buried in roads and ditches without prayers or the attendance of priests.

Not unnaturally, John struck back, arguing that since the clergy were no longer performing their functions the property given to them for this purpose now stood forfeit. Roger of Wendover, a partisan witness, made the most of his fellow clerics' sufferings:

> The king of England, being greatly enraged on account of the interdict, sent his sheriffs, and other ministers of iniquity, to all quarters of England, giving orders with dreadful threats to all priests . . . the kingdom immediately . . . he also gave all the bishoprics, abbacies, and priories, into the charge of laymen, and ordered all ecclesiastical revenues to be confiscated . . . the corn of the clergy was everywhere locked up and distrained for the benefit of the revenue; the concubines of the priests and clerks were taken by the king's servants and compelled to ransom themselves at a great expense.

John still refused to accept Archbishop Langton and Innocent III was finally forced to impose his ultimate sanction. In November 1209 King John was excommunicated.

This was a far more serious matter than the interdict. John was now a religious outlaw, whose subjects were thereby absolved from their oaths of loyalty to him and whose fellow monarchs had the right, if not the positive duty, to attack his kingdom to bring him back to allegiance to the church.

John remained unmoved. During 1210 he conducted a successful campaign in Ireland but it was to be remembered chiefly for a hideous act of cruelty; failing to catch one of his bitterest enemies, William de Braose, he shut up de Braose's wife and son together in Corfe Castle and starved them to death, a process described by the chroniclers in gruesome detail. In the following year he had some success in Wales, but he began a further planned campaign, in September 1212, with another much talked of display of malice:

> On his arriving with his army at Nottingham, before he either ate or

drank, he ordered twenty-eight youths, whom he had received the year before as hostages from the Welsh, to be hung on the gibbet, in revenge for the above-mentioned transgressions of their countrymen.

The murder of the Welsh hostages became the third such charge to be laid against John both by contemporary public opinion and posterity. Such action was not really new; in a sense it was what hostages were for. These, however, were young – perhaps mere children – and John's obvious relish in the deed caused general disgust, for after it he sat down to his delayed dinner with appetite unimpaired.

Then, as if in a medieval morality play, Nemesis threatened, as Roger of Wendover describes:

> While he was, after this, sitting at table, eating and drinking, there came a messenger from the King of Scotland, who delivered letters warning him of premeditated treachery against him; soon after which there came another messenger from [his] . . . daughter . . . the wife of Leolin [i.e. Llywelyn], King of Wales; this second messenger brought letters . . . to one and the same effect, which was that, if the king persisted in the war which he had begun, he would either be slain by his own nobles, or delivered to his enemies for destruction. The king was greatly alarmed on learning this; and, as he knew that the English nobles were absolved from their allegiance to him . . . wisely changing his intention, he ordered his army to return home.

Late in 1212 Stephen Langton and two other English bishops arrived in Rome to press for decisive action against the excommunicated monarch. Urgency was lent to their pleas by the death of Archbishop Geoffrey of York, 'who,' as Roger of Wendover dolefully recorded, 'had been an exile for seven years owing to his defence of the rights of the church and his maintenance of justice'. With Innocent III's agreement, Langton and his colleagues now sought international support against their sovereign:

> In the month of January, in this same year [1213], Stephen, Archbishop of Canterbury, and William and Eustace, the Bishops of London and Ely, returned from the court of Rome, and . . . made known the decree which had been sent forth against the English king . . . to the king of the French, to the French bishops and clergy, and to the people in general.

News of the Langton mission to France was not long in crossing the Channel:

> King John, learning by means of his spies what was going forward in the transmarine provinces, prepared to make the best defence he could against the plans prepared against him; he therefore ordered a list to

be made of all the ships in each of the ports in England, by a warrant which he sent to each of the bailiffs of the ports.

Two weeks after the date fixed for the assembly of the British fleet, on a solemn day, the Monday in Holy Week, 3 April 1213, King Philip Augustus of France held a council at Soissons at which the pope's letter denouncing John was read and Stephen Langton and his colleagues underlined its message:

> In the name of our lord the pope, they enjoined on the king of the French, as well as all others, that, as a remission of their sins, they should all unitedly invade England, depose John from the throne of that kingdom, and appoint another, under the apostolic authority, who should be worthy to fill it.

Never since 1066 had any king received a clearer mandate to attack another, and only one dissenting voice was raised, that of the Count of Flanders, who formally renounced his allegiance to Philip, a most important defection. Philip, who had long dreamed of making England a vassal kingdom under his son Louis, was undeterred, however, and soon France, like England, was alive with military activity on a scale unknown since 1066. Roger of Wendover sets the scene:

> The king of the French, seeing what he had long desired come to pass, made his preparations for war, and ordered all his subjects alike, dukes, counts, barons, knights and attendants, equipped with horses and arms, to assemble in force at Rouen in the octaves of Easter [i.e. on Sunday 21 April 1213], under penalty of being branded with cowardice, and of incurring the charge of treason. He likewise ordered all his own ships, and as many others as he could collect, to be well supplied with corn, wine, meat and other stores, that there might be abundance of all necessaries for so large an army.

John, meanwhile, was calling out his forces, through writs to the sheriffs:

> Give warning by good agents to the earls, barons, knights and all free and serving men, whoever they be . . . that . . . they be at Dover at the end of the coming Lent, [i.e. by Easter Sunday, 14 April 1213] equipped with horses and arms, and with all they can provide, to defend our person and their persons, and the land of England, and let no-one who can carry arms remain behind under penalty of being branded with cowardice, and of being condemned to perpetual slavery; and let each man follow his lord; and let those who possess no land, and who can carry arms, come to take service with us as mercenaries.

John's call to arms produced a massive turn-out; unpopular though he was, no one wanted to be ruled by a foreign king. Roger of Wendover confirms the success of the mobilization:

> On these letters being spread abroad throughout England, there assembled at the sea-ports in different parts which most attracted the king's attention, such as Dover, Faversham and Ipswich, men of divers conditions and ages, who dreaded nothing more than the name of coward; but after a few days, on account of their vast numbers, provisions failed them, therefore the commanders of the army sent home a large number of the inexperienced men, retaining only at the coast the soldiers, attendants, and freemen, with the crossbow men and archers . . . When the whole of the forces were assembled at Barham Down, the army was computed to consist of sixty thousand strong, including chosen knights and their followers, all well armed; and had they been of one heart and one disposition towards the king . . . there was not a prince under heaven against whom they could not have defended the kingdom of England.

The village of Barham lies roughly halfway along the 14-mile [22-km] Roman road that runs north-west from Dover to Canterbury. Caesar's legions probably had camped on the high ground around it and it was to give temporary shelter to many later armies. John still hoped, however, to avoid a fight: 'The king determined to engage his enemies at sea, to drown them before they landed, for he had a more powerful fleet than the French king, and in that he placed his chief means of defence.'

Even while Stephen Langton was encouraging Philip II to prepare to invade England, Innocent III had sent a papal legate, Pandulf [or Pandulph], to England to make a final bid for a peaceful solution. Seldom can an ambassador have had an easier mission. Bereft of allies, with the loyalty of his own troops suspect, John was negotiating from a position of fatal weakness. At Dover, on Monday 13 May 1213, John agreed to accept Stephen Langton as Archbishop of Canterbury, to receive back, without reprisal, all the clergy who had gone into exile, with compensation for their losses, and to grant an amnesty to the other clergy who had defied him. Two days later, on his own initiative, he made over his kingdom to the pope, to be held in return for the modest annual rent of 1000 marks, and – like the rulers of Sweden, Denmark, Poland and Sicily – became a papal vassal.

Pandulf, returning to France, now proved as powerful an emissary on John's behalf as on the pope's:

> He earnestly advised the French king, who had made preparations to invade England by force, to desist from his purpose and to return home in peace; for he could not, without offending the supreme

pontiff, attack England, or the king himself, since that monarch was ready to give satisfaction to God, the holy church, and its ordained ministers . . . The French king was much enraged when he heard this, and said that he had already spent sixty thousand pounds in the equipment of his ships, and in providing food and arms, and that he had undertaken the said duty by command of our lord the pope.

The situation for John had now been transformed. When Count Ferrand's envoy arrived, on 25 May 1213, the English army was still massed on Barham Down and the fleet at Portsmouth.

The French ships said by a French eyewitness to number 1700, many heavily laden with stores, were lying unprotected on the beaches or riding at anchor in the estuary of the River Swein, waiting to attack John's ally, Ferrand of Flanders. The unexpected opportunity was eagerly seized:

> When the chiefs of the English army learned this they flew to arms, fiercely attacked the fleet and, soon defeating the crews, they cut the cables of three hundred of their ships loaded with corn, wine, flour, meat, arms and other stores and sent them to sea to make for England; besides these they set fire to and burned a hundred or more which were aground, after taking all the stores from them. By this misfortune the French king and almost all the transmarine nobility lost all their most valuable possessions . . . on learning which King Philip retired in confusion from Flanders with great loss to himself and to his followers.

The Battle of Damme, then the port for the city of Bruges near the mouth of the River Zywn, about 70 miles [110 km] from the English coast, was fought on Saturday 30 May 1213 and proved an even greater victory than at first appeared; on 2 June King Philip ordered the surviving ships to be burnt, seeing no prospect of their safely setting sail again. It had been a classic example of the use of seapower in an anti-invasion rôle, and opened the way to an effective counter-offensive:

> The English king, on hearing what had taken place in Flanders, was greatly rejoiced and in the joy of his mind at knowing that the approach of the French king was suspended at least for a time, he ordered the nobles and the whole army which he had collected near the sea-coast for the defence of their country to return to their homes.

John planned to follow up his naval victory with a land campaign and assembled a new army at Portsmouth for the purpose, but 'the English nobles', Roger of Wendover recorded, 'refused to follow him unless he was previously absolved from the sentence of excommunication.' This was now formally done by Stephen Langton at Winchester, on 20 July 1213, along with the lifting of the interdict on England. On 2 February 1214 John was at last able to set out on a fresh attempt to regain the lost Angevin empire. It ended in failure, when at Bouvines, between Tournai and Lille, on 24 July 1214, Philip Augustus crushingly defeated all his enemies in one of the decisive battles of the Middle Ages, on a hot summer afternoon, when the dust rose so thickly that the contending armies could scarcely make out the opposing front line. The Emperor Otto of Germany, unhorsed, narrowly escaped capture; the Count of Flanders was wounded and taken prisoner; and the Count of Boulogne and the Earl of Salisbury, in command of the English contingent – John himself was elsewhere – both fell into the hands of warrior French bishops. In Paris the university students, observed a French chronicler, 'indefatigably for seven successive nights . . . did not stop feasting, leaping and dancing and singing.'

In England, to which John returned on 15 October 1214 after concluding a truce with Philip supposed to last until Easter 1220, there was no rejoicing. The justiciar John had chosen had ruled ruthlessly in his absence and military humiliation in France merely added to the long catalogue of tyranny, extravagance and general misrule of which the barons complained. Disaffection now gave way to conspiracy and conspiracy to rebellion. Both sides sought foreign help. John brought in large numbers of Flemish and German mercenaries; the barons appealed to Philip Augustus for reinforcements. Finally, with Stephen Langton acting as intermediary, the barons were established at Staines, King John at Windsor, a few miles away. At Runnymede on the banks of the Thames, on Monday 15 June 1215, the king accepted the document drafted by the barons to restrict his arbitrary powers, known then and ever since as Magna Carta, the Great Charter. Few of its 61 clauses, using the modern classification of them, bore even indirectly on defence, and Magna Carta is important in invasion history only because of its immediate consequences. True to form, John had not the slightest intention of abiding by the Charter he had signed, or of listening to the council of 25 barons set up to enforce it. He had already, in his self-chosen rôle of papal vassal, sought the protection of Innocent III and the weapon of excommunication, so recently used against himself, was now turned against his enemies. The 'guilty' barons were excommunicated on 7 July 1215 and when Stephen Langton delayed promulgating the sentence he was suspended. The country stood once again on the brink of civil war, a civil war in which foreign troops were certain to be involved.

During the summer of 1215 the battle-lines – barons plus promised French aid, king plus continental mercenaries, 'loyal' citizens and the pope – were drawn up. Serious fighting was unlikely to begin before the harvest had been brought in and, though he also visited Canterbury, John spent most of September at Dover, supervising the reception of the reinforcements now pouring in by the boatload.

Apart from his growing army, King John's greatest strength lay in the 150 castles, scattered about the country, still held by his supporters. The barons had already laid siege to two of strategic importance, at Northampton and Oxford, but their principal concern was to protect their main stronghold and headquarters, London, against the powerful force now mustering in Kent. If Rochester Castle could be seized and held it could prove the rock to dam the advancing royalist flood. The opportunity came with the arrival from the Midlands of one of 'the 25' with a great military reputation. Roger of Wendover tells the story:

> In the meantime, the noble William d'Albini [or Albiney or Aubigny], after frequently receiving letters from the barons at London . . . at length, at Michaelmas [i.e. around 29 September], furnished his castle of Belvoir [in Nottinghamshire] with a sufficiency and even a superabundance of provisions and arms, and . . . then went to London and was received there with great joy by the barons, who immediately communicated to him a plan . . . to block up the road against the king, so that no way of approach might be open to him . . . to lay siege to the city of London. They therefore picked out a strong body of troops and appointing William d'Albini to the command of them . . . sent them to occupy the town of Rochester.

Taking the town was of no consequence; it was the castle that counted and for reasons never explained, its custodian, Reginald of Cornhill, simply handed it over intact as d'Albini's little force approached. Its loss on, or about, 11 October infuriated John, who immediately set out to regain it.

The siege of Rochester became a classic of its kind, conducted by John with ruthless determination. 'As soon as he had arrayed his petrarias and other engines, he severely annoyed the besieged by incessant showers of stones and other weapons,' comments Roger of Wendover. The real danger to d'Albini's little garrison of 95 knights and 45 men-at-arms lay in the defences being mined and John issued orders as soon as the siege began that 'all the smiths in Canterbury' should devote themselves 'day and night' to making pickaxes.

The barons believed Rochester Castle could hold out till St Andrew's Day, 30 November, by which time they hoped an invading French army would have taken John in the rear, but they had reckoned without John's unbending resolution. He brought up more troops and kept up a

constant bombardment from five great siege engines as Roger of Wendover describes:

> When the king learned how pompously the barons had
> approached . . . and how basely and ignominiously they had
> returned, he became bolder, and sent out foragers in all directions to
> collect provisions for the support of his army, and yet did not allow
> the besieged in the meantime any rest day or night, for amidst the
> stones hurled from the petrarias and slings and the missiles of the
> crossbow men and archers, frequent assaults were made by the knights
> and their followers, so that when some were in a measure fatigued,
> other fresh ones succeeded them in the assault . . . The besieged, too,
> despairing of any assistance from the barons, endeavoured to delay
> their own destruction, for they were in great dread of the cruelty of
> the king; therefore . . . they . . . hurled stone for stone, weapon for
> weapon, from the walls and ramparts on the enemy; at last, after
> great numbers of the royal troops had been slain, the king . . .
> employed miners, who soon threw down a great part of the walls . . .
> The soldiers of the king now rushed to the breaches in the walls and
> by constant fierce assaults they forced the besieged to abandon the
> castle, although not without great loss on their own side.

The whole siege had been a textbook affair on both sides, with assaults
keeping up the pressure while mining was in progress, and with the
defenders retreating to the keep when expelled from the rest of the castle.
The keep walls, 12 feet [3.6 m] thick, easily withstood all the boulders
hurled against them, so John summoned his 'underwallers', who had
already brought down the bailey wall. The garrison, probably from
weakness, had not even attempted the prescribed counter-measure of
breaking into, or flooding, the workings through another tunnel dug
from within. Now John selected as the most vulnerable spot a corner of
the keep where the underlying layer of chalk came closest to the surface
and here, beneath the square south-western tower, the usual network of
underground galleries, their roofs shored up by timber, was constructed.
On 25 November he issued to the justiciar a famous order for 'forty fat
bacon-pigs, the least good for eating, to help fire the material we have
gathered beneath the tower'. The burning pork-fat did its work, as
remains evident today, where the circular south-western tower, built to
replace the one brought down by John, contrasts with its original, square
neighbours, but still the defenders fought on, retreating behind a strong
wall which protected an intact portion of the keep. Hunger, however,
was now doing its work. According to the same chronicler, the garrison
'were obliged to eat horses and even their costly chargers' but when, to

stretch the rations further, the sick and wounded were pushed outside, they had their hands and feet cut off.

Three times during the siege of Rochester the barons had made overtures to the king for a negotiated settlement, the last occasion, on 9 November, involving the mayor and some leading citizens of London, but another party within the baronial ranks was not prepared to accept John at any price. They had, during the summer, floated a scheme, for which no constitutional precedent existed, for electing a new king 'by the common consent of the whole realm', and now they sent a deputation across the Channel to Prince Louis, 'begging and praying him that he would come with a mighty arm to pluck them out of the hand of this tyrant', and promising that 'if he would pack up his clothes and come, they would give him the kingdom and make him their lord'.

Louis's father, Philip Augustus, held aloof, unwilling to compromise himself with the papacy with which he had recently made his peace, but Louis himself assembled a force of 140 knights, with a supporting retinue of supporters and foot soldiers, who around the end of November, just as Rochester was capitulating, landed at the mouth of the River Orwell and made their way to London. The size of this first contingent, as so often with medieval statistics, is uncertain. One authority speaks of 'about seven thousand men' but another estimate, which puts the total strength of the French contingent at 240 knights and about the same number of crossbow men and other foot soldiers by 7 January 1216, seems more probable. Everyone agrees that they proved more of a liability than an asset. 'They were,' explains the author of the *History of the Dukes of Normandy*, 'very well received and led a sumptuous life; only they were there in great discomfort because they ran short of wine and had only beer to drink . . . Thus they remained all the winter.'

With the barons still inactive, on 6 December 1215 John led his army away from Rochester on a roundabout route probably designed to overawe the maximum number of potentially rebellious citizens. He first marched right across Kent and Surrey to Guildford and then on into Hampshire, spending 12-14 December at Winchester, and then turning back and making his way north-east to Odiham, and Windsor, and thence, avoiding London, into Hertfordshire. He reached St Albans on 18 December and here, if they had not done so earlier, the two knights he had sent earlier to Rome to represent him brought what Roger of Wendover calls 'the agreeable news' that 'the barons of England were excommunicated' and 'the archbishop of Canterbury suspended'. John's response was swift:

He at once moved his camp and proceeded in all haste to St Albans. On his arrival at the place, he went to the chapter house in the presence of the monks, and ordered the letters about the suspension of the archbishop of Canterbury to be read and at once demanded . . . that a confirmation of the aforesaid suspension under their seal should be sent to all the churches of England . . . to be made publicly known.

His spiritual flank secure, John at once called a council of war:

> Immediately after the chapter he retired with a few of his advisers into the cloister and devised plans for overthrowing his enemies . . . At length the king disposed his army in two parts, that with one he might check the irruptions of the barons who were staying in the city of London, whilst with the other he could go himself to the northern parts of England to ravage the whole country with fire and sword.

John had often made much of Christmas but this year he spent it, one of the chroniclers comments, 'not in the usual manner, but as one on the warpath', in Nottingham Castle, and it clearly brought no lessening of his revengeful spirit, for on 26 December he moved on again to the village of Langar, about 16 miles [26 km] east of Nottingham, close to Belvoir Castle, the seat of the man who had thwarted him so long at Rochester. William d'Albini had left it well provisioned and garrisoned, as described earlier, and it could no doubt have held out indefinitely had not John undermined the defenders' will to resist with a timely reminder of what had happened to earlier opponents of his. Roger of Wendover learned the facts of this shameless episode:

> This castle was in the charge of Nicholas, a clerk, son of William d'Albini, and the knights William de Studham and Hugh de Charneles, who immediately asked the opinion of their fellow knights as to what should be done; for they had been told on behalf of the king that if he received a single refusal to surrender the castle, W. d'Albini should never eat again . . . The besieged were thus in a perplexity . . . and did not know what to do; at length, however . . . they agreed to save their lord from an ignominious death by surrendering the castle rather than, by retaining it, to lose their lord as well as the castle. Then Nicholas d'Albini and Hugh de Charneles . . . went to the king at Langar and surrendered the castle to him on the condition that he would deal mercifully with their lord.

John then resumed his march northwards, dividing his forces, since no real resistance seemed likely, so they could achieve even greater destruction. Chaos had come again to the north, at the hands of an alien rabble commanded by an English king.

> After this he separated his wicked army, and took his march towards the northern provinces, burning the buildings belonging to the barons,

making booty of their cattle, plundering them of their goods and destroying everything they came to with the sword. The whole surface of the earth was covered with these limbs of the devil like locusts, who assembled from remote regions to blot out every thing from the face of the earth, from man down to his cattle; for, running about with drawn swords and open knives, they ransacked towns, houses, cemeteries and churches, robbing everyone and sparing neither women or children; the king's enemies wherever they were found were imprisoned in chains and compelled to pay a heavy ransom.

The barons had already proved unable to defeat the king by their own efforts and late in 1215 they sent another two-man embassy to Philip Augustus 'urgently imploring the father that he would send his son to reign in England'. In response, Philip sent a second contingent of troops, who reached London around 7 January 1216, though the 240 knights, plus about the same number of infantry and crossbow men who made up the force were hardly enough to guarantee John's defeat – and the barons, fearful of John's vengeance, were unwilling to take the field until victory could be virtually guaranteed. Louis, with a throne on offer, was notably more keen to invade England than his father and contended, not very convincingly, that he had a legitimate claim to the crown of England, because he was married to Henry II's grand-daughter, Blanche. More valuably, he promised to be on the French coast, ready to cross the Channel, by 20 January 1216, with 'a great multitude of people' to follow him.

18

AN ARDUOUS EXPEDITION

As his own departure on such an arduous expedition could not be effected in a hurry, he sent messengers in advance to give the barons hope.

Roger of Wendover writing of Louis of France, 1216

Around the end of February 1216 Innocent III's formal pronouncement of excommunication of John's opponents, dated 16 December 1215, was published in England. A list of the guilty barons, identified by name, followed, and 'those citizens of London who have been the chief promoters of the aforesaid crime' were also excommunicated. The sentence made little immediate difference to the situation, since, as Roger of Wendover admits, it was largely ignored:

> When these sentences of excommunication and interdict were published throughout England, and became known to all, the city of London alone treated them with contempt, inasmuch as the barons determined not to observe them, and the priests not to publish them; for they said amongst themselves that all the letters had been obtained under false representations and were therefore of no importance.

The barons must also have taken comfort from the arrival in London of a third contingent of troops from France, sent by Louis as an earnest of his sincerity, since his army had failed to materialize in January as promised:

> As his own departure on such an arduous expedition could not be effected in a hurry, he sent messengers in advance to give the barons hope . . . All these with a large retinue of knights and followers came by the river Thames and, to the great joy of the barons, arrived at London on the 27th of February.

A letter cast in highly encouraging terms and naming a new date for the promised invasion followed:

> Louis, eldest son of King Philip, to all his friends and allies in London,

health and sincere affection. Rest assured that on the approaching Easter Sunday [i.e. 10 April 1216] we will be at Calais ready under God's favour, to cross the sea. Inasmuch as you have conducted yourselves strenuously and bravely in all my affairs, we return you abundant thanks; and we earnestly ask and require that, as you have always done, you will continue to conduct yourselves with courage. We also wish you to be assured that in a short time you will have us to assist you.

John's position, when Easter Day, Sunday 10 April 1216, dawned with no sign of an invading fleet in sight, was a strong one. A few potentially dissident spots remained, but virtually the whole western half of England, to the left of a line from Richmond in Yorkshire to the Sussex coast near Arundel, was loyal to the king, and most of the north and east was cowed into temporary submission. The only significant baronial stronghold remaining was London. John did not feel able to risk a frontal assault on it, nor did the barons feel strong enough to challenge his armies away from it. All now depended on the attitude of France and John, fearing the worst, began directly after Easter to make active preparations to defend his unhappy kingdom against a seaborne invasion. On 14 April he issued orders to 21 coastal towns to send all the ships they could muster to the mouth of the Thames; on the 17th he ordered the sheriffs throughout England to summon everyone who had been in arms against him to join him within a month after Easter, or lose their lands for ever. On 20 April he was back at Windsor, to issue further orders, then travelled through Surrey to Rochester and Canterbury, from which he issued orders to his forces to follow him immediately 'wheresoever he might be'.

On that same day events in France reached their climax. Both John and the barons had been dispatching frequent letters and ambassadors to the French Court, soliciting respectively Philip's and Louis's support, the fiction that the latter's proposed expedition was nothing to do with the former being carefully maintained. More important, however, was the rôle of the papal legate, Gualo, dispatched from Rome expressly to forbid Philip to allow his son to attack John, who was, on the contrary, to be given every support.

At Melun, 30 miles [48 km] south of Paris, on 25 April 1216, the decisive conference began. Gualo did his eloquent best, but after two days of intense discussion it was clear that he had failed, as Roger of Wendover records:

On the following day . . . Louis went to his father at Melun and begged of him not to obstruct his proposed journey; he also added that he had given his oath to the barons of England that he would

come to their assistance, and therefore he would rather be excommunicated by the pope for a time than incur the charges of falsehood. Louis
then sent messengers to the court of Rome, there to set forth in the
presence of the pope the right which he claimed for himself to the
kingdom of England and then, in company, with his earls, barons,
knights, and numerous followers, he made all haste to the sea-coast
that he might reach England before the legate . . . When they all
reached the port of Calais, they found there six hundred ships and
eight cogs, all well equipped, which Eustace the monk had collected
there against Louis's arrival.

Three weeks had now elapsed since the conference at Melun and John
had spent them in visiting the various key points of the defence, at
Sandwich, Dover, Folkestone and Romney, from his headquarters at
Canterbury. He still put his chief faith in his fleet, assembled at Dover
ready for a pre-emptive strike across the Channel, when on the evening
of Wednesday 18 May 1216 the sky suddenly clouded over, the wind
began to howl through the rigging of the waiting ships and the waves to
batter them mercilessly at their moorings. By the morning, after one of
the worst storms in living memory, John's navy was scattered up and
down the Channel, much of it crippled. As his enemy's captains
struggled to limp back to their stations Louis, on the night of Friday 20
May, defying the still stormy seas, decided to seize his chance of catching
his enemy off guard. The crossing took much longer than usual due to
the unfavourable winds and Louis himself is said to have landed several
hours ahead of the rest of his force, at Stonor, a spot no longer
identifiable, in the Isle of Thanet.

He had been beaten by a short head by the papal legate Gualo. On the
morning of Saturday 21 May the unfortunate emissary, whose hostile
reception at the French court had been followed by a rough crossing,
finally got ashore at Romney. News of his arrival reached the king at
Canterbury, but just as John was setting off to meet him another
messenger arrived hotfoot from Thanet to report that his coastguards
had sighted a large fleet in the distance. John went on, however, to meet
Gualo, an impressive figure in his scarlet cardinal's robes, mounted on a
white horse, and the two men dismounted and embraced. John broke
the news of the French approach, whereupon Gualo obligingly
pronounced an on-the-spot excommunication of Louis, and the two
returned to Canterbury, from which John on the following day, Sunday
22 May 1216, hurried to Sandwich to confirm with his own eyes the
enemy's strength.

He now faced the classic defending commander's dilemma, whether
to retreat and husband his forces or make an all-out effort to throw the

invader back into the sea as he came ashore. John's instinct, both on temperamental and tactical grounds, was to give battle at once. The troops were mustered on the shore or very close to it; the trumpets rang out, instructing them to prepare for combat. But as the French ships crossed Pegwell Bay and prepared to run ashore, John was persuaded by his chief adviser, William the Marshal, first Earl of Pembroke, to order instead a general withdrawal.

Now well into his sixties, or even older, William the Marshal was already a legend★; a long metrical *History of William the Marshal*, written about 1226, is the major source for this period. Advancing years may, by May 1216, have made him cautious, but at all events John, faced with an invading army, let it come ashore unchallenged, as Roger of Wendover describes:

> King John was then at Dover with his army, but as he was surrounded with foreign mercenaries and knights from the transmarine provinces, he did not venture to attack Louis on his landing, lest in the battle they might all leave him and go over to the side of Louis. He therefore retreated before Louis, leaving Dover Castle in charge of Hugh de Burgh, and continued his flight till he arrived first at Guildford and afterwards at Winchester. Louis, finding no-one to oppose him, disembarked at Sandwich, and soon subdued the whole of the district, with the exception of the castle of Dover.

Louis's first act on landing was to issue a proclamation to the English clergy setting out his claim to the throne and urging them to disregard anything they might hear from the papal legate whom, he said, some-what unfairly, had been brought to England merely 'by the suggestions and bribes' of its king. He seized some ships sheltering at Sandwich, plundered the town, and marched on Canterbury, the ill-starred Gualo being forced to abandon his lodgings in St Augustine's abbey and the citizens throwing open the gates to the invader. Louis's next appearance, at Rochester, provided another triumph. The castle which had resisted John for two months capitulated within a week, on Whit Monday 30 May 1216, and on 2 June 1216 he entered London.

No one seemed in the least troubled by the solemn excommunication of Louis which Gualo, in the presence of the English bishops, had pronounced in Winchester cathedral three days before, nor by the interdict laid upon the city of London. The populace turned out to cheer him, the canons of St Paul's received him with a festal procession.

Louis's arrival, as the barons had anticipated, had transformed the

★The custom that the Marshal should throw down the gage at the king's coronation to indicate his readiness to fight anyone who challenged his right to succeed had in 1206 only recently been established, but still survives today.

situation; everyone now wanted to be on the winning side. As Louis set out from London, on 6 June 1216, for John's temporary, and the nation's ancient, capital of Winchester, castle after castle – Reigate on the 7th, Guildford on the 8th, Farnham on the 10th – was abandoned or surrendered on his approach. To add to John's worries, he was now running short of funds. By definition, a mercenary had to be paid to fight and as William the Marshal's biographer put it: 'When the king had no more money, most of those who served him for wages went off with what they had earned.' John had left Winchester on 5 June, after entrusting its defence to Savary de Mauléon, in command of the still-loyal contingent from Poitou, and thereafter travelled 19 miles [30 km] north-west to Ludgershall in Wiltshire, then a further 17 miles [27 km] to Devizes. The next two or three weeks he spent in Wiltshire and Dorset, inspecting royal castles to see that they were properly garrisoned and trying desperately to drum up support both at home and overseas. The loyal town of Bayonne was ordered to despatch its galleys 'for the annoyance and confusion of our enemies', safe-conducts were offered 'to all who might choose to return to the king's service' in England and an approach was even made to the new head of the de Braose family, offering him his lands back in return for military aid. Finally he reached Corfe Castle where his family had been sent for safety, and made it his headquarters, while organizing its defence and that of the surrounding area.

Louis's progress at this time seemed rapid and remorseless. On 14 June 1216, while John was on the road south-westwards, he marched unopposed into Winchester after de Mauleon and his Poitevins, apparently while trying to destroy their stores, had set fire to a large part of the city. Its two castles, however, still held out, despite one, at the western end of the city, being subjected to a ten-day bombardment, and both only surrendered after John had sent them his licence to do so – a necessary precaution against a subsequent charge of treason.

Static defence, with the enemy army unbeaten in the field, has seldom been regarded as a desirable strategy, but it was this which saved John from defeat. The fleet had failed him; many of his mercenaries had deserted him; but in the north Barnard Castle, at the place subsequently named after it, Carlisle Castle and Durham Castle stood firm; in the Midlands, Nottingham and Newark; in East Anglia, Lincoln. Above all, the south could not be considered conquered so long as the great fortresses at Dover and Windsor remained in his hands. Philip Augustus is said to have criticized his son for attempting to conquer England without first securing its key, Dover Castle, a description often quoted later, but Louis's failure was not for want of trying. Virtually his whole army was encamped outside the walls on the landward side, while out at sea the French fleet, untroubled by John's navy, prevented relief or escape by water, and Roger of Wendover reveals his determined attempts to capture it.

> In the same year on the day of the nativity of St John the Baptist [i.e. 24 June] Louis, with a powerful force of knights and soldiers, laid siege to Dover Castle, having first sent to his father for a petraria. . . . called . . . *Malvoisin* and the French having disposed this and other engines before the castle, they began to batter the walls incessantly; but Hubert de Burgh, a brave knight, with a hundred and forty knights and a large number of soldiers who were defending the castle, destroyed many of the enemy, until the French feeling their loss removed their tents and engines farther from the castle; on this Louis was greatly enraged and swore he would not leave the place till the castle was taken and all the garrison hung.

Louis, who had returned to London after his earlier successes in Surrey and Hampshire, moved to Dover on 25 July 1216 to direct operations in person, in accordance with the best military doctrine of the time. First an outwork, with a ditch and palisade, known as a 'barbican', was captured, then a wooden tower whose top was level with the battlements was brought up, and regular assaults were made by battering ram, protected by a roof and sides, on the north gate of the outer bailey. When all this failed, a tunnel – still in existence today – was driven through the solid chalk and duly brought down one of the gatehouse towers. The garrison, who had kept up a constant pressure on their assailants through frequent sorties, manned the resulting breach so effectively that the French were driven back and the hole was made good with stones and tree-trunks. The invaders then settled down to starve the defenders out, rubbing in the contrast between the two sides' situation in a highly unkind fashion:

> They [the French] therefore, to strike terror into them, built a number of shops and other buildings in front of the entrance to the castle, so that the place appeared like a market; for they hoped that they would, by hunger and a protracted siege, force them to surrender, as they could not subdue them by force of arms.

Windsor was meanwhile proving almost equally troublesome, being defended by 'a man well tried in war, who was stoutly attended by sixty knights with their retainers . . . These,' Roger of Wendover acknowledges, 'stoutly defended the castle against their enemies.' This siege, too, showed every sign of dragging on. 'Long were they there and little did they gain,' commented a Flemish chronicler, observing that 'the host dwindled marvellously' as many of Louis's followers grew bored and went home.

The attack which in May had seemed to be carrying all before it had lost its impetus and the presence on English soil of a foreign army and a foreign prince was serving to revive the spirit of patriotism which John's misdeeds had almost destroyed. It was not the great noblemen, who seemed to emerge with fortune intact however often they changed sides, that formed the new resistance movement, but the freemen of the lesser ranks, and the citizens of the ports, among whom John had always been popular. The Cinque Ports had been forced to acknowledge their loyalty to Louis, but still harried French shipping when they got the chance and some remnants of John's navy were still, on a freelance basis, carrying on the fight at sea. On land, opposition to the French was sufficiently widespread for John, on 3 September 1216, to write a letter of thanks for their continuing loyalty to the men of Kent, Sussex and Hampshire.

John's gratitude was always a doubtful quantity, but at least one guerrilla leader continued to fight the French throughout the summer, as Roger of Wendover learned:

> Here [i.e. in Sussex] a young man named William, refusing to make his fealty to Louis, collected a company of a thousand bowmen, and taking to the woods and forests with which that part of the country abounded, he continued to harass the French during the whole war and slew many thousands of them.

William of Kensham, or Cassingham, was royal bailiff of Marden in Kent, a village seven miles [11 km] south of Maidstone, but he was responsible for royal estates in the adjoining area of East Sussex. His knowledge of the countryside seems to have been supplemented by a natural talent for irregular warfare and he became a notorious thorn in the flesh of the occupying power, earning immortality with the affectionate nickname of 'Willikin of the Weald'. More will be heard of him later.

On 16 July 1216 John lost his most powerful ally with the death of Innocent III, but his successor, Honorius III, continued his predecessor's policy. Louis meanwhile had other worries. The barons could not win without French help but they resented, naturally enough, the arrival of French knights and other noblemen who expected to be rewarded with offices and estates; the more Frenchmen that arrived, the more the apprehension of Louis's English followers grew. The young prince, still only 28, did his best to please both parties, transferring the title of 'marshal of the host', or commander-in-chief, from a Frenchman to an Englishman, but awarding Marlborough Castle to his own cousin instead of to William the Marshal junior, who thereupon abandoned Louis and made his peace with King John. So, too, did John's own half-brother, the Earl of Salisbury, and sundry other great magnates, the king's warm welcome, free of recriminations, encouraging others to follow them. This seepage away of support was self-sustaining for inevitably, as it continued, Louis came to rely increasingly on French advisers and to exclude Englishmen from his immediate circle. A speedy, overwhelming victory might have removed all doubts, but none occurred. As the summer wore on the French continued to besiege Dover; a joint French and baronial force was investing Windsor, and a wholly baronial one Lincoln Castle, while numerous other strongpoints, and most of the south-west, remained loyal to the king. About two-thirds of all the barons still supported Louis and their supporters held most of the south-east, the eastern side of the country as far as the Scottish border, and London.

The many castles which were not threatened by the invader now demonstrated their secondary value, as a reservoir of manpower, as Roger of Wendover explains:

> As soon as John learned that the castles of Dover and Windsor were laid siege to, he assembled a large army of the garrisons of his castles, followed by whom he overran the lands of the earls and barons at harvest time, burning their houses and crops and doing great damage to his enemies.

The vengeful king now spread destruction far and wide, marching, on 2 September 1216, from Cirencester, on the Gloucestershire/Wiltshire border, to Burford in Oxfordshire, and thence, after three days in Oxford itself, moving down the Thames Valley to Wallingford and Reading, which he reached on 6 September, then staying from the 8 to 13 September at the riverside village of Sonning. It seemed as though he intended to relieve Windsor Castle and John made a highly effective feint in its direction with his new allies, the Welsh, who 'came by night to shoot into the host and gave them a great fright'. John had in fact always intended to re-assert his authority in East Anglia, and on 15 September he was on the move again, marching to Aylesbury and thence to Bedford and Cambridge.

John easily outmanoeuvred the barons and was able to wreak his vengeance on the Midlands and East Anglia unchallenged. Starting at Rockingham in Northamptonshire on 21 September 1216, he cut a wide swathe of destruction eastwards to Oundle and then, moving north-east, to Crowland, on the Lincolnshire/Cambridgeshire border, where he stood gleefully watching the village go up in flames. His chief instrument and lieutenant, Savaric de Mauléon, was moved by the monks' piteous pleas for mercy, and a timely bribe, to spare the abbey itself, but John was furious when this was reported to him; abusing de Mauléon and seizing a torch himself, he ran up and down in a frenzy setting fire to the standing corn until the whole estate was a blackened desert. From Lincoln, which he reached on 28 September, he went on to Stow, nine miles [14 km] further north, sending his mercenaries into the Isle of Axholme, 15 miles [24 km] further on, around present-day Epworth, to do as much damage as they could, while he marched relentlessly on to Grimsby, on the Humber estuary 31 miles [50 km] north-west of Lincoln. Finally he turned back to Spalding, 55 miles [88 km] due south, leaving behind him a triangle of ruin.

A few people do seem to have been genuinely pleased to see John. On 9 October 1216 he was given a rapturous reception at King's Lynn, at the south-east corner of the Wash, one of the five busiest ports in the kingdom. Savaric de Mauléon was instructed to fortify and hold it, while, on 11 October 1216, the king himself made the 12 mile [19 km] journey south-west, to Wisbech, from which, on the following day, he crossed the swampy country intersected by rivers emptying into the Wash between Wisbech and the Abbey of Swineshead, 25 miles [40 km] north-west of Wisbech and about seven miles [11 km] due west of the present town of Boston.

The loss of King John's baggage in the Wash is one of the great legends of British history, and an important incident, in its consequences, in the record of foreign invasions. Roger of Wendover sets it in context:

> While Louis was continuing the siege at Dover for a length of time and without success, John with a large force had been committing terrible ravages in the counties of Suffolk and Norfolk . . . He then took his march towards the north, but in crossing the River Wellester, he lost all his carts, waggons and baggage horses, together with his money, costly vessels and everything which he had a particular regard for; for the land opened in the middle of the water and caused whirlpools which sucked in everything, as well as men and horses, so that no-one escaped to tell the king of the misfortune. He himself narrowly escaped with his army and passed the following night at a convent called Swineshead.
>
> He felt such anguish of mind about his property which was swallowed up by the waters, that he was seized with a violent fever and became ill; his sickness was increased by his pernicious gluttony, for that night he surfeited himself with peaches and new cider, which greatly increased and aggravated the fever in him.

John may perhaps have remembered as he lay on his sickbed at Swineshead how the unrestrained Angevin appetite, though for lampreys rather than fresh fruit and cider, had killed his father, but next morning, though in pain, was up before dawn and made his way to Sleaford. Here his condition worsened, and when he at last reached the Bishop of Lincoln's palace at Newark on the afternoon of 16 October 1216 a local monk with a great reputation for his medical skill was sent for. His efforts proved unavailing, as Roger of Wendover records:

> His disease gained ground, and he confessed himself and received the eucharist from the abbot of Croxton. Afterwards he appointed his eldest son Henry his heir and made his kingdom swear allegiance to him . . . After this, on the night next after St Luke the Evangelist's Day, he departed this life.

19

CHASING OUT THE FRENCH

The land is lost for Louis and in a short time he and his supporters will be chased out of it.

King Philip II of France to his courtiers, 1217

King John died on 18 October 1216 at the age of 49, while an angry wind howled round the palace which sheltered him, leaving his country in confusion and with a large foreign army encamped on its soil. A rapidly summoned council at Gloucester unanimously agreed to send for his nine-year-old son to succeed him and the new king was summoned from Devizes Castle, where he had been placed for safe keeping, and met outside Malmesbury by William the Marshal. A solemn, dignified little boy, with a beautiful face and golden hair, Henry responded to the Marshal's greeting with a grave little speech: 'Welcome, sir! Truly, I commit myself to God and to you, that for God's sake you may take care of me,' rather spoiling the effect, when the Marshal replied in similar vein, by bursting into tears, in which both the Marshal and the bystanders joined. This lachrymous start to the reign was rapidly followed, at Gloucester cathedral on 28 October 1216, by the coronation of the 'pretty little knight, clad in his little royal robes', followed by an exceptionally small-scale coronation banquet. In the middle of it arrived a messenger appealing for help from the custodian of a royal castle only 12 miles [19 km] away, which supporters of Louis had just started to besiege, and the proceedings, out of deference to the royal bedtime, ended early. Next day came the selection of a regent, 'a valiant man to guard king and kingdom'. William the Marshal, the obvious candidate, wanted to decline the honour, declaring that he was too feeble and broken, but he was overruled and became in the current phrase, *rector* of king and kingdom.

His acceptance of his onerous, thankless task – 'By my faith,' he acknowledged, 'I have embarked on a wide sea where, cast about as one may, neither bottom nor shore can be found' – was received with rejoicing, and the Marshal made an early bid for baronial support by reissuing on 11 November 1216 a modified version of Magna Carta. John's death had also, unexpectedly, led to a revival of morale among the royalists. 'All the nobles and castellans who had served his father,' explains Roger of Wendover, 'adhered more firmly to him, because they all thought that the sin of the father ought not to be charged to the son.'

The new spirit was immediately in evidence at Dover, where at John's death a truce was in force, the likely prelude to complete surrender. The besiegers were now to be sadly disappointed:

> When Louis and the barons who were besieging Dover Castle received news of the death of King John, they were all greatly pleased, as they confidently expected that they now had the kingdom of England in their own power. Louis then summoned Hubert de Burgh, constable of Dover Castle, to a conference and said to him, 'Your lord King John is dead, and you cannot hold this castle against me for long, as you have no protector; therefore give up the castle, and become faithful to me, and I will enrich you with honours.' To this offer Hubert is said to have replied, 'Although my lord is dead, he has sons and daughters, who ought to succeed him' . . . He then returned to the castle and told his friends what Louis had said to him, but they were all unanimous in refusing to surrender it to him . . . When this was announced to Louis and the barons, they determined to reduce the smaller castles throughout the country, that, after the lesser fortresses were in their power, they might attack the larger ones; then they raised the siege and returned to the city of London. Directly after their retreat, the knights who had defended the castle sallied out and burnt the houses and buildings which Louis had erected in front of the castle and then, ravaging the country, they procured a plentiful supply of necessaries for the garrison.

What happened after his abandonment of the siege of Dover offered a foretaste, if Roger of Wendover's account is accurate, of events to come:

> After this, Louis marched on the morrow of St Martin's Day [12 November 1216] with a large army to the town of Hertford, and laid siege to it, arranging his engines of war round the castle to batter the walls; but . . . a brave knight . . . defended it with his soldiers, and caused a great slaughter amongst the French. However, after the latter had, at great expense, protracted the siege from Martinmas [11 November] till the feast of St Nicholas [6 December], the town was surrendered to Louis, saving the garrison, their property, horses and arms.

The royalists had thus lived to fight another day and the aftermath of the victory involved one of those embarrassing French *v* English arguments which revealed, incidentally, how well-founded were the barons' fears of their allies:

> The town being thus given up, Robert FitzWalter made a demand of it, saying that the charge of it belonged to him by old right; Louis then asked the advice of the French knights on the matter, who told him that the English were not worthy of holding charge of such places, as they were traitors to their own sovereign. On this, Louis told the aforesaid Robert to wait patiently till the kingdom was subdued, when he would give everyone his rights.

Another eminent baron had meanwhile changed sides. William d'Albini, who had defended Rochester castle against John, now 'did homage to King Henry, who delivered into his custody the castle of Lafort [i.e. Sleaford], which he vigorously maintained.'

Few sieges were a walkover and Louis's next effort, at Berkhampsted, to which he moved his artillery the moment Hertford had fallen, provoked a vigorous reaction:

> Whilst the English barons, after pitching their tents, were employed in setting them in order, the knights and soldiers of the garrison made a sally, seized the baggage and conveyances of the barons and gained possession of the standard of William de Mandeville, with which they returned to the castle . . . On the same day, whilst the barons were sitting at table, the knights and soldiers of the garrison again made a sally, and, in order to put the barons in confusion, they carried before them the standard which they had taken a short time before, and thought to come upon them unawares; but the latter were forewarned of this and drove them back into the castle. When the following day dawned Louis ordered the petrariae and other engines of war to be erected round the city, which being done, they kept up a destructive shower of stones; but Walleran, a German, well tried in warfare, made a brave resistance against them and caused great slaughter amongst the excommunicated French. However at last the aforesaid Walleran, after a protracted siege, by command of the king, surrendered the castle to Louis, saving their horses and arms on the 20th of December.

The most striking French progress during the winter was in East Anglia, where Louis succeeded in capturing royalist-held castles at Pleshey and Hedingham in Essex and Orford in Suffolk, along with those at Norwich and Cambridge. William the Marshal was following a skilful policy of consolidation, withdrawing the garrisons from exposed areas to concentrate them in the really decisive theatre of the south-east, but the price was high, for it gave Louis an uninterrupted sweep of countryside from the Thames estuary to the Scottish border – uninterrupted, that is, except for the powerful fortress at Lincoln, safe, it was believed, in the hands of a 'good dame', Nicola Haye, an elderly but resolute woman who had shown unfaltering loyalty to King John throughout his reign.

The real focal point of English resistance that winter was the Cinque Ports, less out of loyalty to the English crown than because of the constant depredations their trade suffered from the activities of French privateers. Their particular enemies were those based on the smaller Channel Islands – the islands as a whole remained loyal to the crown – under the command or encouragement of Eustace the Monk, who had organized the invasion fleet of 1216. It was along this strip of Kentish and Sussex coast that opposition to the French now rallied, both by land and sea. In mid-December 1216 'the brave men of Ireland who are with their ships on the coasts of Normandy' had been offered generous rewards to report to Winchelsea by 13 January 1217. Many responded, and were joined by an English fleet collected locally and from the Channel Islands, whose governor, Philip d'Aubigne (or de Albini or de Aubeny or Daubeny) took over its command. Inland the resistance leader Willikin of the Weald was still harassing the French at every opportunity, breaking down the bridges, blocking the paths through the woodland and cutting off the head of any invader whom they caught.

Philip d'Aubigne was a passionate and brave royalist who later became Henry III's private tutor. He set up his headquarters at Rye, midway between Hastings and Dungeness, less than 20 miles [32 km] from the base of Willikin of the Weald at Marden and the two, along with the royalist-held Dover Castle, helped to make the enemy hold on the whole, key, area uncertain, as Louis discovered to his cost when, during January 1217, he decided he must make a visit home. He was in urgent need of reinforcements and according to Roger of Wendover, 'the messengers of Louis who had gone on his behalf to the court of Rome' had 'brought word to him, that unless he left England the sentence of excommunication which the legate Gualo had pronounced against him, would . . . be confirmed'.

Having landed the previous May without opposition Louis now, eight months later, had to fight his way out of the country:

> The Marshal reassembled all the men who held loyalty to this [i.e. the king's] side, and made his way to Chertsey. Louis, on his part, made his way to Winchelsea, where he had not the chance to embark with his following because he found the road to the sea closed. The Marshal having consulted his allies had the town of Rye occupied by Philip de Aubeney and a sufficient troop of knights and sergeants. Then he sent

round to the seaward side a well-equipped fleet. Next he rode towards Louis and pressed him so hard that he no longer knew in which direction to turn, since he had the Marshal on one side, Philip de Aubeney, who was killing many of his men, on the other, and the fleet in front of him. Furthermore, Willikin of the Weald was harrying him.

Louis now found himself far worse off than he had been in London. The hungry, hemmed-in French had to send to London for help, but the reinforcements sent to rescue them dared not risk the passage through the guerrilla-infested Weald, and the main road from Canterbury was blocked at Rye. Louis's men now appealed to the governor of Boulogne for ships to rescue them, but according to William the Marshal's biographer, 'Thus hemmed in, Louis lost a good thousand of his men . . . The troop of ribalds who boasted of conquering England was almost destroyed there.'

Eventually the rescue fleet, said to have consisted of 200 ships, duly arrived but, having got safely into Dover, it could progress no further for adverse weather kept it shut up there for a fortnight. Only one vessel, probably captained by the legendary Eustace the Monk, managed to claw its way along the cost to Winchelsea, but his arrival had an immediate effect and the short siege of this small town was to witness some of the most unusual operations of the whole war. Eustace built on the largest of the English ships captured in the harbour a 'castle', or large fighting platform, 'so big,' a French chronicler declared, 'that everyone stared at it with wonder, for it overpassed the sides of the ship in every direction.' Eustace's invention rapidly fell victim, however, to an old-fashioned cutting-out expedition. At dusk one day a party of English seamen slipped aboard the unwieldy vessel, towed or sailed it a suitable distance off shore and then chopped the offending castle into fragments in full view of its builders. This humiliating mishap was blamed by the French viscount responsible for the guard on his men's refusal to keep watch at night because of hunger, whereupon Louis offered to take over the duty himself; he had perhaps more of the attributes of a popular commander than his English critics, who called him arrogant, admitted.

But the besiegers did not have things all their own way. Louis had set up on the shore at Winchelsea two stone-throwing trebuchets which bombarded the English ships in Rye across the channel separating the two towns, and Eustace erected a third on a ship in the harbour, designed to engage the English fleet. In the end Louis got away thanks to an accident, for the very morning after the destruction of the 'big castle' ship the French fleet managed to get out of Dover and sail along the coast to Winchelsea, while the two leading English ships which came out to intercept it collided. In the resulting confusion the French got safely into Winchelsea, from where they were able to ferry its hard-pressed and hungry garrison back to Rye which the English troops, heavily outnumbered, now evacuated. On 27 or 28 February 1217, having left his nephew in charge in England with instructions to defend London 'and not stir thence upon any account', and installed a French garrison at Rye, Louis at last managed to sail from Dover.

His absence, and his orders to his deputy to remain on the defensive in London, had clearly had a disastrous effect upon the invaders' fortunes, combined as they were with an upsurge of loyalty to the new king and William the Marshal's military ability. The castles held by pro-Louis sympathizers at Winchester, Southampton, Rochester and Marlborough were all captured and as Roger of Wendover makes clear: 'He never again had the goodwill of the barons of England, as he had formerly; for of that party . . . many . . . at once returned to their allegiance to King Henry and . . . Louis's party was in a great measure broken up.'

Louis returned to England on 23 April 1217 and at once set about recovering the situation, as William the Marshal's biographer reports:

> When Louis learnt that the castle of which he thought himself master had surrendered he was displeased. Having assembled a large number of carters, sergeants, crossbowmen and ribalds, he went by Farnham without stopping to lay siege to it and came straight to Winchester. In a little while, he had restored the tower and the high walls with stone and mortar and had the breaches repaired. He left the count of Nevers on the spot, a cruel, proud man, with a strong garrison . . . On leaving Winchester, Louis divided his great army into two bodies. With one he went to besiege Dover, and he sent the other to Mountsorrel, which the Earls of Chester and of Ferrers held under siege.

'The Army of Louis and the barons of England' as Roger of Wendover neatly describes it, now made its riotous way northward, its mere approach proving sufficient to accomplish its purpose for, 'believing that Louis in person was descending upon them', the two mighty earls encamped outside Mountsorrel 'raised the siege and retired to Nottingham'. The relieving expedition now swung north-eastwards towards Lincoln. The city's strategic importance had been recognized since Roman times and William the Marshal was determined that it, too, should not be feebly abandoned, as his biographer describes:

> When the Marshal learned that the siege of Mountsorrel had been raised, he was greatly distressed . . . He was no less annoyed to hear that the French had made their way to Lincoln and that Louis was not

with them. He himself was at Northampton with the royalists the day before Pentecost [i.e. Saturday 13 May 1217]. God inspired them to a marvellous enterprise from which they earned great profit and honour.

The 'marvellous enterprise' was nothing less than a major counter-offensive designed to end for ever the nuisance of the French invasion; and the Marshal launched it with an inspiring speech:

> 'Hear ye, true and loyal knights!' said William the Marshal. 'At a time when, to preserve our reputation, to defend ourselves, our wives, our children, our friends and our land . . . we support the burden of arms, beware that there is amongst you no coward! A portion of our enemies have gone to Lincoln to besiege our castle but . . . Louis is elsewhere . . . We should indeed be soft if we did not take vengeance upon those who have come from France to rob us of our heritage. They desire our destruction. For God's sake, let us make a great effort . . . Their host is divided; we shall overcome it more easily than if it were united . . . We must open the way with iron and steel. No more threats, but attack them!'

Their spirits high, the Marshal's followers marched to Newark where they waited for two days while they were joined by as many men as could be spared from the royal garrisons scattered around the countryside, as Roger of Wendover describes:

> Whilst these events [the French advance on Lincoln] were passing . . . William Marshal, the guardian of the king and the kingdom, by the advice of Gualo the legate, Peter, Bishop of Winchester, and others by whose counsels the business of the kingdom was arranged, convoked all the castellans belonging to the king, and the knights who were in charge of castles in different parts of the kingdom, ordering them, on the command of the king, to assemble at Newark on the second day in Whitsun week [i.e. Tuesday 16 May 1217] to proceed together with them to raise the siege of Lincoln Castle.

The final advance on Lincoln now began:

> After all had received absolution and the blessing of God, they flew to arms, mounted their horses at once and struck their camp rejoicing. On their arrival at Stow, nine miles [14 km] from Lincoln, they there passed the night without fear. In the morning, seven dense and well appointed battalions were formed and they marched against the enemy, only fearing that the latter would take to flight before they reached the city; the crossbow men all the time kept in advance of the army almost a mile; the baggage waggons and sumpter-horses

followed all together in the rear with the provisions and necessaries, whilst the standards and bucklers glittered in all directions, and struck terror into those who beheld them.

The cavalry, not mentioned by Roger of Wendover, rode between the archers and the baggage-train, which was well escorted by infantry, and looked more dangerous than it was 'for each of the nobles had two standards, one . . . following the troops at a distance in the rear, with the baggage, and another preceding the persons of each of them, that they might be known when engaged in battle.' This sensible precaution was to have unforeseen consequences. As the advancing army approached Lincoln, the French commanders refused to accept the estimates of its strength made by their allies. 'You have reckoned them according to your own opinion,' they told the English barons, according to Roger of Wendover. 'We also will now go out and count them in the French fashion.' The result illustrated how misinterpreted information was worse than none at all:

> They then went out to reconnoitre the coming army of the king, but when they saw the waggons and baggage in the rear of the army, with the guards who followed the squadrons which were already disposed in order of battle, they thought that this was an army of itself, because they beheld there a great multitude of men with standards flying . . . and the Count of Perche with the mareschal, being thus deceived, returned in a state of uncertainty to their companions. On their return into the city they proposed . . . to divide the nobles that the gates might be guarded and the enemy prevented from entering by some, until the others had taken the castle, the capture of which would soon be effected. This plan was approved of by many, but several disagreed with it. Then they secured the gates, appointed guards to them, and prepared for a defence.

While the French were throwing away the overwhelming advantage in numbers they enjoyed, the English army was being admirably handled by William the Marshal, as his biographer makes clear:

> The Marshal delegated the command of the crossbowmen to the noble Bishop of Winchester, Peter, who knew what he was about, advising them . . . to marshal themselves in an extended line in order to kill the horses of the French as they charged. Next he ordered two hundred sergeants to be prepared to kill their own horses to serve as barriers should they be needed.

The defensive battle contemplated by William the Marshal was never fought, for the French having 'barricaded themselves within the town' forced him on to the attack. His enemy held a strong position. Lincoln sloped southward down a hill to the river Witham, with, near its summit, the castle, on its north-west corner, and at its base the river, crossed by, in 1217, the Wigford Bridge. Protected by water to their rear and the city walls to their flanks, the French settled down to bombarding the south and east curtain walls of the castle, which were already beginning to crumble when the relieving army came in sight.

The Marshal's army, having spent the night in the villages of Torksey and Stow, respectively about 10 and 9 miles [16 and 14 km] north-west of Lincoln, had climbed the adjoining ridge along which the Roman Ermine Street ran and advanced due south towards the city. No doubt because any assault on a city at this time was almost invariably preceded by a long siege, the French do not seem to have taken seriously the prospect of being immediately attacked. The city gates were guarded, but not the further approaches to the castle to the north and west and the French were taken by surprise when a small group of horsemen led by the Earl Marshal's nephew, John, suddenly appeared at its postern gate, the minor 'back door' of the fortress, and was admitted. They did pursue him when he re-emerged but he got away safely, bearing the important news that the garrison was in sad shape and the relief operations should be launched very soon.

John Marshal's uncle now decided that a weightier military assessment of the situation was needed and sent off the best of his subordinate commanders, Peter, Bishop of Winchester, one of the late King John's foreign-born favourites, to make a closer inspection of the defences:

> The Bishop of Winchester went off to reconnoitre with a troop of crossbowmen. He told them to wait for him and penetrated into the castle with a single servant . . . He saw the walls and the houses knocked down by the trebuchets. People begged him to take shelter because of the mangonels and the trebuchets which were destroying everything in the vicinity and he went into the tower . . . The bishop did not stop there long; he went out on foot by a postern into the town and as he was examining it, he noticed an old gate that had allowed communication between the castle and the town but which had been walled up in former days. He had it knocked down to give entry to the host. The bishop rejoined his men, who came to meet him singing as though they were already victorious. Laughingly the bishop said to them that they must save the bishop's house for him since he had been responsible for the entrance by which his men would get in.

What the sharp eye of the Bishop had discovered was not the main West gate but its pre-Norman predecessor, disused after the castle had been built by William I. While it was being cleared, the royalists in the castle, on Bishop Peter's advice, launched a diversionary attack as William the Marshal's army prepared another assault against the North gate of the city, which was evidently in poor condition or badly guarded. The sally from the castle was led by Falkes (or Fawkes, or Fulks) de Bréauté, whom Roger of Wendover knew as Falcasius (or Falkasius), and was skilfully coordinated with the main assault:

> The whole body then marched to the northern gate and endeavoured to force it open, the barons, notwithstanding this, continuing to cast heavy stones from their petrariae against the castle. But during this time Falcasius entered the castle with the company of troops under his command, with the crossbowmen, and stationed them on a sudden on the roofs of the buildings and on the ramparts, whence they discharged their deadly weapons against the chargers of the barons, levelling horses and riders together to the earth, so that in the twinkling of an eye they made up a large force of foot-soldiers, knights and nobles. Falcasius then, seeing a great many of the more noble of the enemy struck to the earth, boldly burst forth with his followers from the castle into the midst of the enemy; he was, however, made prisoner by the number who rushed on him, and carried away, until he was rescued by the bravery of his crossbowmen and knights.

Seldom can bowmen have been more skilfully handled, for they cleared the way, according to the classic tactics of the time, for a major assault by the knights and spearmen:

> The great body of the king's army having . . . forced the gates, entered the city and boldly rushed on the enemy. Then sparks of fire were seen to dart, and sounds as of dreadful thunder were heard to burst forth from the blows of swords against helmeted heads; but at length, by means of the crossbowmen, by whose skill the horses of the barons were mown down and killed like pigs, the party of the barons was greatly weakened for, when the horses fell to the earth slain, their riders were taken prisoners, as there was no-one to rescue them.

This force seems to have got in via the newly cleared West gate and to have taken the defenders, already thrown off balance by Falkes's arrows, totally by surprise. Some of the intruders now managed to attack the North gate from the flanks and the rear, enabling a third royalist force to push its way inside. A fierce struggle followed as the three groups of attackers surged forward down the narrow streets and lanes of the city, many of which were barely wide enough to take three or four foot soldiers abreast, but now filled with battling knights, wildly fighting swordsmen and even archers and artillery-men still trying to find worth-while targets.

Eventually a pattern began to emerge from the series of small, uncoor-dinated actions which had followed the eruption of the royalists into the city. The defending troops found themselves driven out of the whole upper area near the castle, one group, fighting all the way, being pushed steadily downhill along the widest street leading to the Wigford Bridge and the South gate, the other, which included the best of the French knights led by the Count of Perche, falling back towards the north-east corner of Lincoln, where they made a stand in the open space in front of the cathedral, adjoining the monastery.

The way to safety for the fleeing French now lay through the South gate, or Bar gate, an apt name if Roger of Wendover's version of events is correct:

> The French battalions, seeing the fall of their commander, took to flight, both horse and foot soldiers, with great loss; for the flail of the southern gate through which they took their flight had been replaced in a transverse way across the gate, which greatly impeded their flight, for when anyone came up and wished to go out at that gate, he was obliged to dismount from his horse and open it and after he had passed the gate was again closed and the flail again fell across it as before, and thus this gate was a great trouble to the fugitives.

The Battle of Lincoln, fought on Saturday 19 May 1217, was according to Roger of Wendover all over in little more than six hours. 'It commenced,' he says, unlikely as this seems in view of the long approach march, 'between the first and third hour and was finished by these good managers before the ninth 300 knights were taken, besides soldiers and foot, not easily to be counted', a remarkable proportion of the 600 knights on the French side, and the resulting ransoms must have been the making of many a fortune.

The victory at Lincoln was also rich in more conventional, inanimate, booty, earning it a famous nickname, preserved by Roger of Wendover:

> After the battle was thus ended, the king's soldiers found in the city the waggons of the barons and the French, with the sumpter-horses, loaded with baggage, silver vessels and various kinds of furniture and utensils . . . Having then plundered the whole city to the last farthing, they next pillaged the churches throughout the city, and broke open the chests and store-rooms with axes and hammers, seizing on the gold and silver in them, clothes of all colours, women's ornaments, gold rings, goblets and jewels. . . . When they had thus seized on every kind of property . . . they each returned to their lords as

rich men, and peace with King Henry having been declared by all throughout the city, they ate and drank amidst mirth and festivity. This battle . . . in derision of Louis and the barons, they called 'The Fair'.

What provided glad tidings for the ten-year-old Henry made bitter hearing for his 29-year-old rival:

Louis was greatly distressed when he heard that his men had been utterly defeated at Lincoln . . . Abandoning the siege of Dover, he made his way to London at full speed, fearing that the city would be taken by the royalists, by main force or surprise, and he sent to France for help.

If William the Marshal's biographer can be believed, Philip Augustus had remained astonishingly ignorant of recent events across the Channel:

When King Philip learnt of the defeat of his men, he was heartbroken and asked if King John were dead. 'Yes,' he was told, 'his son is already crowned and the Marshal has vowed to defend him.' 'Then,' [replied King Philip] 'we have nothing to gain in England. The land is lost for Louis and in a short time he and his supporters will be chased out of it, as the Marshal has taken the matter in hand.'

In France it was now the king's daughter-in-law, Princess Blanche, clearly a woman of iron resolution, who set out to save the situation:

As the king was afraid to give assistance to his excommunicated son . . . he laid the burden of the business on the wife of Louis, who was not slow in fulfilling the duty imposed on her, but sent off to her husband's assistance three hundred brave knights, well equipped with supplies for war, and attended by a large body of soldiers . . . She went at her task so energetically that if all those she assembled had come in arms to London, they would have conquered the whole kingdom.

Louis's wife had soon assembled a respectable, if not formidable, force. One of Louis's kinsmen, Robert de Courtenai, who had already fought alongside him in England, was in command of a motley force of knights and followers, some of high rank, drawn from those useful reservoirs of martial talent, Boulogne and Artois. The fleet had been assembled, and was commanded, like that of the previous year, by the curious, colourful figure of Eustace the Monk, who soon after his death became the subject of an admiring, semi-fictionalized biography, which credited him with near-magical powers. Eustace had been brought up in a monastery, before becoming seneschal, i.e. royal steward, of Boulogne, but had found his true vocation as a privateer. He had worked in turn for, and quarrelled with, the Count of Flanders, Philip Augustus and King John, impressing the last-named so much that he had given him a palace in London. By 1210 Eustace was well established in his career as a maritime entrepreneur, assembling fleets when required, and by 1215 had become John's determined enemy. In the following year he commanded the fleet which got Louis safely into Kent. He had by now become a legend on both sides of the Channel, described by the contemporary English chroniclers as 'a master of pirates' and 'a black monk who had become a blacker demon'. By the royalists he was regarded with hatred as a turncoat and a traitor.

In response to Princess Blanche's solicitation, and cash, Eustace brought together at Calais ten large vessels, four earmarked to carry knights and six their men-at-arms, plus a supporting fleet 70 strong, laden with arms and other supplies. The number of troops on board is uncertain, but if the figure of 32 knights in one vessel can be trusted, an estimate of 150 to 200 knights seems reasonable, plus an appreciably larger number of artillery-men, Eustace's speciality, and foot soldiers.

After Lincoln, that part of the Marshal's army which had not gone home laden with loot had moved to Oxford and then along the Thames to Chertsey, 21 miles [34 km] from London, before moving into Kent. The news that the French fleet had sailed found the Marshal himself steadfast as a rock and eager for action. He spent the night of Wednesday 23 August 1217 at Canterbury, though he and the 'good knights' with him 'slept little', waking early to a clear, bright day with a 'soft and pleasant' on-shore wind, which had brought the enemy fleet safely across the Channel until it was now in sight of the Isle of Thanet, making for the mouth of the Thames.

> The Marshal promptly made for the coast with such forces as he could assemble . . . He had a strong desire to measure swords with the French, but he was not allowed to embark. People remonstrated with him, saying that he ought to remain on land, for if by chance he was killed or captured, who then would defend the country?

Not all those under his command seem, however, to have shared the elderly warrior's fighting spirit:

> The Marshal . . . summoned the mariners of the Cinque Ports and by dint of bribes and promises, he induced them to go and meet the French . . . The Marshal so exerted himself that he soon had 22 ships armed . . . When they saw the large French fleet approaching they went to meet it . . . but, having no leader, they panicked, in utter

bewilderment, abandoning their ships, with the sails still set, and taking refuge in their boats.

The Marshal . . . succeeded by his encouragement in restoring their confidence, showing them that they were accompanied by good knights and sergeants and that he himself would readily have hazarded himself with them if his men had allowed him to do so. For if this fleet managed to land, it would be the end of England.

Above all, he brought them reinforcements, and new commanders. His own knights filled one ship, under his nephew John, who had made his name at Lincoln. In another went William d'Albini, the stalwart defender of Rochester; in a third embarked one of King John's illegitimate sons, Richard. And in supreme command the Marshal placed the most famous warrior in England after the Marshal himself, the justiciar Hubert de Burgh, who had successfully defended Dover Castle for more than a year. He now arrived from there in 'a fine ship' which immediately took the lead as the little English fleet, probably consisting of around 20 fair-sized ships and about as many smaller ones, again cast off and stood out to sea.

Still ringing in the ears of the men on board was a timely reminder the Marshal had delivered of the English triumph, against far less promising odds, at Lincoln. 'God has given us one victory over the French on land,' he told them. 'Now they are coming again, to claim the country against Him. But He has power to help the good on sea as well as on shore.' Roger of Wendover confirms the effect of these words on the English seamen: 'By the event which had taken place at Lincoln, in which a few had triumphed over a great many, they were inspirited and boldly attacked.'* Both wind and tide favoured the incoming fleet and the earlier English retreat had made the French, always inclined to arrogance, openly contemptuous of their opponents, as the Marshal's biographer recounts:

The French saw them come out of the harbour but despised them. The clewed up their sails [i.e. fastened them to the yards, to keep on their existing course], saying 'It's only foot; [i.e. lowly-born infantry] there's not a knight amongst them. They are ours. A happy chance has sent them to us; they won't be able to resist us. They'll pay our

---

*The accounts given by both the sources quoted are hopelessly muddled. Roger of Wendover clearly intends to say the French had 80 ships, the English 40, but gets the figures the wrong way round. William the Marshal's biographer has him arriving in Sandwich twice over. The secondary sources also disagree, but I have followed Kate Norgate, p. 51, in assuming only Hubert de Burgh's ship joined the fleet from Dover, not 36 vessels, as accepted, though with some misgivings, by Brooks p. 218 fn 1.

expenses. We'll take them with us to London or else they'll fish for flounders in the sea.'

As the leading English ship, no doubt beating against the wind, drew near the French fleet only to sheer away again, she was greeted with derisive shouts: 'Sir Robert de Burgh's ship advanced ahead of the others as if to attack. But she passed by under full sail without giving battle. The French ribalds, full of bravado, yelled out "La hart! La hart!" '

'La hart!' was the cry which huntsmen used to direct their hounds towards their quarry. But Hubert de Burgh had not been running away, merely seeking the right moment to attack. Now his little fleet swung round, and wind and tide carried them remorselessly down upon the French, manoeuvred onto a lee shore with the sun in their eyes.

Eustace the Monk's ship, grossly overloaded, was the first target:

> The great ship of Bayonne, which the king's treasure was in, was ahead of the others . . . Sir Richard, the son of King John, steered towards this ship to attack it. But he had little effect till he was rejoined by the cog carrying the sergeants [i.e. the knights' men-at-arms]. The castle [of the cog], being lightly loaded, was high above the water, whereas the Monk's ship was so low that the water was almost coming in. It was carrying the trebuchet and the valuable horses sent to Louis.

Soon the whole hitherto tranquil patch of sunlit sea was alive with ship-to-ship duels, as Roger of Wendover makes plain:

> Philip d'Albini with his crossbow men and archers sending their missiles amongst the French, soon caused great slaughter . . . They had moreover galleys peaked with iron, with which they pierced the ships of their adversaries and sank many of them in an instant; they also threw hot lime-dust on the sea, which, being borne by the wind, blinded the eyes of the French . . . the crews were struck down by the weapons and arrows of the English sailors, who . . . pierced them with their javelins and arrows, or cut them down with swords and lances, whilst others bored holes in their ships' bottoms and sank them.

The French flagship, which had on board the military commander, Robert de Courtenay, as well as the dreaded Eustace, had meanwhile been boarded, with conspicuous gallantry:

> Renaut Paien of Guernsey, a valiant sergeant, leapt from the cog into the ship. In his fall he knocked over Guillame des Barres and Robert de Courtenay and sent Raoul de la Tournelle spinning. He attacked this last so energetically that he ended by taking him prisoner. After

Renaut, Thébaut and others leapt in their turn. All on board the ship were captured.

Eustace the Monk's end was ignoble, though Roger of Wendover felt little sympathy for him:

> That traitor to the king of England and wicked pirate, Eustace the Monk, after being long searched for was at last found, and dragged forth from the hold of one of the ships; and when he found himself a prisoner, he offered a large sum of money for his life and bodily safety and promised for the future to fight faithfully for the English king.

But he had changed sides once too often, and even the mention of 10,000 marks – the Marshal's biographer identifies the amount – did not save him from being presented with a grim alternative:

> There was one Stephen of Winchelsea, who reminded him of the miseries he had inflicted on him on land and at sea, and gave him the choice of having his head cut off either on the trebuchet or on the side of the ship.
>
> In the ship were 32 knights who would have suffered the same fate, had the English knights not prevented it. And they had a hard job to do so. When this great ship had been captured, our men fought with such courage that the French retreated. Our fleet kept in close pursuit and routed them. When they captured a ship they did not fail to kill all they found on board and threw them to the fishes, leaving only one or two . . . alive. They pursued the French in this way nearly to Calais. . . . According to witnesses of the affair, we can say that a good four thousand men were killed, without counting those who leapt into the sea and were drowned.

Although the figure of 4000 dead was certainly exaggerated, the slaughter, even after the actual fighting was over, was appalling. The Marshal's biographer tells of a man picking up a boathook with, he thought, 'a fine coverlet of scarlet', only to find it coated in congealed blood, while the severed head of the arch-enemy, Eustace, was hoisted on a pole and paraded through the Cinque Ports. Only 15 French ships, mainly the largest and fastest, got back to Calais, and though a few were sunk most were captured. Here was the seaman's equivalent of the 'Fair of Lincoln'. 'The King's followers,' says Roger of Wendover, 'then collected all the spoil from the French ships consisting of gold, silver, silk cloths and arms.' The Marshal's biographer describes what happened to some of the captured clothing:

> One ought to have seen, the next day, the sailors coming and going dressed in scarlet and silk, and outdoing one another in boasting: 'My

robe is worth two of it,' said one. 'Bah!' replied another, 'mine is all cisemus fur, cote and surcoat, mantle and cape . . .' 'And mine,' said a third, 'is all ermine edged with gold.' And as they provoked each other in this wise, the others dragged provisions out of the ships, meat, wine, corn, and iron and steel utensils from which the whole country benefitted.

The Battle of St Bartholomew's Day, also known as the Battle of Sandwich, made Louis's position in England untenable. His father's not very helpful reaction was to say 'I told you so.' 'My lords, did I not say that if the Marshal came into this, Louis and his enterprise would be ruined?', Philip Augustus asked his counsellors.

While both sides had awaited the arrival of the French fleet the siege of London had been directed by the legate Gualo from Kingston, conveniently close to Windsor Castle, where the young Henry had been placed for safe keeping. With most of the English forces down on the coast, however, there had been insufficient troops available either to invest it effectively, or to take it by storm, though Louis was apprehensive enough to move into the Tower. The French, for their part, were too weak to create an effective diversion to support the relieving fleet, but strong enough to mount one 'very fine raid', which drove Gualo, in his turn, scurrying back to the safety of Windsor Castle. News of the crushing defeat of his countrymen at Sandwich reached Louis late on the evening of Saturday 26 August 1217. On the Monday his representative rode out, under a safe conduct, from London, which was still in French hands, to discuss terms with the Marshal, now at Rochester.

The Treaty of Kingston was signed on Tuesday 12 September 1217 on an island in the Thames, Louis being rowed from one bank and Henry III, the Marshal and the papal legate, resplendent in scarlet, from the other. The boy monarch, in one of his first public appearances, promised, along with his adult companions, to keep to its terms; Louis did the same:

> The king of England, with the legate and the marshal, swore on the holy gospels that they would restore to the barons of England and all others in the kingdom, all their rights and . . . liberties . . . on account of which the dispute had arisen between King John, King of England, and the barons . . . All those who had . . . ransomed themselves . . . should not recover what had been paid; but from whatever remained to be paid should be entirely released. All the prisoners taken at Lincoln, or in the seafight near Dover, should be everywhere immediately set free . . . without any ransom or tribute.

The following day the legate and his supporting bishops, in their

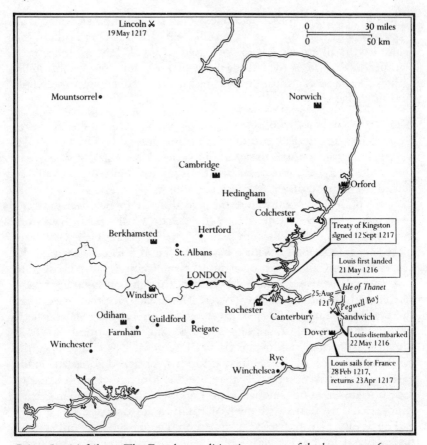

Prince Louis' failure. The French expedition in support of the barons, 1216–1217.

finest silken copes, returned to the island in the Thames to receive the humiliated French prince, barefoot and clad in the rough woollen garb of a penitent. On 14 September 1217 peace with France, and within England, was officially proclaimed and soon afterwards Louis received the first instalment of a promised £7000, to encourage him to leave at once. A novel precedent had been created; an *unsuccessful* invader had been paid to go away. On 28 September 1217, 16 months after Louis's arrival in England as its would-be king, the final act in the drama was played out, as Roger of Wendover recounts:

> Then, under the conduct of the grand marshal, he went with all speed to the sea coast, and thence, in lasting ignominy, crossed to France.

20

THE KING WENT TO WALES

Having therefore raised an army, the king went in person to Wales.

The Chronicle of Lanercost, *describing 1282*

The long reign of Henry III, once the French had been expelled in 1217, was not to witness the landing of any further foreign army on English soil. He died on 16 November 1272. His heir, Prince Edward, was in Sicily, recovering from a stab wound received on crusade while disarming a would-be Moslem assassin, when he learned of his father's death. By the time he reached England, after a leisurely journey, in August 1274, he was 35. So tall that he stood out in any crowd – hence his nickname Longshanks – with handsome features, black hair and a fluent and persuasive tongue, Edward I looked and sounded every inch a king. He was, declared the contemporary minstrels, 'the best lance in all the world'.

Edward I's reign was to be dominated by the twin problems of Wales and Scotland and it was for his achievements there that he was principally to be remembered. The entry which appeared in the *Chronicle* of the Augustinian priory of Lanercost in Cumberland for 1282 was typical of many:

In the unlucky course of that year the Welsh nation broke over their borders carrying fire and sword among the people . . . Their prince Llywelyn, deceived by the advice of his brother David, fiercely attacked his lord the king . . . Having therefore raised an army, the king went in person to Wales, accompanied by gallant men.

This campaign, and another in the following year, were sufficiently successful to make possible what was in effect the enforced union of Wales with England. On 19 March 1284 the Statute of Wales was issued from Rhuddlan, with a pious preamble:

Divine providence, which is unerring in its notions, among other gifts with which it has of its dispensation deigned to honour us and our kingdom of England, has now of its grace wholly and entirely converted the land of Wales previously subject to us by feudal right with its inhabitants into a dominion of our ownership, every obstacle being overcome, and has annexed and united it to the crown of the said kingdom to be a constituent part of it.

In case divine providence should have second thoughts, the statute now introduced English courts and law, with some exceptions, and the whole system of English sheriffs and other officials throughout the entire former principality. More persuasive still, Edward now devoted a vast amount of effort and money to covering the country with such a straitjacket of castles as would make another major rebellion impossible. Existing castles that had been badly damaged or, even worse, been captured, as at Aberystwyth, were so radically rebuilt as to be unrecognizable and everywhere the work was on a vast scale. Caernarvon, where, most appropriately, a son was born to Edward and Eleanor on 25 April 1284, a mere month after the Statute of Wales, was of a size and grandeur sufficient by itself to make any potential rebel hesitate. A Welsh Westminster and Tower of London combined, Caernarvon was unique, with its polygonal instead of rounded towers, and its patterned masonry incorporating bands of stone of different colours, justifying its contemporary description as 'the fairest fort man ever saw'. The remaining seven castles built by Edward were strictly functional but no less impressive. The massive walls of Harlech, on a steep, rocky-sided crag, originally washed on two sides by the sea, must have seemed impregnable; at Conway a Cistercian monastery was moved to make room for the new castle and the town which, as in other places, was planted around it, on the model of the *bastides*, or fortified towns, of Aquitaine. Given the charters and privileges of boroughs, and sometimes with the mayor doubling as castellan of the adjoining castle, the new towns were (on the Roman pattern) originally English settlements, intended to demonstrate to the rowdy, rural Welsh the benefits of peaceful urban life.

The conquest of Wales was rounded off in February 1301 by the formal designation of the king's 16-year-old son and heir, Edward of Caernarvon, as Prince of Wales, henceforward the traditional title of the king's eldest son. (The story that he had been presented at birth to the Welsh by the king in fulfilment of a promise that he would give them a ruler, born in their country, who spoke no word of English is, alas, a myth first recorded 300 years later.)

Edward I was a notably open-minded commander and his Welsh campaigns seem to have convinced him of the importance of the bow in

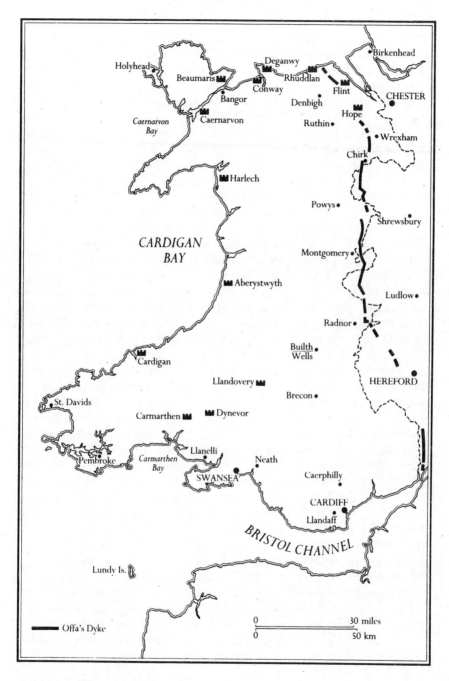

Holyhead

Deganwy

Birkenhead

Beaumaris

Rhuddlan

Conway

Flint

CHESTER

Bangor

Denbigh

Hope

Caernarvon Bay

Caernarvon

Ruthin

Wrexham

Chirk

Harlech

Powys

Shrewsbury

CARDIGAN BAY

Montgomery

Ludlow

Aberystwyth

Radnor

Builth Wells

HEREFORD

Cardigan

Llandovery

Brecon

St. Davids

Carmarthen

Dynevor

Pembroke

Llanelli

Carmarthen Bay

Neath

Caerphilly

SWANSEA

CARDIFF

Llandaff

BRISTOL CHANNEL

Lundy Is.

Offa's Dyke

| 0 | | 30 miles |
| 0 | | 50 km |

Wales and the Marches 43 AD–1603.

all its forms. As already mentioned both the chroniclers and subsequent historians have tended to use the terms 'bowmen' and 'archer' indiscriminately. Strictly speaking, however, 'bowman' meant a man firing a crossbow, a mechanically operated weapon firing a bolt, or 'quarrel', a square-headed missile with great stopping power. The commoner, 'one-foot', version was loaded by the soldier putting one foot in a stirrup to haul back over a trigger the cord which drew back the bowstring. There was a heavier, 'two-foot', variety and, used specifically on board ship in static defence, a mechanical one which required a winch to operate it and was really a small piece of artillery. Crossbows were relatively dear: from 3s to 5s [15-20p] for the 'one-foot', 5s to 7s [20-35p] for the 'two-foot' and 9s [45p] for the winched *balista ad turnum*. The ammunition was ordered in vast quantities; 15,000 bolts for 'one-foot' crossbows and 50,000 for 'two-foot' in March 1277 for coming operations in south Wales, and, during the rising by Rhys ap Mareddud ten years later, two consignments of crossbows and 26,000 quarrels were sent from Bristol to Carmarthen. The cost had fallen as production increased, averaging around 10s [50p] per 1000 for the iron heads attached to the quarrel shafts, and only 1s 2d to 1s 4d [7-8p] for the shafts themselves. Arrows with pointed heads *could* be fired from crossbows but were relatively rare. In 1283 the troops in the Anglesey campaign were issued with 240,000 quarrels but only 16,000 arrows.

The crossbow was a very effective distance weapon and, for military purposes, had the advantage of a roughly standard range, and, owing to the limitations of the 'loading' mechanism, a consistent rate of fire. As the bow was bent mechanically, the strength of the individual user counted for little. The rate of fire was, however, slow due to the need to wind up the string to the necessary tension with a handle or a pulley and stirrup and it required a high degree of training; hence crossbowmen tended to be professionals. It was also troublesome to carry and load, but its missiles had remarkable penetrating power. The Welsh-born chronicler Giraldus Cambrensis recorded seeing in 1188 arrow heads that had 'penetrated . . . the oaken portal of the tower, which was four fingers thick' at the siege of Abergavenny a few years before. Another arrow had plunged straight through the 'thigh and the armour with which it was cased on both sides' of one unfortunate soldier, before it went on to pierce his wooden saddle and 'mortally wounded the horse'. 'What more,' asked Giraldus, 'could be expected from a balista? Yet,' he pointed out, 'the bows used by this people are not made of horn [or] ivory. . . . but of wild elm; unpolished, rude and uncouth . . . not calculated to shoot an arrow to a great distance, but to inflict very severe wounds in close fight.'

The pre-eminence of the Welsh with the bow was sometimes attributed to the wooded nature of much of their country, which provided both ample raw material and excellent moving targets, in the shape of game. It is possible, however, that Giraldus was not referring to the crossbow at all, but to what can conveniently be called the shortbow, similar in shape to the crossbow but drawn back by hand only as far as the chest and firing a lighter arrow. This had been in use since Saxon times, but after Hastings had fallen out of favour. It had the advantage of cheapness and ease of use, but tended to be regarded as an amateur weapon, fit only for poachers. It was not mentioned at all in the Assize of Arms of 1181, and Richard I, no mean expert, John and Henry III had all vastly preferred the crossbow, despite its disadvantages. It was not until a New Assize, of 1252, that archery received official recognition with the requirement that when there was a muster 'all who own more than forty and less than a hundred shillings in land' should 'come bearing a sword and a bow with arrows and a dagger'. Even poor men, worth less than this, were called on to bring bow and arrows if they had them, the normal rate of 'ready' ammunition being 25 arrows in a quiver.

Both shortbow and crossbow were now to be outclassed, and in England at least virtually replaced, by one of the most influential inventions in the history of warfare, the longbow. The French, fortunately for England, never took to it, for the best of reasons: French peasants were forbidden to possess arms, for fear they would be used against their masters. Similar laws in England, designed to protect the nobility's deer and boar from being shot rather than the landlords themselves, had by around 1300 ceased to be enforced; instead, ordinary citizens were first encouraged, then ordered, to practise archery, traditionally on Sundays after church, in preference to private 'games of no value' like dice, quoits and, especially disliked because they so often degenerated into brawls, team games like handball and football.

From the fourteenth century onwards the butts on the village green became a familiar feature of English village life. Who invented the longbow is unknown, but it lent itself to competitive sport, for all depended on the strength and skill of the individual. By the time it reached perfection, around 1350, the standard bow was made of yew, maple or oak and was six feet [1.8 m] in length, but light enough for a man to take several on campaign, in case a string should break. As so often, a weapon that looked right also functioned well. Instead of the clumsy struggling with wheels and stirrups demanded by the crossbow, the new-style archer stood sideways on to his weapon, using the full muscular strength of his back, shoulders and arms to draw back the string with his right hand while thrusting the bow forward with his left; the ideal gap, almost impossible to achieve, was a full yard [0.9 m]. Then, in perfect coordination of hand and eye, the long, slim, almost elegant, arrow was released to fly to its distant target. By Tudor times the minimum length for a practice range was 220 yards [200 m]. An unaimed arrow, where a whole contingent was firing at a mass of soldiers, might find a mark at 290 yards [265 m]; even 400 yards [365 m] was often reached under good conditions, with sufficient force to penetrate chain-mail. Most of the longbow's execution, however, was achieved against unarmoured targets or vulnerable spots left unprotected, like the faces of Scottish men-at-arms, whose helmets rarely possessed a visor, or knights who had briefly lifted it to avoid stifling on a hot day. The longbow could not be fired from horseback and though archers were sometimes mounted for additional mobility most marched into battle, sometimes, like Roman legionaries, carrying pointed stakes which they planted in the earth in front of them. They commonly fought in alternate ranks, one reloading as the other aimed and fired and the rate of fire was devastating. A top-class archer, paid in Edward II's time the very high wage of 6d [2.5p] a day, could discharge an arrow every five seconds, five or six times as fast as a crossbow-man. To be at the receiving end of a salvo from a well-trained contingent was terrifying. A nineteenth-century officer in India, one of the few men then alive who had experienced both types of bombardment, testified that to have a flight of arrows fall all round one was more unnerving than a shower of musket balls, no doubt because one could see and hear the former coming, so that even if not hit a man was likely to halt in his advance, or fall back bewildered*.

Even though Wales was peaceful the outbreak of war with France in May 1294 exposed England once again to the threat of invasion and opened up the possibility, so dear to every potential attacker, of her having to fight a war on two widely separated fronts. On 5 July 1295 her old enemies, France and Scotland, entered into a formal agreement whereby John of Scotland's heir, Edward Balliol, was betrothed to Philip IV's niece, Joan. This was the start of the famous 'Auld Alliance' between two countries which had nothing in common except their hostility to England, and on 23 October 1295 it was formalized in a new treaty for mutual support. Edward I's response was the 'Model Parliament' which met on 27 November 1295, a landmark in the development of the institution. It included not merely representatives of nobility and clergy, but what was later known as 'the commons', consisting of two knights from each shire and two burgesses from every borough – although the three groups met separately and voted different amounts. Edward's writ of summon made clear, however, that national

*See Colonel Norgate (ed.), *Sepoy to Subadar* p. 23, cited by J. E. Morris, *The Welsh Wars of Edward I*, p. 103, fn. 1.

defence was no longer a mere matter of feudal obligation but something which concerned every citizen:

> Inasmuch as a most righteous law of the emperors ordains that what touches all should be approved by all, so it evidently appears that common dangers should be met by remedies agreed upon in common. You know well how the King of France has . . . beset my realm with a great fleet and a great multitude of warriors and proposes, if his power equal his unrighteous design, to blot out the English tongue from the face of the earth.

Long before the Model Parliament met, anti-invasion preparations had begun, though it is difficult, in the case of naval affairs, to distinguish between the fleet required to maintain an army overseas and that mobilized primarily for home defence. The backbone of the fleet for all purposes was invariably formed by the 57 ships, manned by 1245 men, which the Cinque Ports were required to provide, though they were often allowed to send fewer, or sometimes none at all, to avoid overburdening them. The crews had to work for two weeks free, but thereafter were paid at the same rate as the men collected, with their vessels, from other ports, i.e. 3d a day for an ordinary sailor and 6 d for the shipmasters. This fleet was supplemented as necessary from other sources. In November 1294 ships began to be requisitioned from ports like Great Yarmouth, to supplement those already assembled for the expedition to France, and a major building programme was put in hand. Thirty galleys were ordered from yards all round the coast at a cost of around £205 each. They were equipped with sails as well as oars and the requisitioning writ sent to the bailiffs of Newcastle-upon-Tyne still exists:

> Whereas we have of our counsel provided that galleys be built for the defence of our realm and the safety of the sea; we do command you, and strictly charge you on the fealty in which you are bound to us, that on the sight of these presents you cause to be made at Newcastle upon Tyne one good galley of six score oars so that it be ready and prepared in all things that pertain to such a galley about Christmas next.

During 1295 another significant development occurred: the term 'Admiral' was used for the first time to describe the single captain, William Leyburn, placed not merely in overall command of the Cinque Ports and their fleet but of all places 'where ships ply within the kingdom and our authority, including Bayonne, Ireland and Wales'. Leyburn was also made responsible, along with the constable of Dover, for organizing a system of coastal guards, and the approach of the 'invasion season' led to the sheriffs of the coastal shires being instructed in April 1295 to assemble ships at Portsmouth and Harwich as well as further north. A typical squadron, of eight ships, patrolled the coast from King's Lynn to Berwick during the summer and autumn, including the brand-new galley from Newcastle, finally delivered in June.

Philip IV was under no illusions about the difficulty of invading England and looked to a combination of overwhelming force and treachery to succeed where others had failed. In addition to the alliance with Scotland, he began to negotiate one with King Eric of Norway, offering him £50,000 annually to supply 100 large ships for four months of each year that the French war with England lasted. The German emperor was persuaded in the same way to forget his plans to invade France and the Counts of Flanders and Holland, both regularly involved in any serious invasion attempt, agreed to desert Edward for Philip. Even Spain was now brought into the secret coalition, the King of Aragon being promised that, once England was conquered with his help, Edward would become his personal prize. By bringing shipbuilders from Genoa to work at Marseilles and in Normandy, hiring 30 galleys from Mediterranean ports, and the wholesale requisitioning of merchantmen, a fleet 300 strong was assembled in the Channel, superior, at least in number, to any likely to oppose it.

What marked out the 1295 invasion attempt, however, from its predecessors was Philip IV's reliance on a traitor within the English gate. An otherwise obscure Welsh knight, Sir Thomas Turberville (or Turbeville), captured at Rioms in Gascony, and apparently possessing all the eloquence of his race, had suggested to Philip that he should be sent back to England, posing as an escaped prisoner. He was then to infiltrate himself into King Edward's confidence and, having obtained control of the Kent and Sussex coast, would hoist his banner above that of the king as a sign the French could land in safety. Philip agreed and Turberville, as good as his dubious word, duly gained an audience with his sovereign, but his lying tongue was not plausible enough to convince Edward that he should be put in charge of coastal defence or the fleet. He reported encouragingly, however, to France, that if the Scots attacked England the Welsh would start a fresh rebellion, and also assured Philip that the south coast defences could easily be overcome and that the Isle of Wight was undefended.

On 2 August 1285 the French commander, tired of cruising aimlessly off the English coast, and still waiting to sight Turberville's promised signal – he had in fact been detected, and was later executed – detached five galleys to go closer inshore and investigate. They, or some of them – the accounts are contradictory – attacked Dover, where an elderly and saintly monk (though similarly pious geriatrics appear suspiciously often in such accounts) is said to have been butchered at the altar while his younger brethren had shut themselves in the priory tower. The townsfolk rapidly drove the invaders out, however, with heavy loss. Meanwhile the crew of another of the galleys, which had come into harbour at Hythe, were encouraged to advance inland by a feigned retreat – another familiar feature of these incidents – until the whole force, numbering 240, were cut off and killed, and the galley was burnt, causing the remaining four to put hastily to sea.

The burning of Dover was rapidly followed by a far more destructive reprisal raid against Cherbourg and the next French venture, a raid on Winchelsea, was abandoned when a fleet from Great Yarmouth appeared in time to protect – perhaps with some reluctance – their traditional enemy, the Cinque Ports, whose own ships were apparently elsewhere. The discovery of Turberville's plans, which had included a proposal to seize the king when he visited Canterbury in mid-September for the enthronement of the new archbishop, Robert Winchelsey, encouraged the government to intensify its anti-invasion measures. The whole machinery for raising and calling out the reserve forces was overhauled, with every village and hundred being assessed for the purpose and officers nominated to take charge of each ten-man unit. The number of full-time soldiers was also increased. The city of London, for example, supplied 20 men-at-arms for four weeks' service in Kent, at 20 marks a head, much above the going rate, and by April 1296 there were some 500 infantry in Hampshire alone and 76 fully armed cavalry on the Isle of Wight.

The main emphasis was very rightly, however, on intercepting the invaders before they landed. In January 1296 one 'captain' was authorized to raise a fleet of 100 ships from all the ports between King's Lynn and Berwick, and another mustered 94 vessels, manned by 3578 men, an average complement of 38, from those between King's Lynn and Harwich, of which 43 came from Great Yarmouth. A brief panic developed in July following a report of a French plan to stage a cutting-out expedition against Yarmouth by warships disguised as fishing-boats, but it never materialized and during the following year the front line was pushed even further towards France. In March 1297 ten well-armed ships were assigned to watch the French coast, and in July a second line of defence was created of two squadrons, six and twelve strong respectively, to guard the coast north and the south of the Thames. Kent and Sussex, not East Anglia, were clearly regarded as the likeliest target areas, but the modest numbers compared to the 134 ships being employed in the Irish sea in operations involving Scotland, and the 50 from the Cinque Ports employed on the Gascony run, suggest that the threat was not considered to be very serious.

Around 1300 Winchelsea became the headquarters for a new admiral, a baron of the Cinque Ports, with a useful reputation as a merchant-cum-pirate, who was made responsible for the coast from Dover to Cornwall. Other commands were added a little later, one covering the stretch from the Thames to Berwick-on-Tweed, another, based on Ireland, what later became known as 'the western approaches', i.e. the Atlantic and the Irish Sea.

Technological development lagged behind organizational improvements. Neither the size nor the appearance of ships changed much at this time though minor improvements occurred in rigging and gear. The average size of ships engaged in the Gascon wine trade, the main cross-Channel traffic, was only about 100 tons, so that they could sail up rivers like the Garonne. Nor was any real distinction yet made between warships and merchantmen, fore and after castles being added to the latter to convert them to a military role, sometimes with a 'fighting top', a small platform to support a bowman or slingshot thrower at the masthead. The French experimented with a more substantial version, slinging the ship's boats halfway up the mast to accommodate five or six men, but the idea does not seem to have caught on.

Much of Edward I's reign was spent in resisting Scottish incursions into England or in attacking these troublesome neighbours in their own country. During a stay at Berwick, he added a new and deeper ditch and wider and stronger earthworks to the castle's defences, himself trundling a wheelbarrow as an example to the large pioneer force of ditchers, masons and carpenters he had taken with him to Scotland. They were now employed, as at Caernarvon, and Winchelsea, in laying out a whole new town, intended to be the financial capital of Scotland as well as a great commercial centre for the loyalists he planned to settle there. He did not, however, attempt in Scotland the same policy of subjugation by castle-building which he had practised in Wales, because of the cost, and the much larger area to be covered, though some existing castles were given better external defences, and some extensions were built on existing sites. It was while being raised in bed to begin yet another day's campaigning that the old warrior died, aged 68, at Burgh-on-Sands in the Solway Firth, on 7 July 1307, having left instructions that his tomb was to be opened and his funeral winding sheet was to be re-waxed every two years, to prevent his body decaying, until Scotland had finally been conquered.

Two months after his father's death, the new king, Edward II, abandoned the Scottish campaign and travelled south. Edward II, aged 22 on his accession, was a man of many gifts, but an aptitude for war was not among his talents.

The root cause of his failure, however, the fatal flaw which thus becomes a factor in the invasion history of England, was his homosexuality, most notoriously manifested in his infatuation with the son of a Gascon knight, Piers Gaveston. In June 1312, to universal rejoicing, and the king's inconsolable grief, Gaveston was seized by one of the barons he had insulted and beheaded. Even with this source of friction between king and barons removed Edward still proved incapable of protecting either his English subjects or his Scottish territories. On 23 June 1314, at Bannockburn, two miles [3 km] south of Stirling, he presided over the worst-ever defeat England ever suffered at the hands of the Scots and in 1323 he became involved in a dispute with Charles IV of France.

Incapable as he was of defending Northumbria, the prospect of the king keeping the French out of Kent, if they chose to cross the Channel, seemed remote. But the king's wife, Isabella, was Charles IV's sister, and in March 1325, perhaps pleased to have her safely out of the way, Edward sent her to France to negotiate with her brother, taking with her their eldest son, the young Edward, aged 13. Too young and inexperienced to assert herself during the humiliating 'Gaveston' years at the start of her marriage, Isabella was now a mature and self-confident frustrated woman of 29. She now scandalized all around her by entering into a flagrantly open affair with another resident at the French court with as much reason as she to detest Edward and his current favourites, Roger Mortimer, eighth Baron Wigmore and first Earl of March, a thoroughly manly figure about eight years her senior. This formidable pair, spurned wife and aggrieved subject, had on hand the obvious candidate to replace Edward II on the throne and Isabella suspected that the king's current male favourite, Hugh Despenser the younger, was intriguing to have the young Edward disinherited.

Edward II's reign had begun disastrously because of his sexual deviance; these same inclinations, combined with his wife's vigorous heterosexuality and blatant adultery, were now to expose his country to the risk of foreign invasion. A French expedition in support of the queen, designed to put her son, Charles IV's nephew, on the throne, seemed an imminent possibility.

The usual anti-invasion precautions were now put in hand. A number of castles, including the Tower, were hastily put in repair, a coastal watch was set up, with a beacon system to signal the approach of enemy ships, vessels entering English ports were searched for letters to potential traitors, French residents in England were interned and commissions issued for mustering troops in the threatened counties. But Edward lacked that surest shield of any sovereign, his people's trust and affection, and a contemporary London chronicler observed, 'the English sailors did not wish to prevent the arrival of the queen and her son and their company by reason of the great hate they had towards Sir Hugh Despenser.'

The queen's efforts to secure her brother's active support had, owing to her scandalous private life, been a failure. She found a more responsive ally in William II, Count of Hainault, Holland and Zealand, and Isabella enterprisingly negotiated a betrothal agreement between his daughter Philippa and the teenage Edward, in return for an unusual, advance, dowry of soldiers from Hainault to help the would-be bride gain her future kingdom.

The force of 700 men, under the command of Roger Mortimer and the Count of Holland's brother, John, which sailed from near present-day Rotterdam on 23 September 1326, must have been one of the smallest invasion armies ever to approach the British Isles. The French chronicler, Jean Froissart, writing from hearsay about this period – in 1361 he came to England to serve as the then queen's secretary and becomes a more reliable authority – gives a typically colourful account of the start of the voyage:

> And when they were all departed from the haven of Dordrecht, it was a fair fleet as for the quantity, and well ordered, the season was fair and clear and right temperate, and at their departing with the first flood they came before the dikes of Holland; and the next day they drew up their sails and took their way . . .

Froissart then describes a totally fictitious storm and supplies a distinctly misleading description of the invaders' arrival after being blown off course:

> So it was that about the end of two days the tempest ceased, and the mariners perceived land in England and drew to that part right joyously, and there took land on the sands without any right haven or port at Harwich . . . and so abode on the sands three days with little purveyance of victual, and unshipped their horses and harness, nor they wist not in what part of England they were in, other [i.e. whether] in the power of their enemies or in the power of their friends.

Isabella's ships in fact appear to have had a smooth, and certainly undisputed, passage, and to have made landfall at the mouth of the River Orwell, equally unopposed, on Wednesday 24 September 1326, though whether on the Suffolk side, near Landguard Point, or on the Essex side, near Harwich, as Froissart contended, is uncertain. Certainly they knew very well where they were, for Isabella and her entourage immediately moved on to a friendly house, Walton Castle, belonging to the Earl of Norfolk, whose special duty it was, by a pleasing irony, to protect the realm as hereditary Earl Marshal. Her choice of East Anglia had caught her husband on the wrong foot; he was watching the south coast, but now hurried back to issue orders and direct operations from the Tower of London, with the Despensers beside him.

The small army of foreigners who had accompanied Isabella were rapidly outnumbered by the Englishmen of all ranks who flocked to her standard, as she moved on from Cambridge to Baldock in Hertfordshire, from Baldock to Dunstable, and thence, skirting London, since it was by now solidly on her side, to Wallingford, which she reached on 15 October, the day the capital declared for her. From here she went to Oxford. The deposition of the king was now clearly in the air and on 16 November Edward was captured at Neath Abbey in Glamorgan. Hugh Despenser the younger, seized with him, was executed four days later.

On 16 January 1327, faced with a threat that his son might be disinherited, Edward, tearfully and reluctantly, agreed to renounce the crown, and on 1 February Edward III, a handsome 14-year-old, was crowned in Westminster Abbey. The deposed Edward II was now hurried from place to place to make rescue difficult and, harsh efforts to bring about his death through maltreatment having failed, he was murdered on 21 September 1327 at Berkeley Castle in Gloucestershire in a particularly brutal fashion, 'with a hoote broche [i.e. red-hot rod] putte thro the secret place posterialle'. No one believed the official story that, a healthy 43, he had died of natural causes, but Edward III later erected a splendid tomb for his father in the abbey church – now the cathedral – at Gloucester. It was a worthier memorial than was merited by the man who, a chronicler records, 'neither knew how to rule his kingdom, nor how to defend it'.

In October 1330 Edward III, now almost 18, at last became sovereign in reality as well as in name. The sinister Mortimer was immediately tried and executed and Isabella herself consigned to obscurity. (She lived until 1358, and late in life became distinctly pious.) The young king soon showed himself to combine proficiency in the conventional royal occupations – hunting, hawking, handling weapons and military command – with a less usual affability and cheerfulness; he was, it was said, 'not accustomed to be sad'. No scholar or statesman, he was nevertheless, as few of his predecessors had been, fluent in English as well as French and Latin.

The Scots soon became aware that times had changed since 1314. At Halidon Hill, three miles [5 km] north-west of Berwick, on Monday 19 July 1333, Edward, still only 20, achieved his hoped-for 'day of revenge' for Bannockburn. Scotland was nevertheless to remain for the rest of Edward III's reign, and indeed for centuries, the so-called 'postern gate', i.e. back-door, into England and a major factor in English defence policy whenever the French, for their own purposes, felt inclined to invoke the 'auld alliance'. The rest of Edward III's long reign was, however, to be dominated by the danger from France.

21

LORD OF THE ENGLISH SEA

The Kings of England have before these times been Lords of the English Sea on every side.

Instructions to his admirals issued by Edward III, 18 August 1336

On returning to Perth in August 1336 from his latest, unproductive, foray into Scotland Edward III received some highly disquieting news. Twenty-six galleys, claiming to be serving King David II of Scotland, but undoubtedly with French connivance if not with French crews, had attacked the Channel Islands and the Isle of Wight. They were now said to be sailing towards Scotland, but Edward rightly judged that the real danger to his kingdom lay in the south. Philip VI, the king told the Archbishop of York that summer, was clearly assembling a fleet to invade England on the pretext of assisting Scotland. That August, Pope Benedict XII postponed *sine die* a new, long-planned Crusade and immediately Philip VI moved the vast fleet he had assembled at Marseilles to the ports of Normandy. What destination could they have except England? On 18 August 1336 Edward III issued orders to his two admirals, responsible respectively for the waters north of the Thames and those in the south and west, to get their ships to sea in thoroughly uncompromising terms:

> Our progenitors, the Kings of England, have before these times been Lords of the English Sea on every side; and . . . it would very much grieve us if, in this kind of defence, our royal honour should (which God forbid) be lost or any way diminished in our time.

Here was a simple statement of the principle which later generations of Englishmen were to take for granted and England's maritime neighbours were always to find arrogant and offensive: that England, as an island, had a special right to control the seas around her shores. Sometimes, it seemed to other nations, she even implied that because of her unique situation, dependent on free access to salt water, her sailors enjoyed a form of overlordship on all the oceans of the world. In 1336 the lordship of the sea, even though confined to the waters that washed King Edward's shores, was already a highly sensitive subject and one regularly embittering Anglo-French relations.

An additional source of grievance, and potential *casus belli* between the two neighbouring countries, was the assertion that the king of England was also entitled, by right, to be king of France. The argument went back to 1328 when Charles IV had died without leaving a son. Edward III was then only 15 , but his mother, Isabella, had put in a somewhat half-hearted claim to the succession on his behalf. Isabella was herself the daughter of an earlier king of France, Philip IV, and under the so-called Salic Law could not inherit the throne 'because' as had been said on similar occasions in the past, 'of the imbecility of the sex'. It was contended by some authorities that a woman might none the less form, in a phrase of the time, 'the bridge and plank', by which her sons might succeed. As Edward's lawyers later pointed out, Christ himself was linked to the House of David only through his mother, the Virgin Mary. If a woman *could* pass on the right to the French throne then Edward III's claim to it, as the last king's nephew, was considerably stronger than that of Philip of Valois, his cousin.

There remained one further source of argument, which centred on the precise nature of the homage which Edward while still a boy had rendered to Philip, as overlord of his, Edward's, territories on the continent. Over the years between 1327 and 1337 there were endless negotiations on the subject and even a private meeting between the two kings, but the truth was there could be no real peace between the two countries while an English king still owned lands subject to the king of France. This was the real cause of what became known as the Hundred Years War, which was to dominate English defence policy for the next century.

Early in 1337, Edward moved the seat of government back from York to London, where it had been based during the Scottish campaign, and on 28 August he issued a detailed manifesto to be read in every shire setting out his case against Philip VI.

On 7 October 1337 Edward III publicly asserted his claim to the French throne and around this time – the precise date is uncertain – the French struck the opening blow of the Hundred Years War by landing at Portsmouth, under cover of false English flags. The ships of the Cinque Ports, which should have protected it, were absent, apparently engaged in their old feud with Yarmouth, and a large French force got ashore and burned the town, leaving only the church and hospital standing. The townsfolk finally rallied and mounted a counter-attack, which inflicted heavy casualties, but the bulk of the raiders got away.

At the request of the pope a truce in the still undeclared war was agreed, to run from Christmas 1337 to March 1338 and then to midsummer, but the French regarded themselves as still free to attack the English coast. That spring a French fleet, after parading up and down the Channel, launched a series of raids on the Channel Islands, leaving French garrisons in total possession of all except Jersey, where Castle Gorey still held out.

With his eyes set firmly on the Continent, Edward gave little priority to defending his own kingdom. A beacon system to spread the news of French landings, and a warning to able-bodied men in the coastal counties to be ready to turn out at short notice, formed the sum total of anti-invasion preparations in 1338 and these were soon found inadequate.

That spring the Isle of Wight was plundered and much of Portsmouth burnt down, causing Edward to declare, on 6 May 1338, that the truce with France had ended. On 12 July, leaving his officials to defend the homeland, in the name of his eight-year-old son, Edward Duke of Cornwall, he sailed from Orwell in Suffolk for the Scheldt, to seek allies in Europe.

At Coblenz in September the German emperor, Louis, appointed him 'Vicar-general of the Empire' and pledged himself to a seven-year alliance against the King of France. As a direct reprisal the French contemplated an invasion of England but settled instead for the most serious raid yet on Southampton, as Froissart describes:

> And as soon as Sir Hugh Quieret, Sir Peter [in fact Sir Nicholas] Behuchet and Barbevaire . . . who lay and kept the straits between England and France with a great navy, knew that the war was open, they came on a Sunday in the forenoon to the haven of Hampton, while the people were at mass; and the Normans, Picards and Spaniards entered into the town and robbed and pillaged the town, and slew divers [people] and defiled maidens and enforced [i.e. raped] wives, and charged their vessels with the pillage, and so entered again into their ships. And when the tide came, they disanchored and sailed to Normandy and came to Dieppe; and there departed and divided their booty and pillages.

This raid was, by any test, a disgrace. The town's defences proved totally inadequate, the militia failed to turn out, and the French were left in unchallenged possession of Southampton for 24 hours during which time apart from the offences described by Froissart, they hanged the townsfolk they caught from the gables of their own houses and carried off all the wool and wine in the local warehouses along with – as a final gesture of contempt – the scales from the Customs House. What they could not remove they destroyed, along with many houses. Only as they were re-embarking was an adequate force assembled, when 300 of the raiders are said to have been killed, some by a rustic wielding a flail.

The attack on Southampton in 1338 prompted the first account in English of an enemy raid of the kind, written about ten years later by the poet Laurence Minot, who specialized in describing battles and was probably himself a soldier:

At Hampton, as I understand,
Come the galleys unto land,
And full fast they slew and burned
But not so much as some men said . . .
Some were knocked upon the head,
That their body lay and bled.
Some lay stranded on the stones,
And some lay there with broken bones.
With them there was no other glee,
But they were fain to turn and flee.*

Edward III ordered an enquiry into what was described as a 'disgraceful neglect of duty' by those responsible and construction of a stone wall round Southampton began, to give time in future for the defending forces to assemble.

What had happened at Southampton in October 1338 was soon to be repeated elsewhere, though details are sadly lacking and the dates are often confused; Froissart, the fullest source, attributes to 1340 a whole series of attacks probably spread over the preceding two years. It is clear, if only from the official response, which is fully documented, that enemy raids on England from 1338 onwards presented a serious problem and roused a well-founded fear that a full-scale invasion might follow.

On 28 July 1338 two new vice-admirals were appointed to the northern and south and western commands, but were so far from securing mastery of the adjoining waters that on 4 October they were ordered to send the shipping in their harbours out to sea, for fear of it being seized at anchor. The French had now brought together a formidable force of sailors from Genoa and Spain, as well as from Normandy, Brittany and Picardy, under the command of such distinguished seamen as the Doge of Genoa's brother, Barbenoire (Barbevoire or Barbevaire), who, as already mentioned, had taken part in the raid on Southampton, and was to be immortalized in seafaring legend as 'Blackbeard'. On 15 October 1338 the English vice-admirals were warned that 'aliens and pirates', in their galleys, had already made many, unspecified, landings in England and had killed the king's subjects, burnt their houses and stolen their property. On the twenty-third the mayor and sheriffs of London were

*This is my own, very free, rendering of the original, barely intelligible, medieval English, to consult which see Note on Sources.

instructed to enclose the city on its riverward side with stone and timber and to drive piles into the Thames. Everywhere within seven leagues of the sea, although a solitary church bell might still be rung, a full peal was banned, this being reserved as an anti-invasion signal, on hearing which every able-bodied citizen was to assemble to defend the coast.

Late in 1338 or early in 1339 a further escalation occurred in the naval war. On a date and at a place unknown, but most probably soon after the attack on Southampton, around October 1338, near Middelburg, later the capital of Zeeland, on Walcheren Island, near Flushing, a French force of around 50 galleys, plus smaller craft, encountered a much weaker English fleet. This probably included, however, the two finest ships that Edward possessed, the *Edward*, named in his honour, and the great *Christopher*, which was armed, in addition to the usual mangonels and trebuchets, with three cannon, their first known appearance on an English vessel.

According to the poet Minot, Edward himself led his men, outnumbered by a hundred to one, in the fierce fight that lasted all day and into the night, leaving the gallant English beaten, but only after they had killed 60 Frenchmen for every ten of their own dead:

> They fought full fast, both day and night
> As long as any with strength might,
> But galley-men were so many,
> That Englishmen waxed all weary.
> Help they sought, though there came none,
> But since the time that God was born,
> Were never men better in a fight
> Than Englishmen while they had might.*

The Battle of Middleburg, or Armouth, as Minot describes it, apart from being probably the earliest occasion on which gunpowder was used by British ships, was also the first of the epic 'David versus Goliath' sea fights which were to stir English hearts over the centuries and this became a factor in promoting hostility to France. For the moment the English fleet was tied up in escorting troops across the Channel and the coast remained at the mercy of hit-and-run raids, as Froissart, referring, it seems likely, to 1338-9, makes clear:

> They did that winter great damage to the realm of England. Sometime they came to Dover, Sandwich, Winchelsea, Hastings and Rye and

---

*This is also my version, which retains as much as possible of Minot's original, including its imperfections of style. Although a useful, since unique, source, one must hope that he was a better soldier than poet.

did much sorrow to the Englishmen, for they were a great number, as forty thousand men.

According to the chronicler Henry Knighton, writing about 20 years later, at least one raid approached the scale of an invasion. In April 1339, he asserts, 20 ships, carrying 4000 men, appeared off Southampton and called on it to surrender to the Duke of Normandy, the title resumed, significantly, by the king of France's eldest son. The inhabitants replied by suggesting that the Normans should come ashore and rest for two days and then fight them on a one-to-one basis, in whatever strength should be agreed. The French declined this sporting offer and sailed off elsewhere, probably to Hastings, where, on the 27th, some fisherman's huts were burnt and several people killed. 'Like thieves', it was said, they now moved up and down the coast, causing trouble in the Isle of Thanet and at Dover and Folkestone, where the chief sufferers were the poor, whose simple homes and possessions, like fishing nets, provided easy, undefended targets. Another force of 'pirates', as they were known, were meanwhile causing trouble in the south-west. On 20 May 1339 Plymouth was the target for 18 French and Genovese galleys and pinnaces. Then, or on a second raid a little later, seven ships whose home port was Bristol were burnt in the area known as the Catwater, along with some others, and houses on the foreshore were set on fire. The inhabitants put up a stout resistance, in which 500 Frenchmen were said to have been killed for the loss of 89 Devonians; the veteran Hugh de Courtenaye, Earl of Devonshire, aged almost 80, led a counter-attack which 'chased the residue of impudent varletry back to their ships'. Undiscouraged, the French were back two days later and burnt all the ships in the harbour that had escaped their earlier attentions and many houses on shore, but disappeared hurriedly when a larger army assembled to attack them. From Plymouth they sailed back to Southampton, for another daring, or cowardly, raid, burning two more ships before vanishing once again into the Channel mists.

July 1339 brought a notable demonstration of the French tactics of only fighting when they enjoyed local superiority. Having appeared off Sandwich in overwhelming strength, with 32 galleys and 35 other vessels, the enemy commander stood out to sea again on discovering the inhabitants ready to give him a hot reception, and made instead for Rye, a 'soft' target, where much damage was caused.

In spite of some effective reprisal raids on the French coast parliament was growing increasingly restive. But when the king, in October 1339, asked in a message to members how the coast could be protected, they respectfully professed ignorance of the subject, merely recommending that the shore should be policed by local guards, under the direction of duly appointed keepers so long as this involved no public expense. As for strengthening the fleet, it was, argued the Commons, up to the barons of the Cinque Ports, in return for their many privileges, to provide the ships needed, without expecting the nation, who already bore the financial burden of the land forces, to pay their seamen's wages.

Parliament now began, however, to show for the first time that special concern with naval matters which it never subsequently lost and when it met again, in January 1340, agreed to pay half the cost of the 30 ships the Cinque Ports were getting together, not as a precedent but from 'special grace'. The western ports were meanwhile required to find another 70 ships of 100 tons and upwards, partly at the national expense. Southampton was to have a permanent garrison of 50 men-at-arms and 100 archers, with two light pinnaces at their disposal. The Bishop of Winchester, who owned land in the area, was warned to be ready to defend it, and the people of the Isle of Wight told to anticipate more enemy raids, the king's butler being made personally responsible for seeing that the troops holding Carisbrooke Castle were kept supplied with wine and coal.

When parliament assembled on 29 March it readily granted the king an unprecedented 'ninth' for two years, to finance a major ship-building programme and to purchase stores of all kinds, including 32 tons of gunpowder; a large fleet was assembled for a new expedition, artillery being installed on the larger vessels, and food stockpiled at Southampton and Sandwich. Crews, made up to strength when necessary by impress-ment, were recruited, and soldiers, usually about 25 per detachment, assigned to protect them. Conscription even extended to ships' cats, each captain being by law required to carry one, to keep down vermin. Then came alarming intelligence. The largest French fleet ever known was reported to be waiting at Sluys at the mouth of the River Zwin, 400 strong, and including ships of 300 tons or more, with two or even three masts; the standard English merchantman, converted for the moment to naval use, had only one. Edward's admiral of the northern waters confirmed the unwelcome news by a last-minute reconnaissance, while one of Edward's new allies in the Low Countries reported that the French admirals had sworn to deliver him to their true sovereign in Paris, dead or alive.

If Edward was decisively beaten at sea England would be wide open to invasion. His own admiral, Sir Robert Morley, pleaded with him not to take the risk. But Edward was adamant. 'Ye and the archbishop have agreed to tell the same story to prevent my passage; though ye be unwilling, I will go,' he replied, 'and ye who are afraid where there is nothing to fear, may remain at home.' Edward did, however, agree to collect more ships and eventually some 200 were got together.

The English fleet, with Edward nominally in command, sailed from the River Orwell early in the morning of 22 June, making its rendezvous about noon next day ten miles [16 km] west of the mouth of the Sluys, with Sir Robert Morley's 50 vessels, which had sailed independently. Although there are the usual variations in contemporary estimates of the size of the French fleet, from 140 large ships to 400, Edward himself later put the total of major vessels at 190. They included some from Genoa and some Spanish vessels, though the great majority were French.

Edward spent Friday 23 June 1340 deciding on his tactics. 'Anchoring in the sea,' according to the contemporary chronicler Geoffrey le Baker, 'he deliberated the whole day what it would be best to do,' though the explanation he put about was that he did not wish to fight on a Friday, traditionally sacred. By Saturday morning he was ready:

> After nine o'clock, when he had the wind and the sun at his back, and the flow of the tide with him, with his ships divided into three columns, he gave his enemies the challenge they wished for. A terrifying shout rose to heaven above the wooden horses . . . an iron shower of quarrels from crossbows and arrows from long bows brought death to thousands of people; all those who wished or dared to do so fought hand to hand with spears, battle-axes and swords; stones hurled from the turrets of masts dashed on to the brains of many . . . There was joined without any doubt a great and terrible naval battle.
>
> The greatness of the Spanish ships foiled many a stroke of the English, but at last the French ships were overcome and the first contingent of vessels emptied of men, and the English seized the craft. The French ships were chained together, so that they could not be torn from one another; so a few English guarded one group of the captured ships; the others charged the second contingent and with great difficulty thrust home the blow. This contingent was, however, more easily emptied than the first, because the French, deserting their ships, for the most part leapt overboard without resisting. The first and second squadrons of ships were thus captured, and dusk was falling, so the English lay off until morning, because the night was so dark and they were so weary.

As dawn broke over the sea off Sluys the full scale of the English victory became apparent, and Edward did his best to follow it up:

> At daybreak, when the king realized that 30 ships had fled, he sent 40 well-armed ships to follow them, under the command of John Crabbe, who the English accounted very experienced in naval matters and very informed about the French harbours; but what was the effect of

this pursuit is not known . . . The number of warships captured in the main battle . . . amounted to 200 and the number of barges taken was 30. The number of enemy killed and drowned exceeded 25,000; of the English 4000 were slain.

Next day, Sunday 25 June 1340, the leading men of Bruges, vastly relieved that they had backed the right horse, came on board to congratulate Edward and he then went ashore to attend a thankgiving mass, his overwhelming victory being widely interpreted as a divine endorsement of his claims to the French throne. With the French fleet destroyed – the final tally was 230 ships, including most of the largest, captured – England was secure from invasion and on 28 June the king sent the glad news of his success to his son, Edward, Earl of Cornwall, in an affectionate private letter, along with a formal announcement of the victory addressed to the Archbishop of Canterbury and designed to be read publicly, with suitable thanksgiving prayers, by the clergy everywhere:

> You and our other faithful people know with what storms of war we have been and are distracted, and, as in a great sea, tossed about by the boisterous waves. But . . . God our hope, in a hard fought conflict, granted us to prevail, with no small slaughter of the enemy, and the capture of nearly all the said fleet . . . and thus the passage across the sea will hereafter be safer for our faithful people and many other benefits are likely to accrue therefrom . . . whereof the fairest hope already smiles.

Philip VI, if a later English chronicler is to be trusted, learned of the destruction of his fleet in a very different way. His courtiers, not daring to break the news to him direct, arranged for his jester to remark repeatedly on the cowardice of the English and when he asked what his fool meant he received the reply, 'Because they dare not leap into the sea, as our gentlemen of Normandy and France did.'

Edward III, no mean warrior on land, remained inordinately proud of this naval success, and several years later issued to commemorate it his first gold coin, the noble, worth half a mark [6s 8d (0.33p)]. Intended to provide a coin common to England and Flanders, it rapidly came to have a symbolic significance. On the front Edward was shown standing in his flagship, the *Thomas*, with sword and shield, the latter bearing the arms of both France and England; on the back a Latin inscription implied divine support for Edward's claims. 'Jesus crossing,' runs the translation, 'he passed through the midst of them.' A century later the significance of this famous coin was correctly interpreted by an English poet in an equally famous rhyme:

Four things our noble showeth to me,
King, ship, and sword, and power of the sea.

22

DESTROYING THE ENGLISH

And upon this was shown an ordinance made by the enemy . . . to destroy and abolish all the nation and language of the English.

Rolls of Parliament, September 1346

For 20 years after Edward III's great naval victory at Sluys the shores of England remained inviolate. Under papal pressure a peace treaty was signed with France at Malestroit, near Vannes, on 19 January 1343, and when it expired three years later, Edward III launched a major cross-Channel expedition, which landed unopposed at St Vaast de la Hogue on the east side of the Cotentin peninsula, captured Barfleur, from which William the Conqueror had sailed nearly three centuries earlier, and, in the subsequent march along the coast destroyed 61 large ships and many smaller ones. On 26 July 1346, after the first real resistance so far encountered, Caen was captured, yielding an unexpected prize: the plans drawn up for the invasion of England in 1339 or 1340. These were shipped back to England to be read out in parliament in September, and at St Paul's Cross, their impact being increased by misleadingly suggesting that the invasion was contemplated for that very year, instead of six or seven years earlier.

The Rolls of Parliament record how this unusual document, the earliest surviving plan for the invasion of England, was presented to the House, in words calculated to generate patriotism if not panic:

> And upon this was shown an ordinance made by the enemy and various Frenchmen and Normans to destroy and abolish all the nation and language of the English. And to execute his ordinance, the enemy had appointed the Count of Eu and the Chamberlain de Tankerville, with a multitude of men-at-arms, Swiss [i.e. Genevois] and foot soldiers to come over. But, as God wished, the said count and Chamberlain were taken at Caen, and many of their men killed and others captured, so they failed in their plan, thanks be to God.

The operation order which followed, while describing how the troops were to be raised and financed, was suspiciously vague on how the invaders were to get ashore and defeat the enemy army.

The French plan had certainly turned up at a remarkably convenient moment for Edward III, so convenient that some authorities dismiss it as a forgery. If forged, however, it had clearly been done with some care, as the detailed rates of pay which it included indicate, and it seems readily to have been accepted as genuine at the time. Before parliament could meet, however, Edward III at last achieved the major victory he was seeking. At the village of Crécy-en-Ponthieu, ten miles [16 km] north-east of Abbeville, on Saturday 26 August 1346, the two sides finally faced each other in the first of the great land battles of the Hundred Years War. The result demonstrated once again the effectiveness of the English archers, their skill being aided by the weather. A violent thunderstorm left the Genovese crossbowmen with damp bowstrings; the English longbowmen had successfully protected their weapons, while the Genovese found what bolts they did manage to fire falling short. A novelty, its importance missed by both participants and chron- iclers, was the presence of three small cannon, the first field, rather than siege, artillery, dragged all the way from St Vaast. Edward now led his army on towards Calais, which after he had been forced to interrupt the resulting siege to return home to deal with another Scottish offensive, finally capitulated on 4 August 1347. England had henceforward a powerful bulwark against invasion on the far side of the Channel.

During what was nominally a period of truce, fighting never completely stopped, and on New Year's Day 1350 a French captain made a determined attempt to recover Calais by stealth, offering the Italian mercenary Edward had left in command of the galleys there a bribe of 20,000 gold crowns to admit a French force into the courtyard. The Italian took the money but betrayed the plan, which was thwarted by the king in person, dressed as an ordinary knight. That night Edward threw a great feast for his captives, at which the English waited on them and toasted their bravery.

This was the very essence of chivalry, the elaborate code of knightly behaviour epitomized by Edward himself, which helped to encourage men to fight for their country, and other nations to respect the land he ruled. Aptly, perhaps, the whole system rested on a mythical foundation, belief in King Arthur, who was credited with establishing a Round Table of ideal knights – round to demonstrate their equality, with the king as first among equals★. Edward III's personal contribution to the chivalry tradition began with the holding of a Round Table at Windsor

★As pointed out earlier (see page 82) if Arthur did exist he was probably a Romano- British prince fighting to maintain what was left of Roman rule against the Saxon and other invaders.

in 1344. In 1347, probably at a ball to celebrate the fall of Calais, occurred the famous incident, first described 200 years later by Elizabethan chroniclers, when a garter fell off the leg of a lady guest – the queen herself, according to one story, the self-same royal mistress whose attributes kept him in Calais, acording to another. The king thereupon picked the garter up, commenting as he did so: 'Honi soit qui mal y pense': 'Evil be to him who evil thinks', and on his return to England in June 1348, instituted the Order of the Garter, or 'the fraternity of St George', the patron saint of all warriors. Edward now appropriated St George, whose very existence is doubtful, for the English, and the chapel of St George was established at Windsor in August 1348 for the 26 founder members, who wore a blue garter on the right leg and vowed:

> To be united in all chances and various turns of fortune; copartners both in peace and war, assistant to one another in all serious and dangerous exploits; and thro' the whole course of their lives to show fidelity and friendliness one towards another.

Although exploits at sea rated much lower in the knightly scale of values than victories on land, in 1350 Edward III achieved a notable naval success in the affair of *Les Espagnols sur Mer* as it was then known, or 'The Spaniards at Sea' or Battle of Winchelsea, to use its later name. A famous freebooter called Don Carlos de la Cerda had, in November 1349, seized some English wine ships off Bordeaux and murdered their crews and from May 1350 onwards Edward was busy collecting a fleet to secure his revenge. In July la Cerda was at Sluys, boasting, according to the proclamations which Edward sent to the two archbishops on 10 August, that he would destroy the English fleet, obtain dominion over the English sea and then invade England and exterminate its people. The clergy were ordered to mobilize divine support with special services and processions while Edward embarked at Winchelsea with a huge turnout of great lords, among them 400 knights.

The king conducted himself with cheerful insouciance as an eyewitness informed Froissart:

> He was dressed in black velvet and wore on his head a small hat of beaver which became him very much. He was that day as joyous as ever he was in his life, and ordered his minstrels to play before him a German dance, *Sir John Chandos*, which delighted him greatly.

La Cerda's 40 large ships, 'so strong and so handsome,' Froissart was told, 'that it was a pleasure to look at them', greatly outclassed the English fleet of 50 assorted vessels, many of them very small. He also controlled a far larger force of bowmen and infantry, who crowded the decks and 'castles', stocked with great heaps of stones, flints and iron bars. With a north-east wind behind them the Spaniards could have outrun the English ships lying in wait for them but 'by pride and presumption,' it was said, 'they deigned not to pass them by without speaking.'

At 4 o'clock in the afternoon on Sunday 29 August 1350, the lookout on the king's ship, the *Thomas*, hailed the deck below. 'Ho! I see something coming, which seems to be a Spanish ship.' As the minstrels fell silent the same voice reported, 'I see two,' then three, then four, until finally he burst out, 'I see so many as, may God help me, I cannot count them!' The trumpets sounded 'Action stations!', or its medieval equivalent, Edward called for wine and, with his knights, drank a toast to the coming battle, and then they solemnly put on their helmets. The impression of a tournament afloat was heightened by the king's order to the helmsman, 'Lay me against that Spaniard who is coming, for I wish to joust with him' and almost immediately the two ships collided. The shock carried away the mast of Edward's ship, with the men in the 'fighting top', and caused the *Thomas* to spring a leak, but as the Spanish vessel drew away the king shouted, 'Grapple my ship to that, for I wish to have her.' Edward's entourage, knowing the *Thomas* was in a bad way, dissuaded him: 'Let her go, you shall have a better' – and so he did. The next Spaniard which approached was grappled, boarded and captured, whereupon the king moved across to her and made her his flagship.

This success set the pattern for what followed and there was an almost equally famous action involving the king's 20-year-old-son, Edward, Prince of Wales, 'the Black Prince', so called for the colour of his armour, who was accompanied by his ten-year-old brother, the future John of Gaunt. The princes' ship was badly holed and men were pouring onto it from the Spanish vessel grappled to it, when rescue arrived in the nick of time as the Earl of Lancaster attacked the Spaniard on its other quarter, leading the boarding party with stirring shouts of 'Derby to the rescue!' Then, like his father before him, the prince abandoned his sinking ship, its decks awash, for the enemy one which rapidly surrendered, 'not one' of its crew, it was recorded, 'being taken to mercy'; dead, wounded and prisoners alike being flung overboard, as, curiously, the rules of chivalry permitted.

To mark the occasion, and perhaps to demonstrate the enhanced status of naval warfare, Edward now raised 'eighty noble imps', as the Elizabethan chronicler John Stow describes them, to the order of knighthood, while the verse-chronicler Laurence Minot, with more patriotism than poetic talent, described the trouncing of the Spanish fleet at Winchelsea as he had that of the French at Sluys:

Brave men with their weapons
And worthily clad,
Their deeds all forgotten
Are suddenly sad.
They sail in the sea-ways
The fishes to feed,
Many fishes they feed,
Despite every great deed . . .
Boy with thy black beard,
I advise you begin
To seek heaven's forgiveness
For your recent sin
Make war on England
And you'll never win.*

In the summer of 1355 the war with France was resumed after peace negotiations had broken down. A year later the armies of the two nations faced each other at the battle of Poitiers, on 19 September 1356, fought in fact at the village of Maupertus six miles [10 Km] to the south-east of that town. Once more victory went, decisively, to the English and to the Black Prince, who was undoubtedly the hero of the occasion, for the battle ended with the inglorious flight of his 'opposite number', the 19-year-old heir to the French throne, Charles, the Dauphin, and the capture of the French king John II, an unheard-of prize. He was taken back in triumph to Bordeaux, and in May 1357 was led by his captor through the streets of London to splendid lodgings in the borrowed riverside palace of the Savoy.

In October 1359 yet another English expedition landed at Calais, followed in November by the king himself. Edward planned to have himself crowned King of France at Rheims, packing a gold crown in his luggage for the purpose, but found its gates barred against him.

The French now showed that they were far from beaten by a sudden descent on England. Edward had half-anticipated this might happen and, before he left, parliament had voted a special tax to maintain a fleet at sea and the militia had been alerted. On 2 March 1360 a general muster was ordered, since a French fleet was cruising unchallenged in the Channel, apparently making for Southampton, Portsmouth or Sandwich. The Council's inglorious response was to order that all vessels should be drawn up above high-water mark, to make it harder for the French to remove them, and the attack when it came, on 15 March

*This is my very free rendering of Minot's text but retains his original rhyme scheme. 'Blackbeard' was not present at Winchelsea but the name had become a synonym for 'pirate'.

1360, was on Winchelsea. Like the raid on Southampton 22 years before, it was delivered on a Sunday morning while most of the inhabitants were at mass. This time the church was stormed and a gang of French soldiers raped and murdered the most attractive young woman present in front of the rest of the terrified congregation. Nine other women were carried off, never to be heard of again. The French succeeded in landing cavalry as well as infantry, and men, women and children were all butchered without mercy or exposed to even more hideous atrocities. Too late, the defenders arrived and drove the intruders back to their ships, with the loss it was said, though the figure seems very high, of 400 men.

The raid on Winchelsea, delivered while the enemy king was actually a prisoner on English soil, caused something like panic among council and public alike. Every large ship in the vulnerable southern ports was immediately requisitioned and sent to patrol the seas west of the Thames estuary, equipped with 40 seamen, 60 archers and 40 other soldiers, while vessels already in Flanders were summoned back for home defence. Troops were raised in the Midland counties and sent to London, while several castles in the south – at Old Sarum and Malmesbury, a fair way inland, as well as at Pevensey and Southampton on the coast – were made ready for action. To make his rescue more difficult, the royal prisoner, John II, was moved from Somerton to Berkhampsted, and then to the Tower, though accorded every respect and comfort.

In October 1360 he was released, with great ceremony, on payment of the first instalment of his unprecedented ransom of three million gold crowns (£500,000). He was not at liberty for long, for his second son, left behind as a hostage till the balance of the ransom was paid, broke his parole and escaped, and his father insisted on returning in his place, so that he died in exile in London in April 1364.

In 1360 English prestige in Europe reached its peak. 'When the noble Edward gained England in his youth,' wrote the French chronicler Jean le Bel, 'nobody thought much of the English . . . Now they are the finest and most daring warriors known to man.' Parliament, so often critical of the costly military aspirations of past monarchs, was fulsome in its praise. 'Sire,' the knights of the shire and burgesses resolved, 'from their hearts entirely thank God who has given them such a lord and governor, who had delivered them from servitude to other lands and . . . from the charges suffered by them in time past.' Even the ordinary man outside Parliament was touched by the glory Edward had brought to all things English. 'To live,' wrote an ecstatic chronicler, 'was as if to reign; and his fame sprang so far that it came into heathendom and Barbary, showing and telling that in no land under heaven has been brought forth so noble a king.'

High noon must, alas, be followed by evening. In 1369 the war with France was officially resumed, following French incursions into English provinces on the Continent. Once again invasion seemed likely; on 20 March 1369 men between the ages of 16 and 60 were ordered to equip themselves to defend the realm, and on 28 April a new admiral was appointed for the fleet to the west of the Thames, and sailors began to be impressed for the king's principal ships. On 15 August 1369 troops were indeed ordered to be sent to the Isle of Wight and the Southampton area, but the French instead, probably around mid-September, struck against Portsmouth, burning whatever of the town remained, or had been rebuilt, after earlier raids. Enemy raids had now become such a routine affair that no English chronicler even recorded the event; it is known only from a reference in a contemporary letter to the inability of the inhabitants to pay the usual rent to the crown. Thereafter matters got no better; three years later the population were exempted from taxation altogether because of the frequent devastation of their town.

At sea, where earlier in the reign success had followed success, the power of England was now visibly waning. In July 1370 a force of 30 French vessels, half of them galleys, landed at Gosport and set fire to it and troops were hastily ordered to Dover, where a full-scale invasion was anticipated. Between September and November 1370 invasion panic again gripped the country. The year 1371 began alarmingly, with urgent measures to defend the Isle of Wight, in January, and the mustering of a fleet at King's Lynn, followed by a statement to parliament on 17 February that the king of France had assembled a fleet strong enough to sweep the English navy from the seas and then to bring men to occupy England. In April 1372 another invasion alarm developed. A trusted nobleman was ordered to set up his headquarters in Kent to organize the nobility to repel an attack, and in June the troops were called out, though the enemy failed to appear. In August came the near-capture of Guernsey, allegedly by a Welshman, Evan, who claimed to be the son of a Welsh prince whom Edward had put to death, but was probably an impostor. With the help of 3000 French troops Evan defeated the governor of the island and might well have seized Cornet Castle, where the governor had taken refuge, had he not been summoned back to help his own ally the King of Castile.

Parliament was already more navy-minded than the court and after granting another subsidy to enable the king to keep a fleet at sea, the Commons delivered, in November 1372, a grand remonstrance against the recent neglect of the nation's defences at sea:

Twenty years since, and always before that time, the navy of the realm was so noble and so plentiful in all ports, maritime towns and rivers, that the whole country deemed and called our Lord 'KING OF THE SEA' and he and all his country were the more dreaded both by sea and land on account of the said navy. And now it was so decreased and weakened from divers causes, that there was hardly sufficient to defend the country in case of need . . . whence there was great danger to the realm.

Little seems to have been done to put matters right and Genoese war galleys had to be hired to protect the coast against the expected arrival, in the winter of 1372-3, of a combined French and Spanish force, which was expected to include the ubiquitous Evan of Wales among its commanders. In the event it never appeared, but there was another invasion alarm in April 1373, sufficiently serious for the Bishop of Winchester to be instructed to arm his clergy and muster them at Southampton and the adjoining towns. Once again the enemy fleet failed to show up, but, even though on 27 June 1375, a one-year truce with France, later extended, had been concluded at Bruges, coastal defence measures were again ordered in March and April 1376.

From now on it was downhill all the way. Almost senile, Edward fell under the sway of a universally hated and unscrupulous mistress, and in June 1376 his famous heir, the Black Prince, died of the most unromantic of ailments, dropsy. A year later, on 21 June 1377, Edward himself was dead. Few reigns had seen so sharp a decline from a promising beginning, as an Elizabethan chronicler adapting a fourteenth-century original, commented:

Then folk thought that a new sun was rising over England, for the abundance of peace, the plenty of possessions, and the glory of victory . . . As in his beginning all things were joyful . . . when he drew into age . . . good fortune and prosperity decreased and mishapped, and unfortunate things . . . with many evils, began . . . and, the more harm is, continued long time after.

23
A JOURNEY TO ENGLAND

The major part of the knights of France expressed themselves thus: 'Why don't we for once make a journey to England?'

Froissart's Chronicle, *describing 1386*

Hardly had the body of Edward III been laid to rest in Westminster Abbey than England was subjected to the worst series of French attacks that it had ever experienced. The moment the existing truce expired on 24 June 1377 a fleet of 100 galleys set out from Harfleur, assisted by the Spaniards, taking revenge for John of Gaunt's intervention in Castile. Froissart, though he confuses this with a second expedition a little later, describes the raid which followed:

On the feast of Saints Peter and Paul [i.e. 29 June] the French landed at Rye, a port in the county of Sussex, near the borders of Kent, a fair-sized town of fishermen and sailors. They pillaged and burnt the whole town, then took to their ships and sailed off towards Southampton, without, however, approaching it. As they sailed along the coast of England, Jean de Vienne and Jean de Rye, the French admirals, and the Spanish admiral, harried the land and made every effort to force a landing for their own advantage. They came shortly before a considerable town near the sea called Lewes, where there is a very rich priory. The people of the surrounding country had taken refuge there with the prior . . . The Earl of Salisbury and his brother were unable to get there in time, because of the rough roads and difficult going between Lewes and the country they were in.

The French reached the port [i.e. Newhaven, the port for Lewes] which they entered in formation, bringing their ships as close to the land as they could; they effected their landing in spite of the English defenders . . . As they entered Lewes there was a deal of fighting, and many French were wounded by arrows; but they were so numerous that they drove back their enemies, who gathered in a convenient square in front of the monastery to await the foe approaching in close order for a hand-to-hand fight. Many noble feats of arms were performed on both sides, and the English defended themselves very well considering their number, for they were very few in comparison with the French. For this reason they exerted themselves all the more, while the French were all the more eager to inflict losses on them. Finally the French conquered the town and dislodged the English; two hundred of them were killed and a large number of the more important men taken prisoner . . . the prior and the two knights were also taken. The whole town of Lewes was ransacked and burnt or destroyed, together with some small villages round about. By high tide the French were already back in their ships and they set sail with their booty and their prisoners.

The coronation of the ten-year-old Richard, son of the dead Black Prince, on 16 July 1377, was overshadowed by the grim reports from the coast:

When the news reached London, where all the country was assembled to crown the young King Richard, everyone was horror-struck and they all said: 'We must hasten to crown our king, and then set off against these French before they do further damage.' . . . Immediately after the ceremony orders were made for some to go to Dover to guard the straits, and some to other parts; the Earl of Cambridge and his brother the Earl of Buckingham were to go to Dover, with a good four hundred men-at-arms and six hundred archers, whilst the Earl of Salisbury and Sir John Montagu his brother went to . . . Poole with two hundred men-at-arms and three hundred archers.

Four days after the coronation the French sacked Folkestone, followed by Portsmouth and then – inaugurating an era when the western ports became their chief targets – paid brief but destructive calls on Dartmouth and Plymouth. By early August de Vienne was back in Harfleur, but after only a short rest the fleet, around the middle of the month, set out again. The attacks now entered a new and more serious phase, with the realization of a long-standing nightmare, the use of Britain's largest offshore island as an enemy base, as Froissart records: 'The French . . . had landed in the Isle of Wight and set up camp there with their cavalry to launch attacks on the coast.'

The landing on the Isle of Wight had been anticipated. All those owning land there had been ordered to return to it by 1 April, and the keeper of Carisbrooke Castle had been forbidden to allow anyone already on the island to leave even to attend the justices' court. On 7 August the Bishop of Winchester formally summoned the clergy on the island to take up arms. Nevertheless the French, again under Jean de Vienne, and the Spaniards, commanded by Juan de Raux, successfully got ashore on 21 August 1377.

The French disembarked unopposed on the north coast and rapidly overran most of the island, which measures approximately 23 miles [37 km] from east to west and about 13 [21 km] north to south. Newport, in the very centre, was so badly damaged that it remained uninhabited for the next two years, documents were looted from Arreton, midway between there and Sandown on the south-east shore, Newtown, near the north-west coast, was destroyed, and the church at Yarmouth, near the narrowest stretch of the Solent, burned. Elsewhere the islanders are said by the chronicler Thomas Walsingham to have paid 1000 marks 'protection money' to stop their homes being burned, and the only place which put up an effective resistance was Carisbrooke Castle, which remained in English hands even when the rest of the island had been occupied.

The French fleet now felt secure enough to attack Winchelsea and Southampton, but here they received their first rebuff, as Froissart describes:

> They calculated to arrive there on the next tide, and reached the harbour, where they gave signs of making a large landing. But Sir John Arundel and his men were informed of their arrival, having watched them at sea making for the harbour, and were drawn up in armed array to meet them. There was a small skirmish, and the French, realizing that they would make little advance, withdrew to their ships, and sailed along the coast of England towards Dover.

Resistance was, at last, beginning to stiffen as the French soon discovered:

> Their course brought them . . . to Poole, which is an important town, and there they tried to make a landing; but William Montagu, Earl of Salisbury, and his brother John, had drawn their men up in battle order and were ready for them. Another small skirmish ensued, of no great importance, and the French took to sea again and sailed back along the coast towards Dover. Several coastal villages in these parts would have been burnt and despoiled, had the Earl of Salisbury not followed them along the coast with his cavalry; for whenever they made a show of landing the earl was there beforehand to defend the coast, showing the French that he had valiant and disciplined men-at-arms to preserve the honour of their country.

Events at Dover finally confirmed that the defence was now beginning to gain the upper hand:

> All the English from round about were assembled at Dover, where

the two uncles of the king, the Earls of Cambridge and Buckingham, were stationed with a good four hundred lance and eight hundred archers, and they would gladly have seen the French come in to make a landing there. They had agreed not to oppose a landing, so that they could more readily engage battle, for they considered themselves strong enough to deal with the French; they therefore remained quietly in battle order within the town, from where they saw Jean de Vienne's fleet coming straight towards Dover with the tide. All the English were overjoyed to see them approach and to know there would be a fight; but when the French had come close to the entrance of the harbour they decided not to make a landing there and sailed on the tide to Calais, where they anchored.

When Parliament met on 3 October 1377 the chancellor, the Archbishop of Canterbury, announced that the main reason it had been summoned was the need to provide for the future safety of the realm. 'The kingdom,' the speaker of the Commons agreed, 'had . . . lately suffered great infamy and outrage from the enemy in different parts, and would probably suffer more unless God provided a remedy in its government.' The members attributed this, he explained, to the neglect of chivalry in recent years, and voicing a familiar grievance, to the government's attempts to assemble a fleet instead of leaving it to the merchants. The king, the Commons were assured, would take the advice of his great council, but in practice all that was done was to resort to the old tactic of reprisal raids, which, even if successful, merely prompted more counter-attacks.

At the end of June 1378 John of Gaunt's fleet sailed from Dover and Sandwich for Brittany but in September, after quarrelling with his subordinate commander, the Duke came ingloriously home. As his venture had only been financed by heavy new taxation, including a poll-tax of 4d [2p] a head, public disappointment was acute and dissatisfaction mounted still higher when a number of Spanish galleys were able to attack Cornwall unchallenged. Fowey, about 20 miles [32 km] west of Plymouth Sound, although much smaller, rivalled Plymouth in the number of ships based there and in the still smaller ports that lay on either side of it:* Looe and Polperro to the east, towards Plymouth, Par and Mevagissey to the west, towards Falmouth. Fowey was protected by two castles, a longbow shot apart, on either side of the narrow river entrance, but lacked a protective wall and the enemy may have stormed the town from the landward side. All that is known for certain is that during the summer of 1378 it was set on fire and that other Cornish

---

*Fowey sent 47 ships and 770 men on the Crecy expedition in 1346, Plymouth 26 ships and 603 men.

towns, unidentified by the chroniclers, were raided. All this led up to an alas all-too-familiar complaint from the whole Commons:

> In times past the land of England was so well furnished with a navy, as well large ships as small, that the country had been thereby greatly enriched, and surrounding nations greatly intimidated. But since the beginning of the war with France the navy had been so often seized for expeditions to France and elsewhere, that the owners of the ships had suffered such heavy losses and expenses, . . . without receiving any compensation from the king or the realm, that many of them were utterly ruined, and the navy almost destroyed throughout England, to the great damage of the king, the complete impoverishment of the owners of the ships, and to the great satisfaction of all the enemies of England.

During 1379 the French were known to have seven large barges under construction, with 14 others enjoying a major refit; Richard II's fleet at this time – as distinct from the privately-owned ships requisitioned for national purposes – numbered only five. In January 1380 the government at last agreed that the owners of such vessels should receive adequate compensation, but around June an expedition to Brittany could only be mounted thanks to the generosity of the London merchant John Philpott, who not only paid for some of the troops concerned to redeem their armour, pawned for food, but provided several of the vessels to carry them across the Channel. Ships for home defence were non-existent. The citizens of Hull and Newcastle found themselves, in spite of the heavy taxation of recent years, forced to equip warships at their own expense to keep the approaches to their ports clear. The summer brought the usual melancholy tale of coastal raids. Winchelsea was again for a time in enemy hands and though the Abbot of Battle hurried to its defence he was repulsed. Gravesend, half-way up the Thames towards London, was sacked and burned. Eventually the French and Spaniards overreached themselves. On 10 June 1380 they were routed, with Irish help, off Kinsale in County Cork while attempting to raid Ireland, the admiral of France and 20 of his ships, including many previously taken from the English as prizes, being captured. This rare victory, however, failed to prevent continuing minor descents on the south coast, now too routine an affair for the chroniclers to provide details, but when parliament met in November, the Chancellor called for a large subsidy for galleys to prevent a similar experience in the coming year.

The year 1381 saw the great Peasants Revolt, sparked off by the poll tax. The rising broke out in June and was rapidly quelled, but for a month the government was barely in control in southern England and

East Anglia. The peasants' leaders remained, however, patriots first and rebels second, for at the very height of the disturbances they ordered their supporters in the coastal districts of Kent, the county most affected, not to leave their homes to march on London for fear of a French attack. The Speaker of the Commons, explaining the revolt to the subsequent parliamentary inquest, singled out the government's failure to protect the coast as one of its principal causes. 'The common people,' he complained, 'have not been succoured against the enemies of the realm; for they and their homes have been pillaged and robbed and burned . . . for which no remedy has been or is yet provided.'

Throughout the 1380s the French remained in command of the Channel. In 1381 they managed to reach the very heart of the Solent and sail up the River Medina as far as Newport in the centre of the Isle of Wight, where they wrecked the priory of St Cross and destroyed its watermill. In 1382 the Abbott of Quarr and Rector of Arreton were ordered to see that all its clergy, aged from 16 to 60, should be ready armed to defend it, though a force of men-at-arms was also permanently stationed in the island; the captain of Carisbrooke received £45 for their wages in November 1384, and £26 to reimburse him for his payments to its six gunners, each responsible for eight cannon between them. Dover Castle in May 1385 rated 12 guns, with 100 lbs of newly-purchased powder and 120 stone cannon balls presumably to supplement those already in stock. Rye put its faith in more traditional means. Its fortifications were restored from the proceeds of a levy of 3d [1.5p] on every boatload of fish landed in Kent and Sussex, and a permanent watch was mounted in the Ypres Tower. When the alarm was given by the great bell hung in Watchbell Street, the local defenders were required to heat up the *machicoulis*, a fearsome mixture of molten lead and boiling oil, and to prepare the flaming tow and powdered lime which would be poured and dropped through holes in the ceiling on any intruders who broke into the ground floor of the Tower.

A truce with France, from 26 January 1384, was extended until 1 May 1385, though broken by the usual conflicts at sea, whose perpetrators could always be disowned as 'pirates', and by a raid, of which no details survive, on the Isle of Wight. Around this time, there was an attack on Stonor [or Stonar] on the Kent coast, opposite Sandwich at the mouth of the Stour, notable for the vigorous defence – which did not save the town from being burned – led by the Abbot of St Augustine's Priory, Canterbury. During 1384 the French also sent an advance party of troops to Scotland as the first step towards the invasion on two fronts of which they had always dreamed.

On 1 May 1385 hostilities were resumed with both Scotland and France. This new phase of the war began with the English being

outmanoeuvred at sea. While Richard's fleet was looking for him elsewhere in the Channel Admiral de Vienne got safely out of Sluys and
across the North Sea to Leith where he unloaded 1200 suits of armour,
1000 'lances', i.e. men armed with these weapons, and other military
stores, along with large sums of money, and the 'auld alliance' was
reconsummated in a joint Franco-Scottish raid into Northumberland.
The usual 'harrying' took place as far as Morpeth, when the Scots
insisted on retiring, much to the disgust of the French, on hearing that
an English army was approaching.

In March 1386 Richard II formally recognized his uncle John of Gaunt
as King of Castile, and in July Gaunt set sail from Plymouth to seek his
kingdom, and, incidentally, pose a powerful threat to France's southern
flank. His departure removed from England her most experienced
commander and 7000 of the country's best troops just as a major attack
on her shores again became a very real danger.

Rumours of an impending French invasion had begun to circulate in
May 1386 but it was only in August that it was realized that Charles VI
had cast himself in the role of a new William of Normandy. The new
Count of Flanders, Philip, Duke of Burgundy, was also hostile to
England. A passionate desire to avenge the humiliations suffered at the
hands of Edward III now swept the French court and aristocracy, as
Froissart makes clear:

> The young King Charles had a great desire to invade England with a
> large force of ships and men, in which he was supported by all the
> knights and squires of France, particularly by his uncle the Duke of
> Burgundy [and] the Constable of France . . . These lords, with the
> major part of the knights of France, expressed themselves thus: 'Why
> don't we for once make a journey to England to see the country and
> the people to get to know our way about, just as the English in their
> time have done in France?'

Froissart, like all the other chroniclers, stresses the vast scale of the
preparations, more thorough even than those of 1066:

> Thus it happened that in the year 1386 the largest and finest ships ever
> known in France were constructed, with the double purpose of
> breaking the force of the Duke of Lancaster in Galicia and Castile by
> causing his men to be withdrawn thence, and of instilling fear into the
> hearts of the English when they learned how the French could wage
> war . . . All that summer until the month of September they were
> busy milling flour and baking bread and biscuit in Tournay, Lille,
> Douai, Arras, Amiens, Bethune, Saint-Omer and all the towns in the
> neighbourhood of Sluys, for it was the intention of the king and his

council to embark at Sluys and from there invade England and lay waste the country. The richest men in France were taxed a third or a quarter of their wealth to provide sufficient ships for this expedition. Many of the poorer folk paid more than their income to provide the cost of men-at-arms. From Seville in Spain as far as Prussia there was no ship of any size on which the French could lay their hands but it was commandeered for the king and his men . . .

Anyone who was at that time at Bruges, Damme or Sluys would have seen how busily they were filling the ships large and small with trusses of hay in barrels, biscuit in bags, garlic, onions, peas, beans, barley, oats, wheat, wax candles, tallow candles, hose, shoes, long-boots, boots, spurs, knives, axes, wedges, picks, mattocks, wooden pegs, boxfuls of ointment, tow, bandages, quilts for sleeping on, horsehoes and shoeing nails, bottles of verjuice [i.e. the juice of unripe fruit] and bottles of vinegar, goblets, drinking-horns, bowls of tin and wood, candlesticks, basins, earthenware pots, kitchen implements, butlers' utensils and tools for every other kind of job imaginable to serve mankind, all packed in barrels or some other container. Anyone seeing all this would have been so entranced and oblivious of every-thing else that if he had a fever or the toothache he would have forgotten his malady . . . To judge by the conversation of one Frenchman to another, they thought England would be ruined beyond measure, all the men slain and the children under military age brought to France in slavery.

Charles VI displayed great energy in overcoming the usual bottleneck in any large-scale invasion, finding the necessary shipping:

From St John's Day [presumably 27 December 1385] men were sent into Holland, Zeeland, Middelburgh, Dordrecht, and all the other ports on the sea or estuaries to gather all the large ships that could be useful, and all were brought to Sluys . . . Never since the beginning of time had so many great ships been seen together as there were that year in the harbour of Sluys and off the coast between there and Blankenberge, for in September they numbered 87; their masts seemed like a huge forest reflected in the sea. This was without counting the ships of the Constable, Sir Olivier de Clisson, who was preparing his own fleet at Tréguier in Brittany.

The Constable of France was also responsible for the one great innovation of the expedition:

At the same time he was having constructed in Brittany a palisade of heavy timbers, to be set up wherever they chose when they had landed in England, so that the lords could withdraw there for the night, and avoid the danger of alarms and disturbances. When they moved from one place to another this 'town' was so constructed that it was joined by pivots . . . and could be reassembled section by section. A large force of carpenters had designed and constructed it and . . . they were retained at a very high wage.

This pre-fabricated house–cum–castle fascinated other writers besides Froissart and Thomas of Walsingham describes it as being 20 feet [6 m] high and 3000 paces long, with towers ten feet [3 m] higher at regular intervals, each capable of holding ten gunners. The cost must have been enormous but by now the French nobility were eagerly outdoing each other in the ostentation of their contributions:

Meanwhile preparations were being continued at Bruges, Damme and Sluys, the like of which were never known in the memory of man or recorded history. Money was no more spared than if it had rained from the skies or been drawn up from the sea. The chief barons of France had sent their men to Sluys to prepare and load their ships and provide them with everything that was needed, for they all wanted to go across with the army. The king, young as he was, was more anxious to do so than all the others . . . All the great lords made a common effort to stock their ships well and to have them painted and coloured, emblazoning them each with their own arms and devices. The painters had a fine time of it . . . The masts were painted from top to bottom, and some, in a display of magnificence, were covered with gold leaf, the arms of the owner being fixed at the head.

The government was singularly slow to respond to a major threat to the homeland; even if Calais was, as ministers suspected, intended to be the initial target its fall was all too likely to be followed by a cross-Channel assault of vast dimensions. On 9 July the noblemen who were to muster the men-at-arms and archers to serve under the two admirals responsible for maritime defence were nominated, but it was only on 9 August 1386 that a commander, the Earl of Arundel, was appointed for the defence of Kent and Sussex, followed by similar appointments for other counties. There was, however, no real sense of urgency, and the most widespread precautionary measure, if cheap, was of a distinctly unmartial kind: 'In the cities and large towns, processions of bishops and congregations were ordered to be held three times a week in a spirit of devout contrition; prayers were offered to God to deliver the country from this peril.'

During September orders were issued for ships at Great Yarmouth to stay within the chains protecting the port, and later that month vessels elsewhere were seized for home defence. Troops were collected for the south-east from other parts of the country but the funds raised were inadequate to pay them and they were soon roaming the home counties in search of food and loot. Above all what was lacking was firm and inspiring leadership from the top. Richard II was still, at 19, hopelessly immature and totally dominated by a group of unpopular ministers and extravagant favourites.

Parliament, when it met on 1 October 1386, was unwilling to vote the necessary funds unless the king agreed to change his ministers. Richard replied intemperately 'that he would not remove the meanest scullion of his kitchen at their bidding' and talked wildly of treason. The Lords and Commons retorted by pointed references to the fate of Edward II and in the end Richard was forced to replace his chancellor and treasurer and submit to the supervision of an eleven-man council acceptable to parliament. With a new government in office, belated preparations were at last made to defend the country, as Froissart records:

> Orders were now given for the protection of all English ports where it was thought the French might attempt a landing. The Earl of Salisbury, because his lands stretched to that part of the coast opposite the Isle of Wight, which faces out to Normandy . . . was ordered to that island with men and archers from the county of Chester. The Earl of Devon was to guard the haven of Southampton, with 200 men-at-arms and 600 archers. The Earl of Northumberland was to guard the port of Rye with the same numbers; the Earl of Cambridge was sent to Dover with 500 men-at-arms and 1200 archers, while his brother the Earl of Buckingham went to Sandwich with 600 men-at-arms and 1200 archers. The Earls of Stafford and Pembroke were to guard the port of Orwell with 500 men-at-arms and 1200 archers. Sir Henry Percy and his brother Sir Raoul Percy were ordered to Yarmouth with 300 men-at-arms and 600 archers . . . Every harbour from the Humber to Cornwall was garrisoned with men-at-arms and archers, or their garrisons increased.
>
> Guards were posted on all the hills overlooking coasts opposite France and Flanders. They had Gascony wine-casks filled with sand and fastened one on top of the other, and on the topmost was constructed a platform where there were men looking out to sea by day and by night; from this position they could command a view of seven or more leagues. These guards had orders that if they saw the French navy approaching the coast of England they were to light a fire and torches on the spot, and large beacon fires on the hill-tops to warn the people to assemble in the place where the fires were lit. Orders were also given that the King of France and his men should be allowed to land unmolested and to remain on English soil for three or

four days; before any attack was to be made, they were to go and destroy all the French ships and their provisions. After which they would still not engage the French in battle, but harass their army so that they could not go foraging . . . All the productive land would first have been laid waste . . . In this way the French would be starved and destroyed without battle . . . The bridge at Rochester was ordered to be destroyed . . . There were gathered in England at that time 100,000 archers* and 5000 men-at-arms in spite of the great army that had been taken to Castile by the Duke of Lancaster.

No doubt the total strength mentioned by Froissart was exaggerated; the detailed dispositions he mentions add up to 6800 men. But the priority given to archers seems probable enough and here, for the first time was a coherent, pre-planned strategy, even if a questionable one; if the French army was as well furnished with stores as contemporary accounts suggest, the English 'scorched earth' policy would have been slow to take effect. Had the French arrived, as intended, in mid-August, the crops would still have been standing in the fields. By early October the nation's wheat was safely under cover and could readily have been moved inland.

Still the great fleet was not quite ready. One of the king's uncles, the Duke of Berry, remained in his own country making his preparations and that ingenious pioneer of prefabrication, Sir Olivier de Clisson, 'was still in Brittany, ordering the preparation of his fleet at Tréguier, and especially the portable fortifications in wood.' Whether or not the English knew why the French were delayed is uncertain, but a rudimentary system did exist for collecting information about enemy dispositions and intentions and was operated by the very type of scholar-soldier for whom military intelligence work seemed designed. Sir Simon Burley, now aged around 50, was much respected in the world of chivalry and had fought alongside the Black Prince, but was also a man of learning; he had served Richard II as his personal tutor, and later had become chamberlain of his household. Burley at least had no doubt of the seriousness of the danger from France:

> Sir Simon Burley, as governor of Dover Castle, was in a position to receive news from France through the men in Calais or through English fishermen who had often to go as far as Boulogne or Wissant [ten miles [16 km] south-west of Calais] to get good fishing. They brought information back to Sir Simon at his request, for French fishermen they met at sea would readily tell them all they knew – and

*This 'rounding up of the figure is typical of the unreliability of medieval chroniclers when estimating the size of an army.

even more than they knew; whatever war may be afoot between the two countries, fishermen would not engage in any hostilities, but would help each other if need arose and sell fish to the other at sea if one had a better catch . . . From the Dover fishermen Sir Simon Burley learned that the King of France was certain to come and that the French would indeed make landings, one at Dover and the other at Sandwich, in great numbers. Sir Simon believed all these reports, which were also accepted throughout England.

The real reason why the original target date of mid-August, itself quite late in the invasion season, was missed and why thereafter one postponement followed another, was simply that, as other would-be conquerors had already discovered, mounting a cross-Channel expedition was more formidable than it seemed. The problem of finding enough shipping had, however, been triumphantly overcome. According to Froissart 'when their ships had been taken the Dutch and the Zeelanders said: "If you want us to support and serve you, you must pay now or we will not budge" ' and 'They were paid at once.' He put the overall total, with suspicious precision, at 1387, while another chronicler, the Monk of St Denys, estimating the number at more than 900, noted that they were mainly long vessels with prows and two sails, i.e. much larger than the normal coastal cob or barge. They offered, too, evidence of that ingenuity which marked all the best invasion attempts, some of the larger ships, designed to carry horses, having doors cut in the stern for easier loading and disembarkation.

After, in early October, Charles VI reached Sluys all those assembled there were anxious to set off, especially as the days were growing shorter and the Channel was likely to become rougher:

> In Flanders and Artois they kept saying: 'The king will embark on Saturday, or Thursday, or Wednesday.' Every day of the week it was reported: 'He will sail tomorrow, or the day after that.' Several . . . great lords of France stayed in Bruges in order to have better lodgings, and went now and then to Sluys to find out from the king when they should embark. They were told: 'In three, or four, days; or when the Duc de Berry has arrived; or when the wind is favourable.' There was always some excuse, and all the time the weather was getting worse; the days grew shorter and colder, the nights longer and many lords grew discontented at the delay in embarking, for provisions were running short.

The key role, however, in deciding the fate of the expedition was played not by the weather, since the wind was bound to change eventually, but by the Duc de Berry who, having spent five years in England as a hostage, was considered an authority on all things English. He seems all along to have been half-hearted about the invasion, and at a council of war called by the king, around the end of October, effectively killed off the whole huge and costly enterprise:

> Turning to his brother, the Duke of Burgundy, he addressed himself only to him and said: 'If you would wish to make such an expedition as this for which we are here assembled, it should be done not in winter but in the summer, when the sea is calm and the weather fair, and when the horses can have the grass of the fields for fodder . . . My advice is that we should go no further with our plans at this late season, but reassemble the fleet and all our men here or at Harfleur next summer.'

When the news that the great invasion was finally off reached London 'great festivities were arranged to which were invited all the lords who had been in charge of the defences at the harbours and coasts,' the start of a City tradition of honouring successful military commanders. At Christmas Richard II held his own feast at which he created two of his uncles Dukes, of York and Gloucester respectively, so that they now ranked with the great John of Gaunt, Duke of Lancaster.

Although the cynics declared that the whole invasion scare had been a put-up job to bring Gaunt back from Castile the public as a whole were delighted to have seen off the French without a battle: 'The feasting continued with great revelry, for all the people of England believed that they had been saved from great danger . . . Many . . . declared that they would never fear the vainglory of the French.'

During the summer the French again went through the motions of planning to invade England, This time a joint landing was said to be contemplated, with the Constable of France, apparently without his prefabricated fortress, leading 4000 men-at-arms and 2000 archers from Sluys to Orwell in Suffolk, while another army sailed under the Admiral of France from Harfleur to Dover. The council took the threat sufficiently seriously to issue orders, on 14 and 26 July, to 'arrest' – i.e. keep in harbour for possible anti-invasion duties – all ships between Southampton and Mousehole in Cornwall, and on 3 August 1387 appointed as captain of the men-at-arms and archers in the fleet the most famous young soldier of the day, Sir Henry Percy, son of the Earl of Northumberland and already, at 23, a Knight of the Garter, better known as Harry 'Hotspur'. He had little to do for the whole venture collapsed, the Constable's chief supporters somewhat feebly exclaiming, 'Our expedition is at an end; let us hasten to Paris and learn what the king would have us do,' which was apparently nothing.

One military problem remained; Ireland was still unsettled, a perpetual threat to English security. In October 1394 after a slow progress through Wales and a crossing from Haverfordwest Richard landed at Waterford with a large army designed to overawe rebellious elements in the country. In May 1395 he was, however, recalled, most unwillingly, to London by the council, concerned about a possible new rising in Scotland and, it seems likely, the spread of Wycliffism (though John Wycliffe himself had died in 1384) and Lollardry★. Both, challenging as they did the wealth and authority of the church, posed a major threat to civil stability and international peace. Later, anti-papal sentiment was to become patriotic but for the moment heresy was akin to treason. Meanwhile, however, another important source of national strength was already emerging, in the English language. Although the court remained bilingual Richard II probably spoke English for preference.

After his return from Ireland Richard II became increasingly despotic. When in March 1399 John of Gaunt died, Richard went back on an earlier promise and declared all his vast estates forfeit to the crown, thereby depriving his son Henry, now Duke of Lancaster, whom he had already banished abroad, of his inheritance. It was a provocative act, generating much sympathy for its victim, and Richard seems by now to have been degenerating into megalomania. He would sit for hours on a lofty throne, silently watching all around him, and requiring any who caught his eye to genuflect. But, regardless of the discontent he was leaving behind, on 29 May 1399 Richard II set sail from Milford Haven for Ireland, determined to suppress a major rising by the King of Leinster.

The Irish campaign which began at Waterford on 31 May 1399 proved a disaster and ended abruptly on 10 July, when a messenger arrived with an alarming dispatch: Henry of Lancaster, whom he had sent into exile nine months before, had returned to England and was challenging Richard II's right to the throne.

This was a wholly English invasion. Henry had declined offers of French help when he set out from Boulogne and having crossed to Pevensey, where he put in briefly, presumably for supplies, he sailed on up the east coast to Ravenspur on the far side of the Humber estuary, where he landed on or about 4 July 1399. A contemporary chronicler put his force, in three ships, at 'scarce three hundred followers', a modest army with which to seize a kingdom, but by landing in Yorkshire he had immediately placed himself among friends, many of them his family's former tenants.

The elderly Duke of York, left in charge in the king's absence, had

---

★The word is supposedly derived from *lollen*, a Dutch word meaning 'to mumble', applied contemptuously to heretics alleged to mutter private prayers.

strengthened the defences of Rochester Castle and Queensborough Castle, but he had been out-manoeuvred. From Ravenspur the invader marched north, as far as Pickering, then swung inland before turning south at Knaresborough. On 27 July 1399 the armies led respectively by the Dukes of Lancaster and York came into contact between Bristol and Berkeley. After a minor skirmish the Yorkist army, with no stomach for the struggle, either deserted or, along with its commander, marched into the enemy camp. Bristol declared for Henry and Henry himself now made his way back through the border country, via Ross, Hereford, Leominster, Ludlow and Shrewsbury towards Chester, an impressive march of 160 miles [256 km] in ten days.

Richard II had no more aptitude for generalship than for kingship and was persuaded by advisers already intending to betray him first to delay leaving Ireland and then to divide his troops. One detachment was sent ahead to north Wales while Richard himself, around 27 July, sailed for Haverfordwest, from which he trailed around the coasts, past one after another of the great castles established by Edward I – Carmarthern, Aberystwyth, Harlech, Caernarvon and Beaumaris – to Conway, which he reached on 11 August. By now his leading supporters had largely deserted him, and the king of England's territory had dwindled to this single fortress manned by barely 100 men. He was induced to leave this sanctuary by the most solemn of promises, sworn by one of his own earls on the sacred Host, but was immediately ambushed, taken to the Tower of London and, on 29 September, forced to agree to abdicate. On the following day a great meeting in Westminster Hall agreed that he should be deposed and his nephew rose to claim the crown 'as by the right blood coming of King Henry, and through that right that God of His grace hath sent me, with the help of my kin and my friends, to recover it.' Thus dramatically, by a wholly bloodless invasion and an almost bloodless campaign on land, Henry IV, at the age of 32 or 33 – the date of his birth is uncertain – became king of England. Risings in support of the deposed king were still a real possibility, but some time between late January and mid-February he was murdered. According to the chronicler Adam of Usk, a canon lawyer well placed to observe events, he died from being 'heart-broken, fettered and denied common nourishment'. Few doubted that the new king was responsible but, with the cynical effrontery typical of the times, that March Henry IV assigned £16.13s 4d [£16.66] to be spent on 1000 masses for the repose of his predecessor's soul.

24

BURSTING IN BY NIGHT

The Armorican Britons, with their allies the French, came to the town of Plymouth . . . bursting in by night.

Chronicler Thomas of Walsingham, recalling August 1403

The king had changed; the nation's enemies remained the same. As, in January 1400, King Henry IV made a triumphal procession through London, the crowds clamoured for glory. 'God bless our King Henry,' they shouted. 'Now we will wage war with all the world, except the Flemings!' The king, in his early thirties, though 'of mean stature', according to a contemporary, was 'well-proportioned and compact', with auburn hair and russet-brown beard, in disposition, according to Froissart, 'liked by all, gracious, sweet' and 'courteous'. Henry IV had already, in October 1399, instituted a new knightly order, the Order of the Bath, with his four sons among its 40 founder members, and in the following month came the first of a long series of military challenges from outside when the Scots attacked Wark Castle. They were beaten back, and on 17 August 1400, Henry, a veteran of many wars, led a large army across the Scottish border, with the usual fleet at sea on his flank. A notable feature of the campaign was the appalling weather, with almost continuous rain from May till the end of September. By 29 August, when Henry squelched his way back across the border, en route for Newcastle upon Tyne, nothing had been achieved and future disorder was only kept within bounds by the border castles.

Trouble now arose unexpectedly in quite another quarter, a boundary quarrel between a member of his council, Reginald, Lord Grey of Ruthin, who was a large landowner in Wales, and his Welsh neighbour, known to the English as Owen Glendower, to the Welsh as Owain Glyn Dŵr, or Glyndwrdwy. Glendower, now aged about 40, was provoked into rebellion; on 16 September 1400 he had himself proclaimed Prince of Wales, the title already held by Henry's son and heir, and his family and associates swore, at a secret meeting, to make war against the English.

For Wales to be in a state of rebellion was nothing new. What made the affair far more serious was the intervention of the French. Long accustomed to help the Scots when it suited them, they now began to reinforce the Welsh. It was probably in late July, 1403, when, according to the French chronicler Monstrelet, whose figures may be suspect, the Admiral of France himself took command of 120 ships which, after a 15-day wait for a fair wind, carried 1200 Frenchmen from Brest to Haverfordwest. Here they landed and burnt the town, inflicting heavy casualties on the inhabitants, before sailing on to join Glendower at Tenby. The invaders' fate thereafter is uncertain, but it seems likely that, on learning of Henry's victory at Shrewsbury, they returned to France.

Another enemy landing, in England, followed. On 9 August 1403 a powerful Breton force of 30 ships and 1200 men-at-arms approached Plymouth under the command of a Breton nobleman, the Sieur du Chastel (or Cassils, or Castyl), the owner of Château Neuf near St Malo, whose lands had suffered at the hands of 'pirates' from Devon.

The attack had been expected, as Thomas of Walsingham describes:

> When the hostile fleet was seen to approach, the patriots ran to the town, wishing to defend it. But the men of Plymouth, as if unworthy of so much kindness offered to them, soon doubled the price of victuals in the town. When the patriots asked why they did it, they replied that they had no need of such help, and had sufficient resources of their own. When they had been given such an impudent answer, those who had come to help went away again.

Another, less sympathetic, account suggests that the newcomers had merely crowded into Plymouth for their own protection and were made unwelcome as 'useless mouths' but, whatever their motives, the alarm they had raised was ignored. The enemy ships were not challenged offshore and were allowed to sail quite unchallenged up Plymouth Sound, though they were prevented from sailing into the Sutton Pool, which led deeper into the town, by a massive chain dragged across the entrance. This was one of the earliest known examples of boom defence of a harbour though later in the century a grant from the local customs was allocated to providing a similar barrier at Dartmouth and the housings for it can still be seen at Dartmouth Castle. The attack on Plymouth in 1403 was probably also the first occasion on which land-based cannon were used in English coastal defence, as the guns of Castle Quadrante overlooking the harbour, and others dragged down onto the Hoe, bombarded the enemy vessels with moorstone projectiles. They apparently did no damage, and the French ships then anchored in the Cattewater, an obvious affront to both the town authorities and the government, for Plymouth was the fourth city in the kingdom, its population of 7000 being exceeded only by London, Bristol and York. No attempt to use fireships or to cut the enemy ships adrift under cover of darkness seems to have been made and the Bretons now began lowering small boats, obviously preparing to attack the town from the weaker side. Still unchallenged, the French 'landed within a myle of the toune', as one chronicler recorded, and 'with a great companie . . . lodged there all night'. Some of the invaders entered the town via the 'bak haf', since identified by a local historian as the Coxside district, and spent the whole of the short August night robbing the neighbouring houses and setting them on fire, 600 being burned to the ground. With the coming of dawn, the locals at last rallied and a bitter hand-to-hand struggle developed in the road still known as Breton (or Briton) Side, fought bravely but Du Chastel's men failed to make much headway along the edge of Sutton Pool towards the castle, or up the hill towards St Andrew's Church and around 10 a.m., taking many prisoners with him, he ordered a retreat. According to a no doubt imaginative stained glass window later commissioned for the Guildhall, but, sadly, destroyed in 1941 by another enemy, the Breton commander stood with his standard-bearer on a jetty opposite the Castle while his troops struggled to re-embark under a hail of arrows from the Castle garrison, half-blinded by the smoke from the burning ruins behind them.

The French had done more damage than Plymouth was to suffer in any later seaborne attack but were not pursued; they felt secure enough to stop on the way home to plunder an island in the mouth of the Kingsbridge estuary, in defiance of Salcombe castle, on the adjoining headland. Only on their cross-Channel return voyage did the invaders suffer any serious loss, when a dozen vessels foundered, apparently with all hands; the rest got safely back with their spoils into St Malo.

Thomas of Walsingham justly described the attack on Plymouth as 'this disaster':

> The Armorican Britons [i.e. Bretons], with their allies the French, came to the town of Plymouth . . . with a big fleet, and, bursting in by night, attacked the unwary townsmen and oppressed them and burnt the town and plundered the whole night . . . with no-one coming to help.

Avenging the insult offered to the Devon coast was left to private initiative. It proved highly effective. A large squadron of ships carrying, a French chronicler claimed, 5-6000 men, crossed the Channel in November 1403 under the command of a Devon squire, Sir William Wilford, taking the Bretons by surprise. The operation which followed was a classic of its kind, 40 ships, most of them filled with wine from La Rochelle, being captured and as many more destroyed, while a force of

4000 men was landed at Penmarch (or Penmark, or Penare or Penmarks) near Quimper, and spread a swathe of destruction six miles inland. The expedition ended with the stalwart knight, as Thomas of Walsingham records, giving a distinctly dusty answer when challenged by the French:

> The Captain of Brest and many other Breton leaders . . . sent a sergeant at arms to ask if he was prepared to make satisfaction for the damage he had done to the region, to which our admiral replied that he wished to burn half of Brittany for satisfaction, and that they should have no other recompense . . . So they came back home . . . bearing joyful news to their country, and leaving Brittany sad.

Even before the Brittany raid, an enemy attack on Hampshire had been feared, and directions for Southampton to be fortified were issued on 7 September 1403. On 20 October more general orders were given for Commissioners of Array to have local levies ready to march to the coast, with the usual beacons being prepared on the hills. As the autumn gave way to winter reports reached England that Count Waleran [or Walerand] of St Pol (or Count Waleran de Pol), in the Pas de Calais, who had long been carrying on a private war against English shipping, was now planning a freelance invasion of England, with the support of the duke of Orleans, brother of king Charles VI, who had become insane.

Such operations gave the French the opportunity to attack England while still nominally at peace with her, as a British mission vigorously protested to the Duke of Burgundy, the Duke of Orleans' great rival, on 4 December 1403:

> It is a grievous thing, absurd, dishonourable, inconsistent, unreasonable and amazing, that . . . this Duke and this Count should be allowed to make war, by land and by sea, against the English on the pretence of their own private and personal quarrels against the English King, and to have the whole kingdom of France, with all its wealth and all its people, at their back, like an embattled castle, under the protection of which they may break treaties and violate their oaths.

The Duke of Burgundy had, however, no power to intervene and St Pol's men, 1600 strong, after assembling at Abbeville, marched to that traditional jumping-off point, Harfleur, but he denied himself the advantage of possible surprise by a formal message of defiance to Henry IV, who was holding a Great Council, an assembly of about 140 representatives, much smaller than the usual parliament, at Coventry. The French heralds' appearance prompted an enthusiastic declaration of support for the king, but on 6 December 1403 or a little later Count

Waleran's forces arrived unopposed, as Thomas of Walsingham briskly describes:

> A few days before Christmas the French, accompanied by a crowd of warriors, landed in the Isle of Wight, intending to celebrate Christmas there, in spite of the king. When a thousand had landed, and had already chased flocks and herds, so that they could return to the sea with a small booty, a force of militia met them, and they were compelled to relinquish their booty and rush to the ships, not without ridicule and loss.

The French chronicler Monstrelet shows his countrymen in a somewhat different light. The retreat has mysteriously become an advance. Each man, he claims, was armed with a sharp, strong battle-axe hanging at his side, and held in front of him a spear, with handle cut down, for ease of carrying, to five feet [1.5 m]: 'They advanced handsomely, at a slow pace; it was a fine sight . . . for the French were in such close order that one could scarcely throw a tennis-ball among them without its falling on a helmet or lance.'

Both sides agree that the action of a local priest – brave and resourceful in English eyes, cunning and deceitful according to the French – was decisive. He offered to collect a handsome ransom if only the French would spare the villagers' farms and sheepfolds, thus gaining a four-day respite. This gave time for a relieving force to arrive from the mainland, at the sight of which St Pol hastily re-embarked. As it was the French succeeded only in capturing a few fishermen, with their nets and tackle, along with some livestock, and in covering themselves with derision, for St Pol had knighted some of the young noblemen he had brought with him, a traditional preliminary to some major military exploit.

On 13 December 1403 most of the sheriffs were told that the precautions recently ordered could be relaxed, and parliament, so often critical of the king on defence matters, was delighted. The Chancellor reflected its mood when, on 14 January 1404, he reported that the French, appearing on English soil uninvited, had 'neither ventured to wait nor to stay'. The consequences for the Count were less happy. He spent his Christmas in Paris, digesting the news that his lands near Calais had been ravaged by a sortie by its English garrison, and fending off the complaints of his followers that they had invested large sums in the recent expedition without any return.

In late April or early May 1404 200 Norman noblemen, with an unknown number of followers, set out on a trouble-seeking voyage and were carried by chance rather than design to the island of Portland, in Dorset. After doing their customary damage they were surrounded by 1000 peasants, brandishing bows and farm implements, and laid down their arms without a fight. Soon afterwards another raid took place near Weymouth, in which many Frenchmen were killed or taken prisoner, but no other details survive.

About the middle of May – it is first mentioned in a royal letter of the 23rd – a far more serious assault was delivered against Devon*. The initiative was taken by the Bretons, 'stung by the English piracies and provoked by feelings of revenge' for the previous year's raid, according to the contemporary *Chronique de Saint Denis*, but they prudently sought the support of the Duke of Orleans:

> When the Bretons had received a favourable answer, they collected 300 ships, selected pilots and skilled oarsmen and embarked at Saint Malo crossbowmen, light troops and two thousand knights and men-at-arms, commanded by the Lords de Chateaubriand, de Jaille and du Chatel.

'Du Chatel' (or du Chastel) had led the attack on Plymouth the previous year but was now saddled with two fellow-commanders and, as the chronicler comments, 'a multiplicity of leaders is contrary to all military discipline.' The results were soon apparent in the behaviour of both troops and seamen:

> Each was free to do whatever seemed good to him. Thus, on the very first day . . . having met some Spanish wine vessels, they attacked them, regardless of the alliance between France and Spain, and ill-treated their crews. Some of the company remonstrating with the culprits, there followed a quarrel, in consequence of which they separated, and different parts of the fleet made their own course towards the harbour of Dartmouth.

On arriving off the Devon coast the French admiral anchored for six days, presumably to allow the missing vessels to catch up, giving the Earl of Warwick, in command on shore, a veteran of such raids, ample time to collect his troops together. The harbour itself, protected by a castle on the western side and some other, unknown, defences to the east, where Kingswear Castle later stood, was clearly felt to be secure and the real point of danger was judged to be Blackpool [or Black Pool], about two miles [3 km] south of Dartmouth towards Slapton Sands, where deep water led up to a steeply shelving beach. The Dartmouth men themselves, though reinforced from the surrounding neighbour-

*T. F. Jacob in *The Fifteenth Century* (1961) p. 56, implies that the raid was in August, but this is contrary to all the other secondary sources and seems contradicted by the letter referred to above.
J. H. Wylie, *History of England under Henry the Fourth*, Vol. I, p. 435, places it on 15 April but this would put it before the Portland raid when it clearly occurred after it.

hood, were mustered by its most famous citizen, John Hawley, a local shipmaster who had represented Dartmouth in parliament and served for ten years as its mayor. He had played a leading part in the raids against Brittany and now, under the overall direction of the Earl of Warwick, formed a strong defensive position at Stoke Fleming, barring the way from Blackpool towards the town. The chronicler of Saint Denis records the result:

> The English, forewarned of the French attack, had gathered together 6000 men to oppose the landing, and to make approach more difficult had contrived by the shore a deep ditch, which allowed only a narrow crossing, entrusted to a guard of their bravest men. But, on the morrow, when they saw the French advancing in battle order preceded by their archers, the English were reassured by the fewness of their enemies, who were barely two hundred strong; and they moved up to the ditch, which the tide had filled, resolved there to make their stand.

The size of the French force had probably been understated and that of the defenders grossly exaggerated, but the moral advantage undoubtedly lay with the latter. While an invasion bound together with a common purpose all those on shore, it often seems to have had a reverse effect on the attackers as now happened at Dartmouth:

> At the sight of the enemy, Du Chatel and de Jaille, who commanded the Bretons, conferred together. They were of opposite opinions. William du Chatel impetuously urged an immediate attack without waiting for the crossbowmen and their companions, but added that 'If we thus decide, it is by the flank and not by the front that we must attack, for the position is very strong.' De Jaille . . . despising what he called a rabble of peasants . . . looked on it as the depth of dishonour to retire, even for a moment, and called on his colleagues not to be afraid. Du Chatel, piqued by this mortal insult, replied emphatically: 'God forbid, that the heart of a Breton should know so disgraceful a sentiment! Convinced as I am that we march to death rather than victory, I will take the chance of a battle; let the die be cast, for I vow to God I will not this day be put to ransom.'

Du Chatel then leapt ashore, killing the first three men to attack him, and was speedily followed by his men, until they had established a foothold on the beach. But the defence rapidly rallied:

> The speed of the Breton disembarkation had much alarmed their enemies. But when they saw that, contrary to the French practice, they advanced without a screen of crossbowmen . . . they took

courage, and hardily sustained the charge of the French, raining on them a dense cloud of arrows.

A fierce battle was now joined, a classic encounter between invaders trying to force their way off the beach and a resolute army determined to bar their way inland:

> The Bretons first attacked those who were charged with the defence of the crossing. The defenders, continually reinforced, soon established an impenetrable front. Then many of the Bretons, willing to display their courage, tried to cross the fosse at some distance away from the causeway, although they did not know the depth, and so to take the defenders in flank. Some were dragged down by the weight of their armour, but others reached the far bank by swimming, and valiantly threw themselves upon the ranks of the enemy, though covered with mud from head to foot. As for those who had made the direct assault, seeing that they could not escape and must fight for their lives, they sustained for long every effort of the English and killed about fifteen hundred men. William du Chatel, the flower of chivalry, distinguished himself above all others in this mêlée. His great axe swept right and left; and as he was tall and very strong, all that he struck were slain or mortally wounded. In the end, worn with fatigue and unable to fight, but refusing to surrender, he fell pierced with wounds. His comrades, discouraged, wavered and gave ground. They were all slain or compelled to surrender.

The Dartmouth men were unable to prevent the French ships getting away, but they left behind them a scene of carnage. According to an English chronicler, the Devon women joined in the slaughter with their menfolk, pelting with stones any Frenchman within range. Thanks to the robust English indifference to foreign languages, the Devonians killed most of those abandoned on the beach, interpreting their offers to surrender as shouts of defiance, though the total casualty figures on either side remain uncertain.

Those taken prisoner at Dartmouth included three lords and 22 knights and their defeat by a band of Devonshire rustics and their womenfolk did wonders for popular morale. 'The crows have pecked the eagle' ran the catchphrase, quoted by a chronicler, and Henry IV, delighted at his subjects' success, attended at Edward the Confessor's shrine in Westminster Abbey to join in a service of thanksgiving. On 25 May 1404 the mayor of Dartmouth was instructed to bring to the king at Nottingham the chief prisoners of the hundred or so taken – they included two of du Chatel's brothers and a Welsh squire – so that the king might discover the 'secrets and intentions' of the enemy. The early

English historian, John Speed, two centuries later recalled the profitable sequel: 'A boisterous group of plain Western men went to the King in London with their prisoners and he, in delight, stuffed their purses with gold.'

The 'discomfiture at Blackpool' as one of the men responsible, John Hawley, described it, did not deter the French for long, if a French chronicler, the monk of St Denis, is to be trusted – though he probably is not, since he is not supported by any English source. According to him, however, another of du Chatel's brothers assembled 400 men and made a second, totally unexpected, descent on Dartmouth, four weeks after the first, which took its inhabitants by surprise and left the town in ruins; an eight-week reign of terror along the south-west coast followed. No other evidence of this attack has survived, but there is confirmation, of a kind, of enemy activity in the area from instructions issued on 27 June 1404 to the towns of Weymouth and Falmouth, as well as Dart-mouth, not to permit any foreign prisoners to leave the country.

If, on the whole, the south-west coast was now being successfully defended, the story in Wales was very different. On 14 October 1404 one of the King's Commissioners wrote from Calais to the mayor of London to warn him that 15,000 men were said to be ready at Harfleur, with six months' supplies, ready to reinforce Glendower in Wales, and a similar number were at Sluys, *their* objective being Sandwich or some-where on the east coast. On 26 October 1404 sheriffs throughout the country were ordered to have their forces ready to resist an invasion, but the autumn storms, which did great damage all along both coasts, seem to have disrupted the French preparations and made the French commander, the Count de la Marche, hesitate. In the end the great fleet dwindled to 20 ships and some 1000 fighting men and the invasion to a mere raid. The crossing must have been slow and disagreeable, for it took eight days for the two contingents, from Brest and Harfleur, to reach their objective, Falmouth, during November 1404 and the oper-ation which followed was ignored by the English chroniclers. It was left to a French monk to record that de la Marche's men got ashore unchallenged, burnt the town, but were forced to abandon most of their loot and to re-embark in haste. On the way home one vessel was wrecked near St Malo, all its contents being lost. The 'gentlemen' on board were saved, but the crew drowned, there being no room for them in the lifeboats.

25

ALONG THE COAST

So they went along the coast, each day burning and pillaging.

Spanish eyewitness, Diez de Gamez, describing raids on England,
Summer 1405

For Henry IV's government Wales was always the most troublesome
military problem but the second half of his reign also saw an unprecedented number of attacks, some exceptionally serious, on the whole
stretch of coast fronting the Channel between the Thames estuary and
Land's End. The most persistent series of raids yet began during the
summer of 1405, and involved a joint 'freelance' force of Frenchmen and
Spaniards under two experienced and daring commanders, distinguished
respectively on land and sea. Charles de Savoisi (or Savoisy), a rich
French nobleman and royal official, frequently in disgrace for his turbulent behaviour, had an international reputation in the jousting lists and
had visited England for friendly combat with English knights. He fitted
out two galleys at his own expense, so elaborately that the pennons
alone were said to have cost as much as equipping any ordinary ship,
and joined forces with an equally rich Spaniard Don Pero Niño, a great
favourite of King Henry III of Castile, who had made his name, although
still only 27, pursuing Mediterranean pirates. Pero Nino contributed
three more galleys and the little fleet set sail across the Channel around
July 1405 to stir up the English, whom they criticized for being addicted
to drinking, gluttony and – a curiously harmless activity one might have
thought – playing bowls. Savoisi's and Nino's subsequent adventures
are, with one brief exception, totally ignored by the English chroniclers
and only cursorily mentioned by the French, but very well documented
by Nino's standard-bearer, Gutierre Diez de Gamez, who provides that
rarest of sources, a detailed account by an educated eyewitness*.

---

*Nicholas, Vol. II, p. 374 clearly views, this account, first published in England in
1833, with some suspicion, but there seems no good reason to doubt its authenticity
and Wylie, Vol. II, p. 317, wholly accepts it.

After a false start, during which the ships were separated and blown back to Brittany, they tried again, under perfect conditions:

> The galleys set out thence and had a calm sea and a good wind for their passage. They sailed under the great sail and mizzen sail, rowing at times for a day and a night. The next morning England was sighted and by the hour of vespers they had drawn in close to the land. There were along the coast many boats out fishing; the galleys captured a few of them. Through them they were able to get information and to ascertain the state of the country and of each place.

Diez de Gamez does not mention that, their usefulness ended, the captured crews were simply flung into the sea, and operations now got under way in earnest:

> The land which the galleys approached is called the country of Cornwall; and as soon as they had information about this country the galleys made their way to the shore with the tide, up a river . . . Within there was a harbour, well sheltered and shielded from every wind, and a town . . . having perhaps about three hundred inhabitants. This town was not fortified; it was set out in terraces on the slope of a hill and all the streets went down to the sea . . . There the galleys drew in to land.

The Spaniards called this first target 'Shuta', which Diez de Gamez's most recent translator interprets as St Ives, but it may have been either a now vanished town near Looe or East Looe itself. Whatever its identity, the town was taken by surprise:

> The galleys drew in to land . . . The . . . men . . . threw down gangways and all landed with the captain, who drew up his troop in good order. He set in the front a pavisade [i.e. wooden shelter] and behind it the crossbowmen . . . There was a rough fight . . . and at the last the English were driven in and many among them killed or taken. The captain commanded that the standards and the men-at-arms should remain in good array outside the town, so that they should not be surprised if the English came up in greater force, and that the oarsmen and crossbowmen should enter the city to sack it . . . When everything had been carried off he set fire to the town and burnt it all; all this was done in the space of three hours. The trumpets sounded; everyone went back on board and the galleys set out again, taking with them two sailing ships that were in the port.

Getting away proved considerably more hazardous than getting in:

> The tide then began to fall and the galleys went out on the ebb and

towed the ships out. When they were at the mouth of the harbour, many English were already gathered together there and the passage had become very narrow; on one side there was a very high rock which towered above the galleys and there fell on them from either shore a hail of stones and arrows, and if the English had been gathered together at the first in as great numbers as they were then, the descent on shore would have been very perilous.

In spite of their narrow escape the two commanders were encouraged by this initial encounter, and having sent the captured ships back to Harfleur with a prize crew, set out to cause more mischief:

Pero Nino and Messire Charles agreed to the plan of going along round the coast of England. They came to a great seaport, which is called Dartmouth. All over the countryside they saw fair troops of soldiers and archers coming up on all sides to defend the shore. And the captain said to Messire Charles: 'There is a fair place for a fight, and what is more, we have need of water; let us go against those men.' Messire Charles answered: 'My lord, there are more men there than you have; it is not a good place for so few men as we are.' Whereupon they had that day, on the question of this landing, some words of discord.

Later historians have concluded that the raiders were in fact approaching not Dartmouth but Falmouth, but in any case de Savoisi's caution prevailed and the little fleet sailed on, either to Plymouth as Diez de Gamez's translator believed, or possibly, as an English historian concluded, to Saltash, then a separate port on the River Tamar, four miles [6 km] further inland, also approached via Plymouth Sound:

When the captain Pero Nino and Messire Charles were of one accord again, the galleys set out from Dartmouth and kept out at sea eleven nights, in great fear of meeting with the English fleet. When day broke they rowed along the coast to Plymouth . . . There were many sailing ships or other vessels lying in the river, but as soon as they sighted the galleys, they were all hauled up close [to] the bridge. The galleys entered the river to take some of these ships and burn them. They fired so many bombards and bolts from the town, that those in the galleys thought they would be sunk; there was one stone which went twice the height of a tower and fell into the sea nearly half a league off.

Diez de Gamez's reference to heavy guns may be merely a face-saving excuse, for the invaders withdrew without going ashore and turned back up-Channel, narrowly escaping disaster when a sudden strong wind nearly wrecked the whole fleet on a rocky shore. However, thanks, as the crews believed, to divine intervention, they survived to continue their work of destruction:

> That night they passed at sea; the next day, they came to an island which is called Portland . . . quite close to the coast of England. At low tide, men pass from one to the other; at high tide they cross in boats . . . It contains a township in which dwell about two hundred inhabitants. The captain Pero Nino sent some of his men with his standard to sack this town and carry off the flocks on the island; and Messire Charles did likewise. They themselves remained with the rest of their men, hoping that when the tide went down some English troops might appear. Those who went on the island fought for a while with those they met; but these were all ill-armed and few in number and soon took to flight. There were many caverns in the rocks near the sea-shore . . . which were entered down narrow little paths . . . The townsfolk had seen the galleys earlier, when they were skirting round the island and for the most part had taken refuge in the caverns with their wives and children, so that very few of them could be taken prisoners and our men had to fall back on plundering the township. While our men were on the island, the trumpets sounded on board the galleys to recall everyone to the ship.

According to Diez de Gamez the invading forces now fell out among themselves, like their commanders before them, in this case because the French wanted to burn down the thatched houses while 'the Castilians had no heart to ravage the town further, having pity on the poor folk.' This may have caused a dangerous delay, while the tide turned, enabling help to arrive from the mainland and, not a moment too soon, the raiders began to retreat:

> Our men took their way back to the galleys, and by the time they reached them many English men-at-arms and bowmen had already crossed over with the ebb. The captain Pero Nino and Messire Charles were already engaged with the English; these fought to cross over to the defence of the island . . . while our men fought to prevent their passage. The number of the English grew with every minute; and . . . as the tongue of sand was wide, while they [the Spaniards] were engaged with some, others slipped by on to the island. The men who were marching with the captain's banner had reached the high part of the island and thence they saw . . . that many men were coming against them. They set themselves in good array . . . hastened their steps, went to meet the English and threw themselves upon them very roughly; but the English stood firm.

In this crisis previous disagreements were forgotten and the men who had stayed with the boats went to the aid of their comrades on shore:

> Messire Charles went into the battle leading his men and fighting like a good knight. He had with him his standard and the most part of his men. The captain took his standard, which had been brought back from the island, rallied his men, had a pavisade set before his crossbowmen and called near him . . . his men-at-arms. He said to them: 'Look at the French, they are fighting like brave men, and can do no more. We must bring them help . . . It is for you to aid them.' So speaking they went against the English and attacked them fiercely with darts and with arrows; and the captain came up with his banner. There was there a fierce fight in a very small space. In the end the English had to give up their position . . . and withdraw to the mainland. At this moment the tide came in, and separated the combatants from each other . . . The land which was covered again by the tide was as wide as a stone can be thrown from the land; and the English from the other side sent so many stones and arrows that it seemed as if it snowed, and a great quantity reached those who were on the island . . . This exchange of arrows lasted a long time, until night brought it to an end. Our men withdrew to their galleys, tended their wounded, ate and rested.

What had happened at Portland showed what could be done when there was time to summon help and thereafter resistance seems to have stiffened:

> On the morrow the galleys left there and went along the coast seeking the ports. Men from the galleys landed to get water and wood, and seeing herds of cows and sheep they laid hands on them and killed as many as they needed. So they went along the coast, each day burning and pillaging many houses, carrying off goods and apparel; and they had frequent skirmishes with those who dwelt in those parts.

The desire for reprisals prompted Nino to make an attack which the more prudent de Savoisi tried to discourage. The particular target was a Dorset landowner, Sir Henry (or Harry) Paye (or Pay), a name often corrupted by foreigners into 'Arripay'. Diez de Gamez describes Paye's notorious reputation:

> This Harry Paye had many times come to the coasts of Castile, whence he had carried off many boats and ships; he cruised in the Flanders Channel with such powerful forces that no ship could pass into Flanders without being taken. This Harry Paye had burnt Gijon and . . . carried off the crucifix of St Mary of Finistere, which was

famous as that held in the most devotion in all the county . . . and he wrought much other havoc in Castile . . . and although other armed ships came forth out of England, it was he who the most often made folk talk of him.

As Diez de Gamez observed, 'this town of Poole is some distance from the sea,' so that the galleys may well have been spotted on their way in. At all events, de Savoisi's caution soon proved justified:

The Castilians set fire to it and burnt a great part of it; but so many English came against them, that they could not make a stand . . . but withdrew slowly and in good order towards the sea. The captain, seeing his men giving way and leaving the town, was much vexed and ordered more men to land; meanwhile the others fought and defended themselves until the reinforcements came up. Fernando Nino, the captain's cousin, led these and had with him the standard and the men-at-arms; he ranged his men and gave the order to go back and destroy the town . . . The banner was set outside the town, with the men-at-arms round it. The captain had ordered that they should take no plunder for fear that the soldiers should be hampered by the booty, but that they should set fire to everything. So in a little time the town was altogether burnt, except for one fair and great dwelling, which was defended by many men who had taken refuge therein; but the Castilians were so determined that they forced an entrance into this house also, and those who were within escaped by the back; they found therein a quantity of all manner of arms, bolts, rigging, sails and all the furnishing of ships-of-war. They carried off as much as they could of these things and then fired the castle.

The 'great dwelling' and 'castle' seem in fact to have been a large warehouse and the defenders' stand there had given other troops in the area time to rally against the invaders:

This affair ended, they came back towards the galleys, still fighting with the English; and as they began to board the galleys there came up a great number of English on foot and on horseback. The horsemen dismounted, went forward on foot, and made a fair array of men-at-arms and bowmen; and they were so near them that they could easily tell the fair men from the dark. They had with them house doors, which they set upon the ground, propping them up on stakes . . . for fear of the arbalests, which used to kill many of them.

The archers were following the tactical doctrine of the time, advancing in pairs under cover of impromptu shields, as recommended in a military manual of the period: 'If yomen made them a good pavise of bordes . . .

on [one] may hold it while the other doth shete [shoot].' The technique proved highly effective:

> They held the higher ground and the Castilians the lower; and the arrows were so many and came so thick that the crossbowmen did not dare to stoop to bend their bows. Many were already hit by these arrows, and there were so many, that those who wore leather jerkins or surcoats seemed all stuck with arrows. The standard and he who bore it [i.e. Diez de Gamez himself] were likewise riddled with arrows and the standard-bearer had as many round his body as a bull in the ring, but he was well shielded by his good armour, although this was already bent in several places. The English are experienced in war and, to get to grips with the Castilians, they waited until the crossbowmen should by dint of shooting, have emptied their trusses [i.e. quivers].

At this turning point in the battle, the French commander, who had been against the landing from the start, felt compelled to go to the rescue of his allies: 'At this moment, Messire Charles came ashore, leading many knights and gentlemen in armour; they appeared in another part of the field, richly apparelled in surcoats and other ornaments of gold and silver.'

The French had left it very late, so late that only one of them took any real part in the fighting, and he was killed. The mere appearance of this third contingent, however, was sufficient to cause a general retreat by their opponents:

> In such sort had the English been beaten and vanquished that not one of them appeared again, but they let the Castilians get aboard their galleys again at their ease, without a conflict. These tended their wounded and ate and rested, for they had need to . . . When the battle was ended the arrows lay so thick upon the ground that no man could walk without treading on arrows in such numbers that they picked them up in handfuls.

Although the value of armour had been demonstrated once again in the battle, so had its great disadvantage, for de Savoisi admitted that his men's delay in arriving on shore was because 'these knights were overlong in arming themselves.' A great debate then followed as to their next move, in which in the end the professional caution of the sailors who manned the ships prevailed over the soldiers' ardour for more combat:

> And the pilots and masters of the oarsmen said: 'My lords, ye have been long enough upon these coasts and have done many fine things here; you carry away from this land much honour and likewise profit.

We are at the beginning of winter. These seas are very stormy, and especially evil for galleys, and it is time that ours should be repaired; they lack many things that they have lost in the gales. Moreover this country is very cold and men suffer here if they be not warmly clad. Our counsel is that you leave England and that you go to winter in some port of France.' All agreed that the counsel was good and that it must be followed.

Sadly reflecting that with 20 more galleys they would have been able to do 'marvellous things' the intruders prepared to leave English waters, but before doing so made one or two final forays further up the Channel. That favourite target, the Isle of Wight, now proving so conveniently close, Nino and de Savoisi could not forbear from attacking it.

This is the one episode of Nino's voyage for which other accounts exist and they are, perhaps predictably, contradictory. A French chronicler paints his countrymen's role in a more heroic light than Diez de Gamez. *He* says they landed bravely in the face of the enemy and dispersed them, leaving 22 Englishmen dead, and then advanced inland and set fire to a large village before re-embarking unharmed. The chief English version of these events is different again and shows the islanders as unquestionably the victors. At the sight of the French and Spanish they are said to have drawn up, 400 strong, on the shore, waving their caps defiantly and shouting 'Come out of your galleys!', before chivalrously offering the French a six-hour truce to rest and prepare to fight on equal terms. The enemy, perhaps recalling how a similar delay on an earlier occasion had been used to bring troops from the mainland, and fearing an ambush, declined. A third account, by another contemporary, an Austinian friar, John Capgrave, then a child, may refer to some other landing altogether but seems most likely to describe this one, which probably, though not certainly, occurred in 1405*.

> In this same time the Frenschmen came to the Ylde of Wite askynge tribute of the dwelleres for the sustentation of Queen Ysabelle, and they of Wite answered that King Richard was ded, the queen pessably sent home, wherfor they wolde not pay; if thei cam to fite thei shuld be welcome, and thei shuld gyve them leve to entyre the lond and rest there iii days before the batayle. The Frenschmen herd this answere and sayled away to their contree.

If Nino did now make for his own 'contree' it was probably only after

---

*Walsingham (paraphrased by Myers, p. 195) attributes this raid to 1404, Nicholas Vol. II, pp. 358–9, to 'about February' 1404, Hockey p. 103, to 'the summer' of that year. Wylie, Vol. I, p. 445, placed it shortly after 27 May 1404, but in Vol. II, p. 326, fn 3, decided he had been wrong and that it belonged to the Franco-Spanish expedition of 1405, a conclusion followed here.

seeking more mischief in a diversion through what is now Chichester Harbour to Havant, about five miles [8 km] from the open sea, though the evidence rests on other sources than Diez de Gamez. The raiders found stakes driven into the mud to prevent their landing, but managed to get past them in their small boats to fire the town before re-embarking unscathed.

The task force seems to have returned to Harfleur in September 1405 to lay up its ships for the winter, which Nino, 'ever-valiant and well-reputed in love', spent enjoying himself, after what had clearly been a highly successful trip, in Rouen and Paris.

The raids by Nino and de Savoisi had been only a nuisance, though a nuisance on a considerable scale. Glendower's rebellion, which still did not seem to have reached its peak, was another matter entirely. The French, it seemed, were at last about to respond to his appeal for help, and on 22 July 1405, after waiting 15 days for a favourable wind, the French fleet that was supposed to restore his fortunes at last set sail from Brest. The fleet, 120 strong, of which 16 were classed as 'large', encountered stormy weather, but disembarked its cargo of 800 men-at-arms and 1800 infantry under the Marshal of France, at Milford Haven on the western tip of Pembrokeshire, between 1 and 7 August, to be welcomed by an enthusiastic crowd led by Glendower himself.

The new alliance was immediately sealed by successfully attacking Haverfordwest, seven miles [11 km] inland to the north, though the castle held out. They next marched on Tenby, 14 miles [22 km] west of Milford Haven, devastating the countryside as they went, but while they were thus occupied the English fleet put in a belated appearance at Milford and, as Thomas of Walsingham records, 'burnt fifteen of their ships in the same harbour'. A follow-up force also suffered badly: 'At the same time fourteen ships were captured . . . while they were sailing towards Wales to help Owen. With these ships the Seneschal of France and eight other captains were taken.'

From Tenby the invaders might have advanced along the coast to Kidwelly, and extra wooden towers to provide additional fighting-platforms were hastily added to its stone defences, but Glendower's army instead made its way inland: 'The Frenchmen laid siege to the town of Carmarthen and took it, having first allowed the defenders the right to keep all their goods and chattels and transfer themselves whithersoever they pleased.'

The Franco-Welsh army now advanced towards the English border, beyond which the government had long been making preparations to repulse them. Urgent efforts had been made to raise money to pay the troops, and a thousand Yorkshire sheep had been requisitioned to supply the commissariat, though they proved insufficient for the numbers called out to join the king, first at Worcester, then at Hereford, on Friday 4 September. Various individuals were assigned the task of subduing specific areas and getting supplies into the castles, notably at Coity near Bridgend in Glamorgan, in most immediate danger of being starved out.

At last the elusive Welsh were assembled in strength and, by the end of August 1405 had penetrated as far as Woodbury Hill, eight miles [13 km] north-west of Worcester, occupying an ancient British encampment later known as Owen's Camp; the English army took up its position on the opposite side of the valley. There for eight days they confronted each other, both reluctant to risk an engagement, while around 200 on both sides were killed in minor skirmishes, and a larger number wounded. Eventually, their supplies running out, the Welsh and their allies withdrew, the English letting them slip away unchallenged. The miserable weather had probably weakened the spirits of both sides; it was difficult to anticipate the joys of battle on a windswept hillside shrouded in mist with the rain descending in torrents.

During November 1405 another invasion panic developed, with reports, no doubt encouraged by the recent raids in the south-west, that this time the French were planning to land in Cornwall. In fact they already had their hands full in Wales, which they turned out to like no more than the English had done. They were unused to fighting in such unpromising terrain, found Glendower's cautious tactics hard to accept, loathed the climate and detested the diet of mutton and barley bread. The better-off left in November 1405, the ordinary infantry in March 1406, when they had to endure a disastrous voyage in which 14 ships were sunk by the English, now fully alert, and another eight lost on the coast of Brittany.

In spite of its occasional successes, the traditional system of naval defence, in which requisitioned merchant ships supplemented the few vessels owned by the king himself, had obviously failed and in the spring of 1406 a new scheme was tried. A group of merchants and ship-owners undertook to supply as many ships as might be needed, with the necessary crews and from 1000 to 2000 fighting men, according to the season, in return for a levy on wool and wine exported or imported respectively, a guaranteed share in prize and ransom money, and an advance against these earnings of £4000. The contractors were allowed to nominate their own admirals, with full legal powers, but the arrangement was never put to a full-scale test, for after it had run for only six months of the intended period, from 1 May 1406 to 29 September 1407, it was abandoned.

There was in fact an invasion alarm at the very start of the contract period, for on 22 May 1406, the usual pre-invasion warning calling out the local forces was sent to Kent, Hampshire and Suffolk. In mid-June that troublesome partnership, Nino and Savoisi, this time with their crews paid by the French government, again put to sea, though under less happy auspices than the previous year, for as they stood out from the Seine in the early morning of Wednesday 16 June 1406 a total eclipse caused the crews, no longer able to see each other, to protest that the sun was dying, clearly an appalling omen. Nino reassured them, but reports of a 200-strong English fleet lying in wait for him off Plymouth caused him instead to make for Orwell, on the Suffolk coast, which he approached during the night, planning to land at dawn. Not for the last time, however, England's much-maligned climate came to the island's rescue and a sudden off-shore gale forced the French and Spaniards out to sea again, and, after blowing them helplessly about the North Sea, finally drove them into harbour at Sluys.

After dropping off de Savoisi, Nino now made an attack on the Channel Islands, much valued by the English as a useful victualling station on the passage to Bordeaux, and currently about to be reinforced by troops from Weymouth and Poole. The extra men had not yet arrived and Nino encouraged his own soldiers to extra effort by with-drawing their ships as soon as they were ashore on Jersey. The Jerseymen, whose traditional boast was that they had never been subdued either by the French or the English, fought desperately but were forced to pay a ransom of 10,000 crowns to get rid of the intruders, and to endure the loss of many of their cattle, though the five strong castles on the island, manned by English garrisons, remained untaken. Peace then descended on the Channel Islands and Nino is last heard of spending Christmas 1406 at home in Madrid.

From 1406 onwards England's military situation steadily improved. The greatest and most lasting success was in Wales. The premature departure of their allies had taken the heart out of the rebels and thereafter Glendower's support was steadily eroded, less by any single offensive than by steady pressure exerted by Prince Henry, and his readiness to let bygones be bygones. Glendower's son-in-law died during the siege but his daughter and most of his family and treasure and military stores were captured, several of the children dying soon afterwards while in captivity in London; Glendower was not to found a new Welsh dynasty. Henceforward a fugitive, he was still at liberty when Henry IV himself died on 20 March 1413, aged about 46. Three years later Glendower, too, was dead. One day, it was whispered, he would return from the cave where he was sleeping to expel the English. No longer a prince, he had become what the Welsh valued even more, a legend.

26

HONOURABLE VICTORY AND GREAT TRIUMPH

If they labour to disturb us of our journey, we shall escape their malice with honourable victory and great triumph.

Henry V, preparing to march through France, October 1415

No medieval monarch was to enjoy a reign so full of military glory as Henry V, but it was glory gained exclusively outside the British Isles. Henry had hardly, at 25 and already a veteran of many battlefields, succeeded to the throne, on 21 March 1413, when he reasserted the long-standing English claim to the crown of France. The war between the two countries had now dragged on, with various, ill-observed, truces, ever since May 1337, but the time was propitious to resume it. Charles VI of France was still intermittently mad, his bouts of insanity being worst during the campaigning season in the summer, and the country was torn between two bitterly contending factions. On the one side were the Burgundians, led by John the Fearless, Duke of Burgundy, on the other the Orleanists, followers of the Duke of Orleans, generally known after 1415 as the Armagnacs, and from 1418 as the Dauphinists, whose head was the Dauphin or heir to the French throne*.

The campaigns which Henry V conducted in France, the techniques he adopted and the weapons and equipment his armies used illustrate better than any domestic operations the state of the military art at this time. They also demonstrate what an invading enemy, if led by a commander of Henry's charismatic personality and strategic brilliance, might have accomplished. Henry V was master alike of the war of movement and of the set-piece siege. There was no feature of waging war at which he did not excel, from – the rarest of talents in medieval times – logistical skill in organizing the movement and supply of vast forces, to ingenious, life-saving inventions on the battlefield and, not least, inspiring the humblest soldier to fight passionately for king and country.

*Confusingly, there were three different Dauphins during Henry V's reign, John, who died in 1415, Louis, who died in 1417, and Charles.

Henry V's first campaign in France began at the fishing village of Chef de Caux, on the northern bank of the Seine estuary, about three miles [5 km] from his first objective, Harfleur, on Tuesday 13 August 1415. After it capitulated, on 27 September, 1415. Henry insisted on marching to Calais, the only other English bridgehead in France beside Bordeaux, although it lay 150 miles [240 km] away, and, allowing for diversions, probably involved a journey of 200 miles [320 km], through hostile territory, intersected by rivers. To all protestations he replied, according to an Italian then resident in England, 'If they laboure to disturbe us of our journey, we shall escape there mallice with honnorable victorie and greate tryumphe.'

And so it proved. On Friday 25 October 1415, near the village of Agincourt, about 30 miles [48 km] south-east of Boulogne, Henry routed an army estimated at ten times the size of his own, inflicting losses exceeding 6000 for fewer than 300 English casualties.

Henry landed at Dover, on 16 November 1415, after a rough crossing which left his French prisoners saying they would rather be back at Agincourt, while the king was unaffected: most unusually for an English sovereign he was a good sailor. Yet, master of the battlefield as he might be, Henry was still far from secure in the Channel. Only six months after Agincourt a fleet was being assembled in the River Orwell to repel an anticipated French invasion, and on 14 May 1416 men liable to home defence duty in Hampshire, Wiltshire and Dorset were put on alert. That month the French were again in Southampton Water, attempting, though with little success, to sink or carry off any ships they encountered. One of their carracks ran aground on a sandbank and was set on fire by the crew, who got away. The intruders next went on to much-harassed Portland, the inhabitants fleeing at their approach and only returning, to the ashes of their homes, when a friendly fleet, commanded by the king's brother, put in a belated appearance. This may also have been the occasion for yet another raid on the Isle of Wight, during which the invaders were attacked while they were re-embarking and forced to abandon their booty, with some casualties, though a local historian attributes this incident to the following year.

On 30 July 1417 Henry was able to lead another fleet out of Southampton for his second French campaign, which began at Toques, near modern Deauville, and ended in the capture of Rouen on 19 January 1419, an achievement in the field of static warfare comparable to Henry's victory at Agincourt. On Tuesday 21 May 1420 the Treaty of Troyes was formally proclaimed in that city. By the Treaty everything Henry had fought for was achieved, and 1066 avenged. Charles VI was to retain the title of king until his death but Henry was to act as his regent, and would on Charles VI's death become King of France, being in the meantime married to his daughter Catherine.

Like that other absentee monarch, and great soldier, Richard I, Henry V had been content to leave the defence of his own kingdom to others and even his vast reputation on the continent was not sufficient to prevent the customary invasion alarms on the coast. On 3 March 1419, while the king was approaching Paris, the familiar warning was issued in Hampshire and Wiltshire, apparently in anticipation of a Spanish descent on Portsmouth and Southampton, and a similar alert was issued in July and August. Some anxiety also existed that the Spaniards might encourage the Scots to new activity and on 12 August 1419 Cornwall and Devon were required to supply a dozen ships to intercept them, but the expected danger never materialized.

Henry V's only real interest in maritime matters lay in finding ships to transport and supply his armies to fight in France and his reputation as a great naval monarch rests on his policy of building, and buying, more and larger vessels than any previous ruler, and on attempting, through regular retainers, to keep a small nucleus of experienced ship-masters ready to serve him when needed. The amounts were not large: 10 marks [£6.66] for the captains of the largest ships, 5 marks [£3.33] for the smallest and 100 shillings [£5] for those in between, but the number of ships was impressive, totalling 38, all Henry's private property, by the end of the reign. Of these, three were exceptionally large for the time, including the great *Jesus*, rated at 1000 tons, constructed at Smallhithe in Kent, and the *Holigost*, a Spanish ship rebuilt for English use. Henry also owned eight carracks, large, rather clumsy, transports of about 500 tons; six somewhat smaller ships; nine 'balingers', a term usually denoting a shallow-draught, small ship powered by either oars or sails, and a dozen other vessels. Southampton, rather than Portsmouth, was the headquarters of Henry's navy and a Keeper of the King's Ships was appointed there in 1413, with responsibility for supervising the building programme, fitting out the finished vessels and paying their crews. A dock and storehouse was built at Southampton, with other warehouses at Hamble. Bursledon, between the two places, contained Henry's least successful vessel, the 1400-ton clinker-built *Grace Dieu*, which proved unseaworthy and was left to rot on the mud until destroyed by lightning 20 years later.

A ship's fighting capacity still mainly depended on its men-at-arms and archers; the balingers which sailed on the Agincourt expedition in 1415 had ten of each, the larger ships 26. Increasingly, however, cannon, both of brass and iron, and shot, whether iron or stone, were also carried; the *Holigost* is known to have mounted six, manufactured in English foundries in Sussex and the Weald at a cost of £496.

The standard textbook on naval tactics in use in the fifteenth century, itself part of a general treatise on waging war, had been written by a Roman author nine centuries earlier. The author, Vegetius, assumed that any commander's aim was to close with the enemy as a preliminary to boarding her. 'Distance' weapons included projecting inflammable mixtures of oil, pitch and burning tow, to set his craft on fire, and arrows to pierce holes in its sails; for closer combat, Vegatius suggested ramming the enemy ship with a metal beam fixed to the mast, using a sickle to cut any ropes within reach, and sending divers over the side to bore holes in the enemy hull, as well as such well-tried devices as blinding your opponent with pots of lime, all, by the 1420s distinctly primitive.

The scientific study of war on land had made more progress. Here, too, the standard work was the classical textbook, *De Re Militari*, just quoted, but it had been recently updated, in an English translation, issued in 1408, which included new but already old-fashioned material on such matters as how to put on a knight's armour, and a French one, prepared about the same time by an Italian woman, Christine de Pisan. Christine, venturing into a specifically male domain, pointed out that war had its goddess, Minerva, as well as its god, Mars. She quoted examples from other works on siege-warfare and assembled some useful material on cannon, her book proving so popular that it was later selected for printing, in an English version, by Caxton, half a century later.

Henry V, a master of siege warfare, may perhaps also have been familiar with *Bellifortis*, written in 1405 by a German, Conrad Kyeser, who offered practical, illustrated, advice on the design of transportable bridges, collapsible scaling ladders, a machine designed to pull down city gates and even an early armoured fighting vehicle, a metal protected cart.

The really important innovation was cannon, which Kyeser barely mentioned. Henry V ordered at least five different varieties for his expeditions to France, but often their names – bombards, culverins, serpentines and the rest – are used interchangeably. The great weakness of the early cannon lay in the barrel, commonly made of iron bars soldered together and then bound with iron rings. No accurate guide existed as to the charge required, though a pound [0.45 kg] of powder to a nine-pound [4 kg] stone ball was the usual ratio. Loading took a long time as the barrel had to be carefully cleaned after every shot – a lingering spark could cause a fatal, premature explosion – and the powder was then poured down the barrel from the muzzle. Accurate aiming was impossible, since the barrel was never really smooth and straight, and no effective sights had been devised. True field artillery was unknown as no adequate gun carriage yet existed, and such guns as did appear in encounter battles, as at Agincourt, were really siege weapons, hoisted from the carts in which they travelled on to solid firing frames.

No one had yet succeeded in producing a remotely effective hand-gun and the English victories in France, especially Agincourt, had been gained by the famous longbow, able to deliver six arrows a minute at a range of 200 to 300 yards [180–275 m], a distance and rate of fire far exceeding the capacity of the out-moded crossbow, with its clumsy rachet and stirrup. During Henry V's reign English confidence in the longbow reached its peak and the king's preparations for his first expedition had been felt in farmyards throughout the land, as the sheriffs were ordered to impose a levy of six feathers on every goose in their counties to provide flights for the archers' arrows and foresters were instructed to reserve ash for making bows and not to squander it on peasants' clogs.

The archers commonly outnumbered the men-at-arms by three to one, and the latter term, if used precisely, meant a fully armour-clad horseman, only one step socially below a knight. He would be attended by at least one, and probably more, squires, or esquires, and one, or several, pages. The whole section he headed was known as a 'lance', but the term also sometimes referred to a single individual so armed. The well-turned-out knight or man-at-arms insisted on plate armour, which had largely replaced the earlier mail. On his head was an egg-shaped helmet, with vizor, on his feet pointed metal shoes, and in between small metal sections overlapping each other and presenting a curved surface from which a sword thrust was likely to glance off.

Archers, quick moving and firing from a distance, tended to suffer little from cannon-fire; at Agincourt only one is recorded as having been killed 'with a gun'. Not so the knights, and the new school of military writers, instead of exploring the tactical possibilities which the coming of gunpowder opened up, tended to view it, mainly, no doubt, because it was new, with deep distrust. At least one argued that it was blasphemous to imitate God's thunder and another saw in cannon an obvious work of the devil. But it was the threat to the social order, at its most rigid on the battlefield, that caused most concern. Could it be right, one anguished commentator asked, for some distant gunner, of lowly birth, to be able to kill a knight in armour, who had spent good money equipping himself to fight like a gentleman?

27

CONQUERED BY ALL

We who used to be the conquerers of all peoples are now conquered by all.

English chronicler, c. 1450

Henry V died, still only 35, on 31 August 1422, and was succeeded by his six-months-old son by his French bride, Catherine. A mere seven weeks after Henry V, Charles VI of France also died. The infant Henry VI, under the Treaty of Troyes, thus also became King Henry II of France. The Burgundian party supported his claim but the Dauphin's adherents insisted that the latter was now sovereign of France, as Charles VII, the start of a new, and from the English point of view, increasingly frustrating phase of the Hundred Years War. Soon afterwards the whole military situation in France was transformed by the appearance at the court of Charles VII of the 'Maid of Orleans', Joan of Arc, an illiterate 17-year-old peasant girl who claimed to have a divine mission to deliver France from the English and to see Charles crowned in Rheims. The latter aim she rapidly accomplished, to the former she made an enormous contribution, though it was only to be achieved completely after her death – she was burned as a heretic – in May 1431.

In 1438 Henry VI, now 16, declared that henceforward he would rule in fact as well as name, but he rapidly proved to have little aptitude for kingship. He had scant interest in government and even less in war, and when, reluctantly, persuaded to put on armour he refused to use his weapons against his fellow Christians. Other manly qualities were also conspicuously lacking. His harshest oath was 'Forsooth!' and he ran in horror from a state ball crying, 'Fy, for shame!' at the sight of the women's low-cut dresses. Henry might have made a competent schoolmaster or monk but he was no king, much less a warrior, and a desolate, sour, period in English history now began. The suppression three years before, in 1450, of the most serious popular rising since the Peasants Revolt, Jack Cade's rebellion, which had substantial middle-class support, and was aimed largely at oppressive royal officials, had left a legacy of ill-feeling and there was a widespread feeling of national humiliation at the disasters in France. Political satires multiplied. One bitterly summed it up:

> Our enemies laugh at us and say 'Take the ship from your precious money' [i.e. the noble] and stamp a sheep upon it, to signify your sheepish minds. We who used to be the conquerers of all peoples are now conquered by all.

The English mainland had in fact remained inviolate; the French were too busy on land to contemplate invading England. Around 1436, however, the first reasoned case had been made for the country to recognize that its security lay in sea-power in a long poem destined to become a classic, the *Libelle of English Polycye*, written with a view to 'exhorting all England to keepe the sea, and namely the Narrowe Sea; shewing what profite commeth thereof, and also what worship and salvation to England and to all Englishmen'. Commonly, though perhaps wrongly, attributed to the future Bishop of Chichester, Adam de Moleyns (or Molyneaux, or Molins), the *Libel*, to adopt the later spelling – the word means merely 'little book' – was sent to the king's council whom it pointedly reminded of Henry V's achievement in building up a powerful navy:

> And if I should conclude all by the King,
> Henrie the Fifth what was his purposing,
> When at Hampton he made the great dromons,
> Which passed other great ships of all the commons . . .
> What hope ye was the King's great intent
> Of thoo shippes, and what in mind he meant?
> It was not ellis [else] but that hee cast to bee
> Lorde round about environ of the See.

The author, contemplating Edward III's famous noble, lamented the decline which had since set in:

> Where be our ships, where be our swords become?

He summed up his advice in a famous couplet, constantly quoted later:

> Cherish merchandise, keep the admiralty,
> That we be masters of the narrow sea. *

England was now to experience the same bitter rivalry between two

---

*The original is equally striking, if less readily intelligible:

> Cheryshe marchandyse, kepe thamyrolte,
> That wee be maysters of the narowe see.

factions contending for the throne, occupied by a weak and frequently insane king, from which France had just emerged. The rival claimant in this case was Richard, Duke of York, who became a popular hero principally because he was opposed to the king and his advisers, and the king's immensely forceful French wife, Margaret of Anjou.

With the birth of an heir to Henry VI, on 14 October 1453, apparently depriving the Duke of York of any prospect of the succession, the stage was set for the great feud between the two royal houses of York and Lancaster known as the 'Wars of the Roses', although the white rose was only one of the emblems of the Yorkists and the red rose was never the badge of the Lancastrians.

After many months of unrest and disorder, serious fighting between Yorkists and Lancastrians began with the Battle of St Albans, on 22 May 1455, at which Henry VI was wounded and captured. Released soon afterwards, he was nominally responsible for the country's defences when, in August 1457, a French and Breton fleet 60 strong was able, unopposed, to land 1800 men at Sandwich. Although recent efforts had been made to strengthen its defences the town was rapidly sacked in the old, familiar way. The Bretons then went on to attack another ancient enemy, Fowey, which suffered an old-style attempt to burn it down, and the French remained off the coast causing general unease until October.

Queen Margaret, the effective sovereign, was forced to appoint, to 'keep the sea' for the next three years, her arch-enemy the legendary Richard Neville, Earl of Warwick, nicknamed 'the kingmaker'. Still only 29, Warwick had been made captain of Calais after displaying outstanding ability at the Battle of St Albans and now, briefly, he regained command of the Channel. From his base at Calais Warwick managed to bring over to Kent, unopposed, a force of 200 lances and 400 archers to take part on the Yorkist side in the first major campaign of the civil war, and back in Calais he learned that a massive expeditionary force was being assembled in Kent to dispossess him of his position as its captain. Warwick, very typically, decided to strike the first blow, sending a cutting-out party, 800 strong, to Sandwich, which now earned the distinction of having been raided by the English as well as the French. Coming ashore between 4 and 5 a.m. on 15 January 1460 the Yorkists captured the Lancastrian leaders in their beds and carried them off along with all the ships, obligingly made ready for sea, in the harbour. The Yorkists scored another success in June 1460 when, for the second time, they struck a pre-emptive blow at Sandwich. In spite of the presence of 200 men-at-arms and 200 archers, waiting to sail to attack Calais, Sandwich was again captured and the Lancastrian commander kidnapped, the Yorkists feeling sufficiently confident to leave most of their men behind to maintain a bridgehead on the coast of Kent.

On 26 June 1460 'the three earls', as the triumvirate supporting Richard of York were known, namely Warwick himself, his father the Earl of Salisbury, and Richard's son, Edward, Earl of March, led some 2000 men ashore there and immediately set off inland for Canterbury. On 10 July 1460, at Northampton, Henry VI was taken prisoner and borne back in triumph to London, and in September Richard of York landed, near Chester, – unopposed – to claim the throne. He was, however, destined never to be king. On 30 December 1460 he was killed in the battle of Wakefield, fought outside Sandal Castle, two miles [3 km] south of that town, in west Yorkshire, leaving his eldest son, Edward, aged 17, to carry on the struggle as the new contender to succeed King Henry VI, whose cause seemed lost. On 4 March 1461 Edward IV, formerly Earl of March, was proclaimed king in London and Henry VI was deposed. The new king soon had to fight for his throne, not only against the many surviving Lancastrian sympathizers but, after 1469, against his own former ally, the Earl of Warwick, who, resentful of all the favours shown to others, changed sides. Calais now became a base for a Lancastrian offensive against the Yorkists, instead of vice versa, actively aided by King Louis XI of France, who had succeeded Charles VII in 1461. On 7 September 1470 Edward IV warned the nation that 'oure ancient enemyes of Fraunce and oure outward rebelles and traitors' were about to invade the country and on 9 September Warwick led his invasion fleet, provided by the French, out of Barfleur and La Hogue. Warwick's usual good fortune stood by him and the wind carried the 'Kingmaker', now about to try to unmake the king he had made, safely across the Channel. Not a shot was fired on 13 September 1470 as his 60 ships put into Dartmouth and Plymouth, before disembarking their passengers and turning for home, again unchallenged. Edward IV narrowly escaped being captured in bed at Doncaster, making one of those romantic royal escapes so frequent in English history. This began prosaically with the king 'feigning to make his water' and then slipping away on his best horse on a breakneck dash for the Lincolnshire coast, and, after a false start because of a storm, he duly escaped to Holland, with 800 men who owned nothing but the armour they stood up in.

On Saturday 6 October 1470, while Edward IV was still tossing unhappily on the North Sea, Warwick made a ceremonial entrance into London, claiming that he had come to restore King Henry VI. The 48-year-old monarch had now been a captive for five years, and although not at that moment actually insane had little idea what was happening. A pale, shambling figure with shoulders bowed and a lowered voice, he appeared as he was led through the streets on Saturday 6 October 1470 'a mere shadow and pretence of a prynce' and when literally restored to his throne he sat limp and helpless, incapable of any effective intervention in affairs. He must have cut a poor figure compared to the so-recently departed Edward IV, who, now 28, stood an imposing 6ft 3in [1.9 m] tall and whom the chroniclers describe as 'of comely visage, pleasant look, broad-breasted' and as 'of most elegant appearance and remarkable beyond all others for the attractions of his person'.

Parliament met on 26 November 1470 to confirm that Henry VI was now king again and to brand Edward IV a usurper. His supporters were well aware, however, that Edward IV, who had taken refuge in the Hague, was likely to attempt an invasion. In December 1470 the Archbishop of York, Warwick's half-brother, was sent to muster every man he could raise in the north, where the landing was anticipated, and, as the enemy fleet began to assemble around Walcheren, a naval force was assigned to patrol offshore and keep an eye on it. In command was Warwick's nephew from the wrong side of the blanket, known in the forthright medieval fashion as Thomas the Bastard, or, even more simply, 'the Bastard of Fauconberg' (or Falconberg).

Edward IV had assembled some 1200 men at Bruges, perhaps 500 of them English, the rest 'Duchemen', i.e. Flemish or German mercenaries, of whom 300 were armed with the new hand-guns.

After nine highly uncomfortable days on board waiting for a storm to blow itself out, Edward's 36 ships at last left the shelter of Flushing on 11 March 1471 undetected. Edward himself, like Henry V, seems to have been impervious to sea-sickness. Thomas the Bastard, no great sailor, having abandoned his blockade of the port to run for shelter was still in harbour, waiting for calmer seas to return. So fierce was the wind that within 24 hours the invading fleet had sighted the coast of Norfolk, though already one ship, with a valuable load of horses, had been lost. Two knights, sent ashore at Cromer, returned to report that the local inhabitants were too terrified to let them land and camp. There was nothing for it but to put to sea again, and once again the wind dictated their landing place, for after two days of being driven northwards they chose the first possible port to get ashore. It turned out to be Ravenspur on the north shore of the Humber estuary near Spurn Head in Yorkshire, where Henry IV had landed after *his* spell in exile. Edward IV dutifully knelt to thank God for his safe arrival, but found his already meagre forces reduced to a mere 500, though 300 more turned up the following day and the rest on the 15th, having been scattered by the gale over a front of 13 miles.

This stretch of the coast, much further north than Edward had been expected, or planned, to land, was undefended, but the local gentry were not at all pleased to see him, as a ballad of the period recorded:

Lord, the unkyndnes was shewid to Kynge Edward that day!
At his londynge in Holdyrnes [Holderness] he had grett payne:
His subjectes and people wolde not hym obey,
Off hym and his people thay had grett disdayne,
There shewid him unkyndnes, and answerid him playne,
As for kynge he shulde not londe there for ẃle ne wood [wile or
woe].
Yett londed that gentill prynce, the will of God was soo.

With his men still weary from their stormy crossing Edward decided
not to risk striking southwards, but, most unusually for an invader, to
go north. Hull, however, refused him leave to rest within its walls, and
a locally raised force soon afterwards barred his way, while he was only
allowed to enter York with a token force and after claiming that he had
come merely to recover his estates as Duke of York. During the next
few days, as he began to march south and large forces flocked to join
him, Edward abandoned all pretence and openly proclaimed himself the
rightful King of England and – for good measure – of France.

On Thursday 11 April 1471 Edward IV entered his capital unopposed,
was hastily re-crowned, without the usual formalities, and was embraced
by the harmless Henry VI, who allowed himself to be ousted without
protest. Thus ended the 'Readeption', the reign of Henry VI Part II. It
had lasted exactly six months.

Seldom had any invasion so rapidly succeeded in securing both capital
and throne, but the main Lancastrian army and its formidable general
were still unbeaten and as they approached London Edward IV led his
troops, now well fed and rested, out to meet them. He took with him
the monarch he had replaced, Henry VI, whose slumped, dejected figure
contrasted strikingly with that of the tall and handsome Edward. (It was
said that the ladies of the land, captivated by his charms, had encouraged
their husbands to desert to him *en masse*.) In the resulting Battle of
Barnet, on 14 April 1471, Warwick was killed and the Lancastrian
triumph seemed complete, but the bloodletting was still not over. On
the very evening of the Battle of Barnet the 'elder statesman' of the
Lancastrian cause, Henry VI's wife, Margaret of Anjou, landed at
Weymouth, bringing with her his son, Edward, Prince of Wales, the
new Lancastrian claimant to the throne if his father were held to be unfit
to hold it, and, at 17, just becoming dangerous.

This Lancastrian invasion, like the Yorkist one a month earlier, had
been delayed by bad weather, which had kept Queen Margaret waiting
to embark for 17 days and when she eventually left Honfleur, on 24
March, it took another three weeks before she finally landed at

Weymouth, on 14 April 1471. Other ships in the little party came ashore at various points between there and Portsmouth.

Margaret first established herself at Cerne Abbas, in Dorset, and then, by a roundabout route, gathering support as she went, made her way towards the Welsh border, hoping for the support of Jasper Tudor, Earl of Pembroke, who had fought alongside Henry VI at St Albans in 1455 and had landed with Warwick in 1470. She eventually faced Edward IVs army at Tewkesbury in Gloucestershire in an exceptionally bitter battle in which the king and the Yorkists were again victorious. Prince Edward, his would-be rival, fell on the battlefield and most of his leading supporters were either killed in the fighting or subsequently executed, while Margaret of Anjou, shattered by the death of her son, was subsequently captured and spent four years as a prisoner, before being ransomed by the King of France.

On Tuesday 14 May 1471 Edward IV, who was at Coventry assembling a fresh army to deal with possible further risings, learned that he now faced a fresh invasion in Kent. The notorious Thomas, Bastard of Fauconberg, who was basically a pirate but popular among seafaring men, had got together a terrifying army of escaped criminals, desperate refugees with nothing to lose, and men with a grievance, who, though indifferent to England's dynastic squabbles were excited by the prospect of sacking London and enjoying enormous loot and unlimited rape. Proclaiming himself 'captain of the navy of England' and 'leader of our liege lord King Henry's people in Kent', Fauconberg sailed from Calais to Sandwich early in May, hoping to take advantage of Edward's enforced absence from London.

Fauconberg's invasion was on a large scale, and attracted considerable local support from the Cinque Ports. His band of foreign adventurers was rapidly reinforced by contingents from Dover, New Romney, Hythe and Lydd, as well as from Sandwich itself, and others came in from many inland places, including Canterbury.

What had begun as an invasion had thus also become a rebellion, but Fauconberg's operations are of exceptional interest since they provide a detailed picture of what happened when a hostile army attacked London, which was every invader's first, or final, objective. What happened was all the more revealing because Fauconberg, not a Neville for nothing, displayed considerable strategic ability and the force he raised was one which, under other circumstances, might have achieved a very different result. Fortunately for Edward IV, Fauconberg must have landed in Kent, although the exact date is uncertain, just about the time that the Lancastrians were being routed at Tewkesbury, Saturday 4 May 1471. His biographer estimates Fauconberg's army at 16-17,000 and though this is probably an exaggeration it clearly posed a very serious threat, especially with most of the royal forces far away in Gloucestershire and not yet recovered from the recent battle.

On Wednesday 8 May 1471 Fauconberg reached Sittingbourne, 25 miles [40 km] from Sandwich, still without a hand having been raised against him, and from there addressed a letter to the municipal authorities in London demanding an unhindered passage through the capital to attack Edward's army, in return for a promise to abstain from pillaging. Confident that the lack of opposition would continue, Fauconberg arrogantly demanded that a reply be sent to him by 9 a.m. the following Friday, 10 May, at Blackheath, the traditional assembly point for armies attacking London. He duly received it. On Thursday the 9th the mayor and the aldermen composed their answer, informing Fauconberg that they intended to hold London against all comers and forwarding to him a copy of Edward's dispatch reporting his victory the previous Saturday at Tewkesbury.

The attack on London was three-pronged, with the Essex dissidents advancing on the far side of the Thames estuary, the joint force of foreigners and Kentish men marching up the main road from the coast to the south of the river, and Fauconberg himself leading his fleet up the Thames in between. By Sunday 12 May he had established both armies near Southwark and moored his fleet near the Tower. A journal maintained by the City recorded their preparations to meet the challenge:

> The mayor and aldermen with the assent of the common council fortified the banks of the river Thames from Castle Baynard as far as the Tower of London with men-at-arms, bombards and other implements of war to prevent an attack by the seamen who had brought a large fleet of ships near the Tower, and the bank was held by the aldermen and the rest of the citizens in great numbers.

The defence were not short of men or weapons and posted men-at-arms and bombards, a form of cannon, all along the river bank on the north side, building bulwarks to hold extra guns. London Bridge itself, the key point in the whole system, became a strongpoint. Its drawbridge was raised and held up by strong ropes while the wooden base, now upright, was pierced by three holes as gun apertures. Those manning it were protected with bags of stones and wool, brought from Leadenhall, and sheets of canvas soaked in vinegar were hung over the bridge to prevent 'wildfire', the combustible mixture often used in sieges, being used effectively against it, with basins of water on hand to extinguish any blazes that were started.

Fauconberg had moored his ships at St Katherine's Wharf on the south side of the river and opened his attack with a bombardment by guns taken from them directed against London Bridge and the section of the city facing him across the river, namely Bishopsgate and Aldgate. He did some damage to both, while his arrows also caused heavy casualties. The more numerous, heavier, and more professionally handled, artillery in the Tower and at the Bridge responded with some vigorous counter-battery fire and had the better of the duel. The City journal briefly records this opening round in the engagement: 'On Sunday [12 May] . . . Kentish men and others, rebels of the lord the king, made an attack on London Bridge and on the new gate there and set fire to divers houses . . . near the hospital of St Katharine.'

Being under fire seems to have united the citizens of London, many of them often only too ready to join in any disturbance that was going, against Fauconberg. Up to that time some anxiety had existed that the poorer citizens would gladly have welcomed the rebels in, anticipating a breakdown of law and order in which 'they might get their hands deep into rich men's coffers'. Now all classes were at one and Fauconberg, abandoning his attempt to storm London Bridge, announced that he would outflank the defences, leading his army twelve miles [19 km] westwards, to Kingston Bridge and then sweeping back through Westminster to take the City from the flank.

When he returned from his abortive foray westwards Fauconberg, on Tuesday 14 May 1471, launched a full-scale assault on London, bombarding the positions on the north bank from the Southwark side and then, around 11 a.m., sending in his infantry armed with bows and hand-guns as well as other weapons, against London Bridge. He also ferried 3000 Kentishmen and others across the Thames to join the Essex contingent in a mass attack, said by the City chronicle to involve 5000 men, against Aldgate and Bishopsgate. Bishopsgate itself was set on fire, as was Aldgate, where the attackers also entered the main bulwark and it required another sortie from the Tower, involving 400-500 soldiers, along with a general attack by the citizens led by the mayor, to drive them out. At last the Bastard's forces were forced out of Aldgate, and several hundred were killed and others captured as they made for their boats, to join the main detachment south of the river, which had abandoned the attempt to capture London Bridge.

Fauconberg having mustered his depleted forces in another of London's regular assembly areas, St George's Field, now withdrew them to Blackheath, three miles [5 km] to the south-east, where on 18 May 1471 they dispersed, the backbone, the men from Kent, returning to their homes. On Tuesday 21 May Edward IV entered London in triumph, the mayor, recorder and other heroes of the siege being knighted, and the captured mayor of Canterbury being hanged, drawn and quartered. Fauconberg himself, in return for a promised pardon, surrendered himself and his fleet to Richard of Gloucester on 27 May, but in September he was beheaded and his head placed on London Bridge, 'looking,' the chronicler noted, 'towards Kent'. That summer and autumn commissioners moved through Kent and Essex seeking out former rebels. 'Such as were rich,' commented one cynical chronicler, 'were hanged by the purse, and the others . . . by the neck.' Only Jasper Tudor, Earl of Pembroke, with whom Margaret of Anjou never had succeeded in joining forces, remained secure in Pembroke Castle and in September he escaped with his nephew, Henry Tudor, Earl of Richmond, now the Lancastrian claimant for the throne, not to France, as intended, but, due to the changeable winds, to Brittany. Duke Francis refused to give them up, and there they remained, a potentially troublesome presence in the wings.

Fauconberg's invasion claimed one final, and innocent, victim. According to Edward's apologist in the *Arrivall*, on learning that the Lancastrian cause 'was extinct and repressed for ever, without any hope of revival . . . the said Henry, lately called king' died 'of pure displeasure and melancholy' on 23 May 1471. Other chroniclers believed, however, that he had, two days earlier, been 'stabbed with a dagger by the hands of the Duke of Gloucester' and that the sad, mad monarch was murdered can hardly be questioned.

The chief irritant to coastal tranquillity over the next few years – the nuisance could hardly be rated higher – was John de Vere, thirteenth Earl of Oxford, the most active Lancastrian still at large. After the Battle of Barnet he had escaped to Scotland and then to France, from which, with Louis XI's help, he made a series of raids against English-held territory, first in the Calais area, then against the mainland of England. On 16 April 1473 Sir John Paston wrote to his brother from Canterbury: 'Item, the Earl of Oxford was on Saturday at Dieppe and is purposed into Scotland with a dozen ships.' The proposed landing in Scotland never materialized, but de Vere did turn up with a small force at St Osyth's in Essex, just west of the present-day Clacton, on 28 May 1473. On encountering resistance from the local nobility he immediately put to sea again but was later sighted off Norfolk and the Isle of Thanet. De Vere spent the summer harassing English ships in the Channel and then, on 30 September 1473, seized the castle on St Michael's Mount, just east of Penzance on the Cornish coast, described by a contemporary chronicler as 'a strong place and a mighty. If it be well victualled, twenty men may keep it against the world.'

De Vere's force, transported in several ships supplied by the French, was 400 strong and the missions, rather than raiding-parties, he sent ashore were well received by the ordinary people, while the local commander, supposed to enforce a strict blockade, remained curiously inactive. Three ships patrolled offshore to prevent reinforcement by sea, but the invaders were allowed to leave their gates and fraternize with the besiegers on land and even to top up their falling supplies. Eventually the king angrily dismissed the man responsible and sent the sheriff of the county with 900 men in four ships to tighten up control of the siege, along with additional guns. It remained, however, a most sloppily conducted affair, with the occasional skirmishes punctuated by rest days when the dead were buried and the wounded cared for and a general atmosphere of *bonhomie* prevailed between besieged and besiegers. Although two ships sent with extra provisions by the King of France never arrived, one skipper jettisoning his stores overboard during a storm, and the other being intercepted by Edward's patrols, the whole episode, with such a trivial force defying the whole might of the royal forces, was an embarrassment to Edward. In the end the garrison's strength was eroded by offers of free pardons, and even rewards, if they would desert, and on 1 February 1474 de Vere himself capitulated, being down to a mere eight or nine men, to save himself being kidnapped by this disillusioned rump and handed over against his will. His life was spared and after ten years as a prisoner he survived to die a peaceful death in 1513.

The Wars of the Roses had been basically an old-fashioned affair, fought largely with the old weapons and the familiar tactics. The chief organizational innovation was in the raising of what were really private armies through the livery and maintenance system, under which the knights and squires living in a particular locality entered into a written contract with the major landlord of the area to support him on the battlefield with all the retainers, often their own tenants, they could muster. They wore their lord's livery, or badge – Warwick's ragged staff was the classic example – and he undertook to 'maintain' them, not financially but by supporting them in their claims and disputes. Large numbers of men could be collected in this way; one Westmoreland squire had undertaken in 1452 to follow the Earl of Salisbury with nearly 300 men, about half being bowmen and half billmen, or ordinary foot-soldiers, about half the men in each category being mounted.

The chief technical change was the increasing use of hand-guns, which were beginning to take on their later appearance, consisting as they did of a metal tube, with a touch-hole, fired from the shoulder, but still very slow to load and hard to aim. Their outstanding disadvantage, however, was their susceptibility to wind and rain, which rendered match and powder unusable, but foreign mercenaries were armed with them by the second Battle of St Albans in 1461 and Edward IV was lent some from France ten years later. Long after improved versions were in use on the Continent, however, the English still clung to their trusted longbow.

Cannon, first developed overseas, were slowly making headway in England, and their value as a weapon of static defence was beginning to be appreciated. In 1481 Edward IV's fear of an invasion by Henry Tudor led to the construction of the first coastal defence works specifically designed to use artillery, at Dartmouth. The guns were set low down, to hole enemy vessels on the waterline, not in the high embrasures usual in contemporary castles, and the loopholes were wide enough, 2ft by 2ft 6in [60 by 75 cm], to give a respectable field of fire. Above the main battery was another floor accommodating eleven smaller, square gun ports, housing guns known as 'murderers', intended to harass the crews on the enemy deck and in the rigging. The cannon installed had inadequate range to cover the harbour entrance and could not be adequately traversed and elevated, the barrel, as in the case of the field artillery described earlier, being mounted only on a clumsy wooden 'sledge'.

The royal forces in England, in contrast to the Continent, had no specialist, permanent corps of artillery. The nation's new ruler, however, took the new arm more seriously than any of his predecessors had done and developed the manufacture of cannon in the Tower, though he had to go abroad, to Flanders, to recruit his chief gun-founder and cannoneer, as well as many craftsmen, who were expected both to manufacture the weapons and use them, though still civilians, on the battlefield. The handling of artillery was considered far beyond, or beneath, the comprehension of ordinary knights or soldiers, but no tactical doctrine had yet been developed either for using guns independently or to assist infantry or cavalry. There were signs, however, that the times were changing and during the invasion alarm of 1484, to be described later, 20 guns were hurriedly purchased from overseas, plus two smaller 'serpentines'.

Edward IV having been taken ill, possibly with a chill, possibly from over-enthusiastic indulgence in a Lenten diet of fruit and vegetables, died on 9 April 1483, still only 40, leaving his twelve-year-old son to succeed him, as Edward V. The effective ruler was the dead king's 30-year-old brother, the new king's uncle, Richard of Gloucester, who became Protector.

Having emerged on top at the end of decades of unprecedented bloodshed, Richard of Gloucester soon succumbed to the temptation to make himself king, in name as he was already in fact, and thus started a chain of events with vast and unforeseen consequences. Hitherto a loyal subordinate and successful military commander, Richard lacked, both physically and morally, the expected attributes of kingship. He was not a hunchback, or 'crouchback' as he was subsequently labelled, but he did have one shoulder higher than the other, probably the right, as a result of constantly exercising his 'sword arm' in its heavy armour during boyhood. Once in power he soon showed himself a ruthless tyrant. He rapidly had all the loyal members of the Council seized; some were beheaded and others locked up. The boy-king, Edward V, was already, quite reasonably, lodged in the Tower waiting to be crowned, and his mother, much against her will, was now persuaded to let her other son, ten-year-old Richard, Duke of York, join him. On 26 June 1483 their uncle announced that the reign of Edward V was over and himself assumed the throne as Richard III. The princes in the Tower, or, more accurately King Edward V and Prince Richard, were last seen alive that summer and by the spring of 1484 their disappearance was attracting comment, as *The Great Chronicle of London* records:

All the winter season . . . the land was in good quiet, but after Easter there was much whispering among the people that the king had put the children of King Edward to death . . . Some said that they were murdered between two feather beds, some said they were drowned in malmsey, and some said that they were pierced with a venomous potion. But, howsoever they were put to death, certain it was that . . . they were departed from this world.

28

A JUST QUARREL

If ever God gave victory to men fighting in a just quarrel . . . He . . . will this day send us triumphant victory.

Speech attributed to Henry Tudor before the Battle of Bosworth,
22 August 1485

The realization that the physically repellent, obsessively secretive despot who had usurped the throne was also a child-murderer had a decisive effect upon public opinion. Few wanted to see a revival of the Wars of the Roses, but, by happy chance, there was both a credible, Lancastrian, contender for the throne, and a means of uniting him with the Yorkist line and thus ending the disastrous feud for ever. The monk responsible for continuing the long-established chronicle of the abbey of Croyland recorded the great events which Richard III's brutality had set in train:

> A rumour was spread that the sons of King Edward . . . had died a violent death but it was uncertain how . . . In order to deliver them from this captivity, the people of the southern and western parts of the kingdom began to murmur greatly, and to form meetings and confederacies . . . All those who had set on foot this insurrection . . . turned their thought to Henry, Earl of Richmond, who had been for many years living in exile in Brittany. To him a messenger was accordingly sent by the Duke of Buckingham . . . requesting him to hasten over to England as soon as he possibly could, for the purpose of marrying Elizabeth, the eldest daughter of the late king, and, at the same time, together with her, taking possession of the throne.

Richard already had his eye on this 17-year-old girl as a possible wife, who would regularize his own position, and he had given orders that none of Edward IV's surviving daughters should be allowed to leave the country so that, if necessary, they could be disposed of as their brothers had been. By the end of September, however, Buckingham was already in contact with Henry Tudor, and the first disturbances must have begun during the next few days, for on 10 October the Duke of Norfolk wrote to John Paston, from London, 'The Kentishmen be up in the Weald and say that they will come to rob the city.'

Simultaneous risings, as near as possible to Saturday 18 October, the official starting date of the rebellion, were planned for Kent, centred on Maidstone, Berkshire and Wiltshire, based on Newbury and Salisbury, and the western counties, centred on Exeter. Meanwhile Buckingham would raise an army at Brecon and cross the Severn.

The rebellion-cum-invasion was a total failure. In mid-October violent storms, followed by flooding, burst upon Wales and the West country, slowing down Buckingham's progress along the Wye Valley and preventing his crossing the Severn to join the main rising in the south-west, where a little prematurely, Henry Tudor had already been proclaimed king at Exeter and Bodmin.

'The Great Water', or 'Buckingham's storm', as it was long known, washed away the rebels' support. Many of the expected recruits stayed at home or were unable to reach the planned rendezvous, and the damp and disappointed Duke was forced to abandon those who turned out and seek refuge in a cottage in Herefordshire, where, the Croyland chronicler learned, he 'was at last discovered . . . in consequence of a greater quantity of provisions than usual being carried thither'. He was taken to Salisbury, where Richard had assembled his main army, and executed in the market-place on 2 November 1483.

Richard III now made a vengeful progress through Devon, killing all the leading rebels he managed to catch and driving others, like the Bishop of Exeter, who had proclaimed Henry Tudor king, into exile in Brittany. The greatest prize, however, still eluded him:

> While the matters . . . mentioned above [by the Croyland chronicler] were going on here and there in the western parts, and the king was still in the said city of Exeter, Henry, Earl of Richmond, being unaware of these disturbances, had set sail with certain ships, and arrived with his adherents from Brittany, at the mouth of Plymouth harbour, where he came to anchor, in order to ascertain the real state of affairs. On news being at last brought him of the events which had happened, the death of the Duke of Buckingham, and the flight of his own supporters, he at once hoisted sail, and again put to sea.

Other chroniclers tell a slightly different story, but about the main outlines of the invasion, and its outcome, general agreement exists. The venture was financed by Francis, Duke of Brittany, to the tune of 10,000 gold crowns, and a force later put at 15 ships, which is probably correct, and 5000 men, which seems far too many for a fleet of this size, assembled. Henry set sail on either the 10th or the 19th October, only to suffer from the same storm which was disrupting the rebels' plans in

Wales. Most of his fleet was driven back to Brittany or Normandy and only Henry Tudor's own ship and one other eventually sighted the English coast, whether at Poole or Plymouth is not clear. Henry may have intended to land at Poole but been forced by adverse weather, or the sight of soldiers on shore, to move on to Plymouth. One version, highly probable in view of his prudent nature, recounts that he sent a boat ashore while waiting for the rest of his ships to catch up with him and that its crew reported that they had met some soldiers on shore, who had claimed to be the advance guard of the Duke of Buckingham's army and suggested that Henry should land and join them. Rightly suspecting a trap, however, he had immediately hoisted sail and put out to sea again. When Henry learned for certain that the rising had failed is also uncertain, but the most authoritative story suggests that, lacking any firm information, he returned to Normandy and waited three days for his missing ships to appear, only learning later, while marching through Normandy back to Brittany, that Buckingham was dead.

Henry Tudor was not discouraged by the failure of his first attempt to obtain the throne. He immediately appealed to the Duke of Brittany for funds to underwrite a second attempt and during the winter refugees from Richard III's tyranny flocked to join him, until there was at Rennes an English colony several hundred strong. It was headed by a regular council with Henry increasingly taking on the character of a sovereign in exile. In a solemn ceremony in Rennes cathedral he publicly proclaimed his determination to reclaim the crown and, when he had done so, to marry Elizabeth of York, his followers rendering homage as though, a chronicler noted, 'he had bene that tyme the crowned kynge and anoynted prince'.

The council decided that Henry's next landing should be on friendly territory, in Wales, and news of this intention seems to have reached Richard III, for the castles at Pembroke, Tenby and Haverfordwest were put on alert to watch for 'Henry Tydder' and a fleet was stationed at Southampton in hopes of intercepting him en route. Both France and Brittany were now on Henry's side, and the young man was said to have been 'ravished with joy' when he was joined at the French court by a group of experienced soldiers led by John de Vere, Earl of Oxford, who had commanded the expedition to St Michaels's Mount ten years before, but had now escaped, after ten years imprisonment near Calais. Hitherto Henry Tudor had been strong in goodwill, but distinctly short in military expertise. Now he had with him, as he gladly acknowledged, a veteran warrior to whom he could 'safely commit all things'.

Richard III was now making active preparations to meet the expected invasion. On 8 December 1484 he sent out 'commissions of array' for the shire forces to be registered, following these ten days later by a demand for returns showing how many men could be called out on a half day's notice. Even while Richard III was taking part in the usual Twelfth Night jollification, spies arrived to confirm that Henry was definitely planning an invasion. 'Nothing,' according to the Croyland chronicler, 'could have been more pleasing to him than this news.' No coward whatever his faults, Richard may well have been genuinely eager to get to grips with his rival.

All that winter rumours circulated that Henry was already at sea with a French fleet but still he did not appear, causing more embarrassment by his absence than if he had landed, for by now Richard had so often called out the levies and requisitioned ships that he was forced to resort to the always unpopular expedient of raising forced loans to keep the defences up to strength. On 16 March 1485 Queen Anne died, after a long illness. Chroniclers in the next reign alleged that Richard had poisoned his wife to clear the way for marrying his niece, who had been seen 'arrayed like a second queen' during the Christmas festivities at court. They were probably unjust, but Richard, always secretive, now became for a time almost a recluse and a prey to what sounds like paranoia, as eyewitnesses later told the historian Thomas More, then a child of seven:

> He was never quiet in his mind, never thought himself secure. When he went abroad his eyes whirled about, his body was privily fenced [i.e. protected by hidden armour], his hand ever on his dagger, his countenance and manner like one always ready to strike again. He took ill rest at nights, lay long waking and musing; sore wearied with care and watch . . . his restless heart continually tossed and tumbled with the . . . stormy remembrance of his most abominable deeds.

Richard's period of isolation was followed by one of feverish activity. In April one trusted supporter, Sir George Neville, was put in command of a fleet protecting the coast of Kent and patrolling the Channel. In May, another, Lord Lovell, was assigned the southern counties as his province, based on Southampton. The Duke of Norfolk and his son had Essex in their charge; the Constable of the Tower, which had recently received reinforcements of cannon, was to protect the capital. The West country was considered reasonably safe after the fiasco, and subsequent executions, there two years before, but Wales was a more dubious proposition, though numerous local noblemen supported the king including the chieftain of South Wales, Rhys ap Thomas, who boasted that Henry Tudor would have to pass over his body to penetrate the country. The powerful Stanley family, in the shape of Lord Stanley and his son, Lord Strange, largely controlled Cheshire and Lancashire, which could bar the way into England if Henry did land in Wales, while

Shropshire and much of Denbighshire was dominated by Lord Stanley's brother, Sir William Stanley, the Chief Justice of North Wales.

His dispositions made, Richard III travelled about the Midlands, moving through Kenilworth, Coventry and Leicester until setting up his headquarters at Nottingham Castle, killing time and animals by hunting in Sherwood Forest while he waited.

Henry had, since the Christmas ceremony at Rennes, been treated by his entourage like a ruling sovereign, and already dubbed himself Henricus Rex in the letters he was now secretly sending to possible supporters which contained a hint of solid rewards to those who joined the winning side:

> Being given to understand your good . . . intent to advance me to the furtherance of my rightful claim and lineal inheritance of the crown, and for the just depriving of that homicide and unnatural tyrant which now unjustly bears dominion over you, I give you to understand that . . . upon the instance of your sure advertise [i.e. report] what powers ye will make ready and what captains and leaders you get to conduct, be prepared to pass over the sea with such forces as my friends here are preparing for me. And if you have such good speed and success as I wish . . . I shall ever be most forward to remember and wholly to requite this your great and most loving kindness in my just quarrel.

One such message had a particularly important result. Henry learned that the powerful Rhys ap Thomas in south Wales was intending to defect to him, along with other influential Welshmen, and this finally settled the destination of the expedition. The Welsh bards, anticipating the liberator's arrival, now burst into a frenzy of literary creativity in which the red dragon of Wales and the black bull of Jasper Tudor were depicted as challengers to Richard III's white boar.

Some writers chose to see in Henry the *Mab Darogan*, the Son of Prophecy, marked out by destiny as his nation's deliverer, who would restore its lost independence not by separating Wales from England but by placing England under a Welshman, so that the conquered became the conqueror. He might even be the reincarnation of the great Owen Glendower, long expected to return in his countrymen's hour of need. As the author of an *Ode to St David* put it:

> And the city of England will be reduced under thee;
> The world will be driven, the Boar made cold.

The Tudors were in fact an ancient Welsh family of impeccably nationalist credentials. Henry's paternal grandfather had been beheaded at Carmarthen after one Lancastrian defeat; his father had died in captivity there after another. Indeed it was to Henry's uncle and mentor, Jasper, who had brought him up, that another poet looked, rather than to the young prince himself:

In what seas are thy anchors, and where art thou thyself,
When wilt thou, Black Bull, come to land?
How long shall we wait?
On the Feast of the Virgin★, fair Gwynedd [i.e. Wales] in her
singing,
Watched the seas.

On a purely practical level, Henry Tudor was all that a claimant to the throne needed to be. An ideal age, 26, young but mature, he was a personable figure, athletic and a good horseman, fond of music, adequately pious, and believed to be tough and determined. An eyewitness described him, a little later in life, in favourable terms: 'His body was slender but well-built and strong; his height above the average. His appearance was remarkably attractive and his face was cheerful, especially when speaking.'

Henry did in fact have a strong claim to the throne. Through his mother, Margaret, he was a great-great-great-grandson of John of Gaunt, son of Edward III, and his father, Edmund Tudor, was the son of Henry V's widow, Katherine of France, by her second marriage to Owen Tudor. His father had died before his birth and his mother had married again and been parted from him, so that Henry had been brought up in the Welsh household of his uncle and guardian, Jasper, who, as mentioned earlier, had carried him off to safety on the continent after the Yorkist victory at Tewkesbury. Now, after the false start of two years before, had come the moment to return.

Henry Tudor had moved his headquarters to Rouen in the spring of 1485 and, partly with money provided by the French government, began fitting out a fleet in the Seine estuary. He hoped to find most of the men he needed in Wales and England but had managed to assemble some 2-3000 to go with him to secure the initial beachhead. Although the commanders, the Earl of Oxford and Jasper Tudor, were highly experienced, the quality of the rank and file was not impressive. Several hundred consisted of English and Welsh exiles or other expatriates, including a contingent of English students from the university of Paris, but the bulk of his forces, numbering perhaps 1800 or 2000, were French mercenaries, released from jail in return for 'volunteering', and described by a French chronicler as 'of the very worst kind one could find'. They

★The Virgin Mary qualified for nine different feast days. The annunciation, on 25 March, or the salutation, on 25 June, seem the most likely to be referred to here.

were under a Breton commander of some local standing and the fleet, its size unrecorded, had a French admiral in command.

The invasion had been carefully planned and only set sail after a favourable last-minute report from a friendly clergyman in Wales. Henry left Harfleur on Monday 1 August 1485 with a 'soft southern wind' speeding his fleet along the Breton coast and then, in a broad sweep northwards, made his way into the Bristol Channel, thereby evading the opposing fleet. Just before sunset on Sunday 7 August 1485 they entered the great bay of Milford Haven. Precisely where he then landed has been the subject of much speculation by Welsh historians, but local tradition suggests Mill Bay, the first small cove on the north side as one enters the Haven from the sea, and about a quarter of a mile [400 m] south of the present-day Brunt farm. Some authorities attribute its name to Henry having remarked 'This is brunt', i.e. difficult, as he clambered over the sandstone rocks, though others contend that the name was a long-standing one; about Henry's reaction on setting foot on his native Wales there is no dispute. He crossed himself, kissed the ground and, kneeling, began to recite the psalm *Judica me deus, et discerne causam meam* – 'Judge me, O God, and uphold my cause.'

The site for the landing, if it has been correctly identified, had been carefully chosen. It was out of sight of the nearest village, Dale, about two miles [3 km] away, and of Dale Castle, just beyond it, in the centre of the 'neck' of the promontory which ended in St Ann's Head. According to the chronicler Polydore Vergil, 'certain companies of his adversaries had had their station . . . to have kept him from landing', but evidently they had been withdrawn for no opposition was encountered and the king's party, once ashore, advanced as far as Dale and spent the night there. A second detachment may have been put ashore at West Angle Bay on the far side of Milford Haven to seal off Pembroke Castle, but in the event its garrison did not challenge their arrival.

Henry Tudor avoided the mistake of so many invaders of lingering near the shore instead of exploiting the advantages of surprise and an unopposed landing. Before dawn on Monday 8 August 1485 he set off from Dale for Haverfordwest, twelve miles [19 km] away, where according to Polydore Vergil, 'he was received with great goodwill by all men' in that town. Good news also came in from Pembroke, where the townsfolk professed themselves ready to serve their 'natural and immediate lord'; Pembroke Castle, where he had spent much of his youth, remained an unknown quantity, but the invaders kept well clear of it by marching north-east, towards Cardigan, 26 miles [42 km] away, over the Prescelly (or Preseli) Hills. The night of 8 August was probably spent at Nevern, just off the main road, about seven miles [11 km] short of Cardigan. So far only a few recruits had come in and that night wild

rumours circulated that one expected supporter was instead on his way
to attack the column 'with a huge army' and, even worse, that the
powerful Rhys ap Thomas, whose assistance was crucial, was planning
to stay loyal to Richard III. Possibly these stories were put about to
discourage Richard from intervening until it was too late, but Henry
also made a timely offer to Rhys ap Thomas of the future lieutenancy –
in effect the viceroyship – of Wales, and the latter now set out with his
retainers on a cross-country march from Carmarthen and thence to
Brecon, Builth, Llangurig and Newtown to Welshpool.

Perhaps because the invaders found it reassuring to have some means
of escape if things went badly, Henry stayed close to the coast on his
steady march, to which there was still no response from the English
government. On 9 August he passed through Cardigan with not a single
sortie against him from its great castle and pressed on to Llwyndafydd,
four miles [6 km] from modern New Quay, where he was so lavishly
entertained that, if legend can be trusted, he later sent his host a
commemorative drinking horn; the Welsh gentry, all accounts agree,
were solidly on his side. After a further 16-mile [26-km] march to
Llanilar, four miles [6 km] south of Aberystwyth, he is said to have
spent another comfortable night as a guest in a local mansion, untroubled
by the royal garrison of Aberystwyth Castle, and the following day, 11
August, his troops began to swing inland, first north-east, then due east,
heading for Shrewsbury and the Severn. The night of 11 August he
probably spent in another country house, near Machynlleth in Montgomeryshire, after another encouraging but otherwise uneventful day.

For Richard III it had been very different. This was the day that he
learned of the landing at Milford Haven and he immediately dispatched
urgent messages to various trusted counsellors to call out their forces,
long in readiness for this moment, to join him at Leicester. One of the
recipients was the Duke of Norfolk, who wrote 'in hast', as he put it, to
John Paston in that county, probably on Saturday 13 August:

> Well-beloved friend, I commend myself to you, letting you to under-
> stand that the king's enemies be a land, and that the king would have
> set forth on Monday, if it had not been Our Lady's Day [i.e. the Feast
> of the Assumption, on 15 August]; but he will go for certain upon
> Tuesday . . . Wherefore, I pray you to meet with me at Bury [i.e.
> Bury St Edmunds], where, by the grace of God, I intend to lie on
> Tuesday night, and that you bring with you such company of tall
> men as you may be able to supply at my cost and charge, as well as
> those you have promised the king.

John Paston did not respond to this plea; nor was he alone. Twenty-
eight peers, whose rank imposed far higher obligations than Paston's,

also failed to appear at the rendezvous. Henry Tudor's adherents, mean-while, were, in Wales at least, coming out into the open. On 12 August he moved on to Castle Caereinon, four miles [6 km] west of Welshpool, and on the following day, with the recruits now flowing in from all sides, his force was united with that of Rhys ap Thomas, accompanied, according to the chronicler Polydore Vergil, by 'a great bande of soldiers'. Having decided to desert Richard III, Rhys ap Thomas had done so in style, using a system of warning beacons – perhaps the very ones built by the king in anticipation of Henry's landing – to call out his men to meet him along his pre-planned route. He rode at their head on a great warhorse, known as Grey Fetterlocks, preceded by his banner displaying a black raven. When he finally joined Henry, on Long Mountain, beside the Severn, facing Welshpool, he is said to have lain on the ground and asked Henry to step over him, to fulfil the letter of his oath to the king that any pretender, would have 'to make entrance' into Richard's kingdom, 'over his bellie'*. Ap Thomas's defection had, as Henry had anticipated, proved crucial in attracting popular support, as a contemporary ballad recorded:

Then Sir Rhys ap Thomas drawes Wales with him,
A worthy sight it was to see
How the Welshmen rose wholly with him,
And stogged them [i.e. trudged] to Shrewsbury.

After camping for the night on Long Mountain Henry's rapidly swelling army now moved on to face its most formidable obstacle yet, a further crossing of the Severn, this time inside England. That day they secured Montford Bridge, four miles [6 km] west of Shrewsbury and Forton, just north of the river, designed to guarantee them a route into the Midlands if they should be unable to take the town. The senior magistrate did indeed refuse Henry entry, the first rebuff he had encountered, but this was a face-saving manoeuvre for on the next day, after spending the night near Forton, they were allowed in, and were soon acquiring recruits from the townspeople. An agreeable story attributes to this period the emergence of the leek as the Welsh national emblem. When Henry Tudor's men, it is said, met soldiers of whose allegiance they were uncertain they would pull up this humble vegetable, or, in its absence, a hyacinth, daffodil or onion; to display the white root, accepting the strangers as of the same persuasion if they did the same.

Richard III must have received early news of the fall of Shrewsbury for he had appointed a body of mounted scouts, known as 'scurriers' to

---

*Another version has him crouching under a bridge while Henry led his army across it. The later replacement for the bridge featured in the story was still being pointed out to visitors in September 1987, when I visited the area.

shadow Henry's army, whose ultimate direction was still uncertain. On 16 August the invaders made a further 20-mile [32-km] march to Newport, and on the 17th he camped at Stafford, about 18 miles [29 km] further on, where he met Sir William Stanley, a member of the powerful Cheshire and Lancashire family for whose support both sides were eagerly bidding.

On 18 August Henry Tudor turned south-east, causing Richard III to suspect that he might after all be heading for London. That day Henry passed through Rugeley, camping that night outside the walls of Lich-field, and the following morning, 19 August, entering it to a rapturous welcome. He moved on to Tamworth, where the castle immediately surrendered, probably augmenting his artillery train with its heavy guns.

Apart from a day's relaxation hunting in Sherwood Forest while he waited for his troops to assemble, Richard III stayed at Nottingham, until on the morning of Friday, 19 August he left for Leicester in a column described by the chronicler as 'square battayll', i.e. with cavalry on either side of the central formations, with Richard and his household troops in the front, the baggage in the middle, and a miscellaneous assembly of other soldiers, largely from the north, in the rear. The two armies were now on a near-collision course. Richard took up his lodgings in an inn in the High Street of Leicester, renamed the White Boar in his honour, and next day, Saturday 20 August 1485, supervised the organization of his forces as men arrived from all over the country. On Sunday morning the whole host marched out towards Kirkby Mallory, about nine miles [14 km] from Atherstone and Leicester on a direct line between them. After a halt for a meal it went on to the village of Sutton Cheny, five miles [8 km] west of Kirkby Mallory, while news reached him that Henry Tudor was on the move down Watling Street, crossing Witherley bridge, and pitching camp for the night of 21 August on Whitemoors plain, between the villages of Shenton and Stoke Golding. Halfway between them, about one mile [1.6 km] to the north lay Ambion [or Ambien] Hill, two miles [3 km] south of the village of Market Bosworth.

'Bosworth' is a later name for the site known at the time, from the colour of its soil, as 'Redmoor'. The four armies, counting those belonging to the two Stanleys as separate, were spread over a roughly elliptical area about two miles [3.2 km] wide by one mile [1.6 km] deep, with Ambion Hill near the centre, stream and marsh at its foot and to one side, an open area with few trees so that the combatants were in full view of each other.

No eyewitness account of the battle exists, but the Italian Polydore Vergil was commissioned 20 years later by the victor to write a history of his triumph, and it seems as objective as could be expected in the

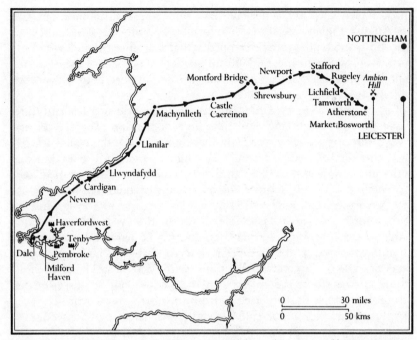

Henry Tudor's triumph. The future Henry VII's march from Milford Haven to Market Bosworth, 1485.

circumstances. (The many diagrams and maps since drawn to explain what happened are imaginative rather than trustworthy.) According to Polydore Vergil Monday 22 August 1485 began badly for the Yorkists:

> It is reported that King Richard had that night a terrible dream; for he thought in his sleep that he saw horrible images as it were of evil spirits hovering clearly about him, as it were before his eyes and that they would not let him rest . . . His heart told him upon this that the result of the following battle would be grievous, and he did not buckle himself to the conflict with such liveliness of courage and countenance as before.

Richard's adversary was in better spirits:

> In the meantime, Henry having returned from the conference with his friends, began to take better heart, and without any delay encamped himself near his enemies where he rested all night, and early in the morning commanded the soldiers to arm themselves, sending as well to [Sir] Thomas Stanley, who had now approached the place of fight, as in the mid-way between the two battles, that he would come with his forces.

The 'Stanleyans' were at this point still nominally loyal to the king but their presence, about a quarter of a mile [400 km] away on his right flank meant that Richard had constantly to be looking in that direction instead of to his front, while his rear 'battle', under the Earl of Northumberland, was preoccupied in protecting the king from these uncertain allies. Numbering perhaps 4000, they could decide the fate of the battle, once they had decided which side, or sides – since the two brothers acted independently – they were on. Keeping an eye on the Stanleys tied up perhaps 3000 of Richard's total force of around 9000, though the remainder still comfortably outnumbered Henry's estimated 5000 troops.

When it came to morale the position was reversed. About the loyalty of his army to Henry Tudor there could be no question and it also included many who, as Polydore Vergil testified, detested Richard III 'worse than all men living'. In the king's ranks meanwhile, matters were very different: 'Many more forbore to fight, who came to the field with King Richard for awe [i.e. out of fear], and for no goodwill, and departed without any danger, as men who desired not the safety but destruction of that prince whom they hated.'

Bosworth was to be no exception to the long tradition which required the historians of battles to put elegant speeches into the commanders' mouths before battle was joined. Polydore Vergil spared his readers any such invention, but the gap was made good by another writer, Edward Hall, in a work first published nearly 80 years after the battle, who at least indicates what one chronicler felt Henry ought to have said:

> If ever God gave victory to men fighting in a just quarrel . . . He of his bountiful goodness will this day send us triumphant victory and a lucky journey over our proud enemy and arrogant adversary . . . For what can be a more honest, goodly, or godly, quarrel than to fight against a captain being an homicide and murderer of his own blood and progeny . . .
>
> For long we have sought the furious boar, and now we have found him. Wherefore, let us not fear to enter into the toil, where we may surely slay him . . . If we win this battle, the whole rich realm of England, with the lords and rulers of the same, shall be ours, the profit shall be ours, and the honour shall be ours.

Deployment of the troops had begun before dawn, but it was not till perhaps nine o'clock that actual fighting began, with an advance by Henry's archers up the hill, which prompted Richard to order a counterattack:

> When the king saw the enemies past the marsh [on Henry's right], he commanded his soldiers to charge against them. They made suddenly

great shouts and assaulted the enemy first with arrows; their foes were not at all loth to fight and began also to shoot fiercely, but when they came to hand strokes the matter then was dealt with by blades.

In this type of hand-to-hand fighting the numerically weaker side usually came off worst but the Earl of Oxford had wisely ordered his men not to move more than ten feet away from their standards so that they presented an impenetrable front. Richard now determined to settle the dispute with his rival in personal combat. He had earlier called for volunteers with keen sight and a good knowledge of armorial bearings to pinpoint the Tudor coat of arms, and now he led his best knights in a fierce onslaught towards them:

> After drawing nearer he knew . . . perfectly by evident signs and tokens that it was Henry. Wherefore, all inflamed with ire, he struck his horse with the spurs, and ran against him out of his own army ahead of the vanguard . . . King Richard at the first brunt killed some men, overthrew Henry's standard, together with . . . the standard bearer. Then he matched himself against John Cheney, a man of much strength, far exceeding the common sort, who strove with him as he came; but the king with great force drove him to the ground, making way with his weapon on every side.

Now came the long-anticipated intervention by the Stanleys:

> Henry abode the brunt longer than ever his own soldiers would have thought, who were now almost out of hope of victory, when suddenly William Stanley with 3000 men came to the rescue.

While the fierce battle was still going on around the person of Henry Tudor the Earl of Oxford, on his right, launched a simultaneous counter-attack against the enemy front line. Those around Richard, seeing that the day was now irretrievably lost, begged him to escape while he could, but his response was manly and royal:

> He . . . is said to have answered that that very day he would make an end either of war or of life . . . wherefore, knowing certainly that that day would either yield him a peaceable and quiet reign thenceforth, or else perpetually bereave him of the same, he came to the field with a crown upon his head, that thereby he might either make a beginning or end of his reign.

It was, as it proved, an end:

> Then truly the remainder in a moment all fled, and King Richard was killed fighting manfully in the thickest press of his enemies . . . When

his men forsook him, he preferred rather to take death with the sword, than by foul flight to prolong his life.

Another chronicler describes the unheroic sequel to this heroic end:

> And Richard, late king, as gloriously as he in the morning departed that town, [Leicester], so as irreverently was he that afternoon brought into that town. For his body was despoiled to the skin, and nothing was left about him so much as would cover his privy member, and he was trussed behind a pursuivant . . . as a hog or other vile beast. And so all bespattered with mire and filth he was brought to a church in Leicester for all men to wonder upon, and was there finally irreverently buried.

The actual fighting during the Battle of Bosworth lasted only two or three hours; by 11 a.m. it was all over, at relatively low cost: perhaps 1000 Yorkist dead, no more than 200 in Henry's army. According to tradition, the victor took up his post afterwards on an eminence just south of the battlefield, towards Stoke Golding, still known as Crown Hill. Polydore Vergil describes the scene: 'After the victory was obtained, Henry gave forthwith thanks unto Almighty God for the same; then afterwards . . . the soldiers cried "God save King Henry! God save King Henry!" and with heart and hand uttered all the show of joy that might be.'

The crown which had fallen from King Richard's head during his last desperate struggle was found, if legend can be trusted, under a hawthorn bush, probably hidden as plunder to be collected later. A London chronicler described the scene which followed, later commemorated in the window of the memorial chapel built in Westminster Abbey:

> Sir William Stanley, who won the possession of King Richard's helmet with the crown being upon it, came straight to King Henry and set it upon his head saying, 'Sir, here I make you King of England'*.

Thanks to the successful invasion and a campaign which had lasted, from the fleet's first landfall to the army's final victory, a mere 15 days, the Wars of the Roses were over at last. On 30 October 1485 Henry Tudor was crowned king, as Henry VII, in Westminster Abbey. By later convention, the death of Richard III marked the end, too, of the Middle Ages in England. Not merely a new reign, but a new epoch of English history, less credulous, less barbarous, less treacherous, with a new sense of national identity and national purpose, had begun.

*The ceremony was probably in fact carried out by the senior peer present, Sir William's brother, Earl Stanley.

BOOK 3
ENGLAND VERSUS ROME

29

THE COUNTERFEIT KINGS

This was a finer counterfeit stone than Lambert Simnel.

Francis Bacon, writing about Perkin Warbeck's arrival in 1491

Henry VII had won his throne by a successful invasion; it was not long before he was forced to fight to hold it against a succession of other invaders all claiming to be its rightful occupant. On 30 October 1485 he was crowned with magnificent ceremony and on 18 January 1486 the 28-year-old king was married to the 20-year-old Elizabeth of York, a tall and beautiful blonde whose attractions he had already found irresistible: their first child was to be born only eight months later. Although happy, the marriage failed in its aim of forestalling further trouble from the Yorkists. The first challenge to his right to his crown, if it had not involved the death of many misguided adventurers, would have been ludicrous. During 1486 a hitherto obscure priest in Oxford decided that if he could make his own protégé king he could claim the archbishopric of Canterbury as his reward, and selected as his candidate the son of an organ-builder, a presentable youth called Lambert Simnel. It suited all who opposed Henry VII to pretend to believe in the imposter, but the real driving force was Margaret of Burgundy, sister of Edward IV and widow of Charles the Hardy, Duke of Burgundy, as Henry VIII's first biographer, the great writer and statesman, Francis Bacon, described in his *History of the Reign of King Henry VII*, published in 1662:

> This princess, having the spirit of a man, and malice of a woman, abounding in treasure . . . and being childless, and without any nearer care, made it her design and enterprise to see the majesty royal of England once again replaced in her house; and set up King Henry as a mark, at whose overthrow all her actions should aim and shoot; insomuch as all the counsels of his succeeding troubles came chiefly out of that quiver.

The murders of Richard III's reign had created the ideal conditions for any would-be pretender to the throne, but it was finally decided to pass off Lambert Simnel, now aged around ten or eleven in 1486, not as the dead Edward V or his brother Richard, but as the live but imprisoned Earl of Warwick, the eleven-year-old nephew of the dead Richard III, who was both the right age and might conceivably have escaped from the Tower. This was the more attractive because the earl's father had been born in Ireland, where a reservoir of discontent towards the English crown always existed, and he could thus be described as 'an Irish Prince'.

Francis Bacon describes the development of the conspiracy:

> And upon counsel taken with the Earl of Lincoln, and the Lord Lovel, and some other of the party, it was resolved with all speed that two lords, assisted with a regiment of two thousand Almains [i.e. Germans], being choice and veteran bands, under the command of Martin Swart, a valiant and experimented [i.e. experienced] captain, should pass over into Ireland to the new king; hoping, that when the action should have the face of a received and settled regality . . . the fame of it would embolden and prepare all the party of the confederates and malcontents within the realm of England to give them assistance, when they should come over there.

Martin Swart [or Schwarz, or Schwartz or Swarte] was one of the most famous freelance captains of the time and his little force of battle-hardened veterans was got together at Tournai in Flanders, while Lambert Simnel and the young priest who had discovered him went ahead to Ireland. The reception they received won over the doubters, as Bacon observes:

> After they were come into Ireland, and that the party took courage, by seeing themselves together in a body, they grew very confident of success; conceiving and discoursing amongst themselves, that they went in upon far better cards to overthrow King Henry, than King Henry had to overthrow King Richard; and that if there were not a sword drawn against them in Ireland, it was a sign the swords in England would be soon sheathed or beaten down.

On 2 February 1487 Henry VII, who was well informed about what was happening, called a conference at Sheen to discuss defence measures. It had two immediate consequences. The genuine Earl of Warwick was taken from the Tower and paraded through the streets to St Paul's to demonstrate that he was still alive, and the Earl of Lincoln fled to Tournai, bearing with him all the secrets of the recent council.

At this stage Henry anticipated a two-pronged invasion of the kind that every ruler dreaded, as Bacon records:

And first he did conceive . . . that he should be assailed both upon the east parts of the kingdom of England, by some impression from Flanders, and upon the north-west out of Ireland. And therefore, having ordered musters to be made in both parts, and having provisionally designed two generals, Jasper [Tudor], Earl of Bedford, and John, Earl of Oxford, meaning himself also to go in person where the affairs should most require it, and nevertheless not expecting any actual invasion at that time, the winter being far on, he took his journey himself towards Suffolk and Norfolk for the confirming of those parts.

Henry's strategic problem was enormously simplified when, at the end of April, the more formidable of the two threatening armies, that in Flanders, instead of crossing to East Anglia, made the week-long voyage to Ireland, where it landed, to an enthusiastic reception, on 5 May 1487. On 24 May, Ascension Day, Lambert Simnel was crowned as King Edward VI in Christ Church, Dublin, though as the new monarch lacked any crown jewels a gold circlet had to be borrowed for the purpose from a statue of the Virgin Mary. The new boy king was then hoisted onto the shoulders of the tallest man in Ireland so that his new subjects could acclaim him and an Irish parliament was summoned in 'King Edward VI's' name.

Henry's best soldier, the Earl of Oxford, had already been assigned to protect the north-west coast and Henry now sent a court official to survey the Lancashire ports to see if they could handle ships of the tonnage needed to carry Lincoln's troops. His report confirmed that they would be adequate for the purpose and after spending a relaxed Easter – Easter Day was on 5 April – at Norwich, Henry moved on, by way of Cambridge, to Coventry, setting up his headquarters at Kenilworth Castle on 8 March 1497.

Meanwhile, as Henry no doubt learned, the Earl of Lincoln had assembled a numerically formidable force, far larger than that Henry had commanded two years earlier. To Swart's well-trained and competently-commanded Germans, numbering around 2000, had been added double that number of Irishmen, spoiling for a fight, but ill-equipped. Half-naked, wearing kilts, and barefoot, the Irish lacked armour, except for a home-made wooden shield, and weapons, except for darts, daggers, and a knotted cord, used to garrotte a fallen opponent. The combined army sailed from Howth, just north-west of Dublin, on Sunday 3 June 1487, and landed unopposed on Monday 4 June 1487 near Furness, later Barrow-in-Furness, on the northern side of the entrance to Morecambe Bay, at a spot variously described as 'the pyle of Fowdrey, 'the Pile of Fouldry'. and Fouldrey'.

Lincoln had expected that his forces would be swollen by floods of eager recruits pouring in, but was to be sadly disappointed as Francis Bacon describes:

> The rebels took their way towards York, without spoiling the country or any act of hostility, the better to put themselves into favour of the people . . . but their snowball did not gather as it went. For the people came not in to them; neither did any rise or declare themselves in other parts of the kingdom for them; which was caused partly by the good taste that the king had given his people of his government . . . and partly for that it was an odious thing to the people of England, to have a king brought in to them upon the shoulders of the Irish and Dutch [i.e. Germans and Flemish], of which their army was in substance compounded.

After marching due east for about 80 miles [28 km], as far as Masham in north Yorkshire, a summons was issued to York, 30 miles [48 km] to the south-east, to surrender to 'Edward VI', but the city had recently been reinforced by 400 men and was aware that a large army was also on its way to the rescue. The demand was ignored and the invaders now turned due south, camping for the night on Bramham Moor, twelve miles [19 km] south-west of York. That same night, 10 June 1497, Lord Clifford, having left York in pursuit of the rebels, had camped with his men at Tadcaster, four miles [6 km] to the west, and was taken unawares when a rebel force launched a night attack, capturing much of his baggage. It was first blood to Lincoln and soon afterwards the royalists withdrew to York, while the rebels moved south towards Doncaster. From Kenilworth Henry VII had meanwhile moved north-east to Leicester.

As Bacon comments 'the relations that are left unto us are . . . naked and negligent', but the king's army when the two sides finally came face to face undoubtedly outnumbered Simnel's with perhaps 12,000 royal troops confronting 8000 on the other side, Lincoln's progress through the north having ultimately brought in a sizeable number of Yorkist sympathizers. The site was where the village of East Stoke now stands, three miles [5 km] south of Newark in Nottinghamshire, the rebel army being deployed along a ridge, with the River Trent on their right flank and covering part of their rear, a classically strong position but one making escape difficult.

On the morning of Saturday 6 June 1487 the Earl of Oxford's 'battle' coming up into position on the left of the line, was heavily attacked by the Earl of Lincoln's men and suffered heavy casualties, so that some of his troops fled in panic. The situation was restored by the arrival of the king's 'battle' and his third division and a violent struggle ensued, with the rebels, though outnumbered and outclassed, fighting bravely, as Edward Hall makes clear:

> And so both the armyes joyned and fought earnestly and sharply, in so muche that the Almaynes [i.e. Germans] beynge tryed and expert menne in warres and marciall feates, were in all thynges, as well in strengthe as pollecye egall and equyualent with the Englishmen; but as for Martyne Swarde theyr chiefe capitayne and leader, not many of the Englyshemen, bothe for vauyuant courage of a stoute stomack and strengthe and agylyte of body was to be compared or resembled with hys manhoode. Of the other syde, the Iryshemen, although they foughte hardely and stucke to it valyauntly, yet because they were after the manner of theyr countrey almoste naked, without harneys or armure, they were stryken downe and slayne lyke dull and brute beastes, whose deathes and destruccyons was a grat discouragynge and abashement to the residue of the company.

For a time the issue was in doubt, but eventually superior numbers and equipment triumphed. Total losses were estimated at perhaps 2000 in Henry's army, and double that number among the rebels, many of the dead being Irish trying to escape across the river at a point later known as 'The Red Gutter'. The Earl of Lincoln and Martin Swart died on the battlefield, the priest who had put Lambert Simnel up to the whole costly imposture was, according to Francis Bacon, 'committed close prisoner and heard of no more', while Simnel himself, still only aged about eleven, suffered a pleasanter, if more humiliating, fate:

> For Lambert, the king would not take his life . . . thinking that . . . being kept alive, he would be a continual spectacle and a kind of remedy against the like enchantments of people in time to come. For which cause he was taken into service in his court to a base office in his kitchen so that . . . he turned a broach [i.e. spit], that had worn a crown.

Only four years after the crushing defeat of the Simnel invasion another pretender, clearly contemplating a similar venture, appeared in Ireland, thanks, as Francis Bacon explains, to Margaret of Burgundy's vendetta against Henry VII:

> The lady Margaret . . . stirring both heaven and hell to do him mischief . . . did continually, by all means possible, nourish, maintain, and divulge the flying opinion that Richard, Duke of Yorke, second son to Edward IV, was not murdered in the Tower, as was given out, but saved alive. For that those who were employed in that barbarous fact, having destroyed the elder brother, were stricken with

remorse and compassion towards the younger, and set him privily at liberty to seek his fortune . . . She had some secret espials [i.e. spies] . . . to look abroad for handsome and graceful youths, to make Plantagenets and Dukes of York. At the last she did light on one, in whom all things met . . . to serve her turn for a counterfeit of Richard of York.

Perkin Warbeck [or Osbeck] – his first name was a shortened version of Peterkin, the diminutive of his real name, Peter – was, when he made his public debut in Ireland in 1491, a young man of about 16. His father, according to Perkin's later confession, was a minor official, probably a boatman turned customs officer, of Tournai, but the family lived for a time in London where Warbeck senior supplied carpets to the royal court. Back in Flanders he mixed with many English residents and at about 14 became footman to a leading Yorkist family, from whom he absorbed a good knowledge of English affairs as well as aristocratic manners. By 16 or 17 he was working for a Breton merchant trading with Ireland, being employed as a male model to show off his master's wares and his rich silk outfits, good looks and dignified bearing set tongues wagging in Cork to suggest that he was of princely blood.

The Warbeck conspiracy was a much more serious nuisance than Simnel's, as Francis Bacon explains:

> This was a finer counterfeit stone than Lambert Simnel . . . he was a youth of fine favour and shape . . . He had such a crafty and bewitching fashion, both to move pity, and to induce belief, as was like a kind of fascination and enchantment to those that saw him or heard him. Thirdly, he had been from his childhood such a wanderer . . . as it was extreme hard to hunt out his nest and parents . . . he did so flit from place to place.

Warbeck was most effectively coached for his imposture by his supposed aunt, Margaret of Burgundy, who speedily 'recognized' him as her nephew Richard, whom she had last seen at the age of seven. By 1493 he had established himself in near-regal state in Antwerp, where he took over the vacant house of the Merchant Adventurers as his palace, and held court under the royal coat of arms, which angry expatriates pelted with mud and stones.

Although Henry VII professed to despise 'the boy who calls himself a Plantagenet', or 'the French lad', as some other sceptics described him, Warbeck had already caused a rupture with Flanders, and a steady trickle of warriors crossed the Channel to put their swords at 'King Richard's' disposal. As the Warbeck plot thickened Henry faced, just he had in Lambert Simnel's time, the danger of a simultaneous invasion from

Flanders and Ireland. This latter was the real seed-bed of conspiracy and during 1494 the king took energetic pre-emptive measures, as Bacon describes:

> Meanwhile the king did not neglect Ireland, being the soil where these mushrooms and upstart weeds [of rebellion] that spring up in a night, did chiefly prosper. He sent therefore from hence, for the better settling of his affairs there . . . Sir Edward Poynings, with a power of men, and a martial commission, together with a civil power of his lieutenant, with a clause, that the Earl of Kildare, then deputy, should obey him.

Poynings, a distinguished soldier whom Henry had already employed on the mission to try to dislodge Warbeck from Flanders by diplomatic means, landed at Howth in October 1494 with a retinue of Englishmen earmarked to take over the chief posts in the country, and 1000 English soldiers, supposed to create the conditions under which this could be done.

Poynings's legislative work, through the Irish parliament which met at Drogheda on 1 December 1494, was to earn his name immortality through what Francis Bacon described as 'that memorable act, which at this day is called Poyning's Law, whereby all the statutes of England were made to be of force in Ireland', a landmark in the long process of trying to integrate Ireland into the kingdom of England.

Perkin Warbeck meanwhile, as Bacon records, had decided that the time had come to make his name, not in Ireland but in England:

> Perkin Warbeck finding that time and temporising did now, rather make against him . . . resolved to try his adventure in some exploit upon England; hoping still upon the affections of the common people towards the house of York. Which body of common people he thought was not to be practised upon [i.e. deceived], as persons of quality are; but that the only practice upon their affections was to set up a standard in the field. The place where he should make his attempt, he chose to be the coast of Kent.

Warbeck had by now mustered sufficient men to fill 14 ships, presumably therefore totalling at least 2-3000 soldiers, and on Friday 3 July 1495 they appeared off Deal: Warbeck had opted for the obvious 'front door' approach which Henry himself, faced with a similar problem, had rejected:

> He cast anchor, and to prove the affections of the people, sent some of his men to land, making great boasts of the power that was to follow. The Kentish men, perceiving that Perkin was not followed by any

English of name or account, and that his forces consisted but of strangers born, and most of them base people and freebooters, fitter to spoil a coast, than to recover a kingdom; resorting unto the principal gentlemen of the country, professed their loyalty to the king, and desired to be directed and commanded for the best of the king's service. The gentlemen entering into consultation, directed some forces in good number to shew themselves upon the coast; and some of them to make signs to Perkin's soldiers to land, as if they would join with them; and some others to appear from some other places, and to make semblance as if they fled from them, the better to encourage them to land. But the wily youth would not set one foot out of his ships, till he might see things were sure. Wherefore the king's forces, perceiving that they could draw on no more than those that were formerly landed, set upon them and cut them to pieces, ere they could fly back to their ships.

According to a more detailed story the victims were originally enticed on shore by a single horseman, who persuaded the first contingent to invite others to disembark while he went off to fetch his comrades and a supply of beer for a welcome party. Instead the invaders found themselves surrounded by archers and swordsmen and were cut to pieces, 150 being killed and 159 captured. The latter, Bacon testifies, had a wretched end:

> They were brought to London all railed in ropes, like a team of horses in a cart, and were executed some of them at London and Wapping, and the rest at divers places upon the sea coast of Kent, Sussex and Norfolk, for sea-marks or lighthouses, to teach Perkin's people to avoid the coast.

Rebuffed in Kent, Warbeck's next move could have been predicted:

> Perkin, advised to keep his fire, which hitherto burned as it were upon green wood, alive with continual blowing; sailed again into Ireland, whence he had formerly departed, rather upon the hopes cf France, than upon any unreadiness or discouragement he found that people. But, in the space of time between, the king's diligence and Poyning's commission had so settled things there, as there was nothing left for Perkin, but the blustering affection of wild and naked people.

Warbeck's campaign in Ireland began with an attempt to capture one of the most loyal cities in the whole province, Waterford. On 23 July his remaining eleven ships, one having been captured and two more blown off course, sailed up-river into its splendid harbour to blockade it by water while 2000 men under a rebellious local earl besieged it by land. After eleven days there was no sign of its yielding, and the besiegers were in danger of being overwhelmed by the hastily summoned forces of Sir Edward Poynings, so on 3 August 1495 Warbeck abandoned the attempt and made for Cork.

For a time Warbeck disappears from view, being credited by legend with surviving a shipwreck, crossing the Irish mountains in disguise before taking ship for Scotland. Here his luck changed. The young King James IV of Scotland, at 22 little older than Warbeck himself, took an immediate liking to him when they met in the grand presence chamber of Stirling Castle on 27 November 1495. The penniless castaway was decked out in lavish clothes, given the handsome maintenance allowance of £1200 a year, and taken on a triumphal tour of Scottish towns as if he were already a reigning monarch. He was also found a suitable bride, Lady Catherine Gordon, described by Bacon as 'a near kinswoman to the king himself and a young virgin of excellent beauty and virtue'; she was also very rich. Warbeck's smooth tongue found congenial new employment in singing his wife's praises. Her eyes, he wrote, 'brilliant as the stars, make all pain to be forgotten and turn despair into delight; whosoever sees her cannot choose but admire her, admiring cannot choose but love her, loving, cannot choose but obey her.' While the young couple enjoyed a blissful honeymoon in the early months of 1496 Warbeck's new ally, James IV, busied himself in preparing for a great expedition into England to put 'Richard IV' on its throne.

Perkin Warbeck was well aware that in entering England with a foreign army he was prejudicing his own appeal to his supposed countrymen, and in a long proclamation tried to forestall such reactions, repeating his claim to be the rightful king of England and explaining that he had only accepted Scottish help in order to secure his inheritance, but the smooth tongue which had captivated James IV failed to impress the sturdy peasants of Northumberland, as Francis Bacon makes clear:

Perkin's proclamation did little edify with the people of England; neither was he the better welcome for the company he came in. Wherefore the King of Scotland, seeing none came in to Perkin, nor none stirred anywhere in his favour, turned his enterprise into a rode [i.e. raid] and wasted and destroyed the country of Northumberland. Hearing that there were forces coming against him, and not willing that they should find his men heavy and laden with booty, he returned into Scotland with great spoils, deferring farther prosecution till another time.

The rumours of an approaching English army were in fact false, but, perhaps disappointed at the lack of local support, James IV seems to have tired of the whole enterprise and by 21 September 1496, four days after they had set out, the invaders were back on the Scottish side of the border at Coldstream Castle. They had destroyed two watch-towers and advanced a mere four miles [6 km] into England.

The raid had unforeseen consequences. Henry VII used it to secure from parliament in January 1487 a promise of taxation to finance 'a substantial war to be continued upon the Scots' and this in turn provoked a serious rising in Cornwall, only ended with the routing of the rebels, who had got as far as Blackheath, on 17 June 1497. The Cornish rebellion may have attracted Perkin Warbeck's attention to that part of the country, and already his prospects were looking brighter for he was now invited by Sir James Ormond to try his luck once more in Ireland. Early in July, on a ship provided by James IV and aptly named the *Cuckoo*, the pretender sailed from Ayr, complete with wife and 30 followers. On 16 July 1497 he landed at Cork and was well received by the mayor.

Henry VII is said to have known as early as 5 August 1497 that Warbeck's next destination was Cornwall and to have made his dispositions accordingly. Lord Daubeny, who had led the attack on the rebels at Blackheath two months before, was sent west, to take command of the levies raised by Rhys ap Thomas in South Wales and Gloucestershire and gathered from the loyal counties of Wiltshire, Hampshire, Somerset and Dorset, while Henry himself assembled at Woodstock a second army to lie across the rebels' route to the capital. The West Country gentry, who had failed to prevent the earlier rising, now poured men into Exeter, which was made ready to resist a siege. Warbeck's army was by contrast more farcical than formidable. Bacon describes him as 'having with him only some six score or seven score fighting men', but he was not deterred. Around the third week of August, or a little later, two small Breton or Spanish sailing ships, attended by an even smaller pinnace, crept down-river from Waterford into the Irish Sea, to be rapidly detected and pursued by four – some accounts say seven – ships lying in wait for him. According to one story, Warbeck's ship was overtaken and searched but the crew had hidden him in a wine cask and refused a bribe of 2000 nobles [£667] to betray him. Another account, less colourful but more likely, states that Warbeck's ships outran Henry's and all are agreed that on Friday 7 September 1487 Warbeck invaded England for the third time, landing at Whitesand Bay, a mile or two north of Land's End. He sent his young Scottish wife, who seems to have been admirably supportive through all his adventures, to the safety of the monastery at St Michael's Mount, scene of an earlier invasion, on the other side of the peninsula, and set out on the long slog up through the south-western counties towards London, 290 miles [464 km] away.

His first rallying point was the town, 50 miles [80 km] from Whitesand Bay, where the June rebellion had begun, as Bacon describes:

> He . . . forthwith came to Bodmin, the blacksmith's town [one leading rebel had been a smith] where there assembled unto him to the number of three thousand men of the rude people. There he set forth a new proclamation, stroking the people with fair promises, and humouring them with invectives against the king and his government . . . entitling himself no more Richard, Duke of York, but Richard IV, King of England. His council advised him by all means to make himself master of some good walled town; as well to make his men find the sweetness of rich spoils and to allure to him all loose and lost people, by likes hopes of booty' as to be a sure retreat to his forces, in case they should have any ill day, or unlucky chance in the field. Wherefore they took heart to them, and went on, and besieged the city of Exeter.

The rebel army was in good heart. During the 55-mile [88 km] march from Bodmin it had met no resistance and had been well supplied with food by the locals, making plundering, about which Warbeck was very sensitive, unnecessary. But no hope existed of battering down the walls and he knew the royalist armies might appear at any moment, as Francis Bacon explains:

> Perkin also doubted [i.e. had no doubt] that succours would come ere long; and therefore resolved to use his utmost force to assault the town. And for that purpose having mounted scaling-ladders in divers places upon the walls, made at the same instant an attempt to force one of the gates. But having no artillery nor engines, and finding that he could do no good by ramming with logs of timber, nor by the use of iron bars, and iron crows [i.e. claw-headed crowbars], and such other means at hand, had no way left him but to set one of the gates on fire, which he did. But the citizens well perceiving the danger, before the gate could be fully consumed, blocked up the gate, and some space about it on the inside, with faggots and other fuel, which they likewise set on fire, and so repulsed fire with fire; and in the meantime raised up rampiers [ramparts] of earth, and cast up deep trenches, to serve instead of wall and gate.

What followed is vividly described by Edward Hall, on whose account Bacon's is clearly based:

> The cytezens perceaving their towne to be envyronned with enemies and lyke to be enflamed, beganne at ye first to be sore abashed, and let certeyn messengers by cordes downe over the walle which shuld

certefie ye kyng of all their necessitee and trouble. But after that, takyng to theim lusty heartes and manly courages they determined to repulse fyer by fier, and caused faggottes to be brought to yet inward part of the portes and posternes and set theim all on fier, to thentent that the fier being enflamed on bothe the sydes of the gates, might as well exclude their enemies from entryng, as include ye citezens from ronnyng or fliyng out, and that they in the meane ceason might make trenches and rapayres [i.e. ramparts] to defende their enemies in stede of getes and Bulwerkes. Thus all the doynges [doings] and attemptes of the rebellious people had evell successe in their first entreprice; And thus by fyer the citee was preserved from flame and burnynge.

Warbeck was by now becoming desperate. According to an Italian observer the pretender had on landing attracted 'eight thousand peasants . . . ill disciplined and without any gentlemen'. The number of these adherents was dwindling, as Edward Hall records:

When the pore and nedy people sawe the great defence which was made at Excetter, and that no men of honour nor yet of honestie drewe to hym . . . they withdrewe theim selfes . . . providying their awne savegarde. Which thinge when Perkyn perceaved, he put small trust and lesse confidence in the remnant of his army . . . because the moost parte of his souldioures were . . . never exercised in warre nor marciall feates but only with the spade and shovell.

During the 20th, Warbeck learned that Lord Daubeny's army was near Glastonbury, only 20 miles [32 km] away to the north-east, and Daubeny's advance guard encountered some of the rebels, killing or wounding 24 of them. The king's main force, Warbeck must have suspected, was unlikely to be far behind and a royal fleet was probably already at sea to cut off his escape by ship. A single vessel might, however, still slip through and Warbeck, possibly after consulting with his council and perhaps in order to save his followers' lives, though his motives remain uncertain, decided to get away while he still could. His opportunity came during the night of 21 September, as the Milanese ambassador later described:

At the fourth hour of the night he silently departed from the camp, with some ten persons and at dawn the next morning the unfortunate Cornishmen discovered their plight and took to flight, to such an extent that by the third hour of the day not one was left in Taunton.

Warbeck was probably making for Southampton Water and having, according to Edward Hall, 'made such haste with the swiftnes of his horse and sharpenes of his spurres that . . . no person could tell tydynes of him', did well to reach Beaulieu Abbey, just short of it, nearly 75 miles [120 km] from Taunton. His departure presented the king and his council with something of a dilemma, for they were, as Bacon explains, 'divided in opinion; some advised the king to take him out of sanctuary perforce and to put him to death . . . Others were of opinion . . . that it was not worth the exposing of the king to new scandal and envy.' In the end, to everyone's relief, Warbeck and his associates gave themselves up and on 5 October the pretender knelt before the monarch he had tried to overthrow, at Taunton, and pleaded for forgiveness, later making a full, indeed fulsome, confession, revealing his true origins. As with Lambert Simnel, Henry had wisely decided that mockery was more effective than murder in discrediting the would-be usurper and Warbeck was taken back to London and 'conveyed leisurely on horseback, but not in any ignominious fashion, through Cheapside and Cornhill, to the Tower, and from thence back again to Westminster with . . . a thousand taunts and reproaches.'

Henry was even more generous in his treatment of 'Queen Catherine', now demoted again to her previous status, once satisfied that she was not pregnant, and 'received her not only with compassion, but with affection'.

Warbeck's deluded followers, who were surrounded by Lord Daubeny soon after Warbeck had deserted them, also got off lightly:

> The King, who commonly drew blood, as physicians do, rather to save life than to spill it, and was never cruel when he was secure, now he saw the danger was past, pardoned them all in the end, except some few desperate persons, which he reserved to be executed, the better to set off his mercy towards the rest.

Warbeck's end was sad, if almost inevitable. A year after being captured, he climbed through a window, at midnight on 9 June 1498, and made a somewhat half-hearted attempt to get to the coast, before surrendering himself to the abbot of the monastery at Sheen after travelling a mere ten miles [16 km]. For punishment he was made to sit in a pillory, on a scaffold derisively constructed of 'pipes [i.e. wine barrels] and hogsheads' outside the Palace of Westminster, before being returned to the Tower and a much more rigorous regime in a cell where, it was related, 'he sees neither sun nor moon'. His fate was finally sealed by the appearance of yet another pretender, a 19-year-old London shoemaker's son, Ralph Wilford [or Wulford] who masqueraded as the still-imprisoned Earl of Warwick, but was speedily caught and executed. This episode seems to have exhausted Henry's patience and, probably through an *agent provocateur*, both Warbeck and the wholly innocent young Earl of Warwick were encouraged to plan an escape, caught and executed,

Warwick being beheaded on Tower Hill a fortnight after, on 16 November 1499. Warbeck had been hanged, drawn and quartered at Tyburn. It was a sad end to a colourful career, but by early December a Spanish envoy, sent to England to secure closer relations between the two countries, was able to report to King Ferdinand of Aragon, that 'not a drop of doubtful royal blood' remained in England! Warbeck's widow, universally admired for her loyalty to her husband as well as for her looks and demeanour, went on to marry another three times but caused the king no more trouble.

Henry VII's reign not merely saw the Tudor dynasty firmly established; it also marked a new stage in the nation's consciousness of its own identity. A major factor was the rapid spread of printing, which helped the English language to triumph over its rivals. In 1484 Caxton published *The Canterbury Tales*, in 1485 an English version of Sir Thomas Malory's classic *Morte d'Arthur*, containing 'the noble hystoryes of . . .' those great folk heroes 'Kynge Arthur and of certeyn of his knyghtes' and in 1497 a *Description of England*, based on a Latin original and some of the early English chronicles. Already continentals were complaining of the assumption of the English that they were innately superior to other nations, like an Italian who came to London on an official mission in 1497:

> The English are great lovers of themselves, and of everything belonging to them; they think that there are no other men than themselves; and whenever they see a handsome foreigner they say that 'He looks like an Englishman', and that 'It is a great pity that he should not be an Englishman' . . . They have an antipathy to foreigners and imagine that they never come into their island, but to make themselves masters of it, and to usurp their goods.

Henry VII's reign was a watershed in the formation of the country's future defence policy. The king appreciated that no fighting fleet could be mobilized in wartime unless a strong merchant marine existed in peacetime and the building of large commercial vessels, i.e. those over 80 tons displacement, was encouraged by a government bounty from 1488 of up to 5s [25p] a ton to owners who commissioned such vessels or bought them from abroad, often paid in the form of a 'custom's credit' whereby duty was remitted on goods brought in on the ship's first voyage. The allowance was generous, representing £30 off the cost of a standard 120-ton craft valued at £110. The numerical strength of the navy did not increase during Henry's reign; at its peak, under Henry V in 1411, it had consisted of 34 vessels, and Edward IV in 1481 could boast of 15; in 1509 Henry bequeathed to his heirs a mere seven. But in size and quality the first Tudor warships were infinitely superior. The

Sovereign, built at Southampton in 1489-90, had a far larger sail area than its predecessors, carried on four masts, displaced from 600-700 tons, and was armed with 225 serpentines, weighing 250 pounds [114 kg] each, breech-loading guns with a range of 1300 yards [1188 m] but only effective against sails and rigging, and firing only two shots an hour; the *Sovereign,* with 600 soldiers and sailors aboard, required only 40 gunners. The *Regent,* even bigger than the *Sovereign,* cost almost £1000, when delivered in 1490, but had only 141 serpentines, and a complement, naval and military, of 700. The slow and inaccurate cast-iron serpentines were, however, slowly being replaced by much superior brass versions; the *Regent* by 1501 had 24 compared with 117 of the earlier type.

Henry VII also appreciated the need for an effective, fortified, base for the fleet. Work began early in the reign on 'building a tower and bulwark' at Portsmouth and in May 1496 the first-ever dry-dock in the British isles was opened there. But progress on coastal defences was slow. At Dartmouth a strongpoint began to be built 'on Kingswer syde', opposite the main castle, to cover the part of the entrance the castle guns could not reach, but the iron guns soon rusted once exposed to the sea air, and were later replaced by brass cannon.

Henry VII's reign saw some important changes in England's international situation. The union of Brittany with France in 1491, already mentioned, presented an unbroken, potentially hostile coastline on the far side of the Channel, Calais alone excepted, while the growth of the port of Antwerp made it a major potential threat to England if the Low Countries fell into unfriendly hands. A more immediate danger was the emergence of Spain as a major maritime power; Columbus had made his epic transatlantic voyage in 1492. Spain featured large in Henry VII's diplomacy and it was a great triumph when on 14 November 1501 the daughter of King Ferdinand of Aragon and Queen Isabella was married to Henry's heir, Arthur, Prince of Wales. Less than six months later, Arthur died, aged 15, on 2 April 1502, the marriage probably unconsummated. King Henry VII himself died early at 52, on 21 April 1509, and on 11 June his second son married his dead brother's widow, Catherine of Aragon. Two weeks later, at their coronation banquet, no voice was raised on behalf of any Yorkist pretender when the King's Champion challenged 'any person . . . that will say or prove that King Henry VIII is not the rightful inheritor and King of this realm'. The Tudor dynasty seemed at last secure.

30

ANCIENT ENEMIES

The French king, ancient enemy to this your realm of England, daily obtains with great strength and power many great cities, towns and countries.

Preamble to Act granting Henry VIII a subsidy for military purposes,
February 1512

The reign of Henry VIII was to prove the great watershed in military as well as religious history but it began conventionally enough. Aged just under 18 when he ascended the throne on 22 April 1509, the young man seemed all that a monarch should be, with 'his goodly personage, his amiable visage, his princely countenance'. A Spanish observer described the new king as interested 'only in girls and hunting' but this did not displease his subjects. 'All the world here is rejoicing in the possession of so great a prince . . . his life is all their desire,' wrote an English nobleman when the new reign was but a month old.

Underlying English foreign policy from 1509, as it had for centuries, was the fear of France, especially France in alliance with Scotland. The English presence in Calais, the still unabandoned claims to the rest of France, and disputes over the Narrow Seas provided a permanent *casus belli.* Henry VIII, who had an instinctive understanding of his subjects, realized this very well. Even a formal profession of goodwill sent to the King of France on his behalf provoked his indignation. 'Who wrote this letter?' he angrily asked his officials. '*I* ask peace of the King of France, who dare not look me in the face, still less make war on me!' Already some saw, however, that the national destiny lay elsewhere than the Continent. When, soon after Henry had come to the throne, the proposal for the usual war with France came up some unknown members of the king's council advised against it. 'Let us in God's name leave off our attempts against *terra firma,*' said one. 'The natural situation of islands seems not to comport with conquests in that kind. England alone is a just empire, or when we enlarge ourselves, let it be in that way . . . to which it seems the eternal providence hath destined us, which is by sea.'

Such pleas, as usually happens to the voice of reason, fell on deaf ears. War was the natural occupation of kings, at least outside the hunting season, a jousting session writ large. Spain was later to become an even greater threat to England, as will be described, but for the moment the potential enemy was France. Her acquisition of Brittany, as noted earlier, had provided the king of France with a splendid new source of ships and seamen and a whole series of harbours, including the great port of Brest, at the western end of the Channel, opposite Falmouth. To this, as will be mentioned later, was to be added a new port, half-way up the Channel facing Portsmouth, Le Havre. In supporting Spain against France Henry could be said to be acting in the national interest, but he always tended to equate what he desired with what the country required. Later he was often to be compared with the 'ideal ruler' of Niccolo Machiavelli's classic work of statecraft, *The Prince*, published (in Italian) in 1532, which argued that a ruler's maintenance of authority was the supreme good, justifying any deception of other nations and any oppression of one's own subjects.

Machiavelli, then a busy Florentine diplomat, would certainly have approved Henry's first diplomatic moves. On 23 March 1510 he renewed the existing treaty guaranteeing peace with France for another year, and on 13 November 1510 signed another, with Spain, undertaking to attack France, as part of the Holy League formed by Venice and the papacy, before the end of April 1512.

The parliament which assembled on 4 February 1512* was on 19 February told the 'secret reasons' which had led the king to resolve on war, and both Lords and Commons readily voted two full 'tenths' and two full 'fifteenths', extremely lavish provision. The reasons were set out in the preamble to the first Subsidy Act, which linked together the intrusion of France into Italy with the danger from Scotland:

> The Frenshe Kyng, auncient enemye to thys your Realme of England, dayly opteigneth with grete strength and power many grete Citees, Townes and Countries in the parties of Italie and other parties beyond the See . . . The Kyng of Scotts, very homager and obediencer of right to your Highnesse, daily prepaireth grete number of habilimentes of Werr and kepeth no parfite leje and amytie with your Grace.

The only indirect anti-invasion measure passed by this session of parliament was designed to encourage 'shooting in longe bowe' and to discourage other sports which might encroach on the time available for archery practice. Soon after parliament had adjourned in April a diversionary fleet was sent to harass French shipping and threaten a landing on the coasts of Normandy and Brittany, followed in June by a

---

*Not 1511, as wrongly stated by H. A. L. Fisher, p. 173, a mistake made clear by the printed Rolls of Parliament, which I have consulted.

major land expedition to Fuenterrabia, near San Sebastian in Spain, in support of an anticipated invasion of France, which was to restore Guienne, the province around Bordeaux, to England.

The land expedition was a failure but the operations off Brittany resulted in the first Battle of Brest. The French fleet, said to number 39 ships, was led by the *Cordelière*, 'a strong ship furnished in all poyntes', in Edward Hall's phrase; the English ships, 25 strong, under the Lord Admiral, Sir Edward Howard, included the equally powerful *Sovereign* and *Regent*. Both sides, as Hall makes clear, were eager to get to grips:

> The Frenche kyng hearyng what dammage thenglishmen had done in Britaine [i.e. Brittany], strongly furnished his Navie and so thei set forwarde out of Brest the x. daie of August, and came to Britayne Bay, in which place the self same day . . . the English navie was arrived. When the Englishe menne poerceived the French Navie to be out of Brest haven, then the lorde Admirall was very joyous, then every man prepared according to his duetie, the Archers to shote, the Gonners to lose [i.e. loose off their cannon], the men of Armes to fight, the Pages went to the toppe Castle with dartes: thus all thynges beyng provided and set in ordre, the Englishe men approched toward the Frenchemen, whiche came fiercelsy forwarde, some levying his Ancre, some with his foresaile onely to take them moste avauntage: and when thei wer in sight, thei shot ordinaunce so terrebly together, that all the sea coast sounded of it.

One inconvenient consequence of gunnery now became apparent:

> By . . . smoke of the ordinaunce or otherwise, the *Sovereign* was cast at the sterne of the Caricke, with which avauntage the Frence menne showted for joye . . . ;
> The fight was very cruel, for the archers of the englishe parte, and the Crossbowes of the Frenche part did their uttermoste: but for all that the English men entered the Caricke [i.e. the *Cordelière*], whiche seyng a varlet Gonner beyng desperate put fire in the Gonne powder as other saie [i.e. as some say], and set the whole ship on fire, the flame wherof set fire in the *Regent*, and so these twoo noble shippes which were so crappeled together that thei could not part, wer consumed by fire. The Frenche navie perceivyng this fled in all hast, soem to Brest, and soem to the Isles adioynyng.

The simultaneous loss of the *Regent* and the *Cordelière* with, according to Hall, 900 Frenchmen and 700 Englishmen 'drowned and brent', strikingly demonstrated the additional danger that gunpowder had added to naval actions, but this first Battle of Brest, on 10 August 1512, must be accounted a victory for Henry VIII since after it the French retreated into harbour. On 4 November 1512 the parliament which had adjourned in March reassembled, with the Battle of Brest fresh in its memory. The French development of that port, and their possession of Brittany, had created fears of an imminent descent on England, or at least of raids on Cornwall, and the result was the first major act of parliament concerning coastal fortifications, in the form of temporary, locally-planned, field works. The reasons for action were admirably set out in the preamble to the first statute, 4 Henrici VIII, Chapter i, credited to this session, which ended on 20 December 1512:

> Prayen the Comons in this present parliament assembled, that for asmoch as the land of Bretayne and also the haven of Brest lyeth streight ayenst the South see costes of the Countie of Cornwall and that the Frenchemen or auncien enemyes and Bretyanes [Bretons] enemyes by reason of theire fysshyng upon the see costes knowe aswell evy haven and creke within the sayde Countie as evy landyng place in as large maner as any subgiett of our Sovaigne Lorde the Kyng dooth; And that the said Countie is thre score and ten myle in length and the substaunce therof right litle more than six myle in brede from the Southsee to the Northsee, by reason wherof they also knowe that grete mulititude of people can not shortly resort to put theym of at theire landyng; And that in divers and many of the seyd landyng place nother pile blockhouse nr Bulwork is made to greve or annoye theym at their landyng; Whiche consideracions unto our sayd enemyes grete audaciite comfort and corage gyveth to arrive and land in the same parties.

The proposed remedy was next set out in detail:

> Therfor be it enacted . . . that the Justices of the Peace and Shiref of the sayd Countie do ride and viewe all the sayd Southcost from Plymmouth Westward, to the Landes ende. And that doone incon-tynent to appoynt within theym self such boroughes Townes and Parisshens as they shall think resonable to make Bulwerkes Brayes Walles Diches and al other fortificacions . . . as shalbe thought by theire discrecion in every of the sayd landyng places betwene this and the first day of Marche next now comyng.

Not merely the planning but the execution of the necessary works was to be left to the local authorities and the penalties provided for non-compliance were severe. Anyone failing to give his labour when ordered, or to provide a substitute, could be sent to jail for up to ten days, while a mayor or constable who was negligent could be imprisoned for a month. More surprisingly, in view of the sacred rights of land-ownership, it was laid down that defence works could be built 'in every mannys grounde of what estate or degree he be . . . without any intupcion or lett of any pson or psones [interruption or hindrance by any person] beyng Lord or Lordes of any such grounds . . . and without any maner of payment to be demanded', an early example of the conscription of property, as well as manpower, for defence purposes.

The Act, it was specifically laid down, would extend only till the next parliament, and it seems unlikely that most of the trenches and ramparts erected by amateur labour on sites selected by the local gentry survived much longer. In any case, Henry VIII was for the moment on the offensive. On 10 April 1513 Lord Admiral Howard led out of Plymouth an advance force of 24 ships, carrying 2880 seamen and 4650 soldiers intended to pen up the French navy in Brest, or inflict crippling losses upon it. It achieved little, except to cost Howard his life, when he heroically led a little force of 17 men on to the enemy flagship before they were overwhelmed, and to prompt the usual reprisal, as Edward Hall describes:

> The Frenche Navie perceivyng that the Englishmen made toward England, came out of their havens, and Prior Ihon [i.e. Admiral Prégent]* coasted over to the coast of Sussex and all his compaignie, and landed on the sea coast, and set fire on the poore cottages. The gentlemen that dwelte here, shortely reised the countrey, and came to the coast and drove Prior Ihon to his Galeis. This was all the hurt that this stout capitain of so great fame did to England, savyng that he robbed certein poore Fishermen of Whitynges.

English hostility to the Scots was as deep-rooted as their distrust of the French. 'Under the sun live not more beastly and unreasonable people' wrote Henry's envoy from Edinburgh later in the reign, and King James IV of Scotland, who had supported Perkin Warbeck against Henry VII, in March 1513, rejected an offer of perpetual peace with England on the grounds of a prior obligation to his French ally. James's invasion of England, however, ended in disaster, and his own death, in the Battle of Flodden, fought on Friday 9 September 1513 near the Northumbrian village of Branxton, about five miles [8 km] south-east of the border town of Coldstream. Scotland henceforward presented no real danger to Henry VIII.

The French now rudely demonstrated that, whatever his triumphs elsewhere, Henry VIII was still unable to guarantee the safety of his own shores. In February there was another humiliating excursion against Sussex, undertaken, it seems, rather in the spirit of a cross-Channel

---

*Admiral Prégent (or Jean Piere) de Bidoux was nicknamed 'Prester John', which the English chronicler renders as 'Prior Ihon'.

shopping trip, with all the purchases free. Edward Hall seems to place it in the spring, but it was in fact in February 1514:

> About this time, the warres yet contynewynge betwene England and Fraunce, prior Ihon [i.e. Admiral Prégent] . . . great capitayne of the Frenche navy, with his Galeys and Foystes [smaller vessels] charged with great basylyskes and other greate artilery came on the border of Sussex and came a land in the night at a poore village in Sussex called bright Helmston [Brighthelmstone, subsequently Brighton] and or [before] the watch coulde him escrye he sett fyer on the towne and toke suche poore goodes as he founde; then the watche fyred the bekyns and people began to gather, whiche seynge prior Ihon sowned [i.e. sounded] his trompett to call his men aborde, and by that tyme it was day; then six archers whiche kept the watche folowed prior Ihon to the sea and shott so fast, that they bett the galyme [beat the galleys] from the shore and prior Ihon hym selfe waded to his foyst, and Thenglishemen went into the water after, but they were put back with pickes or els they had entered the foyst, but they shott so fast, that they wouded many in ye foyst and prior Ihon was shott in the face with an Arrow and was likely to have dyed*.

In August 1514 Henry's first French war was victoriously wound up with a treaty under which Louis promised to pay a huge indemnity of a million gold crowns, the twice-yearly instalments, to rub salt in the wound, to be handed over in Calais. At the same time Louis was married by proxy to Henry's sister, Mary, much against her will: her new husband was an elderly invalid, three times her age. The reluctant wife, to her great relief, rapidly became a widow and on 1 January 1515 Louis XII was succeeded by his nephew Francis I. At 20 the new king of France was three years younger than Henry, whom he resembled in his good looks, athleticism and licentiousness, and an intense personal rivalry developed between the two. Henry would seek reassurance from visitors that his height and figure compared favourably with those of Francis, even opening his doublet to show that his leg and calf were the more shapely. Until Queen Catherine made him shave it off he also grew a red-gold beard to challenge the French king's. Below the surface a more bitter struggle developed, each nation trying to damage the other while professing friendship. The French had long had a pretender to the English throne ready for use when required, the son of Edward IV's sister, Richard de la Pole, who had thrown in his lot with the French. During 1515 Francis I toyed with sending 'White Rose', as he was code-

*A picture of this raid survives, the first known drawing of any English coastal town. See illustration No. 33. The original is incorrectly dated 1545, but clearly depicts the events of 1514.

named by Henry and his agents, to invade England with 15,000 soldiers, or alternatively, to Scotland, but in the end the last Yorkist pretender was killed ten years later, fighting for his adopted country in Italy.

31

DIVERS BULWARKS AND FORTIFICATIONS

And in all such doubtful places his Highness caused divers and many bulwarks and fortifications to be made.

The chronicler Edward Hall, recalling 1539

Although he did much less actual fighting than many of his royal predecessors, Henry VIII was fascinated by all things military. Fine uniforms, noisy cannon, mighty warships, massive fortresses, all made a great appeal to his flamboyant temperament and ingenious, innovative mind, and no sovereign did more to strengthen the nation's defences and to cast off in such matters the stifling, precedent-ridden mental miasma of the Middle Ages.

The service which benefited first, and most, from his attention was the navy. On his accession in 1509 it consisted of only seven ships, five of them large; by 1512 it already numbered 19, including the first *Mary Rose*, of 600 tons, a name later transferred, as constantly happened, to a quite different ship, and the *Peter Pomegranate*, of 450 tons, both laid down on Henry's orders. Far more significant, however, was another vessel, commissioned by Henry as a direct result of the loss of the 1000–ton *Regent*, at the first Battle of Brest, as Edward Hall describes:

> The king of England, heryng of the losse of the Regent, caused a greate shippe to be made, suche another as was never seen before in Englande, and called it *Henry Grace de Dieu*.

The *Great Harry*, as the *Henry Grace-à-Dieu* was popularly known, was magnificent in its size and appearance, but was to have an inglorious career afloat. It looked impressive, however, being a carvel-built [i.e. without overlapping planks] four-master, displacing 1500 tons and carrying a huge spread of sail including 'topgallants' for extra speed. Contemporaries marvelled at the materials required which included more than 3700 tons of timber, 56 tons of iron, 565 stones [3591 kg] of oakum and 1711 pounds of flax. The cost was officially said to be £8708, including three much smaller craft built at the same time, but was rumoured to be £14,000. The number of decks has been variously put at seven or eight and the number of guns at 182–4. They were, as was usual in Tudor warships, a job lot of various types and calibres, but on the evidence of those recovered later from the *Mary* [or *Marie*] *Rose*, the largest were probably brass breech-loaders, 8 ft 6 in [2.6 m] long, and 8.54 in [21.7 cm] in calibre, firing a shot weighing 60 lbs [27 kg]; the smallest were 5-in [12.6-cm] basilisks', loaded with a 15-lb [6–8 kg] projectile. The range is uncertain, documents of the time using an undefined unit of measurement, 'the pace', but was probably, for the heaviest guns, around 250 yards [256 m] for an aimed shot, with a maximum of about 1 mile [1.6 km] for a 'random' one.

Henry VIII delighted in naval affairs. Before his first French expedition sailed in 1513 he constantly visited the docks to monitor progress and acquired a suitably imposing nautical uniform, consisting of a vest of gold brocade reaching to the middle of the thigh, breeches of cloth of gold and scarlet hose. He was also the proud possessor of the traditional symbol of maritime command, an 'admiral's whistle', a somewhat impractical object, a yard [0.9 m] long made of gold encrusted with jewels, and suspended from his neck on a gold chain. Whenever he got the chance, 'he blew near as loud' on it 'as on a trumpet or clarinet', an eyewitness observed.

The real significance of the first *Great Harry*, launched in 1514, was that she marked the debut of a new generation of ships, designed around the guns they were to carry, rather than expected to accommodate any cannon that happened to be available. Light guns continued to be mounted on or above the deck to destroy the enemy sails and rigging, but much heavier calibre weapons were now mounted low down near the waterline, with the enemy hull as their target. The idea of the broadside, with a number of heavy guns firing simultaneously, had been born, and the 83,720 lb [38,008 kg] of ordnance mounted on the first *Henry Grace-à-Dieu* could deliver a formidable weight of shot. Gunports were now cut in the side of the hull, protected by hinged shutters, and Henry's ships also carried 'armour', in the form of thicker baulks of timber, low down inside the hull, to prevent its being holed by enemy fire.

About more fundamental weaknesses Henry could do little. The Tudor navy, like earlier fleets, suffered badly from the use of unseasoned timber, which once exposed to dampness rapidly rotted, so that ships were constantly out of action while the infected timbers were replaced. The difficulty of transporting English oak meant a heavy demand on forests near the coast and in 1544 the first act was passed for conserving and replacing woodland in such areas. To guarantee the supply of other items was more difficult; the best anchors were made in the Bay of

Biscay, the best rivets in Florence, the most dependable armour and bowstaves in Milan, while brass cannon were not cast in England until 1521. A highly credible story claims that Henry put to the test some new 'bombards' brought from Belgium for naval use by having part of the village of Houndsditch on the eastern edge of London cleared of its inhabitants and used for target practice, with suitably destructive results.

Between 1509 and 1547 no fewer than 106 ships were added to the navy, the vast majority, 62, being specially built, with purchased vessels and prizes supplying the rest. This resulted in a vast expansion of the country's strength at sea. Henry had inherited five good-sized ships. By 1513 'king's ships' numbered 23, supported by 21 hired and converted merchantmen and 15 small victualling craft, the royal ships being manned by 3982 seamen and 447 gunners. By 1545 the king's ships totalled from 50 to 60, and the total fleet amounted to 80, while another 60 privateers ranged the Channel, a valuable floating reserve. Two years later, on Henry's death, he owned 53 seaworthy ships, with a total tonnage of 11,268.

Henry VIII's navy was not intended to be ocean-going. The area of operations for the larger ships lay between Brest and the Thames estuary; the East Coast was the preserve of smaller vessels, used on campaigns against Scotland. Portsmouth remained the main base, but was slow to attract sufficient population to make it more secure. The traveller John Leland observed about 1540, 'The town is bare and little occupied in time of peace . . . There is much vacant ground within the town wall.' A good deal less exposed were Woolwich, Erith and Deptford on the Thames which now also acquired royal dockyards where ships could be laid up, often for long periods, while a second dry dock, supplementing the one built by Henry VIII at Portsmouth, was opened at Deptford in 1517. The Thames was now steadily gaining in importance, while the Cinque Ports were losing their old supremacy, as first Hythe and Romney, then Sandwich, silted up, while Henry ordered dredging and building operations to halt the relentless build-up of shingle at Dover, but with only limited success. He also granted, in 1514, a royal charter to the already existing 'Brotherhood of the Most Glorious and Unidvided Trinity of St Clements in the Parish of Deptford', which was made formally responsible for providing lights and pilots and for keeping the Thames clear of obstructions. Trinity House, as it became known, also encouraged moves to improve the rates of pay and working conditions for seafarers. A flourishing merchant marine remained the chief source of trained seamen in time of war. The sailor still tended, however, to regard his first loyalty as being to the sea, not his sovereign, and one sturdily independent mariner told an Admiralty court that if the Grand Turk would give him a penny a day more, he would serve him.

Any regular full-time naval career or command structure was still lacking, a Lord High Admiral, not necessarily with seagoing experience, being appointed as required. By the end of Henry VIII's reign, however, a permanent administrative organization had been created, under a Keeper of Storehouses, who later became Treasurer of the Navy, and a Comptroller of the Ships, responsible for provisions. They were later joined by a Master of the Ordnance, who supplied the guns, and a Surveyor of the Ships, who directed the construction programme. These with two other officials, a Clerk of the Ships, and a Lieutenant of the Admiralty, were known as the Principal Officers of the Navy and met regularly as the Navy Board. No doubt ever existed as to the country against which the new navy was to provide protection. 'This King of France is indeed a worthy and honest sovereign,' Henry VIII told the departing Venetian ambassador in March 1515, 'but he is nevertheless a Frenchman and not to be trusted.' Officially, however, his policy was one of friendship and this reached its ostentatious climax at the Field of the Cloth of Gold, so-called from the costly material of which the 200 tents erected for a 17-day meeting between the two monarchs at Guisnes, near Calais, in June 1520 were made. Henry, with three English knights, met Francis I in friendly combat in a tournament and then the two kings engaged in a private wrestling match; Henry lost, a defeat on which the English chroniclers are tactfully silent. The professions of undying affection and enduring peace which the two men exchanged were worthless.

So far England had stayed aloof from the great rebellion against the authority of the pope, and secession from the Church of Rome, begun by Martin Luther in 1517, which led, in December 1520, to Luther's excommunication. Now she was to become caught up in this movement for reasons which had nothing whatever to do with religion, but which were to expose her to her greatest danger since 1066. Henry VIII was by instinct and background a passionately loyal son of the Church and in August 1521, after Luther's doctrines had been denounced at St Paul's Cross and his works had been solemnly burned, Henry's *The Defence of the Seven Sacraments*, supposedly his own work but possibly 'ghosted', was sent to Rome. He was rewarded, in October 1521, with the title *Defender of the Faith*, still used by his successors, who are pledged to protect the very doctrines that Henry denounced. In 1527, still a loyal Catholic, Henry convinced himself, with good reason, that he needed a male heir to guarantee the succession, and, with less reason, that he had never been validly married to his wife, Catherine, because of her prior marriage to his dead brother. In fact, as indicated earlier, Catherine's marriage to Arthur had almost certainly never been consummated, so she and Henry *had* been free to marry.

22 'The key to England'. Dover Castle, built by the Normans
23 'Harry's Walls'. St Mawes Castle, built by Henry VIII

24   The Tudors. *Above left:* Henry VII
25   *Above right:* Henry VIII
26   *Below left:* Edward VI
27   *Below right:* Mary I

28   Queen Elizabeth. The 'Armada portrait' commissioned in celebration of her victory.
29   England's enemy: Philip II of Spain
30   England's defenders. *Left to right:* Sir John Hawkins, Sir Francis Walsingham, Sir
31,32 Francis Drake

33 Attack: A French raid on Brighton, 1514
34 Defence: A survey of possible enemy landing places in the Isle of Wight, drawn in 1587

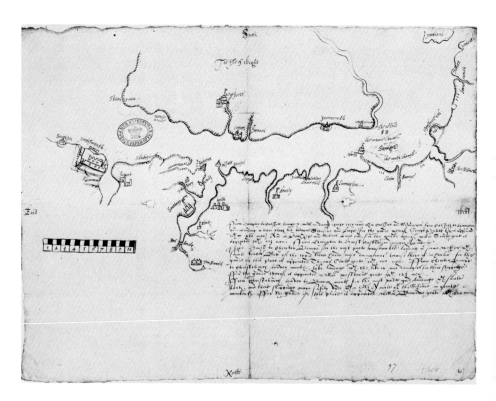

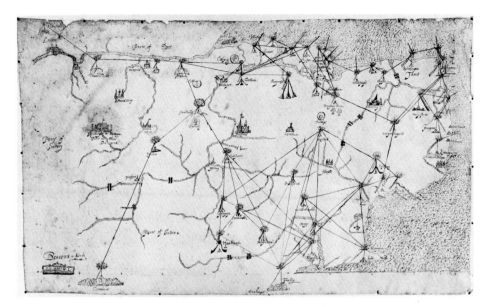

35 Preparations. *Above:* A map of the beacon system in Kent
36 *Below*: Pikemen and harquebusiers, a drawing made at
37 Sir Philip Sidney's funeral in 1587

38 The fortifications erected at Weybourne, Norfolk

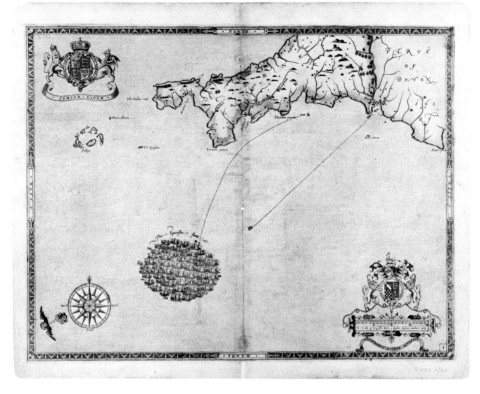

39   In fighting order.   The Armada off Land's End
40   The two fleets confront each other off Portland Bill

41 'The invincible'.   The Armada under full sail
42   The English fire-ships at Calais

The Prince of Parma
coming to Dunkerk with his
Army but too late is received
by the Spaniards with reproach

The Lᵈ Admirall Howard
Knighting Thomas Howard,
the Lord Sheffeild, Rogʳ Townſenᵈ
Iohn Hawkins, and Martin
Forbiſher for their good ſervice

43   Fruits of victory. Four of a set of playing cards
44   prepared soon after 1588, or early in the
45   next century, to commemorate the routing
46   of the Spaniards.

The Spaniſh Ships loſt
on the Coaſt of Scotland
and 700 Souldiers and
Marriners caſt a Shoare.

Spaniſh Comanders taken priſo=
ners & brought into England.

This at least was the pope's judgement and in November 1532 he formally forbade Henry to divorce his wife. When in January 1533, Henry none the less married the young woman on whom his fancy had lighted, Anne Boleyn, a breach with Rome became inevitable.

During 1536 Henry grasped another long troublesome nettle, that of Wales. Although the process was not completed till 1543, from 1536 onwards Wales was systematically incorporated, for legal and adminstrative purposes, into England. Henceforward the officials were to speak English, which was also to be the language of the courts, the marcher lordships were broken up and became English or Welsh shires, represented, along with the Welsh boroughs, in parliament, and only Welsh laws and customs specifically approved by a royal commission were to be allowed to continue. Thanks to the intense loyalty of the Welsh to 'their' i.e. the Tudor, monarchy all those changes have been accomplished with remarkably little difficulty.

The rest of Henry's reign was to be dominated by his quarrel with Rome. What became known as the Reformation Parliament met in November 1529 and was not finally dissolved until April 1536. During these years the Church in England became the Church of England, the jurisdiction of the Bishop of Rome, as the pope now officially became known, was wholly extinguished and Henry VIII became the final arbiter of both ecclesiastical appointments and doctrine. The Act of Supremacy, in November 1534, declared that the king 'justly and rightfully is and ought to be supreme head of the Church of England'. Soon afterwards an English Bible was produced, the preparation of an English Prayer Book put in hand and the process begun of closing down the monasteries and confiscating their vast holdings of land and other property, nominally for public purposes, including national defence.

Anne Boleyn herself, to marry whom Henry had been prepared to alienate most of Christendom and to break with Rome, was beheaded, on trumped-up charges of adultery and treason, in May 1536, having presented him, seven months after their marriage, not with the son he needed but with a daughter, Elizabeth. Henry immediately married a third wife, Jane Seymour, who duly bore him a male heir in October 1537, characteristically regarded by Henry as a sign of God's approval of his recent actions, although his wife died in childbirth. The king, however, 'merry as a widower may be', according to one observer, married again, the distinctly plain Anne of Cleves, whom he divorced to marry Catherine Howard. Henry accepted no responsibility for this dismal marital record, merely 'regretting his ill-luck in meeting with such ill-conditioned wives' and in 1543 married his sixth and last wife, Catherine Parr, who survived him, although one unkind Frenchman commented that she was 'not nearly as beautiful as Anne of Cleves'.

Rome's revenge was slow in developing. Sentence of excommuni-cation on Henry had inititally been pronounced on 11 July 1533, but it was not until 17 December 1538, after Thomas à Becket's shrine at Canterbury had been desecrated on the king's orders and 20 cartloads of jewels and other precious objects left there by pious pilgrims had been carried off from it to swell the royal coffers, that Pope Paul III formally promulgated the fearful sentence. Henry's subjects no longer had an obligation to obey him, while other sovereigns had a positive duty to overthrow him. Pope Paul's initial hopes of the international response probably did not go beyond anticipating that other countries might break off commercial and diplomatic relations with England; actual invasion he seems to have regarded as a last resort. The envoy he selected to rally support took from the first a more realistic view. Reginald Pole, educated at Charterhouse School and Magdalen College, Oxford, had been created Dean of Exeter by Henry VIII, but he had turned down the Archbishopric of York rather than desert the old religion. He had gone into voluntary exile, being proclaimed a rebel by Henry VIII, and created a cardinal by the pope. Pole regarded it as his duty to try to bring England back within the Catholic fold even if this meant English blood being shed by foreign swords. Still a mere 35, he entered on his mission enthusiastically, leaving Rome on 27 December 1538 en route for Spain. Three days later, the French ambassador in London wrote encouragingly to the Constable of France about the glittering prospects awaiting a well-coordinated invasion:

> True, there would be a fight, but it would be less dangerous than ever it was before, for the people are inconceivably discontented . . . Make spoil of this country between you. From the Thames the coast adjoins Picardy, Normandy and Brittany as far as Brest, and is furnished with good ports . . . The other side of the Thames likewise lies convenient for the Emperor, adjoining Holland and Zealand. Hand over to the King of Scots the North, which is his ancient right and heritage.

From Rome, the papal officials kept up the pressure. The pope, wrote one cardinal, on 8 January 1539, 'hopes that God will work some good effect for the reduction of that realm'. On 3 March Henry VIII's ambassador in the Netherlands wrote to warn of an impending attack and a spy in France told the king's chief minister, Thomas Cromwell, 'you must fortify your places and harbours.' Ordinary citizens were equally well aware of the increasing danger. 'It is said,' some English Protestants wrote to friends in Germany on 8 March 1539, 'we are to have war with the French, the Italians, the Spaniards and the Scots at once.'

The annual, or more frequent, turn-outs required of the militia had in the past commonly been ill-attended and unpopular but the prospect of action wrought a transformation. In theory any man of 17 and upwards, except in London, where special arrangements applied, or with seafaring experience, which meant that he was earmarked for the navy, could be required to undergo military training and thereafter to serve under arms if required, but little compulsion was needed. A positive passion to shoulder a weapon and – even more – put on a uniform, swept the country, as the newly arrived French ambassador, travelling up from Dover at the end of March 1539, observed:

> In Canterbury and the other towns upon the road I found every English subject in arms who was capable of serving. Boys of seventeen or eighteen have been called without exemption of place or person. On the road, I met a body of men. I was told there were 6000 of them going as a garrison to Sandwich . . . Artillery and ammunition pass out incessantly from the Tower and are dispatched to all points on the coast where a landing is likely to be attempted.

The whole country was now divided for defence purposes into eleven defence zones, plus London, where the Lord Mayor was in charge. The eleven, listed roughly, it seems, in their order of vulnerability, were as follows:

1. The Thames and the East Coast.
2. Suffolk.
3. Norfolk.
4. Kent.
5. Sussex.
6. Hampshire.
7. Somerset, Dorset, Devon and Cornwall.
8. Lincolnshire.
9. Yorkshire, Westmorland, Northumberland, Cumberland, Durham, Derbyshire, Lancashire and Cheshire.
10. South Wales.
11. North Wales.

The first line of defence was the navy. By April 1539 about 150 ships had been assembled, divided between the Thames and Portsmouth. If the enemy broke through this nautical cordon he was to be engaged by the existing coastal forts and by the others now hurriedly being built, of which more will be said in a moment. Until the ring of fortresses was complete temporary field works were to be used to delay the invader's advance and these barricades of earth, turf and stones were in the spring of 1539 hastily flung up at exposed points where the enemy might come ashore: Portsmouth itself, Hurst beach close to the approaches to it, on the Solent, East and West Cowes on the Isle of Wight, and at Harwich, where the whole population turned out to lend a hand. 'Ye should,' wrote the Lord Chancellor to Thomas Cromwell after a tour of inspection on the east coast, 'have seen women and children work with shovels in the trenches and bulwarks.'

By May Day tension was easing all round, although work was still being pressed ahead on the new fortresses. Henry was at last allowed to bring through the Netherlands the gunpowder he had bought in Germany which Charles V had detained in his ports, while Francis I, not to be outdone, now granted a licence for the export to England of another embargoed commodity, sailcloth.

The London armed bands were not to be cheated, however, of their long-planned march through London from Mile End to St James's, as Edward Hall makes clear:

The 8th day of Maie [1539], accordynge to the kynges pleasure, every Alderman in ordre of battell with his warde came into the common felde at Myle ende, and then all the gonnes severed them selves into one place, the pykes in another and the bowmen in another, and likewise the byllmen, and there rynged and snyled, which was a goodly syght to beholde; for all the feldes from Wyte chappell to Myle ende, and from Bednall Grene to Ratclif and to Stepney were all covered with harnesse, men and weapons, and in especial the battell of pykes semed to be a great forest . . . About 8 of the clocke marched forward the lyght peces of Ordinance, with stone and powder, and them followed the Dromes and fyffes . . . Then folowed the Gonners, four in a ranke, every one goyng five foote a sonder, every mans shoulder eve level with another . . . and especially before the Kynges Majestie, whyche at that tyme sate in his new gate house at his Palace at Westminster where he viewed all the whole company. In lyke maner passed the second and third battels . . . the formost Capitayn at 9 of the clock in the morning by the lytle conduite entryng into Paulyls churchyarde, and so directly to Westmynster . . . the last of the Muster entered Pauls churchyarde . . . four of the clocke at after noone.

The most widely visible and enduring of all the preparations that dangerous summer was the great network of castles which was now constructed all around the coast. Henry VIII had already in 1512, as mentioned earlier, secured the act requiring the construction of temporary bulwarks in Devon and Cornwall, but the coastal fortifications now erected stretched over a much wider area and were designed to be permanent. Very few of the huge forts now built, at vast expense, were ever to see a shot fired in anger but this was their finest vindication.

The costly Henrican castles provided that most effective and economical of all weapons, a deterrent.

Three hundred years before, the chronicler Matthew Paris had, in a constantly quoted phrase, described Dover as 'the key of England', but Henry's earliest efforts at fortifications were largely directed to areas further west. Between 1520 and 1537 a number of relatively minor projects were undertaken, including 'Little Dennis', a blockhouse or walled emplacement housing a single battery of guns, at the tip of the Pendennis promontory guarding the entrance to the Garrick Road in Cornwall, a site first fortified in prehistoric times. By 1537 Dartmouth, where the French had actually landed in the recent past, boasted the New Castle, described by the traveller John Leland as 'a fair bulwark', though plans to repair Tintagel Castle, its site once allegedly a stronghold of King Arthur, came to nothing. A castle was, however, built at Portland, where the gently shelving stretch of Chesil Beach gave way to the deep-water anchorage afforded by another often-raided spot, Portland Bill. The Lord Admiral, in 1537, after an inspection on the ground, recommended the erection of a tower on Calshot Point to guard the western entrance to Southampton Water, because 'it woulde there so strengthen all that quarter . . . that none should lie there, neither come to any road or channel thereabouts, unless he come in and go out at the Needles.'

An existing fort at the entrance to the Solent was rebuilt and a new one planned for 'the hard sand' opposite, the origin of Hurst Castle, but the Isle of Wight, the scene of constant French landings over the centuries, presented a more difficult problem. Visiting commissioners reported in 1538, however, that the islanders 'keep their beacons . . . on every hill right well', and that their morale was excellent:

> The people of the Isle of Wight are all, both gentlemen and others, well minded to defend their country . . . saying they will stake their costs and cast their ditches anew towards the low water mark, then, when their enemies land, it shall be dangerous to them.

Something more than stakes and ditches was going to be needed, however, to keep out the massed might of most of continental Europe and Henry VIII now undertook a personal inspection of the vulnerable parts of his kingdom, following news of the alliance now being formed against him, as Edward Hall describes:

> Yhr kynges highnes . . . was lately enfourmed by his trustie and faithful frendes . . . that Archetraitor Reignold Poole, enemie to Godes worde and his natural contry, had moved and stirred diverse great princes and potentates of Christendome to invade the Realme of

England, and utterlie to destroy th nacion of the same; Wherefore his Maiestie in his awne persone, without any deley tooke very laborious and paynefull iourneyes towardes the sea coastes. Also he sent dyvers of his nobles and counsaylours to view and searche all the portes and daungiers on the coastes where any meete or convenient landing place might be supposed, as well on the borders of Englande as also of Wales. And in all soche doubtful places his hygnes caused dyvers and many Bulwarks and fortifications to be made.

The programme was set in motion by a document known as the *Device by the King* drawn up early in February 1539 and probably, at least in part, Henry's own work. It named the commmissioners who were 'to search and defend' 18 named coastal counties, plus South Wales, seeking out sites and preparing plans for the protection of places which seemed at risk. Other individuals were nominated to take charge of actual construction work in those areas needing immediate protection, close to London or in the south-east. These included Gravesend and Milton on the south bank of the Thames, and Tilbury on the North, where the Thames estuary narrowed down towards the vital dockyards at Deptford and Woolwich; Sandown, Deal and Walmer, where the stretch of sea known as The Downs provided a traditionally safe anchorage; Camber, opposite Rye across an even more sheltered inlet, now silted up; and Calshot Point, already identified as requiring protection, at the entrance to Southampton Water. By early April work had already begun at all these places, and at two others not specifically mentioned in the *Device*, Sandgate, between Folkestone and Hythe, and Dover harbour. In March Henry himself visited the three blockhouses already a-building there, and that month *An exhortation to styre all Englishe men to the defence of theyr countreye*, written on the instructions of the Lord Great Chamberlain, Thomas Cromwell – later, like so many of Henry's loyal servants, executed for alleged treason – made the most of the royal endeavours:

Is it possyble that any his gracis suiecte i.e. any subject, can refust peyne, when his hyghness rydeth about haven to haven, from castell to castell, dayes and nightes devisynge all the ways that wytte canne invent, for our assurance, What charges is his grace at, for the . . . repairyng of Dover haven, Dover castell, for buylding bulwarks in the downes, bulwarkes at Folkestone, What a realme woll Englande be, when his grace hath set walles accordyng to the dyches, that runne round aboute us. England wol then be more like a castel, than a realme. His grace hath devised a bulwark in the Camber, a bulwarke at Calshottespoynte, a bulwarke at the East cowe, a bulwarke at the West cow. His highness fortifieth Portismouth, Southampton, Weymouth, Portland rode, Torre baye, Plymmouthe haven, Dermouth haven, Portsmouth haven, Falmouth haven. This ones done, what enemy, be he never so strong, wol thinke he can invade England on those parties of it?

To the commissioners in charge of the various projects Henry must have seemed to be everywhere at once. He is reported to have been seen supervising the builders, at places as far afield as Pendennis, Plymouth and Lyme, as well as in those more accessible, like Calshot and Dover. At Deal he was untroubled by the worst storms ever witnessed on that stretch of coast, but was more concerned about whether the still unfinished bulwarks would stand up to the fierce gales and heavy seas. When he was out in the field inspecting progress he ensured that his ministers were kept up to the mark by a flow of letters and messengers.

During March 1539, a frenziedly active month, Thomas Cromwell drew up a *Remembrance* of 25 sites earmarked for defence works, the first comprehensive list of recognized invasion danger spots. It started in the north, with Berwick, Carlisle, Holy Island, Tynemouth and Hull, then took in East Anglia, with Lynn, Yarmouth, Lowestoft, Aldeburgh, Orwell and Langar [i.e. landguard] Point, before covering the south-east – Tilbury, Gravesend, The Downs, Camber, Calshot, Portsmouth and Southampton Water – followed by the south-west, at Lyme, Tor Bay, Dartmouth, Plymouth, Falmouth and Fowey. The only place on the western coast considered at risk was Milford Haven, from which Henry's father had advanced to claim his throne.

Rendering the island secure was expensive. The old tradition that it was up to the local nobility, with help from the indigenous population, to protect their own areas, was abandoned. Although local assistance was welcomed and often forthcoming in generous measure, the cost of defending the country was recognized as a national responsibility and the bulk of the work done by professionals. To build the most important, and expensive, of the whole chain, the Kentish forts overlooking the Downs, 1400 men were required at the peak. Records kept at one of them show how, after constructing scaffolding and barrows, work began in earnest during the summer, with 500 men employed at a time, dropping to 100 during the winter but rising again to 630 in June 1540; by autumn the whole undertaking was finished. Craftsmen, who formed more than half the total work force, were recruited from all over the country and paid 7d or 8d [3-3.5p] a day, labourers 5d [2p]. In June 1539 there was a strike for higher wages, speedily ended when nine of the ringleaders were sent to jail. Most of the stone was local; bricks and tiles were baked in kilns at Rye and Canterbury, and timber brought from the Weald, but coal to fire the forges had to be brought from the north of England and tents, to house the workmen, and wooden panelling, from London. Considered purely as a work-creation enterprise Henry's castle-building was a great success, recycling into the economy the wealth previously tied up unproductively in the monastic coffers, the principal source of revenue being the courts set up to handle the money previously siphoned off by Rome.

The fabric of the sequestered monasteries also made its own contribution to protecting the schismatic king from the avenging papal armies. The rubble of the demolished Meaux Abbey formed the foundations for the defences of Hull, stone from Beaulieu helped to strengthen the ramparts of Hurst Castle, and lead from its roof became cladding for the gun-platforms at Calshot. But money still had to be raised from taxation and parliament found little difficulty, in April 1540, in voting the king four 'fifteenths' and two 'tenths'. The preamble to the statute granting these unprecedented amounts acknowledged 'the great and most extreme charges, costes and expenses his Majestic hath susteyned, and continueth dailye, in edifieng, new making, buylding, fortyfieng and repairing' existing fortresses and 'the Castelles, Blockhouses and Fortresses newlye made, edyfied and buylded'.

To keep peacetine costs down, the regular garrisons of the new forts were modest. One of the Thames batteries contained only of a captain, deputy, porter, two ordinary soldiers and six gunners, Deal itself only a captain and 34 more, the captain receiving from 1s to 2s a day [5-10p], the deputy and porter, a combined custodian and janitor, 8d [3p], the gunners 6d [2.5p], though the last-named also had to provide a hand-gun at their own expense. Nor was much money spent on making living conditions comfortable. The ground floor of the keep commonly supplied a communal mess hall, kitchen and barrack room with the bastions providing overflow sleeping quarters when necessary. The upper floor was occupied by the captain and deputy and the basement provided storage space. Where space was short, as at Camber, the kitchen was housed in a bastion, the smoke vents in the firing chamber also serving as chimneys for the bakers' oven. Unlike those castles built by his medieval predecessors, which were primarily places sheltering an army of retainers, Henry VIII's forts were designed solely for fighting; cramped, low-roofed, and immensely strong, they subordinated the occupants' needs to operational necessity as much as any fighting ship.

Henry VIII, every inch a Renaissance prince, open-minded, innovative, was always ready to consider new ideas. A master-gunner who had invented a new mortar shell which an English general described as 'a "fantasy" which will please the king', was sent to London to demonstrate it; Henry even financed experiments, apparently unsuccessful, by a 70-year-old Italian who claimed to have invented a mirror which, placed on Dover Castle, would reflect enemy ships as soon as they left Dieppe.

A strong family likeness exists between 'Harry's Walls', as they become known, especially where, as at Deal and St Mawes, the new works were entirely free-standing and did not have to accommodate existing defences. They were the first to be built in England with strengthened, revetted walls, a large number of artillery apertures, well splayed externally to allow the maximum field of fire, and vents to allow the gun chambers to be kept clear of smoke. The basic design, seen best in the 'Downs' group – Sandown, Deal, Walmer, Sandgate, Camber – the 'Southern' group – Calshot, Hurst and Portland – and the 'south-west' pair, St Mawes and Pendennis, was circular, with a round, central keep rising by three to five flat tiers on which artillery could be sited. This was surrounded by a series of interlocking circular bastions, as at Deal, which consists of six altogether, enclosing another six, much smaller, at a higher level, with the circular keep rising above them. Sometimes, as at Pendennis, the other defences took the form of a single curtain wall, possibly with artillery apertures at intervals. To protect individual harbours, or as supporting outworks to a castle, Henry made use of detached, separate, circular blockhouses, designed for all-round defence, and perhaps enclosed by a dry ditch.

A feature of all the forts was the large number of firing apertures, 145 at Deal alone, for an important step forward in military technology had just occurred with the introduction of wheeled carriages, enabling heavy guns to be trundled readily from one firing bay to the next. The main purpose of the Henrican forts was indeed to serve as gun- platforms, the heaviest guns being placed on the roofs of the bastions and the keep to engage approaching ships. The massive walls and low profile of the new fortresses made them much stronger than the old style castles and they included such refinements as inward-sloping battlements, which caused enemy cannon balls to ricochet harmlessly away from the gun crew within. A programme of improvements to existing forts was also put in hand. 'Little Dennis' in Cornwall, barely ten years after its last modernization, now underwent a massive refit, enabling it to mount 30 guns in its keep and 15-sided wall, and to provide more effective support for the new, and far more ambitious fort, St Mawes, recently built across the bay.

If an enemy succeeded in getting men ashore the fortresses had failed in their initial purpose, but all Henry's castles were also equipped for close defence, Deal, for example, having 54 hand-gun apertures covering the outer moat and another 30 commanding the area between the curtain wall and the keep. The standard personal weapon used for local defence was an arquebus, five to six feet [1.5–1.8 m] long, fired by a matchlock.

Wheel-lock pistols, much easier to reload and fire, did exist but were too expensive for general use, while bows and arrows still formed part of the regular equipment of any fort.

The new forts were built round their artillery. The preferred weapon was the culverin, able to fire an 18-lb [8-kg] ball and the two- pounder [0.9 kg] falconet. Occasionally heavier weapons were provided, like the basilisk, with its 25-lb [11.3-kg] missile and the demi-cannon, firing one of 32 lb [14.5 kg]. The basic design and loading procedure were still unsophisticated. Whether of brass or cast iron the guns were smooth-bored and little more than horizontal tubes, with a cartridge of gunpowder and an iron cannon-ball rammed down the barrel. They were fired by setting a lighted match against a touch-hole at the rear, which ignited a train of powder between there and the cartridge. Increasingly, however, Henry was able to make use of guns manufac-tured in England, usually Sussex, and cast in one piece instead of, as formerly, imported ordnance, usually built up of barrel-like hoops.

Two books on military architecture, the first to be printed, had recently appeared, one in Italian, by Machiavelli, in 1522, the other, by Albrecht Dürer in German, in 1527, but they had no apparent influence in England and Henry has been criticized for adopting a 'transitional', basically circular, design, instead of the straight-sided arrow-head pattern already emerging in Italy, where each bastion presented the narrowest possible target to an attacker and enabled any point in the defence to be covered by a single pair of suitably sited guns. The king, however, had to use what knowledge was readily available. The overwhelming need was speed and Henry's castles were so well sited and built that they have either been incorporated, as at Hurst, in a whole series of later developments, or, as at Southsea, have survived to this day.

If the prevailing influence *was* German this is hardly surprising for in so far as the Henrican defence network had a single architect it was Stefan von Haschenperg, described as 'a gentleman of Moravia', who first appears on the South Coast in 1539, but had perhaps learned his trade in Germany; the rounded parapets and smoke vents seen in the Henrican forts had been introduced twelve years earlier when Nurenburg was refortified. Von Haschenperg seems to have been more plausible than talented, for he had hardly joined the royal pay-roll than his recommendations were being questioned. A letter from the com-missioner in charge at Sandgate, to Thomas Cromwell, on 3 September 1539, speaks for itself:

The castle of Sandgate, within your lordship of Folkestone, is well brought forward. Three towers are ready to be covered; which Stephen the Almain, devisor of the said castle, would have covered

with canvas pitch and tar . . . lead would be better, of which there is
enough to cover the whole castle.

By March 1541 he had been left in the North, after a tour with three
royal officials, 'to report about the fortifications to be made and where';
and four months later, on 3 July, the Privy Council decided 'that Stephen
the Almain should alone have the survey of the works at Carlisle.' He
later made a complaint about 'Sir Thomas Wentworth, captain of
Carlisle, for ill-using the workmen' but Wentworth seems to have been
supported by the Privy Council and remained at Carlisle for the next
two years, earning the handsome salary of 4s [20p] a day; the Bishop's
clerk, by contrast, got 8d [3p]. He seems, however, to have been a man
of remarkably little education and not even literate; he signed receipts,
which are still extant, with his mark. In May 1543 he was suspended,
apparently for incompetence, and that July the Privy Council learned
that they had been backing the wrong man:

> Stephen Almain having long had charge of certain buildings and
> fortifications, appeared to have behaved lewdly and spent great
> treasure to no purpose; and as he had before offered to recompense
> the king if he did anything otherwise than reason would he was
> ordered to bring sureties for his performance.

Rather than face the royal wrath von Haschenperg wisely decamped to
the Continent, leaving an Englishman, evidently a rising star in the
fortress world, to replace him. 'His Majesty mindeth,' the Privy Council
recorded, 'after the perfection of the works at Hull, that John Rogers
shall repair as well to Carlisle as to Wark.' The truth seems to be that
von Haschenperg was really a land surveyor but, when military engineers
were in sudden demand in 1539, managed to bluff his way around the
country until, having quarrelled with those who could have covered up
for him, his professional inadequacy was finally revealed at Carlisle.
Supposed experts like von Haschenperg apart, the building of the
Henrican forts seems to have been entrusted, in the fashion of the time,
to individual master masons and similar craftsmen, and they made an
excellent job of it. Often seconded from very different projects, at
Whitehall or Hampton Court, they took to military architecture as if
born to it. Henry's forts, as well as being intensely practical, are as
attractive, even beautiful, as their grim purpose allows, and were
completed with remarkable speed. The most urgently needed castles, in
the south-east, were already garrisoned by the end of 1540; those in the
south-west not long after; the rest, in East Anglia and the north, within
another year or two. The cost was not excessive: £500 for a small
blockhouse, £5000 for a medium-sized castle, about £27,000 for the

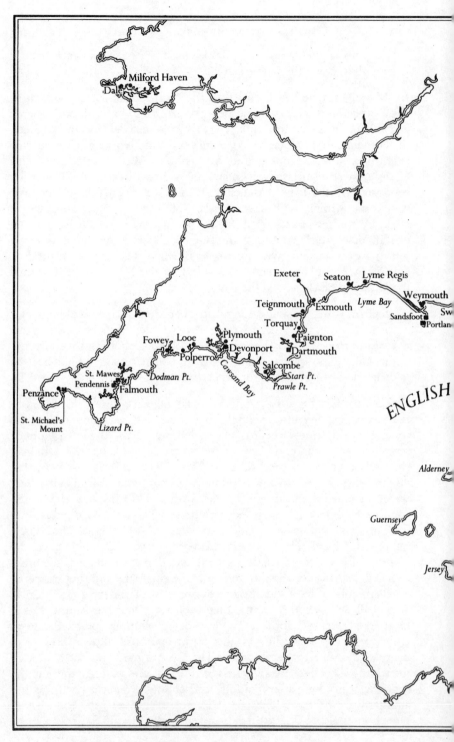

Milford Haven
Dale

Exeter
Seaton
Lyme Regis
Teignmouth
Exmouth
Lyme Bay
Weymouth
Torquay
Sandsfoot
Sw
Portlan
Paignton
Fowey
Looe
Plymouth
Devonport
Dartmouth
Polperro
Salcombe
St. Mawes
Dodman Pt.
Cawsand Bay
Start Pt.
Pendennis
Prawle Pt.
Penzance
Falmouth
ENGLISH
St. Michael's
Mount
Lizard Pt.
Alderney
Guernsey
Jersey

Harry's Walls. How Henry VIII protected the coast 1539–1545.

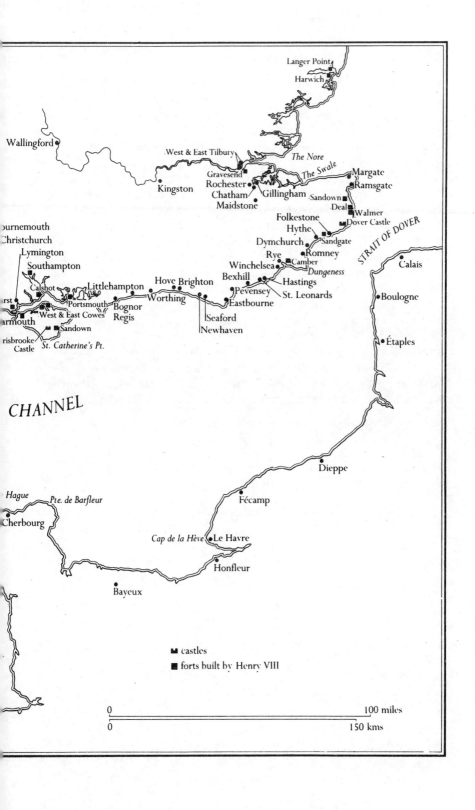

Wallingford

West & East Tilbury
The Nore
Gravesend
Rochester
Chatham   Gillingham
Maidstone
Kingston   Sandown
            The Swale   Margate
                           Ramsgate
                    Deal
Folkestone   Walmer
Hythe   Dover Castle
Dymchurch   Sandgate
Rye   Romney
Winchelsea   Camber   STRAIT OF DOVER
Bexhill   *Dungeness*   Calais
        Hastings
Hove Brighton   St. Leonards
Littlehampton   Pevensey   Boulogne
Worthing   Eastbourne
Bognor
Regis   Seaford
        Newhaven   Étaples

urnemouth
Christchurch
Lymington
Southampton
Calshot
rst
Portsmouth
West & East Cowes
armouth
Sandown
risbrooke
Castle   *St. Catherine's Pt.*

CHANNEL

                                          Dieppe

Hague   *Pte. de Barfleur*
                            Fécamp
Cherbourg

        Cap de la Hève Le Havre

                    Honfleur

    Bayeux

Langer Point
Harwich

◣ castles
◼ forts built by Henry VIII

0 ────────────────────────── 100 miles
0 ────────────────────────── 150 kms

pride of the series, the fortresses along the Kent coast. Minor additions and improvements continued to be made for the next few years but by January 1547, after seven years, the total expenditure was still only £376,000, and there was far more to show for it than for the usual futile foreign expeditions on which earlier kings had squandered their subjects' money.

The new professionalism which had now entered the nation's military planning was demonstrated in the collection, for the first time, of proper intelligence for defence purposes. Systematic maps and surveys of the threatened coastline were prepared, along with statistics about winds and tides and information on the navigability of the various channels in Southampton Water and other danger spots under different tidal conditions. Henry also commissioned the first set of drawings of the English coastline, the whole Channel, plus Calais, being covered, giving an invader's eye view of beaches and ports, as if from a height of some hundred feet a mile or two out to sea. At last a proper, centralized, systematic defence of the whole country was being attempted, instead of the muddled, piecemeal, localized efforts of the Middle Ages.

The king's achievement was admiring expressed in the inscription which the traveller John Leland drafted for one of Henry's finest creations, Mawes Castle, which still stands today. Translated it reads:

Henry, thy honour and praises will remain for ever.

32

BEACONS ON THE HILLS

Inland, in places where the beacons on the hills may be seen . . . set one beacon.

Privy Council instructions, 12 January 1545

Henry VIII's closing years were marked by war abroad and bloodshed at home. In July 1540 his chief minister, Thomas Cromwell, was beheaded on highly dubious charges of treason, and on the same day Henry married again, only to send this new wife, Catherine Howard, to the block two years later. Henry was now aged 50, enormously fat – 54 in [137 cm] round the waist – and plagued by a painful leg, which contributed to his irascibility and indecisiveness. But he remained a formidable figure and, in spite of his vast bulk and swollen legs, crossed the Channel on 14 July 1544 and, dressed in full armour, rode towards Boulogne, which was captured on 14 September, after a six-week bombardment during which 100,000 rounds were fired against it. On 30 September Henry returned to England, having refused all offers from Francis I to buy it back, thereby making a continuation of the war inevitable.

On 3 January 1545 Francis I proclaimed his intention of invading the British Isles that summer, in order both to regain Boulogne and to set free Henry VIII's subjects, supposedly groaning under his brutal and what was worse, Protestant, oppression. The Privy Council had antici-pated a new invasion attempt and on 12 January issued detailed instruc-tions for re-establishing the beacon-warning systems, in which great faith had been placed for centuries:

1. Below in the valleys, next the sea, place three beacons, where all three may be seen from the place of the next three.
2. On adjoining hills place two beacons visible both to seaward and landward.
3. Inland, in places where the beacons on the hills may be seen, and the inner parts of the shire warned, set one beacon.

4.   Appoint wise and vigilant persons to watch and keep the said
     beacons by turns.

The document went into great detail to ensure that the maximum
amount of information was transmitted by the beacons. A single lighted
beacon, for example, meant merely that suspect ships had been sighted,
while two confirmed that they were within four miles of the coast,
'whereupon the men of that part of the shire shall resort to a place
appointed'. A three-beacon alert signified a major emergency:

8.   When the keepers of the three beacons in the valley see the
     enemy land in greater number than the men assembled there
     can resist they shall in haste fire all their three beacons;
     whereupon both beacons on the next hill must be fired . . .
     and all inland beacons, and every man shall resort towards the
     hill where the two beacons burn.

The instructions concluded with a warning against false alarms, which
in May was re-issued – 'Men shall not rise to defend the coast except
that they see two fires to burn at once and . . . the watchmen set no
beacon afire except it be well known that there be ten sail of French on
the coast.' Inevitably mistakes did still occur, but the intention of the
plan, to assemble an overwhelming force while an enemy was still
disembarking, was sound, and the ambassador of the emperor Charles
V reported in June 1545 that the authorities had great faith in their plan:
'By means of beacons, the English say that they can anywhere muster
25,000 to 30,000 men in two hours, and they are confident in their
strength and delighted to see their enemy near.'

   Although, thanks to Henry's great fortress building drive of six years
before, the country's fixed defences were much stronger than they
had ever been, much remained to be done. The government feared a
simultaneous attack from Flanders into East Anglia, across the Scottish
border, and across the Channel into southern England, and all these
areas were now re-examined for signs of weakness. These were soon
forthcoming. The Duke of Norfolk wrote from that county to complain
that the defences of Yarmouth were inadequate:

It is walled on all sides save towards the haven, but so weakly that a
few shots of demi-cannon would make sufficient breach to some.
There are many small towers and evil [i.e. weak] walls, with neither
bulwark outside nor rampart within, and the tower walls not above
six feet [1.8 m] thick; so that it is the weakest walled town he ever
saw.

The officials sent to inspect the older castles at Berwick, Wark and

Carlisle complained that they 'have been kept more like gentlemen's houses' than fortresses, and improvements were rapidly put in hand, while 'four bulwarks to flank it' were also erected at Kelso. The Lord Admiral was brought back from Boulogne to survey the defences at home and another engineer recalled from Calais to strengthen Queenborough Castle on the Isle of Sheppey and the other defences of the Medway, before being hurriedly sent on to Tynemouth and Berwick. Much had to be left to local effort. Blockhouses were built and town walls strengthened at places as far apart as Lowestoft, Rye, Plymouth and Falmouth, and constructing 'field works' provided an outlet for patriotic fervour. 'Lords and commoners here are all diligent for the defence of the country,' wrote Lord Russell from Cornwall. 'It is marvellous what a number of bulwarks, ditches and trenches they have made.'

Henry's navy had so far failed to justify the money devoted to it. All told perhaps 12,000 men were now at sea under the Lord Admiral, many of them conscripted fishermen, whose nets were taken over by women and boys. One major pre-emptive strike was attempted, in June 1545, against the main French invasion port, Le Havre, known, confusingly, to the English chroniclers as New Haven, but it accomplished little, as even Edward Hall, a great admirer of Henry VIII, reveals:

> In June the lord Lisle, Admiral of Englande, wyth thenglyshe flete entered the mouthe of the river of Sain, and came before Newehaven, where the great army of Fraunce laie, which were 200 sayl of shippes and 26 galies of Force, wherof the Bishop of Rome had sent 20 wel furnished wyth men and money, to ayde the French king. Thenglyshemen beyng but an 160 sayle and all great shyppes, did not determine to set on the whole navie, but shot certayn peces of ordinaunce at theim, which caused the Galies to comne abroade, and shot at the Englyshmen whiche Galies had great advantage, by reason of the calme wether: twyse eche part assauted other with ordinaunce, but sodainly the wynd rose to greate, that the Galies could noit indure the rage of the seas; and thenglyshmen were compelled to entre the main seas . . . and so sayled unto Portesmouth, where the kyng then laye.

It was probably this experience that convinced the king that the English navy, contrary to its long tradition, and the trend of the times towards relying solely on sails, required galleys for inshore defence. He is credited with having personally devised, probably against professional advice, a hybrid 'rowbarge', powered by both oars and sails, carrying a forward-firing gun, or bowchaser and a modest 'broadside' of one or two guns in the half-deck. His fleet also contained a number of galleasses, up to 450 tons in burden, which carried oars for use when becalmed. By July he was able to assemble about 80 ships, 40 of them vaguely described as 'large', at Portsmouth; 20-30 of them were requisitioned merchantmen, the rest royal property. The king could also call on the services of about 60, mainly small, vessels, licensed to sail as privateers.

Everywhere morale was high. A 'voluntary' loan was readily subscribed in response to an appeal from the Privy Council. 'If this be too little, His Grace shall have more,' offered one group of willing givers. No sympathy was forthcoming for a solitary dissident, a London alderman who, having refused to contribute, was ordered by the Council to join the northern army, so 'he may feel what pains other poor soldiers abide abroad in the King's service and know the smart of his folly and sturdy disobedience.' The ordinary citizen, if East Anglia was typical, was eager to get to grips with the French. 'My lord,' the local militia begged the Duke of Norfolk, 'if they come, for God's sake bring us between the sea and them.'

A warning issued by the king in April had named the second week in May as the start of the danger period, and during June and early July expectation of the enemy's coming reached its peak. At three-mile intervals all along the coast the watch-fires, of 'a barrel of pitch and tar with flax', waited to be lit, whereupon 'all gentlemen, burgesses and peasants' were 'to be ready with arms to join the standards', ready for their hour of glory. Henry was anxious to stiffen these enthusiastic amateurs with some veteran mercenaries. Charles V successfully prevented some German 'hagbutters', i.e. musketeers, and a party of Italian professional soldiers reaching England via the Netherlands, but Henry did succeed in bringing in 1300 Spaniards to reinforce the northern army at Newcastle. They proved a great nuisance, insisting on purchasing their own food and cooking it themselves to the disgust of their landladies who complained that they had been ousted from their own kitchens.

On 15 July Henry moved down to Portsmouth with the Privy Council to take personal command of the anti-invasion forces. He hunted during the day, despite his poor physical condition, but devoted his evenings to meeting his council and dealing with dispatches. On Saturday 18 July 1545 he entertained Charles V's ambassador to dinner on board the *Great Harry*, indignantly rejecting the suggestion that he should secure peace with France by surrendering Boulogne. That very evening the French fleet appeared off the Isle of Wight, anchoring for the night off Bembridge and Ryde. Sunday morning dawned windless and sunny, perfect weather for galleys but useless for sailing ships. With his ships drawn up just outside Portsmouth harbour, protected to the west by dangerous shoals and to the east by his imposing new row of forts, the king felt confident enough to join his Lord Admiral, Lord Lisle, for dinner on his flagship –

or, according to another version, the *Mary Rose*, his second-largest vessel – when news was brought that the French were attacking. The king hurriedly went ashore, to seek a grandstand view of the coming engagement from Southsea Castle, while the sailors made ready for action★.

The Battle of Portsmouth, the climax to months of preparation on both sides, proved a low-key affair that caused more irritation than casualties. The French plan, drawn up in May, had envisaged the assembly of a large fleet in the harbours of Normandy, an unopposed crossing with a favourable wind which would also keep the enemy in harbour. Both these requirements, with a model two-day passage from Le Havre, had been achieved. The French scenario now called for the decisive defeat in its own waters of the English fleet. The Channel was then to be held a month, during which another French force would build a powerful fort opposite the mouth of Boulogne harbour, to prevent its being reinforced by sea, while Francis I led a large army to overwhelm it. Portsmouth, in other words, was not the real objective but, the key to Boulogne, and the target there was not the dockyard but the fleet.

So far everything had favoured the French and their commander, Admiral d'Annebault, now sent in his 25 galleys, each with a single gun mounted in the bow, but, though they concentrated on the *Great Harry*, they did little damage and after an hour withdrew. They were pursued by the new rowbarges, but apparently escaped unscathed.

The wind now changed and the British fleet weighed anchor and prepared to sail out to challenge the French, who withdrew along the Sussex coast. The sole serious casualty of the whole battle now occurred. The *Mary Rose*, hurrying out into the Solent with her guns primed for action, suddenly heeled over and capsized while attempting to turn, as the water poured in through the gun-ports, which were a mere 16 in [41 cm] above the waterline. The great ship, which had never fired a shot in anger, immediately foundered in full view of the royal party watching from Southsea Castle, taking to their death all but 35 of the 600–700 men aboard her, including the Vice-Admiral, Sir George Carew. The cause of the catastrophe was probably a combination of overloading, her normal complement being only 415, and gross mishandling, Lord Russell, a week later, attributing it to 'rasheness and great negligence'. Henry could ill afford her loss, and that of the 91 heavy guns aboard her. He immediately put salvage operations in hand but the remains of the *Mary Rose* were destined not to be raised until 1982.

Admiral d'Annebault was later to be heavily criticized by his

---

★The secondary sources are more than usually contradictory on these dates and events, Fisher, *England*, p. 467, even placing most of them on a non-existent day, 'Monday the 19th'; the 19th was a Sunday.

countrymen for not having achieved more with the splendid force at his disposal. He excused himself, somewhat feebly, on the grounds that if he had landed any significant number of men he would have been too weak to resist the English fleet – which in fact he outnumbered – and that a council of all the ships' pilots, with expert knowledge of the area, had advised against a direct attack on Portsmouth. It was, d'Annebault was told, almost unassailable by sea because of the adjacent shoals, the unpredictable currents, which exposed a ship anchoring in the tideway to English fire, and the narrowness of the entrance, which might be blocked if a single ship in the assaulting force were to be sunk. None of this would have deterred a determined commander but d'Annebault was clearly a somewhat reluctant warrior. He made no effort to land in force at any point on the mainland, directing his attention instead to a softer target, the Isle of Wight.

Although the channel separating it from the mainland was, at its narrowest spot, Hurst Spit, a mere 1400 yards [1280 m] wide, the island, in spite of its three towns sending members to parliament, had always seemed remote from the rest of Hampshire. In 1545 there was still no regular postal service to London, the 'coneyman' who came to buy rabbits for the London market also carrying any mail, and no coach had yet been seen there. The largest town on the island had fewer than 2000 inhabitants, out of its total of 15-16,000, and the residents tended to pride themselves on being different from their countrymen as a future deputy-lieutenant, born later in the century, observed in his *Memoirs*. 'It is an onnor for oure island to have neyther ffoxe or Papist in it, so it is an imputation or taxe that is layed on it, never or seldome to be guiltie of bredinge a hansom woman or horse.'

If it seemed appallingly vulnerable to the English government, and irresistibly inviting to a potential attacker, the island had some natural defences of its own. The narrow, western waterway was flanked by the dangerous Shingles shoal to the west and the potentially deadly Needles rocks, projecting out into the passage underwater, to the east. The tide raced between at three knots or, during the peak Spring tides season, at six, a constant hazard to sailing ships, although the speed, and the local phenomenon of double high tides, with two separate high water periods only an hour or two apart, could also aid an intruder by sweeping him rapidly past the batteries on the shore. Wisely, however, the French had settled for the longer but safer eastern route, through Sandown Bay and past Bembridge to St Helens, to which, on the evening of Tuesday 21 July 1545, having failed to take Portsmouth by assault or tempt out the English fleet into a decisive battle, they now retired, anchoring offshore and dispatching small parties of men inland.

For defensive purposes the island had been divided into ten 'centons',

under a resident landowner as 'centoner', aided by 'hobblers', watchmen
mounted on 'hobbies', i.e. small horses, to act as scouts. The centoner
was responsible for exercising his men once a month, and they seem, in
1545, to have reached a high pitch of efficiency for the French soon
found they had encountered more than they had bargained for. With the
help of the regular troops already on the island or, possibly, reinforcements from across the water, the 3000 or so soldiers and militia were
rapidly mobilized, outnumbering the small parties d'Annebault, still
afraid to commit his whole force, sent ashore. The terrain, broken up by
streams, with low-lying woodland providing cover for archers, also
favoured the defence.

A large invading army could, however, almost always obtain local
superiority in numbers and belatedly displaying some tactical sense,
d'Annebault ordered three simultaneous landings on a front of more
than ten miles [16 km], at Nettlestone Point (near Seaview), near
Sandown and near Bonchurch, midway between present-day Ventnor
and Dunnose. At Seaview the assault achieved some success, the local
fort being captured and the garrison forced to retreat into Prior Wood,
the victorious French burning Nettlestone. At Sandown the militia
managed to hold the French and finally to drive them back to their ships.
At Bonchurch the Hampshire militia came off worse, and were forced
back. Another, apparently independent, landing was then made at
Whitecliffe Bay, where the French fought their way to the top of the
surrounding downs, only to be ambushed there, with heavy losses, and
driven back.

Henry VIII was kept well informed about the progress of the fighting
and on his orders the British now carried out a general withdrawal to the
River Yar, which runs into the sea at Bembridge, at the eastern tip of the
island. The intention was to entice the enemy forward, before launching
an overwhelming counter-attack. The French, however, were not to be
tempted. D'Annebault had contemplated leaving 6000 solders to hold
the island indefinitely, with a further 6000 pioneers to build fortifications,
providing a fortress on the enemy doorstep and a permanent base for
attacking Portsmouth. But again his natural caution prevailed. 'Here,'
commented one of the island's chroniclers, 'was such a chance as had
not offered itself for a long time', but the French let the opportunity slip
and, having done little more than burn a few houses and kill or wound a
handful of militia, withdrew. D'Annebault had probably hoped that the
sight of the columns of smoke rising from the ravaged Isle of Wight
would goad the English commander, Lord Lisle, into a major engagement, even though outnumbered, off St Helens, but if so was disappointed. Lisle proved as cautious as d'Annebault himself and bided his
time. The French could still have achieved some substantial result, for

they had provisions for two months and a large force of still unblooded soldiers and horses, but their apathetic commander lacked the drive and vision to make effective use of them. On Saturday 25 July 1545 they appeared at Seaford, some 50 miles [80 km] away on the Sussex coast, setting fire to the town and to the house of a local nobleman at Firle. The neighbourhood's defence plan worked perfectly. 300 English rapidly assembled, including 20 archers, and killed 100 Frenchmen, while three beacons were lit on the adjoining hills, just as the instructions laid down, and levies from all over Kent and Sussex moved towards the mobilization point at Uckfield. By the time they arrived they were no longer needed. The French had already re-embarked, and, collecting on the way the forces left behind on the Isle of Wight, had sailed for France, the last ships having left English waters by Tuesday 28 July. The great invasion had turned out to be only a ten-day wonder.

Henry VIII left Portsmouth for Petworth on 1 August, in charge to the last; as he rode over Portsdown Hill, a marvellous vantage point from which the whole of Portsmouth Harbour is spread out below, he commented critically on the distribution of the warships in the harbour and ordered them to be moved. He boasted, however, of his 'great joy that he had been able to measure his strength against that of his enemy' and reaffirmed his confidence in the 'valour and affection of his subjects'. When another envoy from Charles V caught up with him at Guildford, where he was hunting and hawking without, it seemed, a care in the world, Henry told him he had no fear of the King of France, who had proved unable to invade England even though the weather had been so favourable to him that people in England had complained that God seemed to be French.

Although the winds had certainly helped the French the intense heat of that August had caused the sailors on both sides to suffer 'the corruption of their victual', with a resultant epidemic of stomach disorders, a major factor in d'Annebault's decision to withdraw. The invasion of 1545 had been beaten as much by diarrhoea as by English valour, but, understandably, this explanation was not much heard at the time.

What followed proved equally unheroic. After recrossing the Channel d'Annebault disembarked part of the army which had been intended to conquer England at Boulogne, to assist in the siege there, and, with the same purpose in mind, again laid course for England. During his absence Lord Lisle had been reinforced by additional ships from the West Country, although so little was another landing feared that already the troops of men responding to the beacon summons from the inland counties of Oxfordshire, Berkshire and Wiltshire had been stopped en route and sent home. The earlier Battle of Spithead (as the skirmish off

Portsmouth became known) was now followed, on Saturday 15 August 1545, by the Battle of Shoreham, an equally unmemorable action, though, another vindication for Henry VIII's foresight, the proportion of oar-powered ships had been increased.

The English fleet was divided into three 'battles', with 24 in the van, 40 in the main force, under Admiral Lisle, and 40 on one wing. It was this last which saw most of the action when on a calm sea, with a light south-easterly breeze – fine 'galley-weather' – the French sent their galleys against it. It was a small-ships' battle, merely watched by the larger vessels, as Lisle reported to the king:

> The *Mistress*, the *Anne Gallaunt*, the *Greyhound*, with all your majesty's shallops [dinghies, sometimes with a fore and aft sail] and rowing pieces did so handle th galleys as well with their sides as their prows [i.e. with gunfire as well as attempted ramming] that your great ships had little to do.

That night the two fleets anchored three miles [5 km] apart, with Lisle preparing for a general action in the morning, but during the hours of darkness the wind freshened and the dawn showed the French fleet in full retreat, with a line of ships five miles [8 km] long heading for the horizon with all sails set. It had unquestionably been another English victory, though, as a month before, the credit lay rather with the plague virus than Henry's navy. An English spy at Le Havre reported that the fever-and dysentery-racked sailors who stumbled ashore almost aroused his pity. For France the two non-battles, of Spithead and Shoreham, had been a disaster. 'The poor fishermen,' Lord Lisle informed Henry, quoting the usual source of intelligence about the enemy, 'say that there was never journey so costly to France as this has been nor [one with] more shame spoken of among themselves.'

Henry was under great pressuure from his council to make peace with France, even at the cost of surrendering Boulogne. 'Every counsellor saith Away with it,' wrote one court official in November 1545, 'and the king . . . saith, We Will keep it.' What the king said, very naturally, prevailed, but his ministers had good reason to be concerned. The cost of his wars over the previous two years was put at £1,300,000, only met by constant debasement of the coinage, followed by runaway inflation, which at one time touched 100 per cent. Henry had already issued new coins, the first sovereign and half-sovereign, both containing gold worth substantially less than their nominal value, and had authorized a search for new gold and silver mines in Cornwall. More despairingly, he commissioned two alchemists to seek a way of transmuting base metals into gold and silver, though specifying that they must employ only the 'pure science of philosophy' and not 'necromancy'.

More practical measures were also tried. Attempts to hold down wages led to mass desertions from the labour force working on castle building on the Isle of Wight, but the fort at Sandown, intended to prevent a landing on the east coast, was none the less completed in September 1545. Henry, with his usual open-mindedness, was still improving on existing designs. At Portsmouth, where a strengthening of the defences followed Henry's visit in July 1545, Italian-style angled bastions, the advantages of which have been described earlier, began to be incorporated, and, an even more novel idea, earthen ramparts. Earth was also employed to strengthen the small harbour of Ambleteuse, near Boulogne, after its capture in March 1546.

The use of earth for major, permanent, fortifications as distinct from temporary field-works thrown up in emergency, marked both a regression to an earlier age and an anticipation of much later thinking. Its great advantage was that it reduced the effects of artillery fire, since earthen ramparts could absorb a heavy bombardment without breaches being made, and without scattering potentially lethal fragments of masonry in all directions. It was also a far cheaper material than stone, universally available, from which defences could rapidly be erected by unskilled labour. The great drawback of earthern walls was that they could, especially when incomplete, be weakened by rain, and thus required constant repair, the solution being a covering of turf – such as the earliest Britons had used in their hill forts – or, in smaller-scale works, a layer of stone cladding.

Henry VII's wars with France came to an end on Monday 7 June 1546 at Camp, now Campagne-les-Guines, a mere mile from the site of the Field of the Cloth of Gold. The negotiations were conducted, like the Battles of Spithead and Shoreham, by the respective Lord Admirals of France and England and this time the Englishman unquestionably came off best. The French, it was agreed, were to have Boulogne back, but not till 1554 and on payment of two million crowns, i.e. about £300,000.

Less than a year later, 'Old Harry', as his subjects had come affection-ately to describe him, was dead, aged 55. For all his excesses – he had once admitted, 'I never spared men in my anger, nor women in my lust' – he had founded a church, established a dynasty and built a secure kingdom. Edward Hall was amply justified in entitling his account of these achievements *The Triumphant Reign of Henry VIII*.

33

A DIFFICULT REALM TO INVADE

We assure you that England is one of the most difficult realms to set foot on land for a foreign prince.

English commanders in Boulogne to French officer, April 1547

Henry VIII was 55 when he died, a giant among princes. He was succeeded, on 28 January 1547, as he had planned, by his son Edward, an intelligent boy, but at nine years of age if not a pigmy, emphatically a child. The real ruler of the country until late in 1549 was Edward VI's uncle, Edward Seymour, Earl of Hertford, brother of Jane Seymour, who now became Duke of Somerset and Protector of the Realm. Only two months after Edward's accession Henry's old rival, Francis I of France, was succeeded by *his* son, Henry II of France, a vigorous and ambitious 27-year-old, fiercely anti-Protestant and determined to regain both Boulogne and Calais and to make use of the Scottish alliance to embarrass England. Somerset, meanwhile, wished to revive the planned union between his new royal master and the four-year-old Mary, Queen of Scotland, which the Scots had rejected. This he saw as a means towards creating an empire covering the whole of Great Britain, which 'should neither in peace be ashamed nor in war afraid of any worldly or foreign power' and 'having the sea for a wall' would be secure against attack.

Henry II of France had quite different plans for Queen Mary. Scotland was daily coming more and more under French domination. Their troops were to be seen in the streets of Edinburgh; and in March 1547 twelve Gallic galleys reached the Firth of Forth. If Edward VI died young, without an heir, as was widely expected, and Henry VIII's two other children, Princess Mary and Princess Elizabeth, were rejected as illegitimate, as the Catholic world regarded them, Mary of Scotland would become the strongest claimant to the English throne, even though Henry VIII's will had expressly ruled her out of the succession. And thus Mary's husband would become king of England, with the two nations united under a single, French, sovereign. This ambitious scheme, and English determination to frustrate it, underlay many of the events of the next forty years. For the moment, however, the Scots proved unable to defeat the English in the field. In what became known, from a feature of the local landscape, as the Battle of Pinkie, fought near Musselburgh, about seven miles [11 km] east of Edinburgh on Saturday 10 September 1547, they suffered another crushing defeat. This failure was, however, almost outweighed by a dynastic coup.

In July 1548 Mary, Queen of Scots, now all of five-and-a-half, was whisked away to France via Dumbarton and the Irish Sea. Ten years later she duly married the Dauphin, having conveyed to her husband her rights to the thrones of both France and Scotland should she die childless, the very situation Henry VIII and Somerset had been eager to prevent.

Somerset was to be preoccupied for the next two years with domestic matters, especially in securing a generally acceptable religious settlement by establishing a truly national, distinctively English church. In May 1545 Latin had ceased to be used in St Paul's and in the royal chapel at Westminster and in January 1549 an Act of Uniformity was passed making the use of the new Book of Common Prayer compulsory from the following Whit Sunday, 9 June. With only minor modification the new Prayer Book, one of the greatest glories of English prose and a magnificent demonstration of the English genius for compromise, was destined to survive for 400 years, until destroyed, in our own day, by linguistic vandals indifferent to, and unworthy of, its beauty and splendour.

The first forebodings about a new French invasion attempt were expressed early in the reign. On 18 April 1547 the two noblemen in charge at Boulogne, Lord Grey and Sir Thomas Palmer, both soldiers of great experience, reported to London an alarming conversation they had had with a French officer who had been present at the attack on the Isle of Wight two years before. His professional opinion was that if the landings had been properly directed the island's defences must have been overwhelmed, and he had added, for good measure, his belief that 'all the other forts of the country were of equal strength'. The two Englishmen, realizing that their reaction would be passed on to the French court, had done their best to change his mind, and now repeated to Somerset what they had said:

We assure you that England is one of the most difficult realms to set foot on land for a foreign prince . . . for he cannot come to the shore without likelihood of great loss in the landing, and when he is landed, he must come as to the [as]sault the first day; and after that, if he pass it, he must yet look to fight every day, and to have battles offered to him without end. And as our fortifications are not so easy to be beaten as you think, so though they were never so strong, it is not England's profession to trust in lime and stone.

The government seems, however, to have regarded at least the Isle of Wight as vulnerable, for between May and November 1547 Yarmouth Castle was built on the island to supplement Hurst Castle on the mainland, and, facing it even more directly across the Solent, a small, 60-feet [18-m] wide, diagonal blockhouse at Sharpenode, specifically intended to cover the approaches to Portsmouth and the transport of reinforcements from there. Triangular bastions projected from the southern and eastern corners and it was the first fort in England that provided for batteries to flank the adjoining walls, a recognition that – a recurring preoccupation in the Isle of Wight – it might be stormed from the landward side.

A minor invasion scare occurred in March 1548 when the British ambassador in Paris learned that 'a French painter named Nicholas has given the French King pictures of all the havens in England', and some hurried repairs to fortresses in the south of England followed.

Risings against the abandonment of the Latin mass occurred on a large scale in Devon and Cornwall in June 1549 and the 'Prayer Book Rebellion' was only suppressed in mid-August after Exeter, that inde-pendent-minded city, had withstood a six-week siege by German and Italian mercenaries. Almost simultaneously a far more serious outbreak, provoked by the policy of allowing the rich to enclose common land, began in Norfolk and rapidly spread to many other areas.

On 8 August 1549, seeing the English government fully stretched in dealing with the Prayer Book and enclosure rebellions and with trying to retain a toehold in Scotland, Henry II of France declared war on Edward VI. His objective was to regain Boulogne without waiting for the already agreed hand-over date of 1554 and he had soon captured the outer adjoining fortresses of the English settlement at Ambleteuse and elsewhere. Soon afterwards the Protector Somerset was overthrown, for a variety of reasons, his place being taken by John Dudley, Earl of Warwick, who later became Duke of Northumberland, though he refused the title of Protector.

On 14 October 1549, while the new government was still settling in, Haddington, the last major outpost in Scotland, was evacuated, and in January 1550 negotiations began to surrender Boulogne, completed by a treaty there on 29 March, the great fortress being handed over for a mere 400,000 crowns. Everywhere the policy was one of retrenchment. As early as 1545 there was a shortage of gunpowder in the north, because 'When the fortresses are furnished withe the powder which was sent hither, little remains for the field' and in February 1551 the Council recorded its concern that 'the Kings ordonance was so dispersed for the furnyture of them [i.e. the new castles] that presently he hathe no ordonance for the felde'.

Plans to build fortifications in Ireland were now dropped, and very little was done to protect the Channel Islands, a possible French base. Henry VIII had also included the Scilly Isles in his defensive plan, a valuable outpost from which advance warning could be given of any approach towards Cornwall, but the fort only just begun at St Mary's was abandoned half-finished. A search for other economies was also undertaken, an enquiry in Kent, in May 1552, being followed by cuts in the garrison of several fortresses further west, at Portland, Sandsfoot (commanding the entrance to the Portland peninsula), St Mawes and Pendennis. During 1553 the guns were removed from seven bulwarks in Essex and shipped to the Tower, for the field army.

Little more effort was made to maintain the fleet. Edward had inherited 53 ships, of which 13 were large and 14 were galleys, but by 1552 the French were able to defy a request to render the customary salute when they appeared in strength off the Isle of Wight. That October defences all along the coast were being abandoned, or – as at Berwick, Calais and in Ireland – stripped of many of their men. The Council, in granting a subsidy early in 1553, made its position clear. The dead Somerset, it complained, had erected 'sumptuous endles vayne Fortifications', on which 'no smalle sommes of treasure were . . . wasted'.

Edward VI himself took a different view. The journal which he kept from 1550 onwards, when he was 13, shows more than the normal boy's interest in military matters. By 1552, aged 15, he was expecting to be consulted on detailed matters of fortress layout and one of his last appearances in public was at Portsmouth, in August 1552, when he criticized the existing defences as 'well repaired, but ill fashioned, ill flanked and set in unmeet places'. A radical rethink of the whole defensive plan, he suggested in a letter, was required:

> The town [is] weak in comparison of that it ought to be, too hugely great (for within the walls are fair and large closes and much vacant room) the haven notable great, and standing by nature easy to be fortified. And for the more strength thereof, we have devised two strong castles on either side of the haven, at the mouth thereof. For at the mouth, the haven is not past ten score [presumably yards] over, but in the middle almost a mile over and in length . . . able to bear the greatest ship in Christendom.

Edward's own brief voyage was almost complete. On Thursday 6 July

1553 he died, of tuberculosis. In his will, dictated from his deathbed, he laid upon his successors a charge more pious than realistic:

> In the young years of any of my heirs, my executors are not to enter upon any wars, except on occasion of invasion, nor to suffer religion to be altered.

The dying king had agreed, on his deathbed, to exclude from the succession the rightful heir, his half-sister Mary, notorious for her Catholic sympathies, and to substitute his first cousin, once removed, Lady Jane Grey, grand-daughter of Henry VIII's sister, Mary. Within nine days of the reluctant usurper being proclaimed queen, on 10 July 1553, most of her supporters had deserted her, thanks to a popular outcry, especially in London, and on 3 August 1553 Mary entered her capital in triumph, accompanied by her 19-year-old half-sister, Elizabeth.

Mary was 37, a plain, unsmiling woman of medium height, with large-boned features and a masculine voice. At 25 the French ambassador had reported to his master, 'her beauty, Sire, is mediocre,' while other ambassadors observed that her court gave the impression of being in perpetual mourning and she was for ever ill, with headaches and palpitations which bleeding did little to relieve.

But this ill-favoured, unappealing woman had one great consolation: her religion. She observed every fast or feast with passionate devotion and sometimes heard mass nine times in a single day. She regarded herself as God's chosen instrument to root out heresy and reunite England with Rome. On 12 August 1553, she banned the use of the word 'Papist' in sermons and next day, a Sunday, there was a riot when the queen's own chaplain denounced the official religion of the country in a public service in London. The following Sunday 200 guardsmen 'strode about the pulpit with their halerds' to protect the preacher, while Mary herself required 1000 men and eight cannon to protect her palace at Richmond. On 24 August the Latin mass was again sung in St Paul's; and Oxford vestments and chalices reappeared as if by magic from their hiding-places. In the last two weeks of August a leading Protestant was arrested nearly every day, culminating in the detention on 14 September 1553 of Thomas Cranmer, who had been appointed Archbishop of Canterbury by Henry VIII and was the real architect of the English Reformation. From 20 December 1553 parliament tamely restored the mass throughout England, while suppressing Cranmer's great Book of Common Prayer, and making attendance at Protestant services illegal.

The first armed resistance was provoked not by these religious changes but by the announcement, in October, that Queen Mary planned to marry Prince Philip of Spain, son of the emperor Charles V, whom she had always regarded as her mentor. She had hoped to die in that holiest of female states, virginity, but to bring her people back within the fold of the true faith Mary was prepared to sacrifice her personal inclinations. Her only objection to her proposed groom was that he might, at 26, as she told the emperor's ambassador, be 'disposed to be amorous' while 'such was not her desire'.

The majority of the nation, a few extremists apart, might have accepted a return of the mass, and even reunion with Rome, if sensibly handled; a Spanish king they were totally unwilling to tolerate. The crudest xenophobia was rampant, a substitute for the anti-papal sentiments it was already dangerous to express. 'Jack Spaniard' was accused on all sides of 'pomping pride' and it was predicted that once the nation had a Spanish king London would be full of 'beggars, slaves and all kinds of wretches', all demanding that the English address them as señor. The mayor and aldermen of Plymouth, steadily being driven, like the rest of Devon and Cornwall, from its traditional Catholicism to a fierce Protestantism, asked its French ambassador to put the town under French protection should the Spaniards attempt to seize it. The emperor's ambassador was told by a French spy that Henry II of France was planning to open a second front on the Scottish border as soon as fighting broke out in England, that French agents had already been sent to England to distribute white badges to English captains ready to assist the French, and that 24 French ships and 18 companies of infantry were waiting in Normandy to sail to England at a few hours' notice.

The threatened invasion never materialized but a serious rising did occur, led by Sir Thomas Wyatt, son of the poet of the same name, who declared that the threatened Spanish occupation was already beginning. Wyatt's rebellion was suppressed, after a fierce battle in the streets of London on Ash Wednesday, 7 February 1554. Mary's vengeance followed. Thirty new gallows had to be set up, and at least 250 men were executed 'There has never been such hanging as has been going on here every day,' wrote the French ambassador.

The rebellion also sealed the fate of the innocent Lady Jane Grey. Still only 16, she showed great courage when beheaded with her husband, Guildford Dudley, on 12 February 1554. Her father, Henry Grey, Duke of Suffolk, ignominiously detected by a dog while hiding in a hollow tree on his own estate, also went to the block, followed, on 11 April 1554, by Sir Thomas Wyatt. He had been kept alive in the vain hope that he would incriminate others, especially the heir to the throne, Elizabeth, but after being detained for two months she was released in May.

The French ambassador, Antoine de Noailles, rightly believed to have encouraged the recent plot, survived; he was more use to Mary's ministers where he was, for they had, as he suspected, acquired the key to his ciphers and were intercepting his dispatches. They had also, which he did not know, suborned his spies into becoming double agents. He was, however, made physically uncomfortable, being offered the house formerly occupied by the emperor Charles V's ambassador. His diplomatic colleague had, on vacating it, removed all the doors and windows, but did leave behind a servant who reported on his successor's movements.

The Spanish marriage turned out as disastrously as everyone had predicted. Philip, following his arrival in July 1554, did his best to be conciliatory but the foreigners' mere presence gave offence, it being said that there were 'so many Spaniards in London, that a man should have met for one Englishman, above four Spaniards'. The visitors, for their part, complained that they were jostled in the street and that English women were either ugly or, if attractive, behaved immodestly, hoisting their skirts as they walked. Philip was probably glad to leave for the Netherlands in September 1555, where he became regent, and subsequently, in January 1556, on his father's abdication, also King of Spain. He returned to England in March 1557, but left again in July, for good.

Mary, having come to the pleasures of matrimony late in life, became bitterly frustrated at being deprived of them. She sat up late writing to Philip, endured vivid sexual dreams, and twice falsely believed herself pregnant. A male heir, which she passionately desired, might have mellowed her temperament and restored her popularity. As it was, she became more embittered, and her subjects more contemptuous.

On 20 November 1554 Cardinal Reginald Pole, the 'arch-traitor' of a few years before, returned to London as papal legate to arrange the readmission of England to the Roman church. On 30 November 1554, with every peer and member on his knees before the pope's representative, the nation was formally absolved from the sin of schism and readmitted to mother church, a day known as the Feast of the Reconciliation.

A reign of terror now began, of a kind commonplace in other Catholic countries but unique in British experience. Mary and Pole seized their opportunity with the mad enthusiasm of religious zealots. The first Protestant martyr was a non-political scholar, John Rogers, who had edited Tyndale's English translations of the Bible; he was burnt at Smithfield on the afternoon of Monday 4 February 1555. His wife and ten children were present, as was a large crowd, who cheered him. Rogers met his end bravely, as did almost all those who endured the same terrible death during the next few years; usually a merciful bag of gunpowder was attached to the victim's neck but without it the torture might last for a full 45 minutes. In March five laymen were burnt, as well as a priest and the much-loved former Bishop of St David's. In April a City poulterer who had robbed a Spaniard caused a great stir by comparing his crime, as he stood waiting to be hanged at Charing Cross, with those of the pope, whom greed led to 'sell his masses', and read out as his dying declaration an apposite quotation from the Litany:

> From the tyranny of the Bishop of Rome and all his detestable enormities, Good Lord deliver us.

On 23 August 1555 the first woman was burnt, one of 60 members of her sex to suffer. Youth was no protection; at least one victim was an apprentice described as 'a boy'. Nor was pregnancy; one woman is said to have given birth as the flames licked round her.

On 16 October 1555 the frail, 70-year old Hugh Latimer, long since retired as Bishop of Worcester, was led to the stake in Oxford, at the site now marked by the Martyrs' Memorial. The Bishop of London, Nicholas Ridley, was burnt with him and Latimer addressed to his companion, still in his mid-fifties, words destined to become immortal:

> Be of good comfort, Master Ridley, and play the man. We shall this day light such a candle, by God's grace, in England, as I trust shall never be put out.

On 21 March 1556, almost defying belief, Mary burned the senior churchman in England, Thomas Cranmer, Archbishop of Canterbury, who added to the legend of Anglican heroism by publicly renouncing his earlier recantations before he died and thrust into the flames the hand that had signed them. The following day Mary appointed her partner in the enforced reunion of England with Rome, Cardinal Pole, to succeed him.

Still the slaughter continued; 90 were burnt in 1557 alone. Eventually, in just under four years, the figure reached 300 while perhaps another 100 died in prison. By Catholic standards these were trivial totals; in Philip II's Netherlands, with its much smaller population, 1900 a year was routine. England, however, as its people were fond of insisting, was not the Continent and though there *had* been burnings in the past they had been rare events. Mary I was responsible for more deaths in four years than Henry VIII had been in 38, or her successor was to be in 45. The numbers seemed even larger than they actually were because they were concentrated in a small area of London, the southern counties and East Anglia. Edmund Bonner of London was the most zealous persecuter of heretics and became known to Protestants as 'bloody Bonner', a description he was soon to share with his sovereign. His ruthlessness outraged even Catholics. 'You have lost the hearts of twenty thousand that were rank papists within this twelve months,' wrote one to Bonner during 1555. Almost as dangerous in the long term as these opponents were those who professed compliance to the restored religion but were inwardly unconvinced, as the Venetian ambassador reported to his government:

> With the exception of a few most pious Catholics, none of whom, however, are under thirty-five years of age, all the rest make this show of recantation, yet do not effectually resume the Catholic faith . . . They discharge their duty as subjects to their prince . . . believing what he believes . . . to avoid incurring his displeasure rather than from any internal zeal. They would do the like by the Mahometan or Jewish creed.

Directly after Mary's accession 800 leading Protestants had fled abroad, largely to France and the Rhineland. They were supported by British merchants trading abroad, especially those in the increasingly Protestant and anti-Spanish West Country. The exiles wisely resisted all of Mary's attempts to induce them to return and fired off a salvo of propaganda against the new regime, including John Knox's *First Blast of the Trumpet against the Monstrous Regiment of Women*, which, somewhat unfairly, blamed Mary's whole sex for her misdeeds. To be found in possession of this and other proscribed books became a capital offence, punishable by summary execution without trial.

The assistance the exiles gave to any foreign monarch who opposed Mary, notably Henry II of France, posed a permanent threat to the nation's security. English sailors, in French vessels, sailing from French ports, cheerfully plundered Spanish shipping, refusing to acknowledge that the King of Spain was also the King of England. Encouraged by a Frenchman living in London, who may in fact have been on the English government's payroll, plans were made for Sir Henry Dudley, a dashing figure who had formerly been captain of the guard at Boulogne, to cross to France to collect an army from the English expatriates there, with the French king's help, take it back to occupy the Isle of Wight as a base and then seize Portsmouth. The key figure was Richard Uvedale, captain of Yarmouth Castle on the island, who had helped Dudley to cross the Channel in January 1556, on the plausible pretext that he needed desperately to flee the country. Dudley, having revealed his true purpose, addressed Uvedale in manly terms difficult to resist. 'Thou wilt do like a good fellow and help me . . . ' he urged. 'Provide so that the ordnance there [at Yarmouth] may be pegged up [i.e. made unusable] against I come, and by God's blood, I will drive out this Spaniard or I will die for it.'

The Dudley invasion plot was full of agreeable and romantic, and sometimes absurd, details. Dudley's initial imposture, as a defaulting debtor, accorded ill with his black velvet coat, trimmed with fur, while the conspirators' plot to steal the recently raised £50,000 subsidy now lying in the exchequer and hide it 'in some secret place, as under the water by the Bridge', seems distinctly optimistic. The conspiracy also featured private recognition signs, like a coin broken in half, a secret hoard of 'harness, shirts of mail and other for a hundred men', and, to be kept ready at Southampton, 'so many shovels, spades and poles for ships as came to £6 or thereabouts', a somewhat modest sum on which to finance a revolution. (The man invited to go fishing on a boat where these were stored observed that they were 'no fit tools to catch fish withal' and declined.)

The ultimate aim of the plot was to bring back the Earl of Devon, currently in exile, a distant descendant of Edward IV, now aged around 29, marry him to Elizabeth and put them both on the throne in place of Philip and Mary. Inevitably, it now seems, it was betrayed. One of its joint leaders, an obscure 28-year-old called John Throgmorton, after being put on the rack, told his fellow-prisoners, 'I do assure you it is a terrible pain,' but held his tongue. Others were less heroic. By late July 1556, though Dudley was safe in France, those involved had all died, making this yet another invasion that never was. Elizabeth had, happily, been unaware of the conspiracy, though her servants were questioned to try and establish her complicity. The Earl of Devon, though quite willing to marry her, remained, homesick and discontented, in Brussels and then Italy, where, soon afterwards, he died, after catching cold during a storm off Venice, Mary, characteristically, greeting the news with the comment that God had once again showed his justice. (The cynical French suggested that 'there was more in it of human help than divine', i.e. that Edward Courtenay had been helped on his way at Mary's instigation, but this was probably unjust.)

In January 1557 France and the papacy on the one side became involved in a war with Spain and various Italian states on the other. The quarrel had nothing to do with England, but in March 1557 Philip of Spain returned to seek British help, his reappearance making his wife ecstatically happy but spreading gloom among his English subjects. Earlier fears of a Spanish take-over had proved unfounded. Although the minutes of the Council, which also disliked the proposed war, were now kept in Spanish or Latin – King Philip could not speak English – a proposal to leave Spanish diplomats to represent English interests abroad had failed. But everyone could see the absurdity of Mary burning those who refused to acknowledge the supremacy of the pope while her husband was at war with him.

While Mary was bullying her unwilling Council into sacrificing the nation's interests to her husband's wishes a new 'friendly invasion' was attempted in the north. In April 1557 Thomas Stafford, a distant descendant of Edward III, aged around 26, sailed from Dieppe in two ships provided by Henry II of France, with a mere 40 followers. The *Fleur de Lys* and its sister-ship, having disembarked Stafford and his men at Scarborough, sailed on with a detachment of French soldiers bound for Scotland, on which Henry II's real hopes were set; with 3000 Frenchmen just across the border and the northern counties in friendly hands, a new, pro-French, King Thomas I might conceivably have been set on the throne of England.

Stafford's proclamation, denouncing the 'unrightful and unworthy Queen of England', whom, he alleged, loved the Spaniards, hated her own people, and planned to hand over twelve castles to Philip on the day of his coronation – though recognized as king, Philip had not yet been formally crowned – produced no response. The town of Scarborough was captured, but this was the most pro-Catholic part of England, where no burnings had occurred, and the local militia under the Earl of Westmorland easily took the invaders captive; 27, among them Stafford, were later hanged. Henry II of France disclaimed responsibility but the episode was sufficient to produce a general invasion scare. In May the alarm beacons were re-erected on their familiar sites, 'watchers' were appointed, and at Poole, Southampton and the Isle of Wight local commanders were ordered to be on the alert. On 7 June 1557 came the formal declaration of war on France, Henry II cutting the proceedings short on the grounds 'that as the herald came in the name of a woman it was unnecessary for him to listen to anything further' and laughingly remarking, 'Consider how I stand when a woman sends to defy me in war!'

Defence in Mary's reign had enjoyed little priority but her people had inherited a powerful system of fortifications, as an appreciation written for Philip II in 1556 confirms:

> They fear no foreign power because the places where ships can land are well fortified and guarded, and those that are not guarded are protected by high and strong cliffs. In addition the kingdom is strong because of the provision it makes against unexpected attacks, so in time of danger the whole country can quickly take up arms.

No new fortresses were built in Mary's reign, although some repair work was done during the invasion alarms of 1557 and 1558, and the navy was also neglected. The *Great Harry*, burned by accident soon after her accession, was not replaced and the 23 'great ships' which had formed the backbone of the fleet in 1553 were allowed to decay, a process encouraged by corrupt management, in which fervent Catholicism was more important than honesty or competence. By 1555 ships were being sold off at knockdown prices; one, a 450-tonner, which had cost £1500 ten years before, fetched a mere £35, others going for £8 or £10. In 1557 a quarrel with the Hanseatic League, which controlled supplies from the Baltic, made matters worse, depriving the nation of pine trunks for masts, pitch for making hulls watertight, flax for canvas and hempen rope. The dockyard stores were empty and reserves of gunpowder almost non-existent.

The defences of Calais had suffered like those of the homeland. This English outpost consisted of a strip of territory about 25 miles [40 km] long by, at its widest, six miles [10 km] deep, about 120 square miles [310 sq. km] in all. It was well protected by a series of forts, and up to now had always been considered impregnable. The defences, however, though work was started that summer on a programme of extra walls and ditches were not really adequate to withstand the latest cannon.

Henry II of France now assembled, with great strategic skill and in almost unprecedented secrecy, an overwhelming force of around 30,000 men. Calais itself contained only around 800, with smaller forces in the other supporting fortresses. Five English ships, with some 400 men, were supposed to police the Channel but totally failed to prevent, or even detect, the dangerous French build-up.

This great fortress, the last English territory on the Continent, a source of pride to every patriotic citizen, was now to be lost with humiliating speed. The first assault went in during the early hours of New Year's Day 1558; by 20 January it was all over. It had taken Edward III eleven months to capture Calais and successive sovereigns had held it since then for 211 years; Mary had lost it in three weeks. The shock was enormous and her unpopularity reached new heights. Few recognized that the place had been a costly incubus, useful only as a base for aggressive wars which England no longer had any need to fight, and ineffective, as had often appeared, in preventing invasion.

Inevitably, the loss of Calais led to reports of a threatened French landing on the south coast, but they failed to produce a patriotic response, the nation having concluded that a foreign landing offered the best opportunity for its hated sovereign's overthrow. It needed only the crews of four French ships to step ashore, thought the leading Spanish nobleman resident in England, to start a revolution. The signs of disgruntlement were everywhere. The West Country sheriffs argued, most unconvincingly, that there were no arms and armour in their area, and everywhere 'divers absented themselves' from the muster. Money was found, however, to buy gunpowder, armour and weapons in the Low Countries and some repairs were made to the coastal forts. In February parliament passed two Acts to strengthen the country's armed forces, specifying in detail, as will be described later, what arms and armour every citizen was expected to provide and imposing heavy penalties on muster masters who accepted bribes from men evading their obligations.

As during earlier crises, the vulnerable parts of the country were divided up into ten lieutenancies, covering various sub-divisions of the north, East Anglia, the south, and south-west. The reports they sent in were far from reassuring. The Lord Warden of the Cinque Ports protested that Kent had never been so open to an enemy, while Earl Montague, responsible for Sussex, said the inhabitants were already withdrawing inland since 'for five or six miles from the sea coast there is only plain downs, without stick of woods'. The usual instructions were issued, for 'watchers' to be ready day and night beside their beacons, but the justices were also ordered to earmark fast horsemen to ride inland with detailed intelligence, while the main body of defenders, breaking down bridges and blocking roads as they went, withdrew to the nearest town.

On 13 July 1558 Philip of Spain used the British fleet to support, with its guns, another of his ventures, a land attack on a French army at Gravelines, but no attempt was made to follow up this victory and a futile raid on the coast of Brittany, where 'a great abbey and many pretty towns and villages thereabout' were devastated, merely provoked a reprisal, the seizure of the Channel Island of Alderney, Mary deciding that its three square miles [9 sq.km] were not worth defending. It was the loss of Calais that really rankled, however, not least with the queen herself, as her reply to a courtier who asked if her 'much sighing' was due to her husband's protracted absence revealed:

Indeed (said she) that may be one cause; but that is not the greatest wound . . . When I am dead and opened you will find Calais lying in my heart.

On 10 November 1558 five more Protestants were burned at Canterbury; on 13 November Mary roused herself from the sickbed where she was prostrate from 'melancholy' to sign the warrant for the execution of two more. They were to outlive her, for early on Thursday 17 November 1558 'Bloody Mary' died, followed to the grave that same evening by her fellow fanatic, Cardinal Pole. The day was to be celebrated for years to come and a London diarist witnessed the first rejoicing that evening:

All the churches in London did ring and at night [men] did make bonfires and set tables in the street and did eat and drink and make merry for the new queen.

34
YOUR GOOD QUEEN

Be ye well assured I will stand your good Queen.

Queen Elizabeth on the day before her coronation, January 1559

Queen Elizabeth was 25 when she ascended the throne: tall, handsome with a great shock of bright auburn hair, accomplished, and, above all, Protestant. As she rode through London on Saturday 14 January 1559, the day before her coronation, she received a rapturous reception from the crowds. At Temple Bar a child recited verses that summed up the nation's hope:

Farewell, O worthy Queen! . . . our hope is sure
That into error's place thou wilt now truth restore

to which Elizabeth replied, 'Be ye well assured I will stand your good Queen.'

This was the start of a partnership between sovereign and ministers, monarch and people, never before experienced, and never since surpassed. 'She is much attached to the people,' wrote a hostile witness, the Spanish ambassador, after visiting her just before her accession, 'and is very confident that they are all on her side; which is indeed true.' Contemporaries would not have been surprised that she would prove to be the first British sovereign to give her name to a whole epoch. 'It is,' wrote one foreign visitor, 'more to have seen Elizabeth than to have seen England.'

The religious issue dominated all others. Elizabeth's own views were close to her father's – Henry VIII was always her hero – and she detested extremism, whether papal or puritan. In May 1559 the Church of England was restored without bloodshed by the Act of Supremacy and a new Act of Uniformity made attendance at Anglican services compulsory though for many years it was barely enforced. Only a tiny number of clergy, perhaps 200 out of 8000, remained loyal to Rome. Even more influential in encouraging generations of Englishmen to hate the very name of Rome was a long and detailed record of Mary's crimes first published in 1563. John Foxe was a former fellow of Magdalen College, Oxford. From exile in Strasbourg he had issued in 1554 a Latin history of the early Christian martyrs, linking them to all those who in the previous 200 years had suffered in England for opposing the Church of Rome. In its updated, English form, Foxe's *Book of Martyrs* was an immediate best-seller and it was now permanently available in every parish church, chained up alongside the English Bible.

Mary's other legacy, the war with France, was also rapidly wound up. On 2 April 1559 France and Spain concluded the Treaty of Cateau-Cambrésis, with England as very much a minor, third party. Elizabeth was forced to agree to the loss of Calais and although the French promised to return it in eight years, or pay half a million crowns for it, everyone knew that such long-term agreements were never kept. Calais had gone for good.

Elizabeth realized that the country could not afford simultaneously to be on bad terms with both Spain and France. As one observer had commented when she came to the throne, 'England is as a bone thrown between two dogs', but the traditional enemy was France. 'When the Ethiopian is white, the French will love the English' ran a contemporary proverb. But if France was disliked, Spain, thanks to Mary, was detested and the Spanish ambassador received a cool reception at the new court; he was refused a room in the Palace of Whitehall and ignored 'as if', he complained to his royal master, 'I were the devil'.

The English, Philip's ambassador now suggested, could only be dealt with 'sword in hand'. Elizabeth's government was already reaching a similar conclusion about Spain. The invasion scare of early 1558 had revealed the country's military weakness and had led, as mentioned earlier, to two important acts, laying down the mobilization machinery, with the scale of arms and armour each eligible male was expected to provide, under pain of a £2 fine or ten days' imprisonment. Responsibility now rested not on the sheriff or the Commissioners of Array but on the Lord-Lieutenant of the county, an *ad hoc* temporary post which by the end of the reign had become permanent. He appointed the officers of the militia and, with the help of local commissioners, often the justices, laid down the number of men to be supplied by each parish. The demands made by the Act were substantial. A man who admitted to an income of £1000 or more a year was expected to produce 16 horses, 80 suits of light armour, 50 metal helmets, 40 pikes, 30 longbows, 20 bills or halberds and 20 arquebuses. The lowest rated category, earning £5-10 a year, was supposed to find a coat of plated armour, a bill or halberd, a helmet and a longbow. In between were eight other levels of equipment, according to the owner's annual income. Some quaint tests were imposed to prevent evasion, so that, for example, a man whose wife was seen in a velvet kirtle [i.e. gown] was assumed to be able to supply a fully equipped light horse.

The original requirement was that all men who qualified, which meant all but the very poorest, between the ages of 16 and 60 should attend, but from the 1570s only 'able men', presumably the younger and more physically fit, were summoned to the muster, then being further divided into trained and untrained.

The muster was not primarily intended to provide training itself, but to ensure that men had the required equipment, and could be called out when needed. The deputy-lieutenants, each in charge of part of a county, passed an order to the high constable of each hundred naming the time and place of a muster; it might also be announced in church. The 'petty constable' of each parish received a list of assessments within it to jog the memories of those who preferred to 'forget' their obligations.

The general muster for a county was as much a social as a military occasion, with much beating of drums and displaying of colours. It was usually held in the summer; only emergency justified calling men out when the weather was bad and the nights long. The traditional times, encouraging the holiday atmosphere, were Easter, Whitsun and Michaelmas, a muster sometimes extending over four days. Unless everyone was required to parade simultaneously items tended to be lent from one man to another, which defeated the whole object of the exercise, but the offenders could hardly be blamed for equipment was expensive: by 1600 a caliver, or light musket, cost from 13s 4d to 26s 6d [66p – £1.32], a corslet, i.e. breastplate, 33s 4d [£1.66]. Privately owned armour was a sign of wealth, and a man of substance might possess 20 full sets of armour and 15 cases of pistols, kept in his private armoury. To supply those who could not afford to equip themselves many parishes, or even whole counties, had common armour, perhaps maintained by a full-time employee, though excessive zeal could mar efficiency; it was found at the Tower of London, in 1569, that some armour had been weakened by being too frequently scoured with sand.

The council laid down that every man should accustom himself to wearing his armour by marching in it for up to six miles [10 km], under penalty of four days in jail, and one enthusiastic peer in 1569 commended his unit for covering twelve miles, but admitted that they were worn out by the end of the exercise. On the Isle of Wight another fire-eating nobleman suggested that militia-men too idle to turn out in full battle order ought to be 'debarred the credit of wearing any armour and . . . degraded to the pickaxe and shovel amongst the pioneers'. But one unit on the mainland went to war like gentlemen, leaving their armour and weapons to be transported on carts or packhorses, much to the authorities' disgust, since not only did this leave them not ready to fight, but bumpy roads often damaged the 'cockes and springs and stocks and ramming sticks' of the firearms. An unmilitary note was also struck by the men who added lace and ribbons to their uniforms, for which there was as yet no common pattern. The diocese of St Albans provided uniforms for the contingent it financed, specifying the cut and colour of the coats, and the London livery companies also set a high standard of turn-out. In 1559, as her father had done a few years before, the queen watched an impressive demonstration in which they marched before her with their guns and pikes, to the music of drums, fifes and trumpets, and received the royal thanks.

Elizabeth's Principal Secretary, or chief minister, Sir William Cecil, who in 1571 became Lord Burghley and in 1572 Lord High Treasurer, was 38 in 1558, the Cambridge-educated son of a Northamptonshire landowner who had made his fortune under Henry VIII. He was to serve the queen with unfailing competence and loyalty for almost the whole of her reign, amply fulfilling her comment when appointing him that 'This judgement I have of you . . . that you will be watchful to the state and that without respect of my private will you will give me that counsel that you think best.' Hardly less important at first was the government's chief financial adviser and negotiator, Sir Thomas Gresham, then around 40, who in 1559 was sent to the Netherlands on a munitions purchasing mission. Gresham's philosophy, rare among bankers, was 'Fare well the penny that saves one hundred' and he was soon employing agents all over the Netherlands and Germany. A report from the Master of the Ordnance on Elizabeth's accession had painted an alarming picture. Some guns in the coastal forts, themselves neglected, had been dismounted, and there was a desperate shortage of small-arms, pikes, bow-staves, body-armour and, above all, gunpowder. Regulations existed in Philip of Spain's Netherlands forbidding the export of arms through Flemish ports but Gresham overcame all difficulties, seeking out willing manufacturers and bribing customs officials not to make awkward enquiries about suspicious-looking boxes and bundles labelled 'velvet'. In October 1559 alone £48,000 worth of arms was imported and in the next year £296,000 was spent; one dealer's account alone reached £109,000. Gresham acquired almost all the saltpetre in Germany, but his masterstroke was to obtain armour from Spanish stocks in Belgium. 'I will confess here,' he admitted to Sir William Cecil, 'that by trickery I have drawn 2000 corselets from the royal arsenal at Malines and they are now in England. You will understand that their disappearance has created no small stir among the officers.'

Gresham was only able to outbid all competitors because of the reform of the national finances which, with Cecil's help, he now put in hand. The value of the currency was restored – his name is still immortalized in the famous 'law' he propounded about bad money driving out good – and he succeeded in simultaneously securing highly favourable rates of exchange and loans at a lower rate of interest than any other kingdom in Europe. While Gresham was obtaining the weapons, Cecil was mobilizing the men to use them. Professional muster-masters, paid by the government, were sent out to train the vast numbers who regularly assembled, and for a time local turnouts took place weekly or even daily in particularly threatened areas. The Council had set up two committees responsible respectively for defence preparation on the south coast, especially around Portsmouth and the Isle of Wight, and the Scottish border. In 1558 a full-scale reconstruction of the defences of Berwick was put in hand based on five large bastions which completely covered each other, separated by a 100-foot [30-m] curtain wall between them, a basic design which was to influence British fortress building for centuries to come.

Mary Stuart had, as mentioned earlier, become Queen of Scots when a week old. In June 1558, aged 15, she married the Dauphin of France, heir to the French throne, to which her husband succeeded in June 1559, making him Francis II and Mary Queen of both France and Scotland. In December 1560, Mary's husband died, and in August 1561 the 18-year-old widow returned to Scotland, the Catholic monarch of a fiercely Protestant country. It was, however, her disorderly private life which finally sealed her fate. Infatuated by one unsuitable lover after another, she finally married, as her third husband, the suitor universally suspected of murdering her second. In July 1567 she was forced by her irate people to abdicate in favour of her one-year-old son, now James VI of Scotland, and in May 1568 escaped from prison and made a dramatic dash on horseback across the border, to seek safety in England.

The presence of this young, 25-year-old, troublemaker, and claimant to her own throne, was to prove a source of endless problems to Elizabeth, as the queen herself foresaw. Mary was a natural focus for internal, Catholic, dissent, an ally for every would-be invader. Mary herself showed little gratitude to her protector, and less sense. By January 1569 she was already sending a message to Philip II's envoy: 'Tell the ambassador, that, if his master will help me, I shall be queen of England in three months and mass shall be said all over the country.' The English government knew of some of her treasonable activities, and suspected more, but Mary was unquestionably a member of the royal sisterhood. As one of Elizabeth's noblemen put it, 'One that has a crown can hardly persuade another to leave her crown because her subjects will not obey.' But this attitude did not eliminate feminine rivalry between the two women. As Henry VIII was anxious to be assured that he cut a finer figure than Francis I so Elizabeth demanded to know whether she or Mary had the finer hair and complexion and, on learning that the then Queen of Scots was taller than she, commented sharply, 'Then she is too high.'

Mary's arrival was followed, in November 1569, by a serious rebellion in the north, led by the old Catholic families who wanted to see her restored in Scotland and recognized as heir apparent in England. They failed to liberate Mary, who had been moved further south at the first sign of trouble, but Hartlepool was seized, giving rise to the fear that it would become a bridgehead through which Philip's troops could pour into the country. Catholics predicted that the Spanish general, the Duke of Alva, would celebrate Candlemas, a feast day abandoned by the Anglican church, in St Paul's*, but the government crushed the rising with unusual severity, including some 800 executions.

On 25 February 1570 Pope Pius V issued his bull *Regnans in Excelsis*, formally excommunicating the queen as a heretic, like her father before her, and repudiating her 'pretended right' to the throne of England. The consequences were the same as in Henry VIII's day. Invasion and insurrection were now inextricably linked and patriotic backwoods Catholics, wishing only to be left in peace, were pushed towards unwanted martyrdom. The death penalty was inflicted, however, not for rejecting the established church, as in Mary's time, but for high treason, a significant difference, if not one readily apparent to the victim. The law was immediately enforced. An English Catholic who obtained a copy of the bull from the Spanish ambassador's chaplain and fixed it to the Bishop of London's door, in May, was tortured on the rack, to make him reveal any fellow conspirators, and put to death.

This reaction, if cruel, was understandable. England that summer was in the grip of a new invasion scare, part well-founded, part irrational, following the arrival in the Spanish Netherlands of Philip II's best general, and most ruthless governor, the Duke of Alva (or Alba) who had been sent there to stamp out all resistance to Spanish rule and the Roman church. In the Low Countries, already well developed industrially, nationalist and libertarian ideas went hand in hand with Protestant beliefs, one reason why Catholic monarchs were determined to root out doctrinal dissent. The Netherlands, originally independent states but now under the control of Philip II, covered roughly the area of the future Holland and Belgium. The ten southern states, still Catholic, might have accepted Spanish rule; the seven northern ones were

*This festival, officially the Purification of the Blessed Virgin Mary after childbirth, was particularly objectionable to Protestants, as an example of the Mariolatry they had rejected.

unflinchingly hostile to it, and had found a leader in the Prince of Orange, known as William the Silent for his ability to keep a secret. William, after vainly opposing the Spaniards' oppression of the Dutch people, had become a fervent Protestant, the champion of his people against Alva's 'Bloody Council'.

The struggle for the unity and independence of the Netherlands was to be fought simultaneously with Queen Elizabeth's fight to protect her kingdom. Alva's tyranny and the exploits of the 'Holy Office' of the Inquisition, which tried to eradicate heresy by torture and burning, drove large numbers of Flemish Protestants – merchants, mechanics, weavers, artisans of all kinds – to seek refuge in England, one estimate, no doubt excessive, putting the total at 100,000. They revived memories of Queen Mary's recent terror and the Pope's award to Alva, in recognition of his services, of a consecrated hat and sword in 1568, made him even more of a bogeyman in England. He was undoubtedly a brilliant general but was even more proud, as he later boasted, of having executed no fewer than 18,000 men in his six years in Holland and Zeeland.

Alva had at his disposal at least 10,000 Spaniards, plus an even larger number of German mercenaries and locally recruited Catholics. He had no illusions, however, about the difficulty of invading England and when approached to send troops from Antwerp to assist the northern rising in 1569 refused. Alva's attitude, endorsed by Philip II, was that the time to send an army into England was when the Catholics had already staged a successful rebellion there, but so long as his huge army lay just across the North Sea no English government could feel secure.

In February 1570 the English ambassador in Paris warned that 'all men's mouths' were 'full of the invasion of England', with a French force from Brittany descending on Dumbarton to put Mary back on the throne of Scotland as a first step. Elizabeth commented that, 'It were a great folly and . . . against common sense to restore the queen of Scots,' but great preparations were being made without concealment to escort Philip II's new (and fourth) bride-to-be, Anne of Austria, from Flanders to Madrid. The English government suspected that under cover of these innocent activities the Spaniards might be planning a sudden descent on England. By July a full-scale anti-invasion alert was in operation. The defence scheme worked out at the start of the reign was now put into force. The beacon system was activated, the muster system tested and hackbut practice on village greens became a regular feature of rural life. The French ambassador in the previous year had put the numbers involved at 6000 harquebusiers, 6000 pikemen with armour, and 12,000 others, but these were only a fraction of the total who could be called on if required; Gloucestershire alone, in 1569, claimed an available strength of 6250 men, all properly trained.

During the summer of 1570 the fleet was mobilized off Kent under the Lord High Admiral, while his deputy, William Lord Howard of Effingham, was assigned the ten best ships to guard the Channel. Small vessels were also sent to patrol the far shore while Sir John Hawkins, of whom more will be heard later, kept watch at Plymouth in case of a sudden supporting strike direct from Spain. In fact the Spanish ships sailed down-Channel without incident, duly responding when – as the government had specifically ordered – Howard called upon them to make the customary salute as they passed along what the English described as 'Her Majesty's stream'.

The following year, 1571, brought a new invasion alarm with the Ridolfi plot, named after its author, a Florentine banker and business man now resident in England. Like other foreigners who mixed chiefly with English dissidents, Ridolfi grossly overestimated the degree of opposition to Elizabeth, estimating that at least 60 peers would join in a rising and would muster an army of 39,000 in support of Mary Stuart, marrying her off at the same time to the leading Catholic layman in England, the Duke of Norfolk.

Ridolfi was persuasive, plausible and diligent. In April 1571 he travelled to the Netherlands to obtain from the Duke of Alva a promise of military support, but the Duke would only promise to send an army to Harwich, which the rebels were supposed to seize and hold as a bridgehead, once the Duke of Norfolk was already in the field, a condition Ridolfi concealed. Meanwhile the Spanish ambassador was committing his master, without authority, to send an army to the West Country, an equally imaginary force.

The oddest feature of the whole affair was that the Spaniards actually believed they had suborned one of the most fiercely anti-Spanish and militantly Protestant of all Englishmen, William Hawkins (or Hawkyns), of Plymouth, brother of Sir John Hawkins. With the approval of Cecil and the queen, Hawkins offered the Spanish ambassador, in exchange for various rewards, including a pardon for his alleged offences against Spanish colonies in the West Indies, to leave the west coast open to invasion and to take his fleet across to the Netherlands to escort Alva's forces into East Anglia. The Spaniards naïvely swallowed this preposterous proposal, enabling Lord Burghley (as the former Sir William Cecil had become in February 1571) to learn the date proposed for the invasion, the late summer or early autumn of 1571, and though King Philip, to whom Hawkins sent a private emissary, did not disclose the identity of the English traitors involved, Cecil had little difficulty in piecing the whole picture together from other sources. He persuaded a reluctant Elizabeth that Norfolk should be executed, a sentence carried out in June 1572, but she refused, despite pressure from him and from parliament, to send her fellow monarch, Mary of Scotland, to the scaffold. Thereafter, however, there was a notable hardening of her attitude to potential traitors, among whom increasingly every 'recusant' who still practised the old religion came to be counted.

In April 1572 a revolt broke out against the Spanish government in the Netherlands. The inhabitants of Flushing, Rotterdam and other places expelled their Spanish garrisons and four provinces, including Holland, proclaimed their independence under William of Orange. With the Netherlands in turmoil, the French seized their opportunity, occupying Walcheren, which controlled access to the whole country, and menacing Flushing, whose deep-water harbour protected the entrance to the Scheldt. Flushing in French hands was even worse than Flushing in Spanish possession and a force of English volunteers was sent, with official encouragement, to protect it, though the Duke of Alva soon expelled the French and set about restoring the Spanish grip on the whole area.

While Alva was doing his worst, new proof of Catholic perfidy was provided by the Massacre of St Bartholomew's Day, 24 August 1572, when thousands of Huguenots throughout France were suddenly and brutally murdered, ostensibly because of a plot – wholly fictitious – to kill the king. Perhaps 10,000 men, women and children were butchered in a few days, a foretaste of what English Protestants might expect. The Catholic response to this monstrous deed caused almost as much offence as the massacre itself. Pope Gregory XIII ordered celebratory bonfires at the Castle of St Angelo, and a joyful *Te Deum* was sung in St Peter's. 'While I write,' observed the Spanish ambassador in Paris two days after the killings began, 'they are casting them out naked and dragging them through the streets, pillaging their houses and sparing not a babe. Blessed be God who has converted the princes of France to his purpose!' Philip of Spain, who had never before been known to smile, was said to have laughed aloud when he heard the news. Elizabeth's government managed to restrain the public outcry that demanded revenge, but the Massacre of St Bartholomew was not to be forgotten, being added to that long account with the Catholic powers which would one day have to be settled in blood.

35

THAT GUILTY WOMAN OF ENGLAND

*That guilty woman of England . . . Whosoever sends her out of the world . . .
does not sin but gains merit.*

Secretary to Pope Gregory XIII, December 1580

Rivalry at sea widened the gulf which religion had created between
England and her neighbours. Both in France and the Netherlands
persecution on land had encouraged independent-minded men to attack
their enemies at sea, half-patriots, half-pirates. From 1567 the leaders of
the Protestant party in France, known as the Huguenots, the Prince de
Condé and Admiral Coligny, had made the great port of La Rochelle
their headquarters and naval base, issuing commissions to adventurers
of all nations to make war on 'all the enemies of God otherwise called
papists'. By the end of 1568 50 ships, 30 of them English, were sailing
under this dubious authority. Several came from Plymouth, which also
served, along with Southampton, as the main market-place for the
captured goods.

The semi-privateers based at La Rochelle caused a sharp deterioration
in Anglo-Spanish relations in November 1568, when they chased a small
force of unarmed Spanish ships into Fowey, Plymouth and
Southampton. The ships were carrying 450,000 ducats [£100,000],
borrowed from Genovese bankers, to pay Alva's army in the Netherlands, and when the Spanish ambassador asked for an English escort to
take the money safely to Antwerp, Elizabeth declined, well aware that it
was probably destined to finance an invasion of England. Instead she
held on to the treasure and agreed with the bankers to whom it still
legally belonged to borrow it instead.

The French, too, had much to complain about. That La Rochelle
should remain in friendly, i.e. Protestant, hands, became a central feature
of English defence doctrine, and rather than see the port captured by the
French government, Cecil, in December 1568, sent a consignment of
guns, followed in May 1569 by food, ammunition and a force of
volunteers. They included the 17-year-old Walter (later Sir Walter)

Raleigh (or Ralegh), who had come down early from Oxford to take part in the adventure. La Rochelle provided a convenient base for anti-Spanish as well as anti-French government operations, and further up the Channel vessels belonging to the Catholic powers had to run a second gauntlet, from the impudently-named *Gueux de Mer*, or Sea Beggars, whom, from 1569 onwards, William of Orange had licensed, with English connivance, to harass them. Queen Elizabeth insisted that neither the Sea Beggars nor the Huguenot privateers operating from La Rochelle were any concern of hers, as the Spanish ambassador reported to Madrid:

> The whole Channel from Falmouth to the Downs is infested . . . They assail every ship that passes, of whatever nation, and after capturing them equip them for their own purposes, by this means continually increasing their fleet, with the intention on the part of the queen thus to make war on his majesty through these pirates without its costing her anything, and under the specious pretence that she is not responsible.

Friction in the Channel was exacerbated by bitter hostility, partly religious but basically commercial, in the distant waters of the Caribbean and Pacific. Elizabeth's reign saw a vast expansion of trade in every direction, but it was in the West Indies and along the Spanish Main, the strip of coast between Panama and the mouth of the Orinoco River, beyond Trinidad, that the real challenge to the pope's ruling, arbitrarily dividing the Americas between Spain and Portugal, was to be made. Two natural leaders and seamen of genius, both from Plymouth, were to become national heroes as a result. The first, John (later Sir John) Hawkins (or Hawkyns), still only 34, returned in January 1569 from his third voyage to the area, with a mere 15 of his crew of 100 still alive, and with a horrifying tale of being treacherously attacked by a Spanish fleet without provocation in the port of San Juan de Ulua, in 'New Spain', now Mexico. Almost simultaneously his subordinate commander, Francis, later Sir Francis, Drake arrived home after a narrow escape in the same attack. Another Devonian, Drake was already, at 28, familiar with both African and West Indian waters, and he was now sent to London to be interrogated by the Privy Council. In the next three years he made three more voyages to the West Indies, inflicting considerable damage on the Spaniards, and finally sailed round the world between December 1577 and September 1580, returning with his ship, the *Golden Hind*, ballasted with silver taken from a Spanish treasure ship and giving his backers, who included the queen, a return of 4,700 per cent on their investment. The Spaniards' demands for Drake to be punished fell on deaf ears and instead, in the following year, the queen knighted him on his own quarterdeck.

The navy had been by no means neglected during Elizabeth's earlier years on the throne, though her inclination had been to rely on privately-owned merchantmen to provide much of the nation's potential defences. The emphasis, so far as the queen's ships were concerned, was on quality rather than quantity. The navy on her accession in 1558 numbered only 22 vessels of 100 tons or more; a further 12, considered 'of no continuance and not worth repair', were scrapped. A committee appointed by the government systematically listed all the country's naval resources and its report, *The Book of Sea Causes*, was a pioneering document, based on the assumption that ultimately the navy, not the army, would be the country's chief means of defence.

For the first time vessels now began, at least unofficially, to be properly classified. 'First-rates' came to means ships of 600 tons and upwards; 'second-rates' from 400–600 tons, 'third-rates' 200–400, 'fourth-rates' 100–200, 'fifth-rates' 50–100, and 'sixth-rates' anything below 50. John Hawkins attributed the unseaworthiness of the ships he and Drake had taken on their expedition to the West Indies, which had forced them into a Spanish harbour, to their being unfit for prolonged deep-sea, ocean-going work. Hitherto English ships had been built for the Channel, with a harbour and repair yard never far away. Hawkins and Drake had a wider vision, of ships operating thousands of miles away and staying at sea for months. This meant smaller vessels, lacking the heavy superstructure which made the great ships of Henry VIII's time, built for summer campaigns close to home, so vulnerable to both sea and shot.

The real preference of both Hawkins and Drake was for 'second-rates' of around 450 to 500 tons, like the famous *Revenge*, built under Hawkins's supervision in 1577 and later serving as Drake's flagship. She was the first of a whole class of similar vessels, which carried further the idea already introduced under Henry VIII of the ship as gun-platform; one whole gun-deck was built solely for that purpose. With the slimming down of ships, and the removal of the old top-heavy castles, there was no longer room, or need, for the large contingents of soldiers who had dominated sea warfare all through the Middle Ages. The ill-fated *Mary Rose* had carried roughly two soldiers to every sailor; the first *Victory*, in 1558, had 100 soldiers to 168 sailors, the *Triumph*, by 1603, no more than 120 to 340, just over one in three. And 'soldiers' now included gunners who were, before long, the only non-mariners aboard. The reduction in numbers left more room for carrying stores, and the diet and health of crews actually improved at this time despite much longer voyages.

While Drake was setting off on his greatest voyage, in 1577, John Hawkins was writing a report on the existing defects in the navy, caused by a mixture of extravagance and corruption, such as charging for worn-out materials as if they were new, and paying wages to non-existent employees. Hawkins's paper, *Abuses in the Admiralty touching her Majesty's Navy*, submitted to the Lord Treasurer, Lord Burghley, led to his own appointment as Treasurer of the Navy, but provoked strong opposition from Admiral Sir William Winter who, as Surveyor and Master of the Ordnance of the Navy, had proved a poorer administrator than operational commander. Winter bitterly resented Hawkins's criticisms but Hawkins enjoyed the confidence of both Burghley and the queen and pressed on with his reforms, himself contracting to undertake the whole annual maintenance of the fleet for a mere £5714 a year. He managed to obtain an overdue rise in the basic seaman's rate of pay, from 6s 8d to 10s [33p to 50p] a month, though they were still ill-rewarded (a discrepancy which was to continue for centuries) compared to the shipwrights safe on land, who, from 1588, received from 1s to 1s 6d [5-7.5p], plus lodging, victuals and 'as much beer as would suffice'. Later, Hawkins and Drake established the Chatham Chest*, for the 'perpetual relief of such mariners, shipwrights and seafaring men as by reason of hurts or maims received in the service are driven to great distress and want', an elementary insurance scheme to which the categories covered made a monthly contribution from their pay.

Elizabeth's reign was marked by a significant development of the West Country ports and the Thames Estuary area at the expense of Portsmouth and other south coast harbours. A register of shipmen, compiled late in the reign, credited Hampshire with a mere 342 against Devon's 1100; by 1582 Devon and Cornwall together accounted for one-third of all the seamen in the country. Within those two counties Plymouth, the home port of Drake and Hawkins, both of whom served it as a Member of Parliament, was easily predominant over its former rivals Fowey and Dartmouth. The threat from Spain, making it the first major port which an approaching enemy fleet would encounter, further enhanced its importance.

London was the greatest mercantile port, with, in 1573, the largest number of shipowners and of merchant ships (135) of 500 tons and more, so that the chronicler Camden wrote of the Thames resembling 'a very wood of trees . . . so shaded is it with masts and sail'. Hawkins, however, developed the Thames as a naval base, less exposed to French intervention than Portsmouth. It was here that Francis Drake, though born in Devon, had begun his seagoing career, for his father, a

*The box which gave the fund its name is now in the National Maritime Museum.

clergyman, had become vicar of Upchurch, near Gillingham, and his son after living 'in the hull of a king's ship' bedded in the mud of the Medway had first gone to sea as an apprentice on a local coaster.

Chatham had only acquired its first naval store shed in 1547 but its growth thereafter was rapid, so that by 1550 it was being ordered that 'all the kinges shippes should be harborowed in Jillynhgam Water, saving only those that be at Portsmouth,' and by the end of the century it had overtaken Deptford as the most important dockyard. The sheltered waters of the River Medway, free of shoals, rocks and dangerous currents, made it ideal for laying up ships, and its soft mud banks, with a substantial tidal rise and fall, made it admirable for the careening of hulls, then a constant necessity. It had easy access, via Sheerness, to London, to the open sea, and to the sheltered anchorage behind the Goodwin Sands known as the Downs, though it was not until 1567 that it became known as Chatham rather than Gillingham. That year the Navy Board began to meet there and soon afterwards the queen herself arrived to inspect the ships in the Medway and to order the building of a fort at Sheerness.

The expansion of Chatham made possible the building and refitting of vessels on the lines already described. When funds did not allow a brand-new ship to be built Hawkins ingeniously had the old carracks, with their excessive beam, cut in half, so that a new section could be inserted. The removal of surplus superstructures and the improvement of the crew accommodation – though it remained primitive enough – went on apace. By 1585 even the feud with William Winter was made up and Winter was making his own contribution by replacing the old mixed bag of cannon with a standardized culverin, which could project a 17 or 18-lb [7.7-8.2-kg] iron shot, albeit inaccurately, one and a half to two miles [2.4-3.2 km] and was deadly at 300 yards [270 m].

Chatham's local defences were not neglected. A guard-vessel to be manned, he specified, by '25 extraordinary men', was stationed permanently at Sheerness, 'four nimble pinnaces' were to patrol the moorings each night, to guard against sabotage, and a boom, in the form of a heavy chain, was fixed across the river at Upnor. By 1585 the rebuilt and extended dockyard, with, as a great wonder of the times, a large crane, was turning out its first new ship, a 50-foot [15-m], 50-man pinnace.

The worst defects in the land forces had been made good earlier in Elizabeth's reign but the government was well aware that it was effective fighting strength which mattered, not the numbers on paper. The counties were now given two different assessments, the total of men to be mustered and those, selected from the total, who were to be fully trained and equipped. Yorkshire in 1584, when war was beginning to be regarded as inevitable, was expected to muster 42,000 men, of whom 10,000 were required to be fully trained, a ten-fold increase in the past decade, reduced, when the lord-lieutenant protested that the new total was unrealistic, to 6000.

The government now discovered that officers with sufficient military experience to supervise training were very unevenly distributed throughout the country. In Cambridgeshire only a single prominent member of the gentry was so qualified and another company had to make do with a commanding officer resident fourteen miles [22 km] away who was also 'old and, by an issue in his leg, unable'. Suffolk seemed to attract retired military men and could supply 44, but Somerset had no more than 17 and Kent only eight. But a determined, centrally-directed, search worked wonders. By 1587 a list existed of more than 200 good captains, all unpaid volunteers, assisted by professional muster-masters, no doubt old soldiers, who were paid from £29 to £38 a year for from 58 to 78 days' service, a charge eventually transferred to the counties.

The policy of weeding out the ineffective, training vigorously those who remained, and reorganizing the whole force into an efficient fighting machine, worked wonders. In Buckinghamshire the nominal muster strength of 7400 was in 1581 reduced to 5100, the other 2300 having been 'refused as not serviceable, some for want of strength, some for want of spirits and liveliness and some for wretchedness of their persons'. Nationally the force which had numbered just under 60,000 in 1570 and then, by the early 1580s, had reached more than a million, was by 1588 no more than 300,000 strong, all physically first-class, though only 112,000 were so far fully trained.

The transformation of the militia into a competent, if part-time, army, had a marked effect on morale. By the late 1580s it was being reported from Cornwall that 'those that erst . . . would have given good sums of money to have been exempted from the service, rejoice in that they have profited by this training.' A fierce unit loyalty developed, with strong resistance to the replacement of a familiar officer by a more experienced outsider, or the transfer of a company to a new command. Bitter quarrels occurred between neighbouring gentry over who should command a particular unit, or the 'poaching' of men from another unit's catchment area, and in Essex one zealous militia member ended up in jail after interfering with the training provided by a rival commander.

Unlike France and Spain, England, apart from a few royal bodyguards, had no regular, standing army, raising troops *ad hoc* for foreign expeditions from volunteers, 'rogues and vagabonds' and a few unfortunate dragged in by a press gang from 'alehouses, inns and such places', to quote from an instruction given to the justices of Middlesex and

Surrey. The militia, who could not be ordered to serve outside their own county except in case of invasion, were therefore the country's main line of defence and were deeply caught up in the great military controversy of the age, whether firearms had made other weapons obsolete.

The English found it hard to accept that the day of the longbow as master of the battlefield was now over. When Elizabeth came to the throne all able-bodied men under the age of 60 were still required by law to possess a bow, and to give a suitably child-sized one to their sons as they reached the age of seven. Periodic efforts were made to enforce regular archery practice and to ensure a supply of reasonably priced bows, the cheapest, of English yew, being priced at 2s [10p], but those of the best foreign materials at 6s 8d [33p]. The reasons were more sentimental than economic. As a preamble to an Act of 1570 put it. 'The use of archery not only has ever been, but also yet is, by God's special gift to the English nation, a singular defence of the realm.' A contemporary writer, William Harrison, author of the *Description of England*, complained that, thanks to the decline of archery, German and French soldiers no longer went in awe of the longbow:

> [Now they] turn up their tailes and cry 'Shoot, English!' . . . The breech of such a varlet should have been nailed to his bum with one arrow and another feathered in his bowels before he should have turned about to see who shot the first.

The militia themselves were not at all eager to be re-equipped, since a firearm, as mentioned earlier, was much more expensive than a bow, and while arrows could be re-used, gunpowder and bullets, once fired, were gone for ever. The counties also dragged their feet, aware that the powder, match and bullets for a single training session cost 8d [3p] a man. Finally guns were considered, with reason, to be dangerous and unreliable. They had, their opponents argued, only succeeded against the Scots by frightening them with their noise and they were intrinsically inaccurate. In this, too, there was some truth, especially where the standard hand-gun, the harquebus, or arquebus, was concerned. Officially it had a range of 150-200 yards [140-180 m] but only a highly skilled shot was likely to do any damage at that distance. At Portsmouth, in 1571, out of a specially selected contingent of 23, 'not five of them shot within five foot [1.5 m] of a mark being set within four score yards [73 m] of them'. Even loading and discharging a harquebus or caliver – the superior matchlock musket was not yet in general use – was, some commanders thought, beyond the clumsy fingers and low intelligence of the 'rude ploughman'. 'We esteem his service of little worth,' confessed one nobleman from Shropshire at this period, 'until he come to the hewing strokes and knocking down.' This was also the government's view. 'The strongest and best persons,' should, it was suggested, 'be pikes' while 'the least and nimblest should be turned to the harquebuses.'

In all the circumstances it was remarkable that the great revolution from bow to firearm was accomplished so rapidly. Partly it was due to far-sighted individuals like Sir Thomas Gresham, who urged, from early in the reign, 'Spare the bows and arrows for they are of no force against an armed man,' partly to the militia themselves who, their fears and prejudices once overcome, began to enjoy musketry practice. From about 1570 onwards the bow had clearly had its day. In 1572 Bristol reported, 'This year the house in the marsh was builded for practice of shooting with guns with bullets,' and shooting competitions were subsequently held on Midsummer's Day and St Bartholomew's Day [24 August]. The next year, of 400 men who gave a display before the queen 300 carried firearms and only 100 pikes.

In 1577 the Council, in its orders to the lords-lieutenant, was still fighting a rearguard action on behalf of archery:

> You shall signify to the people that it is not meant by the latter orders for training of shot (also a meet and necessary weapon for service) that the reputation of the bow should be in any way obscured or taken away.

But the battle was now really over. The local gentry, who should have been enforcing the official policy, were enclosing traditional archery practice grounds for cultivation or parkland, and from around this time gunpowder appears as a regular item in parish accounts. Suffolk decided, in 1578, that the militia 'should spend their time principally in the shot with the bullet'. By now the Council was bowing to the inevitable. The first day of a two-day muster, it suggested should be devoted to weapon-training, the second to 'skirmishing', and it began to encourage competitions to promote marksmanship with guns as well as bows; in 1580 three bowmen received silver prizes in the presence of the queen, but there was also a 'gilded gun' for the best shot.

The prevailing interest in all things military was reflected in the appearance of the first comprehensive book on the art of war to be written in English: Thomas Digges's *An Arithmetical Warlike Treatise named Stratioticos, compendiously teaching . . . so much of the Rules and Equations Algebraicall and Art of Numbers . . . as are requisite for the Profession of a Soldier.* which was to be several times reprinted over the next two centuries. Digges was a Cambridge mathematician of some standing and an M.P. Nor was he a mere amateur strategist: later he served as muster-master-general, i.e. chief administrative officer, of the English forces in the Netherlands. What gave his book its enduring value was its discussion of that recurring strategic question whether or not an invader should be attacked immediately piecemeal or allowed to get ashore while an overwhelming counter-offensive was prepared. Digges looked first at the arguments advanced by the 'immediate attack' school of thought:

> First, the furie of the Countrey upon the first fyring of the Beacons is great, everie man . . . violently running downe to the sea side to repell the disordered Enimie at the first confused landing: which furie, if we suffer to grow cold, we shall not too easily enflame againe.
>
> Secondly everie man knoweth how great advantage they have that have firme footing on land to encounter an Enimie that must land out of boates in confused stragling manner . . . whereas if you suffer the Enimie to land and put himselfe in Militaire order, he becommeth more terrible unto us.

Digges then, with scrupulous fairness, set out 'Another Opinion':

> Some other hold that . . . running to the sea side to be a barborous Custome, void of order, and warlike Discipline, verie perillous to our felues [fellows], not hurtfull to the Enimie . . .
>
> First, it is said the invading Enimy bringeth a select companie of disciplined and well trained souldiers, whom we seke to encounter with a confused multitude of men untrained. In which match there is no comparison, but losse certaine. Again, it is said An Enimie of force meaning to land will do it in despite of us, and then the Countrey offering to repell him, and finding themselves not able, grow much more fearefull then [than] if quietly without resistance we had suffered the Enimie to land. Againe, while we suffer the Enimie to land, we may drive away all Cattle, and provision farther into the Countrie, and then maintaine straights [i.e. narrow defiles] and passages wel fenced and fortified, so as the Enimie shal be force to approch us upon our oune strengthes and Fortifications, to his great perill and daunger.

What was needed, the writer concluded, was a delaying action on the beaches while the counter-stroke was prepared:

> My meaning is to have such provision in everie shire as we may be able readily on any sodaine to give the Enimie all annoyance possible, before and at the landing, while the inward forces of our countrey may the better assemble and put themselves in Militaire order, to proceed as shall be found most convenient.

Thomas Digges had pointed out that, 'There is in this Realme (as in all States divided in religion) no small numbers of traitorous minds, who having time to confere, and seeing an Enimie of force already landed, may and will then discover their malice', and this warning at least, though they hardly needed it, Burghley and his colleagues took to heart.

Pope Gregory XIII, who had succeeded Pius V in 1572, encouraged the activities of the college set up at Douai, in Flanders, in 1568, to train young Englishmen, aged from 14 upwards, for the priesthood, each student taking a vow to 'return to England for the salvation of souls, whenever . . . the superior of this college . . . order me to do so'. Here, and in the similar establishments set up soon afterwards in Rome and elsewhere, the young men were prepared for their coming ordeal with strict discipline; at Douai the only pictures on the walls showed scenes of torture. The first 'seminarists', as they became known, arrived in 1574 and by 1580 at least 100 were active in England.

The newcomers were not, they insisted, traitors but men of God, concerned to see that the old religion did not die out through the lack of priests to celebrate mass, and from April 1580 onwards they came equipped with a 'licence to be loyal', or *Explanatio*, which authorized English Catholics not to rebel against Elizabeth, in spite of the still valid bull excommunicating and deposing her. This would, it was hoped, protect the laymen who sheltered them from being charged with treason, but the priests themselves were remorselessly tracked down and, in many cases, executed, among them, in December 1581, the most famous of Catholic martyrs, Edmund Campion, a saintly scholar, formerly of Oxford, already aged nearly 40 when ordained*.

The persecution of the Catholic missionaries, as they hurried from one 'priest's hole' to the next, was encouraged by the realization that the pope was actively organizing military attacks on Elizabeth's possessions like any temporal monarch. An English Jesuit professor, Nicholas Sanders, derided by Anglicans as 'Dr Slanders', one of many exiled writers whose works were smuggled into England, admitted candidly: in 1577, 'The state of Christendom dependeth upon the stout assailing of England' and that very year the assailing began, though not very stoutly. Ireland was the chosen theatre and Pope Gregory first appointed a prominent Irishman, James Fitzmaurice, to lead a holy war against 'that woman who . . . has been cut off from the church'. Fitzmaurice, having collected some 80 Spaniards and Portuguese, duly set sail from Lisbon but got no further than St Malo in Brittany, which was not even in the right direction, before his ship's captain refused to go any further.

In February 1578 the pope tried again, commissioning a renegade English knight, Sir Thomas Stukeley, to act as his avenging angel. He succeeded in collecting 600 Italian mercenaries and a shipload of arms,

---

*187 Roman Catholics were executed for treason in Elizabeth's reign, an average of four a year. This compares with 56 a year, burned solely for heresy, under Mary.

but on reaching Lisbon decided his ships were too unseaworthy to face the Irish Sea, and was persuaded – fatally as it turned out – to attack Morocco instead.

A more serious attempt, with Spanish help, was launched in June 1579, once again under Fitzgerald. One of King Philip's envoys described the Irish as 'a sort of beggarly people, great traitors to one another, and of no force', but the chance of raising a holy war against England was not to be missed. On 17 June 1579 an international force containing Italians, Spaniards, Portuguese, Flemings and Frenchmen, as well as a few Irish and a papal legate – the English Catholic Nicholas Saunders now doing some 'assailing' himself – set sail from Lisbon, and, having captured two English ships on the way, appeared in Dingle Bay off the coast of Kerry on 16 July. A follow-up force in two galleys was intercepted and though Fitzgerald himself was killed soon after landing a further contingent of Italians and Spaniards arrived in September 1580. Once the English had begun to exert their full strength the invasion-cum-rising was speedily crushed. The final stronghold, the Fort del Ore, to the north of Dingle Bay, succumbed in November 1580 after Sir William Winter had arrived with an English fleet to blockade it, while the English artillery battered its walls for two days from the landward side.

In December 1580 the papal secretary answered an enquiry from two English noblemen as to whether it would be a sin to take Queen Elizabeth's life, in unmistakable terms:

> Since that guilty woman of England rules over two such noble kingdoms of Christendom and is the cause of so much injury to the Catholic faith, and loss of so many million souls, there is no doubt that whosoever sends her out of the world . . . not only does not sin but gains merit, especially having regard to the sentence pronounced against her by Pius V of holy memory. And so if these English nobles decide actually to undertake so glorious a work, your lordship can assure them that they do not commit any sin.

The papal message was soon widely known and was interpreted by the government as not merely a licence but a positive incentive to kill. Sir Francis Walsingham, formerly Elizabeth's ambassador in Paris, who had since 1573 been her Principal Secretary of State, second only to Lord Burghley, was already inclined to see plots against the queen everywhere and, through a most efficient secret service, set up at his own expense, had proved remarkably successful in detecting those that really did exist.

The successive attempts made from 1580 onwards to overthrow, or kill, Queen Elizabeth were all linked to a possible invasion by Spain. Philip II's leadership of the Catholic world was established beyond question when in April 1581 Portugal, following the death of its childless king, was forcibly incorporated with Spain, making her not merely master of the whole peninsula but also doubling the Spanish empire overseas. The old idea of the French for a roundabout approach to England across her northern border was now replaced by dreams of a direct landing, using Spain's great fleet. 'It appears to me,' wrote the Spanish ambassador in Paris in August 1582, 'that the true road to success is by England rather than by Scotland.' James VI of Scotland, now 16, was indeed not only a Protestant but England's ally. The recovery of England for the faith, the Spaniards now realized, would depend on themselves alone.

The plan at this time was for 4000 to 5000 men to be ferried across from the Netherlands, where the Duke of Parma had replaced the hated Alva as governor. Ten thousand English Catholics were expected to rise in their support, and once the operation had succeeded the foreign troops were to be withdrawn. The Spanish ambassador, who had been in England since 1574, was deeply involved in the planning, and was in contact with Mary via an English Catholic, Francis Throckmorton, a nephew of Elizabeth's former ambassador in France, Sir Nicholas Throckmorton. Throckmorton was caught and under torture incriminated his associates, while another of Mendoza's messengers, disguised as a dentist, was caught crossing the Scottish border with a secret letter hidden at the back of a mirror, which rapidly yielded its secrets to Walsingham's cipher-breakers. Throckmorton was executed at Tyburn and on 9 January 1584 Mendoza was called before the Council and given fifteen days to leave the country, much to his indignation, as his report to the Spanish Secretary of State indicates: 'The insolence of these people has brought me to a state in which my only desire to live is for the purpose of avenging myself upon them, and I pray that God may let it be soon and will give me grace to be His instrument of vengeance.'

Fears of another assassination attempt increased after, on 10 July 1584, William the Silent was shot by a man who had wormed his way into the Orange household specifically to murder him. During the autumn a vast national upsurge of loyalty to Elizabeth found expression in a Bond of Association, drawn up by the Privy Council, under which thousands of ordinary citizens undertook to prevent the succession of any person in whose interest an attempt on the queen's life should be made. Everyone knew that Mary Queen of Scots was the beneficiary referred to and she was now removed into much more secure custody, with a strict puritan jailer.

That summer relations with Spain deteriorated still further with the seizure of a number of English corn-ships in Bilbao harbour and the imprisonment of their crews, by soldiers disguised as merchant seamen, and it was to revenge this outrage, and release the captured seamen, that Drake set sail on 14 September 1585 with his largest fleet yet, of 30 sail, for the plundering of the Indies already described.

War had still not been declared, but in the Netherlands the Orange cause seemed likely to founder without English help. Early in August Antwerp was lost and on 10 August 1585 Elizabeth entered into the Treaty of Greenwich with the Dutch, under which she promised to supply them with £15,000 a year – half the regular royal income – as well as troops, some of whom would occupy Flushing and Brill as 'cautionary towns' until the money was repaid. This was the first major British commitment on the continent since the loss of Calais and marked a significant change of policy, as Lord Burghley explained in a memorandum to the queen:

> Although Her Majesty should thereby enter in a war presently, yet were she better to do it now, while she may make the same out of her realm, having the help of the people of Holland and before the King of Spain shall have consummated his conquests.

Here was a classic statement of what was to become a basic principle of British defence policy, that if one *had* to fight it was better to do so on someone else's soil, and to forestall an attack before it developed. In practical terms this now meant sending an expeditionary force of 6000 foot and 1000 horse to Flushing, under the Earl of Leicester, who set sail in December 1585. The campaign was a failure, due partly to Leicester's own personality, partly to divisions among the Dutch, and in November 1586 the remnants of the force were withdrawn. The adventure did, however, give the English people a new folk-hero. Sir Philip Sidney, already a notable poet, achieved immortality by declining the water offered to him as he lay mortally wounded, in September 1586, insisting that another man's need was even greater than his.

During the summer of 1586 the existing friendly relationship with Scotland had been confirmed by the Treaty of Berwick, signed in July, under which James VI agreed to assist England in the event of an invasion by an outside power in return for an annual pension. The winter brought Elizabeth's ministers another success which in their eyes outweighed the recent military defeat in Flanders. For months past Walsingham's spies had been reading the clandestine correspondence reaching Mary Queen of Scots in her captivity at Tutbury in Staffordshire, the letters being hidden in a waterproof packet inside the barrels of beer delivered from a brewer in Burton-on-Trent, her replies leaving inside the 'empties'. Tempted by a suggestion from a former page, now the 25-year-old Anthony Babington, Mary injudiciously agreed to a proposal to murder Elizabeth and put herself on the throne. Thereafter a great fleet was to arrive from Spain to protect the Catholic restoration. Mary later claimed that she had been 'framed', but the expelled Spanish ambassador, Mendoza, now based in Paris, wrote to Philip II, 'I am of opinion that the Queen of Scotland must be well acquainted with the whole affair' and Mary's guilt is now generally accepted. Babington and the rest were executed in September 1586 and Mary herself on 8 February 1587 after her ministers had sent off to Fotheringay Castle, in Northamptonshire, the warrant signed by Queen Elizabeth before, as had so often happened before, she could change her mind. As the messenger bearing the news rode to London to confirm that the deed was at last done bells pealed in celebration and bonfires sprang into flame behind him. It was the most joyous day since that other Catholic Mary had died, 34 years earlier.

36

MIGHTY PREPARATIONS

We have intelligence by many ways out of Spain that there are mighty preparations of a navy and army.

Lord Burghley to the British agent in the Netherlands, 10 October 1587

Although an invasion of England from the Spanish Netherlands had been discussed for years, it was not until 1583 that a proposal was first put forward for the dispatch of a great fleet from Spain itself. Spain's greatest sailor, the Marquis of Santa Cruz, having decisively defeated a pro-Portuguese force off the Azores, the scattered groups of islands 900 miles [1440 km] west of Lisbon in the North Atlantic, suggested that his fleet should stay together for 'the Enterprise of England'. The effort required would be prodigious and in June 1585 Philip's ambassador arrived in Rome to invite a contribution from Pope Sixtus V, who had succeeded Gregory XIII that April. It was only, however, in December 1586 that, unknown to the English government, the pope finally agreed to underwrite part of the cost of the expedition, though the first half of his promised million crowns would be paid only when the Armada – the Spanish name for an armed fleet – landed in England, the rest being doled out in four-monthly instalments of 100,000 crowns thereafter.

Philip was going to need every penny he could lay his hands on. Two rival plans now lay before him. One, submitted in March 1586 by the Marquis of Santa Cruz, would cost the huge sum of 3,750,000 ducats, equal to about £1,750,000. It had one great advantage. The whole force, soldiers and seamen, was to deliver its attack from Spain itself, avoiding the complications so likely to occur when a fleet had to rendezvous with an army far from its base. The objections were that the Duke of Parma's splendid battle-hardened army, Philip's best troops, would play no part in the operation, while the quantity of shipping, men and supplies needed would be enormous. Santa Cruz's planners estimated that they would need 556 vessels, of which 196 would be major fighting ships, 150 of them sail, 40 oar-powered galleys, and six hybrids with both sails and oars. Forty smaller boats not included in the 556 would be carried by the larger ships, and 200 flat-bottomed landing-craft. The Armada would require 94,222 men, broken down into 58,920 soldiers, plus another 8890 volunteers and non-combatants, such as priests and sutlers, 9400 oarsmen to row the galleys, and 16,612 sailors. 1150 guns would be needed for the ships, with another 130 solely for use on land. The largest single demand for space, however, was for supplies, since Santa Cruz, knowing the uncertainties of wind and sea, had calculated the Armada should have sufficient food and drink for eight months. One of the bulkiest items was water, no doubt mainly for the horses, more than two million gallons [9 million litres] of it, in 20,000 110-gallon [500-litre] 'pipes'. Wine, for the men, took up even more room, with 48,600 pipes, to carry 5,350,000 gallons [24 million litres], 55 gallons [250 litres] per man; the traditional ration of beer for an English seaman was a gallon [4.5 litres] a day. The food included 373,337 cwt [19 million kg] of biscuit, 21,500 cwt [1.1 million kg] of cheese, 22,800 cwt [1.2 million kg] of bacon, and 166,040 cwt [815,000 kg] of salt beef. The quantities of peas, beans and rice were in proportion and, to help make inevitably stale provisions more palatable, a large volume of vinegar and 20,000 strings of garlic were also included.

The sheer scale of this plan caused it to be discarded, but Philip was also unenthusiastic about the more modest alternative drawn up in December 1586 by the former ambassador, Bernardino de Mendoza, a distinguished soldier before he became a diplomatist, who had when expelled from London two years earlier, as previously described, sworn vengeance on the English. Now his chance had come. Mendoza recommended that a small force of soldiers should be sent to help the Scottish Catholics and, if that country were regained and the English Catholics then rose, reinforcements might be sent to secure the whole island. 'It will be no small advantage to your Majesty,' he pointed out, 'that the game should be played out on the English table, just as she [i.e. the queen] has tried to make Flanders and France the arena.' But Mendoza's plan, like Santa Cruz's, failed to make use of the Duke of Parma's army, which Philip had already decided must provide the chief invasion force, and he had already sent orders to Parma to this effect, setting the summer of 1587 as the target date. Walsingham's excellent intelligence service was not slow in detecting the results. Soon his spies were reporting the creation of improvised dockyards in the Low Countries, the building of flat-bottomed boats and the widening and deepening of the canals that linked the Scheldt above Antwerp with Ghent, Bruges and Dunkirk. The vast purchases of naval stores and equipment shipped to Lisbon from all round the Mediterranean and the Baltic could also not be hidden. On 22 February 1587 the Lord Chancellor, Sir Christopher Hatton, warned the House of Commons of the approaching peril, in terms recorded by the deputy clerk:

> The King of Spain's designments are to invade England and Ireland. His preparations: 350 sail of Spain, 80 galleys of Venice and Genoa, 1 galleass with 600 armed [men] from the Duke of Florence, 12,000 men maintained by Italy and the pope, 6000 by the Spanish clergy, 12,000 by the nobility and gentlemen of Spain. It is reported that 10,000 of these be horsemen.

Since his return from the Caribbean in July 1586 Drake had been chafing impatiently ashore, trying to persuade a reluctant Council and an even more reluctant queen to attack the Armada before it sailed. With the execution of Mary Queen of Scots on 8 February 1587 attitudes on both sides of the Channel hardened. 'All the Catholic hopes in England are dashed,' commented the Venetian ambassador in Paris. Mendoza passed the news on from that city to the Escorial, Philip II's just-completed monastery-cum-palace 26 miles [42 km] from Madrid, where it arrived on 23 March. That same month Drake was at last authorized, in the words of the official instructions, 'to impeach the joining together of the King of Spain's fleets out of their several ports, to keep victuals from them, to follow them in case they should . . . come forward towards England or Ireland', and, far more contentious, to 'distress the ships within the havens themselves'.

No sooner had these orders been drafted than the Council got cold feet, or, as seems more likely, went through the motions of withdrawing Drake's authority to wage war in the home waters of a nominally friendly power. On 1 April 1587 new instructions were drafted forbidding Drake 'to enter forcibly into any of the said King's ports or havens, or to offer violence to any of his towns or shipping within harbouring, or to do any act of hostility upon the land', but, as was probably intended, they arrived too late. On 2 April 1587, Drake had sailed from Plymouth, probably, as he feared some change of mind, without completing victualling; the enemy, he was confident, could be made to provide whatever he lacked. Before sailing he dispatched a hurried but highly typical note to Walsingham, which must have crossed with the Council's letter somewhere between London and Plymouth: 'The wind commands me away. Our ship is under sail. God grant we may so live in His fear as the enemy may have cause to say that God doth fight for Her Majesty as well abroad as at home.'

Drake's fleet consisted of 17 sizeable ships, including four belonging to the queen and eight sponsored by London merchants. There were also six pinnaces for use inshore, and ten companies of infantry, intended for operations on land. The departure of such an expedition could hardly be concealed but the Spanish communication system was so slow that Mendoza's urgent warning from Paris that Drake was on his way only reached King Philip after Drake had announced his own arrival, in distinctly less diplomatic fashion.

The campaign which followed was to represent Drake's greatest single service to his country and to mark him out as the most brilliant and daring seaman of the age. The favourable wind soon dropped and he had to struggle towards Spain in the face of a south-westerly gale, learning en route from some Flemish merchantmen that Cadiz harbour, at the very tip of southern Spain just above what is now Cape Trafalgar, was crammed with shipping. The concentration here was second only to that at Lisbon, where many of the ships assembled for the Armada were awaiting new guns, safely inside the estuary of the River Tagus.

On 19 April 1587 Drake called a Council of War, though it was more in the nature of an Orders Group, for he brushed aside the objections of his Vice-Admiral, a member of the Navy Board, ignored the convention of seeking majority support from his fellow captains, and ordered an immediate attack, to take advantage of surprise and the favourable wind.

Cadiz was defended by shore batteries, likely to outclass the smaller weapons on the pitching gun-decks of a warship, and by shallow-draught oar-powered galleys with iron rams, supposedly able to out-manoeuvre any sailing ship in such enclosed waters. The harbour was roughly funnel-shaped, with, at its broad inner end, the city itself, built on an island and connected to the mainland by a bridge. Drake made his way in at 4 o'clock in the afternoon of Wednesday 19 April 1587, getting past the fortress at the entrance by flying French and Flemish colours. When two galleys came out to investigate, his ships hauled down these false flags, hoisted the Cross of Saint George and drove the galleys off with gunfire. He now sailed on into the main harbour where 60 sailing ships were tied up along the quays. Some were loading or unloading, many were waiting for their guns to arrive from Italy, and some were without sails, which had been taken ashore to prevent the owners, from whom the vessels had been commandeered, slipping away if they got an opportunity.

While the nearest nobleman, the Duke of Medina Sidonia, was sending off to Seville and Jerez for reinforcements, and the commander of the citadel was barring his gates to the civilians whom the governor of Cadiz had ordered to seek refuge there, panic seized the tied-up ships and all that could get under way cut their cables and sought safety in the inner harbour. Part of Drake's fleet did as much damage to these as they could while the rest engaged a force of ten galleys which, attacked from the beam, were beaten off by the English broadside long before their own guns could come within range. A 700-ton Genoese merchantman, with

40 guns, provided the only effective resistance, but was eventually sunk after a fierce close-quarter duel.

As night fell, cold and wet, the darkness lit by vessels burning like torches as they drifted helplessly about the outer harbour, and the blazing tar barrels providing light for a working party trying to refloat a galley that had run ashore, Drake's Vice-Admiral urged him to withdraw. Drake refused. Although he had done a great deal of damage he had taken few prizes and he now ordered his ships to anchor in the enemy harbour overnight, in defiance of the now thoroughly aroused defenders. As dawn came up Drake sailed his own flagship, the *Elizabeth Bonadventure*, into the inner harbour, where a splendid galleon belonging to the commander-designate of the Armada, the Marquis of Santa Cruz, laden with wine, was looted and burned, as were several smaller vessels. And then, just as the Duke of Medina Sidonia marched into the town with an avenging force 3000 strong and began to set up culverins along the foreshore, and the galleys, their morale restored, came in for a fresh attack, the wind died away. Drake's fleet was now stationary in a landlocked harbour, with an aroused enemy all round him, beginning to send in that fearsome menace to any sailing vessel, the fireship. Drake took it all calmly. The English cannon beat off the galleys; the fireships were intercepted by longboats and turned back, Drake observing genially, 'The Spaniards are doing our work for us by burning their own ships.' Fortune favoured the brave: at about 2 o'clock in the morning of 21 April 1587, his third day in Cadiz, a brisk offshore wind got up. The English fleet stood out to sea, scornfully replying to a final, ineffective salvo from the guns at the harbour mouth with a derisory salute of drums and trumpets and beating off a final attack from the hopelessly outgunned and outclassed galleys. The English losses had been unbelievably light: one master-gunner wounded, his leg broken by a cannon ball; and five sailors captured.

The great historian Francis Bacon, then a young man of 26, later recalled that Drake jocularly referred to his achievements at Cadiz, as 'the singeing of the King of Spain's beard', and the dispatch sent to the Council a week after the raid, on 27 April 1587, struck just the right note of modest heroism:

The 19th of the month we arrived in Cadiz, where, finding divers huge ships loaded with the King's provisions for England . . . we burnt thirty-two, and sank a great argosy, and carried away four with us. We remained in the Road two days, in which time twelve of the King's galleys sundry times encountered us, in which fights we sank two of them, repulsing the residue with very little loss on our part . . . The ordnance from the shore vehemently thundered at us during our abode there, and the power of the whole country, being raised, resorted in great numbers of their succour, yet (thanked be God) we went thence, in despite of them all, with great honour . . . Now being well furnished with necessary provisions, our intent is (God willing) to impeach the fleet which is to come out of the Straits and divers other places before it join in with the King's forces, in the accomplishment whereof neither willing minds or industry shall be wanting.

Drake proved as good as his word. For three vital summer months, from April to June, he came close to paralysing the customarily busy traffic around the Atlantic coast of Portugal between Lisbon and Gibraltar, his mere presence probably being even more destructive to the Spanish preparations than the actual loss in vessels and stores. From Cadiz he sailed back roughly halfway to Lisbon, to Cape St Vincent, 150 miles [250 km] due west, at the extreme south-west corner of Portugal, and with astonishing effrontery, against the advice of his vice-admiral, whom he eventually court-martialled, set up a base on enemy territory, in the natural harbour of Sagres, a few miles south-east of the Cape. It was commanded by Sagres Castle, which was itself protected on three sides by a cliff which fell sheer to the sea, 200 feet [60 m] below, and on the fourth by a wall 40 feet [12 m] high, but Drake's force of 800 soldiers obtained its surrender within two hours. The castle's cannon, thrown over the cliff to the longboats below, were salvaged to fight in Queen Elizabeth's service.

From his haven in Sagres Drake harassed the local shipping, capturing or burning 47 caravels carrying barrel staves and hoops to Lisbon for the thousands of casks needed to carry the Armada's stores, and destroying so many fishing nets that its food supply was put in danger. He sent home one of the captured boats with a suggestion that his little outpost should be reinforced and a warning that the Armada posed a more serious threat than any England had yet faced:

There was never heard of so great preparation [as] the King of Spain hath and doth continually prepare for an invasion, yet no doubt but this which God hath suffered us to perform will breed great alteration.

The same message contained a famous sentence which his countrymen were to quote again and again in times of peril:

There must be a beginning of any great matter, but the continuing of the same to the end until it be thoroughly finished yieldeth the true glory.

From his base at Sagres Drake now sailed for the mouth of the River

Tagus, which led to Lisbon, but he decided against an attack on the city, aware of the forts lining the estuary, of the presence of the Marquis of Santa Cruz, in charge of the chief fortress, St Julian's Castle, and of the need for special pilots inside the winding upper reaches of the great river. Drake was daring but not reckless and he contented himself with sending a challenge to Santa Cruz via some German merchantmen to send out the galleys assembled to defend Lisbon to fight in the open sea. Not unnaturally, Santa Cruz declined, and Drake returned to Sagres, convincing King Philip, who was suffering agonies from gout and a cataract of the eyes, but trying to control events from his sickbed, that he was planning to attack the next great treasure fleet due any time now from the Indies. Philip ordered a large army to make for Sagres by forced marches from Lisbon, while a fleet of 60 ships was assembled at Cadiz to attack Drake simultaneously from the sea.

Long before they got there, however, Drake had gone, having heard that a richly-laden Portuguese cargo-ship, the *San Felipe*, was on its way from Asia. With his customary mixture of brilliance and luck, Drake successfully intercepted it, off St Michaels in the Azores, on 8 June, thereby amply justifying the whole expedition in financial terms; the *San Felipe* was officially valued at £114,000, of which Drake himself collected £17,000 and the Queen £40,000. He sailed back into Plymouth with his prizes on 26 June 1587, leaving news of his exploits to echo around Europe, though much of the credit was given to the queen. Even in Madrid open admiration of both of them was expressed, as the Venetian ambassador observed:

> There are many remarks current, such as that this woman has shown the world how they can strike at the Spaniard in Flanders, in the Indies, and in his own house; and that these injuries inflicted by Drake will raise many considerations in the minds of other princes and also of the king's own subjects . . . Everyone is amazed to see how cleverly that woman manages in everything.

Pope Sixtus himself was deeply impressed: 'What a valiant woman! She braves the two greatest kings by land and by sea. If she were not a heretic she would be worth a whole world.'

Meanwhile Walsingham's network of spies reported, accurately, that Philip intended to launch the Armada during 1587, with October as the proposed month, though just where the blow was most likely to fall remained uncertain. Sir Walter Raleigh favoured London and the Thames estuary area; the Earl of Essex, who presided over the defence committee set up the previous November, thought Hampshire and the Isle of Wight more likely, with the Isle of Sheppey as the landing site for a follow-up force. Drake, in his dispatch after his attack on Cadiz, had advised

Walsingham: 'Look well to the coast of Sussex.' Thanks to the pioneering work of Henry VIII, model specifications for field works and a list of suitable sites already existed. The Henrican forts already formed a girdle of stone around the coast, but at Great Yarmouth in Norfolk, a likely target for Parma's army, the old medieval walls were hastily modernized by adding arrow-head bastions and were reinforced with frontal ramparts 40 feet [12 m] thick, composed of earth and dung pounded together, 'resistable, by God's help, against any battery whatsoever'. Other fixed defences included booms in the Lancashire ports, at Great Yarmouth, at Upnor and at Gravesend, though the first one installed in the Thames succumbed to the next flood tide.

Exposed beaches were defended by field works. The orders given in the Isle of Wight as long ago as 1583 had laid down that ramparts should be eight feet [2.4 m] thick, of close-packed earth, protected in front by a deep and wide ditch, and at least four feet [1.2 m] high, to shelter the musketeers posted there to 'give some terror to the enemie'. In Cornwall trenches had been dug in all the designated spots by 1586 and in 1587 stakes had been set up on the beaches as anti-landing obstacles. Such defences were supposed to be inspected at least every six months, and manning them provided a regular exercise during training sessions.

Priority in defence spending had been given since 1584 to the so-called 'maritime counties', although not all adjoined the sea and one, Berkshire, was listed both here and in the fourth category, a rare lapse in Tudor civil service efficiency. This first, priority, group also included Cambridgeshire, Cornwall, Devon, Dorset, Essex, Hampshire, Hertfordshire, Huntingdonshire, Kent, Lincolnshire, Norfolk, Somerset, Suffolk, Surrey, Sussex and Wiltshire. From May 1585 the standards of readiness imposed on these areas were extended to 'category two' counties: Derbyshire, Staffordshire, Nottinghamshire, Lancashire and Cheshire. Yorkshire, the largest county, formed its own 'category three', and in 1587 'category one' standards of manning and efficiency were extended to 'category four' counties, i.e. Bedfordshire, Oxfordshire, Buckinghamshire, Northamptonshire and Gloucestershire, and to the lowest, 'category five', areas: Northumberland, Westmorland and Durham.

The least popular, but most essential, part of the anti-invasion preparations was the activation of the beacon system on which alerting the defences depended. Manning a beacon, usually from March to October, was a thankless but not an unpaid job, for the counties which put up the beacons had also to find wages for the watchers, and fuel to warm them, the money being raised by a special rate and disbursed by the churchwardens. The charge was unpopular. The deputy-lieutenant of Hampshire commented that 'the country doth somewhat murmure' against the burden, which even in a 'category four' county was from 10s [50p] to 6d [2p] a head, according to income.

The beacon sites were carefully selected to provide a clear line of vision, not merely to adjoining hills but in the valleys, and the felling of trees for the purpose produced protests from the conservationists, quoting recent legislation against deforestation. 'I think you must set down more than three to a beacon,' wrote one Northamptonshire knight to a neighbour, 'unless your trees be a great deal bigger than ours.' Some of the Midland counties, lying in a plain, were allowed to get away with an iron basket fixed to the church tower, but these tended to be the minor links in the secondary networks, which spread out from the main chain.

The warning system, as in earlier periods, was highly elaborate and conveyed much more information than the mere news of the Armada's approach. The system probably reached perfection on the Isle of Wight, where it also involved the church bells, silenced there ever since 1583 apart from a solitary one permitted for weddings and funerals. If one of the watchers, posted at the ends of the island, saw from six to 20 ships apparently making for the coast, he was to hoist a visual sign, whereupon other watchers were to ring the church bells together and warn the 'searchers', often justices, responsible for confirming the approach of enemy ships. If the latter agreed that 20 to 30 sail were approaching, one beacon was fired, if 30 to 40 two, if 50 all three and the general alarm was then raised.

The three Isle of Wight beacons at Bembridge, Freshwater and the hill above Shanklin could be seen from across the Solent, on Portsdown Hill, 409 feet [124 m] high. From Portsdown the message was picked up at Butser (889 feet [270 m]) and Exton, and thence passed to Burnet, and from there to Crondall and into Surrey. Hampshire had 19 beacons, mainly on the coast, averaging less than 15 miles [23 km] apart, and their message, as each new bonfire burst into life, was passed on to Berkshire and Dorset, and thence to distant counties like Gloucestershire and Worcestershire. The basis of the whole scheme was an elaborate code. A single beacon ablaze on the Isle of Wight, for instance, meant that the Hampshire watchers sent on the news by 'post', i.e. horseback, but did not light their own beacon until they saw two lit across the Solent. They then lit a solitary beacon, to warn Hampshire, Wiltshire, Dorset and Sussex, whose instructions required them to fire one of their beacons and to send their forces towards the coast. If the Hampshire men saw *three* beacons on the island they fired two, which meant that Oxfordshire, Gloucestershire, Berkshire and Somerset were also to send troops. Local commanders, often civilian gentry, knew what captains were to be called out by foot messengers, in response to any particular scale of attack, these messengers being selected as far as possible from men living conveniently near the parish church.

The weakness of the beacon system lay in its vulnerability to bad weather, although the Armada was unlikely to appear in storm or fog, and its dependence on sometimes unreliable watchers. They were selected by the justices from each village in their area in turn, and paid 8d [3p] for each 24 hours on duty, two men being on watch at a time for twelve hours. Fuel and candles were provided but dogs, who might distract them, were banned. When a new shelter had to be erected for the watchers at one Kent beacon it was strictly laid down that it should be 'only to save them from stormy weather, without any seates or place of ease lest they should fall asleepe; only to stand upright in with a hoale towards the beacon'.

Regular – in Hampshire supposedly twice-weekly – inspections, as well as surprise ones, were made to keep the watchers on their toes, one man in Kent being appointed 'scoutmaster' with orders to get rid of idlers and, if an invasion actually began, to prevent any unauthorized bonfires being lit within his area. Guard duty, however, has always been unpopular and tedious, and at Stanway in Essex the beacon went unguarded while its custodians were, it emerged when they were caught, whiling away the time poaching partridges. Far worse were the miscreants who, in Hampshire in 1586, planned to get the local beacons lit on a false rumour, then in the confusion liberate the Catholic 'recusants' from Winchester jail. There were also some well-intentioned false alarms. A report of what must have been a phantom fleet of 120 ships off the Scilly Isles inspired the Council to order preparations to be put under way in the maritime counties but 'with as little . . . trouble to the people that shall be occupied in harvest as may be'. Lord Burghley suggested that the guns captured in the *San Felipe* should be placed in the most threatened places in Devon and Cornwall, Plymouth and Falmouth being regarded as ports 'aptest for landing'. At sea the government was still husbanding its resources. Drake stayed in Plymouth, collecting ships from the smaller ports, like Bideford, for coastal defence, and even taking over five that Sir Richard Grenville was fitting out for a further attempt to found a colony in Virginia, Grenville himself being found useful employment on land.

The threat from the Duke of Parma's army in Flanders the government attempted to counter by diplomatic as well as military means. A second expedition sent to the Netherlands in May 1587 under the Earl of Leicester was not a success and in August Sluys, one of the very ports the campaign was designed to keep in friendly, i.e. Dutch Protestant, hands fell to Parma's troops. Lord Burghley still hoped, however, that Parma might be detached from his loyalty to Philip II to become sovereign of a united, independent Netherlands and on 10 October 1587 urged the British agent there to try a fresh approach to him.

Meanwhile the government made ready for the worst. The expertise of those with personal experience of aggressive amphibious operations was much in demand. The deputy-lieutenants of Devon and Cornwall were instructed to 'confer with Sir Richard Grenville for the trenching of places upon the sea-coast where the most danger is of landing' and Grenville carried out a full inspection before returning to London to report. That month, November 1587, a Council of War was set up in London to finalize anti-Armada preparations, to which both Grenville and Sir Walter Raleigh, another veteran of seaborne assaults, were appointed, and in December Raleigh was sent down to take charge of the land forces in the two westernmost counties, where the government was still apprehensive that the Spanish might try to establish a coastal base.

In its anxiety not to leave the West Country exposed, the government had done little at sea since Drake's return in June. Occasional pinnaces had been sent out on patrol but full mobilization of the fleet, which was bound to be expensive, had not taken place. Now, on 21 December 1587 Charles, Lord Howard of Effingham, the queen's 51-year-old cousin, a sailor of wide experience, was appointed 'commander-in-chief and governor of our whole fleet and army at sea, now fitted forth against the Spaniards', i.e. Lord High Admiral.

By now it seemed likely that, with the winter storms beginning, the great fleet would not appear off Land's End or the Lizard that year. Drake's destruction of the Spanish ships at Cadiz, and of the Armada's intended stores, off Cape St Vincent, had delayed the Spanish preparations. Philip II, at first somewhat cool about the 'Enterprise', was now burning for revenge, and it was his commanders who were losing enthusiasm. Drake had thoroughly demoralized his country's enemies. 'Just look at Drake . . .' Pope Sixtus had commented after Cadiz. 'We have a poor opinion of this Spanish Armada and fear some disaster.' The ordinary Spaniards credited 'The Dragon', *El Draque*, an apt pun on his name, with supernatural powers. He had, they whispered to each other, sold his soul to the devil in return for a magic mirror which revealed to him the dispositions of the enemy fleet.

37

THE TROOPS ARE IN THEIR PLACES

The troops are in their places and the infantry handy

The Duke of Parma to Philip II, 26 March 1588

1588, the soothsayers on both sides of the Channel had long agreed, was bound to be a year of great disaster; indeed one gloomy prophet proved, from scripture, that it would mark the end of the world. In England the Council was sufficiently concerned to suppress a book which mentioned these prophecies and now forbade the compilers of almanacs to refer to them★. Drake was unaffected by these dire forecasts and cheefully told a Spaniard he met in London in December that he would celebrate next Christmas in Lisbon, while Lord Burghley, too, was confident what was coming. 'Our profit and best assurance,' he wrote as the year began, 'is to seek our peace by a determined and resolute war.'

Drake had been appointed vice-admiral under Lord Howard and during January 1588, from his house in Looe Street, Plymouth, directed the fitting out of the 30 ships to be based there, and the recruitment of the flood of eager volunteers who poured in to man them, anticipating another wealth-gathering expedition to the Indies, a rumour which a Spanish prisoner was allowed to go home to report. Meanwhile, on 9 February, the Marquis of Santa Cruz, who had drawn up the original plan for the Armada, died at Lisbon. King Philip, far from mourning his lost commander, observed philosophically that 'God has shown me a favour by removing the Marquis now rather than when the Armada is at sea.' To replace the 63-year-old Santa Cruz the king appointed the Duke of Medina Sidonia Admiral-in-Chief of the Armada and Captain-General of the Ocean Sea. Medina Sidonia was, at 37, the leading nobleman of Spain, and he had made a respectable showing on land at Cadiz, but he had never commanded so much as a single ship, and he

---

★The line between astronomy and astrology was in Tudor times imprecise. One of the seers mentioned had also produced astronomical tables used by Columbus.

did not want either the glory – 'It is enough,' his wife said grandly, 'to be Duke of Medina' – or the responsibility. On 6 February (by the English calendar, 16 February by the Spanish) he wrote to the king's secretary declining the honour:

I first humbly thank His Majesty for having thought of me for so great a task, and I wish I possessed the talents and strength necessary for it. But, sir, I have not health for the sea, for I know by the small experience that I have had afloat that I soon become sea-sick . . . Apart from this, neither my conscience nor my duty will allow me to take this service upon me. The force is so great, and the undertaking so important, that it would not be right for a person like myself, possessing no experience of seafaring or of war, to take charge of it.

The king, however, insisted and was soon sending his reluctant admiral a stream of detailed orders, of which the first on 1 April (English style), summarized the Spanish plan of campaign:

When you receive a separate order from me, you will sail with the whole of the Armada, and go straight to the English Channel, which you will ascend as far as Cape Margate, where you will join hands with the Duke of Parma, my nephew, and hold the passage for his crossing.

A similar flow of instructions was simultaneously being sent to Philip's chosen land commander, Alexander Farnese, Duke of Parma. Parma, now aged 47, was the outstanding general of the time, famous not only for the patience and tenacity which had enabled him to defeat both William of Orange and the Earl of Leicester in unfavourable terrain but also for his mastery of military organization and engineering; his soldiers were said to hold a spade more often than a pike. He had made his name while serving under his other famous uncle, Don John (or Juan) of Austria, and together they had moulded the Spanish army into the most formidable fighting force in Europe. Parma had always been uncertain about a major landing in England involving a separate fleet. He would have preferred a quick dash across the North Sea in barges under his own control but realized that now surprise was lost, this was no longer possible. He covered himself by warning of the risk of failure, even though his letter to Philip II of 26 March 1588 (English style, 5 April Spanish)* began with the usual preliminaries. The Spaniards had already found the perfect scapegoat, for any delay or for an eventual disaster:

Since God has been pleased to defer for so long the sailing of the Armada from Lisbon, we are bound to conclude that it is for His

*See note on dates in Foreword.

greater glory, and the more perfect success of the business . . . The enemy have thereby been forewarned and acquainted with our plans and have made all preparations for their defence; so that it is manifest that the enterprise, which at one time was so easy and so safe, can only now be carried out with infinitely greater difficulty, and at a much larger expenditure of blood and trouble.

I am anxiously awaiting news of the departure of the Duke of Medina Sidonia with his fleet, and am confident that your Majesty will have . . . adopted all necessary measures for the carrying out of the task of protecting my passage across, so that not the smallest hitch shall occur in a matter of such vital importance. Failing this, and the due cooperation of the Duke with me, both before and during the actual landing as well as afterwards, I can hardly succeed as I desire.

Parma then came to the real point of his letter, the need for the Armada to carry a large contingent of Spanish troops to support his own heterogeneous army of Germans, Italians and locally recruited Walloons:

The troops are in their places, and the infantry handy . . . but the cavalry are much scattered, as there was no food for them anywhere nearer; and I was obliged to send them to Hainault and Tournoi. I have done and am doing, everything I possibly can to keep them together, and in good heart . . . but . . . the infantry does not exceed 18,000 men, although some Walloons who had gone to their homes are being brought back again . . . Even if they give me the 6000 Spaniards from the Armada, as no doubt it is intended to do, my force will still be weak, considering that the enemy will be fully prepared.

This letter probably crossed with one from Philip II; each was at least two weeks in transit. The king was, it appeared, already contemplating a secondary objective in case the main plan should fail:

If the principal design should fall through, it would be very influential in bringing them [the English] to . . . the best conditions possible, if the Armada were to take possesssion of the Isle of Wight. If this be once captured, it would be held, and would afford a shelter for the Armada, whilst the possession of it would enable us to hold our own against the enemy. This matter has also been laid before the Duke [i.e. Medina Sidonia].

The Spaniards attempted no concealment of the vast preparations now going on in Lisbon and Elizabeth's Council devoted much effort to deciding when and where the blow might fall. In May it considered a paper entitled *Reasons why the Spaniards should rather land in the Isle of Wight than any other place of England*. The author having tried to put himself in the enemy's place – 'entering into consideration what ports are fittest for his advantage and most dangerous to work our annoyance' – made a convincing case:

> Three things he will principally respect:
> First, where he may find least resistance, and most quiet landing.
> Secondly, where he may have best harbour for his galleys, and speediest supplies out of Spain, France and Flanders.
> Thirdly, where he may most offend the realm by incursions, and force Her Majesty, by keeping many garrisons, to stand upon a defensive war . . .
> What place can be assigned that may stand indifferent from Spain, Flanders and France, but that they are too remote from the one and too near the other, except the Isle of Wight, [South]Hampton or Portsmouth . . . There is no doubt to be made, but landing in the Wight – which with an army of 8000 men, divided into four parts, he may easily do, the force of the Island being unable to resist them with that force – in very short time they may so fortify themselves and possess those parts and places that lie convenient for passing over our supplies, and are by nature more than three parts fortified, that he may keep in safe harbour his galleys to make daily invasion into the firm lands [i.e. against the mainland] . . . So that all the castles and sea towns of Hampshire, Sussex and Dorsetshire will be subject to be burnt.

The Council decided against tying up large forces in the island. Its own militia, 2000 strong, was considered sufficient to hold it until 3000 more men, already earmarked, crossed the Solent to the rescue.

To the sea-captains waiting impatiently for orders in Plymouth it seemed humiliating, as well as poor strategy, to wait passively to be attacked and on 13 April 1588 Drake set out a plea for a more aggressive approach in a letter to the queen:

> If your Majesty will give present order for our proceeding to the sea, and send to the strengthening of the fleet here four more of your Majesty's good ships and those 16 ships with their pinnaces which are preparing in London, then shall your Majesty stand assured, with God's assistance, that if the fleet come out of Lisbon, as long as we have victual to live withal upon that coast they shall be fought with, and I hope, through the goodness of our merciful God, in such sort as shall hinder his quiet passage into England; for I assure your Majesty, I have not in my lifetime known better men, and possessed with gallanter minds, than . . . put their hands and hearts to the finishing of this great piece of work.

While Drake was chafing at the bit in Plymouth the Armada was preparing to sail. That month its officers, accompanied by the 180 priests and friars who were to sail with it, and led by the Duke of Medina Sidonia and Don Alonzo de Leyva, second-in-command of the land forces, marched to Lisbon cathedral in a splendid procession to watch the Archbishop of Portugal consecrate a sacred standard and present it to the Duke. It bore the legend, below a picture of Christ, *Exurge Domine et Vindica Causam – Arise, O Lord and justify our cause* – and was borne solemnly back to the quays where the final embarkation now began. It proved a slow process. Although Santa Cruz's plan of two years before had been radically scaled down, following the decision to ferry the main invading force across from the Netherlands instead of carrying it direct from Spain, the Armada in its final form still consisted of 130 ships, 65 classed as galleons, 25 as store ships, 32 as small ships; there were only four each of the hybrid oar-plus-sail galleasses and oared galleys, in consequence of their poor showing at Cadiz. The fleet was, however, much better-armed than that planned for 1586, another result of the Cadiz raid. It now carried 2431 guns for use at sea – though none for use solely on land – furnished with 123,791 rounds of iron or stone shot. The total complement of men had been cut by two-thirds to a mere 30,656, broken down into 8050 sailors, 2088 rowers, 18,973 soldiers and 1545 volunteers and non-combatants. The reduction in numbers, and the decision to provide supplies for six months, not eight, had made possible a sharp cut in the amounts of food and drink to be carried. There had also been a change in ration scales. The allowance of wine per head had been sharply reduced and that of water doubled, but the total amount was much smaller since Parma was now providing most of the horses. The ships had also been relieved of the dangerous top-hamper of landing craft previously intended; these, too, would be supplied in the Netherlands.

So proud was King Philip of what was officially known as 'The Most Happy Armada' – popular parlance also dubbed it 'The Invincible' – that all attempt at secrecy was abandoned and lists of the vessels, with their armament and stores, were printed and published, copies reaching the Council in London even before the great fleet had sailed.

By Saturday 11 May 1588 (English style), the troops had all made their confession, on the king's express order, and been absolved, the ships being searched for concealed females to remove at least one source of backsliding. (Twenty were found and sent ashore.) Conditions were now ideal. One by one the great ships weighed anchor and, with a light easterly breeze filling their huge sails, began their slow course down river on a falling tide towards the open sea.

Medina Sidonia did not get very far that first day. After a mere seven miles [11 km] the wind backed to north-westerly pinning his splendid flagship, the *San Martin* (appropriated from Portugal), and the 130 vessels following him, inside the Tagus, at whose entrance Drake had hovered, frustrated, a year before. There it stayed, while the sailors grumbled that they had never known such weather at this time of year, and the landlubbers, and especially that reluctant admiral, the Duke of Medina Sidonia, were sadly seasick in the heavy swell. Few ailments are so destructive to morale but the king, when the delay was reported to him, displayed his usual resignation: 'God ordains all things and He has not seen fit to send us weather for the sailing of the Armada. It is as boisterous and bad as if it were December; but He knows best.'

The English fleet could, in theory, call on 197 ships, but many of these were tiny and the real total was probably nearer 140. The queen's Navy Royal consisted of 34 ships, only 21 of them first-class; second-line ships, many of them privately owned, numbered about 40, the other 80 being smaller vessels. Lord Howard had, since his appointment as Lord Admiral, made his headquarters at Queenborough on Thames, leaving a light squadron to patrol the Channel and Drake's deep-sea veterans to guard Plymouth. As news of the Armada's impending departure reached England Howard altered his dispositions, moving his fleet, of 16 warships plus auxiliaries, first to the Downs and then to Plymouth, which he entered on 23 May 1588. The main English fleet, of about 18 large ships, plus some 23 others, was now at Plymouth, while the venerable Admiral Sir William Winter was left in the Downs with five good warships and 16 smaller craft. He would have preferred to be where the main action was likely to be fought, but in his dispatch to the Council that month made the best of things:

> Our ships doth show themselves like gallants here. I assure you it will do a man's heart good to behold them. And would to God the Prince of Parma were upon the seas with all his forces, and we in view of them!

Winter's role was crucial, for if the Armada evaded, or outfought, Drake and Howard, an almost unescorted flotilla might still cross from the Netherlands, and the general opinion among the sailors was that, once on land, Parma's professionals would be more than a match for the Earl of Leicester's militia, as Howard, writing to Lord Burghley from Plymouth on 28 May 1588, made clear:

> My good Lord, there is here the gallantest company of captains, soldiers and mariners that I think ever was seen in England . . . I pray God all things be in best readiness, if the worst do fall out. And God send us the happiness to met them before our men on the land discover

them, for I fear me a little sight of the enemy will fear the land men much.

This opinion was shared throughout Europe. The English army had not been a factor in continental affairs for a long time and had made a poor showing in Flanders under Leicester. The navy's reputation, thanks to Drake, was very different, as the Venetian ambassador in Madrid candidly admitted:

> The Englishmen are of a different quality from the Spaniards, bearing a name above all the West for being expert and enterprising in all maritime affairs, and the finest fighters upon the sea . . . They have no fear that their enemy will be able to come near the English shores.

While Elizabeth and her Council well realized that the proper place to defeat an invasion was at sea, they were reluctant to accept that the effective use of sea-power involved seeking out the enemy at a distance, even if it meant leaving one's own shores unprotected. Howard and Drake therefore had to wait in harbour, not always very comfortably, as Howard's letter to Sir Francis Walsingham of Friday 14 June 1588 made clear:

> We have endured these three days Wednesday, Thursday and Friday, an extreme continual storm. Myself, and four or five of the greatest ships have ridden it out in the Sound, because we had no room in Catwater, for the lesser ships that were there . . . Myself and my company in these ships do continually tarry and lie aboard in all the storm, where we . . . have danced lustily as the gallantest dancers in the court.

On 17 June Howard at last received the longed-for permission, but it was several days more before he could take advantage of it. Whether from meanness, or from a prudent husbanding of resources, his fleet had been kept appallingly short of food. Back in March Burghley had proudly informed the Privy Council of the generous ration scales, which envisaged the sailors enjoying three 'meat days' a week, with 2 lbs [0.9 kg] of salt beef a head, three 'fish days' with '1 quarter of stockfish' and '1 quarter of a pound' [110 gms] of cheese, and a single 'bacon day', with 1 lb [0.45 kg] of bacon and a pint [0.56 litres] of peas, all these being accompanied by 1 lb [0.45 kg] of biscuit and 1 gallon [4.5 litres] of beer. At the end of May, however, Howard was forced, as he informed Burghley, to buy a cargo of rice 'for the better provision and prolonging of our victuals', from a foreign ship detained at Plymouth, and by 22 June he was reduced to making four men's rations feed six. The picture he painted, in his despatch to the Privy Council that day, was a dismal one:

> Men have fallen sick, and by thousands fain to be discharged [and] others pressed in their stead, which hath been an infinite charge [with] great trouble unto us, the army being so great as it is, the ships so many in number, and the weather so extreme foul as it hath been; whereby great charges have risen and daily do. And yet I protest before God we have been more careful of Her Majesty's charges than of our own lives.

Next day his victualling ships arrived and as soon as his store lockers were replenished he put to sea, to patrol the area between Scilly and Ushant, awaiting a sighting, or accurate news of the location, of the Spanish fleet.

While Howard's excellent sea legs had been put to a stern test Medina Sidonia's weak stomach had been facing a far worse ordeal. On 18 May (the 28th by Spanish reckoning) he was still in the Tagus, as he reported to the king:

> The weather is not good and a North-North-West wind is blowing, but I have sent some ships down the river, and some more went down today with a great deal of trouble. They are at anchor on the bar. If a land wind blows tomorrow morning, I will go down with the rest of the fleet. Not an hour has been, or shall be, lost.

Each side was now ready to come to grips with the other, but the wind, once the Armada had got out into the open sea, proved changeable and sometimes died away. Medina Sidonia soon had to reduce speed to accommodate the slowest transport and the 160 sea-miles [184 land miles or 294 km] to Cape Finisterre from the Rock of Lisbon took 13 days. It was now found that much of the food had already deteriorated and, even more serious, that the water emerged green and evil-smelling from its casks. Thanks to Drake's exploits a year earlier, they had had to be made of unseasoned wood. On 10 June the Duke sent a somewhat despairing message to the Duke of Parma, 900 miles [1400 km] away up-Channel:

> What I fear most in the Armada is lack of water. It is true that we carry a six months' supply, but I do not see where we can obtain any more, and it will be advisable for your Excellency at once to consider how we may be aided in this respect, even if it be necessary to transport water in boats from Dunkirk, unless your Excellency knows of any port where both shelter and water may be obtained.

In the end a council of war of all his captains agreed that day that the

Armada should revictual in Corunna, but it was dangerous to attempt to enter the port in the dark and a fierce south-westerly gale blew up during the small hours. Two of the ships which had got into sheltered water collided while those outside were scattered over a wide area. Not till late that afternoon could pinnaces be sent to search for the missing vessels, while couriers were sent along the shore to enquire in neighbouring ports. Medina Sidonia, forced into a command he had never wanted, sent a despairing report to his royal master:

> I expected that on the morning after I entered port with a part of the Armada, the rest would have come in, as it was too late for them to enter that evening. During that night, however, and the next day the weather became so heavy that it is believed that the ships have put to sea. The people of the country say that so violent a sea and wind, accompanied by fog and tempest, have never been seen; and it is very fortunate that all the Armada was not caught outside, and particularly the galleys, which would certainly have been wrecked, and the whole Armada endangered . . . The weather is now moderating and I expect the ships will now make for this port . . . I am very sorry that the bad weather of yesterday had separated the fleet, which will be disabled, and will have to be watered afresh.

Three days later, on 14 June 1588, Medina Sidonia wrote a singularly brave letter to King Philip, virtually suggesting that the whole undertaking should be abandoned:

> Many of our largest ships are still missing . . . whilst on the ships that are here there are many sick, whose number will increase in consequence of the bad provisions. These are not only very bad . . . but they are so scanty that there cannot be more than sufficient to last two months . . . Your Majesty has embarked in this expedition all your resources both in ships and warlike stores, and I can see no means whatever of redressing any disaster that may befall us . . . I have earnestly commended this matter to God, and feel bound to lay it before your Majesty, in order that you may choose the course best for your service while the Armada is refitting here. The opportunity might be taken, and the difficulties avoided, by making some honourable terms with the enemy.

King Philip's reply, sent on 25 June, was uncompromising. The Duke was assured that, if properly husbanded, he should have sufficient supplies and the voyage was to continue as planned, in spite of the delay at Corunna: 'The missing ships should join you there, and when all, or a sufficient number, are united, you may proceed on your expedition.'

If any one factor more than another had upset the royal plans it was the weather, the worst for any June (or July, as it now was according to the reformed Spanish calendar) that anyone could remember. For this only the Almighty could be held responsible but Philip remained confident of His approval. 'For I hope,' he wrote, 'that our Lord will change these difficulties at the start to the triumph of His cause in the end.'

The English conviction of divine support was equally strong, if as befitted Englishmen and Protestants, less ostentatiously expressed. 'God will help us,' wrote John Hawkins confidently that summer, 'for we defend the chief cause, our religion.' The weather remained impartially and unprecedentedly appalling, but West Country seamen were more accustomed to rough seas than the Spaniards, and their ships more seaworthy; Lord Howard stayed at sea while the Spaniards ran for cover. On 5 July 1588 he learned from a bark from Rochelle that the Armada was now sheltering in Corunna and other harbours along the Biscay coast, and at 3 p.m. on the afternoon of 7 July, after a council of war, gave the only possible order: to steer for the coast of Spain and smoke them out, as Drake had done at Cadiz.

Two days and nights of a favourable wind would have been enough to accomplish the business. As it was, 240 miles [380 km] south-west of Ushant the wind changed and, apprehensive of being left off an enemy shore with inadequate supplies, Howard was forced to turn back. After two days of struggling against a severe gale he limped back into Plymouth with nothing accomplished.

On that same Friday (by English reckoning) that Howard and Drake returned to Plymouth, the Armada stood out of Corunna to resume its sadly protracted voyage. The month in harbour had left those who were not ill refreshed; the store barrels were full of fresh food and water; and spread over the ocean almost from one horizon to the other, making its stately, majestic way in bright sunshine across the Bay of Biscay, with an ideal southerly wind filling the great white, cross-decorated sails, it seemed again to merit its favoured nickname, 'The Invincible'. These near-perfect conditions did not last. On the night of 15-16 July, off Ushant, the Bay justified its notorious reputation with a sudden storm that drove 40 ships off course and swamped four galleys, forcing them ashore, where two were wrecked. (The Moslem and Protestant galley-slaves, unwillingly helping a Catholic God, gave thanks to their own deities and decamped.) Medina Sidonia took the chance to put ashore a messenger to let Parma know he was at last on his way, news which reached him eight days later. Then, on 18 July, after the storm had blown itself out, and the missing vessels had regained their stations, Medina Sidonia set sail again, making almost due north. His next landfall would be the Scilly Isles and beyond them lay the coast of England.

38

IN FIGHTING ORDER

Our Armada placed itself in fighting order

The Duke of Medina Sidonia, recalling 21 July 1588

The Armada's unexpectedly slow progress had given the English government ample time to perfect its arrangements on shore as well as at sea. It had been slow to do so for the same reason that had delayed to the last minute the mobilization of the fleet: economy, for once troops passed out of the county which had raised them their maintenance bcame a central government charge. In April 1588, however, the county forces had been put on permanent alert. Already Colonel Sir John Norris (or Norreys), the best of Leicester's subordinate commanders in the Netherlands, was drilling the London trained bands every day and by May a Spanish observer, who had either evaded Walsingham's anti-spy dragnet or, more probably, was operating with his connivance, was reporting that 6000 Londoners were drilling twice weekly. 'They' are, he noted, 'certainly very good troops considering they are recruits, and are well armed.' The shire and provincial towns were all busy buying armour to fill last-minute gaps. Norfolk paid over the odds to the gunmakers for working all night and its county town, operating separately, sent an agent to London who returned with 100 pikes, costing £18 6s 8d [£18.33] and eleven muskets, priced at £14 7s [£14.35].

Other places were concerned to make a colourful showing and bent their minds to the most congenial part of amateur soldiering, choosing a uniform.

One company in Huntingdonshire were decked out in 'popinjay green', trimmed with their commanding officer's colours. In Norwich the tailor attended musters to sell uniforms, the widow Pye was paid for making curtains to cover the newly scoured and oiled armour piled up in the Armoury, and a professional soldier, Captain Suckling, was hired for 50s [£2.50] a day to provide five days' intensive, last-minute training. The financial burden, especially in the maritime counties, was heavy.

Norfolk faced a bill that year for £4240, of which £1186 went on fortifications at Yarmouth and Weybourne, £460 on supporting 300 men in camp at Yarmouth for 35 days, and £700 on ammunition. Much of the total here came from voluntary contributions from the better-off, but in places there were complaints that the rich were not paying their full share. 'If these demands for musters, for powder and new weapons were not demanded of the poor in the towns,' wrote Burghley to Walsingham, 'the matter were of less moment, for the rest may well bear greater.' He was afraid that 'malcontented people will increase to the comfort of the enemy', but even those who grumbled remained fiercely patriotic. The nation's spirit that spring and summer was well expressed by the gout-ridden Earl of Shrewsbury, Lord Lieutenant of Derbyshire. He wrote to the queen assuring her that 'though lame in body, yet was he lusty in heart to lead [i.e. give] her greatest enemy one blow, and to live and die in her service.'

In April 1588 the government appointed a three-man committee of experienced officers, including Sir John Norris, to supervise the preparations of a group of counties and, with their chosen subordinates, to inspect local fortifications and defence forces. Their conclusion was that both were spread too thinly and that it was, for example, impossible to protect every potential landing place in Hampshire, an area considered at even greater risk than either Kent or Sussex. The decision, which Thomas Digges, the amateur strategist quoted earlier, would have approved, was to have only a light screen on the beaches, partly to delay the enemy but, more importantly, to provide accurate information to mount a major counter-attack. The sheer size of the Armada would, it was believed, compel it to seize a large port, and this assumption governed the plans now made.

Concentration was the keynote. The militia of North Wales, if called out, were to converge on Anglesey, those of South Wales on Milford Haven. In the West Country, 19,200 men were to make for Plymouth, 11,000 for Falmouth, 14,000 for Poole. Nearer London, 16,000 would gather to protect Portsmouth, 15,000 for wherever in Sussex proved to be threatened, 10,500 upon the Isle of Sheppey. The rallying points on the east coast were to be Harwich, to which 17,500 men would make their way, with 13,100 earmarked for wherever was attacked in Suffolk, and 13,800 for Yarmouth.

A general call-out of the militia was always regarded as a last resort and in the event the government contented itself with organizing four armies, combining both regular troops, paid veterans recently brought back from the Netherlands, and the most highly-trained of the militia units. One army covering the area from the Scottish border to just north of Harwich, was commanded by the Earl of Huntingdon, based at

Newcastle, and consisted of 12,000 foot from Yorkshire and Durham, 3000 to undertake coast defence, 6000 to defend the country inland, and 3000 forming a mobile reserve. The actual numbers on his strength amounted to 8000, of whom he considered 6000 excellent, plus 400 horses.

A second army was assembled to protect the queen personally. The government talked of its numbering 45,000 and the Dorset militia, burning with loyalty, offered £500 to be allowed to form the royal bodyguard. The actual strength under the queen's cousin, Henry Carey, Lord Hunsdon, was probably nearer 5000 militia-men, plus an unknown number of professionals. A third army, drawn up from the maritime counties, was supposed to move up the coast in line with the Armada, gathering strength as it went. Its strength on paper was 27,000 foot and 2500 horse but little is known of its actual size; in Kent, for example, only half the militia were assigned to move to the coast, the rest remaining in reserve at Canterbury.

London was expected to defend itself with its 10,000 trained men, who would be reinforced if necessary by the fourth and main army at Tilbury, about 20 miles [32 km] down-river from the capital, on the Essex shore, where the Thames narrows and makes a great right-angled bend. A second camp was formed on the other bank, the two being linked by a bridge of boats at Gravesend. Both camps together contained some 17,000 men, including most of the professional soldiers, both foot and horse, under the command of Robert Dudley, Earl of Leicester, newly returned from the Low Countries.

Leicester, now aged around 56, had at one time been a candidate for Elizabeth's hand and despite some distinctly murky episodes and some quarrels with the queen had always returned to her favour. He was a gentleman-adventurer – he had been on one of Drake's expeditions – rather than a true professional and had shown little talent for military command, either operational or logistic. He enjoyed the queen's confidence, however, and it was on his army that the government chiefly depended to defeat Rome. Tilbury had been selected as its base because Burghley and his colleagues believed that the Spanish general would, like any soldier, opt for the shortest possible sea-crossing, from Flanders to Essex, or to the south-east corner of Kent, around Margate.

Since Howard's return to Plymouth the government had received no news of the Armada's progress and they were equally in the dark, because of the adverse winds, about what was happening on the far side of the Channel. Lord Henry Seymour, jointly responsible with Sir William Winter for the fleet near Dover, had a gloomy report to make, on 12 July, to Walsingham:

Such summer season saw I never the like; for what for storms and variable unsettled winds, the same unsettleth and altereth our determinations for lying on the other coast, having of late sundry times put over, with southerly winds, so far as Calais; and suddenly enforced . . . with westerly great gales, to return to our English coasts.

Gradually, however, the weather improved, though the winds were still changeable, and on Thursday 18 July, a bright sunny day, Walsingham received the alarming news, forwarded by the Warden of the Cinque Ports, that Parma's army was reported to have been seen embarking at Dunkirk. The more immediate danger, however, lay in the west, where Howard and Drake were waiting impatiently to put to sea again. The news they were expecting arrived dramatically. Early on the morning of Friday 19 July 1588 Captain Thomas Fleming, posted in 'The Sleeve' or mouth of the Channel for this very purpose, in his 80-ton pinnace the *Golden Hind*, observed a vast and rapidly growing cloud of sails on the distant horizon, immediately put about and, with the wind behind him, made all speed for Plymouth, 100 miles [160 km] away. That afternoon, probably between 3 and 4 p.m., he reported what he had seen to Howard and Drake. The pleasing tradition that they were playing bowls on the Hoe may well be true, since the game was currently popular, it was a fine afternoon, and the story is told as early as 1625 by a Spanish writer. Drake's famous reply, 'We have time enough to finish the game and beat the Spaniards too!' occurs first, with no source identified, in an Anglican bishop's *History of the Reformation* in 1679. However, it may well rest on fact. Such a reaction would have been in keeping with Drake's temperament and he well knew that the Armada could not possibly arrive for at least five or six hours and that, with the wind from the south-west, the English fleet could not get out of Plymouth until the tide began to turn in another hour or so. It was in fact not until well into the early hours of Saturday 20 July that the 90 or so English ships were, on an ebb tide, slowly towed down Plymouth Sound and anchored for the night in the lee of Rame Head, where the Sound reaches the open sea.

While his English adversaries had been painfully working their way out of harbour the Spaniards had been holding a council of war on the *San Martin*, where the bolder spirits urged that they should take advantage of the favourable winds and attack Plymouth. This was exactly what the English government had anticipated, but Medina Sidonia refused. The king had ordered him to press on until the link-up with Parma and the royal instructions must be obeyed. That day he sent an encouraging despatch to Madrid, datelined confidently: 'On board the galleon *San*

Martin in sight of Cape Lizard', and in a later report, written several
weeks afterwards, described the events which followed:

> On the 30th [i.e. the 20th, by English reckoning] at dawn, the Armada
> was very near the shore. We were seen by the people on land, who
> made signal fires, and in the afternoon the Duke sent Ensign Juan Gil
> in a rowing boat to obtain intelligence . . . Ensign Gil returned at
> night with four Englishmen in a boat, hailing as they said, from
> Plymouth. They reported that they had seen the English fleet leave
> Plymouth that afternoon under the Lord Admiral of England and
> Drake.

The calm seas and favourable wind which had carried the Armada
peacefully on the last stage of its journey to England had now changed.
The weather, Medina Sidonia observed, was 'thick and rainy'. The great
fleet was somewhere between Fowey and Plymouth, when the look-
outs on the English ships caught their first glimpse of it through the rain
and mist, stretching in a vast crescent, almost a circle, with the transports
and store-ships surrounded by fighting vessels. During the night, which
was moonlit but hazy, the Spanish look-outs saw distant ghost-like
objects moving across their flank close to the Cornish shore. Only as
dawn broke did they realize that Howard and Drake, by a daring and
masterly piece of seamanship, had, instead of barring the way ahead,
worked their way round behind the Armada, so they enjoyed the
weather-gauge, i.e. stood to windward of it, poised to attack when they
chose. The contemporary chronicler William Camden described the
sight confronting them:

> The English descried the Spanish ships, with lofty turrets like castles
> in front, like a half moon, the wings thereof spreading out about the
> length of seven miles, sailing very slowly though with full sails, the
> winds being, as it were, tired with carrying them and the ocean
> groaning with their weight.

Medina Sidonia recorded his first view of the enemy fleet less graphically:

> On Sunday, the 31st [21 July in England] the day broke with the
> wind changed to the WNW in Plymouth Roads, and eighty ships
> were sighted to windward of us; and towards the coast to leeward
> eleven other ships were seen, including three large galleons . . . They
> gradually got to windward and joined their own fleet. Our Armada
> placed itself in fighting order, the flagship hoisting the royal standard
> at the foremast.

The first shot was fired, apparently as a form of personal challenge by
Howard, from his private pinnace, the aptly-named *Disdain*, and then,

around 9 a.m. on Sunday 21 July 1588, in the vicinity of the Eddystone Rocks, the battle began in earnest. The English tactics, which took the Spaniards by surprise, were for a little group of vessels to make a sudden dash, sailing in line ahead, against a single Spanish ship in an exposed position at the rear or on the flanks, pour in a rapid broadside, at the rate of about five shots to every one fired from their target, and then to veer away, tacking into position to repeat the performance. The English, for their part, had not expected the Spanish fire to be so heavy; their new 50 lb [23 kg] iron roundshot, three times the weight of the ball fired by the English culverins, could, if they struck home, leave an opponent disabled, ready to be grappled and boarded. If this happened the Spaniards, with their higher ships and vast superiority in soldiers, were almost certain to be the victors.

By 1 p.m. when Howard called off the action to conserve his dwindling stocks of powder, honours were fairly even. The English guns caused heavy casualties on the crowded decks of the Spanish vessels, but their shots had proved too light to sink them and the only serious damage occurred during the afternoon and was self-inflicted. Two galleons, in changing formation – 'our Armada continued,' in its commander's words, 'to manoeuvre until four o'clock in the afternoon, trying to gain the wind of the enemy' – collided with each other; later a third, the *San Salvador*, suffered heavy damage from an explosion, popularly attributed later to a disgruntled Dutch conscript, though it may have been due to mere carelessness. Whatever the cause it left 200 dead, and eventually the great ship had to be abandoned. English losses had so far been negligible.

That night both admirals held councils of war. Just ahead lay Torbay, an anchorage big enough to accommodate the Armada, and one of his most experienced officers urged Medina Sidonia to seize this or some secure base nearby before they proceeded any further. The Duke, however, refused to depart from the orders given him by the king. Howard's captains at their meeting also decided not to change their tactics, and so the process of attrition continued. After a squally evening with a choppy sea, conditions improved and during Sunday night and Monday the Armada continued its stately progress towards Start Point. That day Medina Sidonia sent off the trusted Ensign Juan Gil with a letter for Parma which announced his intention to carry straight on up the Channel until they made contact. It contained a significant postscript: 'The enemy continues to harrass our rear, and . . . their ships now seem to have increased to over a hundred sail. Some are excellent vessels and all of them very fast sailers.'

Gil, who spoke good English, duly got through to Dunkirk by adopting Drake-style deception: he flew an English flag and, when he encountered some English fishermen off Rye, was able to convince them that he was on his way to alert Lord Seymour 'to take care that the Duke of Parma did not come'.

During Monday 22 July the *San Salvador* was abandoned by her crew but the enterprising Captain Fleming, who had been the first to sight the Armada, managed to tow her into Weymouth, a valuable prize still containing much of her powder and shot.

That day too, with his usual luck and eye for the main chance, Francis Drake captured a still more important ship, after what seems a flagrant defiance of orders. He had been posted, on the Sunday evening, to lead the English fleet, which was to follow the lantern on the stern of the *Revenge*. but during the night he disappeared and at dawn, by chance according to his story, found himself close to the great 1150 ton (by Spanish measurement) *Nuestra Señora del Rosario* (Our Lady of the Rosary), left behind after being damaged in the accident on the previous day. On board were the vice-admiral in command of one of the Spanish squadrons and 420 men, but they surrendered without a shot being fired at the mere mention of Drake's name. The *Rosario* was to prove the most worthwile prize of the whole campaign, her timbers later being used, in the best 'swords into ploughshares' tradition, to build a gallery in Dartmouth church. Her captain Don Pedro de Valdes witnessed the rest of the action as an honoured guest on the *Revenge*.

Thanks to Drake's freelance treasure-hunting the English fleet was too scattered to accomplish anything more that day, but on Tuesday 23 July, with the Armada sailing across Lyme Bay towards Portland Bill, prompting fears in Howard's mind that it might be planning to put into Weymouth, the fiercest battle yet developed, and lasted all morning. The oldest veterans aboard could not recall such a continuous roll of cannon and rattle of musket fire. The official *Relation of Proceedings*, compiled later, described the encounter as 'a wonderful sharp conflict':

> There was never seen a more terrible value of great shot, nor more hot flight than this was, for although the musketeers and harquebusiers . . . were then infinite, yet they could not be discerned nor heard for that the great ordnance came so thick that a man would have judged it to have been a hot skirmish of small shot, being all the fight long within half musket shot of the enemy.

The Spaniards' constant intention was to tempt the English nearer, denying them the advantage that the 400-pace [approximately 400 yards or 360 m] so-called 'point blank' range of their 17-pounder [8-kg] culverins gave them over their own 50-pounder [23-kg], which were accurate only up to 340 paces [i.e. 340 yards or 310 m]. They had little success. Two main fights developed, in Lyme Bay and under the lee of

Portland Bill where Martin Frobisher may have been trying to lure the Spaniards on to the long, dangerous bank two miles [3.2 km] to the east, called the Shambles. Eventually Howard had to divert some of his main force to rescue Frobisher, who was outnumbered, and a personal duel between the two admirals seemed likely as Medina Sidonia's *San Martin* approached Howard's *Ark* and struck her topsails, in the traditional invitation to an enemy to grapple and board her. Howard's response was a broadside, followed by those of his other ships who repeated the tactics of the first day, and for a full hour the Spanish flagship was fiercely assailed, as Medina Sidonia described:

> When our flagship saw that the flagship of the enemy was leading towards her, she lowered her topsails, and the enemy's flagship passed her, followed by the whole of his fleet, each ship firing at our flagship as it passed. The guns on our flagship were served well and rapidly, and by the time half of the enemy's fleet had passed her the fire became more distant. The flagship was reinforced by [four other ships] . . . although by the time they came up the hottest fury had passed. The enemy then put about to seaward.

During the afternoon fighting died away. It had been inconclusive, which represented a victory for the Spaniards, for the Armada still pressed inexorably on up-Channel. 'From aboard the *Rainbow* at anchor . . . over against Dover, 23 July 1588, at 11 of the clock at night', Lord Henry Seymour wrote to the Council 'humbly praying Your Lordships to send us powder and shot forthwith.' His turn, he clearly foresaw, would be next and, he warned, 'we conjecture still, their purpose may be to land in the Isle of Wight.'

Tuesday 23 July was the day on which the land forces became fully mobilized, as the government called out another 20,000 militiamen to form the field armies; those living near the coast in the south and west had already been assembled. The total finally under arms is hard to establish, though the commander-in-chief, the Earl of Leicester, believed, no doubt correctly, that the country had raised more fighting men that summer than at any time since the Norman conquest. The totals were probably, none the less, smaller than expected. The nobility and principal clergy, required to provide additional soldiers from their own resources, tended to send their own retainers and to withdraw them for the purpose from the militia, although this did not apply to household servants, who did not qualify for it. Nor did all those on the local rolls always turn out. When the very keen Dorset force arrived in Hampshire, for example, it was found to number 2451 instead of the 3000 expected. Nevertheless, the numbers assembled were enormous, totalling at least 8000 infantrymen, plus 400 horses, in the northern army, at least 10,000 for local defence in the London trained bands, another 5000 or more in the army commanded by the queen's cousin, Lord Hunsdon, assigned to protect Elizabeth personally, and probably 16,500 in the main army at Tilbury, and its supporting depot in Kent. These added up to almost 40,000 and the separate, mobile, force supposed to follow the Armada up the coast amounted on paper at least to 29,000, of whom all but 2500 were foot soldiers. Thus that summer something like 60,000 men were under arms, an enormous burden on the country's economy and, for those in the two main armies, on the Exchequer, which explained why the government only mobilized at the last possible minute and was eager to disband its forces the instant it seemed safe to do so.

The call-out arrangements worked admirably. Two companies from Northamptonshire, expected to take six days to cover the 60–70 miles [96-112 km] to London, did the journey in two, thanks to their armour being sent by cart. The catering arrangements were less impressive. The militia in the maritime counties of the south-west, the first to be ordered to report, probably came off best. Their local towns took a pride in sending them off well equipped and adequately fed. The men from Stratton in Cornwall went to their rendezvous at Saltash with beef, bacon, bread, butter and cheese supplied by their fellow townsfolk; those from Dorset, travelling to Hampshire, were accompanied by 'purveyors' who also provided beer, wine and biscuit. The contingents earmarked for the main army, at Tilbury, did less well. At least one regiment of 4000 men was told on arrival that there was not a loaf of bread or pint of beer to be had within 20 miles, while 1000 Londoners in another unit were stopped en route and ordered to stock up with food before going any further. Leicester, however, would accept no blame for these logistic failings, arguing that 'great dilatory wants are found upon all sudden hurly-burlies' and the government tried to prevent overcharging by laying down maximum prices over a 20-mile [32 km] radius from Tilbury: a soldier's supper was to cost no more than 3d [2p] and was to include 'good wheaten bread and drink; boiled beef, mutton, veal or lamb', while a week's lodging, on a feather bed, was to be priced at no more than 6d [2p].

The men's spirits were high, as an eyewitness confirms: 'It was a pleasant sight to behold the soldiers as they marched towards Tilbury, their cheerful countenances, courageous words and gestures, dancing and leaping wheresoever they came.'*

Those militiamen left behind for local defence kept themselves busy by patrolling the streets and, no doubt to the general annoyance, challenging

*One military historian, a former general, comments sourly that 'such a display was a better indication of loyalty than of discipline'.

strangers at crossroads, though anyone who wanted to travel to the coast required authorization from a magistrate. Aliens, however loyal, had a rough time: 'It is easier,' protested one, 'to find flocks of white crows than one Englishman . . . who loves a foreigner.'

No lack of enthusiasm to repel the Spaniards existed, but the government also made a deliberate effort to promote patriotism through propaganda. Lord Burghley had held periodic meetings of justices in the Star Chamber in Whitehall to stress how thorough were the government's military preparations, and he also wrote an open *Letter to Mendoza*, the former Spanish ambassador now collecting information for King Philip in Paris, which made much of the overwhelming reception an invader could expect, with 20,000 men, complete with guns and pioneers, arriving in any threatened county within 48 hours. The Queen, he warned the Spaniards, 'most carefully, by her own frequent directions, caused her whole realme to be put in armes'. Numerous poets wrote English or Latin verses exhorting their countrymen to be as valiant with the sword as they were with the pen, and the Archbishop of Canterbury called for special public devotions on several days each week attended by at least some members of every familly: many people, he complained, were using the national emergency, and the demands of military training, as an excuse to stay away from church. As a further incentive, he forbade the clergy to deliver more than one sermon a day, though some recaptured their missing congregations by holding special services for the militia. One unit in Hertfordshire was treated before starting the day's training to an address on the text 'Dread not, neither bee afraide of them. The Lord your God which goeth before you, he shall fight for you.' Civilians who did still attend church were enjoined to repeat a special prayer, composed by the queen herself:

We do instantly beseech Thee, of Thy gracious goodness, to be merciful to the Church militant here upon the Earth, and at this time compassed about with most strong and subtle adversaries. O let Thine enemies know that Thou has received England . . . into thy own protection. Set a wall about it, O Lord, and evermore mightily defend it . . . Thou art our help and shield. O give good and prosperous success to all those that fight this battle against the enemies of Thy gospel.

39

LET TYRANTS FEAR

Let tyrants fear . . . I am come amongst you . . . to live or die amongst you all.

Queen Elizabeth to her army at Tilbury, 9 August 1588

While the defences on land were being fully mobilized, the fate of the country was being decided in the Channel. After the brisk fighting of Tuesday 23 July, the next day was relatively quiet, though it began with a sharp skirmish, when several ships, probably led by Drake, though the English records are silent about the whole episode, surrounded and attempted to destroy a Spanish straggler. The Spanish rear division, led by Medina Sidonia himself, came to her rescue – she was eventually towed away by one of those useful craft, the galleasses, and settled safely in the middle of the fleet – and a brisk fire-fight developed, lasting perhaps two hours, in which 60 Spaniards were killed and 70 wounded, ten more dead than in the earlier battle off Portland. Sir George Carey, governor of the Isle of Wight, listening in Carisbrooke Castle to the none-too-distant sound of battle, was impressed by the noise – and by the reported absence of any English casualties: 'The shot continued so thick together that it might rather have been judged a skirmish with small shot on land than a fight with great shot at sea. In which conflict, thanks be to God, there hath not been two of our men hurt.'

That afternoon the wind dropped and, their sails flapping idly, the two fleets, south-west of the Needles, briefly drifted within sight of each other. Howard was glad of the lull, for transports now arrived bringing him more shot and powder, and he also called a council at which the command system was overhauled to create four distinct squadrons, under Howard, Drake, John Hawkins and Martin Frobisher; hitherto ships seem to have fought together or independently much as their captains chose.

Thursday 25 July began with another calm, ideal conditions for galleasses and very poor for sailing ships. Hawkins had his ships towed out by their longboats to engage two ships which had fallen astern of the rest, while Medina Sidonia sent his galleasses to their rescue, with some heavier ships in support. Eventually the stragglers were towed away to safety and the English beaten off. Martin Frobisher, lying between the Armada and the shore, had to call for eleven boats to serve as tugs, but at last the wind freshened and he was able to get to grips with the enemy. After doing what damage he could he made his escape, his ship, the *Triumph*, easily outrunning its pursuers, as one of the Spanish captains complained:

> Our flagship and other ships sailed towards her, but she got out so quickly that the . . . the two fastest in the Armada, although they gave chase, seemed in comparison with her to be standing still.

Drake's whereabouts were unknown, but he was probably busy on the seaward side of the Spanish crescent formation, forcing it in towards the centre, where the outermost galleon was driven back towards the main fleet. An anonymous galleon captain recorded the result: 'Seeing that, the enemy took heart and turned with his whole fleet or the greater part of it, and charged upon our wing, so that we who were there were driven into a corner.'

This day's fighting, all around the seaward shores of the Isle of Wight, but probably centring off Dunnose Head, at the south-east corner of the island, was the fiercest so far, as Medina Sidonia's report confirms:

> Whilst the skirmish was going on in the rear, the enemy's flagship, with other large vessels, fell upon our royal flagship, which was leading the vanguard. They came closer than on the previous day, firing off their heaviest guns from the lowest deck, cutting the trice of our mainmast, and killing some of our soldiers.

This was the moment when the Duke had to decide whether to enter the Solent, if he were to do so at all, by the eastern passage, as King Philip had recommended, but he decided to press on, with ahead of him, Howard and Drake permitting, a straight fair run to Calais. The English command seem to have felt that his failure to acquire a port, or land on the Isle of Wight, was a victory in itself. Already the Earl of Leicester at Tilbury seems to have assumed that the English seamen had gained a decisive success, as his letter to Walsingham that day confirms:

> This being true, I would gladly know what Her Majesty will do with me. I have here now assembled in camp 4000 footmen, as gallant and as willing as ever was seen; with the horse yet only of this shire. The lying in camp will do them much good, though it be but for a short time; and in my poor opinion, not good to dismiss them over

suddenly, though the [Spanish] fleet be defeated, till ye see a little also
what Parma will do.

Howard seems to have been even more optimistic. On the morning of
Friday 26 July 1588, on a calm sea and in bright sunshine, he summoned
Hawkins, Frobisher and other senior captains to the *Ark* and, using his
prerogative as Lord Admiral, created them knights, 'as well in reward of
their good services . . . as also for the encouragement of the rest'. With
no large port to attract Medina Sidonia towards Sussex, Howard was
content to shadow the Armada from well astern, but as the wind
freshened, at sunset, the English ships began to catch up and by 4 p.m.
on Saturday 27 July both fleets were approaching Calais. Here the
Armada suddenly lowered its sails and dropped anchor, 'purporting,' an
English observer believed, 'that our ships with the flood should be
drawn to leeward of them'. In such matters, however, Howard and his
colleagues excelled. The Armada came to rest four miles [6 km] short of
Calais; its English pursuers duly anchored, still to windward of their
enemies, a mere mile or so behind.

The decision to halt at Calais was made against the wishes of the
Duke's subordinates, who were all for pressing on to Dunkirk, a mere
24 miles [38 km] further on. His pilots, however, warned him that off
Dunkirk lay a series of narrow sandbanks a mere three fathoms [18 feet
or 5.5 m] deep at low water, far too shallow for the Armada's chief
ships; the only navigable channel was a mere third of a mile [600 yards
or 550 m] across, described by the navigation guide then in use as
'dangerous for great vessels because the waves in the ebbing and flowing
do for the most part set thwart over the shoals'. For 120 large, unwieldy
vessels to attempt such a passage would be to court disaster, especially
without local experts, but these had not been provided, indeed not a
word had been heard from Parma in response to all the Duke's messages.
The other harbours available were also made hazardous by shifting
sandbanks and only Nieuport, besides Dunkirk, was in Spanish hands.
Calais and Gravelines belonged to the French and an English garrison
held Ostend. The Scheldt estuary could have accommodated the
Armada, and the south side of it and the city of Antwerp at its head were
held by Parma, but the north side, and – the real key to the Scheldt – the
port of Flushing at its mouth, were occupied by the Dutch 'rebels'. The
Dutch possessed few large ships but a great number of fly-boats, shallow-
draught, flat-bottomed coastal craft designed specifically to operate amid
the sand-banks off the Flemish coast. They could not have stood up to
larger sailing ships out at sea, but might have done enormous damage
close inshore to deeper-draught galleons in constant danger of running
aground.

As soon as he had dropped anchor Medina Sidonia despatched yet another letter to Parma, by the hand of his secretary. It was couched in sharper terms than any so far:

> I have constantly written to Your Excellency, and not only have I received no reply, but no acknowledgement of their receipt has reached me. I am extremely anxious at this . . . and to free myself of the doubt of whether any of my messengers have reached you safely, I am now sending this boat with the information that I am at anchor here off Calais with all the Armada, the enemy's fleet being on my flank . . . I feel obliged to . . . beg you, if you cannot at once bring out all your fleet, to send me the forty or fifty fly-boats I asked for yesterday. With this help, I shall be able to resist the enemy's fleet until Your Excellency can come out with the rest, and we can go together and take some port where this Armada may enter in safety.

On the following day, Sunday 28 July 1588, Medina Sidonia sent another letter to Parma, even more desperate in tone:

> As the season is so advanced, and my ships so large, I am obliged to be very careful . . . I therefore beg you to hasten your coming out before the spring tides end, as it will be impossible for you to get out of Dunkirk and the neighbouring ports during the neap tides★.

Later that day, he at last received word of what was happening on land. The messenger he had sent to Parma from the Bay of Biscay now turned up at Calais, reporting that Parma himself was still at Bruges, 40 miles [64 km] from Dunkirk, where embarkation had not even begun. Later came a confirmatory message, even more depressing, from Medina Sidonia's secretary, now at that port. Not only had no guns or stores yet been put aboard the barges but carpenters were still working on them and in his opinion they would not be seaworthy for another fortnight at least. He did not mention, as emerged later, that many, intended for river use, were unfit for a sea crossing, or so badly constructed they were not watertight even in harbour, but already Medina Sidonia must have realized that Parma had let him down. The Armada had fought its way through almost to Dunkirk, as ordered, only to find no invasion force ready to be escorted.

During the day both sides held religious services almost within earshot of each other, but the English also finalized the details of the counter-stroke already planned; to attack the Armada in its anchorage and force the survivors out into the open sea. It had been hoped to bring small,

★Neap tides are the weakest, with the smallest change in the water-level. Spring tides are especially high, and occur twice a month.

expendable vessels ready prepared from Dover, but the opportunity had to be seized immediately and during the day, out of sight of the Spaniards, eight of the small ships already assembled off Calais were loaded to the gunwales with firewood and barrels of tar, with guns ready primed to go off when the flames reached them. At midnight a single shot, fired from Howard's *Ark*, gave the signal to the volunteer crews to cast off, towing the dinghies which were to carry them back to safety. The mainsails were set, to keep them on a straight course before the wind, the fuses leading to the combustible contents were lit and the crews took to the dinghies. Then, while still about halfway between the two fleets, the fire ships, larger than the vessels usually employed for such work, burst suddenly into flames. As the tongues of fire licked up the rigging and set the sails ablaze, shot began to pour from the gunports into the protective screen of pinnaces which the Duke had posted in expectation of just such an attack. Their grapnels proved inadequate, however, to halt the remorseless progress of the fiercely burning craft, and their appearance made everyother vessel desperate to get out of the way, their attempts causing far more damage than the fire ships themselves. These indeed sailed right across the anchorage without setting any Spanish ship on fire and finally burned out harmlessly in the distance.

The following day an eyewitness, Richard Tomson, 'Lieutenant of the *Margaret and John*', sent a dramatic account of this soon legendary event, which was afterwards commemorated in a famous painting★, to Walsingham:

> It pleased my Lord Admiral to appoint certain small ships to be fired on Sunday about 12 of the clock at night, and let drive with the flood amongst the Spaniards; which practice, God be thanked, hath since turned to our great good, for it caused the Spaniards to let slip their anchors and cables, and confusedly to drive upon one another; whereby they not only put from their roadstead and place where they were to attend the coming of the Duke of Parma, but did much hurt to one another of themselves.

This was accurate enough, as was a Spanish comment: 'The enemy were lucky; their trick turned out exactly as they had planned. With eight ships they put us to flight, a thing they had not dared to attempt with a hundred and thirty.' Any panic that occurred was among the soldiers and other landsmen on board the Armada. The sailors reacted admirably, cutting their cables, hoisting sails and getting their great ships under way in time to evade the fireships. The only real casualty was a large

★See no. 42 of illustrations.

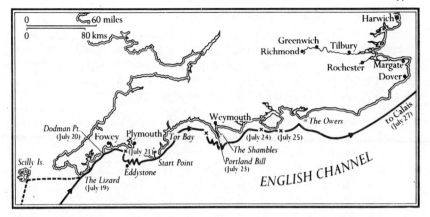

The battleground. The Spanish Armada in the Channel, 19–27 July 1588.

galleass, the *San Lorenzo*, badly damaged when its rudder caught in another ship's anchor cable. But the Spaniard who wrote, 'It was a terrifying spectacle in the night' was right and the operation achieved its purpose, forcing the Armada to scatter in confusion. Medina Sidonia, anchoring again a mile or two offshore, found at dawn only three or four ships of his command anywhere in sight, with the rest spread over a distance of ten miles [16 km], and nearly every ship had lost two anchors, which had serious consequences later.

That Monday was the day of decision for the Armada. Fighting began while Medina Sidonia was still trying to round up the missing vessels, at around 7 a.m, on 29 July 1588, when the tide was at the half-ebb, and about seven miles [11 km] off Gravelines, which was to give the battle its name, though it raged over an area five miles [8 km] in each direction. About 260 ships were involved, but the main action was fought between about 30 Spanish vessels and about 40 English ships.

The day began ingloriously for the English. Howard could not resist sending his longboats to attack the crippled *San Lorenzo* which ran aground off Calais, and they only ceased looting it after the governor of Calais had fired the fort's guns to underline his claim that the wrecked vessel was, by rights, his. By the time they returned Drake had opened the battle with a fierce attack on the enemy flagship, the *San Martin*, with the rest of his ships lining up astern of the *Revenge* to pound the Spaniard in turn. By nine o' clock the main ships of both sides had come up to join in the battle, which was being fought with unusual ferocity and at far closer quarters than in the earlier encounters; one Englishman was so carried away in the excitement that he launched a one-man boarding party against the *San Mateo* and was instantly killed.

For once there was fighting enough for every famous name, whether of captain or ship. Hawkins was there in the *Victory;* so was the latest *Mary Rose* and perhaps the earliest *Dreadnought:* its captain was, incredibly, 89, but had refused to stay on shore and ended what his memorial described as 'his life of honour' at 102. The newly knighted Martin Frobisher was there; so was Drake and Sir William Winter, his long vigil off Dover at last rewarded, as he described:

> My fortune was to make choice to charge their starboard wing without shooting of any ordnance until we came within six score [paces] of them, and some of our ships did follow me. The said wing found themselves, as it did appear, to be so charged [i.e. were so alarmed] as by making of haste to run into the body of their fleet, four of them did entangle themselves one aboard the other.

The English behaved with dash and daring, the Spaniards with determination and courage. Medina Sidonia's own ship and the other principal vessels, on which the attack was concentrated, gallantly came to each other's rescue, even with rigging cut about and pumps overwhelmed by the water flooding in through their peppered sides, constantly coming close enough for musketry fire although they must have long since realized that their great cannon fired too high, and too slowly, to be a match for the English culverins. A Spanish eyewitness described what happened when an Englishman in the maintop of one of the tormentors of the battered, ill-fated *San Felipe,* with her guns dismounted and her rigging destroyed, called on her to surrender 'on fair terms':

> The only answer he got was a gunshot which brought him down in sight of everyone . . . The enemy then retired, while our men shouted out to them that they were cowards, and with rude words reproached them for their lack of spirit . . . calling them Protestant hens.

As the afternoon wore on the Spanish warships, still bravely shielding the small vessels and unarmed transports from attack, began to run short of roundshot or the surviving members of their crews were no longer capable of serving the guns. The English were also in danger of running out of ammunition and when, around 4 p.m., a heavy squall blew up, accompanied by heavy rain, both fleets broke off the action to reduce sail. During the evening and night Medina Sidonia counted up his losses. One galleon, the *Maria Juan,* foundered that evening in full view of the rest of the fleet, with 275 men still aboard. The *San Felipe* and *San Mateo,* already near wrecks, both ran aground near Nieuport and were captured by the Dutch. The *San Martin* itself had taken 107 shot and was hit below the waterline, having suffered 40 dead. Every other galleon was badly damaged, with torn sails, leaking hulls and holds full of shattered casks and wounded men and animals. Some men had had enough and stole a boat to desert, using their shirts as sails. 'They did see through the portholes,' they recounted as they stumbled ashore, 'an Italian ship all full of blood.' Another Spaniard recalled that miserable night as the English still stood to windward and the north-west wind seemed to be forcing the whole Armada on to the Zealand Banks: 'It was the most awful day in the world. Everyone was in utter despair and stood waiting for death.' The official Spanish casualty figure for the Battle of Gravelines was 600 killed and 800 wounded; the English once again had escaped almost without loss.

Howard and Drake did not realize that the decisive battle had now been fought. Howard's report to Walsingham concentrated on his private battle with the galleass that morning and dismissed briefly the main events of the day: 'Ever since we have chased them in fight until this evening late, and distressed them much . . . Their force is wonderful great and strong; and yet we pluck their feathers by little and little.'

Drake was more optimistic:

> God hath given us so good a day in forcing the enemy so far to leeward as I hope in God the Prince of Parma and the Duke of Sidonia shall not shake hands this few days; and whensoever they shall meet, I believe neither of them will greatly rejoice of this day's service.

That afternoon, while the Armada was setting off on its long trek northward, Howard also called a council of war, in which he decided to divide his fleet. The main part would pursue the Armada while the ships commanded by Sir William Winter and Lord Henry Seymour, much to their disgust, were sent back to their former station, 'to guard the Thames mouth,' as Winter reported to Walsingham, 'from any attempt that might be made by the Duke of Parma.' Reluctant but obedient they slipped away 'in the twilight as the enemy might not see our departing'.

On Wednesday 31 July 1588 the chase which had begun off Cornwall continued, though well out to sea, off the eastern and north-eastern counties. Their pursuers had as yet no inkling that the Spaniards had abandoned any hope of making a landing and wanted merely to get away, as Hawkins's letter to Walsingham that day reveals: 'The Spaniards take their course for Scotland; my lord doth follow them. I doubt not, with God's favour, but we shall impeach their landing. There must be order for victual and money, powder and shot, to be sent after us.'

Whatever had happened to his fleet there was nothing wrong with Medina Sidonia's fighting spirit, as his account of why the Armada now broke off the action it had fought, on and off, for the previous ten days reveals:

The Duke wished during this day to turn and attack the enemy with the whole Armada, in order to avoid running out of the Channel, but the pilots told him it was impossible, as both wind and tide were against us . . . They said that he would be forced either to run up into the North Sea, or wreck all the Armada on the shoals. He was therefore utterly unable to avoid going out of the Channel, nearly all our trustworthy ships being so damaged as to be unfit to resist attack, both on account of the cannon fire to which they had been exposed, and their own lack of projectiles.

That Monday 29 July 1588 (English style) knowing nothing yet of the day's events off Gravelines, Parma wrote a long letter of self-justification to Philip II:

The men who have recently come here from the duke, seeing the boats unarmed and with no artillery on board, and the men not shipped, have been trying to make out we are not ready. They are mistaken. The boats are, and have been for months, in proper order for the work they have to do, namely to take the men across. We have not as many seamen as we ought to have, but enough . . . The boats are so small that the troops cannot be kept on board for long. There is no room to turn around, and they would certainly fall ill, rot and die. Putting the men on board these low, small boats can be done in a very short time.

That evening Parma rode to Nieuport to inspect matters for himself. He later claimed that 16,000 troops had already been embarked and everything was ready, once the sea was calm and the promised escort on hand. Next morning he went to Dunkirk where the troops were lined up in the harbour, waiting to embark that evening, and here he met Medina Sidonia's last and most senior messenger, who had been searching for him. This officer, Don Jorge Manrique, Inspector-General of the Fleet, urged, according to Parma, that his troops should be used to help the Armada capture a port, a radical change of plan which Parma, as he reported to the king, could not accept:

Nevertheless . . . I decided to discuss the possibility with . . . practical sailors here, in the presence of Don Jorge Manrique, so that, if it turned out to be impracticable he might be convinced that . . . the most we could hope for from these boats would be in fine settled weather, and with the Channel clear of enemies, to take our men across as had been arranged. The general verdict was that it would be out of the question for them to undertake a voyage of seven or eight days as proposed by the duke.

According to another less partisan witness, the real point at issue was that Don Jorge considered that his authority, and his commander's, extended over Parma's troops and ships, while Parma and his staff contended that they took their orders direct from the king. While this altercation was in progress, and embarkation was still going ahead, news arrived which made the discussion academic. A shivering young man, soaked to the skin, and the most distinguished messenger so far – a prince, Philip's illegitimate son – climbed out of a small boat in Dunkirk harbour, to report that a disastrous battle had been fought the previous day and the Armada was already well past any possible rendezvous point and heading north.

While his emissary had been quarrelling with the Duke of Parma, Medina Sidonia had been grappling with far more immediate problems of his own. By 2 a.m. on the morning of Tuesday 30 July, the day after the Battle of Gravelines, the *San Martin* and the few ships still with her were being driven steadily to leeward, in imminent danger of running aground, as the water beneath the galleons' keels dropped away to seven fathoms [42 ft or 13 m] and then to six [36 ft or 11 m]; the great ships all drew at least five fathoms[30 ft or 9 m]. Just in time the wind changed, but dawn revealed a new danger:

> At daybreak the NW wind fell somewhat and we discovered the enemy's fleet of 109 ships rather over half a league astern of us. The enemy's ships bore down on our flagship, which came round to the wind and lay to; and galleasses placed themselves in front and the rest of our rearguard stood by ready to repel attack, whereupon the enemy retired . . . They saw the Armada was going to be lost; indeed the experienced pilots who accompanied the Duke assured him at this time that it was impossible to save a single ship . . . From this desperate peril, in only six and a half fathoms of water, we were saved by the wind shifting by God's mercy to the SW, and the Armada was then able to steer a northerly course without danger to any of our ships.

With the English still close behind there was talk among the Spaniards of surrender and the Duke's nautical adviser is said to have been threatened with being thrown overboard when he offered this unwelcome counsel. A great grandee like Medina Sidonia could hardly have contemplated such a course, but he did call a council of war to advise him:

> The same afternoon the Duke summoned the generals . . . to decide what should be done. The Duke submitted the state of the Armada, and the lack of projectiles, a fresh supply of which had been requested by all the principal ships; and asked the opinion of those present as to whether it would be best to return to the English Channel, or sail

home to Spain by the North Sea, the Duke of Parma not having sent advice that he would be able to come out promptly. The council unanimously resolved in favour of returning to the Channel if the weather would allow of it, but if not, then that they should obey the wind and sail to Spain by the North Sea, bearing in mind that the Armada was lacking all things necessary, and that the ships that had hitherto resisted were badly crippled.

The chance to turn back, however, failed to come:

On Wednesday, the 10th [i.e. 31 July, English style], the Armada was under way with a fresh SW wind and a heavy sea, the enemy's fleet following us. In the afternoon the violence of the wind abated and the enemy came under full sail towards our rearguard . . . When the enemy saw that our flagship, the galleasses and twelve of our best ships were standing by, he shortened sail and dropped astern without firing at us.

Drake that day was in cheerful mood, as he wrote an accompanying letter to Walsingham when sending his most valuable prisoners ashore:

We have the army of Spain before us and mind, with the grace of God, to wrestle a pull with him. There was never anything pleased better, than seeing the enemy flying with a southerly wind to the northwards.

God grant we have a good eye to the Duke of Parma; for . . . if we live, I doubt it not . . . so to handle the matter with the Duke of Sidonia, as he shall wish himself at St Mary port, among the vine trees.

Two days later, to the Duke's relief, the pursuit was abandoned:

On Friday, the 12th [2 August in England], at dawn, the enemy's fleet was quite close to us, but as they saw we were well together, and that the rearguard had been reinforced, the enemy fell astern and sailed towards England until we lost sight of him.

The two fleets were now roughly level with the Scottish border, but 100 miles [160 km] out to sea. Howard decided that the Armada intended to keep going, and, leaving two pinnaces to follow it and report any change of track, led his ships towards the Firth of Forth, to revictual and rearm. The Armada was, he must have judged, in far worse case for a trail of horses and mules, thrown overboard to save water, bobbed in its wake. Medina Sidonia had already ordered that everyone, irrespective of rank, was to be reduced to a mere pint of water [0.5 litre] a day, plus half a pint of wine and half a pound [0.23 kg] of biscuit. Already 21 days of the

80 days' rations taken on at Corunna had gone and, with the coming voyage likely to last at least a month, it was going to be a close-run thing to get home at all.

As early as Saturday 3 August the government decided that the crisis was past and the shires were instructed to keep their troops under arms but to send no more to Tilbury. Two days later Leicester was instructed to send home two-thirds of those already there, unless he objected, which he did, vigorously, contending that the danger was not yet over. This was true enough. Parma might still attempt the Channel crossing without an escort and the next spring tide, when barges could easily enter Dunkirk to embark troops, was due on Wednesday 7 August. That day, instead, it was Howard's and Drake's ships which made their way, sadly short of food and ammunition, into Yarmouth, Harwich and Margate and other ports close to the Thames. The queen, who had been chafing at her confinement at St James's in London, surrounded by a heavy guard, had, on her own insistence, been allowed to move for a few days to Essex; the Earl of Leicester, in a fulsome letter – 'your person, being the most dainty and sacred thing we have in this world to care for' – agreed to her staying at Havering, provided she went no nearer the coast. Leicester was well aware of the effect a royal inspection would have on his men, and the whole nation: 'You shall,' he wrote to her on 27 July, 'comfort not only these thousands but many more that shall hear of it,' and so it proved. The queen's journey by barge to Tilbury, and her progress through the ranks of her troops, dressed in white velvet with a silver breastplate and marshal's baton, mounted on a white horse, was a triumph. On the second day of her visit, Friday 9 August 1588, after watching a mimic battle, she addressed her army:

> My loving people, We have been persuaded by some that are careful of our safety, to take heed how we commit ourselves to armed multitudes, for fear of treachery. But I assure you, I do not desire to live to distrust my faithful and loving people. Let tyrants fear. I have always so behaved myself that, under God, I have placed my chiefest strength and safeguard in the loyal hearts and good will of my subjects; and therefore I am come amongst you, as you see, at this time, not for my recreation and disport, but being resolved, in the midst and heat of the battle, to live or die amongst you all, to lay down for my God, and for my kingdom, and for my people, my honour and my blood, even in the dust. I know I have the body of a weak and feeble woman, but I have the heart and stomach of a king, and of a king of England too, and think foul scorn that Parma or Spain, or any prince of Europe, should dare to invade the borders of my realm; to which, rather than any dishonour shall grow by me, I myself will take up

arms, I myself will be your general, judge and rewarder of every one of your virtues in the field.

As the queen was dining with Leicester in his tent a report arrived that Parma was preparing to come out at last and it needed a great effort of persuasion by her generals to persuade her to go back to London. But Parma failed to appear and the following day Leicester was instructed to release all but 6000 of his men, the whole camp, including the forces privately raised by the nobility, being dispersed about two weeks later. By around 24 August the danger was officially acknowledged to be over and the militia were stood down.

The wildest rumours had meanwhile been circulating round Europe of a massive English defeat at sea and that Medina Sidonia and Parma had joined hands as planned. The Spanish ambassador to the Vatican demanded that the pope pay the first instalment of his promised contribution as Parma's troops must by now be in England, and requested a special *Te Deum* to be sung in St Peter's; Sixtus, however, wisely insisted on waiting for confirmation from other sources. The Spanish ambassador in Paris, Mendoza, had long had a huge bonfire waiting outside his house and it was duly lit in celebration after a totally false report that Drake had been captured. Mendoza was slow to accept what had really happened and in mid-September (English style) was still sending optimistic reports back to Madrid, until on the last King Philip, who by now knew the real facts, minuted: 'Nothing of this is true. It will be well to tell him so.' Mendoza had already learned the truth, as workmen shouted mockingly after him in the streets of Paris 'Victoria! Victoria!' – 'Victory!' 'Victory!' – while Philip II accepted the foundering of all his hopes with his usual resignation. Once satisfied that no more ships would return he ordered his bishops to stop praying for the fleet and reminded them that 'in the storms through which the Armada sailed, it might have suffered a worse fate, and that its ill-fortune was no greater, must be credited to the prayers for its good success.' Mendoza's absurd optimism had meanwhile been put to good use by the British government, which issued one of his most extravagant accounts of the recent, wholly imaginary, Spanish victories, in a double-column format, with the true facts printed alongside the original claims. Translated into the major European languages, the resulting booklet, entitled *A Pack of Spanish Lies*, had a great success throughout the Protestant world.

What in fact had happened to the Armada since it disappeared into the distance somewhere off the east coast of Scotland? Medina Sidonia's long account of its adventures, sent back to Spain at this point, had ended on an upbeat note: 'We have now, the 20th August [10 August,

English style], doubled the last of the Scottish Islands to the north, and we have set our course with a NE wind for Spain.'

The chief Spanish navigator had plotted an excellent route, round the Shetland Islands, and almost to the coast of Norway, before it turned almost due west well into the Atlantic and then almost due south until it reached the Spanish coast near Corunna. The fleet was intended to keep together but, thanks to battle damage and varied sailing speeds, aided by two weeks of storms and violent head-winds, it was soon dispersed. What became of some vessels is still a mystery. At least three ships were lost off the Scottish coast, including the 650-ton *Gran Grifon*, the crew of which, 300 strong, got safely ashore on little Fair Isle, midway between the Shetlands and Orkneys, where they totally swamped the 17 crofting families who lived there and who had never even heard of Spain. The survivors, their numbers thinned by deaths from sickness, eventually reached the mainland, where a kindly minister described them as 'for the most part young beardless men, silly . . . and hungered, to whom kail, porridge and fish were given'. They eventually got back to Spain. Such treatment was exceptional. The great graveyard of the Armada was the west coast of Ireland, some ships, short of food and water and full of sick and wounded, seeking shelter there, others being driven ashore.

Most of this bedraggled flotsam was clearly no danger to anyone but two Spanish officers ill-advisedly tried to form their men up under arms, if only for self-protection, and one contingent, in Blacksod Bay, County Mayo, established a fortified camp in the ruins of a Celtic castle, with a garrison of 600. In such circumstances the English authorities could hardly be blamed, with fewer than 2000 English soldiers in a largely hostile and overwhelmingly Catholic country, for taking no chances. It was not even certain the newcomers *were* from the Armada, as the governor of Connaught explained in a letter to the Lord Deputy in Dublin: 'Whether they be of the dispersed fleet which are fled from the supposed overthrow in the Narrow Seas, or new forces come from Spain directly, no man is able to advise.'

He failed, however, to give the benefit of the doubt to any of the wretched, half-starved, half-drowned castaways now appearing in his area, as he proudly reported on 21 September:

I dare assure your Lordship now that in the fifteen or sixteen ships cast away on the coast of this province . . . there hath perished at least 6000 or 7000 men, of which there hath been put to the sword . . . and executed one way or another about seven or eight hundred upwards.

Only a handful of those who escaped the perils of the sea ever got home, almost all of them being butchered as they lay exhausted on the rocks or being handed over to the English to be killed. Most of the Irish showed, for once, no reluctance to obey English orders and to murder their co-religionists; one Irishman boasted of having personally killed eight Spaniards with an axe. In England, where the government felt more secure, those aboard the hospital ship, the *San Pedro el Mayor* which turned back up the Channel and was wrecked in South Devon, were decently treated and eventually repatriated; their few minutes of freedom between floundering ashore and being rounded up represented the total extent of the invasion of England in 1588.

Medina Sidonia's *San Martin* reached Santander on 13 September (English style) with 180 men already dead from typhus or other diseases, on top of her battle casualties, and many more died later. Sickness and privation ultimately accounted for more deaths than English cannon-balls; one ship made port having been out of water for twelve days, and another ran aground on entering harbour because its crew were too weak to lower the sails and drop anchor. The deaths continued for weeks, while Medina Sidonia, who had never wanted his command and had shown resource and courage in all the Armada's adversities, himself ill, was smuggled home in a curtained horse-litter, a figure of universal scorn. Eventually 67 ships returned to Spain, only half of the 130 which had set sail back in May – though some estimates put the loss slightly lower. No firm casualty figures exist but probably only about 10,000 of the 31,000 men aboard lived to tell the tale.

The English had lost not a single ship of their 150 and suffered, from enemy action, only 100 casualties. The number who died, or were incapacitated, by sickness was far higher, owing to poor diet and low standards of hygiene. One familiar article, though obviously not the real cause of the trouble, featured in Howard's report of 26 August:

> But, sir, the mariners have a conceit (and I think it is true, and so do all the captains here) that sour drink hath been a great cause of this infection among us; and, sir, for my own part, I know not which way to deal with the mariners to make them rest contented with sour beer.

By now the militia had already been sent home and demobilization of the fleet was in full swing. Its members were very shabbily treated. Like all governments dealing with their fighting men once they are no longer needed, Elizabeth and her ministers subjected Howard and the rest to a penny-pinching inquisition about their recent expenditure. Sir John Hawkins, who had created the navy which had saved the country, complained to Walsingham: 'I would to God I were delivered of the dealing for money,' and Lord Howard found himself forced to pay off the now redundant sailors out of money he impounded, quite irregularly, from Drake's prize the *Rosario*. It was, he wrote, pitiful to see men reduced to beggary and starvation after all they had done for the nation, but, for all his efforts, ill-clad underfed seamen were soon dying in the streets in England as in Spain. Howard himself, establishing a precedent for later commanders who had prevented an invasion, hardly received his due, being blamed rather for not having achieved a more decisive victory; the credit for fending off the Armada tended to go, in the popular mind at least, to Drake.

How well the English army would have acquitted itself if Parma had ever got ashore, one can only speculate. Mendoza, in Paris, had written to Philip II of the 'contemptible English militia'. The militia themselves, as has been seen, were remarkably confident, as men who have never experienced battle usually are, but those who had seen war at first hand knew better. 'They were all wishing to have the Spaniards land, and every man was telling what feats he would,' Sir John Norris, in charge of the army in London, told the queen. 'He was the only man that was trembling for fear of it.' The Earl of Leicester, at Tilbury, who had hitherto only commanded professional soldiers, had shared his fears. 'If her [the queen's] navy had not been strong and abroad . . .' he asked, 'what case had herself and her whole realm been in by this time?'

On 24 August the Council learned that Parma's camp on the Flemish coast had been broken up and his troops had marched inland. They also heard that what was left of the Armada had been sighted off Ireland. The Earl of Leicester hardly lived to enjoy his country's triumph. On 4 September he died, to the queen's great grief, overshadowing for her the round of celebrations which now commenced. Four days later, at a special service at St Paul's, 'eleven ensigns or banners taken from the Spanish fleet . . . were set upon the lower battlements of the church' before being 'hanged on London Bridge towards Southwark'. Tuesday 19 November 1588, just after the anniversary of Elizabeth's accession, was a public holiday, marked by psalm-singing and – this time wholly harmless – bonfires, and on Sunday 24 November there was a great state procession through the City. In Fleet Street the queen was greeted with verses she had written herself:

He made the winds and water rise
To scatter all mine enemies.

Armada medals helped to establish the tradition of the 'Protestant Wind' which kept Britain inviolate, with the inscription *Flavit Deus et dissipati sunt:* God breathed and they were scattered.

Even more pointed was the caption on a cruel caricature of the

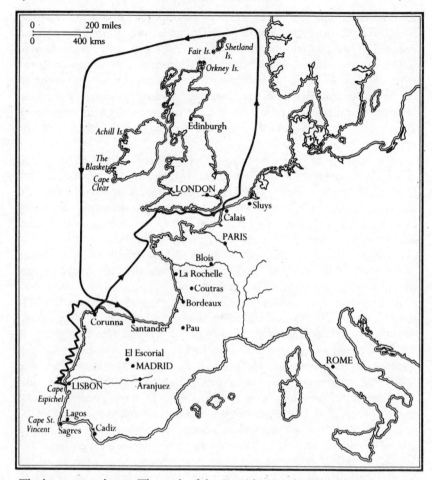

The long voyage home. The track of the Spanish Armada May–September 1588.

Armada, which recalled the boast of England's first invader, Julius Caesar, 'I came, I saw, I conquered'. Now the legend read: 'It came, it saw, it fled'.

40

RAMPANT LIONS

Proud Spain, although our dragon be bereft us,
We, rampant lions, have enough for thee

Charles FitzGeffrey, poem on the death of Sir Francis Drake, *1596*

The defeat of the Spanish Armada did not end the still undeclared war between the two countries. In April 1589 the English government fired the first shots in the post-Armada conflict, by sending an 18,000-men 150-ship expedition to Corunna and Lisbon, under Drake and Sir John Norris, to destroy any surviving vessels which might form the nucleus for another attack on England. They were also, by restoring the pretender Don Antonio, to convert Portugal into a 'Catholic Netherlands'. The force was exceptionally strong, the commanders outstandingly able. However, the harbour at Corunna proved to contain only three ships; only the Lower Town of Corunna, not the more important High Town, was captured and destroyed; and Norris's subsequent march to Lisbon was equally unsuccessful. The Cardinal Archduke Albert, Philip II's viceroy, effectively defended the capital, thereby justifying at least the third part of the *bon mot* attributed to Henry IV, who that year succeeded to the French throne, 'Three things are true but nobody believes them; that the Queen of England is a virgin, that I am a good Catholic and that the Cardinal Archduke is a good general.' Due to adverse winds and that perpetual blight of Tudor navies and armies, sickness, the expedition sailed home after only two months having lost six ships and, from death or desertion, at least 40 per cent of its members. Drake also failed to get to the Azores to set up an 'Atlantic Calais' there and only the dashing 22-year-old Earl of Essex came home with his reputation enhanced, having hung his chain on the gate of Lisbon as a symbol of defiance. The disastrous 1589 expedition not only left Drake personally under a cloud but discredited the whole strategy of attacking the enemy at a distance which he epitomized.

The war against Spanish shipping still continued, but with little success. In 1591 the third attempt in three years to intercept the Spanish merchant fleet near the Azores on its way home achieved little, for Philip II had now realized the value of a convoy system. Seven English ships, waiting at Flores in the Azores for their prey to appear, were surprised by 53 Spanish vessels, sent from Ferrol to escort the treasure ships on the last stage of their journey. Lord Thomas Howard led the rest of the English fleet out to sea, but his vice-admiral, Sir Richard Grenville, chose, or was forced, to stay and fight in Drake's former flagship, the *Revenge*. Grenville was a flamboyant figure, given to ostentatious gestures, and the *Revenge* could probably have got away. In an epic action, lasting for 15 hours from 3 p.m. on 31 August 1591, the small ship held off 16 larger Spanish vessels, including the great *San Felipe*, sinking two of them. With its rigging in ruins, and six feet [1.8 m] of water in the hold Grenville wanted to blow up the ship but the surviving 60 active members of his crew – 40 more were dead and 90 sick – refused, though the battered *Revenge* foundered soon afterwards in a storm. Sir Richard Grenville died of wounds, after some appropriate last words – 'I have ended my life as a good soldier ought to do, who has fought for his country, queen, religion and honour' – and the last stand of the *Revenge* became one of the great English legends, more effective in generating patriotism than a score of victories.

In July 1593 Henry IV of France, anxious to end his country's religious divisions, proclaimed himself a Catholic, on the cynical grounds that 'Paris is worth a mass.' This proved sufficient, however, to unite his country against the Spaniards, who made a determined attempt to hold on to the base they had established at Crozon, commanding the anchorage at Brest. Sir John Norris sent an urgent warning to the queen: 'I think there never happened a more dangerous enterprise . . . than this of the Spaniard to possess Brittany, which . . . I dare presume to say will prove as prejudicial for England as if they had possesed Ireland.'

On 7 November 1594, after a two-month siege, an amphibious force of eight warships under Sir Martin Frobisher (who was killed during the operation) and 4000 men under Norris, stormed and demolished the fort at Crozon, the successful climax of the policy of keeping the Spanish well away from the coast of England.

The danger of invasion remained very real, however. In March 1590 the start of the 'invasion season' saw a revival of drilling by the London trained bands, although by now the smart red coats bought in 1587 were showing signs of wear and everywhere among the militia slackness began to creep in. The better-off now largely boycotted the musters, and sent their servants instead, the latter being glad to deputise, since this removed the risk of being conscripted for service overseas. In 1591 rumours of an impending attack on the Scilly Isles and Cornwall led to some strengthening of the existing defence works there and Drake was made formally responsible for supervising similar construction at Plymouth, resassuring the residents by moving from his country house at Buckland into the city. Drake himself also took the first turn of sentry duty on the newly-refortified St Nicholas Island, now renamed after him.

On 8 February 1593 the Privy Council warned the Earl of Derby, in northern England, that Spanish ships were likely 'to pass the seas betwixt Ireland and England and in their way towards Scotland may surprise the Isle of Man', a new source of anxiety, but when the Spaniards did appear it was at the other end of the country. They still had a foothold at Blavet in Brittany, from which the last British troops had been withdrawn in January 1595 and from there ships were sent out to gather information off Cornwall. On one of these expeditions the Spaniards captured some fishermen from St Keverne, seven miles [11 km] from Falmouth, and when released the Cornishmen brought back the news that four galleys and ten warships had already assembled at Blavet and seven more galleys and another ten warships were expected, their intended destination being the Scilly Isles.

Successive governments had had a somewhat ambivalent attitude to this little group of islands, valuing them as a forward observation post but considering them too exposed to be successfully defended for long. Henry VIII and Edward VI had provided the Scillies with some minor defence works and a small garrison but the emergence of Philip II as the enemy gave them a new importance. The Scillies, as the government's chief informant in the area, Sir Francis Godolphin put it, were 'the fairest inn in the direct way between Spain and Ireland', and in 1593 the government installed six pieces of artillery in a new fort on St Mary's, able to command the little harbour and the sea approaches to it. Its modest garrison, only 27 men in the summer, was reduced to a mere 10 in winter, though another 100 men on the mainland stood ready to go to their assistance when required. Godolphin remained apprehensive, writing to the Earl of Essex on 10 July 1593: 'I rest still of the same mind that it needeth a stronger garrison, for the gathering of those Spaniards seemeth as a cloud that is likely to fall shortly in some part of Her Majesty's dominions.'

But where? All the evidence seemed to point to Cornwall and around 17 July 1595 Spanish galleys were off the north coast at St Eval, near Padstow, a mere ten miles [16 km] by river north-west of the town of Bodmin. Sir Richard Grenville's son assembled the local trained bands and the Spaniards decided not to attempt a landing. Four days later, on 21 July 1595, there was a far more alarming report from St Keverne, on the other side of the peninsula, of '60 sail of ships within the Manacles', the rocks just off the shore, and Godolphin learned next day, 'after sunset, these ships made in to the sea somewhat east of our harbour . . . to the number of twenty sail or upwards and afterwards hovered up and down.' In the end, when the blow finally fell, it was on a much smaller scale and 22 miles [35 km] further west. Shortly after dawn on Wednesday 23 July 1595 four large galleys, part of the force based at Blavet, under the command of Don Diego Borchen, loomed up out of the morning mist off the tiny fishing village of Mousehole [pronounced 'Mowzel'] and landed 200 men, armed with pikes and firearms, an equal number remaining aboard. The landing party set fire to the buildings and those of the adjoining hamlets, and the inhabitants fled ingloriously; Godolphin encountered 200 of them 'naked', i.e. unarmed and unar-moured, on the green outside Penzance, two miles [3 km] to the north. He immediately sent a messenger to Plymouth to alert Drake and Hawkins, then preoccupied with preparing for their next expedition to the West Indies, and bravely announced his intention of expelling the Spaniards once he had mustered sufficient men. 'I attend the coming of more and so to make head towards the enemy.'

The humiliation of Spanish soldiers landing unopposed on English soil so soon after the defeat of the Armada was deeply felt by Godolphin and, later, by the queen herself. Even worse, the locals displayed increasing signs of panic and left the initiative to Don Diego. Having destroyed everything in sight around Mousehole he now re-embarked his men and then landed his whole force, 400-strong, at Newlyn, halfway between Mousehole and Penzance, which was burned, sending a reconnaissance patrol to the top of the nearby hill and deciding, once he learned how weak the opposing forces were, to attack Penzance. The local militia, designed to cope with just this type of situation, melted away at the first shot, including the elite trained bands. 'I speak it to the disgrace of those people,' wrote a local resident to Drake, while Sir Francis Godolphin, trying to make a stand in the market place at Penzance, found himself having to threaten the runaways with his rapier; only a handful of his own servants stood firm alongside him. After Godolphin had been forced to withdraw the Spaniards set fire to Penz-ance and, so it was said, celebrated mass on the hill to the west of the town, swearing to return and build a friary there when they had finally conquered England, before withdrawing to their galleys.

By the evening of 23 July 1585 a fair-sized force had been assembled by Godolphin on the green outside Marazion, three miles [5 km] east of Penzance, anticipating a further landing next day. On Thursday 24 July the Spaniards did approach the west side of Mounts Bay, but retreated at the sight of the force assembled, merely disembarking some English prisoners captured earlier to welcome them. On Friday, not before time, several captains sent by Drake arrived from Plymouth, and some of his ships reached the Lizard, at the eastern end of Mounts Bay, intending to cut off the enemy's retreat. They had only just taken up their station, however, when the wind veered suddenly from south-east to north-west and the galleys seized the chance to make their escape.

The Mousehole landing was a disagreeable shock to the English authorities. The prisoners released by the Spaniards revealed that their captors had intended to go on to attack St Ives and Padstow and after that to ravage the Bristol Channel area; only shortage of fresh water and fear of Drake's fleet had caused a change of plan. They had also hoped to capture the Scilly Isles, news that added strength to Godolphin's pleas for stronger defences there. Far more serious, however, was the timorous conduct of the local militia. As one Cornish nobleman commented, 'The town of Penzance, had the people stood with Sir Francis Godolphin . . . had been saved; but the common sort utterly forsook him.'

Following this shameful episode Lord Burghley himself undertook a new, detailed study of the defences of Cornwall. Sir Walter Raleigh, as Lord-Lieutenant, was sent down to his native country to supervise the training of the militia and his deputy-lieutenants instructed to review arrangements for protecting the numerous small ports, and especially the division of the available manpower into those required for local defence and those earmarked for the mobile force required to respond to threats elsewhere. Large-scale strategic movements were also planned. Devon was to send 4000 men westwards into Cornwall if an enemy appeared there, and similar arrangements for mutual aid were laid down for Somerset and Dorset.

The Spanish fleet did not in fact get off scot-free from the Cornish expedition. On the way home it chased 14 merchantmen described as 'hulks' and in the resulting fight suffered 140 casualties and lost one of the four offending galleys. Drake and Hawkins were meanwhile absorbed in fitting out their ships for the coming voyage to the Spanish Main, although the queen feared that a full-scale invasion might be impending. Eventually she allowed them to go to Puerto Rico, as planned, but only on condition they were both back within six months.

This was one royal command that was not fulfilled. The expedition duly left Plymouth on 29 August 1595, but Hawkins died of sickness that December before its destination was reached, and Drake, still in his fifties, succumbed to a fever, after pleading to be dressed in his armour that he might die like a soldier, on 27 January 1596. He was buried at sea off Puerto Bello in Panama. When the news reached Spain Philip II was said to have smiled broadly for the first time since he had heard of the massacre of the Huguenots, and Seville was illuminated. In England, in which the expedition, having achieved nothing substantial, arrived back during April and May, there was lamentation and dismay. That year the first commemorative poem in Drake's honour was published, striking a suitably defiant note:

> Proud Spain, although our dragon be bereft us,
> We, rampant lions, have enough for thee.

But already Drake's absence was being felt. In March 1596 the Spaniards made another landing in Cornwall, this time on the approaches to Plymouth in Cawsand Bay, where a pinnace landed a small party of men to blow up Cawsand village. Their reception was very different from that at Mousehole, for the appearance of a single man armed with a caliver was enough to drive them off, before they could light the train of powder already laid. The insult, however, was widely felt: 'What a valiant exploit it was,' commented one Londoner, 'to come into our own coast under Sir Francis's nose; and that within one fortnight after they came within twenty miles of Plymouth and there burnt a house, and after came to a gentleman's house and set a barrel of gunpowder to his gate.' This latter reference seems to be to yet another landing, alleged to have taken place in the Pendennis area, where the leading local citizen who also commanded the militia and who had frequently complained to the government about the weakness of the area, was said to have been a target. The fishermen from Penrhyn forced to act as guides to the Spaniards later described the intruders' activities: 'They landed near the castle and tried to fire it . . . They had twelve barrels of like fireworks to [place] gang aboard ships in harbour, and fire another house near, and to carry away Killigrew's wife and children.'

Whatever the truth of this strange story, the Killigrew family escaped the kidnappers, but a little later in 1596 another landing occurred in west Wales. Little is recorded about it, but it appears that, after an unopposed reconnaissance, a second Spanish detachment landed somewhere on the coast of Merionethshire only to be ambushed by a force raised by the local justices, which killed two of the enemy and captured four more. The trained bands, well dug in, were prepared to give a good account of themselves and the defenders fired on the enemy ship and attempted to set it on fire, but thanks to a change of wind it got away, 'leaving us most sorrowful,' one of the defenders recorded, 'that our care and diligence took not better successes.'

During the opening months of 1596 a new armada seemed increasingly likely to appear, perhaps following the same plan as in 1588 but under more favourable conditions, for in April the Cardinal Archduke Albert, Philip II's viceroy in the Netherlands, confirmed Henry IV's belief that he was a good general by capturing Calais from the French after a mere three-week siege. Calais in Spanish hands was even more a threat to

England than Flanders and the government responded with the self-same strategy that had succeeded in 1587, a pre-emptive strike against the home port from which a new armada might sail to this conveniently placed base, Cadiz. The expedition which set sail from Plymouth on 1 June 1596 was the best equipped and best led of the whole reign. In command, on the naval side, were the Lord High Admiral [Charles] Howard, with Lord Thomas Howard as his subordinate; on the military, the 29-year-old Earl of Essex, aided by Sir Walter Raleigh.

The expedition consisted of 82 ships, 17 from the navy, 47 privately owned and 18 Dutch, carrying 6-8000 men. Its arrival at Cadiz, on 20 June, took the Spaniards by surprise. Two galleons of the largest, 'apostles', class were destroyed and two others captured. Even more hurtful to Spanish pride, this time the king of Spain had to singe his own beard, for the Spaniards' offer of two million ducats ransom [£50,000] if the 50 merchant vessels, with cargoes valued at twelve million ducats [£5,640,000] were spared, was refused, and they thereupon set them on fire. Exceeding even Drake's achievements the attackers then captured the town, on the queen's instructions letting the population leave before it was looted and destroyed.

Essex would have liked to keep Cadiz as a permanent English base on Spain's doorstep but he was overruled and after holding it for a fortnight the English left and by 8 August were back in Plymouth, covered in glory.

While Howard and Essex were at sea Elizabeth's ministers had been preparing for home defence. The Lords-Lieutenant and other prominent gentry were ordered to remain in their counties, captains were appointed to put the coastal forts in a state of readiness, government commissioners were sent out to check the muster-books and the previous arrangements for mutual help between the various shires were revived. The dispositions of forces, with armies earmarked to defend London and protect the person of the queen, were also similar to those of 1588 and, learning from the experience of Leicester's camp at Tilbury, for the first time a 'general of victuals' was appointed to oversee the commissariat.

The warning system, although its backbone remained the proven beacon system, was also overhauled. The standing orders for the rousing of the Chatham area were particularly elaborate. A ketch on standing patrol off Sheerness would notify the nearest pinnace, which, having given a general alarm by firing three guns, would then race up-river to Chatham, giving the news en route to Upnor and other fortified spots, and the beacon watchers at Chatham and Barrow Hill. Another ship, waiting at the entrance to St Mary's Creek, would then fire three guns, repeated by the *Mary Rose*, moored at Rochester Bridge. Thereupon the militia were to mobilize at Chatham Church and Upnor Castle, mounted dispatch riders being sent from Chatham to alert places out of cannon or beacon range.

The Duke of Parma had died in December 1592 and his place in the Netherlands had been taken by the Cardinal Archduke Albert, who had successfully rebuffed the Lisbon expedition of 1589. Otherwise nothing had changed, except perhaps for the worse, since the Spaniards now also possessed Calais and Blavet in Brittany. The government believed that, learning from earlier experience, Philip's admiral would this time attempt to seize a base in England, its chief concern being once again the Isle of Wight. In October 1596 six companies of 150 men from Hampshire and Wiltshire were assigned to its defence, though the Captain of the Island, Lord Hunsdon, complained late in November that they were 'unable persons, ill armed and apparelled and', worst of all, 'long a coming'. The Governor of Portsmouth was little more flattering about the 2000 men earmarked to reinforce his regular garrison, for, he told the Council, 'he look'd not to find 600 of them well arm'd, not one leader able to direct or scarce even to obey, nor any of those spirits,' i.e. able and enterprising soldiers, 'who must always be mixed with those companies.' Conditions in the West Country were generally better, thanks to Sir Walter Raleigh's visitation following the Mousehole landing of July 1595, but even here there were still shortages of both cannon and small arms. The local resident responsible for the defence of St Mawes protested that he would not live there himself 'unless I have better supply', asking for another eight pieces of artillery. When, along with Killigrew of Pendennis, survivor of the alleged attempt to kidnap his family in 1596, he assembled 270 men from the five neighbouring parishes, 50 arrived unarmed, while one of the five, Penryn, complained that removing its militia-men left it defenceless. The Privy Council invited Raleigh to settle the dispute, 'not meaning,' they explained, not very helpfully, 'that the said parishes should be utterly disfurnished of their own safeguard or molested unnecessarily with service or attendence on Mr Killigrew.' Killigrew delivered a vigorous riposte, pointing out that, despite his best efforts, 'those five parishes are not prepared for war, nor have provided arms, nor keep watch as they should . . . Thus the castle is in continual danger.' The basic problem, a familiar one, was that everyone wanted strong defences but nobody, least of all the government, wanted to pay for them, and there was the usual resentment of any outsider telling the local men how to do their job. At Plymouth the government did put up £800 to finish the defence works already in progress, but there was a sharp quarrel between the town authorities and the commander of the fort over supervising the actual expenditure.

While the English were indulging in the luxury of squabbling among themselves Philip II had actually launched a second armada, as a direct reprisal for the disastrous attack on Cadiz. On 13 October 1596 a fleet of about 100 ships and 16,000 men set sail from the River Tagus under the governor of Castile, know as the *Adelantado*. It had been hastily raised from inferior troops but these were destined never to challenge the English militia, for the fleet was dispersed by a heavy gale only four days later, off Cape Finisterre; nearly half the ships were wrecked, with heavy loss of life, while the soldiers who survived deserted as soon as they were safe in harbour. Whether the destination was Calais, en route for England, or Ireland, was never discovered, but on 28 November 1596 the alarm was officially acknowledged to be over, Lord Hunsdon being ordered to return his 900 extra soldiers from the Isle of Wight to the mainland.

In January 1597 the English government learned that Philip was forming a new fleet for yet a third armada, and once again the national defences were overhauled. The Earl of Essex, who had played a leading part during the recent alarm and, despite his glamorous reputation, was no mere playboy but a serious soldier, urged that the 'trained band' principle be applied still further, with a much smaller mobile force under regional, not local, commanders, consisting of the 'cream of the cream' among the men, and numbering no more than 5000. The remainder of the militia would need to be stiffened by professionals drawn from the Low Countries:

> Ther numbers do for the most part consist of artificers and clownes who know nothing of the warres and little of the armes they carry, so as, to make them keepe ther orders in embattling or to do ther dutyes ether upon ther gardes or in any service, we must have as many officers as wee have soldiers; ther leaders [are] men of quality dwelling neere, butt as insufficient comonly as ther soldiers; the furniture [i.e. armour] only fitt to hang over the skereene in a halle.

Essex now worked out an elaborate scheme for dividing the country up into districts, which reported in turn to counties or groups of counties, with professional officers in charge, preferably men with local connections acceptable to the resident gentry. He also put in hand a programme of more concentrated training: the Cornish militia, for example, after training at Bodmin in June 1597, were given experience of life in the field by a week's camp at Truro. In October English troops were brought back from France for home defence, and others recalled from Brill, Ostend and Flushing to provide the first line of resistance along the south coast. Essex told Secretary of State Cecil that 100 regular soldiers were worth 1000 trained militia-men, and showed his assessment of the likeliest areas of danger by his allocation of the troops brought back from Europe. A detachment of 200 were sent to Portsmouth, another

200 to Dartmouth, but 900 to Plymouth, now thought to be the likeliest objective, and 200 to Falmouth. Any troops left over could go to the Isle of Wight or the Channel Islands, the poor relation among defence zones.

As always, each local commander tended to think his area was in the greatest danger, and Sir Walter Raleigh, who had begun a detailed study of the defences of Cornwall following the Mousehole fiasco of 1595, pressed its claims hard. Surrounded by the sea and the River Tamar, the county, he pointed out, was almost an island, and sub-divided by three deep estuaries which made internal reinforcement difficult:

> There is no part of England so dangerously seated, so thinly manned, so little defended and so easily invaded, having the sea on both sides, which no other county in England hath, and is withal so narrow that if an enemy possess any of the two or three straits, neither can those of the west repair eastward nor those of the east westward.

Raleigh suggested that Falmouth, the most westerly deepwater port, was even more exposed to attack than Plymouth, 45 miles [72 km] up-Channel:

> [The estuary of the River Fal] is as much of Cornwall as the enemy should need, for within so much as lieth to the west . . . are the best ports, and are very sufficient to receive the greatest fleet that ever swam, and containeth 27 miles [43 km] of length very guardable, which in my simple judgement is every way more to be sought by the enemy than Plymouth.

With rumours reaching Cornwall of a 100-strong armada almost ready to sail, and Spanish warships active in the Channel, to disrupt the enemy's preparations, Essex and Raleigh were, in July 1597, despatched from Plymouth to El Ferrol with 98 ships and 5000 men. Once they had burned the armada in port, or intercepted and destroyed it at sea, they were to steer for the Azores and capture the Spanish *flota*, or annual home-bound treasure fleet. Neither objective was achieved. The English force had hardly got to the mouth of the Channel when it was dispersed by a great storm, the two commanders, appropriately enough as they did not get on, ending up at Falmouth and Plymouth respectively.

On 17 August 1597 they set off again, on the so-called 'Islands Voyage' and would no doubt have wrought great execution if they had ever got to grips with the enemy. Unfortunately, having failed to get to El Ferrol at all, they got to the Azores too late and during October, while they were on their battered and quarrelsome way home, the Spanish commander, the *Adelantado*, had put out of Ferrol with 136 ships and 9000 troops. His destination, exactly as Raleigh had predicted, was Falmouth, where he hoped to set up a Spanish base on English soil. The

immediate Spanish objective was the Pendennis promontory, strategically important since prehistoric times: the name 'Pen Dinas' meant
'fortress headland'. Henry VIII had built a fort there capable of mounting
30 cannon, which was supported by the 'Little Dennis' artillery blockhouse, equipped with a long-range, seaward-facing gun, and these the
Spaniards planned to seize by assault, perhaps making a simultaneous
attack on St Mawes, another Henrican castle, on the other side of the
bay. The two together commanded the entrance to the Carrick Roads
and Falmouth Bay and, once established there, the *Adelantado* planned to
make his position impregnable on the landward side by digging a great
ditch across the peninsula. From this secure haven his ships would be
sent to wait off the Scilly Isles to destroy the returning English fleet,
then, with this accomplished, his troops would march on Plymouth.

The preparations on land revealed many deficiencies. Lord Hunsdon,
in Hampshire, was shocked to find that the trained bands had not been
mustered for the past year and did not even have an adequate list of
qualified pikemen or shot, 'alleging,' he reported to London, 'the usual
exchange and departure out of the country of servants at Michaelmas.'
To get reinforcements to the Isle of Wight would take five or six days,
an absurdly long time. The panic which swept London when, on 23
October 1597, the news arrived via Plymouth that the latest armada was
at sea was well founded – or would have been had not the Spanish fleet
by then, while within two days' sail of Land's End, been scattered by a
sudden storm and forced back to Spain. Only those ships unable to see
the recall signal arrived in sight of the English coast and, finding
themselves alone, hastily turned back.

Raleigh and Essex got home safely soon afterwards from their futile
expedition and threw themselves ostentatiously into strengthening the
defences on land against a danger which their absence had created. Essex,
with his recent miseries on board ship in mind, boastfully declared that
'though we eat ropes' ends and drink nothing but rain-water, we
will . . . make a final end of this proud nation,' while Raleigh, belatedly
remembering that he was Lord-Lieutenant of Cornwall, hastily mustered
500 men to defend Pendennis, which was now discovered – both sides,
had as usual, been thoroughly indiscreet – to have been the Spaniards'
objective. Necessary though this was, it imposed a heavy burden on a
poor and thinly-populated county, as Sir Francis Godolphin pointed out:

> Our country people do and will much repine at the burden of
> maintaining these small forces of 400 or 500 at Penryn . . . What
> speak I of beggarly country [i.e. county] aid against prince's royal
> armies, which cannot but by our prince's purse and munition be
> resisted.

Slowly such ideas were gaining ground, but individual citizens, as well as whole communities, were still encouraged to finance the nation's defences out of their own pockets. A well-off man who lived by the quay at Fowey, midway between Falmouth and Plymouth, built a site for an artillery battery beside his house and himself equipped it with guns, whereupon Sir Walter Raleigh exempted this public-spirited enthusiast from all liability for the usual watching and mustering. He was to be permitted instead to assemble a little private army, drawn from his family, servants and a dozen tenants. Increasingly, too, the sheer cost both of fortifications, no longer, unlike medieval castles, used as residences, and of cannon was forcing the government to accept the whole burden, though they still attempted to provide some of the finance from local resources. The narrow escape of Pendennis had given the government a great shock; 9000 Spanish professionals – some estimates put the total at 20,000 – would surely have been able to drive 500 ill-armed amateurs from the existing inadequate fortifications, and once in possession would have controlled the approaches to Falmouth. As soon as the true nature of the Spanish plan was understood in London, a trusted military subordinate of Essex, Sir Ferdinando Gorges, was sent down to inspect the site. His report added to the existing anxiety: 'It is now the [most] dangerous place that ever I saw, and the worst provided for. If the enemy should descend there before these defences be made, I protest I do not see . . . how without great difficulty they will be gotten out again.'

The government reacted energetically. Four companies of soldiers were despatched to guard Falmouth as an interim measure, the colonel in command being made a deputy-lieutenant of the county, to give him additional status, and new fortifications were commissioned from a specialist engineer. The initial work was financed, as similar construction at Plymouth had been, from a special levy on exported pilchards and by other charges on the customs in the area. The estimated cost of £1000 was soon exceeded, thanks, the engineer explained, to the 'exceeding hardness of the work' which involved employing 400 labourers to build, often on 'main rock', trenches and walls around the whole most exposed area and a bulwark to command the harbour. In the end the estimate was exceeded by 100 per cent and a further £191 had to be found for ordnance.

The continuing threat from Spain, so expensive to the government, at least kept the amateur strategists happy. In 1597 one martially-minded knight, Sir George Knyvett, proposed in a pamphlet, *The Defence of the Realm,* that remedy so appealing to retired military men, that all male civilians should have to undergo compulsory military training, setting the age limits at 18 to 50. But some authors still failed to appreciate the changing nature of war and concentrated on such trivial irrelevancies as the hallowed rituals of siege warfare: the herald demanding the city's surrender, it was explained in one book first published in 1576 and still in use, must sound his trumpet three times, while the defending commander, in declining, must be sure to give him a present. This had been all very well in the Middle Ages when so much fighting was a mere ritualized charade, often between a king and his subjects, and it seemed to matter little who won or lost. Now warfare, like other aspects of life, had come of age and on the outcome of a battle the very survival of the nation might depend. Matthew Sutcliffe, in *The Practice, Proceedings and Lawes of Armes* in 1593, advanced the revolutionary idea that the commanding general, instead of trying to fight on equal terms with his opponent, should give himself every possible advantage, for example by attacking with the wind behind him to blow dust in the enemy's eyes. He even advocated such underhand tactics as smuggling soldiers into a town dressed as clowns sent to entertain the garrison, or women, or hidden under straw in carts, a Tudor variant on that most ancient of devices, the wooden horse, but the guiding principle that Sutcliffe urged on his readers was one valid for military commanders in every century: 'Opportunity to do great matters seldom offereth itself the second time.'

Although even forward-thinking writers like Sutcliffe still gave archers a role on the battlefield, by now the revolution wrought by gunpowder was almost complete; the bow seemed likely to follow the mechanical siege-engine into oblivion. In 1588 the men who turned up so armed at Tilbury had rapidly thrown their bows away as useless and in the following year the Council laid down that the ideal 100-strong company would contain 60 men equipped with firearms, 30 with pikes and ten with halberds or bills. The excuse for not mentioning bowmen was that the bow was such a 'natural weapon of the realm' that archers could easily be formed into separate units, but by 1595 they were being described as 'able men untrained' and were being taught how to use calivers, the standard small-arm, some three-and-a-half feet [1.6 m] long, and muskets, much more unwieldy, as they were a foot [0.3 m] longer and had to be fired from a rest, but far more effective, as their bullets could penetrate armour. By this time, too, the primitive, short-barrelled weapons, the dag and the slightly larger petronel, favoured by cavalry, were being replaced by the longer, and more accurate, carbine. By 1600 the bow was, for practical purposes, a museum piece.

Tactics lagged behind technology. The musket demanded, because of its size and the time taken to load and aim it, an essentially defensive approach, and much smaller units than the massed ranks appropriate for hand weapons, but formations remained large and most training revolved round massive manoeuvres more impressive to admiring civilians than to a potential enemy. But at least the need for field-works on the battlefield, to protect the somewhat immobile arquebusier or musketeer, was understood; by the end of the century every 100 militia-men were supposed to be supported by at least 20 pioneers, as well as the customary smiths, carpenters and wheelwrights.

As the old ways vanished with the dying century the international situation also changed. In May 1598, to Elizabeth's great indignation, Henry IV of France concluded a separate peace with Philip II of Spain in the Treaty of Vervins, though it had its benefits for England since both Calais and Blavet were now restored to France. The Netherlands was now separated from Spain under the Cardinal Archduke Albert, though the seven northern provinces claimed to be an independent, Dutch, state, unrecognized as such by Spain. That year, too, saw the death, in August, of Elizabeth's greatest minister, Lord Burghley, followed, in September, by that of Philip II. His successor, Philip III, continued the war against England and July 1599 brought the most serious invasion threat since the Armada. The new king was said to have assembled 100 sailing ships and 70 galleys, carrying 15-16,000 men, and that month and for much of August all the old precautions were taken. On 1 August 1599 the Council ordered the blocking of the Thames with ships and the mobilization of 3000 men for the immediate defence of London. Ulti-mately it was planned to have 25,000 there by 12 August, raised, by additional volunteers and contingents paid for by the nobility, to 27,000, plus 300 horsemen, and as the men, from 8 August, began to reach the capital they were billeted in the suburbs. There was talk of a new camp at Tilbury, as in 1588, linked to one in Kent, but neither was actually set up, and an attempt to build a bridge of boats across the Thames on the London side of Gravesend, as a combined highway and boom, proved a failure, the local commander settling instead for blocking the river by sinking hulks on the river bed.

The 1599 alarm revealed a different spirit in the country from that of 1588. The heroic attitudes of ten years before had given way to a resentment of the expense and disruption anti-invasion preparations involved and the government over-reacted with wild warnings of the death penalty for people failing to turn out for the muster or to provide arms and armour. In fact all that happened to some wealthy residents who refused to send their servants to Portsmouth was a stiff letter of reproof.

Although the government began standing down the county forces from 17 August, the Devon men being sent home that day, to their great relief, to get on with the harvest, and the Hampshire forces on the Isle of Wight being released on the following day, the alarm was far from over, and rumours of an approaching Spanish fleet led to the

London horse being recalled on 23 August, and the trained bands, much to their discomfort, being kept under arms all day in heavy rain. At 2 a.m. on Monday 27 August 1599, a letter reached one commander in Hampshire ordering him to reassemble the dispersed militia and ship them back across the Solent, grumbling about the alarm which 'disturbed our sleepe and made us to disturbe the moste part of England'. The cause this time was a well-intentioned message from the governor of Brest that he had sighted a Spanish fleet moving up-Channel which turned out to be a harmless convoy of Flemish merchantmen. Less justified were the stories of an impending attack up the Thames by Philip III's galleys, which kept the Londoners training until 4 September. By then the danger was recognized to be over. The 'invisible armada', as it became known, had in fact barely existed.

During 1600 the Council made clear that the danger from Spain was over, the militia being reduced to two musters a year instead of the former minimum of six, and, at most, one or two days' training. England was now to be harassed in a new, but yet all too familiar, quarter. Ever since 1593 unrest in Ireland had been mounting under Hugh O'Neill, Earl of Tyrone, who in that year first approached Philip II for help. For various reasons it was not until September 1601 that 33 Spanish ships carrying a force estimated at from 3–5000 finally arrived at the tiny town of Kinsale in Munster, 14 miles [22 km] due south of Cork and about 150 [240 km] south-west of Dublin.

The campaign that followed ended on 2 January 1602 when the Spanish commander in Kinsale capitulated on condition the English would repatriate his men. He left Ireland without regret, declaring 'This land seems destined specially for the princes of hell.' The rebellion now collapsed and at the end of March 1603 O'Neill himself surrendered unconditionally. For the first time Ireland had been totally subjugated and, it seemed, could now be incorporated for good within the English governmental system.

A few days before O'Neill's submission the great queen had, unknown to him, died on 24 March 1603. She was 69. Within a few hours, without dissension, her chosen successor, James VI of Scotland, who now became James I of England, was proclaimed king. Sixteen hundred years after Caesar's first appearance on its shores and 500 after William the Conqueror's arrival, the British Isles were at last united under a single ruler, with a common, if not yet universally spoken, language. As one of the many writers who suddenly burst into distinction in Elizabeth's reign, Thomas Dekker, observed, the nation 'was almost begotten and born under her'.

In November 1601 Queen Elizabeth had delivered, to her last parliament, what became known as her 'golden speech':

Ireland, 1066–1603.

And though God hath raised me high, yet this I account the glory of my crown, that I have reigned with your loves. I do not so much rejoice that God hath made me to be a queen, as to be a Queen over so thankful a people, and to be the means under God to conserve you in safety and to preserve you from danger.

Here was the sovereign's first duty defined: without freedom from invasion no peace or progress was possible, and that security, it was at last realized in Elizabeth's reign, lay upon the sea. As yet no colonies had been established overseas, but already English seamen had penetrated to Africa and Asia as well as the Americas and, along with the soldiers, given the English race the national heroes – Raleigh, Sidney, Grenville, Drake – who were to inspire future generations and to be remembered whenever some new foreign tyrant threatened.

The other great source of national inspiration bequeathed by Elizabeth's reign was the literature created by the poets, prose-writers and dramatists who in its later years appeared in a profusion and richness unprecedented before and unequalled since, above all William Shakespeare, who was still only 38 when Queen Elizabeth died. Many of his themes were drawn from English history; he made his debut as a writer with *Henry VI Part I*, around 1591. It was in, or about 1595, that an audience heard for the first time the famous lines from *King Richard II*, delivered by John of Gaunt, which have ever since represented the classic statement of their country's unique situation:

> This fortress built by Nature for herself
> Against infection and the hand of war;
> This happy breed of men, this little world;
> This precious stone set in the silver sea
> Which serves it in the office of a wall
> Or as a moat defensive to a house,
> Against the envy of less happier lands.

In the end, as in the beginning, what mattered was the sea.

A NOTE ON SOURCES

The list of books which follows is comprehensive and includes all those, except a few standard reference works, which I have consulted. Those which relate to a specific chapter or subject will generally be self-evident. The chronicler from whom an extract is taken is identified in the text, and where he or she is not named, is the last source cited. By reference to the date it should therefore be possible, even without detailed page references, to trace the original passage without great difficulty. Where no separate text is shown below the extract is taken from the relevant volume of *English Historical Documents* or from one of the other anthologies mentioned. Lack of space has compelled me, reluctantly, to omit the sources of the very brief quotations given in the text but the source is invariably a contemporary, since I have tried to avoid quoting from secondary sources, i.e. other historians writing long after the events described. Similarly, non-historical writers have not been quoted until after the narrative has reached a point where their work would be familiar to contemporaries, e.g. Shakespeare is only drawn on *after* his plays had been performed in public. In quoting sources I have normally used the edition most readily available to the non-academic reader, often a recent paperback. Where there are substantial differences between editions of a book I have indicated both the original date of publication and that of the text I have used. The place of publication is London, unless otherwise stated, or, in the case of the Oxford University Press and Clarendon Press, Oxford.

Acts of the Privy Council 1587–88, Vol. XV, *1588*, Vol. XVI, HMSO 1897.

ALEXANDER, Michael Van Cleave, *The First of the Tudors, A Study of Henry VII and his Reign*, Croome Helm, 1981.

APPLEBY, John T., *John, King of England*, Alfred Knopf, New York, 1959.

ASHLEY, Maurice, *The Life and Times of King John*, Weidenfeld and Nicolson, 1972.

ASHLEY, W. J. (ed.), *Edward III and his Wars 1327–1360*, 1887.

ALCOCK, Leslie, *Arthur's Britain. History and Archaeology AD 367–634*, Penguin, 1971.

BACON, Francis: see LUMBY

BAMFORD, Frances (ed.), *A Royalist Notebook. The Commonplace Book of Sir John Oglander Kt, 1585–1655*, Constable, 1936. [See also LONG for an earlier version of the same memoirs.]

BARBER, Richard (ed.), *The Life and Campaigns of the Black Prince from Contemporary Letters, Diaries and Chronicles, including Chandos Herald's Life of the Black Prince*, Folio Society, 1979.

BARBOUR: See MACKENZIE

BARROW, G. W. S., *Robert Bruce and the Community of the Realm in Scotland*, Eyre and Spottiswoode, 1965.

Bartholomew's Gazetteer of Britain, 1986 edition.

BERNERS, Lord (trans.), *The Chronicles of Froissart, edited and reduced into one volume by G. C. Macaulay*, 1895, republished Macmillan, 1930.

BIRLEY, Anthony (trans.), *The Lives of the Later Caesars*, Penguin, 1976.

BLACK, J. B., *The Reign of Elizabeth, 1558–1603*, Clarendon Press, 1936.

BOUCHER-JAMES, E., *The Isle of Wight. Letters Archaeological and Historical*, Vol. I, 1896.

BOWLE, John, *Henry VIII. A Biography*, Allen and Unwin, 1964.

BOYNTON, Lindsay, *The Elizabethan Militia 1558–1638*, Routledge and Kegan Paul, 1967.

BRACKEN, C. W., *A History of Plymouth and her Neighbours*, Plymouth, 1931.

BRADFORD, Ernle, *Julius Caesar. The Pursuit of Power*, Hamish Hamilton, 1984.

BREEZE, David, *The Northern Frontiers of Roman Britain*, Batsford Academic, 1982.

BROWN, P. Hume, *A Short History of Scotland*, Oliver and Boyd, 1951.

BRYANT, Arthur, *The Story of England. Makers of the Realm*, Collins, 1953.

——, *The Elizabethan Deliverance*, Collins, 1980.

BUSCH, Dr Wilhelm (trans. Alice M. Todd), *England under the Tudors, Vol. I, 1485–1509*, 1895.

Calendar of State Papers, Domestic, 1595–1597, Vol. IV, HMSO, 1869.

Calendar of State Papers, Foreign, Elizabeth I *1586–1588*, Vol. XXI, HMSO 1927–1931.

CAMPBELL, Alastair, *Encomium Emma Reginae*, Camden 3rd series, Voi. LXXXIX, Royal Historical Society, 1949.

CAMPBELL, James, *The Anglo-Saxons, Phaidon Press, Oxford*, 1982.

CAPPER, D. P., *Moat Defensive. A History of the Waters of the Nore Command, 55 BC to 1961*, Arthur Barker, 1963.

CARY, Earnest [sic] (trans.) *Dio's Roman History*, 9 vols, Heinemann, 1961.

CHANCELLOR, John, *The Life and Times of Edward I*, Weidenfeld, 1981

CHAPMAN, Hester W., *The Last Tudor King. A Study of Edward VI*, Cape, 1961.

CHEVALLIER, C. T. (ed.) and others, *The Norman Conquest. Its Setting and Impact*, Eyre and Spottiswoode, 1966.

CHIBNALL, Marjorie (ed.), *The Ecclesiastical History of Orderic Vitalis*, 6 vols, Clarendon Press, 1969–79.

CHRIMES, S. B., *Henry VII*, Eyre Methuen, 1972.

CLARKE, C.P.S., *Every Man's Book of Saints*, Mowbray, Oxford, 1952.

CLIVE, Mary, *This Sun of York. A Biography of Edward IV*, Macmillan, 1973.

COLLINGWOOD, R. G. and MYRES J. N. L., *Roman Britain and the English Settlements*, Clarendon Press, 2dn ed. 1937.

COLVIN, H. M. (ed), *The History of the King's Works*, vols I–IV HMSO, 1963. See also: HALE.

COTTRELL, Leonard, *The Great Invasion. How the Romans Conquered Britain*, Evans Bros, 1958.

CREASY, E. S., *The Invasions and the Projected Invasions of England from the Saxon Times. With Remarks on the Present Emergencies*, 1852.

CRUICKSHANK, G. C., *Elizabeth's Army*, Clarendon Press, 2nd ed, 1966.

D'AUVERGNE, Edmund B., *John, King of England*, Grayson and Grayson, 1924.

DAVIES, J. D. Griffith, *King Henry IV*, Arthur Barker, 1935.

DENHOLM-YOUNG., N. (ed.), *Vita Edwardi Secundi. The Life of Edward the Second by the so-called Monk of Malmesbury*, Nelson, 1957.

DIGGES, Thomas, *Stratioticos. An Arithmetical Warlike Treatise*, 1579, rev. 1590.

DONNELLY, J. A., A Study of the Coastal Forts built by Henry VIII, in *Fort*, Vol. 10, 1982.

DOUGLAS, David C. and GREENAWAY G. W. (eds), *English Historical Documents 1042–1189,* Eyre Methuen, 1981.

DUDLEY, Donald R. and WEBSTER, Graham, *The Rebellion of Boudicca*, Routledge, 1962.

EARLE, Peter, *The Life and Times of Henry V*, Weidenfeld, 1972.

ELLIS, Peter Berresford, *Caesar's Invasion of Britain*, Orbis Publishing, 1978.

ERICKSON, Carolly, *Bloody Mary*, Dent, 1978.

——, *Great Harry*, Dent, 1980.

EVANS, Joan (ed.), *The Unconquered Knight, A Chronicle of the Deeds of Don Pero Nino, Count of Buelna*, Routledge, 1928.

FALKUS, Gila, *The Life and Times of Edward IV*, Weidenfeld, 1981.

FALKUS, Malcolm, and GILLINGHAM, John (eds), *Historical Atlas of Britain*, Grisewood and Dempsey, 1981.

FEILING, Keith, *A History of England*, 1950, Book Club Associates, 1974.

FISHER, H. A. L., *The History of England from the Accession of Henry VII to the Death of Henry VIII, 1485–1547*, Longmans, 1906.

——, *A History of Europe*, Edward Arnold, 1936.

FLOWER, Kenneth (ed.), *The Hundred Years War*, Macmillan, 1971.

FOORD, Edward and HOME, Gordon, *The Invasion of England*, A. and C. Black, 1915.

FORESTER, Thomas (ed.), *The Chronicles of Henry of Huntingdon*, 1853.

——, *The Chronicle of Florence of Worcester with the two Continuations*, 1854.

Fort. Journal of the Fortress Study Group.

FORTESCUE, Sir John W., *A History of the British Army*, Vol. I, *To the Close of the Seven Years War* [i.e. 1713], Macmillan, 1910.

FOWLER, Kenneth (ed.), *The Hundred Years War*, Macmillan, 1971.

FOX, Sir Cyril, *The Boundary Line of Cymru* [i.e. Offa's Dyke], in *Proceedings* of the British Academy, Vol. XXVI, reprinted by Oxford University Press, 1941.

FRASER, George MacDonald, *The Steel Bonnets. The Story of the Anglo-Scottish Reivers*, Barrie and Jenkins, 1971.

FREEMAN, A. Z., *A Moat Defensive. The Coast Defense Scheme of 1295, in Speculum*, the Journal of the Medieval Academy of America, Cambridge, Mass., 1967.

FREEMAN, Edward A., *The History of the Norman Conquest of England. Its Causes and Effects*, 5 vols, plus index, 1867–79.

——, *William the Conqueror*, Macmillan, 1888.

FULLER, Thomas, *The Church History of Britain from the Brith of Jesus Christ until the year MDCXLVIII*, 3 vols, 1868.

GARMONSWAY, G. N. (trans.), *The Anglo-Saxon Chronicle*, Dent, 1953; new ed. 1972.

GILDAS: See: Giles, *Six Old English Chronicles*

GILES, J. A. (ed.), *William of Malmesbury's Chronicle of the Kings of England*, 1847.

Six Old English Chronicles, 1848.

Roger of Wendover's Flowers of History, 2 vols, 1849.

Matthew Paris's English History from the Years 1235 to 1273, 1852.

GILLINGHAM, John, *Richard the Lionheart*, Weidenfeld, 1978.

——, *The Wars of the Roses*, Weidenfeld, 1981.

GIRALDUS CAMBRENSIS: See WRIGHT

GOAD, J. G., *Guide to Battle Abbey*, 1984.

GOLDING, G. F., (trans.), *Records and Songs of Saxon Times*, Bell, 1932.

GOLDINGHAM, C. S., The Navy under Henry VII, in *English Historical Review*, Vol. XXXIII, October 1918.

GRANT, Michael (trans.), *Tacitus. The Annals of Imperial Rome*, Penguin, 1956; rev. ed, 1977.

GRAVES, Robert (trans.), *Suetonius. The Twelve Caesars*, rev. by Michael Grant, Penguin, 1979.

GREEN, E., *The Preparations in Somerset against the Spanish Armada 1558–88*, 1888.

GREEN, John Richard, *The Making of England*, Macmillan, 1882.

——, *A Short History of the English People*, Macmillan, 1902.

HACKETT, Francis, *Henry the Eighth*, Cape, 1929.

HALL, Edward, *Hall's Chronicle, containing the History of England during the Reign of Henry the Fourth and the Succeeding Monarchs to the End of the Reign of Henry the Eighth*, 1809. [Originally published as *The Union of the Two Noble and Illustre Families of Lancastre and Yorke*, 1548.]

HALL, Joseph (ed.), *The Poems of Laurence Minot*, Clarendon Press, 1897.

HALE, J. R., *The Defence of the Realm under Elizabeth I*, in COLVIN, H. M., (ed.), *The King's Works*, Vol. IV, Part 3, HMSO, 1963.

HAMMOND, P. W., and SUTTON, Anne F., *Richard III. The Road to Bosworth Field*, Constable, 1985.

HANDFORD, S. A. (trans.), *Caesar. The Conquest of Gaul*. Revised with a new introduction by Jane F. Gardner, Penguin, 1981.

HANNAY, David, *A Short History of the Royal Navy, 1217 to 1688*, Methuen, 1898.

HARGREAVES, Reginald, *The Narrow Seas. A History of the English Channel, Its Approaches and its Immediate Shores, 400 BC – AD 1945*, Sidgwick and Jackson, 1959.

HARRISON, G. B. (ed.), *The Letters of Queen Elizabeth I*, Cassell, 1935; later edn, 1968.

HAWKES, Jacquetta, *The Shell Guide to British Archaeology*, Shell, 1986.

HENNINGS, Margaret A., *England under Henry III illustrated from Contemporary Sources*, Longman, 1924.

HENRY, L. W., The Earl of Essex as Strategist and Military Organiser, in *English Historical Review*, 1951.

HOCKEY, S. F., *Insula Vecta, The Isle of Wight in the Middle Ages*, Phillimore, Chichester, 1982.

HODGKIN, R. H., *A History of the Anglo-Saxons*, 2 vols, Clarendon Press, 1935.

HOLLISTER, C. Warren, *Anglo-Saxon Military Institutions*, Clarendon Press, 1962.

HOGG, A. H. A., *Hill-Forts of Britain*. Hart-Davis, 1975.

HOGG, O. F. G., *Clubs to Cannon. Warfare and Weapons before the Introduction of Gunpowder*, Duckworth, 1968.

HOWARTH, David, *1066. The Year of the Conquest*. Collins, 1977.

——, *The Voyage of the Armada. The Spanish Story*, Collins, 1981.

HOZIER, H. M., *The Invasions of England*, 2 vols, Macmillan, 1876.

HUTCHISON, Harold F., *Henry V. A. Biography*, Eyre and Spottiswoode, 1967.

——, *Edward II. The Pliant King*, Eyre and Spottiswoode, 1972.

HYLAND, Paul, *Wight*. Biography of an Island, Gollancz, 1984.

INNES, Arthur D. (rev. by J. M. HENDERSON), *England under the Tudors*, 1905; new ed, Methuen, 1950.

JACOB, E. F., *The Fifteenth Century, 1399–1485*, Clarendon Press, 1961.

JOHNSON, Paul, *The Life and Times of Edward III*, Weidenfeld, 1973.

JOHNSON, Stephen, *The Roman Forts of the Saxon Shore*, Elek, 1976.

KEEN, M. H., *England in the Later Middle Ages*, Methuen, 1973.

KENDALL, Paul Murray, *Richard the Third*, Allen and Unwin, 1955.

KEYNES, Simon and LAPIDGE, Michael (eds), *Alfred the Great. Asser's Life of King Alfred and Other Contemporary Sources*, Penguin, 1983.

KIGHTLY, Charles, *Strongholds of the Realm. Defence in Britain from Prehistory to the Twentieth Century*, Thames and Hudson, 1975.

KINGSFORD, Charles Lethbridge (ed.), *The First English Life of King Henry V written in 1513 by an Anonymous Author, known commonly as The Translation of Livius*, Clarendon Press, 1911.

KIRBY, J. L., *Henry IV of England*, Constable, 1970.

LABARGE, Margaret Wade, *Henry V. The Cautious Conqueror*, Secker and Warburg, 1975.

LARSON, Laurence M., *Canute the Great 999–1035*, Putnam, 1912.

LEMMON, Charles H., *The Campaign of 1066*. See Chevallier.

LEWIS, Michael, *The Navy of Britain. A Historical Portrait*. Allen and Unwin, 1948.

——, *The Spanish Armada*, Batsford, 1960; Pan Books, 1966.

LINDSAY, Jack, *Arthur and His Times*, Muller, 1958.

LIPSCOMB, F. W., *The Heritage of Sea Power. The Story of Portsmouth*, Hutchinson, 1967.

LLOYD, Alan, *King John*, David and Charles, Newton Abbot, 1973.

LOADES, D. M., *The Reign of Mary Tudor*, Benn, 1979.

LONG W. H. (ed.), *The Oglander Memoirs*, 1888. [See also BAMFORD]

LOYN, H. R., *Alfred the Great*, Oxford University Press, 1968.

LUMBY, Rev. J. Rawson (ed.), *Bacon's History of the Reign of King Henry VII*, Oxford University Press 1881.

MACKIE, J. D., *The Earlier Tudors, 1485–1558*, Clarendon Press, 1952; new ed. 1962.

MARCUS, G. J., *A Naval History of England*, Vol. I, *The Formative Centuries*, [i.e. c. 1380–1790], Longman, 1961.

MACKENZIE, W. M. (ed.), *John Barbour, The Bruce*, London, 1909.

McKISACK, May, *The Fourteenth Century, 1307–1399*, Clarendon Press, 1959.

MCLYNN, Frank, *Invasion. From the Armada to Hitler, 1588–1945*, Routledge, 1987.

MARKHAM, Sir Clements R., *King Edward VI. An Appreciation*, 1907.

MATTINGLY, Garrett, *The Defeat of the Spanish Armada*, 1959; Book Club Associates, 1983.

MATTINGLY, H. (trans.), *Tacitus, The Agricola and the Germania*, (rev. S. A. HANDFORD) Penguin, 1970.

MINOT, Laurence: See HALL; RITSON

MONSEN, Erling (ed.), *Snorre Sturlason: Heimskringla, or The Lives of the Norse Kings*, Heffer, Cambridge, 1932.

MORRIS, John E., *The Welsh Wars of Edward I*, Clarendon Press, 1902.

MORLEY, B. M., *Henry VIII and the Development of Coastal Defence*, (pamphlet), HMSO, 1976.

MORRIS, William and MAGNUSSON, Eirikr (eds), *The Stories of the Kings of Norway, called the Round of the World (Heimskringla) by Snorri Sturlason*, 6 vols, 1905.

MYERS, Alec R. (eds) *English Historical Documents, 1327–1485*, Eyre and Spottiswoode, 1969.

MYRES, J. N. L., *The English Settlements*, Clarendon Press, new edn. 1986.

NATIONAL TRUST MAGAZINE, No. 53, Spring 1988, articles on *The Spanish Armada* by Mary Connatty, Frank Kitchen and James Mildren.

NEALE, J. E., *Queen Elizabeth I*, Cape, 1934, Pelican edn, 1960.

NENNIUS; See GILES, *Six Old English Chronicles*.

NICOLAS, Sir Nicholas Harris, *A History of the Royal Navy from the Earliest Times to the Wars of the French Revolution*, 2 vols, 1847 [in fact completed only till 1422].

NORGATE, Kate, *John Lackland*, Macmillan, 1902.

——, *The Minority of Henry III*, Macmillan, 1912.

OGILVIE, R. M., and RICHMOND, Sir Ian (eds), *Cornelii Taciti De Vita Agricolae*, Clarendon Press, 1967.

OGLANDER: See BAMFORD: LONG

OMAN, Sir Charles, *A History of the Art of War in the Middle Ages*, 2 vols, Methuen, 1924. [The original edition, published in 1898, ended at 1375. The later edition extends to 1485.]

——, *A History of the Art of War in the Sixteenth Century*, Methuen, 1937.

——, *The History of England from the accession of Richard II to the Death of Richard III (1377–1485)*, Longmans, 1906.

O'NEILL, B. H. St J., Stefan von Harschenperg, Engineer to Henry VIII, and His Work, in *Archaeologia*, 2nd series, xci, pp. 137–55, 1945.

ORDERIC VITALIS: See CHIBNALL

PACKE, Michael, *King Edward III*, Routledge, 1983.

PAGE, William (ed.), *The Victoria County History of Hampshire and the Isle of Wight*, Vol. 5, Constable, 1912.

PAINTER, Sidney, *The Reign of King John*, John Hopkins Press, Baltimore, Maryland, 1968.

PASTON LETTERS: See WARRINGTON

PATON, Lucy A. (ed.), *Geoffrey of Monmouth's Histories of the Kings of Britain*, Everyman's Library, Dent, 1911.

PERROY, E. (trans. W. R. WELLS), *The Hundred Years War*, Eyre and Spottiswoode, 1951, of rev. edn 1962.

PLATT, Colin, *Medieval Southampton*, Routledge, 1973.

POLLARD, A. F., *The History of England from the Accession of Edward VI to the Death of Elizabeth (1547–1603)*, Longmans, 1910.

—— (ed.) *The Reign of Henry VII from Contemporary Sources*, 3 vols, Longmans, 1913–14.

POOLE, Austin Lane, *From Domesday Book to Magna Carta, 1087–1216*, Clarendon Press, 1951.

POPE, M. K. and LODGE, E. C., *The Life of the Black Prince by the Herald of Sir John Chandos*, Oxford University Press, 1910.

POTTER, K. R. (ed.), *The Historia Novella of William of Malmesbury*, Nelson, 1955.

POWELL, Ken and COOK, Chris, *English Historical Facts, 1485–1603*, Macmillan, 1977.

POWICKE, F. M., *King Henry III and the Lord Edward*, 3 vols, Clarendon Press, 1947.

——, Sir Maurice, *The Thirteenth Century, 1216–1307*, Clarendon Press, 1953.

PRESCOT, H. F. M., *Mary Tudor*, Eyre and Spottiswoode, 1952.

PRESTWICH, Michael, *War, Politics and Finance under Edward I*, Faber, 1972.

——, *The Three Edwards. War and State in England, 1272–1377*, Weidenfeld, 1980.

RAMSAY, Sir James H., *The Dawn of the Constitution, or The Reigns of Henry III and Edward I*, AD 1216–1307, Swan Sonnenschein, 1908.

REES, David, *The Son of Prophecy, Henry Tudor's Road to Bosworth*, Black Raven Press, 1985.

RICHARDSON, Oliver H., *The National Movement in the Reign of Henry III and its Culmination in the Barons' War*, Macmillan, 1897.

RICHMOND, C. F., The War at Sea [in *The Hundred Years War*]: see FLOWER

RICHMOND, Admiral Sir Herbert W., *The Invasion of Britain. An Account of Plans, Attempts and Counter-Measures from 1586–1918*, Methuen, 1941.

RIDLEY, Jasper, *The Life and Times of Mary Tudor*, Weidenfeld, 1974.

——, *Henry VIII*, Constable, 1984.

RILEY, H. T. (ed.) *Thomas of Walsingham. Historia*, Rolls Series, Vol. I, 1864.

——, *Thomas of Walsingham, Anglicana*, Rolls Series, 2 vols, 1863.

RITSON, Joseph (ed.), *Laurence Minot. Poems written Anno MCCCLII*, 1825.

ROTHWELL, Harry (ed.), *English Historical Documents, 1189–1327*, Eyre and Spottiswoode, 1975.

ROTULI PARLIAMENTORUM, Edward I to Henry VII, 6 vols, 1783, plus index, 1832.

ROWSE, A. L., *The Expansion of Elizabethan England*, Macmillan, 1955.

——, *Tudor Cornwall*, 1941, Macmillan, 1969.

——, *Bosworth Field and the Wars of the Roses*, Macmillan, 1966.

RUSSELL, Percy, *Dartmouth. A History of the Port and Town*, Batsford, 1950.

SALMON, Arthur L, *Plymouth*, SPCK, 1920.

SALWAY, Peter, *Roman Britain*, Clarendon Press, 1981.

SALZMAN, L. F., *Edward I*, Constable, 1968.

SANDERSON, Michael, *Sea Battles. A Reference Guide*, David and Charles, Newton Abbot, 1975.

SCARISBRICK, J. J., *Henry VIII*, Eyre and Spotiswoode, 1968.

SCOTT, A. F. (ed.), *Every One a Witness. The Plantaganet Age*, White Lion, 1975.

SEELEY, B. B., *The Greatest of All the Plantagenets* [i.e. Edward I], 1860.

SENIOR, Michael, *The Life and Times of Richard II*, Weidenfeld, 1981.

SHERLEY-PRICE, Leo (trans.), *Bede. A History of the English Church and People*, Penguin, 1955, later ed. 1968.

SIMONS, Eric N., *The Reign of Edward IV*, Muller, 1966.

——, *Henry VII. The First Tudor King*, Muller, 1968.

SMURTHWAITE, David, *The Ordnance Survey Complete Guide to the Battlefields of Britain*, Book Club Associates, 1984.

STATUTES OF THE REALM, Vol. III, 1509–1547, part of 11 vol. series published 1810–28.

STENTON, F. M., *Anglo-Saxon England*, Clarendon Press, 1947.

STURLASON, Snorre [or Snorril]: See MONSEN, MORRIS AND MAGNUSSON

TEMPERLEY, Gladys, *Henry VII*, Constable, 1914.

THOMAS OF WALSINGHAM: See RILEY

THOMPSON, Peter E. (trans.), *The Hundred Years War, from the Works of Jean Le Bel, Jean Froissart and Enguerrand de Monstrelet*, Folio Society, 1966.

THOMSON, George Malcolm, *Sir Francis Drake*, 1972, Book Club Associates, 1973.

THORPE, Lewis (trans.), *Geoffrey of Monmouth. The History of the Kings of Britain*, Penguin, 1966.

TOUT, T. F., *The History of England from the Accession of Henry III to the Death of Edward III* (1216–1377), Longman, 1905.

——, *The Place of the Reign of Edward II in English History*, Manchester University Press, Manchester, 1936.

TREVELYAN, G. M., *History of England*, 1926; Longman, 1945.

TYLER, Patrick F., *Life of King Henry the Eighth founded on Authentic and Original Documents*, Simpkin Marshall, 1837.

USHERWOOD, Stephen (ed.), *The Great Enterprise. The History of the Spanish Armada*, 1978; Bell and Hyman, 1982.

VICKERS, Kenneth H., *England in the Later Middle Ages*, Methuen, 1913; later ed, 1950.

VINE, Rev. Francis T., *Caesar in Kent. The Landing of Julius Caesar and his Battles with the Ancient Britons*, 1886.

WACHER, John, *The Coming of Rome*, Routledge, 1979.

WALLING, R. A. J., *The Story of Plymouth*, Westway Books, Plymouth, 1950.

WARNER, Philip, *Invasion Road*, Cassell, 1980.

WARREN, W. L., *King John*, Eyre Methuen, 1961, later ed. 1978.

——, *Henry II*, Eyre Methuen, 1973.

WARRINGTON, John (ed.), *The Paston Letters*, Vol. II, Everyman's Library, rev. 1956.

WATKIN, Hugh R., *Dartmouth. Vol. I. Pre-Reformation*, Devonshire Association, 1935.

WEBB, Henry J., *Elizabethan Military Science. The Books and the Practice*, University of Wisconsin Press, Madison, Wisc. and London, 1965.

WEBSTER, Graham, *The Roman Invasion of Britain*, Batsford Academic, 1980.

——, *Boudica* [sic]. *The British Revolt against Rome*, Batsford, 1978.

WELLESLEY, Kenneth (trans.), *Tacitus. The Histories*, Penguin Books, 1974, later ed. 1975.

WERNHAM, R. B., *Before the Armada. The Growth of English Foreign policy, 1485–1588*, Cape, 1966.

WHIBLEY, Charles (ed.), *Henry VIII by Edward Hall* [i.e. an edition of Hall's Chronicle], 1904.

WHITE, H. T., The Beacon System in Hampshire, in *Proceedings* of the Hampshire Field Club, 1930.

WHITELOCK, Dorothy (ed.), *English Historical Documents, c. 500–1042*, Eyre and Spottiswoode, 1955.

WILLIAM OF MALMESBURY: See POTTER

WILLIAMS, Charles, *Henry VII*, Barker, 1937.

WILLIAMS, C. H. (ed.), *English Historical Documents 1485–1558*, Eyre and Spottiswoode, 1967.
WILLIAMS, Neville, *Elizabeth, Queen of England*, Weidenfeld, 1967.
——, *The Life and Times of Elizabeth I*, Weidenfeld, 1972.
WILLIAMSON, James A., *The English Channel. A History*, Collins, 1959.
——, *The Tudor Age*, Longman, 1979.
WILSON, Mona, *Queen Elizabeth*, Daily Express Publications, n.d.
WORSLEY, Sir Richard, *The History of the Isle of Wight*, 1891.
WORTH, R. N., *History of Plymouth*, Plymouth, 1871.
WRIGHT, Thomas (ed.), *The Historical Works of Giraldus Cambrensis, containing The Topography of Ireland and the History of the Conquest of Ireland, The Itinerary through Wales and the Description of Wales.*
WYLIE, James Hamilton, *History of England under Henry the Fourth*, 2 vols, 1884 and 1894.
——, *The Reign of Henry the Fifth*, 2 vols, Cambridge University Press, 1924.

ACKNOWLEDGEMENTS

Grateful acknowledgement is made for the use of copyright material as follows: to Associated Book Publishers (UK) Ltd and Joan Evans for *The Unconquered Knight*; to Routledge and Kegan Paul Ltd and Lindsay Boynton for *The Elizabethan Militia*; to B. T. Batsford Ltd for Percy Russell, Plymouth, and Michael Lewis, *The Spanish Armada*; to David Rees for *The Son of Prophecy*, published by Black Raven Press in 1985; to Boydell and Brewer Ltd for Alistair Campbell, *Encomium Emma Reginae*, Camden 3rd Series Vol. LXXXIX; to William Collins Sons and Co Ltd for David Howarth, *The Voyage of the Armada*; to J. M. Dent and Sons Ltd for G. N. Garmonsway (trans. and ed.), *The Anglo-Saxon Chronicle*; to the Folio Society Ltd for Peter Thompson, *The Hundred Years War*; to the Hampshire Field Club and Archaeological Society for H. T. White, *The Beacon System in Hampshire*; to W. Heffer and Sons Ltd for *Heimskringla or The Lives of the Norse Kings* by Snorre Sturlason, Edited with notes by Erling Monsen and translated into English with the assistance of A. H. Smith; to the Controller of Her Majesty's Stationery Office for J. R. (Sir John) Hale, *The Defence of the Realm 1485–1963* in *The History of the King's Works*, Vol. IV; to Longman Group UK Ltd for A. F. Pollard, *The History of England 1547–1603*; to Methuen and Co Ltd for M. H. Keen, *England in the Later Middle Ages*; to Macmillan Publishers Ltd for A. L. Rowse, *Tudor Cornwall*; to Oxford University Press for Marjorie Chibnall, *The Ecclesiastical History of Orderic Vitalis*, published 1969–1979;

to Penguin Books Ltd and the individuals specified for the following: *Caesar: The Conquest of Gaul*, translated by S. H. Handford (Penguin Classics, 1951, 1982) copyright the estate of S. A. Handford; *Alfred the Great: Asser's Life of King Alfred and Other Contemporary Sources*, translated by Simon Keynes and Michael Lapidge (Penguin Classics, 1983); *Bede: A History of the English Church and People*, translated by Leo Sherley-Price and revised by R. E. Latham (Penguin Classics, 1955, 1968); *Tacitus: The Annals of Imperial Rome*, translated by Michael Grant (Penguin Classics, 1956, 1959, 1971), copyright Michael Grant Publications Ltd, 1956, 1959, 1971; to the Society of Antiquaries of London for B. H. St. J. O'Neill, *Stefan von Harschenperg* in *Archaeologia*; to Stephen Usherwood for *The Great Enterprise*, published by Bell and Hyman (now Unwin Hyman Ltd), 1982; to A. P. Watt Ltd, on behalf of the executors of the estate of Robert Graves, for *Suetonius: The Twelve Caesars*.

Apologies are offered for any inadvertent breach of copyright where, despite every effort, it has proved impossible to trace a copyright-holder, and amends will gladly be made in any future edition.

ILLUSTRATION ACKNOWLEDGEMENTS

Bibliothèque Nationale, Paris: 21
British Library: 19, 33, 35
Bridgeman Art Library: 28, 41
British Museum: 4, 5, 6, 8, 14
Cambridge University Press: 11
Christ Church, Oxford: 36, 37
Corpus Christi College, Cambridge: 16, 17
Courtauld Institute: 15
Department of the Environment: 22
Fitzwilliam Museum, Cambridge: 20
John Hillelson Agency: 2
Michael Holford: 12, 13, 23
Lambeth Palace Library: 18
Mansell Collection: 3, 7
The Marquess of Salisbury: 38
National Maritime Museum: 30, 31, 32, 39, 40, 42, 43, 44, 45, 46
National Portrait Gallery: 24, 25, 26, 27, 29
Public Record Office: 34
Weidenfeld and Nicolson Ltd: 9, 10
Alan Woolfitt: 1

INDEX